Translated Texts for Historians

300–800 AD is the time of late antiquity and the early middle ages: the transformation of the classical world, the beginnings of Europe and of Islam, and the evolution of Byzantium. TTH makes available sources translated from Greek, Latin, Syriac, Coptic, Arabic, Georgian, Gothic and Armenian. Each volume provides an expert scholarly translation, with an introduction setting texts and authors in context, and with notes on content, interpretation and debates.

Editorial Committee
Sebastian Brock, Oriental Institute, University of Oxford
Averil Cameron, Keble College, Oxford
Marios Costambeys, University of Liverpool
Mary Cunningham, University of Nottingham
Carlotta Dionisotti, King's College, London
Peter Heather, King's College, London
Robert Hoyland, University of St Andrews
William E. Klingshirn, The Catholic University of America
Michael Lapidge, Clare College, Cambridge
John Matthews, Yale University
Neil McLynn, Corpus Christi College, Oxford
Richard Price, Heythrop College, University of London
Claudia Rapp, University of California, Los Angeles
Raymond Van Dam, University of Michigan
Michael Whitby, University of Warwick
Ian Wood, University of Leeds

General Editors
Gillian Clark, University of Bristol
Mark Humphries, Swansea University
Mary Whitby, University of Oxford

A full list of published titles in the Translated Texts for Historians series is available on request. The most recently published are shown below.

For full details of Translated Texts for Historians, including prices and ordering information, please write to the following: **All countries, except the USA and Canada**: Liverpool University Press, 4 Cambridge Street, Liverpool, L69 7ZU, UK (*Tel* +44-[0]151-794 2233, *Fax* +44-[0]151-794 2235, Email J.M. Smith@liv.ac.uk, http://www.liverpool-unipress.co.uk). **USA and Canada:** University of Chicago Press, 1427 E. 60th Street, Chicago, IL, 60637, US (*Tel* 773-702-7700, *Fax* 773-702-9756, www.press.uchicago.edu)

Translated Texts for Historians
Volume 54

Orosius
Seven Books of History against the Pagans

Translated with an introduction and notes by
A. T. Fear

Liverpool
University
Press

First published 2010
Liverpool University Press
4 Cambridge Street
Liverpool, L69 7ZU

British Library Cataloguing-in-Publication Data
A British Library CIP Record is available.

ISBN 978-1-84631-473-5 cased
ISBN 978-1-84631-239-7 limp

Set in Times by
Koinonia, Manchester
Printed and bound by CPI Group (UK) Ltd, Croydon, CR0 4YY

CONTENTS

ACKNOWLEDGEMENTS

I would like to thank all those who have made many improvements to this work, in particular Gillian Clark, John Davies, Mark Humphries, and Mary Whitby. The errors and infelicities that remain are entirely my own responsibility.

ABBREVIATIONS

a.	anno (in the year)
A Abr.	*a Abraham* (from Abraham)
ANF	Ante-Nicene Fathers: The Writings of the Fathers Down to A.D. 325 (ed. A. Roberts and J. Donaldson)
AUC	*Ab Urbe Condita* (from the foundation of the City)
CCSL	Corpus Christianorum: series Latinorum
CIL	Corpus Inscriptionum Latinarum
CSEL	Corpus Scriptorum Ecclesiasticorum Latinorum
fr.	fragment
MGH	Monumenta Germaniae Historica
NPNF	A Select Library of the Nicene and Post-Nicene Fathers of the Christian Church (ed. P. Schaff)
Per.	Periocha
PG	Patrologia Graeca
PL	Patrologia Latina
PLRE	*Prosopography of the Later Roman Empire* (vol.1, ed. A. H. M. Jones, J. R. Martindale and J. Morris; vol. 2, ed. J. R. Martindale)
s.a.	sub anno (in the year)
SHA	Scriptores Historiae Augustae
sup.	supplement

INTRODUCTION

1. LIFE

For an author who was to become so popular in the Middle Ages, there is disappointingly little concrete information about the life of Orosius; even his name is unclear.[1] Jordanes refers to Orosius Paulus,[2] and the fragment of the *Histories* in the *Bibliotheca Laurentiana*, which probably dates to the sixth century, speaks of Paulus Orosius, but earlier sources, such as Augustine and Jerome, and later ones, such as the seventh-century Visigothic bishop of Saragossa, Braulio, simply refer to our author as Orosius.

The date of Orosius's birth is as opaque as his name, nor is anything known of his childhood and upbringing, his own works being almost entirely devoid of autobiographical details. Braulio believed that Orosius had been a follower of the heretic Priscillian who was later brought back to orthodoxy by Augustine.[3] This seems most unlikely and is probably derived from Braulio's knowledge of Augustine's *Book against the supporters of Priscillian and Origen dedicated to Orosius* (*Liber ad Orosium contra Priscillianistas et Origenistas*), but his ignorance of Orosius's own attack on the Priscillianists, the *Commonitorium de errore Priscillianistarum et Origenistarum* which provoked Augustine's reply. Orosius's writings contain quotations from, and, more importantly, adaptations of, Classical authors, showing that he had had a good literary education. From this we can infer that he may well have been a man of some pedigree and have stemmed from a wealthy family. Probably, like his near contemporary, Patrick, he was a member of the curial class, though the two were to have very different lives.

Orosius's entry into the historical record comes in a letter of commendation written by Augustine to Jerome written in AD 415. In it, Augustine

---

1 For an extended discussion of Orosius's life see Vilella (2000).

2 *Getica* 9; the odd order of names here suggests that conceivably Jordanes mistakenly expanded an abbreviation, Orosius P[resbyter], as Orosius Paulus.

3 *Letter* 44 = PL 80 693–94; Riesco Terrero (1975) 170–71.

is at pains to mention Orosius's youth, but gives us no other clues about his background.[4] When Augustine wrote to Jerome, Orosius was already a priest and so must have been towards if not, given Augustine's persistent harping on the theme (it is mentioned on three separate occasions), at the very youngest age at which ordination was possible. According to the letter of Pope Syriacus sent to Evemerius, the metropolitan of Tarragona, and that sent by Innocent I to the bishops of Spain, this limit in the peninsula was 35. However, this age seems to have been the exception not the rule and elsewhere 30 was accepted as the lowest age for entry to the priesthood. Given that this is what would have been known to Augustine, maybe we ought to assume that Orosius was around 30 at the time Augustine wrote to Jerome, making the date of his birth around AD 385.[5]

Although questioned in recent years,[6] Spain remains the clear candidate for Orosius's birthplace. Gennadius refers to him as 'the priest Orosius, of Spanish origins',[7] while Braulio writing to Fructuosus of Braga lists him among the 'most eloquent and learned' products of Galicia.[8] The implications of our ancient sources are supported by Orosius's own writing. He takes evident pride in the resistance to Rome at Numantia, in the fact that Spain has supplied Rome with 'good emperors' such as Trajan and Theodosius the Great,[9] and has eye for details in Spain, such as the lighthouse at Corunna, which is not repeated elsewhere in the empire. To these details can be added his description of the Spanish town of Tarragona as 'our Tarragona'.[10] Therefore, short of an unequivocal statement of the fact, the evidence for Orosius's Spanish origins is as solid as it could possibly be.

Debate has also raged over from precisely what part of the peninsula Orosius hailed. The reference to 'our Tarragona' mentioned above has led some scholars to believe that this was Orosius's hometown. This was certainly the view among many older commentators, such as Baronius and Mörner. On the other hand, in the context where it is used, 'our' could simply mean 'Spanish', and there has also been a long tradition, now supported by the majority of modern commentators, of following Braulio in seeing Orosius's

---

4 Augustine, *Letter* 166 = PL 33 720–21; *CSEL* 44 547–48. Augustine was 60 at the time.

5 See Raymond (1936) 5, following Mörner (1844) 19.

6 See Arnaud-Lindet (1990) xi–xii.

7 *Ecclesiastical Writers* (*De Scriptoribus Ecclesiasticis*), 39 = PL 58 1080–81.

8 *Letter* 44 = PL 80 698–99; Riesco Terrero (1975) 180–83.

9 Numantia 5.5, see also Orosius's description of the Cantabrian Wars 6.21; lighthouse, 1.2.71; good emperors 5.23.16, 7.34.1.

10 7.22.8.

patria chica in the north-west of the peninsula.[11] Braga is often seen as the most likely candidate for Orosius's hometown, above all because he refers to two colleagues named Avitus as *cives mei*, 'my citizens', and Avitus of Braga, who is likely to be one of these two Aviti, later calls Orosius 'my son and fellow-priest'.[12] But these references, while perhaps suggestive, are in no way conclusive. If we are to reject *noster*, when referring to Tarragona, as having a personal reference to Orosius, his use of *meus* here is no stronger, while Avitus's remarks need not imply anything other than affection from one priest towards another. In many ways, Corunna seems a more appropriate candidate for Orosius's place of birth.[13] While lying within Galicia, and so not contradicting Braulio's comments, this town seems to occupy a special place in Orosius's affections; the singling out of its lighthouse in the *Histories* as 'a work with which few can be compared' is particularly striking. Augustine may also give us a hint here when he writes that Orosius has come to him 'from the shores of the Ocean' and 'from the furthest reaches of Spain – that is Ocean's shore'. However, it is worth remembering that Orosius, albeit to produce a forced contrast, is happy on one occasion to refer to Tarragona, located on Spain's Mediterranean coast, as 'the utmost West'.[14] Any speculation on our author's hometown therefore remains, in the last analysis, mere speculation.

At some point in the early fifth century, Orosius was forced to flee from Spain to North Africa. The account of his flight in the *Histories* implies that this was done under duress and placed him in danger.[15] The precise date of his escape is disputed. Some, using Orosius's comment that he fled at the first sign of trouble, have suggested that he left for Africa in AD 409 when the first serious barbarian incursions into Spain began, but this seems unduly pessimistic, and the most likely date for Orosius's flight is AD 411.

---

11 e.g. Corsini (1968) 15. Ibañez Segovia defended this position in 1681 in his *Disertaciones eclesiásticas por el honor de los antiguos tutelares contra las ficciones modernas*.

12 *Commonitorium* 3, *Letter of Avitus to Palchonius* (*Epistula Aviti ad Palchonium*) = PL 41 805.

13 See Javier (1982) 177–78; Torres Rodríguez (1985) 25–27.

14 Augustine, *Letters* 166 and 169 (= CSEL 44); 6.21.19–20.

15 3.20.6–7, 5.2.1. Later in the work, *Histories* 7.41.4–6 suggests that Orosius's flight was relatively easy and this is the view taken by Sánchez Salor (1982) 15. The problem we face here is the degree of rhetoric to be found in the *Histories*. The context of the first two passages is one where an emphasis on the difficulties of flight would be useful for Orosius's argument, while in the final passage Orosius is at pains to emphasise the benefits of the Christian epoch and so may well be downplaying the difficulties involved in flight. The first account appears the more credible of the two, but with no corroborating evidence, it is important to keep an open mind.

This is when the Sueves occupied Braga and, according to Hydatius, 'those parts of the west which lie on the edge of the Ocean' which would include Corunna.[16]

On his arrival in North Africa, Orosius became acquainted with St Augustine, presenting the bishop of Hippo with his *Memoir on the Error of the Supporters of Priscillian and Origen (Commonitorium de errore Priscillianistarum et Origenistarum).*[17] The work suggests involvement in doctrinal disputes in Spain and is a good indication of Orosius's combative disposition. The account of his journey to Africa in the *Memoir* differs from that presented in the *Histories*, and states that he had arrived to consult Augustine on issues of doctrine, coming to Africa 'neither through any wish or my own, nor through compulsion, nor at the suggestion of another, but after being moved by some unknown power'.[18] Given that Augustine had previously criticised priests who had abandoned their flocks in the face of barbarian invasions, it is perhaps not surprising that Orosius chose to make no mention of his flight when writing to him.[19]

Augustine produced his *Liber ad Orosium contra Priscillianistas et Origenistas* in reply to Orosius's work,[20] but was unable to satisfy some of his enquiries. He therefore sent him on to Jerome in Palestine, commending him highly.[21] Orosius may have travelled to Palestine via Egypt, where he speaks of seeing various books at Alexandria, and the Red Sea, where he may have seen what he believed were the wheel ruts from Pharaoh's army preserved under the water.[22] While we have no evidence of how the relationship between Jerome and Orosius worked in practice, the two men's similarity of character implies that they would have got on well together.[23] It is likely that during his stay, Orosius acquired a copy of Jerome's *Chronicle*, which was to be a major source for the *Histories*. In Palestine Orosius soon became involved in the Pelagian controversy, representing the anti-Pelagian

16 Hydatius, *Chronicle*, 17.49.
17 PL 31 1211–16; CSEL 18; Torres Rodríguez (1985) 729–43.
18 *Commonitorium*, 1.
19 See Augustine, *Letter* 228 = CSEL 57 484.
20 PL 42 669–78.
21 Augustine, *Letter* 166 (= CSEL 44 547). Given the tension that at times flared up between Jerome and Augustine, one cannot help wondering whether Augustine's sending Orosius to Jerome was an act entirely devoid of malice.
22 Alexandria, 6.15.32; wheel ruts, 2.10.17.
23 Jerome is certainly complimentary about Orosius in a letter to Augustine (Augustine, *Letter* 122 = PL 33 752; CSEL 56 56–71).

cause at a synod in Jerusalem convened on 28 July 415 by Pelagius's ally, bishop John of Jerusalem. The synod went badly for Orosius and afterwards he was accused by John of denying that man could be free of sin even through the agency of divine grace. To defend himself he wrote his *Defence against Pelagius concerning the Doctrine of Freewill* (*Liber Apologeticus contra Pelagium de Arbitrii Libertate*).[24] Towards the end of 415 a further Council at Diospolis (20–23 December), which Orosius did not attend, gave Pelagius a clean bill of orthodox health.

In this respect Orosius's stay in the Holy Land was not a happy one,[25] but it was perhaps leavened by the discovery on 3 December 415 of the body of the protomartyr Stephen by Lucian of Kaphar Gamala. Avitus of Braga, a fellow Spaniard staying with Jerome, managed to obtain some of Stephen's relics, including, as he proudly says, not just dust, but solid bones,[26] and he gave them to Orosius to take to Palchonius, the bishop of Braga. Orosius had promised Augustine that he would return from the Holy Land via North Africa and so put in on his way home with a letter from Jerome to Augustine, a further letter and some works of Jerome for his pupil Oceanus, the official minutes of the Council held at Diospolis, and a letter from Heros and Lazarus for Aurelius, the bishop of Carthage.[27] He arrived in the midsummer of 416.[28]

While in Africa, Orosius attended the Council of Carthage in 416. He then set out for Spain, but the chaos into which the peninsula had descended prevented him from returning home. He left the relics of Stephen in Magona[29] on Minorca and returned to Africa.[30] This is our last notice of Orosius, apart from the internal evidence of the *Histories* which show them to have been written by AD 418. We have no knowledge of his later life or death. Gennadius merely notes that Orosius won his reputation during the final years of Honorius's reign. We must presume that this reputation was based on the publication of the *Histories*. It seems unlikely that such

---

24 PL 31 1173–1212; CSEL 5 603–64; Zangemeister (1967) 601–64; Torres Rodríguez (1985) 756–880.

25 Jerome, writing to Augustine, describes these as 'most difficult times', *Letter* 134 = CSEL 56 261–63.

26 *Letter of Avitus to Palchonius*, 8 = PL 41 807, 'ossa solida'.

27 Augustine, *Letter* 166 (Orosius's promise); *Letters* 175 and 180 (Orosius's baggage).

28 Augustine, *Letter* 175.

29 The modern Port Mahon.

30 *Letter of Severus* (*Epistula Severi*), 4 = PL 41 823. For a modern edition, see Bradbury (1996). For a discussion of Orosius's journeys and the use of these relics, see Gauge (1998).

a pugnacious character would have rested on his laurels, and it is therefore likely that Orosius met an early death at around the age of 40, probably in North Africa.[31]

2. THE HISTORIES

When then did Orosius write his *Histories*? Again, there is no consensus. According to Orosius, who is our only source of evidence, the *Histories* were commissioned by Augustine after the completion of the first ten books of the *City of God*, and while Augustine was working on the eleventh. The work must therefore have been commissioned after Orosius's arrival in Africa prior to which Augustine had no knowledge of him, but when? A *terminus ante quem* is provided by the death of the Gothic king Vallia in AD 418, as he is the ruling king of the Visigoths at the end of the work.[32]

One resolution to the problem is to see the work as being started soon after Orosius's arrival in Africa, broken off by his trip to the Middle East, and completed on his return. This would have the advantage of giving Orosius time for research, but there is no positive evidence to show that this was the case:[33] Augustine, when commending Orosius to Jerome, makes no reference to any historical work, either commissioned or begun. Another approach would be to see the work completed during Orosius's stay in Africa after his return from the Holy Land, but before his attempted return to Spain.[34] A final solution would be to see the work as being written by Orosius after he had been forced to return to Africa, having failed to return to mainland Spain. Augustine, when speaking of the promise Orosius made to revisit Africa, refers to him returning to Spain, but gives no hint of anything other than a brief stop-over in Carthage. Severus of Minorca, the unexpecting recipient of Stephen's bones, refers to Orosius arriving in Minorca when returning to Spain from Jerusalem. This also implies that Orosius's stay in Africa had been a short one. If this is the case, it is perhaps most likely that the *Histories* are a product of Orosius's exile, written in

---

31 In more apocalyptic fashion Arnaud-Lindet (1990) xx suggests Orosius died in a shipwreck when returning to Africa from Minorca.

32 7.43.10.

33 See Fink-Errera (1954), Lacroix (1965), and Arnaud-Lindet (1990) xxii–xxv.

34 See Sánchez Salor (1982) 15. Penelas (2001) 22 believes that this is when Orosius finished the definitive version of his work, but suggests it may have been begun during Orosius's first visit to Africa.

Africa after he had failed to return home, making them the product of under a year's work.[35]

Either of the final two solutions makes more sense than the first. The main objection to them – that such a lengthy work could not be researched in such a short time – is weak. There is no need to believe that Orosius consulted widely for his work. The bulk of his material is drawn from a small number of standard historical works. Moreover, the *Histories*, though well written, do show signs of misunderstanding of their source material, and while, as will be seen, some of these 'misunderstandings' are deliberate, others are not; and these, along with various lapses in editing, suggest that the *Histories* were composed in haste.[36]

3. INTENTIONS

We have only Orosius's word that Augustine commissioned a work from him, and only deductions based on this statement, and from the work itself, that it was a history that was so commissioned. Specifically, we are told that it was to be a book setting out 'concisely and in order' all the troubles 'found in times gone by that I could discover in all the records of the histories and annals which are to be had at the present time'.[37] Like Augustine, who worried about the danger of becoming a mere compiler of facts, Orosius too wanted his work to have some purpose.[38] What we have therefore is not a mere list of disasters, but a continuous narrative. The commission certainly did not provide the 'essential material' of the *City of God* as Trevor-Roper once asserted: book three of the *City of God*, which contains similar material, had already been written when Orosius began his work.[39] Orosius's end product, however, was unique for its times. While previous Christian writers had composed histories of the Church, Orosius produced a history of the secular world from a Christian perspective, and it was the combination of this subject matter with its new ideological interpretation

35 See Bradbury (1996) 24–25.

36 See, *inter alia*, the conflicting time schemes of 1.1.5–6 and 1.21.20; the curious chapter 'title' at 1.2.91; the division of Valerius Antias into two historians at 5.3.3–4.

37 1 *Preface* 10.

38 Augustine, *City of God* 3.18; 3 *Preface* 3.

39 Trevor-Roper (1955); date of composition, 1 *Preface* 11. Perhaps Trevor-Roper was drawing on Dante, *Paradiso*, canto 10, where the 'defender of the Christian Age whose writings Augustine used for his own betterment', *quello avvocato de' tempi cristiani del cui latino Augustin si provide*, is normally seen as Orosius; see Toynbee (1902) 121–36.

that was to lead to Orosius's work becoming a great success in the Middle Ages.

Orosius took the view that previous historians, because they were pagans, had necessarily missed the underlying message to be found in history: an error that he regarded as his duty to correct.[40] This message was that the unfolding of history shows the unfolding of God's plan on earth, and that the arrival of Christianity therefore necessarily marks an improvement in man's condition regardless of any first appearances to the contrary which, as Orosius is happy to admit, may have seemed to contradict this message unless one looked at the *longue durée*.[41] It is a message that Orosius repeats relentlessly, telling his reader in no uncertain terms that 'you've never had it so good', continually challenging him to find a happier epoch than the present in man's history,[42] and emphasising how trivial present troubles, by the very nature of their being present, always appear much worse to the thoughtless than the major disasters that have occurred in the past.[43]

Moreover, for Orosius the march of history does not merely show God's plan at large; His direct intervention in particular events is also readily discernible. These interventions began with divine punishment for original sin in the Garden of Eden,[44] but can also be seen throughout historical time. Such interventions, which Orosius regards as uncontroversial and incontrovertible, are normally made to punish sin.[45] These sins are both secular and religious. The destruction of a library in Rome by lightning, for example, is seen as punishment for Commodus's murder of part of the Senate.[46] Rituals at Rome that involve burial alive or murder bring outbursts of madness and military defeats.[47] Naturally, Orosius sees the persecution of Christians as immediately bringing down divine vengeance. Nero's execution of Peter and Paul brings a plague and Boadicea's rebellion in Britain in its wake,[48] plague immediately follows Marcus Aurelius's persecution,[49] and rebellion

40 1.1.13.
41 1 *Preface* 13–14. One interesting argument Orosius uses is the success of Claudius's expedition to Britain undertaken after the birth of Christ and the arrival of St Peter to preach in Rome, compared to the previous failure of Caesar's British expedition; see 7.6.11.
42 Above all 7.43.16, but see also 2.11.8, 2.19.4, 2.19.12, 5.18.29, 5.22.5–15, and 5.24.9.
43 See the extended argument/diatribe on this theme at 4 *Preface*.
44 1.1.4, 1.3.1, and 7.1.3.
45 See 7.3.5–6.
46 7.16.3.
47 3.9.5–3.10 and 4.13.3–8.
48 7.7.11.
49 7.15.5.

in Gaul is Severus's reward for his attacks on Christians.[50] Trajan, an
emperor of whom Orosius generally approves, is punished by childlessness
for his attacks on the Church.[51] Heresy too attracts divine retribution.
Constantius's flirtation with Arianism produces a massive earthquake in the
eastern empire, as does the adoption of the Arian Valens as emperor. For
Orosius, this emperor's heresy was also responsible for the military disaster
at Adrianople.[52]

While punishing the wicked, God rewards the faithful. Constantine's
adoption of Christianity is repaid with a major victory over his enemies,
and the rapid growth of his new foundation, Constantinople, is due to its
being a Christian city.[53] The emperor Gratian defeats a large horde of barbarians at Argentaria by placing his faith in Christ.[54] But the best example of
divine favour is that of Orosius's hero, Theodosius, to whom the Goths and
Persians surrender because of his almost Christ-like demonstration of faith
and whose piety brings the divine aid that assured victory at the river Frigidus.[55] Similarly, it is the piety of the current emperor, Honorius, that dooms
the usurpers who rise against him.[56] Orosius is also quick to recruit changes
in fortune to his cause, making the point that defection from God's party
brings a fall in its wake. Arbogastes enjoys success as Theodosius's general,
but fails when he joins the pagan Eugenius, and Mascezil, after a triumphant
campaign against Gildo in Africa, also falls from grace when he begins to
persecute the Church.[57] As well as specific members of the faithful, Orosius
also believes that the very presence of Christians in a community alleviates
suffering, as God is more inclined to be merciful when there at least some
men attempting to follow His will.[58] This view necessarily means that more
suffering was to be found in the pre-Christian era than after the incarnation:
'I found that the days gone by were as fraught as the present, and all the more
horribly wretched as they were further from the salvation of True Religion.'[59]

Such an ideologically orientated interpretation of history carries its
own dangers. While it can be comforting and heartening to read that one is

50 7.17.5.
51 7.33.4 (see Orosius's earlier special pleading for Trajan at 7.12.4).
52 7.29.5, 7.32.5, and 7.33.17.
53 7.28.27–30.
54 7.33.8.
55 7.34.7 and 7.35.15–22.
56 7.42.15.
57 7.35.12 and 7.36.13.
58 2.3.7.
59 1 *Preface* 14.

part of an inevitably triumphant process, it can also be troubling when the historical record fails to meet such expectations. One obvious strategy here for an historian is to avoid any mention of such awkward data, but while Orosius is guilty of this from time to time – the most striking example being his silence over the massacre at Salonica ordered by his hero Theodosius in 390 – normally he is honest enough to record events in the Christian period which do not seem to fit into his plan and express himself to be perplexed. This is how he deals with Constantine's execution of his sons.[60] In the end, Orosius accepts that God moves in mysterious ways and that sometimes His decisions cannot be understood by mere men. Like Alexander Pope, he asks us to accept this problem with faith and believe that 'whatever is, is right'.[61]

The overall structure of the *Histories* shows the influence of Christian apocalyptic thought, though Orosius does not labour this overtly in the text. The seven books of the *Histories* reflect the seven days of creation in Genesis. They also have important implications for Orosius's eschatological beliefs. The final, seventh, millennium on various readings of the Bible is meant to usher in Christ's reign of one thousand years which would be followed by the last battle with Satan, the Final Judgment, and the recreation of Heaven and Earth.[62] This was already a matter of some controversy within the Christian church of Orosius's day. Some Christians looked forward to the coming of the seventh millennium as a cataclysmic event that would augur the end of time, a view normally characterised now as premillennarian. Others, most notably Augustine, were deeply worried by this literalist approach to the Bible and regarded the birth of Christ as heralding the start of the seventh millennium which would then continue with a mixture of good and evil until the Second Coming and Final Judgment, a viewpoint now normally referred to as amillennarian.[63] Orosius, however, seems closer to a third viewpoint, the postmillennarian, where the seventh millennium is again initiated by the birth of Christ, but what follows is a thousand-year reign of increasing peace and plenty as Christianity spreads across the world. The fact that the seventh book of the histories takes its starting point from the birth of Christ is highly suggestive in this respect. Orosius tells us that God has ordained Babylon

---

60 7.28.26.

61 7.43.18; cf. 7.41.10.

62 The seven days of Genesis give a timescale for completeness. This is then combined with Psalm 90.4 and 2 Peter 3.8 where we are assured that a thousand years is a day in the sight of God. The world, therefore, will last for seven millennia. The details of the seventh millennium and the end of the world are described in Revelation 20–21.

63 See *City of God*, 20.7–9.

to rule at the beginning of this world and Rome at its end. His seventh book therefore represents the seventh millennium that will last until the Second Coming.[64] Orosius certainly thought the number seven important; it is the 'number by which all things are judged' and had put an end to both the kingdoms of Macedon and Carthage.[65] Rome too was badly affected by this number, though we are told it escaped harm.[66] Unfortunately, Orosius assumes his readers know why seven is such a dangerous number and so never gives an explicit statement about this matter, but the general sense is that seven is the number of completeness and so marks the end of things.[67]

If this were all that could be found in Orosius's *Histories*, it could be regarded as a worthy but somewhat ineffective work. The symbolism of the seven books would carry no resonance with his non-Christian readers. Perception of divine intervention in the world was by no means unique to the Christian world, and while pagan critics would have had no quarrel with Orosius's methodology, they simply would have argued that it was misplaced. Sadly, Orosius's work has been all too often seen in this light, and much scholarship has been expended quarrying Orosius's sources out of the *Histories* while paying little regard to the work itself.

This is a great pity. Orosius writes well and uses the full repertoire of the rhetorical techniques available to late antique writers. *Recusatio* is deployed on occasions,[68] and Orosius has a particular love of contrast, chiasmus, and verbal puns. He has had a good classical education and the deployment of his learning shows that he is writing for those of a similar background. To understand the *Histories*, it is important to bear in mind that Orosius's career had been that of an ecclesiastical polemicist. His work is not a mere list or chronicle, but a work of polemical history with a specific target – the pagan intellectuals of the day and their argument that Christianity had ruined Rome[69] – and it is designed to face down his opponents in the most effective way possible.

---

64 2.3.5.

65 7.2.9; cf. 4.23.6.

66 7.2.10.

67 This sentiment lies at the back of the 'seven ages of man'. This is found in the Hippocratic work, 'On the Number Seven', for which see Roscher (1913). It is likely to be Orosius's source, as the work was known to the early Church Fathers, see Ambrose, *Letters*, 44. The notion is also found in Ptolemy's *Tetrabiblios*, 4.10, and in early Jewish thought, see Philo, *On the Maker of the World* (*De Mundi Opificio*) 30.89–43.128. It is most famously found in Shakespeare's *As You Like It*, Act II scene vii. For numerology in antiquity in general, see Barry (1999).

68 1.12.3 and 5.1.9.

69 1 *Preface* 9.

When writing to Jerome, Augustine describes Orosius as 'keen-spirited, swift to speak, and full of zeal' and of his wish to become a 'useful vessel... for the refutation of heresies...' The picture thus drawn is one of a highly combative individual. This is born out by Orosius's own self-characterisation as a 'hound of the Lord' found in the *Preface* to the *Histories*.[70] In general, Orosius's instinct when confronted with pagan opposition to his faith was not to conciliate, but to attack. Given his contemporary situation, the most important issue facing him was the sack of Rome at the hands of the Goths and the role that Christianity was perceived as having played in this disaster. The sack certainly had been a shock for the Church and made the early fifth century seem a much darker and more despondent place to most Christians. Jerome was horrified; 'what can be safe if Rome has fallen?' he asks, and elsewhere bewails that, 'the whole world has perished with this single city'.[71] Augustine was to deal with the problem by insisting on the distinction between the earthly and heavenly cities and placing priority on the latter. Orosius, though, was to take a very different tack.

Far from lamenting the sack of Rome, as did his contemporaries, Orosius's solution was to confront the problem it posed for the Faith head on, by denying that there was a problem at all. He makes the bold claim that the sack was of no significance, and goes on to stand on its head the standard pagan view that it had come about because of Rome's neglect of her traditional gods by insisting that its occurrence was, in fact, due to the presence of pagans, not Christians, in the city.[72] The centrepiece of his tactics was to contrast the sack of Rome in AD 410 by the Goths with that of the Gauls in 390 BC. Orosius presents the latter as an unmitigated disaster, compared to which the former is so trivial that it is hardly worth mentioning at all, and in fact brought positive benefits by cleansing Rome of pagan iconography.[73] For Orosius the key difference between the two events is Christianity. The sack of 390 BC was a sack of a pagan city carried out by pagans, but the sack of AD 410 was God's justified chastisement of a partially Christian city performed by Christians (Orosius here carefully forgets that the Christians concerned, Alaric's Goths, were Arians – a heresy upon which earlier

70 Less charitably Kelly (1975) 317–18 describes Orosius as a 'talented, opinionated, narrowly-orthodox, impetuous young man' and 'aggressive and tactless'. This is hard, but probably fair.

71 Jerome, *Letter* 123, see also *Letter* 127; *Commentary on Ezekiel* (*Commentaria in Ezekiel*), prologue.

72 7.37.8 and 7.38.7.

73 2.19.13–15.

in his narrative he has heaped much abuse) and mitigated by the presence of Christians in the city.[74] Other disasters, including natural disasters, are given the same treatment, and again it is Christianity which is presented as the key mitigating factor. An earthquake at Constantinople is avoided by the prayers of the Christian emperor Arcadius, in contrast to the disasters that happened in pagan times at Ebora and Helice,[75] and when Orosius records that a disastrous plague of locusts struck Africa in 125 BC, and he goes on to note that while such plagues still occur in his day, they are now bearable.[76]

4. SECULAR RELIGIOUS HISTORY

The use, or lack of use, of the Bible in the *Histories* also shows the care taken to maximise the impact of the work. Given his career as a controversialist, Orosius had a good working knowledge of the Bible: the *Commonitorium* and *Liber Apologeticus* both contain extensive biblical quotations, and Orosius's stay with Augustine shows that he was intensely interested in biblical exegesis. But Orosius also realised that pagans were unlikely to be impressed by an extended use of Scripture and so knew that if he was to defeat his opponents, he would have to fight on ground that they would accept contained the truth. His technique therefore is to let secular history justify the ways of God to men and show how this fits the Christian message rather than vice versa.[77] An example of this approach is the 'rain miracle' that occurred during Marcus Aurelius's German campaigns. Orosius here uses an unimpeachably pagan source, the letters of the emperor himself, to assert that it was the prayers of the Christians in his army that brought this miracle about and then retrojects the notion of God's protection of the Romans back to the rainstorm that deterred Hannibal from marching on Rome.[78] Similarly, when Orosius synchronises the birth of Christ with the accession of Augustus, it is the miracles attending the latter that he draws on to make the point that this is more than coincidence.[79] While, therefore,

74 2.3.7.

75 3.3.1–2.

76 5.11.

77 The work only contains one extended allegorical passage – the application of the ten plagues of Egypt to Roman history, 7.27.

78 Marcus Aurelius, 7.15.11. For a detailed discussion of Marcus Aurelius's letter, see Kovács (2009) 113–21; for Hannibal, see 4.17.8–9; cf. 5.15.15.

79 6.20; see also Augustus's refusal to be called 'master' at 6.22.4–5.

some biblical quotations are found in the *Histories*, they are far fewer than may have been expected, and in the first book Orosius deliberately emphasises that he will not rely on the authority of the Bible to make his points.[80] One exception to this is the account given of the Exodus from Egypt, but this is done only after an attack on the accuracy of Tacitus and an assertion that pagan historians accept Moses as a good practitioner of their art, which allows the Bible to be presented as a work of history rather than one of religious dogma. This secular approach is also seen in Orosius's use of Jerome. Jerome's Latin version of Eusebius's *Chronicle* contains a large number of notes concerning ecclesiastical history. Orosius, while drawing on the secular notes heavily, scrupulously avoids ecclesiastical material, the use of which would defeat his purpose.

While Jerome's Christian *Chronicle* forms the spine of Orosius's work, the vast bulk of his sources are pagan. This poses a problem for Orosius, but it is one that he turns to his advantage. This is done in two ways. As we have seen, Orosius mines his sources for arguments that his opponents will find hard to gainsay, precisely because they are drawn from pagan writers. But Orosius is also happy to attack such authors. On several occasions, he claims that his researches show his pagan predecessors to be unreliable. The inaccuracy that he detects is normally a failure to agree on figures, and he finds it particularly worrying when this happens for events that were contemporary with the historians concerned.[81] The most innocent reasons he suggests for such errors relate to simple human failings such as a wish to flatter patrons, leading to a tendency to exaggerate success and downplay failure; but at times, particularly with Tacitus, more sinister accusations of deliberately distorting the past are raised.[82] Given that Orosius himself is none too careful with the finer details of his own work, this is hardly a justified approach, but raising doubts about previous historical accounts lies at the heart of all revisionist history. Orosius wishes to undermine the credibility of earlier works in his reader's mind in order to create the impression that there had been no reliable account of pagan history produced by pagans themselves, so leaving his new Christianised account of the past as the most authentic record available.

---

80 1.1.8.
81 See 4.5.10–11, 4.20.6–9, 5.3.3–4 (where Orosius manages to turn one historian into two), and 6.1.30.
82 1.10.5.

5. SOURCES

The sources Orosius used were probably not great in number, though a specious lustre of wide reading comes from his secondary use of the fragments of authors found in the notes of Jerome's *Chronicle*. His main source for Greek history is Justin's epitome of Pompeius Trogus's *Philippic History*.[83] Justin composed his epitome in the second or third century AD, while Trogus's original work dates from the end of the first century BC. Livy, often at second hand via epitomes, the second-century historian Florus, and late fourth-century writer Eutropius form the main base of Orosius's passages concerning the Roman Republic. In the Imperial period, Eutropius's work becomes more prominent along with the now lost fourth-century 'History of the Emperors' or *Kaisergeschichte*.[84] Orosius also shows knowledge of Caesar, Sallust, Tacitus, and Suetonius. His approach to these sources was by no means naive. While at times he takes material verbatim or with very minor alterations, they are more often approached with a careful eye for selectivity. Instances of failed prophecy are seized upon as demonstrations of the folly of pagan religion,[85] while pagan prophecies that seemingly come true are suppressed,[86] as are accounts of successful pagan divine intervention.[87] At times more open manipulation occurs. Leonidas's speech to the 300 Spartans at Thermopylae is carefully edited to give it a sense quite different to the original found in Justin.[88] Similarly, the sack of the Phoceans' temples is portrayed as evidence of the impotence of the pagan gods, but Orosius's source, Justin, presents it as divinely inspired punishment for the Phoceans' earlier blasphemy.[89] Later Orosius tells us that the consul Gurges was defeated after the 'snake of Aesculapius' was brought to Rome, leaving the reader to infer that there is a causal link between

---

83 For a discussion of this work see Yardley and Heckel (1997) and Yardley (2003).

84 The existence of the *Kaisergeschicte* was postulated by Enmann (1883). For modern discussions, see Barnes (1970) and Burgess (1995).

85 e.g. 3.22.3 and 4.13.14.

86 e.g. 4.10.3, where the sacred chickens rightly predict the Roman defeat at the battle of Drepanum.

87 For example, at 2.10, Orosius suppresses Justin's comments that before Salamis Xerxes had sacked Delphi and hence was waging war on the gods as well as the Greeks, as he has no wish to imply that pagan gods could have been a factor in the Greeks' victory at Salamis. He also suppresses the Delphic oracle's comments about the wooden walls of Athens being her salvation.

88 2.9.6.

89 3.12.17; cf. the destruction of the Temple of Vesta at 4.11.9.

the two events. In Livy, however, who is Orosius's source, the two events occur in the opposite order.[90] Pagan sources are used to discredit the oracle of Ammon, and Mithridates' final speech is also recruited to the cause of refuting paganism by a careful misinterpretation of its actual sense.[91] This studied editing of the pagan past is intended to leave the reader feeling that Christianity's critics are refuted by the very authors they would claim as their own.

6. STRUCTURE

The shape of the *Histories* as a whole is also informed by a careful polemical strategy. Orosius begins his work with a description of the world, probably taken from a map.[92] This does describe the known world at the time and its ostensible purpose is to give a geographical context for the rest of the *Histories*.[93] However, no further use is made of it, nor does it describe all the areas later found in the body of the work. It can be seen as establishing Orosius's universalist credentials but, beyond this, it is redundant.[94] It may not even serve that purpose, but merely be a product of Orosius following the historiographical conventions of his day:[95] the full title of Trogus's work is *The Philippic History and the origins of the world and description of the earth*[96] and it may be that this title provided a model for Orosius.

After the curious *geography*, the work continues with the history of the Near East and moves onto the classical Greek period and the Hellenistic kingdoms, but the predominant focus, and main subject, of the book is the history of Rome, 'the head of the world', which Orosius regards as

---

90 3.22.5–6; Livy, *Per.* 11.

91 3.16.13 and 6.14.11–17.

92 See Miller (1896) 4–5.

93 The geography was to become a source for, *inter alia,* the early eleventh-century 'Cotton Map' and the late thirteenth-century medieval *mappa mundi* of Hereford Cathedral which has the inscription 'Orosius's description of the *ornesta* of the world which is shown within'; see Harvey (1996) app. 1. For its impact on medieval geography in general, see Paget (1902) and Moore (1903).

94 For a contrary view, see Merrills (2005). Corsini (1968) 85 speaks of Orosius's universalism in time and space, but a reader will soon notice that this universalism is more apparent than real in the *Histories*.

95 See Cicero, *On the Orator* (*De Oratore*), 2.62–64. The phenomenon of the redundant geography is all too frequently found in modern works of history.

96 *Historia Philippica et totius mundi origines et terrae situs.*

particularly important.[97] While, at first sight, this seems to be a descent into parochialism, albeit an understandable one, as Orosius's readers were subjects of the Roman Empire, Orosius's interpretation of history is more subtle than this. His strategy is to persuade his reader that Rome's history is from the beginning a Christian history and so it is paganism, not Christianity, that is alien and damaging to Rome. To begin this argument, Orosius suggests that just as there is one God in heaven, so there should necessarily be one dominant power on earth – conveniently this turns out to be Rome – and men should have the humility to submit to this power as it is the only way that peace will come about.[98] It is therefore God's design to unite all peoples together under one empire to enable Christianity to spread more rapidly, and his chosen instrument for doing so is the Roman Empire. The history of Rome, then, precisely is universal history and Rome's empire is, unlike those that preceded it, one that has divine sanction.[99] Orosius's Romanisation of the Christian faith is also a clever counter-attack against his opponents who wished, particularly after the sack of Rome, to portray Christianity as alien to Rome. Roman history for Orosius is both universal history and Christian history; the three are inseparable from one another: as he says at the beginning of Book 5, everywhere he goes, he will 'encounter my country, religion, and laws'.[100]

The centrality of Rome in salvation history is therefore a key theme for Orosius and one that reflects his western origins and audience. While intensely proud of his Spanish origins, his pride is in not just in Spain herself, but also in her contribution to the empire at large.[101] He is happy to style himself as a 'Roman and Christian'[102] and to refer to Rome as 'our country'.[103] In short, he agrees with his contemporary Rutilius Namatianus that Rome had 'made a single fatherland from far-flung nations'.[104] As Christianity was historically a religion of the east, its focus on the east and

97 1.12.3 and 2.12.2. At 2.12.1, Orosius says he has no intention of just concentrating on Rome, but this claim to universalism is belied by what follows and the following section shows where his true priorities lie.

98 6.17.9; cf the hostility to the Gauls' resistance to Rome at 6.22.2–7.

99 2.1.2–5 and 6.1.5–8.

100 5.2.1.

101 5.23.16.

102 5.2.6.

103 5.19.22. Orosius would have been quite shocked to read Menéndez Pidal's (1940) xxxvi–xxxvii comments that 'he was the first openly to question the foundations of the Roman state and feel that his homeland was something opposed to it'.

104 About His Return (De Reditu Suo), 63.

its claims made for people there may well have struck much of Orosius's target audience as at best tedious and at worst absurd. By making Rome the clear focus of God's plans for the world, we can see a conscious plan on Orosius's part to adapt traditional Christian apologetics to fit a broader canvas, producing an account which would have seemed more credible and compelling to his Western readers.

7. CHRONOLOGICAL SYSTEMS AND THE ORDERING OF TIME

Given his wish to show that secular events prove the truth of Christianity, it is perhaps not surprising that Orosius uses the common chronological systems of his day rather than one centred on the incarnation. Such a system was not in fact available: the universal Christian chronology used today was devised some 100 years after Orosius's death by Dionysius Exiguus.[105] However, it is noticeable that Orosius chooses not to date events from the birth of Abraham, as does Eusebius/Jerome's *Chronicle*. Rather, prior to the foundation of Rome, Orosius dates events by Olympiads. He then uses, as was common in Roman historiography, the date of Rome's foundation as the starting point for his chronology.[106] Orosius dates the foundation of Rome to 752 years before the birth of Christ, a year which fell in the sixth Olympiad and 414 years after the fall of Troy.[107] The date of the foundation of Rome was subject to some dispute in antiquity. The commonest accepted date was that posited by the late republican scholar Varro – 754/3 BC. However, Orosius's date has official sanction in that it is that which was used by the *Capitoline Fasti*, the official list of Roman magistrates erected in the forum at Rome, and it may be for this reason that he chose it, as it would once again link his account of the Roman past with the 'official' version of the day.

The chronological structuring of the *Histories*, as well as the method of enumerating years, also shows careful thought, but here Orosius is prepared, indeed determined, to use Christian concepts. Nevertheless, in keeping with his overall approach, the two schemes that he uses, while inspired by Christianity, are not presented to the reader in explicitly Christian terms. The first

---

105 See Declercq (2002).

106 Normally such dates are styled *AUC* (*Ab Urbe Condita*), 'from the foundation of the City'.

107 2.4.1; 6.22. Eusebius places Rome's foundation in the fourth year of the sixth Olympiad, 1264 years after the birth of Abraham.

is drawn from the Book of Daniel. Here, Nebuchadnezzar dreams of a statue composed of four different materials that are interpreted as four kingdoms that are to dominate the world in succession.[108] This prophecy, which had originally been a thinly veiled attack on the Hellenistic ruler Antiochus IV Epiphanes, had already been developed to become a standard part of Christian chronology and apologetics.[109] The four kingdoms represented by the statue were normally interpreted by Christian writers as the Babylonian, Medo-Persian, 'Greek', and Roman empires. Orosius accepted that the vision outlined the evolution of historical time, but produced a new interpretation of it, which was much more firmly focused on history as it would have been understood by inhabitants of the later Western Roman Empire. The Persian Empire is collapsed into the Babylonian, leaving Macedon as the second empire. The vacuum created in this way is filled by Rome's great rival, Carthage, as the third empire, leaving Rome as the fourth and final empire.[110] The end result of this revised chronology is the same as the original, but Orosius's new explanation of the vision would have seemed a far more credible version of historical development to his Roman readers than those offered by previous Christian interpretations, mired as they were in a narrow eastern perspective.[111] Orosius's approach to the vision in Daniel is a striking innovation which shows him not as a thoughtless chronicler, as he is too often caricatured, but as a man prepared to look at the basic material of his faith and adopt new approaches to it. Nor should we see this as a mere rhetorical strategy. Though it would have indubitably been useful as a debating tool, it is difficult not to believe that Orosius was entirely sincere in his interpretation. Sadly, this new framework for looking at the world's history is not then exploited to its full potential in the *Histories*, as Orosius's main concern in it simply lies in the way in which can be used to demonstrate that the Roman Empire is the culmination of God's plans on earth. In particular, he presents Rome as the anti-type of the first empire,

---

108 Daniel 2.31–45. For the notion of a succession of kingdoms or *translatio imperii*, in historical thought, see Trompf (1979) esp. 200–49.

109 Daniel's dramatic date is the sixth century BC, but it was in fact written between 167 and 146 BC, as had already been deduced by Porphyry in the third century AD – see Jerome, *Commentary on Daniel (Commentaria ad Daniel),* prologue. = CCSL 75a 617–18.

110 2.1.4–5 and the recapitulation at 7.2.

111 The discussion of the prophecy in Daniel has been the object of much labour, most of it futile, over the centuries. For an introduction to the main issues involved, see Rowley (1935). Oddly, Orosius's version was to fade from memory, leaving the Middle Eastern version as the dominant one in Christian thought; see, for example, the somewhat bizarre comments of the *NIV Study Bible* (London, Sydney, Auckland, Toronto, 1985), 1277 and 1281.

Babylon, which fell through its corruption and paganism, while in contrast Rome has been preserved through her Christian faith.[112]

Orosius's other chronological scheme, of which he makes much more use, is even more firmly centred on Roman history. This is another four-fold division of time:[113] the first division runs from the genesis of man to the reign of Ninus of Babylon, the second begins from Ninus (the point at which Jerome's *Chronicle* and Justin's *Epitome of Trogus* begin) and continues to the foundation of Rome, the third continues from the foundation of Rome to the accession of Augustus, and the fourth takes history down from Augustus's reign to Orosius's own day. These four divisions are treated very unevenly: the first and second are dealt with in Book 1, the third takes up Books 2 to 6, and the fourth is dealt with in the lengthy Book 7. These divisions in themselves show Orosius's desire to place Rome at the centre of history and also his wish to demonstrate the improvement that Christianity has made to the world. This has its beginning with the birth of Christ which is synchronised with the reign of Augustus, so it is natural that the catalogue of disasters, which mankind suffered in the pre-Christian period, the gravamen of Augustine's commission, forms the lion's share of the work.

The synchronisation of Christ and Augustus is a vital feature of Orosius's writing, as it serves to underline his message that Rome is the key part of God's plan for mankind. Christ, the 'prince of peace',[114] is born at the time when Augustus has established for the first time peace across the earth, something that Orosius emphasises is not mere coincidence, but a self-evident part of God's plan.[115] The *Pax Romana* therefore, for those who care to consider the facts fully, is a *Pax Divina*. The Romans in the *Histories* have in many ways supplanted the Jews, who occupy a remarkably small place in Orosius's thinking, as God's mechanism for bringing his plans for mankind to fruition.[116] Like the Jews of the Old Testament, they often lapse from their appointed task and are tried and found wanting, but they

112 2.3; 7.2.

113 This is initially a threefold scheme, see 1.1.5–6, but 1.21.20 implies the fourfold scheme as outlined here.

114 Isaiah 9.6.

115 6.20.4–8 and 6.22.9; cf. 5.1.12.

116 Orosius sees the Jews as once being the people of God, but as having alienated their status through rejecting the Christian message, 7.27.2, not to mention being responsible for the Crucifixion, 7.4.13. Rome, God's new instrument, brings down divine vengeance on them when Titus destroys their temple, 7.9.5–6. Strikingly, the Jews become one of the ten plagues of the Roman Empire, in Orosius's allegorical treatment of the ten plagues of Egypt, 7.27.

nevertheless remain God's chosen instrument. The sack of Rome, or rather, as Orosius would have it, Rome's delivery from a sack, in Book 7 of the *Histories*, takes on the colouring of the Jews' exodus from Egypt in Book 1. The culmination of this process is that Christ chooses to become incarnate as a Roman, thus giving divine sanction to, and Christianising, Rome and, perhaps equally significantly, the Imperial Roman state. This unique assertion that Christ was a Roman citizen is based on a false understanding of the nature of Roman citizenship in the early empire prior to Caracalla's grant of universal citizenship in AD 212. Nevertheless, it shows how Orosius has developed not the pessimistic thinking of his contemporaries, but rather the optimism of a previous generation of Christian writers, and sees the empire as almost the instantiation of heaven upon earth. This can be seen from Orosius's presentation of Rome as the anti-type of Babylon, the archetypal wicked empire of the Bible. The parallels between the two are emphasised, but so is the crucial dissimilarity that while Babylon fell, Rome still stands.[117]

Moreover, the message of the *Histories* is that Rome will continue to stand. Orosius's comments that King Athaulf initially wished to replace 'Romania' with 'Gothia', but then realised this would be impossible and so lent his support to the empire, are important evidence for this belief.[118] Orosius had a visceral dislike, probably based on personal experience, of barbarians and this dislike is occasionally found in his work,[119] but in his more reflective moments he sees the barbarians as Rome's future. The reason for this belief is that Christianity, whose purpose is to unite all peoples, has tamed them. Orosius strikingly declares that the sack of Rome was worthwhile because it led to the conversion of peoples who would otherwise have remained pagan.[120] This is not an assertion that Rome has no worth, but rather a demonstration of divine providence. Paradoxically, for Orosius the sack of Rome did not weaken, but strengthen, the city, as it led to the spread of Christianity and Christianity was to unite all peoples under Rome. Orosius notes that the Burgundians have been tamed by Christianity, continuing, 'they have recently all become Catholics, received priests

117 2.3.2–8.
118 7.43.5–7.
119 For a general dislike see 7.42.2. For specific instances, see the highly suggestive *grand guignol* description of the Scordisci at 5.23.18; the comment that the loss of his hero, Theodosius's, Gothic allies at the River Frigidus was a 'gain' for Rome, 7.35.19; and the description of the Vandals as a 'effete, greedy, treacherous, and sorrow-bringing race', 7.38.1.
120 7.41.8.

from us whom they obey, and live peacefully, calmly, and causing no harm, looking on the Gauls not as their subjects, but as their Christian brothers'.[121] The most important feature of this passage is that the Burgundians' priests have been sent to them from the Roman Empire. Orosius takes the view that a people's coming under the aegis of the Church will naturally entail falling under the influence of Rome. Here we see Orosius's postmillennarian hopes come to the fore: the seventh millennium is already here and it will be one of increasing peace as Christianity spreads across the world, civilising barbarians and bringing them into Rome's orbit.

8. NOTES OF CAUTION

Despite this approving attitude towards Rome, Orosius, informed by his opposition to Pelagianism, is nevertheless at pains to emphasise that the city has achieved nothing worthwhile by herself and that none of her success or destiny is a product of her own doing. Rather it is only Divine Grace that has made the Roman Empire a success, and this has been done often in spite of the Romans, not because of them.[122] At times Orosius can be particularly savage towards Roman failings. It is no coincidence that the sharpest of these attacks comes when he compares the perfidious nature of Rome to the pristine virtues of his provincial compatriots at Numantia.[123] For Orosius this dependence on Divine Grace is true even of the present where it is the faith of Honorius, and indeed that of his enemies, the Goths, not Roman arms that render the sack of Rome in AD 410 harmless.[124]

Famously Orosius combines this lesson with another Christian doctrine, that of the horror of war. Military glory had traditionally been the centre of Roman pride. Orosius disparages this in two ways: first, by emphasising the number of defeats that Rome has suffered but, more notably, by also underlining the tragedy of war.[125] In particular, his descriptions of battles lay stress not on the fame won in them, but on the numbers who died. This emphasis on the suffering of war is a striking contrast to the mainstream of Roman historiography and Torres Rodríguez is right to characterise it as a

---

121 7.32.13.
122 1.16.
123 5.5.
124 2.3.7.
125 3 *Preface* 1

'genuine revolution' in the writing of history.[126] In the same vein, Orosius also underscores that Rome's glory is built on the sufferings of others and that, if in the future Rome is defeated, those who defeat her will be seen not as barbarians, but as great leaders in their turn.[127] These sentiments have led to him being seen as a kind of 'left-wing heretic'.[128] But this is to misunderstand Orosius, who is a highly conservative writer and who, while emphasising the horrors of war, also worries about the enervating effects of peace and comes close to enunciating the traditional conservative Roman argument that war abroad produces moral rectitude and unity at home.[129] His other opinions follow in the same mould: he is in no way disturbed by slavery, and takes an orthodox aristocratic position on the major events of Roman history, being, for example, violently opposed to the Gracchi.

9. OROSIUS'S CLASH WITH AUGUSTINE

Is Orosius therefore guilty of precisely what Augustine warned against – believing it possible to create the City of God in this world and seeing Rome as heaven on earth? This is not an entirely fair accusation. Parts of Orosius's vision of the future are by no means happy: he believes, for example, that a final apocalyptic persecution that will usher in the end of the world lies ahead[130] and, as a good Christian, he does on occasions emphasise the triviality of the earthly life compared to the life to come.[131] Nevertheless, the general tone of Orosius's work does come perilously close to the positions that gave Augustine concern. If not heaven on earth, his postmillennarian views mean that Christian Rome will certainly bring heaven closer to earth as the last millennium progresses.[132] For a moment in Book 2 it appears that he may subscribe to the cyclical theory of history and that Rome will, in her turn, succumb to the passing of time.[133] But it is only a moment. We are

126 Torres Rodríguez (1985) 65, though he goes too far in seeing Orosius as presenting history generally from the point of view of the 'masses'. Orosius's views on most issues, such as slavery, are those of an aristocrat.

127 5.1.4 and 3.20.12.

128 Lacroix (1965).

129 1.16.8, 3.2.1, 3.6.1, 3.8.4, 4.16.21, and 5.8.2.

130 7.27.15.

131 5.2.6 and 7.41.9.

132 For a general discussion of this danger of 'immanentising the eschaton' of Christianity, see E. Voeglin (1952; 1968).

133 2.6.13–14.

also told that God has ordained the Roman Empire for the end of this epoch and so it seems clear that for Orosius the empire will only end when time itself comes to an end at the end of days.[134] Orosius's self-characterisation as a 'Christian and a Roman' is correct; his work is not merely Christian polemic, it is patriotic Christian polemic. This would have appealed to the Roman gentlemen who were his intended audience, but also reflects his own views on the world. Such an outlook may well be the reason for Augustine's later silence about Orosius's work, apart from one oblique attack on it.[135] For Augustine, a millennarian turned amillennarian, the lesson of the sack of Rome is that it has demonstrated the inherent fragility of all human affairs and the folly of thinking that the City of God could be constructed on earth.[136] The relationship between the two men is opaque, but it seems unfair to characterise Orosius as Augustine's 'henchman' who 'didn't understand a tithe of what he said to him'.[137] While Orosius does at times defer to Augustine in the *Histories*,[138] he is equally not afraid to disagree with him.[139] It seems more likely that the young Spaniard did understand the old man he admired, but simply differed with him at a fundamental level about what the future held.

10. LEGACY

Time is not kind to historians who indulge in predicting the future and Orosius's dream of a Christian empire rejuvenated with barbarian blood was doomed to failure. Ironically, he is often now seen as of value for the history of his own day and of nugatory importance for the bulk of his historical work. But this is a modern view. Orosius's Christian interpretation of the classical past, often oddly entitled the *ormesta* or *ormista*,[140] became a standard reference work on antiquity for the medieval world. Already by the end of the fifth century, he had become a Christian classic and his reputation was to

134 2.3.5.

135 At *City of God*, 18.52, Augustine, though mentioning no one by name, attacks the idea that the ten plagues of Egypt are an allegory for later history, an idea that is applied *in extenso* by Orosius at 7.27.

136 See in particular *City of God*, 15–18.

137 O'Donnell (2004).

138 4.20.25.

139 6.20.4; see Mommsen (1959).

140 An enigmatic term. It is probably an abbreviation for Or(osii) m(undi) (h)ist(ori)a. See Crone (1965) 448.

last into the early modern period.[141] More than two hundred manuscripts of Orosius survive and the work was translated into many European vernacular languages including Old English[142] and into Arabic at the court of the Caliphs of Cordoba by Ḥafṣ al-Qūṭī and Qāsim ben Aṣbag, whence it passed into later Arabic historical thinking, most notably being used as a source by Ibn Khaldūn.[143] Orosius was a source for many later historians such as Jordanes (whose *History of the Goths* (*Getica*) begins with an explicit reference to Orosius and a close paraphrase of 1.2.1), Gregory of Tours, Gildas, Bede, and Alfonso X. The *Histories* also provided an important model for how one should go about writing chronicles – Orosius's influence in this respect can be seen in Ranulf Higden's *Polychronicon* and Otto of Freising's *History of the Two Cities* (*Historia de Duabus Civitabus*). He also appears as the 'pleader' found in the 10th Canto of Dante's *Paradiso* and as a strong influence in a popular twelfth-century redaction of the Alexander Romance.[144] His geographical excursus, which circulated independently of the main work,[145] also had a powerful lasting effect, providing not simply material for cartographers but also a model for later geographical writing such as the enormously popular *Image of the World* (*De Imagine Mundi*) of the early twelfth century.[146]

The early modern period saw a strong decline in Orosius's reputation that has not been arrested, and he has now become relegated to the backwaters of history. Hobsbawn remarked of him 'No historian today cares a rap what [he] wrote, [or] thinks [his] views worth a minute's consideration'.[147] Hobsbawn should have been more careful. As a Marxist he wrote with the assumption that history necessarily followed a preordained course just as much as Orosius did. Perhaps the spirit of the Spanish priest is not as dead as many would like to believe.

---

141 Pope Gelasius in AD 494 speaks of Orosius's *Histories* as an 'indispensable work', *Decree of Pope Gelasius and 70 Bishops on Apocryphal Scripture* (Gelasii Papae decretum cum septuaginta episcopis habitum de apocryphis scripturis) = PL 59 161. Nor were his words unheeded: his near-contemporary, the grammarian and mythographer Fulgentius, draws heavily on Orosius as a source for his *The Ages of the World and of Man* (*De Aetatibus Mundi et Hominis*); see Whitbread (1971).

142 Often attributed, but falsely, to Alfred the Great; see Liggins (1970) and Bateley (1970).

143 For manuscripts in general, see Bately and Ross (1961). For Alfred, see Bately (1980); for the Arabic edition of Orosius, the Kitāb Hurūšiyūš, see Penelas (2001) and Christys (2002) ch. 7.

144 The so-called J2 redaction of the translation of Leo of Naples.

145 See Riese (1878) 24–55.

146 See Doberentz (1880; 1881).

147 Hobsbawn (1955).

NOTE ON TRANSLATION

I have normally followed the Budé text established by Arnaud-Lindet, though I have occasionally rejected his readings in favour of those of the Teubner text of Zangemeister. The points of departure are signalled in the notes. Orosius has a great love of chiasmus, assonance, and alliteration that I have endeavoured to preserve as far as possible. Direct and near direct quotations in the text have been italicised, those from the Bible have been given in the Authorised Version translation, those from Virgil, where the sense allows, from Dryden's translation. For ease of reading, other italicisation has been kept to a minimum. The titles of ancient works have been spelled out in full; where a common English version of a title exists, it has been used, for example, Augustine's *City of God*, otherwise the Latin title has been retained.

SYNOPSIS

A brief synopsis of the Histories is given below.

Book One: History before Rome

Preface addressed to Augustine

1   Consensus of when history begins – King Ninus of Assyria
2   The geography of the world
3   The Flood
4   Ninus's conquests and those of his wife, Semiramis
5–6   Sodom; the fate of Sodom compared to that of Rome
7   The war of the Telchines against Argos; the flood in Achaea
8   Moses in Egypt
9   The flood in Greece: Deucalion
10   The 12 plagues of Egypt and the Exodus
11   The crimes of Danaus
12   Lament for the evils of these times
13   War between Athens and Crete; the Minotaur
14   Egypt's war against the Scythians.
15–16   The Amazons
17–18   The Trojan War
19   The fall of Sardanapulus of Assyria; the rise of the Medes
20   The Bull of Phalaris; the crimes of Aremulus, king of the Latins
21   War between the Athenians and Sparta; Sparta's war with the
        Messinians; conflict between Sparta and Athens, the Athenian
        Empire

Book Two: From the Foundation of Rome to the Gallic Sack

1–3   The theory of Four Kingdoms
4   The foundation of Rome
5   Brutus and the establishment of the Republic; Rome's early wars
6–7   Cyrus the Great's capture of Babylon and his death

Book Three: From the Peloponnesian War to the Death of Alexander the Great

Book Four: From the War against Pyrrhus to the Fall of Carthage

Book Five – From the Fall of Carthage to Spartacus's Rebellion

Book Six: From Mithridates to Augustus

Book Seven: The Imperial Period

BOOK ONE

PREFACE

1. I have obeyed your instructions, most blessed father Augustine, and hope that I have done so as competently as I did willingly. However, in either event I hardly feel the urge to explain whether I have done well or badly, **2.** for you have already done the work of assessing whether I could do what you wanted done, whereas I am satisfied with the evidence of obedience alone, provided I have been able to adorn it with will and effort. **3.** For as in the great house of a great squire, although there are many different kinds of animal that are useful to the household, the dogs' task is not the lowliest.[1] They alone have been given a nature which urges them on to carry out willingly the tasks for which they have been trained, and, through some innate disposition towards obedience, hold back, simply showing a disciplined tremor of expectation, until they are sent off with permission to act by a nod or a sign. **4.** They, indeed, have their own special desires, which excel those of the beasts as much as they approach those of rational creatures: namely to perceive, to love, and to serve. **5.** For perceiving the difference between their masters and strangers, they do not hate those they attack, but rather are full of zeal for those they love.[2] And in their love for their master and his house, they keep watch not because nature has endowed their bodies with this ability, but keep their guard through the conscientiousness of a love full of cares. **6.** Whence, in the mystic allegory found in the evangelists, the Canaanite woman did not blush to say that whelps eat the crumbs from beneath their masters' table and that the Lord did not disdain

---

1 This phrase echoes Virgil, *Georgics*, 3.404 'Nor is the care of the dogs your lowliest task'. Virgil's dogs guard the house and are used for hunting. Here Orosius sees the house as the Church and the squire as God, while he is one of the dogs that guard the Church and hunt down its pagan opponents.

2 Orosius sees the dogs as a metaphor for Christian apologists. His ability to live up to this ideal in the *Histories* is mixed.

to hear her.[3] **7.** The blessed Tobit, too, though he had an archangel as his guide, did not refuse a dog as a companion.[4]

8. Thus, bound by special love to that general love which you inspire, I willingly obeyed your will; for since my lowliness owes this act to the instruction that Your Paternity ordered and this work of mine, which returns from you to you, is entirely yours, my only contribution to it is that I did the work willingly.

9. You had instructed me to write against the arrogant wickedness of those who are strangers from the city of God and are called pagans, taking their name from crossroads and fields in the countryside, or otherwise gentiles because they know of the things of this world.[5] These men, as they do not look to the future and have either forgotten or are ignorant of the past, besmirch the present as a time particularly full of evils, far beyond those which are always with us, and do so for this reason alone: because Christ is believed in and God worshipped, while their idols are worshipped the less. **10.** You instructed me therefore to set out in a book, concisely and in order, all the troubles caused by wars, the ravages of disease, the sorrows caused by hunger, the terrible events brought about by earthquakes, the unexpected disasters caused by floods, the terror caused by volcanic eruptions, the savagery of lightning strikes and hailstorms, and the misery caused by parricide[6] and other such crimes, found in times gone by that I could discover in all the records of the histories and annals which are to be had at the present time. **11.** I thought it right that Your Reverence should not be bothered with this slight work while you were working hard to complete your eleventh book against these same pagans, the soaring rays of ten others of which having already swiftly shone across the whole world, as they

---

3 Matthew 15.27.

4 Tobit 5.16. The archangel is Raphael.

5 The use of pagan in this sense was a recent innovation in Christian rhetoric. Orosius here is distinguishing between the pagans of town and country, but also skilfully uses the classical preference for urban life here by contrasting the city of God with the countryside of the pagans. To the ancient mind countrymen were notoriously stubborn and slow-witted and so this contrast also fits with Orosius's claims about pagan blindness in failing to see the obvious truth of Christianity. For further discussion of 'pagan', see O'Donnell (1977).

6 Orosius draws a sharp difference between the killing of family members and of non-family members, regarding the former as a much worse sin. His word for this form of killing is parricide, which, despite its more narrow meaning in modern parlance, has been retained in the translation in order to preserve this distinction.

blazed forth from a watchtower of the church's bright light.[7] **12.** Moreover, your holy son, Julian of Carthage,[8] a servant of God, strongly urged me to carry out his request concerning this matter in a way that would equal his faith in asking me to do it. **13.** I gave myself over to the work and straight away found myself in confusion, for I had often thought that the disasters of our present times seemed to rage beyond what could have been expected. **14.** However, I found that the days gone by were as fraught as the present, and all the more horribly wretched as they were further from the salvation of True Religion. So through this scrutiny it became clear, and rightly so, that Death, greedy for blood, had reigned when there was no knowledge of Religion which keeps bloodshed at bay. For when Religion spreads forth its light, death is confounded; death is imprisoned, when Religion is strong; indeed, in the profoundest sense death will not exist when Religion alone reigns. **15.** An exception, of course, is in those final days at the end of the world when the Anti-Christ will appear and the Final Judgement is held. At that time, Christ the Lord has prophesied through His own words in the Holy Scriptures that there will come troubles the likes of which have never been seen before[9] **16.** and then in the unbearable torments of that time, it will be not in the way which happens now and has always occurred in the past, but, through a much clearer and more serious judgment that the saints will receive their approbation and the wicked their damnation.[10]

1

1. Almost all scholarly writers, both Greek and Latin-speaking, who have recorded in their words the deeds of Kings and peoples for posterity, have begun from the time of Ninus, the son of Belus, the king of the Assyrians.[11]

---

7 A reference to Augustine's *City of God*. Given that Orosius was greatly impressed by the lighthouse at Corunna, see 1.2.71 below, maybe this metaphor is of a lighthouse.

8 Nothing is known of Julian.

9 Matthew 24.21; Mark 13.19.

10 For the notion of retributive justice in Orosius, see Trompf (2000) 292–309.

11 This is of course untrue; however, it is true of one of Orosius's major sources, Justin. Augustine states that Belus was the first king of the Assyrians in his *City of God*, 12.11 and 18.2, though this had not been written at the time that the *Histories* were composed. Ninus may be the Nimrod of Genesis, but neither Orosius nor Augustine makes this identification explicitly. He probably should be identified with the historical King Tukultininurta I (1235–1198 BC) whose name means 'I trust in Ninurta'. Ninurta was the Assyrian god of war. 'Belus' is likely to be a euhemerisation or misunderstanding of 'Ba'al' or 'Lord', a common Semitic religious title for deities

2. Although through blind prejudice they want us to believe that there was no beginning to the world or creation of mankind,[12] they have nevertheless decreed that wars and reigns started at this point, **3.** as if prior to this the human race had lived like cattle and then at this time had woken up for the first time like they had been shaken and roused to a new state of wisdom. **4.** But I have decided to trace the beginning of men's misery from man's original sin, merely gathering together a few short examples. **5.** 3,184 years passed from Adam, the first man, to Ninus, the so-called 'Great', when Abraham was born.[13] These years are omitted by, or unknown to, all historians. **6.** There are then 2,015 years from Ninus, or from Abraham, to the time of Caesar Augustus: that is to the birth of Christ which took place in the 42nd year of Caesar's reign, when peace was made with Parthia, the gates of Janus were closed, and wars ceased all over the world.[14] During this time, every form of action and inaction was ground out either by men of affairs or those who wrote of them. **7.** This is why the matter in hand now demands that a few things be taken, albeit as briefly as possible, from those books which deal with the beginning of the world and which gained credibility in the past by predicting future events which subsequently came to pass. **8.** This is not because I want to insist on their authority to anyone, but because it would be worthwhile to draw attention to the common consensus which I share with everyone else.[15] **9.** First, we hold that if the world and man are ruled by a Divine Providence which is good and hence just, man, who by his fickle nature and through his freedom to choose is weak and insolent, must be guided lovingly, when he needs help, and must also justly be punished when he abuses his freedom to excess. **10.** Anyone who looks at himself, and through himself at mankind, will perceive that from mankind's beginnings this world rightly has been subjected to alternating good and bad times. **11.** Then, we are taught that sin and punishment for sin began in the

12 Orosius here is attacking the cyclical theory of history, albeit he appears to misunderstand it. Augustine, *City of God*, 12.10–11, provides a better Christian critique, though this would not have been available to Orosius when he wrote.

13 Orosius has taken this date from Jerome's *Chronicle*. Jerome in turn took his date from Eusebius. Jerome divides the total into 2,242 years from Adam to the flood and 942 years from the flood to the birth of Abraham (2016 BC) which he then uses as the prime point of dating in his *Chronicle*. In these notes Jerome's dates are expressed as *A Abr.* 'from Abraham'.

14 See 6.22.1, when Augustus closed the Gates of Janus for the third time. The birth of Christ heralds an outbreak of peace in the world, a theme close to Orosius's heart.

15 Orosius's 'books' are those of Old Testament. His tactic by asserting that there is a common consensus about the nature of the world is to demonstrate that the foundations of this consensus can only be rationally held by accepting the truths of Christianity.

time of the very first man.[16] Moreover, we see that even those who begin their accounts in the middle of history and make no mention of previous ages, talk of nothing but wars and calamities – **12.** for what else can wars be called, except disasters that affect one side or the other?[17] Now evils of this type, both those which happened then and those which still happen to some degree today,[18] are without doubt sins made manifest or hidden punishments for sin – **13.** so what should stop me from revealing the cause of the symptoms that other historians have described, or from revealing in a short account that previous ages, which, as we have shown, lasted far longer than our present times, endured sufferings similar to those of today? **14.** I shall, therefore, in as far as I am able to call events to mind, give an account of the quarrels of mankind from the foundation of the world to the foundation of the City, then move on down to the rule of Caesar and the birth of Christ from which time all the globe has remained in the City's power, and then continue down to our own days,[19] **15.** and in doing so will reveal, as if from a watchtower, the diverse parts of the world ablaze with evil after being fired with the torch of lust.[20] But before doing this, I think it is necessary **16.** to describe the globe where man dwells, first in the threefold scheme into which it was divided by our ancestors, and then by regions and provinces, **17.** so that those who are interested when they are told of disasters caused by war or plague somewhere, might learn more easily not just of the event and its date, but also its location.[21]

---

16 The notion that man has always suffered for his sins is a central theme of Orosius's outlook.

17 The suffering caused by war is another persistent theme of the *Histories*.

18 The largest of these is the sack of Rome in AD 410. The triviality of present suffering compared to that found in the past is a theme to which Orosius frequently returns.

19 Orosius's tripartite scheme is not carried out evenly. Book 1 deals with events down to the foundation of Rome; Books 2–6 deal with his second period; and Book 7, the third.

20 The image of the watchtower is perhaps a reference to Isaiah 21, but may equally be drawn from Orosius's own day.

21 cf. Cicero, *On the Orator (De Oratore)*, 2.62–64. Orosius's aim is a noble one, but he never refers back to his geography in the rest of the work.

2[22]

1. Our ancestors divided the whole world, surrounded as it is by the belt of the Ocean, into three rectangular blocks,[23] and called these three parts Asia, Europe, and Africa, although there are some who believe that there are two parts: namely Asia and Europe, including Africa in the latter part.[24] **2.** Asia is surrounded on three sides by the Ocean and extends across the entire East. **3.** To the West on her right she borders Europe, which begins at the North Pole, and to her left Africa, but by Egypt and Syria she is bounded by Our Sea, which is usually called the Great Sea.[25] **4.** Europe begins, as I have said, in the North from the river Tanaïs[26] at the point where the Riphaean mountains[27] facing the Sarmatian Ocean[28] give rise to the Tanaïs. **5.** The Tanaïs flows by the altars set up as boundaries by Alexander the Great in the lands of the Rhobascians[29] and feeds the Maeotid marshes[30] whose immense

22 For a detailed discussion of Orosius's geography, see Janvier (1982), Lozovsky (2000), and Merrills (2005). Orosius may have had access to the anonymous fourth-century *The Divisions of the World* (*Divisio Orbis Terrarum*), but is unlikely to have drawn on Ptolemy; see Merrills (2005) 90. Merrills argues that the geographical excursus is an important part of Orosius's overall project, but it is in fact not referred to in the rest of the work. Similarly he suggests that it is an attempt to escape from a 'Romanocentric' view of the world, yet again Orosius, unsurprisingly given that his target audience is educated Roman pagans, takes precisely such a Romanocentric view; see in particular 6.1.6, 6.17.4, and especially 7.2.16. Lozovsky more plausibly argues that the description serves the purpose of setting the scene for the contemplation of the scale of human suffering and the frailty of temporal power. Orosius carries over his principle of using secular evidence to prove his points into the geography by making no reference to Jerusalem or any of the other holy places of Christianity.

23 This division is found in Pliny, *Natural History*, 3.1, and Pomponius Mela, 1.1. According to Herodotus, 2.16, this tripartite scheme was devised by the early Ionian Greeks.

24 The opinion of Sallust, *The War against Jugurtha*, 17.3; Varro, *On the Latin Language* (*De Lingua Latina*), 5.4; and Lucan, *Pharsalia*, 9.411–13. Augustine (*City of God*, 16.17, which would not have been available to Orosius) inclined to the tripartite view.

25 i.e. the Mediterranean. Left and right are not useful geographical terms and we must assume that Orosius is describing a map, perhaps derived from Agrippa's map displayed in the *Porticus Vipsania* in Rome; see Merrills (2005) 70–73.

26 The Don.

27 The mythical mountains at the end of the world; beyond them were said to live the Hyperboreans. Ptolemy (*Geography*, 3.5.15, 22) places this range in Russia and makes it the watershed for rivers flowing to the Baltic and Black Sea.

28 The Arctic Ocean.

29 Orosius is simply wrong: these are the altars set up on the river Jaxartes (the Amu-Daria) by Alexander. The Rhobascians are the Borusci of Ptolemy, *Geography*, 3.5.

30 The Sea of Azov.

mouth pours its waters into the Euxine Sea[31] by the city of Theodosia.[32] **6.** Thence it flows as a long, narrow channel past the city of Constantinople until the sea, which we call Our Sea, absorbs its waters. **7.** The Ocean by Spain is Europe's Western boundary: more specifically where the Columns of Hercules are to be seen by the islands of Cadiz[33] and where the Ocean swell comes in through the straits of the Tyrrhenian Sea.[34] **8.** Africa begins at the borders of Egypt[35] and those of the city of Alexandria where the town of Parethonium[36] lies above the Great Sea, which washes all lands and shores in the middle of the world. **9.** From there it extends through the area, which the natives call Catabathmon,[37] not far from the camp of Alexander the Great and above Lake Chalearzum.[38] Thence it runs past the upper borders of the Avasitae[39] through the Ethiopian Desert to the Southern Ocean. **10.** The Western bounds of Africa are the same as those of Europe: namely the narrows of the Straits of Cadiz. **11.** However, its uttermost end is Mount Atlas and the so-called Blessed Isles.[40]

12. Now, as I have briefly outlined in general terms the threefold division of the globe, I shall take the trouble to list their regions too, as I promised to do.

13. Asia has in the centre of its Eastern flank the mouth of the River Ganges by the Eastern Ocean. To its left is the promontory of Caligdamana[41] to whose south-east lies the island of Taprobane[42] from which point the Ocean begins to be called the Indian Ocean. **14.** To its right is the promontory of Samara,[43] which belongs to Mount Imavus at the end of the Caucasus.[44] To the north-east of this promontory are the mouths of the river

31 Orosius appears to reserve the term 'Euxine Sea' for the western half of the Black Sea, and to refer to the eastern half as the 'Cimmerian Sea'.

32 Feodosia in the Crimea.

33 Now a peninsula, Cadiz formed two islands in antiquity.

34 The western basin of the Mediterranean Sea.

35 For Orosius, as for other ancient authors, Egypt is part of Asia.

36 Marsa-Labeit.

37 Called Catabathmus by Sallust, *The War against Jugurtha*, 17.4, and Pliny, *Natural History*, 5.5.32. Catabathmon merely means 'canyon'; see 1.2.88 below.

38 The Kattara Depression.

39 Probably Abyssinia.

40 The Canary Islands.

41 Probably the Caticardamma of Ptolemy, *Geography*, 7.1.16, normally identified with Cape Calimere on the Coromandel Coast of India.

42 Ceylon.

43 Perhaps Cape Negrais in Burma.

44 Here the Himalayas.

Ottorogorra[45] from which point the Ocean begins to be called the Chinese Ocean.

15. India lies in this region. Its western boundary is the River Indus, which runs into the Red Sea;[46] its northern boundary is the Caucasus,[47] the rest, as I have said, ends at the Eastern and Indian Oceans. **16.** There are 44 peoples here, apart from those on the Island of Taprobane, which has ten cities, and those on the remaining, and extremely numerous, inhabitable islands.[48]

17. From the river Indus in the east to the river Tigris in the west lie the following regions: Arachosia, Parthia, Assyria, Persia, and Media which are located in a rough, mountainous land. **18.** They have the Caucasus to their north; the Red Sea and Persian Gulf to their south; and through them flow the notable rivers the Hydaspes[49] and the Arbis.[50] 32 peoples live here. **19.** The area is commonly called Parthia, though the Holy Scriptures often call all of it Media.

20. Between the river Tigris and the river Euphrates lies Mesopotamia. It begins in the north between Mount Taurus and the Caucasus. **21.** To its south is Babylonia, then Chaldaea, and finally Blessed Arabia,[51] which extends to the east along a narrow spit of land between the Persian and Arabian Gulfs. **22.** 28 peoples live here. **23.** The land generally called Syria extends from the river Euphrates in the east to Our Sea in the west; and in the north from the city of Dacusa,[52] which lies on the boundaries of Cappadocia and Armenia not far from the spot where the Euphrates rises, as far as Egypt and the Arabian Gulf **24.** which runs southwards in a narrow furrow full of rocks and islands, and then from the Red Sea, i.e. the Ocean, it runs towards the west. Syria comprises the important provinces of Commagene, Phoenicia, and Palestine. Besides these, there are the twelve tribes of the Saracens and Nabateans.

---

45 Perhaps the Tarim, see Janvier (1982) 109–12. The name Ottorogorra is a corruption of the Hindu utopia, Uttarakuru.

46 The Indian Ocean.

47 Caucasus is the generic term used by Orosius for the mountain massif that marches down through Asia from the Black Sea.

48 Perhaps a reference to the islands of Indo-China.

49 The Jhelum.

50 This river is in Gedrosia.

51 Arabia Eudaemon, modern Aden and Yemen. Arabia was 'blessed' because it was the entrepôt for the Indian spice trade; see Miller (1969) chs 1 and 9.

52 See Pliny, *Natural History*, 5.20.84, 6.10.27. Dacusa is possibly the modern village of Pengau in Turkey.

25. Cappadocia is at the head of Syria and has Armenia on its east; Asia on its west; the plains of Themiscyria[53] and the Cimmerian Sea[54] on its north-east; and Mount Taurus to its south, under which lie Cilicia and Isauria, running as far down as the Cilician Gulf which looks over to the island of Cyprus.

26. The region of Asia, or more correctly, Asia Minor,[55] is surrounded by sea except on its eastern side which borders on Cappadocia and Syria. To its north is the Euxine Sea; to its west the Propontis and Hellespont; and to its south Our Sea. Here Mount Olympus is to be found.[56]

27. Lower Egypt has Syria and Palestine to its east; Libya to its west; Our Sea to its north; and to the south is the mountain called *The Ladder*,[57] Upper Egypt, and the river Nile **28.** which seems to rise in a place on the shore at the beginning of the Red Sea called the Trading Post of Mossylon.[58] Then it flows far to the west, creating an island called Meroë in the middle of its stream, and finally turns to the north. When it is swollen with the seasonal rains, it irrigates the plains of Egypt.[59] **29.** Some writers[60] say that it has its source not far from Mount Atlas, is straightaway swallowed up by the sands, **30.** and then, after a small intervening space, bursts forth again in a huge lake. Then, they say, that turning east, it flows through the Ethiopian desert towards the Ocean and after turning once more to its left, descends into Egypt. **31.** Now it is true that there is a great river of this kind which has such a birth and course, and which truly gives birth to all the wonders of the Nile.[61] The natives who live near its source call it the Dara, the remaining inhabitants, the Nuchul.[62] **32.** But this river flows into, and is absorbed by,

53 Terme on the Black Sea in Turkey. Themiscyra was traditionally founded by the Amazons. Given his later interest in this group, it is odd that Orosius is either unaware of this fact or suppresses it.

54 The eastern half of the Black Sea.

55 Orosius is the first attested author to use this term.

56 Not the famous mountain of Thessaly, but the Anadoli Dagh in Bithynia in Turkey.

57 The Greek *Climax*. No mountain of this name fits Orosius's location. Orosius has either misplaced the *Climax* of Ptolemy, *Geography*, 4.5.52, which lies in western Egypt, or perhaps is making a reference to the escarpment by the First Cataract.

58 Ras Antarah.

59 For a detailed discussion of the Nile, see Merrills (2005) 79–87.

60 e.g. Pliny, *Natural History*, 5.10.51, who accepted this view which derives from Juba II of Mauretania.

61 There is of course no such river. For a detailed discussion of the genesis of this theory, see Janvier (1982) 206–12.

62 Both these names appear to be native names for the Nile. Pomponius Mela, 3.96, comments that 'Nuchul' is a barbarian corruption of 'Nile'.

a huge lake in the land of the peoples called Libyo-Egyptians, not far from that other river which, as we have said, has its source on the shore of the Red Sea, **33.** unless, of course, it bursts out in an underground channel into the bed of the river which runs down from the east.

34. Upper Egypt extends far to the east. To its north is the Arabian Gulf and to its south the Ocean. It begins at the border of Lower Egypt in the west and ends at the Red Sea in the east. 24 peoples live there.

35. Now since we have described all the part of Asia, it remains to list the remaining part starting from its eastern end and ending in the north.

36. The Caucasus range first rises among the Colchians who live above the Cimmerian Sea, and among the Albanians who live by the Caspian Sea. As far as its uttermost east, it appears to be one range of mountains, but it has many names.[63] **37.** Moreover, there are many who think that the Caucasus is part of Mount Taurus because it is indeed held that Mount Parchoatras of Armenia,[64] which lies between Mount Taurus and the Caucasus, joins the two together. **38.** But the river Euphrates shows that this is not the case. It has its source at the foot of Mount Parchoatras and runs south, keeping the Caucasus to its left and cutting off Mount Taurus on its right. **39.** Now among the Colchians and Albanians where it has its gates,[65] the Caucasus is called Mount Caucasus. **40.** From the Caspian Gates to the Portals of Armenia, or as far as the source of the river Tigris between Armenia and Iberia, it is called the Acroceraunian range.[66] **41.** From the source of the Tigris as far as the city of Carrhae[67] among the Massagetae and Parthians, it is called Mount Ariobarzanes.[68] **42.** From the city of Carrhae to the town

63 This is the range that Pliny, *Natural History*, 5.27.9, identifies with the Taurus mountains and he uses the same names for its different sectors as Orosius does for the Caucasus. For a detailed discussion of the Caucasus, see Merrills (2005) 87–92.

64 Orosius has either misplaced this range, which is the Parachoathras of Strabo, 11.8.1, and the Choatras of Pliny, *Natural History*, 5.27.98, which lies far to the east and the Parachoathras of Ptolemy, *Geography*, 6.4, which lies between Media and Persia, or he is referring to a different location. Janvier (1982) 94 suggests Murat Nehri in Armenia.

65 Perhaps Pliny's 'Gates of the Caucasus', *Natural History*, 6.12.30. Its most likely location is the Dariel Pass in Georgia.

66 These are probably the hills running from the Koura valley in the Lebanon to that of the Euphrates.

67 If the Carrhae where Crassus was defeated is intended, Orosius has become muddled as this lies well to the west of the area he is describing here. Janvier (1982) 97–100 suggests that Orosius's Carrhae is one of the many settlements called Charax (meaning fortified place in Aramaic) and proposes Charax Cadusiorum, i.e. Kesker.

68 The name probably derives from the mythical Haraberezaite of the *Zend Avesta*. It is probably part of the Elburz range in Northern Iran.

of Cathippus[69] among the Hyrcanians and Bactrians, it is called Mount
Memarmali.[70] Here *amomum*[71] is to be found. The nearest part of the range
to this place is called Mount Parthau.[72] **43.** From the town of Cathippus to
the village of Safris[73] among the Dahae,[74] Sacaraucae,[75] and Parthyenae, it
is called Mount Oscobares,[76] which is where the river Ganges rises[77] and
laser[78] is found. **44.** From the source of the River Ganges to those of the
river Ottorogorra which lie to the north and to where the mountain-dwelling
Paropanisades live, it is called Mount Taurus.[79] **45.** From the sources of the
river Ottorogorra as far as the city of Ottorogorra[80] among the Huns, Scythians, and Gandaridae,[81] it is called the Caucasus. **46.** Finally, among the
Eoae and Passyadrae where the river Chrysorhoas and the promontory of
Samara reach the Eastern Ocean, it is called Mount Imavus.[82]

   47. Between Mount Imavus, i.e. from the depths of the Caucasus, and

69 The *Peutinger Table*, 13.3, has a Catippa in this area. Janvier (1982) 101 proposes that
Cathippus could be the capital of the Hycanians, the Zadracarta of Arrian, *Anabasis*, 3.23.6, in
the Gorgan basin to the south of the Caspian Sea.

70 This is probably another section of the Elburz range.

71 Probably Cardamom. According to Pliny, *Natural History*, 37.78.204, Amomum was the
most expensive product to be derived from shrubs. See also Pliny, *Natural History*, 12.28.48,
and Virgil, *Eclogues*, 3.89, 4.25.

72 Probably to be identified with Isidore of Charax's Parthaunisa (*Parthian Stations*, 12)
and hence the Djaghataï/Kûhhâ-ye-Joghatay range in north-east Iran. See Janvier (1982) 104.

73 Possibly Isidore of Charax's Saphi (*Parthian Stations*, 12) and the Sapham of the
Peutinger Table, 12.3, and hence, perhaps, Shoffri. See Janvier (1982) 101–02.

74 The Däae of Strabo, 11.8.2, a Turkic tribe centred in what is now southern Kazakhstan.

75 The Sagaraucae of Strabo, 11.8.1, a nomadic Turkic tribe whom Strabo says were one of
the tribes which conquered Greek Bactria and originated from the far side of the Jhelum river.
See also Ptolemy, *Geography*, 6.14.4.

76 Probably the Khorassan range in north-east Iran.

77 This is not the case. The Ganges rises some 1,250 miles further east. This error is
perhaps based on Orosius believing that the Sassanid Empire extended as far as the Ganges.
See Ammianus Marcellinus, 23.6.13, for this view.

78 Asafoetida.

79 The Paropanisus of Mela and Ptolemy, namely the mountains of western Afghanistan
from Herat to Koh-i-Baba.

80 Perhaps near Khotan.

81 The region of Gandara lies around Peshawar and Rawalpindi in north-west Pakistan.

82 None of these toponyms is easy to locate. The Eoae may be a tribe of Burma, though
they have also been placed in Tibet. The Passyadrae may have lived in the Ganges valley, but
Assam has been proposed as an alternative. There are several rivers called Chrysorhoas in our
ancient sources, but none in this area. We cannot rule out simple confusion on Orosius's part,
but an alternative would be that he intends the Chrysoanas, see Ptolemy, *Geography*, 7.2.5,
which may be the Irrawaddy in Burma. For a detailed discussion, see Janvier (1982) 113–14.

the right-hand part of the east, where the Chinese Ocean lies, as far as the promontory of Boreum and the river Boreum,[83] and from there up to the Scythian Sea in the north as far as the Caspian Sea in the west and the extended Caucasus range in the south, live 42 Hyrcanian and Scythian tribes. These peoples wander far and wide because of the infertility of the soil. **48.** The Caspian Sea rises on the north-eastern shore of the Ocean and its shores on either side by the Ocean, and the places nearby are deserted and uncultivated.[84] Thence it extends south in a long, narrow channel until, spreading out into a wide expanse, it comes to an end at the foot of the Caucasus. **49.** 34 peoples live in the lands which are bounded by the Caspian Sea on the east and run along the shore of the Northern Ocean to the river Tanaïs and the Maeotid marshes to the west, extending along the shore of the Cimmerian Sea in the south-west to the summit and gates of the Caucasus in the south. **50.** The nearer region is commonly called Albania and the further region, lying beneath the Caspian Sea and mountains, the land of the Amazons.

51. The dimensions of Asia have therefore been briefly outlined. I shall now wander with my pen through what man knows of Europe. **52.** Europe begins in the east at the Riphaean mountains, the river Tanaïs, and the Maeotid marshes. Its border runs along the shore of the Northern Ocean to Gallia Belgica and the river Rhine in the west. It then comes down to the Danube, which is also called the Hister. This river runs from the south towards the east and ends in the Euxine Sea. **53.** On its east is Alania, in its centre Dacia, where Gothia is also found, then comes Germany, the greater part of which is held by the Sueves. In total, 54 peoples live here.

54. Now I shall set out the area that the Danube cuts off from barbarian lands down as far as Our Sea.

55. Moesia has the mouth of the river Danube to its east; Thrace to its south-east; Macedonia to its south; Dalmatia to its south-west; Istria to its west; Pannonia to its north-west; and the Danube to its north.

56. Thrace has the Propontic Gulf and the city of Constantinople, which was previously called Byzantium, to its east; part of Dalmatia and the gulf of the Euxine Sea to its north; Macedonia to the west and south-west; and the Aegean Sea to the south.

57. Macedonia has the Aegean Sea to the east; Thrace to the north-

---

83 Perhaps the river Ili in Kazakhstan.
84 Orosius thinks of the Caspian Sea as an ocean gulf.

east; Euboea and the Macedonian Gulf to the south-east; Achaea to the south; to its west are the Acroceraunian mountains lying by the straits of the Adriatic Gulf – these hills lie opposite Apulia and Brundisium;[85] to its west is Dalmatia; to its north-west, Dardania; to its north, Moesia.

58. Achaea is surrounded by the sea on almost all sides. For to its east is the Myrtoan Sea; to its south-east, the Cretan Sea; to its south, the Ionian Sea; to its south-west and west, the islands of Cephalenia and Cassiopa; to its north is the Corinthian Gulf; and to its north-east, a narrow ridge of land by which it is joined to Macedonia, or rather to Attica. This place is called the Isthmus. Corinth is found here which has Attica, and, at no great distance, the city of Athens, to its north.

59. Dalmatia has Macedonia to the east; Dardania to the north-east; Moesia to the north; Istria, the Liburnian Gulf and Liburnian Islands to the west; and the Adriatic Gulf to the south.

60. Pannonia, Noricum, and Raetia have Moesia to the east; Istria to the south; the Pennine Alps[86] to the south-west; Gallia Belgica to the west; the source of the Danube and the frontier which divides Germany from Gaul between the Danube and Gaul to the north-west; and the Danube and Germany to the north.

61. The land of Italy runs from the north-west to the south-east. To its south-west is the Tyrrhenian Sea and to its north-east, the Adriatic Gulf. The part that joins continental Europe is blocked off by the barrier of the Alps **62.** which rises up by the Gallic Sea on the Ligurian Gulf, cutting off first the territory of the Narbonenses,[87] then Gaul and Raetia, and finally comes down by the Liburnian Gulf.

63. Gallia Belgica has Germany and the river Rhine as its eastern boundary; to the south-east are the Pennine Alps; to the south, the province of Narbonensis; to the west, the province of Lugdunensis; to the north-west, the British Ocean; and to the north, the island of Britain.

64. Gallia Lugdunensis curves in a long, narrow stretch of land, half-surrounding the province of Aquitania. **65.** On its east, it has Belgica; and on its south, part of the province of Narbonensis, where the city of Arles lies and the river Rhône enters the Gallic Sea.

---

85 The range lies in Albania and was a notorious hazard for shipping. See Horace, *Odes*, 1.3.20; Lucan, *Pharsalia*, 5.653; and Silius Italicus, *Punica*, 8.632.

86 The Pennine Alps are a western part of the Alpine range containing the Great St Bernard Pass.

87 Gallia Narbonensis approximated to Provence. Oddly, Orosius here treats it as separate from Gaul, though he then almost immediately includes it as part of Gaul.

66. The province of Narbonensis, which is part of the Gauls, has the Cottian Alps to the east;[88] Spain to the west; Aquitania to the north-west; Lugdunensis to the north; and to the south, the Gallic Sea between Sardinia and the Balearic Islands. Facing it, where the Rhône enters the sea, are the Stoechadae Islands.[89]

67. The province of Aquitania is drawn round in a curve by the flow of the river Loire, which for the most part forms its boundary. **68.** On its north-west, it has the part of the Ocean called the Aquitanian Gulf; on its west are the Spains; to the north and east, Lugdunensis; to the south-east and south it borders the province of Narbonensis. **69.** Spain in its entirety is triangular and is almost an island, being surrounded by the Ocean and Tyrrhenian Sea. **70.** Its first angle, which looks to the east, joins onto the border of Narbonensis, being flanked by the province of Aquitania on the right and the Balearic Sea on the left. **71.** The second angle stretches towards the north-west, where the city of Brigantia,[90] which lies in Gallaecia, has erected a very tall lighthouse looking out towards Britain – a work with which few can be compared.[91] **72.** Spain's third angle lies where the islands of Cadiz, which face Africa, look across to Mount Atlas over a gulf of the Ocean.

73. Hispania Citerior[92] begins at the Pyrenean Passes in the east. Its boundary extends westwards as far as the Cantabrians and Astures. From there its territory passes through the Vaccaei and Oretani, who lie on its western side, to its other boundary, the city of Carthage[93] which lies on Our Sea.

74. Hispania Ulterior has the Vaccaei, Celtiberians, and Oretani to its east; the Ocean to its north; the Ocean to its west; and the ocean strait of Cadiz to its south, whence Our Sea, which is here called the Tyrrhenian Sea, has its inlet.

75. In the Ocean are the islands called Britain and Ireland which lie opposite part of the Gauls, looking towards Spain. These will now be described briefly.

---

88 The Alps between north-west Italy and south-east France, ranging from Mont Cenis in the north to the Maddalena Pass in the south.

89 The modern Îles d'Hyères.

90 Corunna.

91 For details of this lighthouse, see Hutter and Hauschild (1991).

92 Oddly, Orosius uses the divisions of Spain established in the Republican period, rather than the five provinces to be found there in his own day.

93 Carthago Nova, i.e. Cartagena.

76. Britain is an island in the Ocean that extends far to the north; to its south it has Gaul. On the closest shore to which one can cross, there is a city called the Port of Rutupus[94] which looks across to the land of the Menapians and the Batavians, who lie at no great distance from the Morini to their south. **77.** The island is 800 miles long and 200 miles wide.[95]

78. To its rear, where an infinite expanse of Ocean lies open, are the Orkney Islands. Twenty of these are deserted and thirteen are inhabited.

79. Then comes the island of Thule,[96] which is separated from the others by an infinite stretch of water and lies to their north-west in the middle of the Ocean. It is known to very few men.

80. The island of Ireland lies between Britain and Spain, its longer side running from the south-west to the north-east. **81.** Its closer parts, especially from the promontory where the mouth of the river Scena[97] is found and the Velabri and Leuceni live, look south-west across a great expanse of the Cantabrian Ocean towards the Gallaecian city of Brigantia which faces it, looking north-west. This island is nearer than Britain, smaller in size, but more tractable because of the nature of its soil and climate.[98] It is inhabited by Scottish peoples.[99]

82. Nearest to it is the island of Meuania,[100] which is not small in size, and is fertile as regards its soil. It is also inhabited by Scottish peoples. These then are the boundaries of all of Europe.

83. Our ancestors, as I have mentioned, made Africa their third division of the world, following a rule that did not take regard of size, but rather of natural divisions, **84.** for the Great Sea, which has its birth in the Ocean in the west and then turns southwards, narrows the expanse of Africa which lies between itself and Ocean. **85.** For this reason some men, knowing that Africa, while of equal length, was much thinner, thought it wrong to call it a third part of the world, and considered it rather as part of Europe, preferring to call it a portion of this second part of the world. **86.** Moreover, as almost

94 Normally Rutupiae, the modern Richborough in Kent.

95 Orosius has made Britain too long; it is approximately 500 miles long (Orosius has 736). As regards the island's width, the distance from the Welsh to the East Anglian coast is around 300 miles, but many may feel Orosius's figure of 184 miles is a fairer reflection of its average width.

96 Probably Shetland.

97 The river Shannon; see Ptolemy, *Geography*, 2.2.3.

98 A curious comment. Pomponius Mela, 3.53, and Solinus, 22.2, praise Ireland's pasture, but both see its inhabitants as the worst sort of barbarian.

99 For a detailed discussion of this section on Ireland, see Freeman (2001).

100 The Isle of Man.

all living or growing things are more tolerant and resistant to the extremes of cold than those of heat, the heat of the sun has caused there to be much more unknown and uncultivated land in Africa than the freezing cold has produced in Europe. The reason why Africa seems to be altogether smaller in its extent and number of people is that by its very shape it contains less space and that because of its inclement climate it has more deserts. Its description by provinces and peoples is as follows:

87. Libya, Cyrenaica, and the Pentapolis[101] lie in the first part of Africa which begins after Egypt. **88.** This region begins at the city of Parethonium and the Catabathmon mountains.[102] Thence it runs along the coast to the Altars of the Phileni.[103] Beyond this region, and extending as far as the Southern Ocean, live the Libyoethiopians and Garamantes. **89.** On its east lies Egypt; to the north, the Libyan Sea; to the west, the Greater Syrtes[104] and the Troglodytes, opposite whom lies the island of Calypso;[105] and to the south, the Ethiopian Ocean.

90. The province of Tripolitana, which is also called Subventana or the region of the Arzuges (although those living all along the edge of Africa are commonly called Arzuges) and where the city of Lepcis Magna is to be found,[106] has to its east the Altars of the Phileni which lie between the Greater Syrtes and Troglodytes; the Sicilian, or rather the Adriatic, Sea and the Lesser Syrtes to its north;[107] Byzacium as far as the Lake of the Salt-pans to its west;[108] and to its south, the barbarian Gaetuli, Nathabres, and Garamantes who extend down to the Ethiopian Ocean.

101 Orosius is confused here. The Pentapolis is an alternative name for Cyrenaica, see Pliny, *Natural History*, 5.5.31, not a separate set of towns as Orosius appears to think. 'Libya' here is presumably Lower Libya, *Libya Inferior*, as Upper Libya, *Libya Superior*, was Diocletian's new provincial name for Cyrenaica. Orosius could, of course, have created three entities out of one in error.

102 See 1.2.9 above.

103 Two Carthaginian brothers who died to save their country. Their story is told by Sallust, *The War against Jugurtha*, 79. According to Strabo, 3.5.6, the altars themselves had already disappeared in his day, some 400 years before Orosius wrote, but the toponym remained.

104 The Gulf of Sidra.

105 Various candidates have been offered for this island; perhaps the most plausible is Djerba, but Malta and Gozo have also been suggested.

106 The Arzuges appear to have been a border tribe living between Tripoli and Tunis; they are mentioned by Publicola when writing to Augustine (*Letters*, 46) and in the Synod of Carthage (AD 419), *canon* 49.

107 The Gulf of Cabes.

108 Probably the Chot el-Djerid in Tunisia. The *Peutinger Table*, 7.4, notes that a lake lies to the south of the Garamantes and adds, 'there are great salt-pans which grow and decrease in size according to the phases of the moon'.

91. Byzacium, Zeugis, and Numidia.[109] We have found that Zeugis was not in the past a name used of a single region, but applied to the entire province. **92.** Byzacium is where the city of Hadrumetum[110] is to be found; Zeugis is where Carthago Magna[111] is to be found; and Numidia where Hippo Regius[112] and Rusiccada[113] are found. They have the Lesser Syrtes and Lake of the Salt-pans on their east; Our Sea, where it looks towards the islands of Sicily and Sardinia, to their north; Mauretania Sitifensis to their west; and to their south, the Uzarae mountains[114] and beyond these, the nomadic Ethiopian tribes who wander as far as the Ethiopian Ocean.

93. Mauretania Sitifensis and Mauretania Caesariensis[115] have Numidia to their east; Our Sea to their north; the river Malua[116] to their west; and to their south, Mount Astrixis which divides the living land from the sands which stretch away to the Ocean.[117] In this area live the nomadic Gangine Ethiopians.

94. Mauretania Tingitana is the end of Africa. It has the river Malua to its east; to its north Our Sea as far as the Straits of Cadiz, which lie between the two facing promontories of Habenna and Calpe;[118] Mount Atlas and the Atlantic Ocean to its west; to its south-west, Mount Hesperium;[119] and to the south, the tribes of the Autololes who are now called the Galaules and extend as far as the Hesperian Ocean.

95. This is the end of all of Africa. Now I shall outline the positions, names, and size of the islands which lie in Our Sea.

96. The island of Cyprus is surrounded by the Syrian Sea, which men called the Issican Gulf, to its east; by the Pamphylian Sea to its west; by the Cilician Strait to its north; and to its south by the Syrian and Phoenician

---

109 These are names of three of Diocletian's African provinces. This opening 'sentence' appears to be a title for a section for the book, perhaps showing that Orosius had first planned a different way of presenting his geography and has failed to correct himself here.

110 The modern Sousse in Tunisia.

111 Carthage.

112 The modern Annaba in Algeria.

113 The modern Skikda in Algeria.

114 The Aures range in Algeria.

115 These two areas were made separate provinces by Diocletian.

116 The modern river Moulouya.

117 Mount Astrixis appears only in Orosius. Its name is possibly related to the Astacures of Ptolemy, *Geography*, 4.3. Orosius's references to the division of cultivated land from the desert seem to imply that he means the edge of the Erg Chebbi dune fields in Morocco.

118 Ceuta and Gibraltar.

119 The Anti-Atlas.

seas. It is 175 miles long and 125 miles wide.[120]

97. The east of the island of Crete ends at the Carpathian Sea; the west and north at the Cretan Sea; and the south at the Libyan Sea, which men also call the Adriatic Sea. It is 172 miles long and 50 miles wide.[121]

98. The islands of the Cyclades – of which the most easterly is Rhodes; the most northerly, Tenedus; the most southerly, Carpathus; and the most westerly, Cythera – have to their east the shores of Asia; to their west, the Icarian Sea; to their north, the Aegean Sea; and to their south, the Carpathian Sea. In all, there are 53 Cyclades. From north to south they extend for 500 miles and from east to west for 200 miles.[122]

99. Sicily is an island with three promontories.[123] One, which is called Pelorus, lies close by the city of Messana and looks towards the north-east.[124] The second is called Pachynum[125] and looks south-south-east. Beneath it lies the city of Syracuse. The third is called Lilybaeum.[126] It is sited where the city of the same name is to be found, and runs out towards the west. **100.** From Pelorus to Pachynum, there are 159 miles[127] and from Pachynum to Lilybaeum, 177 miles.[128] To the east, Sicily is girt by the Adriatic Sea; to the south, by the African Sea which lies opposite the Subventani and the Lesser Syrtes; to the west and north it is surrounded by the Tyrrhenian Sea, and to the north-east as far as the east, by the Adriatic Gulf which separates the people of Tauromenium in Sicily from the Bruttii of Italy.

101. Sardinia and Corsica are islands divided by a narrow strait of

120 The Roman mile measures only 1,620 yards, but even so, Orosius has inflated the size of Cyprus which in reality is around 140 miles long (Orosius has the equivalent of 161 statute miles) and only around 59 miles wide (Orosius has 115 statute miles).

121 Orosius's measurements for Crete are better than those for Cyprus. He has the length of the island approximately right at 158 miles, but has over-estimated its breadth at 46 miles (in reality the widest part of the island is around 38 miles across).

122 Orosius's choices for the edges of the Cyclades, particularly Tenedos and Cythera, seem odd. His north–south measurement is too great, the distance from Tenedos to Carpathus being some 280 miles as the crow flies (Orosius has 460), but his east–west measurement is much closer, Rhodes to Cythera as the crow flies being 250 miles (Orosius has 230).

123 Oddly, Orosius does not say that Sicily is triangular, though it is much closer to this shape than Spain which he has earlier described in this way.

124 The modern Punta di Faro.

125 The modern Cabo Passaro.

126 The modern Cabo Lilibeo, sometimes known as Cabo Boeo.

127 This is reasonably accurate: the distance as the crow flies is around 115 miles, while Orosius has 106.

128 This is accurate: as the crow flies the distance is around 170 miles, Orosius has 172.

20 miles.[129] Of the two, the part of Sardinia which lies opposite Numidia is dwelt in by the Caralitani, while in the part that faces Corsica live the Ulbienses. **102.** The island is 230 miles long and 80 miles wide.[130] To its east and north-east it is washed by the Tyrrhenian Sea where it lies opposite the port of the City of Rome, and to the west by the Sardinian Sea. To its south-west lie, far away, the Balearic Islands; to its south is the Numidian Gulf; and to its north, as I have mentioned, is Corsica.

103. Corsica is a jagged island with many promontories. To its east it has the Tyrrhenian Sea and the port of the City; to its South, Sardinia; to its west, the Balearic Islands; and to its north-west and north, the Ligurian Gulf. It is 160 miles long and 26 miles wide.[131]

104. There are two Balearic Islands, the Greater and the Lesser,[132] both of which have two cities. The Greater has the Spanish city of Tarragona to its north; the Lesser, Barcelona. Beneath the Greater island lies the isle of Ebusus.[133] To their east they look on Sardinia; to their north-east, the Gallic Sea; to their south and south-west, the Mauretanian Sea; and to their west, the Iberian Sea.

105. These are the islands that lie in the Great Sea starting from the Hellespont[134] and stretching as far as the Ocean which are considered, because of their culture and history, to be the most famous.

106. I have now briefly listed, as far as I was able, the provinces and islands of the whole world. Now I shall set out, to the best of my ability, the specific misfortunes of each people: how they have inexorably arisen since the beginning of the world, of what kind they were, and for what reasons they occurred.

129 This is too great a distance, the Straits of S. Bonafacio are no greater than eight miles across, Orosius has eighteen.

130 Reading 80 with Zangemeister, Arnaud-Lindet reads 280. Though many manuscripts do have 280 at this point, it is difficult to believe that Orosius made an error of this magnitude and a copyist's error following on from the length of the island seems most likely. Orosius has made the island slightly too long, and a little too thin; in reality it is around 175 miles long (Orosius has 211), while its broadest point is around 85 miles across (Orosius has 74).

131 Orosius's Corsica is too long and narrow: in reality, it is around 110 miles long (Orosius has 147) and 50 miles wide (Orosius has 24).

132 Maiorca and Minorca.

133 Ibiza.

134 Which Orosius has failed to mention.

3

1. Therefore after this world had been created and adorned, man, whom God had created righteous and stainless, perverted and besmirched himself and, as a consequence, the whole human race, with lustful sin. Straightaway righteous punishment followed this unrighteous licentiousness. **2.** For all of us, unwillingly though we be, can either feel the force of the sentence of God, the Creator and Judge – which has been established for sinful man and, because of man, for the Earth, and which will endure as long as men dwell on the earth – by denying it, or, by trusting in it, endure it. Those whose obstinate minds are not persuaded by the truth of the Scriptures are branded as guilty by the testimony of their own weakness.[135] **3.** The most reliable authors[136] very clearly state that the sea was poured over all the land and a deluge unleashed upon it, so that the world became entirely sea or sky,[137] and that the human race was entirely destroyed, save for a few kept safe in the ark as a reward for their faith and in order to create a new race. **4.** Even those who know nothing of times gone by, or of the Author of those times, have born witness that this was so, learning of it by putting together the evidence and hints given by stones which we see on far-flung mountains encrusted with sea- and oyster shells and which often show signs of being hollowed out by the waves.[138] **5.** Now, although I could produce more compelling proofs of this sort which are worth relating, let these two principal points be sufficient, *viz.* that concerning the fall of the first man and the condemnation of his offspring and life, and that concerning the damnation of the entire human race which followed from it, **6.** so I shall merely say that if pagan historians have at some point dealt with our theme, these two arguments will be expounded more fully, along with all the others, at the same place in my history where they raise the issue in theirs.

135 The guilty Orosius has in mind are the Pelagians who refused to accept the doctrine of original sin.

136 Orosius means the Bible, here Genesis 6–8. Perhaps there is also an implied criticism of the reliability of pagan authors whom he goes on to attack.

137 cf. Ovid, *Metamorphoses*, 1.291.

138 cf. Ovid, *Metamorphoses*, 15.264, Pomponius Mela, 1.6.2.

4[139]

1. 1,300 years before the foundation of the City, Ninus the 'first' (as they would have it) king of the Assyrians, took up arms out of lust to spread his power abroad and lived a bloodstained life, spreading war across all of Asia for 50 years.[140] **2.** Rising up from the south by the Red Sea, he laid waste and brought under his sway the far-flung shores of the Euxine Sea, and taught the barbarian Scythians, at that time still a peaceful and innocent race, to arouse their slumbering savagery, to know their own strength, and no longer to drink their herds' milk, but human blood: in short, as he conquered them, he taught them how to conquer.[141] **3.** His last deed was to defeat in battle and slay Zoroaster, the king of the Bactrians, whom men say was the discoverer of the art of magic.[142] After this, he was struck and killed by an arrow while attacking a city that had rebelled from him.

4. On his death, his wife, Semiramis, succeeded him. She had her husband's spirit and took on his son's appearance.[143] She led her people, who were already eager to spill blood, in the slaughter of other tribes for 42 years. **5.** Indeed, this woman who was not content to inherit the boundaries which her husband, the only warlike king at that time, had seized in his 50 years of war, crushed Ethiopia in war, drenched it in blood, and added it to her domains. She also waged war on India which no-one save she and Alexander the Great have invaded. **6.** At that time hunting down and slaughtering peoples who lived in peace was a more cruel and serious matter than it is now, because among them there were neither great conflagrations of war abroad nor such a great cultivation of greed at home.[144]

7. This woman, ablaze with lust and thirsting for blood, lived amid

139 This chapter draws heavily on Justin's *Epitome* of Trogus (here after Justin), 1.1–2.
140 Ninus is mentioned by Augustine, *City of God*, 4.6, who also draws on Justin. But while Augustine criticises Justin and Trogus, commenting that 'other more trustworthy documents show that they were guilty of inaccuracy at times', Orosius draws on Justin very heavily throughout his *Histories*.
141 Orosius here notes the contagious nature of sin.
142 cf. Augustine, *City of God*, 21.14. The Zoroaster here is the Persian religious prophet. He and Ninus were not contemporaries, Zoroaster's *floruit* being around 1,000 BC.
143 Semiramis may be Sammuramat, wife of Shamsi-Adad V, the king of Assyria from 824 to 811 BC, and mother of, and perhaps regent for, Adad-Nirari III (809–782 BC). Such an identification would explain the assertion that she took her son's appearance in order to rule. Semiramis was to become a symbol of lust in Christian writing, see Dante, *Inferno*, canto 5 48–62.
144 Orosius's point of comparison here is probably the Gothic sack of Rome which he is at pains to play down throughout the *Histories*.

unending fornication and murder. After she had killed all those with whom she had enjoyed pleasures of the flesh – men she had summoned as a queen, but detained as a prostitute – on illicitly conceiving a son, she vilely exposed him. Then, when she learnt that she had indulged in incest with him, she covered her personal disgrace by inflicting this crime on all her people. **8.** For she decreed that there should be none of the natural reverence between parents and their children when it came to seeking a spouse and that everyone should be free to act as he pleased.[145]

5[146]

1. 1,160 years before the foundation of the City, Cornelius Tacitus, among others, relates that the region neighbouring Arabia which was then called the Pentapolis[147] was set ablaze down to its soil by fire from heaven, speaking as follows: **2.** *Not far away are those plains which men say were once fertile and supported great domains, but which were burnt up by a thunderbolt and they say that traces of this disaster still remain and that the very earth has been made solid and lost its power to be fertile.* **3.** Although here he says nothing about the cities being consumed by fire because of the sins of their inhabitants, as if he were ignorant of this matter, a little later he forgets himself and reveals the facts by adding: **4.** *I grant that these famous cities were indeed once set ablaze by fire from heaven, but believe that it is the fumes from the lake that infected and corrupted the land.*[148] **5.** In saying these things, albeit most unwillingly, about cities that were without a doubt consumed because of the vileness of their sins, he admits that he knows this and holds it to be the truth, and so openly shows that he does not lack belief in what he has found out, but rather the willingness to expound that belief. It is this matter that I shall now set down more fully.

6. On the borders of Arabia and Palestine where the mountains come down on both sides to the low-lying plains, there were five cities: Sodom, Gomorrah, Adama, Seboim, and Segor. **7.** Out of these Segor was only a small town, but the others were large and spacious, for the fecundity of the

145 Orosius here differs sharply from Justin, 1.2.10, who merely says that Semiramis's son killed her after she attempted to seduce him. Perhaps there is a hint here of the whore of Babylon found in Revelation 17.5.

146 The material in this chapter draws on Genesis 14 and 19.

147 The name given to the five towns listed in Genesis 14 in the apocryphal Wisdom 10.6.

148 Both quotations are from Tacitus, *Histories*, 5.7. In the first quotation, our manuscripts of Tacitus have 'cities' for 'domains' and 'roasted' for 'made solid'.

soil and the river Jordan, which ran through the plains and happily breaks up into streams here, helped increase their fertility. **8.** This abundance of things was the cause of evil for this entire region which put these goods to bad use. For from abundance came extravagance, and from extravagance came foul lusts, *men with men working that which is unseemly*[149] without even giving thought to place, rank, or age. **9.** And so God in His wrath rained down fire and sulphur on this land and burnt up the entire region along with its peoples and cities, damning them to eternal perdition that thenceforth they might be a witness to His judgement. **10.** The result is while the shape of the region can still be seen, it is a region of ashes, and the sea has now poured over and covered the middle of the valley that the Jordan used to irrigate.[150] **11.** So greatly was Divine Wrath inflamed over a matter which is thought of little consequence that, because they used good for ill and had turned the fruit of mercy into the nourishment of lust, the very earth on which those cities stood was first burnt up by fire and then, being overwhelmed by the waters, perished into eternal damnation as a warning to us all.[151]

6

1. And so, if it pleases those who spew forth at Christ, Whom we are showing to be the Judge of Ages, all the spittle they have in them, let them look at the crimes and punishment of Sodom and Rome respectively – things which I ought not to set forth again for the simple reason that they are well-known to all.[152] **2.** How happily would I accept their judgement, if they truthfully admitted to what they see to be the case. **3.** For although a few scattered men mutter complaints about these Christian times in odd corners, I do not think that this ought to cause any great annoyance, since the opinion and views of the entire Roman people are clear from the unanimous judgement that they delivered with one voice. **4.** For they gave unassailable evidence that their customary pleasures which had ceased for a short time did so for trivial, inconsequential reasons, when they cried out of their own accord, 'If the circus is brought back, nothing has happened to us' – that is to say they felt the swords of the Goths had done nothing to Rome, as long as the Romans were allowed to watch their circuses.[153] **5.** But, of course, a view held by

149 Romans 1.27.
150 The Dead Sea.
151 Orosius returns here to the theme of 1.3.1 that nature suffers for man's sins.
152 A reference to the sack of Rome in AD 410.
153 Augustine, *City of God*, 1.32–33, talks in disgust of refugees who had fled from the

many people, especially at the present, and after a long period of ease, is that any small trouble which arises is an unbearable burden and so they rank these most merciful warnings by which we are all at some time or other admonished, higher than all the punishments of other peoples about which they have heard or read. **6.** Taking the demise of Sodom and Gomorrah as my example, I warn them that they can learn and understand in what ways God has punished sinners, in what ways He can punish them, and in what ways He will punish them.[154]

7

1. 1,070 years before the foundation of the City, the Thelcises[155] and Carsatii[156] waged a war of aggression with doubtful hope of success and with no fruit of victory against Phoroneus, the king of the Argives, and the Parrhasians.[157] **2.** Shortly afterwards the Thelcises were defeated in war, fled from their homeland, and, being ignorant of the ways of the world, thinking that they were taking themselves off from contact with all human habitation, seized the island of Rhodes, which had previously been called Offiussa, as if it would be a secure possession for them.[158]

3. 1,040 years before the foundation of the City, a severe flood in Achaea laid waste to almost the entire province. This happened in the reign of Ogygius, who at that time founded and ruled over Eleusis and has given his name to both the place and that epoch.[159]

---

sack to Carthage asking for the way to the theatre. This may have been the inspiration for Orosius's moralising here. It is hard not to detect here an allusion to Juvenal's comment about the mob's love of bread and circuses, *panem et circenses*, *Satires*, 10.81.

154 Orosius points to the past as an example of what will happen to Rome if the present, mild warning is ignored.

155 Normally spelt Telchines. Orosius has taken this incorrect form from Jerome's *Chronicle*. The Telchines were a group of craftsmen-magicians/daemons, euhemerised by Jerome and hence Orosius. Mythological accounts speak of them being later destroyed either by Jupiter (Ovid, *Metamorphoses*, 7.367) or Apollo (Servius, *On the Aeneid (Ad Aeneidem)*, 4.377).

156 Normally the Caryates, i.e. the inhabitants of the town of Caryae in Arcadia.

157 Phoroneus was, according to legend, the second king of the Argives. The Parrhasians were the inhabitants of Arcadia. The reference to this war is taken from Jerome, *Chronicle*, *A Abr.* 230, but Orosius dates the war some 36 years earlier.

158 The defeat of Telchines was at the hands of the Caryates. These events are much more separated in Jerome who places the Telchines' occupation of Rhodes 50 years after their defeat, Jerome, *Chronicle*, *A Abr.* 280.

159 'Achaea' is an anachronistic reference to the Roman province of this name. Again, Orosius's date differs from Jerome, *Chronicle*, *A Abr.* 260, who puts the flood 36 years later.

8

1. 1,008 years before the foundation of the City,[160] the historian Pompeius and his epitomator Justin tell us that in Egypt there was first an unaccustomed, and indeed infuriating, glut followed by perpetual and unbearable famine, and that this was alleviated with Divine help by Joseph, a just and wise man.[161] Among other things, this account tells us that: *Joseph was the youngest of his brothers who, fearing his great intelligence, carried him off and sold him to some foreign merchants.* **3.** *He was taken by them to Egypt where, after a short time, because through his shrewd nature he had learnt the arts of magic, he became the king's favourite. For he was the wisest interpreter of prodigies and the first man to establish a system for understanding dreams. Indeed, nothing decreed either by human or divine law seemed unknown to him.* **4.** *Therefore having foreseen the sterility of the land many years in advance, he collected together its produce. Indeed, so great were the proofs of his wisdom that his advice seemed to come not from a man, but from God.* **5.** *Joseph's son was Moses whose beauty, quite apart from his inheriting his father's knowledge, stood him in good stead. But when the Egyptians suffered from scabs and tetter,[162] after being warned by an oracle, they drove him and the sick from the borders of Egypt to stop the plague spreading to more people.*[163] This is Justin's account.

6. But since the very same Moses whom they themselves state to have been a wise and clever man, has written at greater length and more truthfully about these deeds since they were done by himself and his people, our first task is to enlighten the ignorance of these historians using Moses' account which they concede is reliable and authoritative.[164] **7.** Then we must refute the malicious lies of the Egyptian priests who through a use of low cunning, which is absolutely obvious, have tried to erase the memory of the manifest anger and mercy of the True God. They have tried to erase the memory of these events by dispersing it in a garbled account so that they should not be

160 Orosius has diverged in his dates here from Jerome, *Chronicle, A Abr.* 282, who places the period of abundance 18 years earlier than the date given by Orosius.

161 Pompeius Trogus, author of the *History of Philip* which in reality was a universal history. It is now known only through the work of Justin. Pompeius's *floruit* was probably the reign of Augustus. Justin's *floruit* is much disputed: the second and third centuries AD are the main candidates, though the fourth has also been suggested.

162 An unidentifiable skin disease.

163 Taken virtually verbatim from Justin, 36.2.6–12.

164 Orosius's source is Genesis 41–47. Early Christian and Jewish opinion was unanimous in believing that Moses was the author of the Pentateuch.

seen to be denigrating their idols by showing that God, by Whose counsel these ills were foretold and with Whose help they were avoided, should rightly be worshipped. On the other hand, if we were to be more generous, we could assume that they have simply forgotten these facts. **8.** For it was through the foresight of our famous Joseph,[165] who was a servant of the True God and took a pious and vigorous concern for the creatures of his lord, that they had plenty as if they were true priests. But because they were false priests, they did not grieve with the rest of the hungry.[166] Truly *those who receive favours forget them, while those who suffer remember.*[167] **9.** For, although histories and annals are silent, the very land of Egypt bears witness to the happenings of these times. It was at this time taken into royal ownership and leased back to its owners who to this day have continuously paid a fifth part of all their produce over as tax.[168]

10. The great famine occurred in the reign of the Egyptian king of Diopolis[169] whose name was Amosis.[170] He lived at the time when Baleus ruled over the Assyrians, and when the Argives were ruled by Apis.[171] **11.** Before these seven years of famine were seven years of plenty whose abundant produce would have been allowed to perish as carelessly as it grew prolifically had our Joseph not skilfully gathered it up and stored it and hence saved all of Egypt. **12.** He acquired all the money for Pharaoh and all the glory for God, rendering most justly *tribute to whom tribute was due and honour to Whom honour is due.*[172] He took in all the people's herds, land, and wealth, but after making an agreement that they would pay a fifth of their produce in tax, released the Egyptians themselves who had sold their bodies along with their land for a ration of corn.[173]

165 Orosius claims Joseph for Christianity here.

166 Genesis 47.22, states that the priests received a food allowance from Pharaoh. Orosius is suggesting that true priests would have suffered with their flock or distributed their allowance among them.

167 Cicero, *In Defence of Murena* (*Pro Murena*), 20.42.

168 This statement is simply false.

169 Egyptian Thebes.

170 Ahmose Nebpehtire, founder of the XVIII Dynasty (1550–1525 BC). Much ink has been spilt in vain on determining the date of Exodus; see Josephus, *Against Apion*, 1.15, and Theophilus, *Defence addressed to Autolycus* (*Apologia ad Autolycum*), 3.20.

171 Orosius appears to have his chronology wrong here. According to Jerome, Amosis ruled from *A Abr.* 294 to *A Abr.* 318, but according to Orosius's dates, the famine should start in *A Abr.* 263. Jerome dates Baleus's rule from *A Abr.* 264–315 and that of Apis from *A Abr.* 271–305.

172 Romans 13.7.

173 See Genesis 47.14–16.

13. Who would believe that this Joseph, whom God set up as the author of Egypt's salvation, would have slipped from their memory in so short a time that a little later they made slaves of his sons and all his race, afflicting them with burdens, and decimating them with massacres? **14.** So it is no wonder if some can now be found who, although they turned aside *the sword hanging over their necks*[174] by saying that they were Christians, feign ignorance of, or defame, the very name of Christ by Whom alone they were be saved and assert that they are suffering because they live in the times of those by whose virtues they have been saved.[175]

9

1. 810 years before the foundation of the City, Amphictyon ruled in Athens, being the second king after Cecrops.[176] In his time, a great flood destroyed the majority of the peoples living in Thessaly. A few escaped by taking refuge in the mountains, especially on Mount Parnassus, an area where Deucalion was king. **2.** On the twin peaks of Parnassus he received, fed, and fostered those who fled to him on their rafts and because of this, men say that he saved the human race.[177]

3. Plato tells us that at this time there were a great number of plagues and outbreaks of terrible diseases in Ethiopia which was all but consumed by them.[178] **4.** And in case someone thinks that the times of God's wrath and the fury of war are divided from each other by mere chance, it was at this time that father Liber conquered India and left it dripping with blood, full of corpses, and polluted with his lusts – and this was a race which had done no harm to anyone, but was content to live in its naturally peaceful state.[179]

174 Cicero, *Tusculan Disputations*, 5.21.62.

175 Orosius returns to the assertion that the sack of Rome was a trivial event and was so because God mitigated it because of the presence of Christians in the city, see 7.39.

176 Cecrops is normally taken, as here, as the first king of Athens. He was succeeded by Cranaüs and then Amphictyon.

177 Again, Orosius has diverged from Jerome, *Chronicle*, A Abr. 495, who places the flood 41 years later. The narrative of his account draws heavily on Justin, 2.6.9–11. Deucalion is normally presented as the pagan Noah figure. Here while Orosius retains his connection with flooding, he is careful to demythologise him. See also Justin, 2.6.11.

178 Taken from Jerome, *Chronicle*, A Abr. 498, which makes direct reference to Plato. See Plato, *Timaeus*, 22c.

179 The retention of the 'father' element of *Liber Pater* (i.e. Dionysius) emphasises the cruelty of this pagan father as opposed to the mercy of the Christian God the Father. Orosius is again eager to emphasise the innocence of the Indians, cf. 1.4.6.

10

1. 805 years before the foundation of the City, Pompeius and Cornelius tell us that terrible ills and unbearable plagues descended upon Egypt.[180] Now these two, when they both set down what they want to say about the Jews, leave me somewhat confused as they differ from one another. **2.** For Pompeius, or rather Justin, speaks as follows: *when the Egyptians suffered from scabs and tetter, after being warned by an oracle, they drove Moses and the sick from the borders of Egypt to stop the plague spreading to more people. Moses was made leader of the exiles and secretly stole the Egyptians' sacred vessels. The Egyptians attempted to recover these by armed force, but were driven back to their homeland by storms.*

3. However Cornelius speaks in this way about the same events: *A great number of writers agree that when a disease which rotted the body arose in Egypt, King Bocchoris, who had sought a remedy from the shrine of the oracle of Hammon, was ordered to purge his kingdom of that race of men who were hateful to the Gods, and to drive them away to other lands.* **4.** *After this crowd had been sought out, rounded up, and abandoned in the desert, while all the rest of them wept helplessly, one of the exiles, Moses, told them that they could expect no help from gods or men but that they should trust in him as their heaven-sent leader and that straight away with his aid they would put an end to the troubles which then afflicted them.* **5.** So Cornelius says that it was the Egyptians who drove the Jews into the desert and afterwards carelessly adds that it was with the aid of Moses as their leader that they averted the miseries that had befallen them in Egypt.[181]

---

180 Pompeius, see Justin, 36.2; Cornelius is Tacitus, here, *Histories*, 5.3.

181 This passage of Tacitus is notoriously difficult and Orosius's quotation differs from the accepted reading. Tacitus reads: *Sic conquisitum collectumque vulgus, postquam vastis locis relictum sit, ceteris per lacrimas torpentibus, Moysen unum exulum monuisse ne quam deorum hominumve opem expectarent utrisque deserti, sed sibimet duce caelesti crederent, primo cuius auxilio praesentis miserias pepulissent.* Whereas Orosius's quotation of him reads: *sic conquisitum collectumque uulgus postquam uastis locis relictum sit, ceteris per lacrimas torpentibus Moysen, unum exulum, monuisse, ne quam deorum hominumue opem exspectarent sed sibimet duci caelesti crederent, primo cuius auxilio praesentes miserias pepulissent.* First, Tacitus's phrase *utrisque deserti* 'for they had been abandoned by both of them' has dropped out of Orosius's quotation. Second, Orosius's quotation places 'leader' in the dative case, *duci*, hence making this word refer to Moses. However, it is likely that Tacitus's original text read *duce*, in the ablative, which would lead to the phrase meaning 'but they should trust to themselves, as that was to be their heaven-sent leader, through whose help they should first have ended the troubles that afflicted them'. In other words, in the original reading Moses receives no divine sanction. Orosius is either the victim of a corrupt manuscript, or guilty

Therefore it can be seen that he has obscured some of the actions which Moses took great pains to carry out. **6.** Moreover, Justin adds that when Moses was exiled along with his people, he stole the sacred vessels of the Egyptians which the Egyptians tried to recover by force of arms, but were compelled to return home because of storms. So he has added some more of the facts that Cornelius concealed, though not all of them. **7.** Therefore, since they bear witness to the fact that Moses was a great leader, the account that he himself gives of his deeds and words is to be preferred.[182]

8. When the Egyptians were torturing the people of God – that is the race of Joseph, by whose aid they had been saved – forcing them to work as slaves and, moreover, had cruelly ordered them to murder their own offspring, God commanded through His messenger, Moses, that His people should be freed to serve Him. **9.** When He was scorned by the arrogant Egyptians, He inflicted terrible punishments upon them and they, burdened and crushed by ten plagues, finally forced those whom they had not wanted to let go, to make haste to leave them.

10. So, after their rivers had turned to blood, bringing them, as they burnt with thirst, a remedy for their punishment that was worse than the punishment itself; after filthy, vile frogs had crawled everywhere, both clean and unclean; after fiery sciniphes[183] from which there was no escape, made all the air hum; **11.** after dog-flies[184] had crept, wriggling horribly, over their inner members, bringing sharp torments as painful as they were shameful; after the sudden ruin and general slaughter of all their flocks and beasts of burden; after their sores were boiling, ulcers oozing over their bodies, and, as they preferred to put it, 'scabs and tetter' broke out all over them; **12.** after hail mixed with fire had laid low men, herds, and trees alike; after clouds of locusts had eaten up everything, seeking out even the roots of their seedlings; after a nightmarish darkness which was so thick that it could be touched and was funereal in its duration;[185] **13.** and, finally, after the death of all the first-born in the entire land of Egypt in a storm of bereavement that fell on all alike, those who had not yielded to God when He gave His command, now yielded to Him when He punished them. But soon, after falsely repenting, they dared to pursue those they had freed and were to pay

---

of hasty reading and finding that which he wished to find in his text, or, more seriously, of a deliberate manipulation of the text.

182 i.e. that found in Exodus 1–14.
183 An unknown form of stinging insect, see 7.27.6.
184 Probably the stable-fly (*stomoxys calcitrans*), see Augustine, *Sermons*, 8.5.
185 cf. Augustine, *Sermons*, 20, for a similar description of clouds.

the ultimate penalty for their sinful obstinacy.

14. For their king summoned the entire army of Egypt, complete with chariots and cavalry, and led it against the Jews in their wanderings. We can deduce this army's size from this single, but very important, fact – namely that 600,000 men had previously fled from it in terror.[186] **15.** But God, the Protector of the oppressed and the Avenger upon the stiff-necked, suddenly divided the Red Sea. He paralysed its waves, pushing them back on either side, and held its flanks upright like the faces of a mountain, so that, attracted by seeing an unhindered passage, the good should enter onto a road of salvation that they had not seen, but the wicked into a trench of death that they had not foreseen. **16.** So when Hebrews had safely walked over the dry earth, the mass of raised-up water poured back into its place to their rear and all the Egyptian horde, along with their king, were overwhelmed and killed, and this entire province which had previously been wracked with plagues was now emptied by this final slaughter. **17.** Very clear evidence of these events still exists, for the tracks of the chariots and ruts made by their wheels can been seen not only on the shore, but also on the sea bed as far as it is possible to see there. And if this evidence is at any time disturbed, either by chance or human meddling, straight away by God's will the winds and waves restore it to its pristine condition **18.** in order that anyone who has not learnt the fear of God through study of our manifest Religion, will at least be terrified of His anger from this example of the vengeance He has enacted.[187]

19. At this time, a great, unending heat blazed up so that it is said that the sun, carried along an unaccustomed course, did not merely warm the entire world with its heat, but roasted it with fire. This overbearing heat could be endured neither by the Ethiopians for whom it was stronger than usual nor by the Scythians for whom it was completely unusual. Some authors who do not grant God His ineffable might, looking for empty excuses, have weaved out of this event the ridiculous story of Phaethon.[188]

---

186 This is the number of Hebrews who left Egypt, see Exodus 12.37.

187 Orosius is the only author who mentions this phenomenon.

188 In Greek mythology Phaethon was Apollo's son who lost control of his father's chariot causing conflagrations on earth. Orosius has drawn his note from Jerome, *Chronicle*, *A Abr.* 495, but misplaced it. Jerome firmly links the story of Phaethon to that of Deucalion that Orosius has already used at 1.9.3. For a theory that this myth alludes to the explosion of a large asteroid in early antiquity, see Spedicato (2008).

11

1. 775 years before the foundation of the City, 50 acts of parricide were committed in a single night among the offspring of two brothers: Danaus and Egyptus.[189] After this, Danaus, who had devised these great crimes, was driven from the kingdom he had obtained in such a shameful fashion and took himself off to Argos. There he ungratefully persuaded the Argives to rise against Sthenelas, who had taken him in when he was a penniless fugitive, drove him from his kingdom, and ruled in his stead.[190]

2. At the same time, the cruel Busiris, the blood-stained tyrant of Egypt, exercised his cruel hospitality and practised his even crueller religion. He sacrificed the innocent blood of his guests to toast the gods who were accomplices in his crime: a crime that men certainly find execrable, I would inquire whether the gods found it so too.[191]

3. At that time too occurred the parricide mixed with incest of Tereus, Procne, and Philomela, and to this can be added an even more horrible crime than either of these: the banquet of cursed food, when a mother, having learnt of the violated chastity of her sister and how her tongue had been cut out, killed her own little boy and his father ate him.[192]

4. In the same epoch Perseus crossed from Greece to Asia, conquered the barbarian tribes there after a long and bloody war, and immediately after his triumph gave his name to the vanquished – for the Persians are named after Perseus.[193]

12

1. But now I am forced to confess that the goal of bringing to its end an account of the great evils of this time compels me to pass over many more events and to shorten my account of all of them. Indeed, I would be unable

189 Dated by Jerome, *Chronicle*, *A Abr.* 550, 61 years later. In the myth, Danaus's 50 daughters are married to Egyptus's 50 sons and murder them on their wedding night. To increase the horror of pagan times, Orosius suppresses the normal version of the myth, which is given by Jerome, where one of the brides, Hypermnestra, spares her husband with whom she was later happily reunited.

190 Drawn from Jerome, *Chronicle*, *A Abr.* 530.

191 Busiris was a mythical king of Egypt who sacrificed strangers on an altar of Zeus. The altars of Busiris were a byword for cruelty in antiquity; see Claudian, *On the Rape of Proserpine (De Raptu Proserpinae)*, 2.43, for a reference from Orosius's own day. Orosius's notice is taken from Jerome, *Chronicle*, *A Abr.* 558.

192 Embroidered from Jerome, *Chronicle*, *A Abr.* 645.

193 See Herodotus 7.61.7–150.

to pass through such a thick forest, unless I were to fly forward from time to time by leaps and bounds. **2.** For since the kingdom of the Assyrians lasted for 1,160 years down to the time of Sardanapulus,[194] was ruled by almost 50 kings, and since during that time war was almost always being waged either against them or by them, what end would there be to this account, even if we were merely to try to list these matters, not to speak of describing them? **3.** This is all the more true as we must not pass over the history of the Greeks and must give special attention to that of the Romans.

Now it is not my task to list the foul deeds, which have become even fouler in the telling, of Tanatalus and Pelops **4.** in which we learn that when Tantalus, the king of the Phrygians, had scandalously seized Ganymede, the son of Trous, the king of the Dardanians, he kept him in the even viler filth of conjoined combat.[195] These matters are established by the poet Phanocles[196] who records that a great war broke out because of this, **5.** or perhaps he wants this same Tantalus to be seen as devotee of the gods and to have seized and prepared the boy for the lusts of Jupiter as his family pimp. This was, after all, the man who did not hesitate to serve up his son, Pelops, at one of Jupiter's banquets. **6.** It would also be dreary to recount the battles, however large or small, between Pelops and Dardanus and his Trojans. These things are the staple of stories and so not listened to with great attention.

7. I shall also pass over the stories concerning Perseus, Cadmus, the Thebans and Spartans – a tangled tale of alternating grief written about by Palefates.[197] **8.** I shall be silent on the matter of the Lemnian women's crime, pass over the lamentable flight of Pandion, the king of the Athenians, and ignore the hatred, perversion, and parricide, hateful even to heaven, of Atreus and Thyestes. **9.** I omit Oedipus, the murderer of his father, husband of his mother, brother of his children, and stepfather to himself. I prefer to keep silent over how Eteocles and Polynices worked hard to fight each

---

194 The figure of 1,160 is probably a textual corruption; Augustine, *City of God*, 4.6, and Jerome, *Chronicle, A Abr.* 1197, both have 1,240. It is easy to see how a careless scribe, or perhaps Orosius, could have mistranscribed MCCXL as MCLX.

195 A euphemism for sodomy.

196 Phanocles was an elegiac poet of the late fourth century or third century BC. He wrote 'Lovers or Beautiful Boys', a catalogue of the homosexual loves for young boys of sundry gods and heroes. Orosius has taken the reference from Jerome, *Chronicle, A Abr.* 660.

197 A rationalising mythographer of the late fourth century BC whose book 'On Unbelievable Things' attempted to provide rational explanations for myths; for example, Pegasus is explained away as the name of Bellerophon's ship. Orosius has drawn his reference from Jerome, *Chronicle, A Abr.* 700.

other lest one of them should not become a parricide, **10.** and have no wish to recall the deeds of Medea, she who was *wounded by a savage love*[198] and rejoiced in the death of her little children, the pledges of her love, or whatever deeds were done at that time. We might wonder how men could endure that from which they say even the stars fled.[199]

13

1. 560 years before the foundation of the City, there was a horrendous conflict between Crete and Athens. After both sides had suffered terribly, the Cretans used their victory in an even bloodier fashion. **2.** They cruelly commanded that the sons of Athenian nobles be devoured by the Minotaur, which I do not know whether is best described as a bestial man or as a man-like beast, and so fattened this misshapen monster by ripping out the eyes of Greece.[200]

    3. In these same days the Lapiths and Thessalians fought their battles which have too much renown. **4.** Palaephatus[201] states in the first book of his *Wonders* that the Lapiths believed, and therefore called, the Thessalians centaurs because when their cavalry charged into battle the horses and men seemed to possess but a single body.

14[202]

1. 480 years before the foundation of the City, Vesozes,[203] the king of Egypt, attempted to either embroil in war or add to his kingdom regions which were divided by almost the entire heavens and sea. He first declared war on the Scythians, sending ambassadors in front of him to dictate terms of

198 The quotation is from Ennius, *Medea*, perhaps drawn here from Cicero, *On Fate* (*De Fato*), 15.35. See Jocelyn (1967) *fr.* CIII.

199 This long *recusatio* (the discussion of matters through a denial that they will be discussed) shows Orosius's familiarity with ancient rhetorical theory and techniques.

200 An embroidered version of Jerome, *Chronicle*, A Abr. 787, though Orosius dates the story 83 years before Jerome.

201 To be identified with the Palefates of 1.12.7 above. Orosius has drawn his reference from Jerome, *Chronicle*, A Abr. 776.

202 This chapter draws heavily from Justin, 2.3.8–17.

203 A corruption of Sesosis or Sesostris, perhaps the Pharaoh Senwosret III of the 11th Dynasty (1878–1841 BC). Orosius's story combines a distant memory of this king's defeat with the subsequent collapse of Egyptian military power and Egypt's conquest by the Hyksos in the Second Intermediate Period, c. 1640 BC.

surrender to his enemy. **2.** At this, the Scythians stoutly told the ambassadors that their king, a very wealthy man, was a fool to wage war on poor people, for he had more to be afraid of than they, given the uncertain outcome of war, the lack of prizes, and obvious dangers of loss for himself. They added that they would not wait for him to come to them, but would, of their own accord, set out on the road to plunder. **3.** Nor was there any delay; deeds followed words. First, they forced the terrified Vesozes to flee back to his kingdom and then attacked the army that he had deserted, seizing all its equipment for war. They would have laid waste to all of Egypt had they not been forced back by the difficulties caused by the marshes. **4.** They then immediately headed back towards their homeland and forced Asia, where they indulged in endless slaughter, to pay them tribute. They remained there for fifteen years, during which time there was no peace, and were finally summoned back to their homeland by the complaints of their womenfolk who threatened to have children by the men of neighbouring tribes if they did not return.

15[204]

1. During this period, in Scythia two young princes, Plynos and Scolopetius, were driven from their home by a faction of noblemen. They took with them large numbers of the Scythian youth and, after conquering the Themiscyrian Plains, settled on the shore of Pontic Cappadocia by the river Thermodon.[205] Here, after ravaging the nearby lands for a long time, they were killed during an ambush in a plot devised by their neighbours. **2.** The wives of this group, driven hysterical by being exiled and widowed, took up arms and, so that all of them should have the same spirit by being in the same condition, killed the men who had survived. Having inflamed themselves in this way, they avenged with their own blood their slaughtered husbands by exterminating the neighbouring tribes. **3.** When they had obtained peace by force of arms, they lay with foreigners. They immediately killed their male offspring, but carefully reared the females, burning off the right-hand breasts of these young girls in order that they should not be impeded in shooting arrows. For this reason they were called Amazons.[206]
4. The Amazons had two queens, Marpesia and Lampeto, who divided

---

204 This chapter draws heavily on Justin, 2.4.

205 The modern river Terme in Turkey.

206 The derivation of 'Amazon' from the Greek *a-mazon*, meaning 'without a breast', was popular in antiquity, but its validity is dubious.

their army into two and drew lots to take in turn the tasks of waging war and looking after their homes. **5.** Now when they had subdued most of Europe, captured a number of cities in Asia, and founded others including Ephesus,[207] they recalled the main part of their army which was loaded down with the richest booty, but the remaining part, which, along with Queen Marpesia, had been left to watch over their Asian Empire was slaughtered in an attack by their enemies.

6. Marpesia's daughter, Sinope, took her place. She crowned her outstanding reputation for manliness with life-long virginity. **7.** She excited so much fear and admiration among the peoples who had heard of her reputation that Hercules, when he was ordered by his master to produce the queen's arms for him, gathered together the picked youth of all the Greek nobility, as if he had been sent into inescapable danger. He had nine warships fitted out, but was still not happy with this force and preferred to attack the Amazons by surprise and surround them while they were off their guard.[208]

8. At that time, two sisters, Antiope and Orithyia, ruled the kingdom. Hercules, coming by sea, subdued them as they were unprepared, unarmed, and had become slothful from the inactivity which peace brings. Among the great number of dead and prisoners were two sisters of Antiope: Melanippe taken by Hercules, and Hippolyte taken by Theseus. **9.** Theseus married Hippolyte, but Hercules restored Melanippe to her sister, receiving the queen's arms as the price of her ransom.

10. Penthesilea, about whose bravery among men in the Trojan War we have the clearest evidence, ruled after Orithyia.

16

1. O the sorrow caused by the shame of men's errors! Women, who were exiles from their own land, invaded, passed completely through, and laid waste to Europe and Asia – that is the largest and most powerful parts of the world. They held them for almost 100 years, overthrowing many cities, and founding others. Still the burden of these times must not be imputed to men's wretchedness. **2.** The people who were once called the Getae and now are

207 According to Pausanias, 7.2.7, the claim that the Amazons had founded Ephesus was made as early as Pindar. See also Tacitus, *Annals*, 3.61.

208 The Ninth Labour of Hercules. Orosius has not used the common version of the myth where the queen of the Amazons was named Hippolyta.

called the Goths,[209] whom Alexander declared should be shunned, at whom Pyrrhus trembled, and whom even Caesar declined to fight, abandoned their homeland, and on leaving it, all entered the provinces of the Roman Empire with all their force. But though long regarded with terror, they then sought an alliance with the Romans that they could have exacted by arms, by entreaties, and **3.** though they were free to seize as much as of the world that lay subjected beneath their feet as they wanted, they asked for a small home not of their choice, but subject to our decision. The only people whom unconquered kingdoms feared, offered themselves to guard the kingdom of the Romans. **4.** But the gentiles in their blindness, when they do not see things brought about by Roman courage, will not believe that they have occurred through the faith of the Romans nor agree to concede, though they know it to be true, that through the gift of the Christian Religion, which joins all peoples in a family of faith, these men, whose womenfolk laid low the greater part of the world with immense slaughter, have now become their subjects without a battle being fought.

17

1. 430 years before the foundation of the City there took place the Rape of Helen, the alliance of the Greeks, the assembling of the 1,000 ships, the ten years' siege, and, finally, the famous destruction of Troy.[210] **2.** Homer, who is head and shoulders above the front-rank of poets, has made clear in his marvellous poem what nations and peoples this storm swept up and afflicted in the ten years of this, the cruellest of wars. It is not our task now to set this affair out in order once again, for this would be too long for our work and these matters are common knowledge. **3.** Nevertheless, those who have learnt about the length of that siege and the atrocities, slaughter, and enslavement that took place on Troy's fall, might see if they have any justification to be angry with the present state of affairs, whatever it is like, when their enemies,[211] through the workings of God's hidden mercy, pursue them over every sea to offer peace and surrender hostages, although they could have armed themselves for battle and pursued them in war in over every

---

209 There is no justification for the identity of these two peoples, but it was a commonplace in antiquity. It also serves Orosius's purpose to show that the troubles of his day are trivial compared to those of the past and so he adopts it with alacrity.

210 Jerome, *Chronicle*, dates the rape of Helen to *A Abr.* 827 (= 437 *AUC*) and the fall of Troy to *A Abr.* 835. (= 429 *AUC*).

211 i.e. the Goths.

land. Moreover, in case it is thought that they have done this through a love of peace and quiet, they are offering to risk themselves against other peoples to keep the peace for the Romans.

18

1. School exercises have engraved on our memory how a few years later Aeneas, an exile from Troy, arrived in Italy which took up arms against him, the war he waged for three years, and the peoples that he ensnared in hatred and did to death.[212] **2.** In the midst of these times, too, occurred the exile and shipwrecks of the Greeks, the disaster of the Peloponnesians who were broken by the death of Codrus,[213] unknown Thracian tribes rising once more in war, and a general period of instability throughout Asia and Greece.

19[214]

1. 64 years before the foundation of the City, Sardanapulus, the last king of the Assyrians reigned, a man more corrupt than women.[215] Arbatus, his prefect, who was then governing Media, saw him among a crowd of prostitutes dressed as a woman and working purple on a distaff, and cursed him.[216] The Medes rebelled, forcing the king to fight them and on his defeat, he cast himself onto a blazing funeral pyre.[217] From that time the kingdom of the Assyrians passed into the hands of the Medes.

2. Then after the many wars that burst out on all sides and which it does not seem at all useful to describe one by one, power passed in one way or another to the Scythians and the Chaldeans, and then returned once again by the same route to the Medes. **3.** One should reflect on what a short time it took for such ruin and disasters to befall these peoples, and on the changing fortunes in these wars, during which so many great kingdoms were transformed.

212 Virgil's *Aeneid* was a standard school text in Orosius's day.

213 See Jerome, *Chronicle*, *A Abr.* 948. Codrus was the king of the Athenians who engineered his death after an oracle had revealed that in this way Athens would win the war. Orosius has suppressed this pagan element of the legend.

214 This chapter draws on, and abbreviates heavily, Justin, 1.5–1.7.2.

215 Sardanapulus is a difficult figure to identify. His legend does not suggest a memory of the last vigorous ruler of Assyria, Assurbanipal (668–627 BC), though this is often suggested. It is more probable that the far feebler Sinsharishkun (627–612 BC), at the end of whose rule Nineveh fell, is intended.

216 Orosius later, 2.2.2, also spells this name as Arbaces.

217 Jerome, *Chronicle,* dates the death of Sardanapulus to *A Abr.* 1189 = 75 *AUC.*

4. After this, Phraortes ruled the Medes. He spent the 22 years of his reign in almost continual war against the Assyrians and Persians.[218] **5.** After Phraortes, Diocles became king. He was a man with great experience in arms and always at war. Having expanded his kingdom greatly, on his death he handed it over to Astyages.[219] **6.** Astyages had no male offspring, but had a grandson, Cyrus, born among the Persians.[220] But this Cyrus as soon as he came of age gathered together a band of Persians and declared war on his grandfather. **7.** Then Astyages, forgetting the crime which he had once done to Harpalus – when he had killed his only little son and served him up as a feast for his father and, in case happy ignorance should lighten this most horrible of bereavements, taunted him with the vile banquet, showing to the father the head and hands of his son – **8.** forgetting this deed, he made Harpalus his commander-in-chief, who, on accepting the command, immediately betrayed him, and handed over his troops to Cyrus. When he learnt this, Astyages quickly gathered together the troops he had with him, marched on Persia himself, and renewed the conflict all the more bitterly, telling his men that if anyone were to leave the battle in fear, they would meet him, sword in hand. **9.** Now when the army of the Persians was driven back a second time and slowly yielding to the Medes, who fought keenly because of this threat, *the Persians' mothers and wives ran up to them, begging them to return to the battle. When their menfolk delayed, they lifted up their clothes and showing the shameful parts of their bodies, asked whether they wished to flee into the bellies of their mothers or those of their wives.*[221] **10.** Shamed by this display, the Persians returned to battle and launching a charge, forced those who had previously made them flee, to flee themselves. *Astyages was then captured. Cyrus took nothing from him save his kingdom, and put him in charge of the largest of the Hyrcanian tribes. Indeed, he himself had no wish to return to Media. This was the end of the Empire of the Medes.*[222] **11.** But the cities that had paid tribute to the Medes now defected from Cyrus, *something which cost him many wars.*[223]

218 Phraortes ruled from 647–625 BC.

219 Orosius appears to have confused Diocles, normally taken as ruling before Phraortes, with Cyaxares who ruled from 625–585 BC.

220 The son of his daughter, Mandane, whom he married to the Persian Cambyses after an ill-omened dream; see Herodotus, 1.107.

221 Taken verbatim from Justin, 1.6.13–14.

222 Taken virtually verbatim, and with slight omissions from Justin, 1.6.16–17. Astyages ruled from 585–550 BC.

223 This phrase is drawn virtually verbatim from Justin, 1.7.2.

20

1. At this time,[224] the Sicilian Phalaris became tyrant of Agrigentum and ravaged its land. **2.** His disposition was cruel, and he was crueller still in what he practised, working every form of infamy against innocent men.[225] Unjust though he was, he once came across a man whom he punished justly. **3.** A certain bronze-smith, Perillus, feigning friendship with the tyrant, made him a bronze bull, thinking it a fitting present, given his cruel nature. He skilfully set a door in its side as a place to thrust in the condemned. It was designed so that as the man trapped inside was roasted by the fire placed beneath it, the hollow bronze amplified the sound of his tortured voice and, struck by the cries of the dying man, sent forth an echoing sound which seemed, horrific spectacle as it was, more like the lowing of a cow than cries of a man. **4.** Phalaris embraced the artefact, but loathed the artificer. He found a way to exercise both his vengeance and cruelty, for he executed the smith in his own device.[226]

5. A little earlier, King Aremulus ruled among the Latins. He flourished amidst his crimes and impiety for eighteen years, but was finally struck down by a thunderbolt by divine judgement and ended his unripe years with this well-ripened punishment.[227]

6. So let the Latins and Sicilians choose now, if they want, whether they would have preferred to have lived in the days of Aremulus and Phalaris by whose punishments innocent lives were tortured, or in these Christian times when Roman emperors, set right above all by Religion, after suppressing tyranny for the good of the state, do not even punish the injuries done to them by tyrants.[228]

224 Orosius presumably means at the same time as Cyrus took power. This would show him following Jerome who has the two reigns running in parallel (Phalaris, *A Abr.* 1457–65; Cyrus, *A Abr.* 1457–85).

225 The cruelty of Phalaris (c. 570–c. 549 BC) was a topos in antiquity; see Claudian, *On the War with Gildo* (*De Bello Gildonico*), 1.186–89, and *Against Rufinus* (*In Rufinum*), 1.253.

226 See the description in Silius Italicus, *Punica*, 14.213–17.

227 Orosius has embroidered Jerome's (*Chronicle*, *A Abr.* 1142) comment on Aremulus, 'who afterwards died struck by lightning because of his impiety'. Jerome has Aremulus ruling for 19, not 18 years.

228 Probably a reference to Honorius's treatment of the usurper Attalus, see 7.42.9.

21

1. 30 years before the foundation of the City, there was a great war waged with all their body and soul between the Athenians and the Lacedaemonians. In it, both were compelled by the deaths suffered on each side to withdraw from, and abandon, the conflict, as if they had been defeated by one another.[229]

2. Then, the sudden incursion of the Amazons and Cimmerians into Asia caused devastation and slaughter far and wide for a long period of time.[230]

3. Twenty years before the foundation of the City, the Lacedaemonians waged war against the Messenians because their young women had been spurned at a solemn Messenian sacrifice. They fought for 20 years with untiring fury, entangling the entire strength of Greece in their ruin.[231]

4. The Spartans had sworn great oaths, binding themselves not to return home until they had stormed Messena. But after they had been worn out by a long ten-year siege and gained no fruit of victory, they were recalled, troubled by the complaints of their wives who spoke accusingly of their long bereavement and the dangers of sterility. **5.** They held an assembly and, fearing lest their perseverance would result in their loss of offspring rather than the destruction of the Messenians, they picked out the men in army who had come as reinforcements after the oath had been taken, sent them back to Sparta and *allowed them to lie freely with all the women*:[232] an act of licentiousness which was certainly notorious enough, but in fact of no use to them at all.[233]

6. The Lacedaemonians pressed on with their campaign, stormed Messena by trickery, and forced the vanquished into slavery. But they, after

229 This appears to be Orosius embroidering Jerome, *Chronicle, A Abr.* 931, where he notes that 'The Peloponnesians fought with the Athenians'. It is unclear why Orosius has transposed the entry in time, placing it over 300 years later than Jerome.

230 This appears to be an embroidering and transposition of an entry in Jerome, *Chronicle, A Abr.* 940, which reads: 'Asia was invaded by both the Amazons and Cimmerians'. Again, Orosius has post-dated the entry by over 300 years.

231 This appears to be a transposition of Jerome, *Chronicle, A Abr.* 1273, dating nine years *after* the foundation of Rome, which reads 'The Spartans waged war on Messenia for 20 years'. Orosius draws the bulk of his account of the war from Justin, 3.4–5. The First Messenian War is conventionally dated c. 735–715 BC.

232 Taken verbatim from Justin, 3.4.5; the moralising that follows is Orosius's own.

233 Orosius omits the end of Justin's account where we are told that the offspring of these unions were known as the Partheniae, who, on reaching the age of 30, left Sparta and founded Tarentum. Presumably, the useless nature of the act was that it failed to provide Sparta with extra manpower as had been envisaged.

enduring the whips and chains of their bloody servitude for a long time, shook off their yoke, took up arms, and renewed the war.[234] **7.** The Lacedaemonians chose the Athenian poet, Tyrreus,[235] as their war leader. They were put to flight in three battles and made up for their lost army with a band of slaves whom they freed. **8.** But when, while they were still thinking of abandoning the fight from fear of its dangers, their leader, Tyrreus, who was both poet and general, composed a song and recited it at a meeting, they were enflamed once more and soon rushed into battle. The conflict was fought with such determination that rarely has a more bloody battle blazed forth. Victory finally went to the Lacedaemonians.

9. The Messenians however renewed the war for a third time. Nor was there any delay on the part of the Lacedaemonians.[236] Both sides took many troops as reinforcements. Meanwhile, the Athenians prepared to attack the Lacedaemonians on a different front while they were concentrating on events in Messena.[237] **10.** But the Lacedaemonians did not sleep. While they themselves dealt with the Messenians, they sent the Peloponnesians to give battle to the Athenians. The Athenians were weaker than their opponents, because they had sent a small fleet to Egypt,[238] and so were easily defeated in a naval battle. When their fleet returned and their number of troops increased, they challenged the victors to battle. **11.** The Lacedaemonians, postponing their Messenian campaign, turned their arms on the Athenians. There followed a number of serious battles with no clear results and eventually both sides ended the war with the matter undecided.

12. It is very important to realise that Sparta is the same as the city of Lacedaemona and that for this reason the Spartans are called Lacedaemonians.

13. *The Lacedaemonians were recalled to their war against the Messenians and, in order not to give the Athenians any respite, made a treaty with the Thebans to the effect that if they would wage war on the Athenians, Sparta would restore to them the Boeotian Empire which they had lost at the time of the Persian War.* **14.** *Such was the frenzy of the Spartans that*

234 The Second Messenian War, c. 650–c. 620 BC.

235 i.e. Tyrtaeus. Orosius derives his Athenian nationality from Justin, 3.5.5.

236 The Third Messenian War, 464–459 BC. Orosius has compressed his account, giving a false impression that the third war closely followed the second in time.

237 The First Peloponnesian War, 461–445 BC.

238 Orosius has misread, or misunderstood, Justin, 3.6.6, here which reads 'The Athenians had few resources at this time having sent a fleet to Egypt'. Orosius has erroneously read *parcae*, 'few' with *classe*, 'fleet', a grammatical impossibility. The expedition took place in c. 454 BC.

while they were involved in two wars, they did not hesitate to engage in a third as long as they gained enemies for their foes. **15.** *The Athenians, rocked by this storm of war, chose two leaders: Pericles, a man of proven ability, and Sophocles, a writer of tragedies.*[239] *They divided their army and ravaged the lands of the Spartans far and wide, adding many cities in Asia to the Athenian Empire.*[240] **16.** Thence for 50 years war raged by land and sea but never with a clear victory, until the Spartans, whose resources were dwindling and who had betrayed their word, became a disgrace even in the eyes of their allies.[241]

17. But this volume of troubles which beset Greece for so many ages does not count for much today, when it is thought intolerable that pleasure should be interrupted from time to time and that our lusts be hindered for a little while. **18.** The difference between men of that time and those of today is this: they tolerated the intolerable with equanimity because since they had been born among, or rather nurtured by, these events, they had no knowledge of anything better, but the men of today on the other hand, accustomed to a perpetually serene life of tranquillity and delight, are annoyed by every little cloud, however small, that brings unease. **19.** Would that they might pray to Him Who drives away even these small fears and by Whose gift they have this continual peace unknown in other times.

20. Since I remember that when I defined the order of my work in a number of limbs, so to speak, I promised that I would write from the foundation of the world to the foundation of the City, **21.** this is the end of the volume where we have written an account from the foundation of the world. The following volume will begin at the foundation of the City and contain an account of the evils of those times which are more close-knitted as men by then were better versed and more refined in the practice of vice.

239 Sophocles served as a *strategos* (elected general) in Athens' expedition against Samos in 440 BC.

240 Taken virtually verbatim from Justin, 3.6.10–11.

241 The section has been drawn from Justin, 3.7.13–15. The 50 years are those extending from the First Peloponnesian War to the Peace of Nicias. Orosius follows Justin in believing that when they began the Archidamian War in 431 BC, the Spartans broke the terms of the Thirty Years Peace which they had made in 445 BC.

BOOK TWO

1

1. I believe that the fact that God created man in this world can have escaped no one at this present time. From this it follows that because of man's sin, the world is implicated in his crimes, and in order to bring our excesses to heel, the very earth on which we live is punished with all other animals dwindling away and its fields becoming barren.[1] **2.** Now, if we are God's creation, we are rightly subject to His ordinances.[2] For who loves a thing more than He who made it? Who can better order and control it than He who has made and loves it? Who can more wisely and firmly order and control what he has made than He who foresaw what ought to be made and Who has brought what He foresaw to fruition? **3.** Therefore, all power and order comes from God. Those who have not read of this, feel it to be the case, and those who have read it, recognise it to be so.

And if power comes from God, this is especially the case with kingdoms from which all other power proceeds. **4.** So, if there are a number of kingdoms, it is right that there is one supreme kingdom under which all the sovereignty of the rest is placed. In the beginning, this was the kingdom of Babylon, then the kingdom of Macedon, after that the African kingdom,[3] and finally that of Rome, which remains in place to this day. **5.** Through this same ineffable ordering of things, the four principal kingdoms which have been pre-eminent to differing degrees, have occurred at the four cardinal points of the world: the kingdom of Babylon to the east; that of Carthage

---

1 See 1.3.2 and 1.5.9.

2 Augustine also uses the notion of the *dispensatio Dei*, God's conscious ordering of the world. His use of it is, like Alexander Pope's, to argue for a benevolent purpose to history that is indiscernible to human reason. While Orosius does adopt this position on occasions, here his purpose is to demonstrate that Rome's rule over the world is divinely ordained. Unlike Augustine, who argues that history's purpose is radically unknowable, Orosius in the *Histories* wishes to show that God's purpose can be deduced from the past.

3 i.e. Carthage.

to the south; that of Macedon to the north; and that of Rome to the west.[4]
6. Between the first and the last of them, that is to say Babylon and Rome,
just as in the interval of time between an old father and his young son,
come the short-lived and intermediate periods of the African and Macedonian kingdoms. These fulfilled roles like those of a teacher and guardian,
and came into being through force of circumstances rather than from any
right of succession.[5] I shall now take care to expound as clearly as possible
whether this is true.[6]

<h2 style="text-align:center">2</h2>

1. The first king among the Assyrians who was able to gain pre-eminence
over all the rest was Ninus.[7] After Ninus was killed, Semiramis, his wife and
the ruler of all Asia, rebuilt the city of Babylon and decreed that it should be
the capital of the Assyrian kingdom. **2.** For a long time the kingdom of the
Assyrians stood with its power unshaken, but when Arbatus, whom some
call Arbaces, the governor of the Medes and himself a Mede, slew his king,
Sardanapulus, in Babylon, he handed over both the name of the kingdom
and its power to the Medes.

3. So, in the same year in which Procas, the father of Amulius and Numitor
and the grandfather of Rhea Silvia, who was the mother of Romulus, began
to rule among the Latins, the kingdom of Ninus and of Babylon was given
to the Medes.[8] **4.** I can show from the fact that all histories of antiquity begin
with Ninus and all histories of Rome with Procas, that all this came to pass
through the ineffable mysteries and the deepest judgments of God and not
by human action or chance.[9] **5.** Moreover, from the first year of Ninus's

---

4 For a similar argument from cardinal points, see Irenaeus, *Against Heresy* (*Adversus Haereses*), 3.11.8, who uses the four cardinal points to argue for the logical existence of four gospels.

5 i.e. they are not part of the family, just necessary for the son's upbringing.

6 Orosius's theory of the four kingdoms is based on the dreams of Nebuchadnezzar and the prophet Daniel and their interpretation as found in the book of Daniel (Daniel 2.31–45, 7.1–18). For a full discussion of the many problems involved in this book's interpretation, see Rowley (1935).

7 See 1.4. Orosius phrases his statement carefully here, making Ninus not the first king per se, but the first important king.

8 See Jerome, *Chronicle*, *A Abr.* 1198 = 66 years before the foundation of Rome.

9 As regards non-Roman history and Ninus this is true of Orosius's two main sources, Jerome and Justin. Orosius needs to begin his history of Rome with Procas for his parallelism to work, but earlier kings are attested by Jerome (*Chronicle*, *A Abr.* 1142 = 122 years before the foundation of Rome; *A Abr.* 116 = 103 years before the foundation of Rome), Livy, 1.3,

empire to the time when Babylon was rebuilt by Semiramis is a period of 64 years, and there is equally a period of 64 years from the first year when Procas began to reign down to the foundation of the City carried out by Romulus.[10] In Procas's reign, therefore, the seed of the future Rome was sown, although it had not yet begun to germinate, and in the same year of the rule of that same Procas, the kingdom of Babylon fell, though the city of Babylon still stands.

6. When Arbatus defected to the Medes, the Chaldeans, who successfully defended Babylon against the Medes, held on to a part of the kingdom for themselves. **7.** So sovereignty over Babylon rested with the Medes, but possession of the city itself with the Chaldeans. The Chaldeans, however, because of this royal city's ancient dignity, preferred not to call it after themselves, but rather themselves after it. It is for this reason that Nabuchodonosor[11] and all the other kings after him down to Cyrus are not counted in the ranks or line of famous kings, although you may read that they were mighty through the power of the Chaldeans and famous because of the name of Babylon.

9. Therefore we see that Babylon was humbled by its governor Arbatus in the same year when, under King Procas, the seed of Rome was, to speak precisely, sown, and that Babylon was finally overthrown by King Cyrus in the same year when Rome was first liberated from the rule of the Tarquin kings.[12] **10.** So it was at this exact conjunction of time that the one fell and the other rose. The former suffered the heel of foreign domination for the first time, while the latter threw off the haughty rule of her masters for the first time. The former, like a dying man, abandoned its inheritance, the latter, though but a youth, recognised itself as its heir.[13] It was at this time that the Empire of the East perished and that of the West arose.[14]

11. Now, in order not to tarry longer with my words, I shall place myself

---

and Virgil, *Aeneid*, 6.767.

10 Orosius's parallel appears to be original. It cannot be taken from Jerome, who speaks of Babylon being rebuilt 43 years after Ninus's rule began, *A Abr.* 1, and who has a gap of 66 years between the reign of Procas and the foundation of Rome.

11 i.e. Nebuchadnezzar.

12 This synchronism again appears to be original. It is not found in Jerome where Cyrus captures Babylon in *A Abr.* 1457 = 193 *AUC*, but Tarquin is not deposed until *A Abr.* 1505 = 241 *AUC*.

13 Orosius is possibly drawing his reader's mind to the rise of Octavian here.

14 The notion of Rome as a second Babylon is also found in Augustine, *City of God*, 18.2 and 18.22, as is the notion of Rome's rising at the time of Babylon's fall, *City of God*, 18.27.

in the jaws of madmen,[15] but only in order to be freed from them by the truth.[16]

3

1. Ninus ruled for 52 years and, as I have said, his wife, Semiramis, succeeded him. She ruled for 42 years and in the middle of her reign established Babylon as the capital of her kingdom.

2. Almost 1,164 years after its foundation, Babylon was stripped of its wealth, and had its kingdom and its own king taken from it by the Medes and Arbatus, who was king of the Medes and also the governor of Babylon. Nevertheless, the city itself remained unscathed for sometime after this. **3.** Similarly, Rome after the same number of years, namely almost 1,164, was stormed by the Goths and Alaric who was their king and a Count of the City. She was stripped of her wealth, but not her kingdom – for she still remains and rules in safety.[17] **4.** Nevertheless, the order of all these parallels between the two cities, which was brought about by mystic decree, has been kept to this degree: that there the prefect Arbatus invaded the kingdom, and here the City's prefect, Attalus, tried to become its ruler,[18] but here, unlike at Babylon, because of the merits of our Christian ruler,[19] Attalus's attempt was made in vain and came to nothing.

5. I thought that these things deserved recording in order that, above all, those who bicker foolishly about these Christian times might learn from this partial revelation of the great mystery of the ineffable judgments of God that the One God has ordained these events – for the Babylonians at the beginning of the cycle and now for the Romans at its end – and might learn that it is through His clemency that we are alive and that our life is wretched through our own excesses.

---

15 Perhaps a reference to Daniel in the lions' den.

16 cf. John 8.32, 'the truth shall make you free'.

17 This chronological synchronism is essential for Orosius's scheme of the four empires of the world, but Augustine would not have agreed. He believes that Babylon stood for 1,240 years, commenting that 'it endured so long that Rome has not yet reached the same age', *City of God*, 4.6.

18 Priscus Attalus, the *Praefectus Urbi* or Prefect of Rome (essentially the mayor of the city), was proclaimed emperor by the Visigothic leader Alaric in AD 409, allowing himself to be baptised as an Arian in order to further his ambitions. The following year Alaric deposed him in a curious 'uncrowning' ceremony near Ariminium. See 7.42.7–10 for Orosius's account of the attempted usurpation.

19 i.e. the emperor Honorius, AD 395–423. See 7.37.11 for similar comments.

6. Behold, how Babylon and Rome had a similar beginning, similar power, a similar size, a similar age, similar goods, and similar evils, but their ends and decline are not similar. Babylon lost her kingdom; Rome retains hers. Babylon was left an orphan on the death of her king, Rome is secure and her emperor safe. **7.** And why has this happened? Because there punishment for its disgraceful lusts was visited upon the person of the king,[20] but here the restrained moderation of the Christian Religion was preserved in the person of the king.[21] There, where there was no reverence for religion, licentious frenzy eagerly took its fill of desires; here there were Christians who gave pardon,[22] Christians who were pardoned,[23] and Christians through whose memory and in whose memory pardon was given.[24]

8. Therefore let them cease to execrate Religion and exasperate the patience of God through which they have the chance of going unpunished for this vice too, if they were ever to stop their sinning. **9.** Let them recall, along with me, the times of their ancestors, times troubled by wars, cursed by their crimes, soiled by dissension, and continually miserable – times at which they can rightly tremble, because they were so and ought of necessity to ask that they should be so no more: **10.** they surely need to ask the One Sole God, Who, through His hidden justice, once allowed these things to come to pass, but now has revealed His mercy and vouches that they shall be no more.

I shall now set down these past times more fully, starting from the birth of the City and going through its history in order.

4[25]

1. In the 414th year after the fall of Troy in the sixth Olympiad, which is celebrated with competitions and games in the Greek city of Elis every fifth

---

20 i.e. Sardanapulus.

21 Strikingly Orosius is happy to use 'rex' of the emperor, something that would have deeply shocked earlier generations of Romans. The usage allows Orosius to continue with his theme of the four kingdoms. Orosius praises the restraint, *continentia*, of Honorius again at 7.37.11.

22 i.e. the Goths who sacked Rome. Orosius makes great play of the Goths' Christianity, quietly forgetting their Arianism. The point is made more extensively at 7.37.5–11.

23 i.e. the inhabitants of Rome.

24 i.e. the saints, perhaps particularly Peter and Paul, see 7.39.1

25 Orosius's account of the regal period at Rome draws heavily, though in a highly abbreviated fashion, on Florus, 1.1.

year, four having passed from one celebration to the next,[26] the city of Rome was founded in Italy under the twin leadership of Romulus and Remus.[27] **2.** Straightaway Romulus stained his rule with parricide[28] and followed this with an equally cruel act by giving a dowry of their husbands' and fathers' blood[29] to the Sabine women *who had been seized contrary to custom*[30] and shamefully married off. **3.** It was in this way that Romulus, having first murdered his grandfather Numitor,[31] and then his brother Remus, seized power and founded the City. He dedicated his kingdom with the blood of his grandfather, its walls with the blood of his brother, and its temple with that of his father-in-law, and then gathered together a band of criminals by promising them immunity from punishment. **4.** His first field of battle was the forum of the City – a sign that wars, both external and civil mixed together, would never be absent from the realm. **5.** He seized the womenfolk of the Sabines, a people he had seduced by making a treaty and holding games with them, in a fashion as dishonourable as the criminal way by which he then defended what he had seized. **6.** After a long period in which he had fought off by force of arms the Sabines' leader, Titus Tatius, an old man who walked in the noble ways of piety, he made him a partner in his rule, and then almost immediately killed him.[32] **7.** After this, he stirred up a war which is still little known, but was fought with large forces, against the men of Veii and *captured and sacked the town*

26 The Roman dating system uses inclusive dates. Oddly, Orosius speaks as if the Olympics were still being held at the time of writing, whereas in fact Theodosius had abolished them in AD 393.

27 Orosius has contradicted himself, as at 1.17.1 he dates the fall of Troy to 430 years before the foundation of Rome. His date also differs from that of Jerome who places the foundation of Rome in the last year of the sixth Olympiad and for whom the fall of Troy occurred 429 years before the foundation of the city, and from that of Eutropius, 1.1, who places the foundation of Rome on 21 April, in the third year of the sixth Olympiad and 394 years after the destruction of Troy. At 6.22.1 Orosius dates the foundation of Rome to 752 BC. This differs by one year from the commonly used 'Varronian' date of 753 BC.

28 cf. Augustine, *City of God*, 3.6.

29 This is an adaptation of Virgil, *Aeneid*, 7.318, who speaks Lavinia's dowry of Trojan and Rutulian blood. Augustine, *City of God*, 3.13, also makes this point.

30 'Sabine women... contrary to custom' – this is a slight adaptation of Virgil, *Aeneid*, 8.635.

31 An egregious error for Amulius, Numitor's brother; see Justin, 43.2.10.

32 Titus Tatius was killed at Lanuvium while sacrificing. Romulus's decision not to go to war to avenge him led some commentators to assume that he had connived in the murder. Livy, 1.14, is entirely neutral on the subject. Orosius, like Augustine, *City of God*, 3.13, deliberately takes a black view of the matter to support his interpretation of Roman history.

of Canusium.[33] **8.** Once he had taken up arms there was no respite, since he and his men feared that they would suffer from *shameful want* and *dismal famine*[34] at home, if they should ever pursue a peaceful, quiet life.

I will now list, as briefly as possible, these continuous struggles which, given the number of men involved, were always bloody affairs. **9.** Hostilius Tullius devised their way of fighting, and, being confident that he had trained the youth of the City well, attacked Alba.[35] For a long time both sides were uncertain of victory, though certain to suffer disaster. At last, they put an end to these terrible events and their precarious results by a duel fought between three pairs of brothers.[36] **10.** But the peace was broken again and Mettus Fufetius, who was caught while plotting treachery during the war against Fidenae, paid the price for his duplicity by having his body torn apart – it was pulled into pieces by chariots galloping in different directions.[37] **11.** When Ancus Marcius led Rome, the Latins often gave battle and were sometimes defeated.[38] Tarquinius Priscus defeated all his neighbours and the then-powerful twelve tribes of Etruria in innumerable battles.[39] The men of Veii were defeated, but not subdued, by Servius Tullius's continual onslaught.[40] **12.** Tarquinius Superbus obtained the kingdom through the criminal murder of his father-in-law,[41] held onto it through his cruelty

33 Quoted from Florus, 1.1.11. Veii is the modern Isola Farnese some 10 miles to the north of Rome. Canusium is the modern Canosa di Puglia in Apulia.

34 These two phrases are taken from Virgil, *Aeneid*, 6.276 and 3.367, respectively.

35 Hostilius Tullius was the third king of Rome (conventionally 672–641 BC). Orosius has suppressed any mention of the second king, Numa (conventionally 715–673 BC), as his peaceful reign jars with his purpose to depict early Rome as a violent and lawless state.

36 Orosius's account of the reign of Tullus Hostilius is an abbreviated version of that found in Florus, 1.1.3. The three brothers are the Horatii (Roman) and the Curiatii (Alban). While Orosius is emotionally detached as regards the battle, Augustine, *City of God*, 3.14, uses it to demonstrate the horrors of the early Roman state.

37 Fidenae is the modern Castel Giubileo some five miles from Rome. Mettius was king of Alba and hence, given Alba's conquest by Hostilius, a nominal ally of Rome. Orosius's account is again an abbreviated version of Florus, 1.1.3.

38 Ancus Marcius was the fourth king of Rome (conventionally 640–617 BC). He is mentioned by Florus, who does not, however, record Ancus's military exploits. Ancus's campaigns against the Latins are mentioned by Eutropius, 1.5, and discussed at greater length by Livy, 1.33. His campaigns against the Latins are also mentioned by Eutropius, 1.5.

39 Tarquinius was the fifth king of Rome (conventionally 616–579 BC). Orosius's account of his military campaigns is drawn from Florus, 1.1.5.

40 Servius Tullius was the sixth king of Rome (conventionally 578–535 BC), Orosius takes his note from Florus, 1.1.5.

41 Tarquinius Superbus was the seventh and final king of Rome (conventionally 534–510 BC). His murder of his father-in-law is noted by Eutropius, 1.7, and alluded to by Florus, 1.1.7.

towards its citizens, and lost it through the shameful rape of Lucretia. While he indulged in vice at home, he showed outstanding ability abroad[42] – he captured the powerful cities of Ardea, Oricolum, Suessa, and Pometia in Latium,[43] and what he did against the Gabii was achieved through a trick of his own devising, a punishment devised by his son, and the might of Rome.[44]

13. But the number of wrongs the Romans had endured for 243 years under the heel of kings is shown by the fact that they not only expelled one king, but also foreswore the title and power of kingship.[45] **14.** For if they had merely held the arrogance of one man as culpable, they ought simply to have expelled him and kept the honour of royalty for better men.

15. After the Romans had expelled their kings from the City, thinking that they themselves should look to their own interests rather than that some one individual should lord it over their liberty, they created the consuls under whom the affairs of the growing state, as if it had now reached its manhood, were tested in even more daring deeds.[46]

5

1. 244 years after the foundation of the City, Brutus, the first Roman consul, not only equalled the first founder and king of Rome in his acts of parricide, but took care to excel him.[47] He summoned his two adolescent sons and, at the same time, his wife's two brothers, the young Vitellii, before a public meeting on the trumped-up charge that they wished to restore the kings. He had them beaten with rods and then executed with his axe.[48]

---

42 This is the judgment of Livy, 1.53, 'He proved as skilled a leader in war as he was wicked in peace-time'. Augustine, on the other hand, is entirely hostile to Tarquin; see *City of God*, 3.15.

43 Orosius does not realise that Suessa Pometia, a vanished city in Latium, was one town not two.

44 Tarquin took Gabii, a town 12 miles to the east of Rome, by having his son Sextus inveigle his way into its inhabitants' confidence. Sextus became the town's leader and executed its leading citizens, making the city easy to conquer. The full story is found in Livy, 1.53–54.

45 The figure of 243 years is taken from Eutropius, 1.8, and is also mentioned by Augustine, *City of God*, 3.15.

46 These sentiments, and the notion of the Roman state reaching adulthood, are taken from Florus, 1.2.8 and 1.3.9.

47 Sarcasm is a recurrent feature of Orosius's narrative style. Brutus's consulate is normally dated to 245 *AUC*/509 BC.

48 A reference to the *fascis*, an axe surrounded by rods, symbolising the consul's right to inflict corporal and capital punishment. The story of Brutus's sons is taken from Florus, 1.3.9,

2. He himself fell when he met Arruns, the son of Superbus, face to face, sharing a common death with him during the war against Veii and the supporters of the Tarquins.[49] **3.** Porsenna, the king of the Etruscans, was the strongest proponent of royal rule, and marching on the terrified City, terrorised, isolated, and besieged it without ceasing for three years. Had Mucius not moved the enemy to admiration through his steadfast endurance when his hand was roasted, nor Cloelia done the same by the marvellous boldness of her crossing over the river, the Romans would surely have been compelled to suffer either being imprisoned by their tenacious foe or being subjected to slavery once more by the return of their king.[50]

4. After these events, the Sabines gathered their forces from all over their lands and marched on Rome in great military force. In the ensuing panic, the Romans created a dictator whose authority and power outstripped that of the consul, an act that proved to be a great help to them in the war.[51]

5. There followed the secession of the plebs from the fathers.[52] The people, already aroused by a variety of grievances, armed themselves and set up camp on the Sacred Mount when the dictator Marcus Valerius was conducting a military levy.[53] What could have been more horrendous than this wickedness, when a body severed from its head wished to destroy that from which it drew its life?[54] It would have been the end of the name of

where again Brutus is criticised. This is a striking change from the earlier account of the same story by Livy, 2.4–5, where Brutus's sons are assumed clearly to be guilty and Brutus's patriotism in executing them is praised. Augustine also mentions Brutus's consulate in negative tones, *City of God*, 3.16.

49 For this episode see Florus, 1.4.10, and Eutropius, 1.10.

50 The comment about Porsenna and the stories of Mucius Scaevola and Cloelia are told by Florus, 1.4.10. Orosius curiously suppresses the story of Horatius keeping the bridge which directly precedes those of Scaevola and Cloelia in Florus, who firmly links them as the three prodigies (*prodigia*) of Rome.

51 A reference to the dictatorship of Titus Larcius in 501 BC and recorded in Eutropius, 1.12, and Jerome, *Chronicle, A Abr.* 1513 = 249 *AUC*. The dictator held power alone, but his office lasted only six months.

52 A reference to the so-called conflict of the orders. The fathers are the patricians, the hereditary aristocrats of Rome; the plebs, the rest of the population.

53 The Sacred Mount lies three miles from Rome by the river Anis. The dictator concerned is normally known as Manlius Valerius. Orosius may have been working from an already corrupt manuscript or he, or a later copyist of his work, misread the abbreviation M' as M.

54 The first secession of the plebs occurred in the dictatorship of Manlius Valerius in 494 BC. Jerome, *Chronicle, A Abr.* 1523 = 259 *AUC*, notes the secession and describes it as 'sedition'. Eutropius, 1.13, while not mentioning the secession, does speak of 'sedition' – though he notes that it was brought on by the oppression of the Senate and consuls. As usual, Orosius takes the side of the aristocracy in discussing civil strife; this is in contrast to Augustine

Rome because of this wickedness within had not a reconciliation hastened to remove it, before, indeed, secession knew its own name.

6. Apart from the obvious calamities brought by external wars, the City was hard pressed and threatened by a pitiable succession of hidden disasters. In the consulate of Titus Gesonius and Publius Minucius, probably the two most abominable of all ills – famine and disease – seized hold of the weary City, and so, though there was a brief respite from war, there was no respite from death.[55]

7. The people of Veii from Etruria, no mean foe, uniting their neighbours' forces with their own, rose up in war and were met by the consuls, Marcus Fabius and Gnaeus Manilius. After the Romans had sworn a solemn oath, vowing not to return to their camp unless they were victorious, there was so fierce a fight with equal losses for victor and vanquished alike that the consul Marcus Fabius refused the triumph given to him by the Senate on the grounds that since most of the army had been lost and his fellow-consul Manlius and the former consul Fabius had been killed in the fight, there ought rather to be a period of mourning after the Republic had suffered so many losses.[56] **8.** The extent to which the Fabian clan, renowned for its numbers and vigour, orphaned the republic on its fall, after it had been allotted the task of waging the Veientine War, is attested to by the names, infamous to this day, of the river that destroyed them and the gate that sent them forth.[57] **9.** For when 306 men of the Fabii, who were truly the brightest light of the Roman State, asked that the war against Veii be assigned to them alone, their initial advances made this rashly undertaken adventure seem successful at first. But then they were led into an ambush, surrounded by the enemy, and all slaughtered there save one who was spared to take back news of the disaster, in order that their country should have more misery in hearing the news of their losses than the losses themselves caused her.[58]

10. It was not at Rome alone that such things happened. Various

who uses the incident to point to injustices in the early Roman state, *City of God*, 2.18 and 3.17. Orosius's comments about a body severed from its head draws on the parable of the belly used by Menenius Agrippa to persuade the plebs to end their protest, see Livy, 2.32.8–12.

55 492 BC. Titus Gesonius is called Titus Geganius by Livy, 2.34.1.

56 This incident, which occurred in 480 BC, is recorded in full in Livy, 2.45–47.

57 Orosius's comments about the gate are a paraphrase of Florus, 1.6.3.

58 The incident is recorded by Florus, 1.6.12, who correctly names the river as the Cremera (the modern Fosso Valchetta) and the gate as the *Porta Scelerata* (i.e. the *Porta Carmentalis*). Eutropius, 1.16, notes the disaster, but with no mention of the river or gate. For a full account of the episode, see Livy, 2.49–50.

provinces each blazed with their own fires so that what an outstanding poet said of one city, I will say of all the world:

All parts resound with tumults, plaints, and fears
And grisly death in sundry shapes appears.[59]

6

1. At the same time as Cyrus, the king of the Persians, whom I have mentioned previously in order to keep to the correct chronology,[60] was marching in arms through Asia, Scythia, and all the Orient, Tarquinius Superbus was bringing woe to the City either by enslaving it while king, or by waging war on it as an enemy. **2.** Cyrus, as I have said, after defeating all whom he had attacked, marched on the Assyrians and Babylon, the wealthiest people and city of his day. But the river Gyndes,[61] which is the second greatest in size after the Euphrates, stayed his attack. **3.** In a place where dangerous whirlpools are formed along its treacherous river-bed, one of the king's horses, a beautiful white animal, confident that it could cross the river, was caught up its currents, thrust down into its depths, and drowned. **4.** In his fury the king swore that he would be avenged on the river, telling it that though now it had devoured a noble horse, he would leave it so shallow that women would be able to cross it and hardly have to get their knees wet. Nor were his deeds slower than his words. For the entire year he had all his troops dig great ditches and channel the Gyndes into them, so reducing it into 460 streams.[62] **5.** Having turned his men into expert engineers by this work, he then diverted the flow of the Euphrates, a far larger river which ran through the middle of Babylon.[63] **6.** In this way he created a dry path along streams which were fordable and at times even revealed the river-bed, and captured a city which scarcely seemed possible to have been built by human hands or to be brought low by human endeavour.[64] **7.** For this was the Babylon that, according to many authorities, was founded by the giant

---

59 Virgil, *Aeneid*, 2.368–69.

60 1.19.6–11.

61 The modern Diyálah, a tributary of the Tigris in Iraq.

62 Orosius has drawn this tale from Seneca, *De Ira*, 3.21.

63 The minority manuscript reading. The majority of manuscripts read 'Babylonia'; however, Babylon makes more sense here.

64 The account of the capture of Babylon ultimately derives from Herodotus, 1.189–91. Near Eastern tradition speaks of Babylon falling to Cyrus without a fight. For a discussion of these sources, see Briant (2002) 40–44.

Nebrot[65] and refounded by Ninus or Semiramis.

8. It lay, conspicuous from all sides, on a flat plain. Its land was naturally very fertile, and, like a fort, it was square in shape and walled on each side.[66] When they are described, the solidity and size of these walls hardly sounds credible, for they were 50 cubits thick and four times as high again. **9.** Its circumference was 480 stades. This enceinte was made of baked bricks joined together with bitumen. Outside it ran a broad ditch like a river. A 100 bronze gates were built into the walls. **10.** The thickness of the walls accommodated equally spaced turrets for defenders on either side of the wall at the top of the rampart and in the central space there was room for *swift four-horse chariots* to pass.[67] The houses within were of twice-four stories and marvellous for their menacing height.

11. The great Babylon, however, the first city to be founded after the restoration of the human race,[68] was at that time captured and overthrown with hardly any delay.

12. It was then that Croesus, the king of the Lydians, famed for his wealth, came to help the Babylonians, but was defeated and fled back to his own kingdom in panic. Cyrus, after he had come to Babylon as its enemy, cast it down as its conqueror, and arranged its affairs as its king, turned to make war on Lydia where he easily defeated its army which had been terrified by his previous success in battle. He captured Croesus himself and gave his prisoner a present of both his life and his patrimony.[69] **13.** It is not my task here to expatiate on the unstable nature of changeable things: *whatever is built by the work of man's hands, collapses and is consumed by old age*[70]

65 A common belief in the early church based on Genesis 10.10; see Augustine, *City of God*, 16.3.

66 Orosius has in mind the *quadriburgium* of the late Roman army – a square fortification with a square projecting tower at each corner; see Southern and Dixon (1996) 136–37, and Johnson (1983) 253–55.

67 These figures ultimately derive from Herodotus, 1.178–79. The cubit was a variable measure, but normally around 1'6", leading to walls some 300 feet high and 75 feet thick. The stade was 600 feet long, though the foot itself varied through the ancient world. Orosius's circumference is likely to have been 54.5 miles. The phrase 'swift four-horse chariots' is a possible reminiscence of Virgil, *Aeneid*, 8.642. In reality, Babylon was some eight miles in circumference and surrounded by a double wall. The breadth of these walls *in toto* was some 85 feet. For a full account, see Oates (1979) 144ff.

68 i.e. after Noah's flood, see 1.3.

69 Orosius's account of Croesus is a rhetorical embroidery of Justin, 1.7. In Justin's account Cyrus only gives Croesus part of his patrimony.

70 The quotation is taken from Cicero, *Speech in defence of Marcellus* (*Pro Marcello*), 4.11.

as the capture of Babylon shows. Hers was the first and mightiest empire, and so it was the first to come to an end in order that, as if in obedience to some law of the succession of ages, her due inheritance could be handed on to the next generation who would, in their turn, follow this same law of succession.

14. In this way great Babylon and mighty Lydia fell on Cyrus's first attack – the most powerful limbs of the East falling along with its head[71] and collapsing through the outcome of one single battle. And the people of our time are looking round in unreflecting distress and asking whether the once-mighty foundations of the Roman state are now tottering not from the blows of foreign foes, but rather from the weakness of its own old age.[72]

7[73]

1. Immediately afterwards Cyrus waged war on the Scythians. Although Queen Thamyris[74] who at that time ruled this race *could have stopped him crossing the river Araxes, she allowed him to cross*[75] both because of her own confidence and because this gave her a chance to trap her enemy as he would have the river to his rear. **2.** Cyrus therefore advanced into Scythia and pitched his camp far from where he had crossed the river. Afterwards, he cunningly abandoned it, though it had been decked out with food and wine, to give the impression that he had fled in terror. When the queen heard of this, she sent her young son with a third of her army to pursue Cyrus. **3.** Soon, after the barbarians had been overcome by drink, just as if they had been invited to a feast, Cyrus returned and slew them all, including the young boy.

4. After losing her army and son, Thamyris made ready to assuage her sorrows as a mother and as a queen with the blood of her enemy rather than with her own tears. She pretended that she had lost confidence and was despondent because of the disaster, and, by slowly retreating, drew

71 i.e. Babylon.

72 This statement contrasts with Orosius's normal optimism about the future of Christian Rome and appears to be a reversion to pagan theories of cyclical history. There is perhaps here an echo of Tacitus's pessimism when discussing the internal wars of German tribes; see *Germania*, 33.

73 In this chapter Orosius closely follows Justin, 1.8.

74 See Justin, 1.8.2. Herodotus, 1.205, calls her Tomyris.

75 Taken verbatim from Justin, 1.8.2. The Araxes is the modern Syr Darya which rises in the Tien Shan mountains of Kyrgystan and flows west through southern Kazakhstan to the Aral Sea.

her arrogant foe into an ambush. **5.** *Having arranged this in the mountains, she annihilated 200,000 Persians there along with their king – not one survived to report this great disaster, which is the most amazing part of what happened.*[76] **6.** The queen ordered that Cyrus's head be struck off and thrown into a wine skin filled with human blood, cursing it as a man would curse. *'Drink your fill'*, she said, *'of the blood for which you thirsted and with which could not sate yourself* for 30 years.'[77]

8

1. 245 years after the foundation of the City, when Cyrus had been killed in Scythia, after an interval of time, the lot fell on Darius to take possession of his kingdom.[78] **2.** Between the reigns of these two came that of Cambyses, the son of Cyrus. He conquered Egypt and, having a loathing for every aspect of Egyptian religion, put an end to their rites and temples.[79] **3.** After him, the Magi dared to seize the kingdom in the name of a king whom they had killed.[80] They were, however, soon found out and done away with. **4.** Darius, one of those who had put an end to the audacity of the Magi by the sword, was made king with the approval of all.

After he had re-conquered Assyria and Babylon, which had rebelled against the empire of the Persians, he made war on Antyrus, the king of the Scythians.[81] The prime cause of this war was that he had sought, but not obtained, Antyrus's daughter in marriage,[82] **5.** so one can see the great necessity that made 700,000 men be exposed to the threat of death to satisfy the lusts of one man. After making an incredible number of preparations,

---

76 Taken virtually verbatim from Justin, 1.8.11–12.

77 Justin has Thamyris curse Cyrus's head 'upbraiding him cruelly' rather than 'as a man would curse'. However, Orosius has taken the queen's spoken words, save for the addition of 'for 30 years', verbatim from Justin, 1.8.13.

78 Orosius's chronology is awry here. According to Jerome, the temple in Jerusalem was restored in *A Abr.* 1468 and Darius was already on the throne. This year is equivalent to 205 *AUC*.

79 The story of Cambyses is taken from Justin, 1.9. Orosius suppresses Justin's account of how this sacrilege, as he styles it, led to Cambyses' death and how a Persian army failed to destroy the temple of Amon at Siwah as it was driven away from the site by sand-storms. For a discussion of Cambyses' campaigns in Egypt, see Briant (2002) 50–61.

80 The so-called pseudo-Smerdis, see Justin, 1.9.

81 Orosius's account of the rise of Darius is a highly abbreviated version of Justin, 1.9–10.

82 The Scythian king is called Jancyrus by Justin, 2.5.8. The account of the Scythian expedition follows Justin's version closely.

Darius entered Scythia with 700,000 men. His enemy did not give him the chance to fight a set-piece battle, but whittled his troops away with sudden sorties on their flanks. **6.** Fearing that he would not be able to withdraw if the bridge over the Danube was destroyed, Darius fled in panic having lost 80,000 warriors, although he did not count their deaths among his losses and did not feel the loss of a number of men which hardly anyone would have dared to imagine to have in their army in the first place. **7.** After this, he marched on and subjugated Asia and Macedonia,[83] and, after fighting a naval battle, also conquered the Ionians.[84]

He then turned his arms to attack the Athenians because they had sent help against him to the Ionians.[85] **8.** When the Athenians learnt that Darius was coming, although they sought help from the Lacedaemonians, they discovered that the Persians were delayed by a four-day religious observance.[86] Taking hope from this chance event, they marshalled 10,000 citizens and 1,000 Plataean allies, and fell on the 600,000 troops of the enemy on the plains of Marathon.[87] **9.** Their general at the time was Miltiades, who relied more on speed than courage and, by making a swift charge, managed to come to grips with the enemy before his attack could be driven off by their arrows. **10.** There was a great difference in the way they fought in that battle: one group of men came ready to kill; the others seemed like cattle brought to the slaughter.[88] **11.** That day 200,000 Persians died on the Plains of Marathon.[89] **12.** This was a loss that Darius did feel and, after being routed in defeat, he seized some ships and fled back to Persia.

13. He then renewed the war and plotted vengeance against his victors. He died in the middle of his preparations in the 74th Olympiad, that is 275

83 A reference to Mardonius's expedition of 492 BC.

84 The Battle of Lade, 494 BC.

85 Orosius's account of Darius's Scythian expedition, including the numbers of those involved and those lost, and his subsequent actions follows Justin, 2.5.9–13, closely. He has omitted Justin's long anthropological excursus on the Scythians.

86 Having passed over Justin, 2.6–8, this passage follows Justin, 2.9.8ff. Orosius has misread Justin, 2.9.9, where Justin correctly states that it was the Spartans, not the Persians, who were holding a religious festival.

87 490 BC.

88 Orosius's account of the battle, including the numbers involved, draws heavily on Justin, 2.9.9–12. Justin, however, has Militiades 'relying more on his speed than his allies'. Orosius embroiders Justin's observation at 2.9.12 that 'you would think they were men on one side and cattle on the other', but because he has changed Justin's 'allies' to 'courage' his use of this observation is somewhat inept.

89 Justin, 2.9.20, says that 200,000 Persians died at Marathon and in the subsequent sea-battle. For a discussion of Marathon from a Persian perspective, see Briant (2002) 160–61.

years after the foundation of the City, in the same year as the virgin Popilia was buried alive at Rome for sexual misdemeanours.[90]

<h1 style="text-align:center">9[91]</h1>

1. Xerxes succeeded his father Darius on the throne and for five years made preparations for the war against the Greeks that had been begun by his father. The Lacedaemonian Demaratus, who happened to be in exile at the court of Xerxes at that time, treacherously told his people about this on tablets that he first wrote on and then covered with wax.[92] **2.** Xerxes is said to have had 700,000 armed men from his kingdom, 300,000 from his allies, 1,200 warships, and 3,000 transport vessels, so it was justly recorded that the rivers hardly had enough water to drink for such an army of unprecedented size and such a massive fleet, and that there was hardly enough land for his army's advance or sea for his fleet's course.

3. Against this column, whose size would be unthinkable in our day and whose numbers are more difficult to count now than they were to defeat then, stood Leonidas, the king of the Spartans, with 4,000 men in the Pass of Thermopylae.[93] **4.** Xerxes, contemptuous of the small numbers of those facing him, ordered the battle to begin and that it be fought at close quarters. Those whose kin and fellow-soldiers had fallen on the Plains of Marathon were the first to enter the fray and suffer disaster. **5.** Then came a larger, but less enthusiastic, rabble who, since they were neither free to charge forward, nor equipped for fighting, nor able to flee, were simply marched up to be slaughtered.[94] For three whole days there was what was not a battle between two peoples, but simply the butchery of one of them.

---

90 Jerome also links the year of Darius's death with that of Popilia's execution, but these are placed in the 73rd Olympiad in *A Abr.*1531 = 268 *AUC*. Orosius's comments on Popilia closely follow those of Jerome.

91 This chapter omits Justin's account of Xerxes' struggle for the succession to the Persian throne and then draws heavily, albeit in a much abbreviated form, on Justin, beginning at 2.10.12 and continuing to 2.11.18. There is much rhetorical embroidery at the end of the chapter and Orosius has suppressed the Delphic Oracle's prophecy that either a Spartan king or the city of Sparta would perish; see Justin, 2.11.8.

92 Demaratus had been deposed as king of Sparta by Cleomenes in 491 BC and fled to Persia. Orosius is much harsher on him than Justin, 2.10.13, who comments 'he was a better friend to his country after his exile'.

93 480 BC.

94 Orosius has embroidered Justin, 2.11.3, which merely notes 'Greater slaughter ensued with the following, useless rabble'.

6. On the fourth day, after Leonidas saw that the enemy had surrounded him on all sides, he urged his allies to withdraw from the battle, escape up into the mountains,[95] and save themselves for better times,[96] but said that he and the Spartans would have a different fate, for they owed more to their country than to life.

7. When he had dismissed his allies, he warned the Spartans that they could hope for great glory, but that they had no chance of life; that they should not wait for the enemy or daybreak, but break into the enemy's camp by night, exchange blows with him, and throw his columns into confusion; and that they could have no more honourable death than as victors in their enemy's camp. **8.** Persuaded therefore to choose death, they armed themselves to avenge their coming deaths as men who would both bring about their own demise and take revenge for it. Wondrous as it is to relate, 600 men burst into the camp of 600,000.[97] **9.** The whole camp was in uproar, the Persians helping the Spartans by killing one another. The Spartans sought the king, and, on not finding him, slew and laid low everything they found. Ranging through the whole camp, they were scarcely able to pursue the scattered men amid the piles of corpses and would without a doubt have been triumphant, had they not chosen to die. **10.** The battle dragged on from nightfall into the latter part of the following day. Finally, worn down by their triumph, after each of them with failing, tired limbs had taken his fill of vengeance for his own death, weary, they fell down and died among the baggage of the dead and battlefield which was oozing with thick, half-congealed blood.

95 Orosius appears to have misread Justin, 2.11.5, who states that 'Leonidas was told that the heights were occupied by 20,000 of the enemy'.

96 Orosius changes the speech he found in Justin at this point. At Justin, 2.9.5, Leonidas urges his allies to save themselves for 'better times for their country'; however, Orosius suppresses 'for their country' in order to make an ideological point later on in his narrative.

97 Justin, 2.11.15, has 500,000 Persians. Orosius has presumably increased the number to make a more pleasing contrast with the 600 Spartans.

10[98]

1. Xerxes twice defeated on land, now prepared to fight a naval battle.[99] But the Athenians' commander, Themistocles, on learning that the Ionians, because of whom the Persians were now attacking Athens as she had given support to the Ionians in the previous war, had marshalled their fleet in support of Xerxes, decided to draw them onto his side and away from that of the enemy. **2.** Because he had no chance of talking to them, he ordered that signs be made and fixed to the rocks in the places to which the Ionians seemed likely to come in their ships. By means of these signs, he rightly rebuked them on the grounds that they had once been the Athenians' allies and partners in peril, but had now unjustly deserted them. By urging them to remember the solemn vows of their old alliance, he won them over and, above all, told them that when the conflict began, they should stay their oars as if they were retreating and take themselves out of the battle.[100]

3. The king kept part of his fleet with him and stayed on the shore to watch the battle. On the other hand, Artemidora,[101] the queen of Halicarnassus, who had come to support Xerxes, plunged so fiercely among the leaders of the front ranks of the battle that it seemed as if their roles had been reversed, for a feminine caution was seen in the man and a masculine daring in the woman.[102]

4. While the fight was in the balance, the Ionians followed Themistocles' advice and gradually began to withdraw from the battle. Their defection persuaded the Persians, who were already looking round for an excuse for flight, to flee openly. **5.** In the panic many ships were sunk or captured, and more, fearing the wrath of their king as much as the cruelty of the foe, slunk away to their homes.

6. Mardonius came to the king, who was troubled by so many setbacks, and persuaded him that as king he ought to return to his kingdom before news of the reverse stirred up revolution at home. **7.** He said that if the remnants of the army were entrusted to him, he would exact retribution

---

98 This chapter draws heavily, in abbreviated form on Justin, 2.11.19–2.13.12. Orosius suppresses Justin's comment, 2.11.8–9, that Xerxes sent 4,000 men to sack Delphi before the battle of Salamis and so was waging war not just against the Greeks, but also against the gods. He also declines to mention the famous Delphic oracle about the 'wooden walls' of Athens; see Justin, 2.11.13–14.

99 The Battle of Salamis, 480 BC.

100 An abbreviated third-person rendering of a first-person speech in Justin, 2.12.3–7.

101 In fact, the queen's name was Artemisia. See Justin, 2.12.23, and Herodotus, 8.87.

102 This rhetorical flourish has been taken from Justin, 2.11.24.

from the foe and free the royal house from shame, or, if the reverses of war continued, he would fall before the foe, but that this would not involve disgrace for the king. **8.** Mardonius's advice was approved and the army handed over to him.

The king set off with a few men to Abydus[103] where he had built a bridge as if he had conquered the sea, but he found that the bridge had been destroyed by the winter storms, and so crossed over panic-stricken in a small fishing boat. **9.** It was right that mankind should have wondered and grieved at the way things change, using this enormous reversal of fortune as their guide. For a man beneath whom previously the sea itself had hidden itself and, shackled by a bridge, borne its yoke of captivity, was now himself content to lie hidden in a little boat. **10.** The man who now lacked the demeaning help of even a solitary underling was that same man before whose power nature itself had previously yielded when he ordered mountains cut through, valleys filled in, and rivers drunk dry.[104]

11. His foot soldiers too, who had been placed under the command of his generals, were wasting away under the effects of hard work, famine, and fear. Disease spread to epidemic proportions among them and the stench from the dying was so great that the roads were full of corpses, and ill-omened birds and accursed animals followed the dying army, lured by the temptation of finding food.

11[105]

1. Mardonius to whom Xerxes had entrusted the rest of the army was at first puffed up by a brief moment of success, but soon cast down into dire straits. **2.** He stormed the Greek town of Olynthus and advanced on the Athenians, offering them various hopeful approaches to make peace. When, however, he saw their liberty was not for the taking, he burnt down part of their town and took his entire army off into Boeotia. **3.** 100,000 Greeks pursued him thither, gave battle without delay and, after destroying his army and leaving him stripped of everything like a survivor of a shipwreck, compelled Mardonius to flee with a few men.[106] They captured his camp which was full of the king's treasure. This was no a small factor in undoing their previous

---

103 The modern Canakkale on the eastern side of the Hellespont.
104 This moralising is Justin's, 2.13.10.
105 This chapter until section 6 draws heavily on Justin, 2.14.
106 The Battle of Plataea, 479 BC.

work for after this booty was divided up, Persian gold proved the worst corruptor of Greek virtue.

4. Then a final disaster crowned these wretched undertakings, for it happened that on the same day that Mardonius's army was destroyed, part of the Persian army was fighting a sea battle under Mount Mycale.[107] **5.** A sudden rumour came to the ears of the fleets on both sides that Mardonius's troops had been wiped out and that the Greeks had triumphed. O, what a wondrous dispensation of Divine Justice that the result of a battle that had begun in Boeotia when the sun was in the east should become known in Asia on the same day at midday when so great a stretch of land and sea lies between them![108] **6.** The rumour was consistent with fact, because it rendered the Persians, after they heard of the disaster that had befallen their allies and were gripped first by sorrow and then despair, neither fit to fight nor able to flee; while the enemy, now made all the more resolute, fell with complete success on their terrified and broken foe.

7. After he had waged an unsuccessful war in Greece, Xerxes became a laughing-stock to his people. He was trapped and killed in his palace by the prefect Artabanus.[109]

8. O, what times most worthy to remember with nostalgia! What days of peaceful serenity they set before us to look back on from our times of darkness! Days when in the blink of an eye, three wars waged by three neighbouring kings snatched 9,000,000 men from the heart of a single kingdom, not to mention the misfortunes of Greece, where the number of deaths exceeded even this figure: a number which even today leaves us numb.

9. Leonidas, the most famous of the Lacedaemonians, gave this famous encouragement to his 600 men in the war against Xerxes, a war which proved both his and his enemies' last: 'Take your breakfast as if you are going to dine in the underworld', but he mercifully urged his allies, whom he ordered to leave the battle, to save themselves for better times. **10.** Behold, that while he promised better times in the future, men today assert that the past was better than the present, so what can one conclude when both groups detest their own times, except that all ages are good, but never seem so, or rather that none are better in all respects.

---

107 The modern Dilek Dagi, located on the Turkish coast opposite the island of Samos.

108 Justin, 2.14.9, attributes the spread of this news merely to the speed at which rumour travels.

109 This section draws on Justin, 3.1.1–2. For a more favourable assessment of Xerxes, see Briant (2002) 567–68.

12

1. I shall now return to Rome and to that time from which I digressed. It is not any break in Rome's suffering that forces me to look at other peoples, but, as these evils bubble up everywhere and collect themselves together through their actions, so they must be discussed together, given that our task is to collate the history of the world and not to pounce upon the troubles of one part of that history. **2.** At Rome then, 290 years after the foundation of the City, a severe plague put an end to war for a while. Plagues always broke the short truces that Rome made, or compelled her to make such truces. This plague raged fiercely throughout the entire city, so the sky which had been seen burning on fire was rightly seen as an omen of its coming, given that the head of the world was ablaze with such a great flame of disease.[110] **3.** In that year the plague carried off both the consuls, Aebutius and Servilius, and took the lives of most of Rome's soldiers. Its foul decay killed many nobles and even more of the plebs, **4.** though the people had already been ravaged by an outbreak of the plague four years previously.[111]

5. The following year some exiled citizens and fugitive slaves led by Herbonius, a Sabine, attacked and burnt the Capitol **6.** where the Iuniores[112] bravely held out under their general, the consul Valerius. However, the deciding moment of the conflict was so fierce and furious that the consul Valerius was himself killed there and soiled with his death a sordid victory over slaves.[113]

7. There followed a year in which an army was defeated and a consul besieged. For the Aequi and Volsci met and defeated the consul Minucius in battle and then, after he had fled to Algidus,[114] besieged him with hunger and the sword. These events would have turned out badly, had not Quintius Cincinnatus, the famous dictator, defeated the enemy and lifted this close

110 Livy, 3.5.14. Orosius is happy to accept portents of natural disasters. For him these are true signs and caused by God, but often misinterpreted by pagans.

111 Orosius is one year out in his reckoning as this plague occurred in 291 *AUC*/463 BC; see Livy, 3.6. The previous plague occurred in 288 *AUC*/466 BC.

112 The centuries of troops aged between 17 and 46. The title, though with a different meaning, was also in common use in the later Roman army of Orosius's own day.

113 Orosius's chronology is again awry: these events date to 294 *AUC*/460 BC when P. Valerius Poplicola was consul. A full account is found at Livy, 3.15.5–3.18.9, where the slaves' leader is called Herdonius. Again, Orosius's aristocratic tone is noticeable here. The death of Valerius also occurs in a list of disasters found in Augustine, *City of God*, 3.17, which is used to demonstrate the impotence of Rome's pagan gods.

114 L. Minucius Esquilinus Augurinus, suffect consul in 458 BC. Algidus is the modern Monte Campatri on the edge of the Alban Hills.

siege. **8.** Cincinnatus was found in the countryside and summoned from his plough to rule. He accepted this honour, marshalled the army, and soon emerged victorious. He made the Aequi pass under the oxen's yoke and was the first to drive his yoked foes before him, treating his victory as if it was his plough's handle.[115]

13

1. In the following year, which preceded the 300th since the foundation of the City, while the ambassadors who had been sent to Athens to bring back the laws of Solon were still away, famine and plague weakened Roman arms. **2.** In the 300th year since the foundation of the City – that is in the 95th Olympiad – the power of the consuls was given to ten men in order to establish the laws of Attica.[116] This brought great harm to the Republic, **3.** for the leader of the ten, Appius Claudius, extended the duration of his own power[117] after the others laid theirs down. They immediately formed a conspiracy so that they might all indulge in all their individual lusts, ignoring the custom whereby while the emblems of command were given to one magistrate, its power was common to them all.[118] **4.** And so, among the other things that they had all usurped with sheer arrogance, suddenly each one of them began to parade with twelve *fasces* and the rest of a commander's insignia. **5.** After this wicked new order of things had been established, an army of tyrants appeared which ignored the reverence due to the consuls.[119] They added two tables of laws to the old ten tables and carried out many acts with utter arrogance, including parading with the same insignia as ever on the day

---

115 The story of Cincinnatus is found in Florus, 1.5.11–15; Eutropius, 1.17; and more fully in Livy, 3.25–28. He was dictator in 296 *AUC*/458 BC. Livy makes no claim that this was when the custom of forcing enemies under the yoke was first instituted, but does describe the practice here. Augustine, *City of God*, 5.18, regards Cincinnatus as an exemplary role model.

116 Conventionally 451 BC, i.e. 303 *AUC*. Eutropius, 1.18, Jerome, *Chronicle*, *A Abr.* 1566, and Livy, 3.33.1, date the Decemvirate to 302 *AUC*. The story of the decemvirate is found in Livy, 3.33–50. Orosius's synchronisation with the Olympiads is incorrect: the decemvirs date to the end of the 81st Olympiad. For a discussion of the decemvirate, see Cornell (1995) 272–76.

117 Latin, *imperium.*

118 The custom concerned was the practice of the previous decemvirs that only one of them should parade with the *fasces*, Livy, 3.36.3. The 'others' are members of the so-called Second Decemvirate and conspired with Appius Claudius. Orosius appears confused here.

119 This is the so-called Second Decemvirate, conventionally 450 BC.

when it is customary to lay down one's magistracy.[120]

6. It was the lust of Appius Claudius that caused most hatred. In order to rape the maiden Virginia, he first accused her of being a slave. Because of this Virginius, her father, driven by his sorrow at her loss of liberty and by his shame at her disgrace, killed his daughter, who had already been enslaved, in an act of pious murder before the gaze of the people. **7.** The people were moved by this horrible, but necessary, deed, and warned by it that their liberty was in danger, occupied the Aventine Hill in arms. Nor did they cease to guard their liberty with their arms until the conspiracy had dissolved itself and the conspirators laid down their powers.

8. In the 103rd and 105th Olympiads, there were severe and frequent earthquakes in Italy for almost an entire year with the result that Rome grew weary of messages reporting the countless tremors and the continual destruction of farms and towns. **9.** Then there came a long, roasting drought that put an end to any hope of the land yielding crops either in that or the following year.[121] **10.** At the same time, Rome's enemies, the Fidenates, menaced the citadel of Rome, a threat made all the more terrible as they had a huge band of allies with them. But Aemilius, the third dictator, dispelled and cured this great mass of evil by capturing Fidenae itself, albeit with difficulty.[122]

11. So great was the strife and these troubles and dissensions that the wars which poured down on them from abroad erased the memories of internal discord, and, after the losses of war, the following periods of uneasy truce were ruined by the unending outbreaks of plagues which blazed forth from both earth and sky.[123]

---

120 i.e. they refused to lay down office; see Livy, 3.38.1.

121 These two Olympiad dates are 386–389 *AUC* and 394–397 *AUC* and must be an error. The mention of farms derives from Livy, 4.21.5, and dates to 318 *AUC*/436 BC. The later drought may be a reference to Livy, 4.30.7–11, but it seems odd that Orosius has not taken the chance to attack the religious practices mentioned there.

122 Reading *tertius* with Arnaud-Lindet and our ancient manuscripts. Zangemeister corrects the reading to *tertium*, 'for the third time'. In terms of historical facts, Zangemeister is correct: Mamilius Aemilius Mamercinus had been dictator twice before (in 437 and 434 BC) and held the office for the third time in 328 *AUC*/426 BC. However, it seems that Orosius is guilty of a hasty reading of Livy, 4.32, where Mamilius is described as *dictatorem tertium*, and has failed to see that Livy is here using *tertium* adverbially. Fidenae is the modern Castel Giubileo.

123 This material is probably drawn from Livy, 4.30.8, but the pagan content concerning rituals has been suppressed.

14[124]

1. Sicily was at first the land of the Cyclopes and after that has ever been the nurse of tyrants. Often she has been the prisoner of slaves.[125] The first of these groups nourished themselves on human flesh, the second on human torture, and the last on human slaughter. The exception to these times was when the island was considered as booty or a prize in foreign wars. **2.** To put the matter as briefly as possible, the island has known no respite from troubles, save in the present day. Indeed, this is clearly shown by her diverse fortunes – previously, she alone of all nations continually suffered from either internal or external troubles, whereas now she alone never suffers them. **3.** Etna itself gives an example that allows me to be silent about the continual calamities Sicily used to suffer and the peace that she now enjoys. For while in the past the volcano often used to erupt and destroy both cities and fields, now it merely lies there smoking: a harmless witness which serves to make the stories of the past credible. **4.** Now I shall pass over the time of the tyrants and how one after another threw down his predecessor and then soon took his place, and begin in the middle of the period, namely in 335th year after the foundation of the City, when the Regini who live near Sicily were suffering from civil strife which had divided their state into two factions.[126] One faction summoned veterans from the Sicilian town of Himera[127] to their aid. **5.** Soon after these veterans had driven out of the city those against whom they had been begged to fight, they slaughtered those whom they had come to help and seized the city along with the women and children of their 'allies', thus daring to do a deed unequalled by any tyrant. **6.** It would have been better for the Regini to endure anything rather than of their own freewill to have invited in those to whom, after they themselves had been driven into exile, they left their country, wives, children, and household gods as booty.

7. The people of Catina, when they were suffering from the bitter hostility of the Syracusans, asked for help from the Athenians.[128] The Athenians,

---

124 This chapter draws very closely on Justin, 4.2–5.

125 A reference to the two major slave uprisings on the island in 135–132 BC and 104–100 BC. As ever, Orosius shows no sympathy for slaves or hostility to slavery.

126 This date is Orosius's own. The Regini are the inhabitants of Rhegium, the modern Reggio di Calabria.

127 Located near the modern town of Termini Imerese.

128 The modern Catania. Orosius has copied an error from Justin, 4.3. The embassy to Athens came from Leontini with whom the Athenians had had a full military alliance, a symmachia, since the 450s BC, see Thucydides, 3.86. Catania was one of Leontini's allies.

looking more to their interests than those of their allies, marshalled a fleet
and despatched it to Sicily, both with the intention of extending their empire
there and also because they feared that the recently created Syracusan fleet
would come to the aid of the Lacedaemonians. **8.** Since the Athenians who
had been despatched killed their enemies and so enjoyed initial success,
Athens sent more supplies and a stronger army under the leadership of
Laches and Chariades to Sicily.[129] **9.** But the people of Catina were wearied
by the war and struck a treaty with the Syracusans, spurning Athens' aid.[130]
10. Afterwards, however, when the Syracusans, who were planning to
conquer them, broke the terms of this peace treaty, they once more sent
ambassadors to Athens. These ambassadors had unkempt hair and beards
and were dressed in mourning so that they could beg for pity and help both
through their words and by their appearance.[131]

11. A great fleet was marshalled and put under the command of Nicias
and Lamachus, and so the Athenians returned to Sicily in such force that
even those who had asked for them to come were afraid of what they had
requested.[132] **12.** Straightaway, the Athenians fought two successful land
battles, drove the enemy back into their city, and, bringing up their fleet,
surrounded them by land and sea. **13.** But the Syracusans, exhausted and
with their affairs in ruins, sought help from the Lacedaemonians. They soon
sent Gylippus – he came alone, but was worth an entire garrison. On arriving
and hearing that the war was already going badly, he gathered allied troops,
some from Greece, some from Sicily, and occupied positions from which he
could wage war. **14.** He was defeated in two battles, but was unmoved, and
in the third encounter killed Lamachus, put his enemies to flight, and lifted
the siege for his allies.[133]

15. After the Athenians had been defeated on land, they began to try
their luck at sea and prepared to fight a naval battle. On learning of this,
Gylippus summoned the fleet that had been marshalled by the Lacedaemonians, **16.** and the Athenians too despatched Demosthenes and Eurymedon
with reinforcements to take the place of their lost general. The Pelopon-

---

129 In 427 BC.

130 The Treaty of Gela, 424 BC.

131 The successful embassy was in fact from Segesta in 416 BC, Orosius has followed an
error in Justin, 4.4.1–3.

132 Orosius suppresses mention of the third Athenian general, Alcibiades, found at Justin,
4.4.3. The Sicilian expedition took place in 415 BC.

133 Gylippus arrived in Sicily in 413 BC. Justin, 4.4.9, mistakenly places Lamachus's
death after his arrival and again Orosius has followed Justin's error.

nesians also sent a large number of reinforcements to the Syracusans in accordance with a decree approved by many cities. **17.** So in this way, under the pretext of fighting for their allies, they pursued their own quarrels abroad with both sides fighting there at full strength, as if it had been decreed that their struggle be transferred from Greece to Sicily.

18. The Athenians were defeated in the first encounter and lost their camp, and with it all their money, both that belonging to the state and that of private individuals, as well as all the equipment necessary for a long expedition. **19.** After their resources had been shattered and they were reduced to dire straits, Demosthenes urged that they should return home and withdraw from Sicily, while, albeit they seemed in great trouble, everything was not altogether lost. **20.** But Nicias, who had become all the more desperate from shame at having done everything badly from the beginning, argued that they should stay. **21.** They renewed the naval war and soon, because of their ignorance of these waters, were drawn into the narrows of the Syracusan Sea where they were surrounded in an enemy ambush. Eurylochus was the first of their generals to die and eleven ships were set on fire.[134] Demosthenes and Nicias then abandoned the fleet, thinking that they could flee more safely by land. **22.** Gylippus first fell upon the 130 ships that the Athenians had left and then set off to pursue the fugitives themselves, capturing and killing the vast majority of them. Demosthenes spurned the disgrace of enslavement by taking his own life, but Nicias added the disgrace of capture to his unworthy and shameful life.[135]

15[136]

1. The Athenians, after being mauled by the Lacedaemonians in Sicily for two years, though not without inflicting losses on them, were then entangled in other ills at home. For Alcibiades who had once been declared a general in the war against Syracuse, but soon afterwards had been detained for trial on some trumped-up charge, voluntarily took himself off to Lacedaemon

---

134 Eurylochus is either a scribe's error for Eurymedon who is mentioned earlier in the chapter, or Orosius has forgotten himself. Justin, 4.5.7, says 30 ships were burnt.

135 Athens's defeat took place in 413 BC. The final maxim is taken from Justin, 4.5.20. It is surprising that Orosius as a Christian does not disapprove of Demosthenes' suicide. Augustine devotes a long section of the first book of his *City of God* (chapters 17–24), which Orosius would have known, to suicide and concludes that suicide to avoid dishonour is not acceptable.

136 The material in this chapter, including its *sententiae*, draws heavily on Justin, 5.1–2.

into exile.[137] **2.** Here he urged the Spartans to renew the war against the Athenians while they were in difficulties, and crush them rather than allow them a breathing space. **3.** All Greece joined in this project, as if, taking heed of the common good, they had joined forces to put out a fire that threatened them all.

4. Now Darius, the king of the Persians,[138] remembering his father's and grandfather's hatred of this city, made a treaty with the Lacedaemonians through the agency of the prefect[139] of Lydia, Tissaphernes, and promised them that he would pay for the war and give them troops. **5.** Wondrous to relate, the resources of the Athenians were so great at this time that when they, that is one city, were attacked by the forces of Greece, Asia, and all the Orient, they gave frequent battle, never yielded, and seem to have been worn out rather than defeated.

6. At first, Alcibiades forced all the Athenians' allies to defect to the Lacedaemonians, but when the Lacedaemonians too became envious of him and sought to ensnare him, he fled and went off to Tissaphernes in Media.[140] **7.** Because of his adaptable character and tactful eloquence, he became a firm friend of the prefect. He persuaded him not to help the Lacedaemonians so generously, saying that he ought rather to be a judge and spectator of the contest and keep the might of Lydia intact to use against whomever won. **8.** Tissaphernes therefore ordered that part of his fleet along with some troops be sent to Lacedaemon so that they should not have such an abundance of aid that they could fight entirely free from danger, but neither be left completely devoid of help and so give up the conflict which they had begun.[141]

16[142]

1. Although the Athenians had long suffered from internal discord, when danger loomed, the people willingly transferred supreme power to the Senate. For discord is nourished by idleness, but when necessity presses,

137 The incident of the mutilation of the Herms, 415 BC. Oddly, Orosius makes no mention of Alcibiades as a general at 2.14.11 above.

138 Darius II, 424–404 BC.

139 i.e. the satrap. Orosius is presumably ignorant of this Persian title.

140 This detail is not in Justin and presumably is just a reference to the Persian Empire as a whole as Tissaphernes would have been resident in his Satrapy, Lydia, not in Media. Alcibiades fled here in 412 BC.

141 For an account of Persian relations with the Greek states in this period, see Briant (2002) 591–96.

142 The material in this chapter draws heavily on Justin, 5.3.1–5.8.3.

private quarrels and hatreds are put aside for the common good.[143] **2.** Now this policy would have been disastrous for the Athenians, given the innate pride and tyrannical lusts of their race, but finally Alcibiades was recalled from exile with his army and made commander of the fleet.[144] **3.** When this became known, the leading citizens[145] at first tried to betray their city to the Spartans, then, after their plot came to nothing, they went into voluntary exile and Alcibiades, after freeing his country, sailed with the fleet against the enemy. **4.** They came to battle and the Athenians won the victory. The greater part of the Spartan army was killed, almost all their generals were cut down, and 80 ships were captured, quite apart from those that had been fired or sunk in the fight.[146]

5. The war passed to the land again and proved equally unlucky for the Spartans, and so with their affairs in ruins the Lacedaemonians sought peace, but were unable to obtain it. **6.** Moreover, their Syracusan garrisons were summoned back to the island on hearing that a war with Carthage had broken out in Sicily.[147] So Alcibiades ranged through all Asia with his victorious fleet, plundering and laying low everything with war, fire, and slaughter, and captured or retook the vast majority of the cities that had defected from the Athenian alliance. **7.** Having made a great name for himself, he entered Athens in triumph to the admiration and joy of all.[148] **8.** Soon afterwards, he strengthened his forces, increased the size of the army and navy, and set out for Asia once again.

At this point, the Lacedaemonians made Lysander the commander of their fleet and put him in charge of the war.[149] **9.** Darius's brother, Cyrus,[150] was now put in charge of Ionia and Lydia in Tissaphernes' place and reinforced the Spartans with a great number of supplies and troops. Lysander crushed Alcibiades' army in a sudden attack while it was intent on plunder

143 This *sententia* is Orosius's own. Justin, 5.3.4, is a little more equivocal. This is unsurprising as the 'Senate' is the oligarchic Council of 400 instituted in 411 BC, a group normally regarded in a highly negative light.

144 This was done by the Athenian fleet stationed on Samos who were opponents of the 400. Orosius here manages to square the circle of approving of the motives that led to the creation of the 400, while also criticising the behaviour of that body by attacking the Athenians' temperament.

145 i.e. the Four Hundred.

146 The Battle of Cyzicus, 410 BC.

147 409 BC.

148 In 407 BC.

149 In late 408 or early 407 BC.

150 Cyrus was in fact Darius II's son, as is correctly noted by Justin, 5.5.1.

and therefore dispersed, with its men wandering far and wide.[151] In this way, without having to offer battle, he defeated and slaughtered them as they fled. **10.** This was a great disaster for the Athenians and a far more severe blow than that they themselves had inflicted on the Spartans a short time before.

On hearing of their defeat, the Athenians decided that Alcibiades had been minded to avenge the old grievance of his exile through the crime of treachery, **11.** and so they appointed Conon in his place, giving him command over what was left of their troops and the prosecution of the war. **12.** Conon wished to increase the numbers of his depleted forces and enlisted an army by enrolling old men and boys. But this kind of force brought no respite from war, for a war is usually determined by the strength of an army, not its numbers. **13.** Consequently this unwarlike band was at once either captured or killed, and so great were the piles of the slain in that battle that it seemed that it was not merely the kingdom of the Athenians that had been wiped out, but the very name Athenian itself.[152] **14.** In their desperate plight the Athenians decided to entrust their city to foreigners[153] and so they, who shortly before had lorded it over all Asia, now looked to defend their walls and liberty with these dregs of an army. Although they themselves took the view that this group, even when behind the walls, was not strong enough to mount a defence, they nevertheless prepared to make trial of their enemies in a naval battle once more.

15. For frenzy devoid of reason considers grief to be strength and overconfidence promises it can deliver what anger broods upon.

16. When all of this army had been captured or killed, there was nothing left that the remnants could do.[154] Conon was the only general who had survived the war and the people's wrath and he, fearing the vengeance of his fellow citizens, took himself off to King Cyrus.

17. Then Evacoras,[155] the Lacedaemonians' general, detached every

151 This is a highly abbreviated, and somewhat garbled, notice of the Battle of Notium, 406 BC, drawn from Justin, 5.5.2–3. Alcibiades was not in fact present at the battle.

152 The Battle of Mitylene, 406 BC.

153 Orosius has misunderstood Justin, 5.6.5, where *civitatem* means 'citizenship', not 'city' as he assumes.

154 Orosius appears to have conflated the Battle of Arginusae, a naval battle that ended in triumph for Athens in August 406 BC, with the disastrous Battle of Aegospotami in August 405 BC.

155 Orosius has badly garbled the end of Justin 5.6 and the beginning of 5.7 which reads 'He took himself off with eight ships to the *Cypriot* king, Evagoras. But the Spartan commander...' Orosius has taken 'Cypriot' as a noun and assumed that the accusative of Evagoras is a nomina-tive in apposition with 'Spartan commander'.

state from the Athenians, leaving them with nothing but an empty city, and did not even leave them with this for long, for soon afterwards he besieged the town. Hunger, devastation, and disease afflicted the Athenians within, **18.** and after suffering all these horrendous torments, which are terrifying even to relate, and seeing they had no hope but death, they sued for peace.[156]

17[157]

1. At this moment, there was a great debate among the Spartans and their allies. The overwhelming majority of them declared themselves in favour of razing this war-mongering city to the ground and annihilating its hated people along with their name, **2.** but the Spartans said that they would not allow one of Greece's two eyes to be gouged out.[158] In addition, they promised that they would make peace if the fortifications of the port of Piraeus that led to the town were knocked down and if of their own free will the Athenians handed over the remainder of their fleet and would then accept 30 governors[159] chosen by the Spartans. **3.** After the Athenians agreed and succumbed to these terms, the Lacedaemonians appointed Lysander to draw up the laws that the city would have to obey.

4. This year was remarkable for the capture of Athens, the death of Darius, king of the Persians, and the exile of the Sicilian tyrant Dionysius.[160]

5. Now the 30 governors appointed for Athens rose up to become 30 tyrants. They first went out accompanied by 3,000 bodyguards and soon also had by their side 700 soldiers from the victorious army.[161] **6.** After killing Alcibiades, who was burnt alive after being trapped in his room while on the road fleeing from them, they inaugurated an indiscriminate slaughter that would fall on all alike. **7.** For after his death, the Thirty felt sure that there would be no one to take vengeance on them and so drained dry what was left of the wretched city with their slaughter and plundering. As a warning to terrify the rest, they even murdered one of their own number, Theramenes, when they realised that he disagreed with what they were doing.

---

156 404 BC.

157 The material in this chapter until section 14 draws heavily on Justin, 5.8.3–5.10.11.

158 This striking phrase is taken from Justin, 5.8.4.

159 'rectores'.

160 This synchronism is taken from Justin, 5.8.7, but there is no evidence that Dionysius, who ruled from 405--67 BC, was ever exiled.

161 i.e. Spartans.

8. The result was that everyone began to flee from the city in all directions, and when the Spartans forbade that hospitality be given to these exiles in any part of Greece, they all took themselves off to Argos and Thebes. There they received such lavish hospitality that they not only assuaged their grief at losing their country, but even began to hope that they could recover it. **9.** Among these exiles was Thrasybulus, an active man, well-known among them because of his noble birth, and the first to dare to act for his country. The exiles therefore gathered themselves together, seized the fortress of Phyle on the borders of Attica, and then gained in strength as they were reinforced by aid given by many states. The Syracusan orator Lysias sent them 500 men and the wages to pay them, giving aid, he said, to the city that was the common homeland of all who cultivated eloquence.[162]

10. A fierce battle ensued, but, as one side was fighting for their country's freedom and the other to keep it in the power of foreigners, the battle itself gave judgment on their courage and causes. The tyrants were defeated and, on fleeing into the city, removed all those Athenians whom they had previously chosen as bodyguards from guarding the city, as they suspected them of treachery. **11.** They even dared to try to bribe Thrasybulus himself, but after they saw that their hopes were in vain, they summoned help from Lacedaemon and rushed out to wage war again. In the battle, the two cruellest tyrants of all were cut down.[163] **12.** When Thrasybulus realised that the majority of the others who had been defeated and routed were Athenians, he went off in pursuit, shouting out to them. He stayed them with his speech and bound them to him with his entreaties, setting before their eyes those from whom they wanted to flee and those to whom they wished to flee for refuge. He said that he had taken up arms against 30 tyrants, not against the wretched citizenry of Athens, and told them that rather than flee, all those who remembered that they were Athenians ought now rather to follow him and redeem the Athenians' liberty.

13. This speech made such an impression on them that they soon returned to the city and forced the tyrants to abandon their citadel and move to Eleusis. When they had received back into the city their fellow citizens who had been in exile up to that time, they roused the tyrants to war through envy, for to them the liberty of others seemed to be their own enslavement. **14.** Then, after war had been declared, when initially the tyrants came as

---

162 Orosius follows Justin in calling Lysias a Syracusan. Though born in Syracuse, Lysias lived as a metic in Athens. He fled to Megara after the rise of the Thirty.

163 The Battle of Munychia, 403 BC. The two tyrants are named by Justin, 5.9.15, as Critias and Hippolochus.

if to negotiate, they were taken in an ambush and *cut down like sacrificial victims for peace.*[164]

And so after the Athenians were reunited and had wept endless tears of great joy, they renewed the first foundations of their regained liberty, making a declaration under oath that the discord and animosity of the past be consigned to permanent oblivion and everlasting silence. **15.** And, as if they were fashioning a new style of life and a new, happy existence for themselves, they called this kind of agreement an 'amnesty', which means the abolition of grievances.

This would have been a very wise decision by the Athenians, especially after they had gone through so many recorded instances of suffering, had human arrangements the power to endure with men's consent in the form in which they were originally conceived.[165] **16.** But this decree was corrupted almost as soon as the very words of the agreement were spoken, and to such a degree that scarcely two years later the great Socrates, the most famous of philosophers, was driven by the wrongs which he suffered to take his life by poison before their very eyes.[166] Hardly 40 years after this, I pass over other matters, the Athenians completely lost their liberty and ended as the slaves of Philip, the king of the Macedonians.

17. Nevertheless, the Athenians, who were the wisest race of men, learnt well enough from their misfortunes that *through harmony even the smallest affairs flourish, whereas through disharmony the greatest founder.*[167] For seeing that all achievements or failures which happen abroad have their roots in, and grow from, domestic arrangements, they decided to abstain from hatred at home and from war abroad. In this way, they left their descendants the example of their fall and advice on how to recover, if only the feeble fickleness of the human mind could in times of prosperity keep to what it decided on in adversity.

---

164 This strikingly pagan phrase is taken verbatim from Justin, 5.10.9.

165 Orosius's message is that human actions devoid of divine grace are doomed to failure. Compare 7.6.5 for a successful amnesty in the emperor Claudius's reign which Orosius insists was produced by an act of grace on God's part as Christians were by this time present in Rome.

166 This judgment may be Orosius's own, as Justin makes no mention of Socrates and while Augustine approved of him, *City of God*, 8.3, his highest praise is reserved for Plato, *City of God*, 8.11.

167 Sallust, *The War against Jugurtha*, 10.6.

18[168]

1. At almost the same time, a civil war, or rather *a war more than civil,*[169] which took parricide to bring it to a close, broke out among the Persians. On the death of King Darius, his sons, Artaxerxes and Cyrus, fought for the kingdom.[170] The war was waged after great preparations had been made on both sides and brought ruin to both provinces and their peoples. **2.** In this conflict, chance brought the two brothers, rushing together from their different sides, face to face. First, Artaxerxes was wounded by his brother, but escaped death because of the speed of his horse; however, soon afterwards, Cyrus was overcome by the royal cohort and this put an end to the fray.[171] Artaxerxes seized the booty of his brother's forces and his army, and then assured himself of control over the kingdom by killing his brother.

3. So all of Asia and Europe, at times individually and at times joined together, were entangled in slaughter and crime.

4. Behold, how in such a small book and with a scant number of words I have listed the acts of a great number of provinces, peoples, and cities, and how all I have set down has involved great sorrow. For *who could describe the disasters* of those times, *the deaths that occurred, or equal their sorrows with his tears*?[172]

5. But these deeds have been blunted by the passage of the centuries and for us they have become either rhetorical exercises or simply entertaining tales. However, if someone were to pay more attention to these matters and apply himself with his whole mind to these wars and their causes and, as if he had been set on the top of a watchtower, gauge the nature of these two ages, I can easily say that he would judge that past events could not have been so wretchedly troubled and thrown into confusion without God's wrath and hostility, nor the affairs of our own time be so well arranged without God's kindness and mercy.

6. After these events, Sicily was struck by a powerful earthquake and was, moreover, devastated by seething fire and hot ash from Mount Etna which destroyed many fields and farms.[173]

168 The Persian material in this chapter is drawn, in a heavily abbreviated form, from Justin, 5.11.

169 A paraphrase of Lucan *Pharsalia*, 1.1, which is Orosius's own.

170 Darius II who died in 405 BC.

171 The Battle of Cunaxa, 401 BC.

172 Virgil, *Aeneid*, 2.361ff.

173 An embroidered version of Jerome, *Chronicle, A Abr.* 1591 = 327 *AUC*/427 BC, which is too early for Orosius's chronological sequence.

7. Then the city of Atalante, which lay next to the territory of Locris, was cut off by a sudden onrush of the sea and left a desolate island.[174] Plague fell upon the wretched remnants of the Athenians and laid waste to them for a long time.[175]

19

1. 355 years after the foundation of the City,[176] the siege of Veii, which had lasted for ten whole years, destroyed the besiegers rather than the besieged. For the Romans had lost many men to the frequent, sudden sorties of their enemies and were forced to run the risks of war during the winter, spending the winter under canvas and enduring cold and hunger in the sight of their enemies. **2.** They finally captured the town in a surprise attack from tunnels without giving any worthy demonstration of Roman courage.[177]

3. This useful rather than noble victory was followed by the exile of the dictator Camillus, who had defeated the people of Veii,[178] and then by the invasion of the Gauls and the burning of the city. **4.** Let someone dare, if he can, to compare this disaster with any upset of the present day, even though tales of past troubles are not given the same weight as injuries suffered in the present.

5. The Senonian Gauls led by Brennus were laying siege with a large and powerful army to the town of Clusinum, which is now called Tuscia,[179] when they saw the Roman envoys who had come to make peace between the two parties, fighting against them in the front line. Outraged, they lifted the siege of Clusinum and marched on Rome with their entire force.[180] **6.** As they came on, they were met by the consul Fabius and his army, but

---

174 Jerome, *Chronicle, A Abr.* 1592 = 328 *AUC*/426 BC; again this is too early for Orosius's narrative sequence.

175 Jerome, *Chronicle, A Abr.*1587 = 323 *AUC*/431 BC; again too early for Orosius's narrative sequence.

176 399 BC. Livy, 5.23, places the end of the siege in 358 *AUC*/396 BC.

177 Orosius draws on Florus, 1.6.8–9, for his account of the fall of Veii; for a fuller account, see Livy, 5.22–23.

178 Augustine, *City of God*, 3.17, mentions the exile of Camillus as an act of ingratitude at Rome.

179 The Senonian Gauls' original home was by the banks of the Seine, but by this time they had occupied a strip of land by the Adriatic south of Ravenna, known as the Gallic Lands, the *ager Gallicus*. Clusinum is the modern Chiusi, and normally spelt Clusium in antiquity; perhaps Orosius has been confused by Livy's constant use of *Clusini*, i.e. 'the people of Clusium' in his account. Only Orosius asserts that the town was called Tuscia.

180 This story is found in Livy, 5.36.

Fabius did not stop them – rather the enemy's onslaught cut his army down, laying them low, as if they were a crop ready to be harvested, and passed over them.[181] The river Halia bears witness to Fabius's disaster, just as the Cremera does to that of the Fabii.[182]

It would not be easy, even had Rome not been burnt afterwards as well, for anyone to recall a similar disaster to Roman arms. **7.** The Gauls entered the city that lay open before them. They butchered the senators who sat rigidly in their seats like statues, cremated them by firing their homes, and buried them under the fallen gables of their own roofs. **8.** They then laid siege to all the surviving young men of the town whom our sources agree numbered scarcely 1,000 and who were lying low in the citadel on the Capitol Hill.[183] There through hunger, disease, desperation, and fear the Gauls wore them down, subdued them, and finally sold them: **9.** for the Romans made peace by handing over 1,000 pounds of gold as the price for the Gauls' departure. This was not because Rome had such a low reputation among the Gauls, but because they had already ground the town down so much that it was unable to pay more.[184]

10. When the Gauls left, where there had once been a city marked out, there was a horrible heap of formless ruins. On all sides *the sound of echoing voices*[185] of those wandering through the rubble and unknowingly over their own possessions resounded, keeping them on tenterhooks as they nervously listened out. **11.** *Their spirits quaked with horror; even the silence was terrifying,*[186] for small numbers in a great space produce panic. As a result, they contemplated, decided, and, indeed, attempted to change where they lived, dwell in another town, and even to call themselves by a different name.[187]

181 Q. Fabius Ambustus, who was not a consul but one of the military tribunes with consular power who ruled Rome at this time.

182 The account of the battle is taken from Florus, 1.7.7; however, the account of the embassy is not, as Florus, 1.7.6, makes no mention of Roman ambassadors fighting against the Gauls and blames the embassy's failure on Gallic barbarism. The Halia is normally referred to as the Allia, and may be the modern Fonte di Papa, 12 miles from Rome. Fabius was not a consul, an error that Orosius copies from Florus. In fact, three Fabii were present among the military tribunes with consular power, Livy, 5.36.10–11. Florus probably confused Quintus Fabius, one of the ambassadors who fought the Gauls (Livy, 5.36.7) with Quintus Sulpicius Longus, the commander at the Halia, and Orosius has followed this error.

183 This figure and the reference to 'sources' is taken from Florus, 1.7.13.

184 For doubts about the extent of the Gallic sack, see Cornell (1995) 313–18.

185 A slight adaptation of Virgil, *Georgics*, 4.50.

186 Virgil, *Aeneid*, 2.755.

187 A proposal by some of the tribunes; see Livy, 5.49.8.

12. Behold the times to which the present is compared! Behold the times for which nostalgia sighs! Behold the times that demand penance for the religion that had been selected, or rather neglected![188] **13.** In truth, these two sacks of Rome are alike and can be compared with one another.[189] One raged on for six months, the other ran its course in three days. The Gauls exterminated the people, destroyed the City, and pursued the very name of Rome down to its uttermost ashes. The Goths abandoned their intention to plunder and drove columns of confused citizens to safe havens – namely the Holy Places of the City. In the first sack scarcely a senator, even out of those who fled, was to be found alive, in the second scarcely one could be found who had perished, save for some who done so by accident while hiding. **14.** I could safely say that the number that were saved in the first incident was the same as the number who died in the last.

Plainly, as the facts show, and as ought to be stated, during the present disaster God was more enraged than the men involved, for He Himself carried out what the Goths could not have done and so showed why He had sent them. **15.** For since it is beyond human powers to burn up bronze beams and overturn the mass of great edifices, the forum with its empty idols, whose wretched superstition lies about what is God and what is mortal, was cast down by a thunderbolt and all those abominations which the enemy's fire did not reach were overturned by fire sent from heaven.[190]

16. Now since there is an abundance of material, which cannot in any way be dealt with definitively in this book, I have put an end here to this volume so that we may examine what is left in the ones that follow.

188 Orosius has carefully omitted all mention of pagan religious events during the sack by the Gauls that would have undercut his position. These included Juno's geese saving the Capitol from the Gauls and the Pontifex Maximus's sacrifice on the Quirinal Hill; see Livy, 5.41 and 5.47.

189 i.e. the sack of Rome by the Gauls described here and Alaric's sack of Rome described at 7.39. The contrast between the two events is a centrepiece of Orosius's defence of Christianity.

190 See 7.39.18.

BOOK THREE

PREFACE

1. I have already stated in the preceding book, and now, out of necessity, repeat that in discussing the past conflicts of this world in accordance with your instructions, it is impossible to expound everything or go through everything that was done or how everything came to be done. This is because there is a great, indeed innumerable, amount of material written at great length by a vast number of men. These authors, however, do not have the same motive as I do, although they deal with the same affairs – for they unroll the history of wars, while I am unrolling wars' miseries.

2. Moreover, the very breadth of the material about which I am complaining puts me in narrow straits and I am bound all the tighter by this anxiety – namely that if, in my eagerness to be concise, I omit some event or other, it will be thought that I did not know about it or that it did not happen at that time. But, on the other hand, if I gird my loins to speak about everything, not expatiating at length, but just using concise summaries, I would make my work obscure with the result that most people will think that what I have said appears to say nothing at all. **3.** This is of the greatest concern, since I am taking care to do the opposite and give an account of the true forces of history, not a mere picture of the past. For concision and obscurity, or rather, as is always the case, the obscurity of concision, while producing an appearance of knowing the facts, in reality takes away the power of understanding them. Now, although I know both of these vices should be avoided, I will indulge in both of them, so that each might be mitigated by the other and that in this way my account should not seem to omit many events nor to be too cursory.

1[1]

1. 364 years after the foundation of the City, a year which weighed heavily on Rome because of her enslavement, something which she had never known before, but which Greece considered magnificent because of the peace, something which she had hardly known before, while the Gauls occupied and sold a captive Rome reduced to ashes, Artaxerxes, the king of the Persians, through his envoys ordered all of Greece to desist from fighting and live at peace, warning that he would wage war on anyone who broke the peace. **2.** When he gave this order, the Greeks could have stoutly ignored him in the same way that they had often bravely defeated him, had they not drunk down a proffered opportunity of peace, wherever it came from, as eagerly as they had longed for one, (**3.** The fact that they set their wars aside so easily and, indeed, on dishonourable terms, showed with what suffering and misery they had waged them up to this point. For what could be more dishonourable for free and valiant men than to lay down their arms and submit themselves to peace on the command of a man who was far away, whom they had often beaten, who was still an enemy, and, even at this time, still continually threatening them?), had the will to fight not melted away in all their weary hearts merely at the sound of peace simply being decreed, and had this unexpected respite not weakened them while they were dazed and stunned after the effort of standing to arms each day, before a treaty made of their own free will could give them the self-same respite.[2] **4.** I shall now outline, as concisely as possible, whence came such weariness in the hearts and bodies of all the peoples throughout the whole of Greece that it persuaded their wild spirits to acquiesce so easily in a peace that had previously been unknown to them.[3] **5.** The Lacedaemonians, being men, and more than this, men from Greece, the more they possessed, the more they wanted.[4] So, after conquering Athens,

1 This chapter draws heavily on, and abbreviates, Justin, 6.1–6.

2 This is the so-called King's Peace, or Peace of Antalchidas, of 386 BC. For its terms, see Xenophon, *Hellenica* 5.1.34. For a modern discussion of the treaty, see Briant (2002) 649. Orosius is embroidering Justin, 6.6, from whom he takes his synchronism with events at Rome (6.6.5). However, this chronology is awry as the sack of Rome is normally assumed to have occurred in 390/389 BC.

3 For a discussion of the complex relations between Persia and the Greek states at this time, see Briant (2002) 635–46.

4 This *sententia* is drawn from Justin, 6.1, though the addition 'from Greece' is Orosius's own doing, possibly reflecting the tensions of his own day.

they drank deeply of the hope of lording it over all of Asia. **6.** They therefore waged war on all of the East, appointing Hircylides as the commander of their expedition.[5] He, when he saw that he would have to fight against Pharnabazus and Tissaphernes, the two most powerful prefects of Artaxerxes the Persian king, devised a plan as required by these circumstances to avoid the heavy blow of engaging with both of them, and declared war and attacked one of them, while making peace with, and so delaying, the other.

7. Pharnabazus then accused Tissaphernes of treachery before Artaxerxes, their common king, above all because he had made a treaty with the enemy in time of war. He urged the king to appoint in his place the Athenian Conon, who at that time happened to be in exile on Cyprus, and to make him commander of the war at sea. Conon was therefore given 500 talents, summoned by Pharnabazus, and put in charge of the fleet.

8. On discovering this, the Lacedaemonians sent envoys to Hercyion, the king of Egypt,[6] seeking naval support, and received from him 100 ready-equipped triremes and 600,000 *modii* of corn.[7] They also garnered together a great amount of support from their allies on all sides **9.** and unanimously elected Agesilaus the commander of their army.[8] Agesilaus was lame in one foot, but in these troubled times the Spartans preferred to have a lame king rather than a lame kingdom.[9] Rarely ever have two generals so equal in all their efforts confronted one another in a single war. Worn out by the fierce fighting and covered in blood, both retired from the fray as if they were undefeated.

10. Conon then, through his own devices, received another payment from the Great King,[10] returned to his fleet, and invaded the enemy's territory, storming towers, forts, and the other garrisons there. *Like an unleashed storm, he laid low everything wherever he went.*[11] **11.** The Lacedaemonians,

---

5 Perhaps a corruption from Justin, where the name given is Hercyclides. The commander's name was in fact Dercylidas.

6 Hercyion is the Psammetichus of Diodorus Siculus, 14.35. In fact, the king concerned is Nepherites I, founder of the 29th Dynasty (398–392 BC).

7 A *modius* is approximately two gallons.

8 Orosius suppresses Justin's, 6.2.4–5, comment that this was done in response to an oracle from Delphi.

9 This *bon mot* is taken from Justin, 6.2.6.

10 i.e. not via a satrap's intercession. Orosius has omitted Justin's, 6.2.11–15, explanation for this – namely that Conon's men had mutinied because their pay had been sequestered by the two satraps.

11 The phrase is a reworking of poetic vocabulary from Virgil, *Aeneid*, 7.222–23 and *Georgics*, 2.310–31.

afflicted by troubles at home, ceased to ogle at foreign things and cast aside their hopes of mastery now that the peril of slavery loomed. They recalled Agesilaus whom they had sent to Asia with his army, to help defend his homeland.

12. Meanwhile, Pisander, who had been left in command at Sparta by King Agesilaus, had marshalled the largest and best-equipped fleet possible. Moved to emulate the courage of Agesilaus, who was fighting on land, he undertook a naval sortie, ranging along the coast.

13. Now Conon after taking up his commission, began to think about two things: namely how to look after his allies and how to show loyalty to his country – so that he might demonstrate his natural feelings towards the latter, while employing his energy on behalf of the former. In this, he showed himself to be most concerned about his fellow-citizens, as for their peace and liberty he waged a war that spilt foreign blood and fought against their most arrogant enemies at the king's peril, but for a prize that would fall to his homeland.

14. So the two sides fought a naval battle, the Persians commanded by Conon and the Spartans by Pisander. Soldiers, oarsmen, and even the commanders, were all dragged together with equal frenzy to their mutual slaughter.[12] **15.** The scale and savagery of this war is shown by the fact that from this time on the power of the Lacedaemonians declined and never recovered – *From thence the tide of fortune left the Spartans' shore and ebb'd much faster than it flow'd before*[13] – until, exhausted by their rising with pain and their piteous collapse, they lost both their power and their very name.**16.** But for the Athenians this self-same battle was the beginning of recovering power, just as it was the beginning of its end for the Lacedae-monians.[14]

First, the Thebans, bolstered by help from Athens, marched on the Spartans who were crippled and panic-stricken from their previous defeat. They had great confidence because of the courage and energy of their general, Epaminondas, with whom they thought that they could easily gain power over all of Greece.[15] **17.** A land battle took place that the Thebans won with minimal effort.[16] Lysander was defeated and killed in this battle

12 The Battle of Cnidus, 394 BC.
13 A close paraphrase of Virgil, *Aeneid*, 2.169–70 with 'Spartans' substituted for 'Greeks'.
14 A reworking of Justin, 6.4.1.
15 Ancient Thebes' most famous statesman, c. 418–362 BC. Oddly, Orosius makes no mention of his most famous battle, Leuctra, fought in 371 BC.
16 The Battle of Haliartus, 395 BC. Orosius has mistakenly placed the Spartan defeat at

and Pausanias, the other Lacedaemonian general, was accused of treachery and forced into exile.

18. After their victory, the Thebans marshalled their entire army and marched on Sparta, thinking that they would enter a city that was devoid of a garrison with no trouble at all. For they had already destroyed almost all of Sparta's troops, killed her king, and saw that all her allies had deserted her. **19.** The Lacedaemonians, driven on by the threat to their city, held a levy of such untrained troops as they had to hand, and marched out to meet the foe. But after this army had been defeated once, it had neither the courage nor the spirit to face the victors again. **20.** While this slaughter, suffered almost entirely by one side, was going on, suddenly King Agesilaus, who had been summoned from Asia, unexpectedly entered the war. He marched on the Thebans, who had become too confident and too slipshod because of their double victory, and defeated them without difficulty. This was all the easier for him as he had a force that had hardly been touched by battle, but even so he was badly wounded himself.[17] **21.** When the Athenians learnt that the Lacedaemonians had taken heart because of their unexpected victory, trembling in fear because of their previous enslavement from which they had hardly then begun to recover, they gathered together an army and joined it to the Boeotians in their support.[18] They entrusted their force to Iphicrates, a mere youth of hardly 20 years of age, but whose maturity of spirit shored up the weakness of his years.[19] **22.** On hearing of Agesilaus's return, Conon too, since, though in charge of a Persian army, he was an Athenian, also began to lay waste to the Lacedaemonians' land once more. And so the Spartans, surrounded and terrified by the clash of their enemies' arms that encompassed them on every side, languished in almost unplumbed depths of despair.

23. But Conon, after having sated himself by ravaging the enemy's soil, returned to Athens – an event which caused great joy to its citizens, but gave the man himself sorrow when he saw how his city, which had once been adorned by its people and culture, now lay destroyed and was a pitiable, squalid desert of ruins. **24.** And so he engineered a great monument to his piety and loyalty by rebuilding it. For the town that had been pillaged by the

---

Cnidus before this battle, whereas in fact it took place afterwards. Moreover, Epaminondas took no part in the battle.

17 The Battle of Coronea, August 394 BC.

18 An embroidered version of Justin, 6.5.

19 Iphicrates was a major military innovator who substantially lightened the traditional hoplite's equipment and changed his tactics. Cornelius Nepos wrote a brief *Life* of the general.

Lacedaemonians he refilled with plunder from Lacedaemon, and rebuilt a town burnt down by the Persians with Persians as its builders.[20]

25. Meanwhile, Artaxerxes, the king of the Persians, as stated at the beginning of the chapter, commanded, via his envoys, all the peoples of Greece to lay down their arms and live in peace. He did this not because he took pity on their weary state, but in case they were tempted to invade his kingdom while he was occupied with a war in Egypt.[21]

2

1. Therefore, while all Greece relaxed its guard in its much-longed-for peace and grew weak through its inactivity at home, the Lacedaemonians, more through restlessness than strength, and becoming unbearable more from their wild madness than because of their courage, embarked on clandestine warfare, although they had renounced war itself. **2.** For when they saw that the Arcadians were away, they launched a sudden raid and broke into their fortress.[22] The Arcadians were enraged by this wrong and, gathering Theban support, sought to reclaim what they had lost in this razzia. **3.** In the battle that followed, the Lacedaemonian general, Archidamus,[23] was wounded, and after he saw his men being cut down as if they were already defeated, he sent a herald to ask that the bodies of the dead might be buried. Among the Greeks this is the customary sign of admitting defeat. **4.** The Thebans, therefore, content at this concession of victory, gave the order to spare the vanquished and put an end to the struggle.

5. After a truce lasting a few days, Lacedaemonians reverted once more to launching other attacks. The Thebans and their general Epaminondas had the confidence to invade Lacedaemon on the grounds that there would be no danger since the city was deserted. They advanced in silence on Lacedaemon at the dead of night, but did not encounter it as unguarded or without defences as they had anticipated. **6.** The old men, along with the remaining mass of those not yet of military age, had discovered that the enemy was advancing on them and armed themselves. This force stationed itself in the very narrows of the city gates and, though numbering hardly 100 men burdened by old age, charged an army 15,000 strong. This group was

20 The 'Persian builders' may be a reference to the Daric, a Persian gold coin.
21 For this war see Briant (2002) 650–55.
22 The fortress of Cromnus, the raid took place in 364 BC.
23 Archidamus III (360–338 BC).

bearing the brunt of the heavy fighting when the Spartan army arrived and instantly decided to attack the Thebans in open combat.

7. After battle was joined, the Lacedaemonians got the worst of it, until the Theban commander Epaminondas who fought too recklessly, was suddenly wounded.[24] This brought terror born of grief to the Thebans and stunned amazement born of joy to the Spartans; and both sides withdrew by tacit consent. **8.** Epaminondas was gravely wounded and when he heard of his men's victory, he kissed his shield and lifted up the hand that covered his wound, opening an exit for his blood and for death an entrance. His death was followed by the Thebans' decline, for they seemed not merely to have lost their general, but to have perished with him.[25]

9. I have woven this tangled basket of undigested history and, following the evidence with my words, set out the confused cycles of war that were waged hither and thither with insane fury. It seems to me that the more that I have kept to the order of the events, the more disorderly my writing has become.

10. For who could number, place in order, or explain all the incitements to hatred of all kinds and the reasons for these wars that the Lacedaemonians' wicked lust for mastery roused up in so many people, cities, and provinces? They themselves could be said to have suffered no less from the chaos brought about by these wars as from the wars themselves. **11.** Indeed, as this war dragged on without ceasing for several generations, the Athenians, Lacedaemonians, Arcadians, Boeotians, Thebans, and finally Greece, Asia, Persia, and Egypt, along with Libya and the largest of the islands, all waged war by land and sea at the same time in a set of mutually inextricable campaigns. Even if I could list these wars, I would be unable to recount the thousands of men who were slaughtered in them.

12. Now let someone damn the present and praise the past – whoever does not realise that now all the people in these towns and provinces grow old watching games and at the theatre, whereas then they wasted away on military service and in battle.[26] **13.** The most flourishing town of that age which aimed to rule the entire East, the town of the Lacedaemonians, was reduced to barely 100 old men; for surrounded by unending troubles, she

24 The Battle of Mantinea, 362 BC. Oddly, Orosius makes no mention of Epaminondas's victory at Leuctra in 371 BC.

25 Up to this point, the chapter is based on Justin, 6.6–9. The melodramatic account of Epaminondas's death is found in Valerius Maximus, 3.2.5.

26 A strikingly positive assessment of the games and theatre, compared to the attitude expressed below at 3.4.5–6.

wretchedly squandered away her youth. **14.** Do men whose cities today are
full of the old and boys and which grow rich as their youth travels safely
abroad and earns money on these peaceful forays to spend on pleasures
at home, complain about their lot? If they do, perhaps the reason is that
the present always seems worthless to fickle humanity and life itself has
become irksome to those aching to perform, or hear of, novelties.

3

1. 376 years after the foundation of the City, all Achaea was struck by a
most ferocious earthquake and two cities, namely Ebora and Helice, were
swallowed up as the ground gaped open.[27]
   2. But I myself, on the other hand, could have mentioned similar events
that were foretold, began, but did not reach their final end in our own times
at Constantinople, which also a short time ago became a capital of the
world.[28] For after a terrible warning and prescient feeling of its own ills,
the troubled earth trembled from its very depths below, while above there
hung a flame spreading from the heavens. This continued until God, moved
by the prayers of Prince Arcadius and his Christian people, turned aside the
destruction that threatened them, **3.** proving that He alone is the Saviour of
the humble and the Punisher of the wicked.[29] But modesty dictates that I
note, rather than discuss, these matters, so that he who knows of them may
remember them and he who does not may make enquiries about them.[30]
   4. Meanwhile, the Romans who had been hard-pressed and worn down
for 70 years by the continual wars waged by the Vulsci, and also by the

27 Drawn from Jerome, *Chronicle*, *A Abr.* 1637. Orosius's chronology is therefore two
years out as this date in fact coincides with 374 *AUC*. Ebora, normally Bura, and Helice lay
in Achaea on the southern coast of the Gulf of Corinth. They were destroyed in 373 BC. The
event was well known in antiquity; see Diodorus Siculus, 18.48; Strabo, 8.7.2; Ovid, *Metamorphoses*, 1.263; and Marcus Aurelius, *Meditations*, 4.48. Orosius has slipped back in terms of
his narrative sequence.
28 A very western reference to the *de facto* division of the Roman world on the death of
Theodosius in AD 395. The empire was split between his elder son, Arcadius, whose court was
at Constantinople and his younger son, Honorius, whose capital was Rome.
29 The incident occurred in AD 396. Augustine, *On the Destruction of the City of Rome*
(*De Excidio Urbis Romae*) 7–8 = *CCL* 46 258–60 describes the incident at length. However,
Augustine interprets the cloud as a warning from God to a sinful city and His mercy lies in that
fact that He chose to frighten rather than punish the town. Where Orosius has a town protected
by God from a natural disaster because of its merits, Augustine sees a wicked town punished
by divine agency.
30 cf. 6.11.30.

Faliscians, Aequi, and Sutrini, finally, under Camillus's leadership, captured these peoples' cities in the times I have just discussed, and put an end to this recrudescent struggle. **5.** At the same time, under the command of Titus Quintius, at the river Halia they defeated the Praenestines who had reached the gates of Rome with war and slaughter.[31]

4

1. 384 years after the Foundation of the City, in the consulate of Lucius Genucius and Quintus Servilius, a great plague held all of Rome in its clutches.[32] **2.** This was not like a troubled climate when the weather varies a little from what is expected, such as unseasonable dryness in winter, a sudden heat-wave in spring, unaccustomed heavy rain in summer, or the chaotic charms of a rich autumn, to which we can add the poisonous breezes from the groves of Calabria, that bring sudden attacks of violent illness,[33] **3.** rather it had severe, long-lasting effects and spared neither sex nor old or young. For two years without ceasing, it infected all alike with its decay and even those it did not kill, it left with their flesh foully decayed and wasted away.[34]

4. Now I suspect that those who complain about our Christian times would complain, if I happened, at this point, to pass over the ceremonies that the Romans used to placate the gods and alleviate disease. **5.** When the plague grew stronger by the day, their priests were the ones who persuaded them to put on plays, as this is what the gods demanded. So to drive out a plague that afflicted their bodies for a short time, they summoned up a disease that would afflict their souls forever. **6.** Now here is a rich source of sorrow and indignation for me, but, as Your Reverence[35] has already devoted your love of wisdom and truth to this matter, it would not be right for me to dare to speak more about this. Let it be enough for me to have drawn atten-

---

31 The Roman history in this chapter is drawn from Eutropius, 2.1–2. Camillus is Marcus Furius Camillus, military tribune, interrex, and dictator. His activity dates between 401–381 BC. The Praenestines were defeated in 380 BC. 'Quintius' is a misspelling of Quinctius, who is normally known by his *cognomen*, Cincinnatus, see 2.12.7–8, where the same misspelling is found. The Halia is the Allia, a tributary of the Tiber.

32 L. Genucius Aventinensis and Q. Servilius Ahala were consuls in 365 BC, i.e. 389 *AUC*. Orosius's chronology has slipped by five years.

33 A reference to the Atabulus wind, now known as the Sirocco, see Sidonius Apollinaris, 1.5.8, and Sallares (2002) 74.

34 cf. Livy, 7.1.7–8.

35 i.e. Augustine.

tion to it and referred my readers of whatever opinion to depth of discussion found in your reading of these matters.[36]

5

1. The following year a suitably sad prodigy followed on from this pitiable disease and its even more pitiable expiation. The ground suddenly sprung apart in the middle of the City and all at once the gaping jaws of hell were visible in a great chasm.[37] **2.** This shameless cavern in the yawning void remained for many days a terrifying spectacle for all to behold. According to the oracles of the gods, it was required, horrible though it was, that a man be buried alive in it. **3.** Throwing himself into its vile jaws, Marcus Curtius, an armed knight, gave unforeseen satiety to the cruel earth for whom, unless it also tore itself open to suck down the living, the numbers it had taken by the grave through this great plague seemed too few.[38]

6

1. 388 years after the foundation of the City, there was another terrible flood of Gauls who encamped along the river Anio by the fourth milestone from the city. With their weight of numbers and fierce courage, they could, without a doubt, have occupied the troubled City, had they not grown weak through idleness and self-indulgence. **2.** Manlius Torquatus began a savage battle against them single-handedly, and the dictator Titus Quintius brought it to an end with his blood-soaked attack.[39] A great number of Gauls fled from this fight and, after regrouping their forces, rushed once more into battle where they were defeated by the dictator Gaius Sulpicius.[40]
   3. A short time afterwards, a war was fought against the Etruscans under

---

36 Orosius's remarks reflect standard Christian invective against the theatre. He is probably referring to Augustine's attack on the theatre in his *City of God*, 1.32. His comments here sit uneasily with those made at 3.2.12.

37 cf. Virgil, *Aeneid*, 8.243–44.

38 cf. Livy, 7.6.1–6. Curtius here is described as a 'young man distinguished in war' rather than as a knight. Orosius dates the event to 386 BC, but it is traditionally placed in 392 BC.

39 Quinctius's attack took place close to the Colline Gate.

40 The Gallic incursion is normally dated to 361–358 BC, i.e. 393 *AUC*. Manlius fought a Gallic chieftain in single combat. On killing him, he stripped off the Gaul's torque, thus earning himself the name *Torquatus* or 'betorqued'; see Virgil, *Aeneid*, 8.660. Orosius's account is drawn from Eutropius, 2.5, though he has added the moralising note about the Gaul's self-emasculation through idleness and the comment about the bloody nature of Quinctius's attack.

the command of Gaius Marcius – one can conjecture how many men were slain given that 8,000 Etruscans were captured.[41]

4. For the third time in those days, the Gauls poured down to plunder the coast and the lowlands under the Alban Hills. After a new levy had been held and ten legions enrolled, 60,000 Romans marched out to fight them, though the Latins refused to come to Rome's aid. **5.** This battle was brought to its conclusion by Marcus Valerius with the aid of a crow, whence afterwards he was surnamed 'Corvinus'. The Gauls' champion was killed and the terrified foe were brutally butchered as they fled in all directions.[42]

7

1. I believe that the first treaty with Carthage that was struck at this time should also be numbered among Rome's ills, especially because such great troubles arose from it that they seem to have had their beginnings in it. **2.** 402 years after the foundation of the City, envoys were sent to Rome from Carthage and made a treaty. **3.** Reliable histories, the ill-omened places, and the horror of the days in which these things were done all bear witness that the arrival of the Carthaginians into Italy was to bring a hailstorm of troubles and an unending shadow of continual suffering. **4.** For the night seemed to last into the greater part of the day and a hail of stones fell from the clouds, lashing the earth with a veritable stoning.[43]

5. At that time too Alexander the Great, truly a whirlpool of sufferings and ill-wind for the entire East, was born.[44]

6. It was then too that Ochus, who is also known as Artaxerxes,[45] drove great numbers of Jews into exile after a long and bitter war in Egypt and

41 The war is normally dated to 356 BC. Orosius's account is drawn from Eutropius, 2.5.

42 The crow, *corvus* in Latin, perched on Corvinus's helmet as he entered battle, see Livy, 7.26. Orosius's account is drawn from Eutropius, 2.6. Orosius presumably knew of the brief account in Florus, 1.8.20, where the crow is referred to as a sacred bird, but suppressed this fact. The battle is traditionally dated to 349 BC.

43 cf. Livy, 7.27.2. The treaty is normally dated to 406 *AUC*/348 BC. Orosius is ignorant of the treaty recorded by Polybius, 3.22, which was struck in 507 BC, see Cornell (1995) 210–14. The ill-omened day and ground are not, however, found in Livy. The portents mentioned by Orosius are drawn from Livy, 7.28.7, but are dated there to 344 BC and their connection to the treaty with Carthage is found only in Orosius.

44 Jerome, *Chronicle, A Abr.* 1661. For Orosius Carthage and Macedon are the two 'intermediate kingdoms' between Rome and Babylon, see 2.1.6. His mention of Alexander here may be to link the two together in the reader's mind. Alexander was born in 356 BC.

45 Artaxerxes III Ochus (359–338 BC).

ordered them to settle in Hyrcania by the Caspian Sea. There they remain to the present day and have greatly increased in numbers. It is believed that at some time they will burst forth from this place.[46] While waging this tempestuous war, Ochus also destroyed Sidon, the wealthiest town of the province of Phoenicia and, although at first defeated, brought Egypt, crushed and broken by the sword, under the rule of the Persians.[47]

8

1. Immediately after this, the Romans waged a war on behalf of the Campanians and Sedicini against the Samnites, a wealthy and well-armed people. When this war hung in the balance, Pyrrhus, the most formidable of the Romans' enemies, joined the Samnites[48] and the Punic War soon followed on the heels of the war against Pyrrhus. So, **2.** although the ever-open gates of Janus show that from the death of Numa there had been no end to the disasters of war, from this time on the heat of their troubles grew white-hot as if it were emblazoned over all the sky at mid-day.

3. Therefore let anyone who thinks that these Christian times should be disparaged, make enquiries, discover, and publish abroad his findings as to whether after the beginning of the Punic War, wars, slaughter, destruction, and every kind of appalling death have, save in the times of Caesar Augustus, ever ceased. **4.** The one exception is a single year during the Punic Wars which passed by like a flying bird,[49] when the Romans, because

46 Orosius has drawn the story of the expulsion of the Jews to Hyrcania from Jerome, *Chronicle, A Abr.* 1658 = 357 BC. He has then embroidered Jerome's account with a version of the Magog legend, according to which the Jews in this area, sometimes known as the 'Red Jews', will launch an invasion as the world comes to an end. For a full discussion of the legend, see Anderson (1932). Notice of Alexander's expulsion of Jews to Hyrcania only occurs in late sources. Josephus, *Against Apion*, 1.22.194, referring to the works of Hecataeus of Abdera (*floruit* fourth century BC) speaks of expulsions to Babylon, but not Hyrcania.

47 Orosius's source for Artaxerxes' capture of Sidon and Egypt is Jerome, *Chronicle, A Abr.* 1669 = 348 BC. In fact Artaxerxes conquered Egypt in 343 BC. For a discussion of these campaigns, see Briant (2002) 683–87.

48 To preserve his argument Orosius has elided three separate conflicts wars together, creating a picture of sustained warfare greater than is justified. His initial reference is to the First Samnite War, 343–341 BC, which began with a plea to Rome from the Campanian city of Capua for help against the Samnites, Florus, 1.11.16. However, Pyrrhus's arrival in 280 BC substantially postdates not only this, but also the Second (327–321 and 316–304 BC), and Third (298–290 BC) Samnite Wars.

49 The year concerned is 235 BC. Orosius returns to it at 4.12.4–13. Ornithomancy was a standard form of state augury at Rome and Orosius may be sniping at it here.

the gates of Janus were closed when the republic was suffering from fever and disease, were seduced by this fleeting sign of peace, like by the merest sip of cold water, and then, as the fever blazed up again all the worse, found themselves more seriously and badly afflicted.[50]

5. Nevertheless, if there is indisputable agreement that the whole world laid down its arms for the first time in Caesar Augustus's reign, after he had made peace with the Parthians, set aside its quarrels, enjoyed a universal peace and a state of quiet that had been hitherto unknown; that its peoples obeyed Roman ordinances, preferred Roman law to their own arms, and, spurning their own leaders, chose Roman judges in their stead; **6.** and that finally that every race, all the provinces, innumerable cities, countless peoples, and every land had one desire: to cultivate peace freely and honourably and take counsel for the common good (something which previously not even a single city, a single citizen-body, or, what is more, even brothers in a single household had been able to do together);[51] **7.** if it is agreed that these things came to pass in Caesar's reign, it is obvious from crystal-clear evidence that the birth in this world of Our Lord, Jesus Christ, shone its light on Caesar's realm. **8.** And those whom envy drives to blasphemy are compelled to recognise and admit that this peace over all the world and its tranquil serenity came not from the wide rule of Caesar, but from the power of the Son of God, Who became manifest in the time of Caesar, and that the world itself with a universal understanding obeyed not the ruler of a single city, but the world's Creator, Who, just as the rising sun fills the day with light, coming in mercy clothed the world in a lasting peace. These matters will be more fully discussed, when we come, the Lord willing, to that place.[52]

9

1. Therefore, 409 years after the foundation of the City, in the consulate of Manlius Torquatus and Decius Mus, the Romans waged war on the rebellious Latins.[53] In this war one consul was killed and the other committed parricide. **2.** For Manlius Torquatus killed his own son, a young man who had

---

50 This metaphor is repeated at 4.12.8.

51 This purple passage contains slight overtones of Lucan, *Pharsalia*, 1.60–62.

52 See 6.22. Augustine, *City of God*, 3.11, also sees the rise of Augustus as renewing the Roman state, but avoids any imputation that this possessed theological significance.

53 Normally dated to 340 BC, i.e. 414 *AUC*. Orosius remains five years out in his chronology.

triumphantly killed Metius Tusculanus, a noble knight and one of Rome's most provocative and arrogant enemies at that time.[54] **3.** When the battle resumed, the other consul, on seeing that the wing he commanded was being cut down and hard-pressed, fell of his own free will upon the enemy where they were thickest and perished.[55] **4.** Manlius, despite being victorious, did not receive the welcome of the noble youths of Rome which is customarily given on such occasions, as though triumphant, he was a parricide.

5. In the year following this, a vestal virgin named Minucia admitted to sexual impurity, was condemned, and buried alive in the field which is now called the field of wickedness.[56]

10

1. I shudder to recount what occurred shortly afterwards.[57] For in the consulate of Claudius Marcellus and Valerius Flaccus,[58] the matrons of Rome became inflamed with an incredible madness and love of crime. **2.** It was indeed a foul and pestilential year and its slaughtered victims were piled up in heaps on all sides. But everyone in their simple credulity still believed that this was caused by corruption in the air, until a slave-girl came forward and gave compelling evidence after which many matrons were first forced to drink the poisons that they had devised, and then, as they drank them, they perished. **3.** The number of matrons involved in this conspiracy was so large that 370 of them are said to have been condemned at single sitting.[59]

54 This incident is found in Livy, 8.7, where the Latin commander is called Geminus Maecius. Augustine, *City of God*, 1.23 and 5.18, singles out Torquatus's behaviour as exemplary.

55 Orosius suppresses entirely the pagan religious aspects of the consul's death. Decius Mus dedicated himself and the enemy to the gods of the underworld and the Earth in a ritual known as *devotio*. The incident, along with Mus's dedicatory prayer, is recorded by Florus, 1.12.17, and Livy, 8.9.4–8.

56 For an in-depth discussion of the punishment of Vestals and of this priesthood in general, see Worsfold (1934). For the death of Minucia, see Livy, 8.15.7–8, who dates the incident to 416 *AUC*. The field was named for the crime of the vestal, but Orosius wants his readers to believe it was named for the crime of burying Minucia alive.

57 The implication is that the women's madness that Orosius now describes was a divine punishment for the execution of Minucia; see 3.9.5 above.

58 M. Claudius Marcellus and C. Valerius Potitus Flaccus, consuls in 423 *AUC*/331 BC.

59 This incident is mentioned by Augustine, *City of God*, 3.17, Valerius Maximus, 2.5.3, and, at greater length, Livy, 8.18. Valerius Maximus and Livy give the number of the condemned as 180.

11

1. 422 years after the foundation of the City, Alexander, the king of Epirus and uncle of the famous Alexander the Great, brought his troops into Italy since he was preparing to fight against Rome. He was active around the cities neighbouring Rome, trying to strengthen his army and obtain their support, or to detach them from his enemy. However, he was defeated and slain in a great battle in Lucania by the Samnites who gave their aid to the Lucanians.[60] **2.** However, since I have gone forward some way in my account of the disasters that Rome suffered, mentioning this Alexander reminds me to go back a few years and, as far as I am able, I shall gather together in a few words the great deeds of Philip, the king of the Macedonians, who married Olympias, the sister of this Alexander of Epirus, by whom he bore Alexander the Great.

12[61]

1. 400 years after the foundation of the City, Philip, the son of Amyntas and father of Alexander, became king of Macedonia and reigned for 25 years.[62] In this time, he heaped up piles of every kind of sorrow and amassed crimes of every kind. **2.** Before this, he had been handed over as a hostage to the Thebans by his brother Alexander[63] and brought up for three years in the house of the vigorous general and great philosopher, Epaminondas. **3.** After Alexander was criminally killed by his own mother Eurydice, who had already committed adultery, killed another of her sons, left her daughter a widow, and pledged herself in marriage to her son-in-law on the death of her husband, Philip was forced by the people to assume the crown which he

---

60 Livy dates the arrival of Alexander of Molossia in Italy to 414 *AUC*/340 BC. The king went to the assistance of Tarentum in 334 BC. He was killed in 331 BC at the battle of Pandosia, the site of which lies in Bruttium, not Lucania, near the modern Mendicino, see 3.18.3. True to his wish to avoid vindicating pagan oracles, Orosius has suppressed the story that Alexander had been warned to avoid the town of Pandosia by an oracle, but only knew of the Greek Pandosia, the modern Kastri in Epirus, and hence failed to avoid his doom. See Livy, 8.24 and the discussion in Oakley (1998) 664–67, 671–72.

61 This chapter draws on, and abbreviates, heavily Justin 8. Orosius adds some moralising *sententiae* and at times suppresses Justin's paganism.

62 Philip became *de facto* king in 395 *AUC*/359 BC and was acclaimed as such in 356 BC.

63 Alexander II of Macedon, 370–368 BC. Philip was handed over as the result of a war the Macedonians had just lost against Thebes. Philip was in Thebes from c. 368 to c. 365 BC.

was guarding for the young son of his murdered brother.[64]

4. He was beset abroad by attacks on all sides from his enemies and at home by fear of conspiracies which he continually discovered. However, he first attacked Athens **5.** and, on defeating her, marched on the Illyrians and, after slaughtering many thousands of his enemies, captured the glorious city of Larissa.[65] **6.** He then invaded Thessaly, not so much out of a love of victory, as out of a desire to take control of the Thessalians' cavalry and add its strength to his own army. **7.** And so, after he had seized Thessaly by a surprise attack and brought it under his power, he united the most powerful squadrons of cavalry and units of infantry, creating an invincible army.

8. After defeating the Athenians and subjugating the Thessalians, he took Olympias, the sister of Aruba, the king of Molossia, as his wife.[66] This Aruba thought that by making an alliance with the Macedonians by becoming a relative of their king, he would in this way expand his own kingdom. In this he was deceived, lost his kingdom, and grew old as a private citizen in exile.

9. After this, Philip lost an eye to an arrow while he was besieging the town of Methone, but, even so, he soon stormed the town and took it.[67]

10. He went on to conquer by force almost all of Greece which he had already enmeshed in his scheming; for while each Greek city wanted to assume supreme power, they all lost their power one by one, and rushed without restraint to their common doom. Finally, when they were defeated and enslaved, they realised what each of them had lost individually had also perished for them all. **11.** For Philip observed their mad machinations as if he were sat on a watchtower and, a skilled artist in treachery, by always helping the weaker side, fostered the disputes which are the kindling of wars, and then conquered the victors and vanquished alike.

12. What gave him the opportunity to gain domination over all of Greece was the arrogant way the Thebans used their dominant position. For on defeating the Lacedaemonians and the Phoceans and exhausting the resources of these two through their killing and plundering, at the common

64 Philip assumed power in 357 BC, deposing Amyntas IV.

65 This is an error taken from Justin, 7.6.7. In fact, Philip captured Larissa in 352 BC, after his campaigns in Illyricum.

66 Philip married Olympias in 357 BC. Aruba, normally spelt Arybbas, was in fact Olympias's uncle. Molossia lies in modern Albania.

67 In 354 BC. Methone is the modern Methoni in the Greek province of Pieria. Orosius suppresses Justin's comment, 7.6.15, that the wound made Philip no less eager for the fray and did not increase his vindictiveness in victory when he behaved with moderation. Such comments would not, of course, fit with Orosius's picture of Philip as an out-and-out tyrant.

council of Greece they then burdened them with such a great fine that they were unable to pay and forced to take refuge in arms once more.[68] **13.** So the Phoceans under the command of Philomelus and bolstered by assistance from Lacedaemonia and Athens, joined battle and routed their enemy, capturing the Thebans' camp. A second battle followed where, amid heavy losses on both sides, Philomelus was killed. The Phoceans then made Oenomaus their commander in his place.[69]

14. At this point the Thebans and Thessalians did not hold a levy of their citizens, but of their own free will asked King Philip of Macedonia, whom they had previous taken pains to repel as an enemy, to be their leader. Battle was joined, the Phoceans were killed almost to a man and victory went to Philip.

15. But the Athenians, on hearing the outcome of the battle, followed the same plan that they had previously employed during the Persian invasion and occupied the pass of Thermopylae in order to stop Philip from marching into Greece.

16. So Philip, seeing that he was barred from entering Greece by the fortification of Thermopylae, turned the war he had prepared against his enemies on his allies, invading as an enemy and cruelly plundering those cities that had just made him their commander and who opened their gates ready to praise and embrace him. **17.** Completely setting aside any notion of duty towards an ally, he sold all their women and children at auction and destroyed and sacked all their temples – though if the gods were angered by this, he was never defeated for 25 years.[70]

18. After this, he crossed into Cappadocia and waged war there with equal perfidy. He captured the neighbouring kings through trickery, put them to death, and brought all Cappadocia under Macedonian rule.[71]

19. After inflicting this slaughter, arson, and rapine on cities allied to him, he turned to committing parricide against his brothers. He feared his siblings whom his stepmother had borne to his father as they were co-heirs of the kingdom and so set out to kill them. **20.** After he had killed one, the

68 Orosius has elided two events. He is referring to the fine imposed on the Phoceans at the Amphyctionic Council of 356 BC, but the condemnation of Sparta dates to 383 BC.

69 The Battle of Neum, the modern Tithorea, fought in 354 BC. Justin, 8.1.14, gives the name of the new commander as Onomarchus. Orosius is referring to the so-called Sacred War of 356–346 BC.

70 Orosius cannot resist indulging in anti-pagan sarcasm here. To do this, he has inverted Justin's reasoning, as Justin, 8.1.8–8.2.4, presents the Phoceans' sufferings as punishment for their previous sacrilege at the temple of Apollo at Delphi.

71 Orosius has confused Cappadocia with Thrace, see Justin, 8.3.6.

other two fled to Olynthus. Philip soon marched on this most ancient and prosperous town and filled it with blood and slaughter, emptying it of its men and riches. He then dragged out his brothers and brutally executed them.[72]

21. After this, elated by the destruction of his allies and the murder of his brothers, he began to think that he would be allowed to do anything he planned. He attacked the gold-producing regions in Thessaly and the silver mines in Thrace and, so as not to leave any law or custom inviolate, he took control of the sea and indulged in piracy too, sending his fleet out in all directions.

22. Moreover, when two brothers who were kings in Thrace and in dispute about the borders of their kingdom agreed to chose him as their arbitrator, Philip, with his usual cunning, came to give judgment with his army marshalled as if he were coming to battle and deprived the unsuspecting youths of their lives and kingdom.[73]

23. The Athenians, who had repelled Philip's previous incursion by fortifying Thermopylae, sought peace with him of their own free will and by doing so drew their treacherous enemy's attention to the slack state of their guard over the pass,[74] **24.** while the rest of the Greek cities willingly subjected themselves to foreign domination under the pretence of making a peace-treaty so that they had more free time to indulge in civil war. **25.** Above all, it was the Thessalians and Boeotians who asked Philip to come to be their leader against the Phoceans and take the command of the war they had begun. The Phoceans, on the other hand, with the support of the Athenians and Lacedaemonians, were working hard by prayers and payments to halt the war or gain a respite from it. **26.** Philip secretly promised different things to each side. He assured the Phoceans on oath that he would make peace and pardon them, but gave a pledge to the Thessalians that he would soon come with his army. He also forbade both sides to prepare for war. **27.** Philip therefore marshalled his forces, marched safely into the pass of Thermopylae, occupying and fortifying it with garrisons at key points.

28. It was then that not only the Phoceans, but all of Greece first realised that they had been taken prisoner. Philip immediately broke faith with the Phoceans and, trampling his oath underfoot, ripped them apart. He then ravaged towns and lands of all of them so bloodily while he was there that

---

72 The three sons of Amyntas by Gygaea, his second wife. Archelaus was murdered in 359 BC, the other two brothers in 348 BC.

73 The sons of Berisades. Philip took their land in 346 BC.

74 The Peace of Philocrates, 346 BC.

he was feared even in his absence.

29. When he returned to his kingdom, like a shepherd who moves his flocks at times round his summer, and at times round his winter, pastures, he transplanted at whim populations and cities to whatever places he thought should be filled with, or from whatever places he thought should be emptied of, people. **30.** Everywhere woeful sights met the eye along with the harshest kind of woes – the suffering of destruction without invasion, enslavement without war, exile without charge, defeat without a victor. **31.** Amid the barbs of these injustices, despondency spread and crushed them. Their misery was increased by their pretence that it did not exist, and the more it increased, the less able they were to speak of it, fearing that their tears be taken as arrogant signs of rebellion.

32. Philip tore some peoples from their homes and settled them on the borders of his enemies. Others he set down on the furthest-flung frontiers of his kingdom. Yet others whose power he envied, he divided up and added to the cities which he had emptied of their population, doing this to stop them having the strength that it was thought they had. **33.** In this way, having first destroyed its freedom, he cut up the once glorious, flourishing body of Greece into small bleeding chunks.

13[75]

1. When he had done this to some of the cities of Greece, while crushing them all by terror, he worked out from the booty which he had got from a few of them the wealth of them all and came to the conclusion that to devastate them all equally at a useful profit, it would be necessary to gain possession of a maritime city. He judged that the noble city of Byzantium was the most suitable for his purposes, as it could be a base for both land and sea operations. When the town resisted, he immediately besieged it.[76]

2. This town of Byzantium was founded by Pausanias, the king of the Spartans,[77] and afterwards enlarged by the Christian emperor Constantine and named Constantinople. Now it is the glorious seat of imperial power and the capital of the entire East.

---

75 This chapter draws heavily on, and abbreviates, Justin, 9.1–3. The *sententia* at the end is drawn from Justin, 9.3.11.

76 The siege took place in 340–339 BC. Orosius suppresses the fact that prior to this Philip had chosen Perinthus as a base and besieged it in vain.

77 Orosius has copied this error from Justin, 9.1.3. Pausanias governed Byzantium from 477 to 470 BC, but the town was founded from Megara in c. 660 BC.

3. Philip, after a long and futile siege, turned to piracy to recover through theft the money he had lost in the siege. He captured 170 ships full of merchandise and sold them piecemeal.[78] This was the way he replenished to a small degree his desperate poverty. **4.** In order to go plundering and besiege the town at the same time, he divided his army up. He himself set out with his bravest men and captured many cities in the Chersonese, ruining their peoples and stealing their riches. He then crossed over to Scythia with his son Alexander, intending to plunder it too.

5. At that time, Ateas was the king of the Scythians. When he was hard pressed in a war with the Histriani,[79] he asked Philip for help using the Apollonians[80] as intermediaries, but when the Histrian king died and he was freed from the fear of war and the need for allies, he dissolved the treaty that he had made with Philip.

6. Philip raised the siege of Byzantium and turned all his attention to war with Scythia. When battle was joined, although the Scythians outnumbered him and proved the more courageous, Philip still defeated them by trickery.[81] **7.** In this battle, 20,000 Scythian women and children were captured and a great number of cattle driven off, but no gold or silver was found. This was what first gave rise to the belief that Scythia is a poor country. 20,000 thoroughbred mares were sent to Macedonia to breed stock there.

8. The Treballi[82] came out to fight Philip as he was withdrawing. In the battle that followed, Philip was wounded in the thigh: an enemy weapon passing through his body and killing his horse. Everyone thought he had been killed and so fled, abandoning their booty. After this, there was a small pause while he convalesced and recovered from his wound in peace, **9.** but as soon as he had recovered, he declared war on the Athenians. They were placed in such dire straits that they enlisted their one-time enemies, the Lacedaemonians, as their allies and wearied every city in Greece with their ambassadors, asking that Greece might face the foe of all with an army drawn from all. Some cities did join Athens, but fear of war dragged others over to Philip's side. **10.** When battle was joined, although the Athenians were

78 A reference to the Athenian grain fleet returning from the Black Sea which Philip captured in 340 BC.

79 (H)istria is located on the Black Sea coast of Romania.

80 Apollonia is the modern Pojani in Albania.

81 Ateas, normally spelt Atheas, held land in the Dobruja. The Histriani were the people living by the Ister, i.e. the Danube. Philip defeated and killed Ateas in 339 BC. His 'trickery' was a stratagem for dealing with Scythian horse archers that was much admired in antiquity, see Frontinus, *Stratagems*, 2.8.14.

82 A people based around Nis in modern Serbia.

far superior in numbers of troops, they were defeated by battle-hardened courage of the Macedonians.

11. The outcome of the battle shows us that it was infinitely worse than all the wars they had fought before – for on that day there came an end for all of Greece to the glory of the empire she had conquered and to her ancient liberty.[83]

14[84]

1. Afterwards, Philip exploited his victory in the bloodiest of fashions at Thebes and Sparta. He sent some of the cities' leaders to the executioner's axe, others he drove into exile, and he confiscated the wealth of all of them. **2.** He restored those who had been recently exiled by their fellow-citizens to their homelands and out of these exiles chose 300 to be judges and rulers so that they, assuaging their past sufferings with a new lease of power, would not allow these unhappily oppressed peoples a breath of a hope of liberty.[85] **3.** Moreover, after a great military levy had been held over all of Greece to strengthen the king's arrangements,[86] he marshalled 200,000 infantry and 15,000 cavalry besides the Macedonian army and a countless host of barbarians, whom he intended to send into Asia on an expedition against the Persians. **4.** He chose three generals, namely Parmenion, Amyntas, and Attalus, to go as a vanguard against the Persians. While the above-mentioned troops from Greece were mustering, he decided to marry his daughter Cleopatra to Alexander – the brother of his wife Olympias, who was later killed by the Sabines in Lucania[87] – whom he had decided to make king of Epirus as a reward for the buggery he had inflicted on him. **5.** It is said that when Philip was asked the day before he was killed what was the best end for which a man could hope, he replied that the best one was that which could come suddenly and swiftly by the sword from an unexpected quarter to a brave man who was reigning in peace after winning glory through his courage, while he still suffered from no bodily illness or ill-repute. This end soon befell the man himself:

---

83 The Battle of Chaeronea, 338 BC.

84 This chapter draws heavily on, and abbreviates, Justin, 9.5–9.6.5.

85 These sanctions are drawn from Justin, 9.5, but there apply to Thebes alone. Orosius suppresses Justin's, 9.5.1–2, comments that Philip dealt with each town on its merits and that Athens was treated mercifully, Justin, 9.4.4–5.

86 A garbled reference to the League of Corinth created by Philip in 337 BC.

87 See 3.12.8.

6. Not even the angry Gods, to whom he had always paid scant regard and whose altars, temples, and idols he had destroyed, could stop him from obtaining that which he thought the most desirable of deaths.[88] **7.** For when on the day of the wedding, he was walking to the magnificently produced games between the two Alexanders, his son and son-in-law, he was waylaid without his bodyguards in a narrow passage by Pausanias, a young Macedonian noble, and killed.

8. Now let those for whom the worst calamities suffered by others are nothing but sweet stories from the past, assert and proclaim at length that these were the praiseworthy, fortunate deeds of brave men – provided that they never relate their own troubles, if at times they are ever tormented by them, with an excessively tearful tale.[89] **9.** But if they wish those who hear about their own complaints to be affected by the same feelings as they themselves felt when they suffered them, let them first not compare the past with the present, but one deed with another and, having heard them, give judgment between the two like arbitrators who have no part in the quarrel.

10. For 25 years the deceit, savagery, and tyranny of this one king brought about the burning of cities, the devastation of war, the subjugation of provinces, the slaughter of men, the plundering of property, the rustling of herds, the sale of dead men's goods, and the enslavement of the living.

15[90]

1. These notorious deeds of Philip, engrained as they are in our memory, would be sufficient examples of man's misery, even if Alexander had not been the successor to his kingdom. I will now put off for a short time the chronological account of Alexander's wars, or rather of the ills that the world suffered because of them, in order to note at this point what happened at Rome during in this period.

2. 426 years after the foundation of the City,[91] an infamous disgrace suffered by Rome certainly made the Caudine Forks celebrated and

88 Orosius appears to have used a story originally told of Caesar (Suetonius, *Caesar*, 87; Plutarch, *Caesar*, 63) and twisted round its natural irony – that the subject predicted his own imminent demise – into a demonstration of the impotence of the pagan gods.

89 Orosius reverts to his attack that his opponents, while ignoring the great sufferings of the past, magnify those of the present.

90 This material in this chapter is drawn, heavily abbreviated, from Livy, 9.15–16. Livy follows the comments about Alexander with a lengthy comparison, 9.17–19, between Alexander and Rome in which Rome emerges as superior. This is suppressed by Orosius.

91 The incident of the Caudine Forks is normally dated to 433 *AUC*/321 BC.

famous.[92] In the war that had preceded this debacle, 20,000 Samnites had been killed when they came to battle with Fabius, the Master of Horse.[93] After this, the Samnites, acting with greater caution and a better-equipped army, occupied the Caudine Forks. **3.** Here, after their army had trapped consuls Veturius and Postumius[94] and all the Roman troops with them in this pass, their commander Pontius was so sure of his victory that he thought he should ask his father whether he ought to kill the men he had trapped or free them, now they had been defeated – he chose to let them live, but in disgrace. **4.** For it was common knowledge that the Romans had often been defeated and slain in the past, but had never been captured or could be forced into total surrender.

5. So the Samnites after their victory, stripped the entire Roman army, which had been so disgracefully captured, of their arms and even of their clothing – allowing each man only a loin cloth to cover the shameful parts of his body – and forced them under the yoke into slavery, forming them up by ranks in a great procession. **6.** They kept 600 Roman knights as hostages, and sent back the consuls laden only with shame and with nothing else to show for themselves.

7. But why should I try to underline with my words the stigma of that most terrible of treaties,[95] when I would have preferred to keep silent about it? Today, the Romans, if they had, after their defeat, kept to the conditions of the treaty which they made with the Samnites in the way they now require those defeated by them to keep to their treaty obligations, would have either vanished entirely or been the Samnites' slaves.

8. But the following year,[96] the Romans broke the pact they had made with the Samnites and forced them to wage war. This war was started at the insistence of the consul Papirius[97] and caused great slaughter on both sides. **9.** One side fought driven on by anger at their recent humiliation, the other by the glory of their last victory. Finally, the Romans, stubborn to the death,

92 The location of the Caudine Forks is disputed. Traditionally the pass has been identified with the Arienzo-Arpaia valley. See the discussion in Salmon (1967) 225–27.

93 Q. Fabius Ambustus. A dictator's deputy was given this title. The dictator at the time was A. Cornelius Cossus.

94 T. Veturius Calvinus and Sp. Postumius Albinus, consuls in 321 BC.

95 *Foedus* (treaty) *foedum* (adjective meaning foul). This play on words is drawn from Augustine, *City of God*, 3.17.

96 In fact, the war was not renewed by Rome until six years later at the end of 316 BC.

97 L. Papirius Murgilanus Cursor. Papirius was consul on five occasions, once in 320 BC, which may be the source of Orosius's error as to when the war was renewed, but also in 315 BC which is the consulate referred to here.

were victorious. They did not stop slaughtering or being slaughtered until, after defeating the Samnites and capturing their commander, they repaid them by forcing them under the yoke.[98] **10.** This same Papirius went on to storm and capture Satricum, driving out its Samnite garrison.[99]

He was at that time regarded by the Romans as such a mighty warrior that when it was rumoured that Alexander the Great had decided to return from the East first to take Africa by force and then cross over into Italy, the Romans thought that out of all the other capable commanders whom they had at that time in the state, he would have been the best man able to resist Alexander's onslaught.[100]

16[101]

1. 426 years after the foundation of the City, Alexander succeeded to the throne of his father Philip.[102] He gave the first proof of his spirit and courage by swiftly suppressing a rebellion of the Greeks. The ringleader in urging them to break away from the Macedonians' empire was Demosthenes who had been bribed with Persian gold.[103] **2.** Alexander abandoned his war against the Athenians when they recanted, and even freed them from the fear of being fined. He then massacred the Thebans after destroying their town, auctioned what remained of them into slavery, and imposed tribute on the rest of the towns in Achaea and Thessaly. Soon afterwards, he moved the theatre of war to Illyricum and Thrace and subdued them.[104] **3.** Then, as he was about to set off on his Persian expedition, he killed all his nearest male relations.

His army was composed of 32,000 infantry, 4,500 cavalry, and 180 ships.[105] *It is debatable which should be thought more amazing: that he*

98 After the Battle of Luceria.

99 The modern Borgo le Ferriere. In fact, it was Q. Fabius Rullianus who captured the town, see Salmon (1967) 234 n.1.

100 This sentiment is drawn from Livy, 9.16.19.

101 This chapter draws heavily on, and abbreviates, Justin, 11.2.1–11.

102 Orosius's chronology is awry here – Alexander came to power in 418 *AUC*/336 BC. Orosius wants to link the disaster of the Caudine Forks to what he sees as the disaster of Alexander's accession to power.

103 Orosius's source for this allegation is Justin, 11.2.7, but they were also made in Demosthenes' own day; see Aeschines, *Against Ctesiphon* (*In Ctesiphon*), 156, 173, 209.

104 This campaign in fact preceded the rebellion in Greece. Orosius has followed the error he found in Justin, 11.9.

105 These figures agree with Justin, 1.6.2, except that Justin has 182 ships.

conquered the entire East with such a small band, or that he dared to set out on such an enterprise in the first place.[106]

4. In his first encounter with King Darius,[107] *there were 600,000 Persians in the battle line. These were vanquished as much by Alexander's skill as by being turned to flight by the Macedonians' courage. A great slaughter of the Persians ensued. One hundred and twenty of Alexander's cavalry and only nine of his infantry lost their lives.*[108]

5. After this, he besieged, assaulted, and captured the Phrygian town of Gordies which is now usually called Sardis, and allowed it to be sacked.[109] When he was told that Darius was advancing on him with a large force, fearing the enclosed nature of the place in which he found himself, he crossed the Taurus mountains with amazing swiftness and arrived at Tarsus, having covered 500 stades in a single day.[110] There, while he was sweating with the heat, he jumped into the freezing waters of the Cydnus,[111] grew stiff with the cold, and, as his sinews contracted, came close to death.

6. Meanwhile, Darius deployed his 300,000 infantry and 100,000 cavalry into line of battle.[112] This enemy host moved even Alexander, especially when he considered his own small numbers, although from his previous triumph over 600,000 of the enemy with this same small number of men, he had learnt not only not to be afraid of battle, but even to have hopes of victory.

7. After the two armies stood within a spear's throw of one another, the men were eagerly waiting for the signal for battle, and the two generals had rushed back and forth sharpening their enthusiasm in all manner of ways, both sides joined battle in high spirits. **8.** In it, both kings, Alexander and Darius, were wounded. *For a long time the battle hung in the balance, until finally Darius fled and then the Persians were slaughtered.*[113] **9.** On this field, 80,000 infantrymen[114] and 10,000 cavalrymen were slaughtered, and another 40,000 were captured. *On the Macedonian side 130 infantry and*

---

106 Taken verbatim from Justin, 11.6.3.

107 Darius III (336–330 BC).

108 The Battle of Granicus, 334 BC. The italicised passage is taken almost verbatim from Justin, 11.6.11–12.

109 This false identification appears to be Orosius's own. Gordies is Gordium, the modern Yassihüyük in Turkey. Ancient Sardis lies just to the south of Sart Mahmut, also in Turkey. The incident took place in 333 BC.

110 Around 57 miles.

111 The modern Tarsus Cayi in Turkey.

112 Justin, 11.9.1, gives the number of Darius's infantry as 400,000.

113 This sentence is taken verbatim from Justin, 11.9.9.

114 Justin has 61,000.

150 cavalry fell. A great quantity of gold and other riches were discovered in the Persian camp. Among those captured there were Darius' mother, his wife, who was also his sister, and two of his daughters.[115] **10.** When Darius, even after offering half his kingdom, was unable to ransom them, he gathered together for a third time all the might of Persia along with the help he could obtain from his allies, and renewed the war.

11. But while Darius was doing this, Alexander despatched Parmenion with a force to attack the Persian fleet and he himself went to Syria. There out of the many kings who came to meet him of their own free will wearing fillets on their heads,[116] he made alliances with some, deposed others, and yet others he executed. He subdued and captured the ancient and prosperous city of Tyre which resisted him, placing its hopes on support from its kinsmen in Carthage.[117] **12.** Then his insatiable fury carried him to Cilicia, Rhodes, and Egypt.

From there he went on to the temple of Jupiter Hammon[118] in order to erase the shame of the doubts over who had been his father and the disgrace of his mother's adultery by concocting a lie which fitted the occasion. **13.** For, according to what their historians say,[119] he summoned the priest of the shrine and secretly advised him of answers that he wished to hear when he pretended to consult the oracle. So Alexander was convinced, and has shown us, that since the gods are both deaf and dumb, that it is either in the power of the priest to devise whatever answer he wishes or in the credulity of the petitioner to hear what he prefers to hear.[120] **14.** On his return from Hammon to fight his third campaign against the Persians, he founded Alexandria-in-Egypt.[121]

115 The italicised passage is taken verbatim, save for one synonym for 'infantry', from Justin, 11.9.10–12. Orosius suppresses Justin's comment on Alexander's chivalrous behaviour towards Darius's womenfolk. The battle is the Battle of Issus, 333 BC.

116 i.e. they came as suppliants.

117 The siege of Tyre occurred in the August of 332 BC. Carthage was a colonial foundation of Tyre.

118 At the oasis of Siwah.

119 i.e. pagan historians.

120 Justin, 11.11, has the story that Alexander sent envoys to give the oracle the correct replies. Orosius's version is sharper in its anti-pagan rhetoric, yet oddly does not specifically state that the oracle told Alexander that he was the son of Ammon, not Philip, which is found in Justin's version. Nor does Orosius use Justin's comments that it was after this incident that Alexander's arrogance became intolerable.

121 i.e. the modern Alexandria. Alexandria was probably founded before Alexander's journey to Siwah, see Arrian, *Anabasis*, 3.1.5; Plutarch, *Alexander*, 26. Orosius is following Justin's, 9.11.13, error.

17[122]

1. Darius, who had lost any hope of making peace, faced Alexander on his return from Egypt in battle at Tarsus[123] with 404,000 infantry[124] and 100,000 cavalry. Nor was there any delaying the fighting: **2.** all rushed at their enemies' swords in a blind frenzy. The Macedonians were spurred on by the fact that they had beaten their enemy so often before, while the Persians preferred death to defeat. **3.** Rarely was so much blood spilt in a battle. When Darius saw his men being defeated, he prepared to die in battle, but bowed to the persuasion of his people and fled. **4.** This battle was the downfall of the strength and kingdoms of Asia: all the East fell into the hands of the Macedonian Empire, and the confidence of the Persians was destroyed to such a degree in this war that afterwards none dared rebel. So the Persians after holding an empire for so many years, now patiently accepted the yoke of slavery.[125] **5.** Alexander spent 34 whole days cataloguing the booty he found in the camp, then he attacked Persepolis, the capital of the Persian kingdom, a most famous city, full of wealth which had come from around the whole world.[126]

6. When he heard that Darius's relatives had imprisoned him and bound him in golden fetters, he decided to give chase. So, after ordering his army to follow him, he himself set off with 6,000 cavalry. He found the king abandoned by the wayside: he had been stabbed many times and was breathing his last. **7.** In an empty gesture of pity, Alexander ordered that the dead king be taken to, and buried in, the tomb of his ancestors. He kept Darius's mother and wife and even, I should say, his little daughters in cruel captivity.[127]

8. In the midst of such a multitude of evils, it is difficult to speak with credibility. In three battles and as many years, 1,500,000 infantry and cavalry

122 This chapter draws heavily on, and abbreviates, Justin, 11.12; 11.14–15.

123 The Battle of Gaugamela, fought on 1 October 331 BC.

124 Justin, 11.12.5, has 400,000 infantry.

125 Orosius takes these sentiments, which are vital to his interpretation of history, from Justin, 1.14.6–7. Justin makes the collapse of Persia personal, speaking of Alexander seizing the Persians' kingdom and attributes the lack of subsequent rebellions to Alexander's luck rather than Persian demoralisation.

126 Persepolis is now known as Takht-e-Jamshid and lies some 30 miles north-east of Shiraz in Southern Iran. Oddly, Orosius makes no mention of Alexander's destruction of the city.

127 This sharp attack on Alexander's behaviour is Orosius's own and contrasts with Justin's account, 11.15, which portrays Alexander as moved by Darius's fate and acting in a chivalrous fashion towards his womenfolk.

perished,[128] and they came from that kingdom and those peoples where not long before more than 1,900,000 lives are said to have been wasted. **9.** Apart from this tragedy, in those same three years a great number of cities in Asia were crushed, all of Syria laid waste, Tyre uprooted, Cilicia stripped bare, Cappadocia enslaved, and Egypt placed in bondage. In addition, the island of Rhodes, fearing enslavement, surrendered of her own free will and most of the provinces which lie under the Taurus mountains and Mount Taurus itself, conquered and defeated, received the yoke they had spurned for so long.

18[129]

1. In case any one should think that it was only the East that was enslaved by the might of Alexander, or merely Italy that was exhausted by Roman restlessness, we must remember that at that time war was being waged in Greece by Hagis, the king of the Spartans,[130] in Lucania by Alexander, the king of Epirus,[131] and in Scythia, by the prefect Zopyrion.[132] **2.** Out of these, Hagis the Lacedaemonian roused all Greece to rebel with him, met Antipater's powerful army in battle, and fell amid great slaughter on both sides.[133] **3.** Alexander was defeated in Italy by the Bruttii and Lucanians after many costly battles, while attempting to build an empire in the West to rival that of Alexander the Great. His corpse was then ransomed for burial.[134] **4.** The prefect of the Euxine Sea, Zopyrion, mustered an army 30,000 strong and dared to wage war on the Scythians. His army was slaughtered to the last man, and he himself was wiped out along with all his troops.[135]

5. After the death of Darius, Alexander the Great subdued the Hyrcanians and Mandi.[136] While he was fighting there, he was approached along with 300 women by the shameless Amazon Halestris, who is sometimes

128 Orosius has correctly added his casualty figures for the battles of Granicus, Issus, and Gaugamela.

129 This chapter draws heavily on, and abbreviates, Justin, 12.1–6. Justin is critical of Alexander, but Orosius's tone is much more strident in this respect.

130 Agis III, 338–331 BC.

131 Alexander I of Molossia, see 3.11.1.

132 These three examples are taken from Justin, 12.1.4.

133 The Battle of Megalopolis, 330 BC.

134 Alexander died at the Battle of Pandosia in 331 BC, see 3.11.1.

135 The expedition perhaps took place in 325 BC.

136 Alexander made this expedition towards the Caspian Sea in 330 BC. The Mandi are Justin's, 12.3.4, Mardii, who are mentioned as a nomadic Persian tribe by Herodotus 1.125.

called Minothea and who had been aroused by the hope of bearing children by him.[137] **6.** After this, he fought the Parthians. They resisted him for a long time and he almost destroyed them before he finally conquered them. **7.** Then he subdued the Drangae, Euergetae, Parimae, Parapameni, Adaspii, and the rest of the peoples who live at the foot of the Caucasus. Here he built Alexandria-on-the-Tanais.[138]

8. Nor was his cruelty towards his own people any less than his rage against his enemies, as is shown by the killing of his cousin Amyntas, the murder of his stepmother and brothers, the butchering of Parmenion and Philotas, and the eradication of Attalus, Eurylochus, Pausanias, and a host of leading Macedonians. Even Clitus, an old man and an old friend, was shamefully killed. **9.** At a banquet, relying on his friendship with the king, he opposed the king who was saying that his deeds were greater than those of Philip, by reminiscing about Alexander's father. He was run through with a hunting spear by the king who had taken offence for no reason, and, as he died, covered the whole banquet with his blood.[139]

10. But Alexander, whose taste for human blood, either of his enemies or even of his friends, was never slaked, always thirsted for fresh gore. **11.** So he rushed to war and, after hard fighting, received the surrender of the Choarasmae and the Dahae,[140] a people never previously defeated in war. He killed the philosopher Callisthenes, who had been his fellow-pupil under Aristotle, along with many other leading men because they would not honour him as a god and abandon their normal way of greeting him.[141]

137 The story is drawn from Justin, 12.3.5–6. Orosius suppresses Justin's comments that the Amazons provoked universal admiration and that Alexander stayed among them for 13 days during which time Halestris, spelt Thalestris/Minythyia by Justin, got her way.

138 The Tanais is the modern Syr-Darya. For a discussion of the geographical problems here see Bosworth (1993) 109. The town is normally known as Alexandria Eschate, the modern Khudjand/Khudzhand in Tajikistan. Alexander campaigned in central Asia between 330–327 BC.

139 This notorious incident occurred at Maracanda, the modern Samarcand. Orosius suppresses Justin's comments that Alexander bitterly regretted killing Clitus.

140 See 1.2.43. Both tribes were Saca nomads living in Sogdiana – the region lying to the north of Oxus now comprising parts of Tadjikistan and Uzbekistan.

141 A reference to Alexander's attempt to introduce the Persian practice of *proscynesis* into his court and the 'conspiracy of the pages'. The philosopher and historian Callisthenes whom Alexander had invited to accompany him as his official historian was executed in 327 BC.

19[142]

1. After this, he made for India in order to make the Ocean and the furthermost East the borders of his empire. He came to the city of Nyssa[143] and stormed the Daedalian mountains and the kingdom of Queen Cleophyle, who, after surrendering, bought her kingdom back by sleeping with him.[144]

2. After Alexander had crossed and subjugated India, he came to an astoundingly rugged and high crag where many peoples had taken refuge. He learnt that an earthquake had stopped Hercules from storming the crag and so, urged on by a wish to outdo the deeds of Hercules, after great effort and danger he seized the rock and received the surrender of all the peoples on it.[145]

3. Then he fought a bloody battle with Porus, the bravest of the Indian kings, in which Alexander met Porus face to face.[146] His horse was killed and he was thrown to the ground, but his bodyguard rallied to him and saved him from the threat of death; Porus, after being wounded many times, was captured.[147] **4.** As a testament to Porus's bravery, Alexander restored him to his kingdom and founded two cities, Nicaea and Bucephala, there, ordering the latter to be so named after his horse.[148]

Then the Macedonians took the Adrestae, Cattheni, Praesidae, and Gangaridae by storm, slaughtering their armies. **5.** When they came up against Cofides,[149] they fought a battle against 200,000 enemy horsemen. Worn out by their years, sick at heart, and physically weary, after they had, with some difficulty, won the fight, they founded a camp of more than usual

142 This chapter draws heavily on, and abbreviates, Justin, 12.7.4–12.10.4.

143 The location of this city, whose inhabitants claimed to be worshippers of Bacchus, is unknown.

144 For the Daedalian mountains see Tarn (1984) 249–50, though his conclusions about Cretan mercenaries seem fanciful. Justin, 12.7.9, gives the queen's name as Cleophis, she ruled over the Assacenes who lived in the Swat valley.

145 The rock of Aornos, the modern Pir-Sar in the Indus Valley. Orosius manages to engage two targets here: Alexander for his arrogance and the pagans whose gods who are shown to be inferior to mortals.

146 Porus (d. 318 BC) was ruler of the Pauravas who lived between the Jhelum and Chenab rivers.

147 The Battle of the Hydaspes, the modern Jhelum, in the Punjab, fought in 326 BC.

148 Nicaea is probably the modern Jalalpur. The site of Bucephala, founded on the battlefield of the Hydaspes, is unknown.

149 Justin, 12.8.10, calls the king Sophis. He is to be identified with the Indian king Saubhuti, who struck Graecising coins under the name of Sophytes. His realm probably lay in the northern Punjab.

magnificence as a memorial to their victory.[150]

6. Then Alexander advanced to the river Agesis,[151] along which he voyaged down to the Ocean. Here he subdued the Gesonae[152] and Sibi whose founder was Hercules.[153] He sailed hence against the Adri[154] and Subagri[155] who were waiting for him with an army of 80,000 infantry and 60,000 cavalry. **7.** Battle was joined. The fight was bloody and lay in the balance for a long time, but eventually gave the Macedonians a victory that almost turned into tragedy. For when he had routed the enemy, Alexander led his army to their city. He was the first to scale its walls and, thinking that the city was deserted, leapt down into it alone. **8.** When the enemy had surrounded him on all sides with murderous intent, *incredible to relate, neither the numbers of his foe, nor the great violence of their weapons, nor the huge shout that went up from his assailants frightened him, and, though he was alone, he killed and routed many thousands of them.* **9.** *But when he realised that he was being overcome by the multitude that poured round him,*[156] guarding his back by putting it to the wall, he easily beat off his opponents until his entire army broke down the walls and burst into the city, making for where he was in danger and towards the shouts of his enemies. **10.** In this battle, Alexander was shot under the breast by an arrow, but raising himself on one knee, he fought on until he had killed the man by whom he had been wounded.

11. After this, he embarked on his ships, cruised along the shores of the Ocean and came to the city ruled by King Ambira.[157] In storming this city, he lost a great part of his army to the enemy's arrows which were dipped in poison. But after a herb revealed to him in a dream and which, on being

150 Orosius has garbled Justin, 12.8.12, where Alexander's troops complain that their lives will hardly be long enough for them to return to Macedonia. The camp was built at the furthest point east which Alexander had reached. Alexander built twelve altars here to the twelve Olympian gods. Perhaps Orosius has suppressed this information because he did not wish to glorify paganism, but, as Justin makes no mention of the altars, it is more likely he was simply unaware of their existence.

151 Probably the river Chenab.

152 Justin, 12.9.2, calls this tribe the Agensonae.

153 The Sibae of Strabo, 15.1.8–9. They are also found in Nonnus, *Dionysiaca*, 26.218. The deduction that they were a creation of Hercules was derived from the fact that they wore skins and carried clubs. They may in fact have been a caste group rather than a tribe.

154 Justin, 12.9.3, calls this tribe the Mandri.

155 Perhaps a garbled form of Ksudraka, a tribe who lived between the Indus and Hydaspes.

156 Taken verbatim from Justin, 12.9.8–9.

157 Justin, 12.10.2, speaks of King Ambus. Orosius has either misread his manuscript and elided the two words (*Ambi Regis*) or had a corrupt manuscript at this point.

given to them in a potion, cured his remaining wounded, he went on to storm and take the town.

20

1. After turning the corner, so to speak,[158] Alexander entered the river Indus from the Ocean and swiftly returned to Babylon. **2.** Here terrified ambassadors from all the provinces of the entire world were waiting for him. There were ambassadors from the Carthaginians, all the cities of Africa, and also from the Spaniards, Gauls, Sicily, and Sardinia, besides others from most of Italy. **3.** So great was the fear of a leader who ruled the far east among the peoples of the uttermost west that you would have seen delegations drawn from all those parts of the world to which you would hardly have believed that rumours of Alexander's existence could have penetrated.[159]

4. Alexander then died in Babylon while still thirsting for blood with a lust that was cruelly punished – for he drank poison that had been treacherously prepared by a servant.[160]

5. O the hardness of man's mind, and his ever-inhuman heart! Have I, who recount these matters to show how throughout the ages one different calamity has followed another, never filled my eyes with tears while telling of such evil times, when the whole world trembled either from death or the fear of death? Have I never been sick at heart? Have I never, when reflecting on these things, seeing them as the common lot of those who live, made my ancestors' sorrows my own? **6.** When I tell, if I may mention my own life, how I first saw barbarians from unknown lands, how I escaped from their hostility, flattered those in power, guarded myself against those I could not trust, outwitted those who lay in wait for me, **7.** and finally, how, when they pursued me by sea with their rocks and spears, and had almost laid hands upon me, I escaped them when I was covered by a fog which suddenly arose, I would want all those listening to me to be moved to tears and would silently grieve for those who did not grieve for me, considering their hardness to be that of those who do not believe in what they themselves have not suffered.

---

158 The 'meta'. This is a metaphor taken from chariot racing and borrowed from Justin, 12.10.5, where it is made more explicit.

159 The account of the ambassadors is drawn from Justin, 12.13, though the contrast between east and west is Orosius's own. See 6.21.19.

160 Alexander died in 323 BC. Orosius's judgment of him is completely different to that of Justin, 12.16, who describes him as 'a man endowed with mental capacities beyond those of mere mortal ability'.

8. The Spanish and the Morini[161] came to Babylon to grovel before Alexander, and of their own free will sought out this bloodstained warlord through Assyria and India in order to stop him becoming their enemy, scouring the ends of the earth and coming to know in their misfortune both oceans.[162] But the memory of this violent necessity that was forced upon them has either been forgotten altogether, or is little remembered because it happened long ago. **9.** So do we think that we shall set in our memory forever the fact that some fugitive thief managed to plunder one corner of the world, when for the most part it remained free of him?[163] It is as if an Indian or Assyrian asked the Goths and Sueves, not to mention the reverse, for peace, or even a Spaniard who is suffering their attacks. **10.** But if Alexander's life and times are judged to be more worthy of praise because of the courage with which he conquered the whole world than worthy of contempt because of the chaos into which he plunged it, even more men will be found who think the present day worthy of praise because there have been many victories and because they consider the sufferings of others to be their own good fortune.

11. But someone will say, 'But those men are the enemies of the Roman World'.[164] The reply to this is that this is how Alexander seemed to the whole East, and how the Romans too seemed to others, when they made war on unknown, peaceful peoples.[165]

'But Alexander and Rome strove to obtain a kingdom, while the barbarians fight to overthrow them', will come the counter.

However, the destruction wrought by an enemy and the order imposed by a victor are two separate things. **12.** Alexander and Rome first made war on those whom afterwards they brought under their laws. Similarly, the barbarians too are now throwing into confusion as their enemies those whom, if they conquer them, and, may God not allow this to come to pass, they will endeavour to rule after their own fashion, and thus those whom

161 A Gallic tribe found opposite the English Channel and so on the edge of the Ocean. Orosius is here drawing on Virgil, *Aeneid*, 8.727–28, to make his following point about both the Oceans. Given the context, and Orosius's homeland, we should assume that the Spaniards are from Galicia.

162 The image conjured up is one of anti-magi seeking an anti-Christ.

163 This is a reference to Alaric's sack of Rome in AD 410. Orosius is arguing that *sub specie historiae* this is a trivial event.

164 'These men' are the barbarians. Orosius here uses the abstract term 'Romania' to mark out not just Rome's empire but the cultural baggage that went with it. See 7.43.5.

165 See 5.1.1–13. There is perhaps also an echo of Ninus of Assyria/Babylon, see 1.4.1 and 2.3.6.

we now regard as our most brutal enemies, will be considered as great kings by posterity.

13. Now whatever name is given to these deeds, be it courage or suffering, they are fewer in number now compared with those in times gone by. In either case we compare favourably with Alexander and the Persians, for if this is now to be called courage, then that of the enemy is less, if it is to be called suffering, then that of Rome is less.

21[166]

1. 450 years after the foundation of the City, when Fabius Maximus was consul for the fifth, and Decius Mus for the fourth, time,[167] the four most powerful and flourishing peoples of Italy made a treaty and united their armies into one, the Etruscans, Umbrians, Samnites, and Gauls combining their forces in a plot to try to destroy Rome. **2.** The Romans' spirits trembled at the prospect of this war and their confidence was shaken. They did not dare to put all their hope in their own strength, but divided the enemy by trickery, thinking it safer to fight more small battles than a few large-scale ones. **3.** So, after they had sent some of their men to ravage the enemies' fields in Umbria and Etruria, and in this way forced the Etruscan and Umbrian armies to retreat to protect their territory, they made haste to engage the Samnites and Gauls. **4.** In this battle the Romans were pushed back under the onslaught of the Gauls and Decius, the consul, was killed.[168] However, Fabius eventually won the victory after the death of a great number of Decius's troops.[169] **5.** In this battle, it is said that 40,000 Samnites and Gauls were killed, while only 7,000 Romans perished, and these came from the division of Decius who was killed in the battle. **6.** Livy states that apart from the Etruscans and Umbrians whom the Romans had cunningly drawn out of the war, the Gauls and the Samnites

---

166 This chapter is drawn, in a very heavily abbreviated form, from Livy, 10.27–31.

167 Normally dated to 459 *AUC*/295 BC.

168 The Battle of Sentium (near the modern Ancona), 295 BC. For a detailed discussion of the problems involved with our ancient accounts of this battle, see Harris (1971) 69–74.

169 Orosius suppresses the fact that Mus, like his father, died through performing the religious rite of *devotio*, see Livy, 10.28.12–18, and that Fabius, on learning of Decius's death, pledged that he would build a temple to Jupiter Victor and give the god the spoils of battle if he triumphed, Livy, 10.29.14. *Devotio* was the ritual dedication of oneself to the gods of the underworld. The enemy by killing one so dedicated would bring the wrath of those Gods and thus destruction upon themselves.

had 140,330 infantry, 47,000 cavalry, and 1,000 waggoneers in line of battle against the Romans.[170]

7. But – as has often been pointed out, the Romans' high hopes have always been completely checked from all directions, either by having their harmony at home disrupted by war abroad or their foreign adventures made worse by plague at home – **8.** a plague in the city made this sorrowful and bloodstained victory all the worse, and funeral corteges of the dead defiled their triumphal processions. No one could be persuaded to rejoice in the victory, since the entire city was grieving for either the sick or the dead.

22[171]

1. In the following year, the Samnites renewed the war, defeated the Romans, and forced them to flee back to their camp. **2.** After this, the Samnites took new heart and a new form of dress – for they covered their arms and tunics in silver[172] – and marched out to battle prepared to conquer or die.

3. Although the keepers of the sacred chickens and their empty prophecies forbade him to take the field, the consul Papirius[173] and his army was sent out against them. He laughed at the chicken-keepers and in the same way as he had steadfastly begun the campaign, brought it to a successful conclusion.[174] **4.** For it is said that in the battle 12,000 of the enemy were

170 This is Orosius's first direct mention of Livy. He has, however, read a poor manuscript, or badly garbled Livy's account. Livy, 10.29.17–19, gives the casualties as 25,000 for Rome's opponents and 8,700 Romans, the latter comprising the 7,000 of Decius's army mentioned by Orosius and an additional 1,700 from Fabius's troops. Orosius's numbers of those engaged also differs from those given by Livy, 10.30.5, who states that there were 600,000 infantry, 46,000 cavalry, and 1,000 waggons. We must suppose that Orosius was unaware of Diodorus Siculus's, 21.6.1, account drawn from Duris of Samos that gives the Etruscan and Gallic losses as 100,000.

171 This chapter draws in a heavily abbreviated form on Livy, 10.28–42, 11, and 12.

172 A rather garbled reference to the 'linen legion' of the Samnites (Livy, 10.28). The Samnites equipped this legion with bright white linen tunics. Orosius has taken his information from the comments of Papirius (Livy, 10.39.13), but fails to note that this speech itself states that the Samnites had equipped a legion like this as early as 310 BC (see also Livy, 9.40 which Orosius either did not read or has forgotten). Oddly, Orosius also suppresses the account of the lurid pagan rituals that accompanied the creation of the legion which would have served his anti-pagan cause.

173 L. Papirius Cursor, consul in 461 *AUC*/293 BC.

174 Orosius has created a tale about the worthlessness of pagan prophecy here, but is being a little disingenuous. Livy's, 10.40.4–5 and 10.40.10–12, report from which Orosius draws his comments is more ambiguous. Here the chickens give a bad omen, but their keepers send a false positive omen to Papirius. When members of his army reported this to him, Papirius

killed and 3,000 taken prisoner.[175]

But his truly praiseworthy victory which empty prophecies had been unable to prevent was ruined by the sudden onset of disease. **5.** For such a great and unbearable plague then took hold of the city that in their efforts to put an end to it by any means possible, they decided to consult the Sibylline Books and brought over the infamous, vile snake of Epidaurus along with the stone of Aesculapius – as if plague had not died down in the past, or would not arise again in the future.[176]

6. The following year the consul Fabius Gurges[177] fought, but badly, against the Samnites – he lost his army and fled back to the city.[178] **7.** When the Senate was debating whether to remove him from office, his father, Fabius Maximus,[179] while condemning the cowardice of his son, freely offered to serve as his own son's lieutenant, if he were given the chance to purge his disgrace and renew the war.

8. After Maximus had obtained his request and battle was joined, he suddenly saw his son, the consul, fighting with Pontius, the leader of the Samnites, and cut off and threatened by the weapons of the enemy. This dutiful[180] old man then charged into the midst of the fray on his horse. **9.** His actions roused up the Romans who pressed on along all the battle line, until they destroyed the enemy's army, defeating and capturing its leader Pontius. **10.** 20,000 Samnites were killed in this battle, and 4,000 were captured along with their king. The disappearance of their captured leader finally brought to a close the Samnite War that had dragged the Romans through

---

declared that he preferred to believe the positive omen, but nevertheless ordered the chicken-keepers to be stationed in the front line.

175 The battle was fought near Aquilonia. Livy, 10.42.5, gives the Samnite casualties as 12,340 dead and 3,870 taken prisoner.

176 Orosius has a clear message here, namely that paganism does not work, but he has garbled his data. He appears to have confused the cult of Aesculapius that was introduced to Rome in 291 BC (Valerius Maximus, 1.8.2) and was associated with snakes, with that of Cybele and the arrival of the *betyl* (an uncarved sacred stone) of the *Magna Mater* in Rome in 206 BC. Livy, 10.47.7, notes that nothing could be done about the summoning in the year of Papirius's consulate and only a one-day formal supplication, or *supplicatio,* to the god was performed. Augustine, *City of God*, 3.17, also mentions the incident.

177 Q. Fabius Maximus Gurges, consul in 462 *AUC*/292 BC.

178 The ordering of these events by Orosius is highly suggestive – the Romans ignore the instructions of pagan omens under Papirius and are triumphant, then follow them and are defeated. Orosius, either out of guile or careless enthusiasm, has changed their order to bring this about. Livy, *Per.* 11, places Gurges' defeat before the summoning of Aesculapius.

179 Q. Fabius Maximus Rullianus.

180 'Pius' here in the sense of loyalty to one's family.

many a disaster for 49 years.

11. The next year, war was waged against the Sabines under the consul Curius.[181] The consul himself revealed how many thousands of men had been killed and how many captured, for when he wished to announce in the Senate the amount of Sabine land he had seized and the great number people he had captured, the numbers defeated him.

12. 463 years after the foundation of the City, in the consulate of Dolabella and Domitius,[182] the Lucanians, Bruttii, and Samnites made an alliance with the Etruscans and Senonian Gauls in an attempt to renew the war against Rome. Rome sent envoys to urge the Gauls not to join in.

13. After the Gauls killed these, the praetor Caecilius was despatched with an army to avenge the envoys' deaths and put down the enemies' rising, but he was defeated and killed by the Gauls and Etruscans. **14.** Seven military tribunes were also killed in this battle, many noble men were slaughtered, and the 30,000 Roman soldiers laid low in the war.[183]

15. And so whenever the Gauls' spirits became inflamed, Rome lost all. For this reason while we suffer at present from an incursion of Goths, we ought to remember all the more those attacks of the Gauls.[184]

23[185]

1. But now I shall call myself back in order to go through the wars that the leaders of the Macedonians fought among themselves, since these happened at the same time as the Romans suffered from the disasters I have just described, and relate how on the death of Alexander, they drew lots for the various provinces and then destroyed themselves by infighting.

2. I seem to look down on the tempestuous times of these men as if I were to look down by night on a vast camp from the top of a mountain, and

181 Orosius has missed a year – the consul is M'. Curius Dentatus, consul in 464 *AUC*/290 BC.

182 Orosius's chronology is eight years awry, he is referring to P. Cornelius Dolabella and Gn. Domitius Calvinus Maximus, consuls in 471 *AUC* /283 BC.

183 Augustine, *City of God*, 3.17, mentions this battle in his list of times when pagan gods gave no aid to Rome. Significantly, both Orosius and Augustine suppress the fact that soon after this battle the Etruscans were defeated at the Battle of Lake Vadimon by the consul P. Cornelius Dolabella (Florus, 1.8). A further string of Roman victories in 282 and 281 BC are equally suppressed.

184 Again, Orosius wishes to press home to his readers that the troubles of the present are negligible compared to those of the past.

185 The material in this chapter is taken and radically condensed from Justin, books 10–17.

see nothing on the expanse of that great plain but innumerable specks of fire.[186] **3.** At this time the terrible fires of war suddenly blazed forth though all the kingdom of Macedonia: namely all of Asia, most of Europe, and the greater part of Libya. **4.** After these conflagrations had devastated the places where they had flared up, they threw the rest of the world into confusion through, as it were, a thick, black smoke of frightening rumours. **5.** But it will be useless to go through the wars and slaughter that overtook so many kings and kingdoms, unless I first list these realms and their rulers.

6. After Alexander had crushed the trembling world beneath his sword for twelve years, his generals tore it asunder for another fourteen and, like lion-cubs eager to tear apart the rich prey brought down by a great lion, destroyed one another by quarrelling among themselves in their eagerness for the prize.

7. *The first lot allocated Egypt and parts of Africa and Arabia to Ptolemy. Laomedon of Mitylene[187] obtained the province of Syria which lay on Ptolemy's borders; Philotas, Cilici; Philo,[188] Illyria.* **8.** *Atropatus[189] was put in charge of Greater, Perdiccas's father-in-law,[190] Lesser Media. The people of Susa were assigned to Scynus[191] and Greater Phrygia to Antigonus, the son of Philip.[192]* **9.** *Nearchus[193] was allotted Lycia and Pamphylia; Cassander,[194] Caria; and Menander,[195] Lydia. Leonnatus[196] received Lesser Phrygia.* **10.** *Thrace and the area around the Euxine Sea were given to Lysimachus,*

---

186 Perhaps an allusion to the watch fire scene at the end of Homer, *Iliad*, 8.562–63. Homer still featured in the liberal education of the Latin West, see Augustine, *Confessions*, 14. However, there is no firm evidence that Orosius knew any Greek and the relevant section of the *Ilias Latina* appears rather to draw on *Aeneid*, 9.159–60. It is likely therefore that, if this is an allusion to Homer, it is born not of first-hand acquaintance with the text, but via a common cliché of the day.

187 Arrian, *Indica*, 18.4, states that Laomedon hailed from Amphipolis. He was a trierarch in Alexander's fleet and one of his *hetaeroi*.

188 A trierarch in Alexander's Indian fleet. In section 23, he is called Python.

189 A Persian general who defected to Alexander after the Battle of Gaugamela.

190 Orosius has misread his source, Justin, 13.4.13, here. Justin reads 'Pytho the Illyrian was put in charge of Greater Media, and Atropas, the father-in-law of Perdiccas, in charge of Lesser Armenia'.

191 The satrap of Susa at Alexander's death.

192 Antigonus Monophthalmus, 382–301 BC.

193 Nearchus of Crete, Alexander's admiral and author of a lost history of Alexander that is unlikely to have been known to Orosius.

194 Antipater's son.

195 The commander of Alexander's Lydian mercenaries.

196 One of Alexander's 'Old Guard' from the days of Philip II.

Cappadocia along with Paphlagonia to Eumenes.[197] *Command of the army was given up to Seleucus,*[198] *the son of Antiochus; and Cassander, the son of Antipater, was put in charge of the royal retinue and bodyguard.* **11.** *In outer Bactria and the regions of India, the prefects* who had been previously appointed by Alexander *remained in place. Taxiles ruled the Seres who live between the Hydaspes and Indus rivers.* **12.** *Python,*[199] *the son of Agenor, was sent out to rule the colonies established in India. Oxyarches*[200] *received the Parapameni who dwell at the end of the Caucasus mountains, and the Arachossians and Chedrosians were* decreed to belong to *Sibyrtes.*[201] **13.** *Statanor drew the Dancheans and Areans; Amyntas,*[202] *the Atriani. Itacanor the Scythaean*[203] *obtained the Sogdians; Philip,*[204] *the Parthians; Fratafernes,*[205] *the Hyrcanians; Tleptolemus,*[206] *the Armenians; Peucestes,*[207]*the Persians; Archous Pellasos,*[208] *the Babylonians; and Archelaus, Mesopotamia.*[209]

14. Now the cause and origin of these wars was a letter of King Alexander in which he ordered that all exiles be restored to their homelands and set at liberty.[210] The rulers of the Greek states, fearing that when these exiles regained their freedom they would plot their revenge, consequently rebelled against the kingdom of the Macedonians.

15. The first to do so were the Athenians who gathered together an army of 30,000 men and 200 ships and waged war against Antipater who had been

197 Eumenes of Cardia, Philip II's private secretary.

198 Seleucus I Nicator, 358–281 BC.

199 The satrap of India.

200 A Sogdian king and father of Alexander's wife, Roxanne.

201 More usually Sibyrtius. Sibyrtes had made satrap of these areas by Alexander; see Arrian, *Anabasis,* 6.27.1, and Quintus Curtius, 9.10.20.

202 Justin, 13.4.20, has 'Bactrians' for Atrians. This must surely be correct and suggests that Orosius was using a poor copy of Justin. There is a slight confusion in verbs here between Orosius and Justin, which, while not changing the sense of the phrase, also suggests that Orosius's manuscript was corrupt at this point.

203 Justin, 13.4.23, assigns the Sogdians to Staganor of Soli.

204 The satrap of Bactria.

205 A Persian satrap who defected to Alexander.

206 Justin, 13.4.23, has Carmenians instead of Armenians. As Tleptolemus was the satrap of Carmania, it appears that Orosius's version of Justin was corrupt at this point.

207 The satrap of Persia.

208 Another example of Orosius's corrupt version of Justin, 13.4.23. The text reads 'Archon of Pella'.

209 The above, italicised list, apart from a small number of very slight variants, is taken verbatim from Justin, 13.4.10–13.4.24.

210 The so-called Edict of Susa, 324 BC.

allotted Greece. Through the work of the orator Demosthenes, they forged an alliance with Sicyon, Argos, Corinth, and the rest of the Greek states and besieged Antipater.[211] **16.** It was there that their leader, Leosthenes, was killed by a javelin thrown from the walls, but the Athenians attacked Leonatus who was bringing help to Antipater, destroyed his force and killed him.

17. Perdiccas waged war on and defeated Ariaratus, the king of Cappadocia.[212] But his victory brought him nothing except wounds and dangers, for before he broke into their city, all the Cappadocians set their homes on fire and cast themselves and their belongings into the flames.[213]

18. After this, war broke out between Antigonus and Perdiccas, and many provinces and islands were torn asunder for either granting them help, or for refusing it. **19.** After pondering for a long time whether the theatre of war should be moved to Macedonia or to fight in Asia, Perdiccas finally marched on Egypt with a great army. So Macedonia, divided into two by its fractious leaders, turned its arms on its own vitals. **20.** Ptolemy marshalled his Egyptian forces and his troops from Cyrene and prepared to go to war with Perdiccas.

While this was happening, Neoptolemus and Eumenes brought their quarrel to the sword in a bloody encounter. **21.** Neoptolemus was defeated and fled to Antipater whom he urged to crush Eumenes while he was off his guard. Eumenes, however, had anticipated this, and trapped those who would have trapped him. **22.** In this war, Polyperchon was killed and Neoptolemus and Eumenes wounded one another. But while Neoptolemus died, Eumenes emerged victorious.

23. Perdiccas came to battle with Ptolemy in a bitter fight, lost his army, and was killed.[214] Eumenes, Python,[215] along with Illyrius,[216] and Alcetas, Perdiccas's brother, were proclaimed public enemies by the Macedonians, and Antigonus was placed in charge of the war against them.[217]

211 At Lamia in Thessaly, hence the war is known as the Lamian War, 323–322 BC.

212 In fact, the satrap of the area. This campaign took place in 322 BC.

213 Orosius follows Justin, 13.6.1–2, in confusing the capture of Cappadocia with Perdiccas's later attack on Psidia where the holocaust here attributed to Cappadocia took place in the town of Isaura.

214 In fact, Perdiccas was murdered by his own mutinous troops at the Nile Delta in 320 BC. Orosius appears to have embroidered Justin, 13.8.10, to create his battle.

215 This is the 'Philo' of section 7.

216 Orosius has followed an error in his manuscript of Justin, 13.8.10, which has made the adjective 'Illyrian' a noun, producing Python and Illyrius, rather than Python the Illyrian.

217 This was done at the Conference of Triparadisius in 321 BC.

24. So Eumenes and Antigonus, after marshalling enormous armies, came to battle.[218] Eumenes was defeated and fled to an extremely well-fortified stronghold,[219] whence he sent ambassadors to Antipater, who was at that time the most powerful of the warlords, asking for his aid. Antigonus was so terrified on learning this, that he lifted his siege. **25.** Even so Eumenes had no firm hope or guaranteed safety and so, as a last resort, he asked the 'Silver Shields', who were so-called because of their silvered arms – that is, the troops who served under Alexander – to come to his aid. **26.** They listened to their commander's battle plan with contempt,[220] were defeated by Antigonus, had their camp seized, and so lost, along with their wives and children, everything they had gained while serving with Alexander.[221]

27. Afterwards to their shame, they sent envoys asking the victor to return to them what they had lost. Antigonus promised that if they handed Eumenes over to him in chains that he would return their possessions. **28.** Seduced by this hope of recovering their possessions, the Silver Shields performed a disgraceful act of treachery and, while captives themselves, took their commander, under whose standards they had marched but a short while before, captive and brought him loaded with chains to Antigonus. Soon afterwards they were dispersed in deep disgrace among Antigonus's troops.

29. Meanwhile, Eurydice, the wife of the Macedonian king Arridaeus,[222] committed a great number of crimes in her husband's name through the agency of Cassander with whom she had formed an outrageous open liaison. She had promoted him through every distinguished rank to the height of power and he, through a woman's lust, inflicted suffering on many Greek towns.

30. At this juncture, Olympias, the mother of King Alexander,[223] came, on Polypercon's advice, from Epirus to Macedonia, followed by Aecides, the king of Molossia. When she was stopped from entering the kingdom by Eurydice, as she had the support of the Macedonians, she ordered King Arridaeus and Eurydice to be killed.[224]

218 The Battle of Orcynium, 320 BC.
219 The fortress of Nora in the northern Taurus mountains on the borders of Cappadocia.
220 We are told that, as Macedonians, they were unhappy to be commanded by the Greek Eumenes; see Bosworth (1978).
221 The Battle of Gabiene in 316 BC.
222 Alexander's half-brother.
223 i.e. Alexander the Great.
224 The two were killed towards the end of 317 BC.

31. However, Olympias too immediately paid the price that she deserved for her cruelty. For while she was engineering, with a woman's lack of self-control, the deaths of many leading men, she learnt that Cassander was approaching, and, since she did not trust the Macedonians, fled with her daughter-in-law, Roxa,[225] and her grandson, Hercules, to the city of Pydna,[226] **32.** where she was immediately captured and put to death by Cassander.[227] The son of Alexander the Great[228] was sent with his mother to the citadel of Amphipolis to be kept under guard there.

33. After the deaths of Perdiccas, Alcetas, Polyperchon, and of the rest of the generals of the opposing faction, whom it would be too lengthy to list by name, the wars between Alexander's successors seemed to be coming to an end. **34.** But then Antigonus in his lust for power speciously argued that the king's son, Hercules, must be freed from his prison by war. **35.** When Ptolemy and Cassander learnt of this, they formed an alliance with Lysimachus and Seleucus and made vigorous preparations to fight both by land and sea. In the ensuing war Antigonus and his son, Demetrius, were defeated.[229]

36. Cassander who had taken part in Ptolemy's victory, was returning to Apollonia when he fell in with the Avieniatae.[230] This people had abandoned their native soil after suffering from an intolerable plague of frogs and mice, and were seeking a new home and in the meantime were peaceably disposed. **37.** Cassander, knowing that they were a sizeable and courageous race, made an alliance with them and settled them on the furthermost borders of Macedonia in the fear that otherwise they would be forced by necessity to invade and wage war on Macedonia itself.

38. Then, since Alexander's son, Hercules, was already fourteen, Cassander who was afraid that everyone would chose Hercules as their legitimate ruler, saw to it that he was put to death in secret along with his mother.[231]

225 Normally Roxane, see Justin, 14.6.2.

226 Alexander's son by his Persian concubine, Barsine. Orosius, following Justin, 14.6, appears to have confused Hercules with Alexander IV, see sections 32 and 34 immediately below. Pydna is near Katerini in modern Greece.

227 At the beginning of 316 BC.

228 Not Hercules, but Alexander IV, his son by Roxane.

229 Ptolemy defeated Demetrius near Gaza in 312 BC.

230 Justin, 15.2.1, calls this tribe the Audariatae.

231 Orosius has confused (or perhaps elided into one group) Alexander IV and Roxane with Hercules and Barsine. The former were murdered in 310 BC, the latter in 309 BC. While Justin, 15.2.3–5, Orosius's source here, is confused and inverts the order of the murders, he does make clear the fact that there were four, not two individuals involved.

39. Ptolemy fought another naval battle with Demetrius and, after being defeated with the loss of almost his entire fleet and army, fled back to Egypt.[232] **40.** Elated by this victory, Antigonus decreed that he and his son should be called kings. All the others followed his example and usurped royal titles and protocol for themselves.

41. When Ptolemy, Cassander, and the rest of the leaders of the other faction realised that Antigonus was betraying them one by one, encouraging one another with letters, they arranged a time and place to meet and prepared to wage a joint war against him with their combined forces. **42.** Cassander, who was ensnared in wars against his neighbours, sent in his stead Lysimachus, the best of all his generals, and a large body of men to help his allies.[233] **43.** Seleucus too came down from Greater Asia and became a new enemy for Antigonus.

This Seleucus had waged many wars throughout the East with the allies of the Macedonian kingdom.[234] **44.** His first move was to storm and capture Babylon. He then crushed a new Bactrian uprising and **45.** crossed over into India which, after the death of Alexander, had killed his prefects, removing, as it were, and throwing off the yoke from their[235] necks. A certain Androcottus was their leader in this attempt to regain their liberty.[236] Afterwards Androcottus behaved cruelly towards his fellow citizens, making those whom he had previously saved from foreign rule slaves of his own. **46.** Seleucus fought many hard wars against him. Finally, after consolidating his kingdom and making peace, he retired from the country.[237]

47. When Ptolemy and his allies had joined forces, the battle began. It was all the more ruinous given the great amount of preparation for it, for almost the entire strength of the Macedonian kingdom came crashing down. **48.** In this war Antigonus was killed;[238] however, the end of this war was only the beginning of another – for the victors could not agree about the spoils and divided into two parties. **49.** Seleucus allied himself with

232 The Battle of Cypriot Salamis in 306 BC.

233 In 302 BC.

234 Orosius here has shortened Justin's, 15.4.10, phrase, 'He fought many wars in the east after the division of the Kingdom of Macedon amongst the allies'. It is difficult here not to see Orosius as guilty of the worst sort of undergraduate plagiarism as the removal of phrase 'after the division' completely changes the sense of Justin's words.

235 Orosius has forgotten that he is talking about an abstract 'India', not Indians.

236 Justin, 15.4.13, has Sandracottus. This is a mutation of the name of the Maurya king Chandragupta, c. 321–c. 298 BC. See Rapson (1935) ch. 17 and Bhargava (1996).

237 In 303 BC.

238 At the Battle of Ipsus in 301 BC.

Demetrius; Ptolemy with Lysimachus; while the deceased Cassander was succeeded by his son, Philip.[239] And so in this way war came new-born once more to Macedonia.

50. Antipater ran through his own mother, Thessalonice, who was Cassander's wife, with his own hand, even though she pleaded piteously for her life.[240] **51.** His brother, Alexander, was tricked, and then killed, by Demetrius whose help he had sought while he was fighting Antipater in order to avenge his mother. **52.** Lysimachus was unable to fight Demetius as he was involved in a bitter war against the Thracian king Dorus.[241]

53. Elated by taking Greece and all Macedonia, Demetrius was inclined to invade Asia. **54.** However, Ptolemy, Seleucus, and Lysimachus, after having learnt from the last conflict how powerful an alliance could make them, made a treaty once again, united their forces, and took the war to Demetrius in Europe.[242] **55.** Pyrrhus, the king of Epirus,[242] joined them as a colleague and ally in the war, hoping that Demetrius could be driven from Macedonia. Nor was his hope in vain, for after Demetrius's army had been destroyed and he had been forced to flee, Pyrrhus invaded Macedonia.

56. Then Lysimachus killed his son-in-law, Antipater,[243] who was plotting against him, and also slew his own son, Agathocles, whom he hated with an unnatural loathing.[244]

57. At this time, the town of Lysimachia was levelled by a terrifying earthquake and cruelly became a tomb for its afflicted people.[245]

58. Lysimachus, who had stained himself with many acts of parricide, was deserted by all his allies, who defected to Seleucus and urged the king, already so inclined through his envy of the other's kingdom, to wage war on Lysimachus. **59.** The affair was a disgraceful spectacle. The two kings, Lysimachus, aged 74, and Seleucus, aged 77, trying to snatch their kingdoms

---

239 Philip IV, who died soon after, leaving his mother Thessalonice as regent; see Justin, 16.1.1. Orosius's suppression of this fact produces a rather confused account.

240 In 294 BC.

241 Justin, 16.1.10, calls the king Dromichaetis.

242 King of Epirus 306–302, then displaced, but returning as king in 297 and subsequently ruling until his death in 272. For his wars in Italy, see 4.1.5–4.2.7.

243 Pyrrhus's invasion and Antipater's murder occurred in 287 BC.

244 In 283 BC. The sentiment about the degree of hatred shown for Agathocles is taken from Justin 17.1.4.

245 The modern Ecsemil at the northern end of the Dardanelles peninsula. It was founded by Lysimachus in 309 BC. Justin, 17.1.10, notes its destruction as a portent of Lysimachus's demise, a notion which Orosius suppresses.

from one another, stood in the front line dressed in armour.[246] **60.** This was indeed the last battle between Alexander's fellow-soldiers, but it was one specially set aside as an example of man's wretchedness. **61.** For, although 34 of Alexander's generals were already dead and they were the sole rulers of the world, they gave no thought to the tightly narrow limits of their old age and lives, but rather considered that the limits of the whole world were too narrow for their empire. **62.** In this battle,[247] Lysimachus, the last of his line – he had already lost or killed fifteen children prior to the conflict – was killed and so brought the Macedonian War to a close.

63. But Seleucus did not rejoice in his great victory with impunity, as neither did he, after his 77 years, find peace in a natural death, but ended a life which he had the misfortune to be snatched from him, almost, one might say, before his time. **64.** For he was trapped and killed at the instigation of Ptolemy whose daughter had been married to Lysimachus.[248]

65. These then were the dealings between families and friends found among parents, their children, brothers, and allies. Such was the weight of respect due to gods and men that hung upon them. **66.** Let men, who now know that it is only through the coming of the One True Christian Faith and the mediation of sworn oaths that they live with their enemies and suffer no harm, blush indeed to remember these past times. **67.** This is proved beyond all doubt because now they do not as in the past *stand and pledge their troth with the slaughter of a sow,*[249] but rather the Gospels, on which their oath is sworn, ensure a fidelity among the Romans and barbarians when they jointly call on their Creator and Lord, which in the past natural affection could not guarantee even between fathers and their sons.

68. Now let the close of the Macedonian War also be the close of this book, above all because after this point the wars of Pyrrhus begin and the Punic wars soon follow on.

246 The ages of the two kings are taken from Justin, 17.1.10. In fact, Lysimachus was 80 at the time of the battle.

247 The Battle of Curopedium fought near Manissa in Turkey in 281 BC.

248 Seleucus was stabbed while disembarking from a boat by Ptolemy Ceraunus less than a year after the death of Lysimachus.

249 Virgil, *Aeneid*, 8.641.

BOOK FOUR

PREFACE

1. Virgil tells us that Aeneas, after his perils and his men's shipwreck, spoke the following words while consoling his surviving companions:

An hour will come, with pleasure to relate, your sorrows past as benefits of fate.[1]

2. This saying, carefully devised on this one occasion, always carries with it three very distinct senses. First: that the worse events in the past were in reality, the more gratifying they are to relate later. Second: that it is always believed that the future will be better, as our desires for it are brought about by discontent with the present **3.** And third: that while troubles are present, no just comparison of our sufferings in any respect is possible, because the troubles of the present, however trivial they may be, cause much more grievance than those of the past or future, even if they are said to be great, because these are altogether absent when they are being discussed.

    4. For example, if a man who is troubled by fleas at night and kept awake by them, happens to remember some other sleepless nights he once endured when gripped by a burning fever, he will, without a doubt, be more troubled by his present circumstances than the memory of those in the past. **5.** But although everyone can feel like this in the grip of circumstances, surely there is no one who while being plagued by fleas would declare that they are a worse affliction than fever, or agree that it is worse to be kept awake while in good health than not to be able to go to sleep when at death's door?

    6. Since this is the case, I grant that our precious moaners think that the troubles they feel, and by which we are now from time to time chastened as is expedient, are severe, but I will not concur with their assertion that they are the more severe when compared to those of the past.

    7. In the same way, if someone were to get out of his soft bed in a comfortable bedroom one morning and, on going outside and seeing pools

---

1 Virgil, *Aeneid*, 1.203

frozen over after an icy night and plants white with hoarfrost, exclaim, when confronted this unexpected sight, 'It's cold today', I would not think his attitude at all reprehensible, for he would be speaking as men normally do and with the common sense of these words. **8.** But if he were to rush panic-stricken back to his bedroom, cover himself with his blankets or hide himself all the more deeply under the bed-clothes, shouting out that there had never been such cold as this not even in the Apennines when Hannibal was cut off by the snow and lost his elephants, horses, and most of his army,[2] **9.** I would not endure his talking such puerile drivel, but, indeed, would drag him from under his sheets, the evidence of his idleness, out into the crowd in a public place, and, having got him out of doors, show him the children playing in the frost, and because of it enjoying themselves and sweating. **10.** In this way our wordy fuss-pot, corrupted by his delicate upbringing, would learn that his troubles came not from the violence of his times, but from his own idleness, and that, when we judge these matters, it is not that his ancestors endured a small amount of suffering, but rather that he is unable to endure even a small amount.

11. I shall demonstrate this more clearly by bringing to mind the disasters of past times. I shall begin with the war against Pyrrhus, as this is the correct order. Its cause and origins were as follows:

1[3]

1. 464 years after the foundation of the City, while Tarentines were sitting in their theatre, they saw a Roman fleet that happened to be passing their city and launched an attack on it.[4] Only five ships escaped and those with difficulty. The rest were dragged into the Tarentines' harbour and destroyed. The ships' commanders were butchered,[5] everyone of military age killed, and the remainder of the crews sold into slavery.

---

2 See 4.14.8 below.

3 Orosius's main sources here are Florus, 1.13, and Livy, 12–13. However, he has suppressed Pyrrhus's comments on the bravery of the Romans for which see Florus, 1.13.18.

4 This incident is normally dated to 472 *AUC*, i.e. 282 BC. Orosius omits to mention that a treaty made between Rome and Tarentum in c. 303 BC forbade Roman ships from sailing beyond the Lacinian peninsula, near Croton. The vessels attacked by the Tarentines were in clear breach of this treaty. Rome therefore was the provocateur, not the innocent victim of violence in this incident as Orosius depicts her.

5 Orosius may be exaggerating here. Livy, *Per.* 12, speaks of the duovir (a 'two-man', one out of a board of two magistrates) who commanded the fleet being killed rather than the ships' captains.

2. The Romans at once sent envoys to Tarentum[6] to complain about the ill treatment that they had suffered; these were driven away by the Tarentines and so returned with insult having been added to injury. For these reasons a great war broke out. **3.** After they saw who, and how many, the enemy were who had raised their cries against them, extreme necessity forced the Romans to arm and enrol even the proletarians (that is those who were always left in the City to keep up the number of children[7]), since any thought about children would be vain if they did not deal with their immediate circumstances. **4.** The Roman army under the consul Aemilius[8] invaded the entire territory of Tarentum. They laid waste to everything with fire and sword, stormed many towns, and cruelly avenged the arrogant insult that they had received. **5.** The Tarentines were immediately reinforced by contingents from many of their neighbours, but it was Pyrrhus who gave them the most help. Because of the great size of his forces and the scope of his strategy, he took over the running of the war and gave his name to it. **6.** In order to liberate Tarentum which had been founded by Lacedaemon and so was a blood-brother of the towns of Greece,[9] he brought over the entire strength of Epirus, Thessaly, and Macedonia, and even 20 elephants, being the first to bring this animal, previously unknown to the Romans, into Italy. He would have been a terrible foe on land or sea, given his men, cavalry, arms, and beasts,[10] and, above all, his own energy and cunning, **7.** had he not been deluded by an ambiguous reply from that emptiest of spirits and lying slattern, whom they call a great prophet, the Delphic oracle, and come to the same end as someone who had not consulted it.[11]

8. Battle was first joined between King Pyrrhus and the consul Laevinus[12] at the river Siris by the town of Heraclea in Campania.[13] The day was spent

6 The modern Taranto.

7 Orosius is no doubt drawing this definition from Augustine, *City of God*, 3.17. The same etymology is also given by Cicero, *On the State* (*De Republica*), 2.23.

8 Q. Aemilius Papus, consul in 282 BC.

9 Tarentum was traditionally founded in 706 BC by the Spartan Phalanthus.

10 i.e. his elephants

11 The oracle's words are quoted by Augustine, *City of God*, 3.17, as 'Aio te, Aecida, Romanos vincere posse'. This can be read either as 'I tell you, son of Aeacus, that you are able to defeat the Romans' or 'I tell you, son of Aeacus, that the Romans are able to defeat you'. Augustine's source was probably Cicero, *On Divination* (*De Divinatione*), 2.56.116, who dismisses the oracle's authenticity. The line is normally thought to derive from Ennius's *Annals*, book 6 (Skutsch [1985] fr. 167).

12 P. Valerius Laevinus, consul in 280 BC.

13 The Siris is the modern Sinno and Heraclea, the modern Policoro, a Tarentine colony

in bitter strife with both sides fixed on death and heedless of flight, **9.** but when the Romans saw the elephants brought into the fray – animals grim in appearance, foul to smell, and terrifying in size – they were stunned and terrified, especially their cavalry, at this new form of warfare and fled in all directions.[14] **10.** But after Minucius, the chief centurion of the second rank of the Fourth Legion,[15] used his sword to cut off the hand of the beast as it stretched it out towards him,[16] and forced it from battle because of the pain of its wound, making it turn in its rage on its own side who began to panic and became disordered because of its wild onslaught, night brought the gift of drawing the battle to a close. **11.** Their disgraceful flight betrayed the fact that the Romans had been defeated; 14,880 of their infantry are said to have been killed, and 1,310 captured.[17] The figures for the cavalry are 246 killed, and 802 captured. Twenty-two standards were lost.

12. Tradition has not handed down the numbers of Pyrrhus's divers allies who were lost, since it was not the custom of writers in olden times to record the number of dead on the victorious side lest the victor's losses should mar the glory of his victory, **13.** unless by chance so few fell that the small number of his losses should increase the admiration and terror inspired by his prowess. This happened, for example, in Alexander's first battle against the Persians, when men say that while almost 400,000 of the enemy died, only nine infantrymen in his own army perished.[18]

14. However, Pyrrhus himself gave witness to both gods and men about the disastrous blow that he had suffered in this battle, by setting up a plaque in the Temple of Jupiter at Tarentum on which he wrote:

Those men who were previously undefeated, great father of Olympus,
These I have defeated in battle and have been defeated by the same.[19]

---

which in fact lies in Lucania. Orosius has followed the error found in Florus, 1.13.7. The battle took place in 280 BC.

14 For Pyrrhus's use of elephants, see Scullard (1974) 101–16.

15 Orosius calls Minucius (called Numucius by Orosius's source, Florus, 1.13.9) the *primus hastatus*. For a full description of this rank, see Vegetius, 2.8. Orosius has misread his source which attributes Minucius's action to the second battle with Pyrrhus and is perhaps guilty of a pretentious, and incorrect, use of a technical term, as Florus only describes Numucius as an *hastatus*, or 'front-ranker'.

16 i.e. the trunk.

17 Eutropius, 2.11, gives no figure for the dead, but says Pyrrhus captured 1,800 Romans.

18 See 3.17.4.

19 These lines are normally attributed to book 6 of Ennius's *Annals* (Skutsch [1985] fr. 180), see also Skutsch (1968) 88–92.

15. When his allies rebuked him and asked why he said that he had been defeated when he had triumphed, he is said to have replied, 'If I triumph like this again, I shall return to Epirus without a single soldier.'

16. Meanwhile, the Roman army after its defeat fled secretly from its camp and came to believe that the terrible disaster of the battle had been made all worse and aggravated by even more serious portents. **17.** For a storm rose up, as if it too was part of the enemy's army, and with a terrible crash from the heavens seized hold of, and blasted with lightning bolts, a group of foragers who happened to have been sent out in advance of them. **18.** The whirlwind killed 34 of them, 22 were left half-dead, and the majority of their pack-animals were killed or captured, so that it was rightly said that this was not the sign of destruction to come, but an act of destruction in its own right.

19. The second battle between Pyrrhus and the Roman consuls was fought on the borders of Apulia.[20] Here the battle was a disaster for both sides, but especially for Pyrrhus, and victory fell to Rome. **20.** For during a long period while they fell on each other, resolutely indulging in mutual slaughter and the outcome of the battle hung in the balance, Pyrrhus was wounded in the arm and became the first commander to leave the battle. However, the Roman commander Fabricius was also wounded. **21.** In the first battle it had been discovered that elephants could be wounded and forced to flee; in this battle that they could be driven mad by inflicting fire on their rear, tender quarters and that when they panicked in terror and rushed around carrying burning howdahs on their backs, they were lethal to their own side. **22.** 5,000 Romans died in this battle, but 20,000 of Pyrrhus's men perished. The king lost 53 standards, the Romans eleven. **23.** Pyrrhus fell back on Syracuse, broken by the war and after being summoned to the Sicilian empire on the death of Agathocles, the king of Syracuse.

2

1. But the miseries of the Romans did not stop for any peace treaty. The gap between wars was filled by the evils of disease and when wars abroad came to an end, wrath from heaven fell on them at home. **2.** For when Fabius Gurges was consul for the second time along with Gaius Genucius Clepsina, a terrible plague fell upon the City and its lands.[21] It afflicted everyone, but

---

20 The battle was fought near the town of Asculum, the modern Ascoli, in 279 BC.
21 478 *AUC*/276 BC.

especially the women and flocks, killing their offspring in their wombs and destroying the future generation. Strained abortions, putting the mother in danger, were brought forth in premature births and this happened to such a degree that it was believed that posterity had been destroyed and that the race of living things would become defunct because the normal way of giving birth to the living had vanished.[22]

3. Meanwhile, the consul Curius intercepted Pyrrhus on his return from Sicily[23] and a third battle against the Epirotes was waged through Lucania in the fields of Arusia.[24] **4.** As soon as they came to grips with one another, Pyrrhus's troops were thrown into panic by the Romans' onslaught and got ready to withdraw, looking for a way to flee from the battle. Pyrrhus then ordered the elephants to be brought up in support. **5.** However, the Romans were now used to fighting against these beasts and had prepared firebrands equipped with hooked barbs for gripping, wrapped in tow, and smeared in pitch. They set light to these, shot them at the animals' backs and howdahs, and then easily drove back the beasts which were maddened by the flames, turning what had been their enemies' salvation into their annihilation.

6. Men say that the king's army in this battle was composed of 80,000 infantry and 6,000 cavalry. Out of these, it is recorded that 33,000 were killed[25] and 1,300 taken prisoner. **7.** Pyrrhus then left Italy in defeat in the fifth year after he had arrived. After waging many great wars, he was seduced by a desire for the kingdom of Sparta and killed when struck by a rock while in Argos, the wealthiest city in Achaea.[26]

8. At the same time at Rome, the vestal virgin Sextilia, after being accused and found guilty of sexual impurity, was buried alive at the Colline Gate.[27]

3[28]

1. 475 years after the foundation of the City, the Tarentines, after learning of the death of Pyrrhus, searched once more for new arms to take up against the Romans. They despatched envoys to seek aid from the Carthaginians

---

22 This plague is mentioned by Augustine, *City of God*, 3.17.
23 275 BC, the consul was M. Curius Dentatus.
24 Near the modern Benevento.
25 Eutropius, 2.14.5, gives the figure of 23,000.
26 Pyrrhus died in 272 BC.
27 In 274 BC; this note is drawn from Livy, 14.
28 Orosius's source for this section is Livy, 15.

and received it.[29] **2.** Battle was joined and the Romans were victorious. It was at this time that the Carthaginians, although they were not yet considered as enemies, realised that they could be defeated by Rome.

3. In the following year, Rome's stern nature fell upon a great part of her own vitals. **4.** For when Pyrrhus had just arrived in Italy, the Eighth Legion lost hope in Rome's cause and dared to commit a new sort of crime.[30] They slew all the people of Rhegium who had been placed under their protection, and divided up all the booty and the city itself among themselves. **5.** The consul Genucius was ordered to punish this crime on the persons of these criminal defectors.[31] After besieging the town and capturing everyone within, he rightly executed the non-Roman runaways and bandits, but sent the Romans, the troops of an entire legion, back to Rome. Here, by the people's decree, they were flogged to death and beheaded in the middle of the forum.[32] **6.** On this occasion, although she had killed an entire legion of her own, Rome thought that she had been triumphant – she who without a doubt would have been defeated, had she lost this legion in a battle against the enemy.

4

1. 470 years after the foundation of the City,[33] vile, terrible portents were seen, or news given of them, at Rome. The Temple of Health was destroyed by a lightning bolt and part of the city wall in the same place was also struck as they say, 'from the heavens'. **2.** Three wolves entered the city before dawn carrying a half-eaten corpse and left its scattered limbs in the forum after being frightened away by men shouting. **3.** At Formiae,[34] the entire city wall was burnt up and destroyed by lightning bolts. **4.** In the fields of

29 This statement is taken from Livy, *Per.* 14, where we are told a Carthaginian fleet came to the Tarentines' aid.

30 Pyrrhus arrived in 280 BC. The eighth legion was composed of Campanians, rather than Romans proper.

31 L. Genucius Clepsina, consul in 483 *AUC*/271 BC, though according to the *acta triumphalia*, the triumph for the campaign was given to his fellow consul, Gn. Cornelius Blassius.

32 Orosius takes this figure from Livy. However, Polybius, 1.7.7, states that most of the legion, mindful of the punishment they would receive, died fighting, leaving just over 300 men to be executed at Rome.

33 This date is the majority reading of our manuscripts, but it is wrong. If Orosius has the date of Sempronius Sophus's consulate correct later in the chapter, the date here should be 485 *AUC*/269 BC.

34 The modern Mola de Gaeta.

Cales,[35] a flame suddenly burst forth as the ground gaped open. It blazed in a terrible fashion for three days and three nights, and reduced five *iugera*[36] of land to ashes, drawing out all the fertile moisture that lay within. This destroyed, they say, not merely the crops, but even the trees down to their deepest roots.

5. In the following year, the consul Sempronius led an army out against the Picentes.[37] When both battle-lines stood within javelin range, the earth suddenly trembled with a terrible crashing sound, so that each side grew numb in terror and amazement at this omen. **6.** For a long time the stunned men held back on both sides, knowing that the outcome of the engagement had been preordained, but finally they roused themselves to charge and joined battle. **7.** This encounter was so heart-rending that it is deservedly said that the earth had trembled with a horrible-sounding groan because it was going to receive so much human blood. The few Romans who survived the battle emerged as the victors.[38]

5

1. 480 years after the foundation of the City, among many other portents, blood was seen oozing from the earth and milk dripping from the sky. For in very many places blood gushed from fountains and milk came down in drops like rain from the clouds, and these terrible, as they seemed to them,[39] showers inundated the land.

2. At that time the Carthaginians, who had given aid to the Tarentines against Romans, were reprimanded by ambassadors sent by the Senate and then added the shameful disgrace of breaking their treaty to the perjury they had already committed.[40]

3. At this time too, the people of Vulsinii,[41] the richest of the Etruscans, almost perished because of their decadence. For having made licentiousness

35 The modern Calvi.

36 Around three acres.

37 P. Sempronius Sophus, consul in 486 *AUC*/268 BC.

38 Orosius's source for the battle appears to be Florus, 1.14, or Livy, 15 (the battle is noted both by Livy, *Per.* 15, and Eutropius, 2.16, but no details are given). Orosius has suppressed Florus's comment that Sempronius appeased the goddess Tellus after the earthquake by promising to build a temple for her.

39 i.e. the pagan Romans.

40 Orosius is our only source for this embassy which presumably took place in the early 260s.

41 Near the modern Bolsena.

their way of life, they freed all their slaves regardless, admitting them to their banquets, and ennobling them through marriage.[42] **4.** These freedmen, after they had been given a share in power, began to plot how they might criminally usurp it all. For freed from slavery's yoke, they were on fire with a lust for mastery, and now they were free, they cursed their masters whom they had happily cherished when they were slaves, because they remembered that they had been their masters. **5.** So these freedmen formed a conspiracy to carry out their crime (their numbers were so great that they were able to carry out this audacious deed without resistance) and seized the city, making their class its sole rulers. They then criminally seized the possessions and wives of their former masters for themselves and banished their masters, driving them far away. These wretches took themselves off to Rome as poverty-stricken exiles, where after weeping and relating their sufferings, they were avenged and restored to power by the stern rule of Rome.[43]

6. 481 years after the foundation of the City, a great plague flared up at Rome, I am content to mention it in these terms, as I am unable to describe its horrors in words. **7.** If someone asks how long it lasted, its devastation extended for more than two years; if they ask about the death it brought, the census is our witness – it does not record the number of men who perished, but the number who survived; if he asks about the violence with which it raged, the Sibylline Books bear witness to this, saying that the plague was brought about by Divine Wrath.

8. But in case anyone is struck by a specious form of quibbling from the fact that the Sibylline Books say that the gods were angry, while I appear to have described this episode as the result of Divine Wrath, let him hear and learn that although the majority of these things are brought about by incorporeal spirits, they would not come to pass without the consent of Almighty God.[44]

42 Again, Orosius here shows no hostility towards, and perhaps even support for, the institution of slavery.

43 This was done by the consul Fulvius Flaccus in 490 *AUC*/264 BC; see Festus, 228L. Livy, *Per.* 16, notes that 'successful actions were carried out against the Vulsini', but gives no details; Orosius's account may preserve some of the sense of the lost text.

44 The 'specious reasoning' here is to accuse Orosius of trying to suppress the fact that the Sibylline Books refer to the pagan gods. Orosius certainly is placed in some difficulties by his use of the Sibylline Books as evidence, and to escape this accusation is forced into acknowledging the existence of pagan gods, albeit as demons, rather than adopting his normal attitude of dismissing them as non-existent. This approach to paganism is also found in Augustine, *City of God*, 2.24, with which Orosius would have been familiar.

9. At this same time, the Vestal Virgin Caparronia was convicted of defiling herself and died by hanging. Her seducer and the slaves who were his accomplices were executed.[45]

10. Behold, how many great events we have listed as happening unceasingly every single year. It was certainly a rarity, in fact almost never the case, that some tragedy did not occur each year, and this is despite the fact that the writers of the time, whose main task was to give praise, took care to leave out a considerable number of disasters **11.** in order not to offend those for whom and about whom their accounts were written, and not to be seen to terrify rather than educate their listeners with the examples they had drawn from the past. **12.** Moreover, we who live at the very end of these times have no way of knowing of the sorrows of the Romans, save through the accounts of those who praised them. **13.** Given this fact, we can see how much must have been deliberately suppressed because of its horrible nature when so many things of this sort are faintly discernible amid their praises.

6[46]

1. Since the Punic Wars follow on from this point, it is necessary briefly to say something about Carthage, which was founded by Elissa[47] 72 years before the city of Rome, and about the disasters and domestic calamities it suffered, which have been set out in the works of Pompeius Trogus and Justin.[48]

2. The Carthaginians have always suffered from an innate and particular evil among themselves, namely civil strife, a misfortune which dictated that they never enjoyed prosperity abroad or peace at home. **3.** When, among all their other troubles, they also suffered from plague, they resorted to murder rather than medicine, performing human sacrifices and placing small children on their altars, something which made even their enemies pity them.[49]

45 The execution is noted with fewer details by Jerome, *Chronicle, A Abr.* 1752 = 488 *AUC*. The form of Caparronia's death was not that normally prescribed for Vestals convicted of unchastity (burial alive) and has therefore been assumed to be suicide; see Bauman (1992).

46 Orosius, as he himself states, has drawn on, and heavily abbreviated, Trogus's epitome of Justin (18.3–19 and 21–23.3) for the first 33 sections of this chapter.

47 i.e. Dido.

48 See in particular Justin, 18. Jerome places the foundation of Carthage in *A Abr.* 1164, i.e. 100 years before the foundation of Rome.

49 The account of human sacrifice draws very heavily on Justin, 18.6.11–12; the plague occurred in c. 370 BC.

4. I do not know what I best ought to say about this form of sacrifice, or rather sacrilege. If some demons dared to ordain these rites so that human death should be propitiated with human murder, the Carthaginians ought to have understood that they were being engaged as agents and assistants of the plague in order to kill themselves those upon whom it had not taken hold. **5.** For their custom is to offer healthy victims untouched by the plague with the result that they did not cure diseases, but rather anticipate them.[50]

6. So, after the Carthaginians, with the gods against them because of this infamous kind of sacrifice, according to Pompeius Trogus and Justin, or, as we clearly know, because their presumption and impiety had angered God, **7.** had fought a long war without success in Sicily, they changed their theatre of operations to Sardinia where they were defeated after enjoying even less success.[51] Because of this, they ordered that their commander, Mazeus, and the few soldiers who had survived with him, to be exiled. The exiles sent envoys who asked for forgiveness, but this was refused. They then waged war on, and besieged, their own city. **8.** It was then that the exiles' leader, Mazeus, had his own son, Carthalo, a priest of Hercules,[52] killed. He had come out to meet his father dressed in purple as if to taunt him, so Mazeus hung him on a cross, just as he was, in his purple, priestly garb, beneath the eyes of his city.[53] **9.** A few days later Mazeus took the city itself and then, after exercising a bloodstained reign and killing most of the senators, was himself slain. These things happened at the time when Cyrus was king in Persia.[54]

10. After this, the Carthaginian king,[55] Himelcho, lost his army in a

---

50 Orosius chooses his words carefully here. The sacrifices were intended to anticipate plague by preventing it; Orosius, of course, means that they anticipated plague by producing its effects in advance. The question of human sacrifice at Carthage is controversial; for a full discussion, see Barnes (1971) 13–21, and Lancel (1995) 227–56.

51 Orosius has misread his source here, Justin, 18.7.1, which in fact states the reverse – that Carthage fought a long *successful* war and that the displeasure of the gods brought defeat only when they campaigned in Sicily. Over-eagerness to denounce pagan human sacrifice is probably at the root of Orosius's error, rather than a corrupt manuscript.

52 i.e. the Punic god Melqart.

53 Mazeus is called Malchus by Justin, 18.7.2. The name is probably a corruption of the Phoenician title MLK or Lord; see Picard and Picard (1968) 56–59 who are inclined to doubt the historicity of the whole episode, as is Lancel (1995) 111–12.

54 For ideological reasons Orosius, 2.2.9–10, places Cyrus's reign at the time of the fall of Tarquinius Superbus. This allows him to synchronise the rise of Rome and the fall of Babylon.

55 In fact, as Justin, 19.2.7, states, Himelcho, normally spelt Himilcho, was simply a general, not a king. Orosius has suppressed Justin's notice of Malchus's successor, Mago, under whom, according to Justin, 18.7.19, the Carthaginian state prospered.

sudden, terrible plague while waging war in Sicily. **11.** The disease brooked
no delay, the troops died in droves: as soon as a man fell sick, he died,
nor were men buried any longer. After the bearer of these ill-tidings had
filled an astounded Carthage with sudden grief, *her distress was the same
as if the city had been captured.*[56] **12.** Everywhere echoed with cries of
lamentation, doors were shut up on all sides, all public and private business
was forbidden, everyone rushed down to the port and asked the few who
had survived the disaster about their kinsmen as they disembarked from
the ships. **13.** When from these men's silence or groaning, these wretched
folk learnt of the disaster that had befallen their kinsmen, the cries of the
grieving and then the weeping and wailing of hapless mothers were heard
along the whole shoreline. **14.** Amid these scenes, the commander too
disembarked *from his ship in an ungirt, dirty, slave's tunic. On his appearance, the weeping crowds joined together as one and he too lifted his hands
to the sky,*[57] bemoaning and bewailing now his own, and now the state's,
misfortune. **15.** Finally, crying out as he went, he passed through the city,
entered his own house, with his last words dismissed the wailing band who
had followed him, and then, after bolting his doors and barring even his own
sons, put an end with his sword to both his sorrow and his life. These things
happened in the times of Darius.[58]

16. After this, Hanno, a Carthaginian whose private wealth exceeded
the resources of the state, imbibed a great lust of seizing power. To further
this end, he decided to devise a false wedding for his only daughter and
poison the drinks of all those senators whose rank he thought would be an
obstacle to his plans. **17.** The plan was betrayed by his servants and circum-
vented, though no vengeance was taken on the grounds that in dealing with
a powerful man, the plot might cause more trouble when disclosed than it
had when it had been devised. Foiled in this plan, Hanno conceived another
scheme to further his criminal ambition. He inflamed the slaves, intending
to use them to overwhelm the unsuspecting city in a sudden uprising. **18.**
But when, before the day that had been marked down for this slaughter, he
learnt that he had been betrayed and his actions anticipated, he occupied
a strongpoint with 20,000 armed slaves. **19.** *He was captured there while
stirring up the Africans*[59] *and the king of the Moors. First, he was beaten*

56 This phrase is taken verbatim from Justin, 19.2.8. The whole account of the plague
paraphrases Justin very closely.
57 This phrase is taken verbatim from Justin, 19.3.1–2.
58 Darius II (424–404 BC).
59 i.e. the local native tribesmen of the region.

with rods, then his eyes were gouged out and his arms and legs broken, as if to inflict punishment on each of his limbs, and finally he was put to death before the people. **20.** *His body, lacerated from his flogging, was nailed to a cross, and all his sons and male relatives were put to death so that no one from the same family should ever think of imitating, or avenging, him.*[60] These things happened in the time of Philip.[61]

21. After this, the Carthaginians learnt that Tyre, their mother city, had been captured and destroyed by Alexander the Great. Fearing that he would cross into Africa, they ordered a certain Hamilcar who was called 'the Rhodian', a man outstanding in his eloquence and cunning, to look into Alexander's plans. **22.** After being given asylum by Parmenion as if he was a refugee, and then being accepted into the king's service, he informed his countrymen of all the king's plans by writing them on tablets that he then covered over with wax.[62] *After the death of Alexander, Hamilcar returned to Carthage and was murdered as if he really had sold his city to the king. This was done not so much out of ingratitude as out of a cruel sense of envy.*[63]

23. The Carthaginians then waged incessant, but fruitless, wars against the Sicilians. They besieged Syracuse, which at that time was the wealthiest city in Sicily, but they were outwitted by the astounding cunning of Agathocles, the king of Sicily, and brought to the point of complete despair.[64]

24. For while the Carthaginians besieged Syracuse, Agathocles, seeing that he would be no match in battle, given the state of his troops, and that he did not have enough money to pay a garrison to last out a siege, employing a plan that was well conceived and even better concealed, crossed over to Africa with his army.[65] On his arrival, he revealed his plan to his men and told them what had to be done. **25.** Straightaway, and with one accord, they burnt the boats in which they had come so that they should have no hope of returning, and then laid low every site to which Agathocles led them. After

60 The episode of Hanno is drawn from Justin, 21.4. The italicised section is either taken verbatim or is an extremely close paraphrase of Justin. The incident took place in 344 BC.

61 i.e. Philip II of Macedon.

62 The strategy is the same as used by Demaratus to inform the Spartans of Xerxes' plans; see Herodotus, 2.9.1. Curiously, Orosius, who is likely to have known of Demaratus and despite his love of contrast, does not draw attention to the reversal of the barbarians' and Greeks' roles in this later tale.

63 The episode of Hamilcar the Rhodian is taken from Justin, 21.6, the italicised section being drawn virtually verbatim.

64 Agathocles became tyrant of Syracuse in 317 BC, but only began to style himself king in 304 BC after his wars with Carthage.

65 Agathocles landed on the Cap Bon peninsula in modern Tunisia in 310 BC.

they had fired various farms and strongholds, they were met by a certain Hanno with 30,000 Punic troops.[66] Agathocles killed him along with 2,000 of his men, while losing merely two of his own in the battle.[67] **26.** This encounter utterly broke the spirit of the Africans,[68] while raising that of his own men to an enormous degree, and Agathocles went on to storm both cities and strongholds, obtaining a vast amount of booty and killing many thousands of the enemy. **27.** *He pitched his camp five miles from Carthage so that from its walls the inhabitants could see for themselves the destruction of their finest possessions, the laying waste of their land, and the firing of their farms.*[69]

28. A rumour then made the Carthaginians' current plight even worse. It was announced that the army of Africans in Sicily had been destroyed along with its commander. Agathocles's brother, Andro, had crushed it while it was completely off-guard and almost behaving as if it was on holiday.[70]

29. When this rumour spread through all of Africa, not only the Carthaginians' tributary cities, but even the kings allied to them deserted. Among these was Afellas, the king of Cyrene, who made a military alliance with Agathocles as he burned to possess the kingdom of Africa. **30.** However, after they had joined their armies together in a single camp, he was beguiled by the blandishments and trickery of Agathocles and killed.[71]

31. The Carthaginians had now gathered their forces together from all sides and were eager for the fray. Agathocles joined battle with them, having on his side the troops of Afellas, and after a severe battle with much spilling of blood on either side, he emerged victorious. **32.** *At this crucial moment in the struggle, the Carthaginians were so despondent that had there not been a mutiny in Agathocles' army, their general Hamilcar would have*

66 'Poeni'. The translation has endeavoured to retain the variety of words Orosius uses for the Carthaginians, of which this is one. Here Orosius has either a read a corrupt manuscript or misunderstood Justin, 22.6.5, who speaks of 30,000 *pagani* or country-dwellers, who are likely to have been North African tribesmen, and not Carthaginians *per se*.

67 Orosius has misread Justin, 22.6.5, who states that Agathocles lost 2,000 men to Hanno's 3,000.

68 Orosius is using 'African' here as *variatio* for Carthaginian, in his account Justin, 22.6.7, uses 'Punic'.

69 Taken virtually verbatim from Justin, 22.6.9.

70 Agathocles' brother is called Antander by Justin, 22.7.2. He defeated Hamilcar in 309 BC. The moralising comments about Hamilcar are Orosius's embroidery of Justin's account.

71 Afellas is the Ophellas of Justin, 22.7.4. Ophellas was sent by Ptolemy I as governor of Cyrene, where he established a virtually independent fiefdom. He was probably murdered in 309 BC.

defected to him along with his army. Because of this offence, the Carthaginians ordered that Hamilcar be impaled in the middle of the forum to form a cruel spectacle for his own people.[72]

33. After the death of Agathocles,[73] the Carthaginians marshalled a fleet and laid waste to Sicily, but they were then defeated many times on both land and sea by Pyrrhus, the king of Epirus, who had been summoned over from Italy by the Sicilians. After this, they turned again to fighting Rome.

34. O, the suffering that we see here! Do the men who grumble about recent events, read about the past? Indeed, they do, and draw their conclusions from jaundice, not judgment. **35.** They are urged on by a great, ineffable goad, which they themselves do not see – namely, they moan not because our times are bad, but because they are Christian. The product of this ulcer of hatred is that whatever happens in detestable circumstances comes to seem all the worse. **36.** Even in our circles it is often the custom for those who are detested to be seen in their enemies' eyes as doing nothing which is not depraved, nothing which is not shameful, nothing which does not do themselves harm, either by word or deed. And all of this is believed almost without reflection, for hatred grips and twists the heart to such a degree that nothing appears in its natural light. **37.** Our detractors are also among this group's numbers, but they are even more pitiful because they are the enemies of God, and hence the enemies of Truth. We say this weeping with sorrow for them[74] whom, if they could endure it, we would reprove in order that we might heal them. **38.** For they perceive these present troubles with diseased eyes so that what they see seems double to them, and, befuddled by the fog of wickedness, they fall into that state where by seeing less, they see more, since they are unable to see the nature of the things which they see.[75] **39.** They think a beating from their father worse than fires started by their enemy, and call the God Who soothes, admonishes, and redeems them harsher than the Devil who persecutes, enslaves, and slaughters them, **40.** although, if they knew the Father, they would rejoice in His punishments,

---

72 The italicised section is taken verbatim, or virtually verbatim, from Justin, 22.7.7–8. The executed general was named Bomilcar, not Hamilcar, see Justin, 22.7.7–11. Orosius rightly makes Bomilcar a general, not a king as Justin does, but suppresses the point of the execution: according to Justin, 22.7.8, the Carthaginians used the forum so that Bomilcar would be punished where he was previously honoured. The gloss of a cruel spectacle is Orosius's own, and he also suppresses Justin's story of Bomilcar's courage during his crucifixion.

73 Agathocles died in 289 BC, perhaps by poison. Orosius is surprisingly abrupt in bringing his account of the Sicilian king to an end.

74 cf. Philippians 3.18.

75 This argument could, of course, easily be reversed by Orosius's opponents.

and, if they saw the coming fruit of their education, they would find His discipline tolerable, and, because of the hope, which was once denied, but which has now been given, to the gentiles, even if they suffered more than now, they would consider that they suffered less. **41.** Moreover, they can learn to despise suffering from the examples of their own people[76] among whom the greatest troubles were counted as the greatest good, provided that the glory of a famous and outstanding reputation followed on from them. **42.** From these men we can see how much we, to whom a blessed eternity has been promised, should endure for the sake of life, when they were able to endure so much merely for the prospect of fame.

7[77]

1. 483 years after the foundation of the City, namely in the consulate of Appius Claudius and Quintus Fabius, the Romans sent the consul Appius Claudius with an army to the aid of the Mamertines, who possessed the noble town of Messana in Sicily, against Hieron, the king of Syracuse, and the Punic forces allied with Hieron.[78] **2.** Appius defeated the Syracusans and the Punic forces so rapidly that the king, terrified by the scale of these events, admitted that he had been beaten even before he joined battle.[79] **3.** After the destruction of his forces, he lost his confidence and immediately asked for peace as a suppliant. This was granted after he had been fined 200 talents of silver by order of the consuls.[80]

4. The consuls then besieged the Sicilian town of Agrigentum and the Punic garrison there, surrounding the town with siege works and a rampart. **5.** Since the Elder Hannibal,[81] the Punic commander, was trapped in this siege and reduced to dire straits, Hanno, the Carthaginians' new commander,

76 i.e. the pagans.

77 Orosius's main source here is Livy, 16 and 17. This chapter begins Orosius's account of the First Punic War. For a detailed modern discussion of the war, see Lazenby (1996).

78 Orosius has made several errors here. Appius Claudius's expedition took place in 264 BC, i.e. 490 *AUC*; moreover Appius's fellow consul was M. Fulvius Flaccus, not Quintus Fabius who was consul in the previous year.

79 cf. Florus, 1.18.7. Orosius is following the version of Fabius Pictor, probably second-hand via Livy, 16. According to Philinus of Agrigentum, the Romans were defeated.

80 Hieron became the tyrant of Syracuse in 271 BC and proclaimed himself king in 265 BC, reigning until 216 BC. Orosius implies that Appius and Fabius exacted the fine, but in fact this was done by the consuls of 261 BC. The figure of 200 talents is also found in Eutropius, 2.19.

81 Hannibal, the son of Gisco.

made an emergency incursion on his behalf with 1,500 cavalry and 30,000 infantry, as well as 30 elephants. This delayed the storming of the city for a short while, but it was captured straight after this episode. **6.** The Punic forces were defeated, indeed routed, in a great battle and lost eleven of their elephants to the Romans, while the Agrigentines were all sold into slavery. The elder Hannibal made a sortie with a few men and escaped.

7. In the consulate of Cornelius Asina and Gaius Duilius,[82] after the Elder Hannibal had marshalled a fleet of 70 vessels and laid waste the coast of Italy, the Romans decided to construct and fit out a fleet of their own. **8.** This decision was swiftly implemented by the consul Duilius, for within 60 days the trees had been felled and a fleet of 130 ships had been launched and lay at anchor.[83] **9.** The other consul, Cornelius Asina, made for the island of Lipara[84] with 16 ships. Here he was captured by Hannibal who, with typical Punic treachery,[85] pretended to invite him for peace talks, threw him in chains, and murdered him.[86] **10.** After Duilius, the other consul, heard of this, he set out to fight Hannibal with 30 ships. When battle was joined at sea, Hannibal lost his ship, but was taken off by a small boat and fled. Thirty-one of his ships were captured, 13 were sunk, 3,000 of his men were killed, and 7,000 captured.[87]

11. Afterwards, in the consulate of Gaius Aquilius Florus and Lucius Cornelius Scipio,[88] the Carthaginians appointed Hanno as commander of the war at sea in Hannibal's place, with instructions to defend Sardinia and Corsica. He was defeated by the consul Scipio and, after losing his army, hurled himself into where the enemy were at their thickest and was slain there.[89]

12. In the same year, 3,000 slaves and 4,000 of her allied marines[90]

---

82 494 *AUC*/260 BC.

83 See Florus, 1.18.7. Florus says the Roman fleet numbered 160. Orosius suppresses Florus's implication that the preparations were completed so quickly because of divine aid.

84 The present-day Lipari islands.

85 cf. Florus, 1.18.11, and Eutropius, 2.20.2.

86 In fact, Asina survived to be re-elected consul a second time. It is likely that the text has become corrupt with *nexus*, 'bound', being miscopied as *necatus*, 'murdered'.

87 The Battle of Mylae. Eutropius, 2.20.2, has similar figures, but says 14 Carthaginian ships were sunk. The rams of the Carthaginian vessels were used at Rome to decorate a column surmounted by Duilius's statue.

88 495 *AUC*/259 BC.

89 The Battle of Aleria, mentioned on Scipio's epitaph = CIL 1² 2.8 and 9.

90 The phrase 'allied marines' only appears here and in Livy, from whom we must assume Orosius drew the phrase. For a full discussion of the term, see Milan (1973).

plotted to destroy the city of Rome, and, had not the plot been betrayed beforehand, the city, which had no garrison, would have perished at the hands of slaves.

8[91]

1. In the year which followed on from this, the consul Calatinus while marching towards the city of Camerina in Sicily[92] rashly led his army into a pass which the Punic forces had long since fortified. **2.** He had no chance of resisting or escaping from the enemy, and was saved by the courage and vigour of Calpurnius Flamma, who with a band of 300 picked men seized a small hillock which had been occupied by the enemy and by his attack turned the full force of the Punic troops on himself, while the Roman army crossed through the occupied pass without opposition from the enemy. **3.** All 300 were killed in this engagement, except Calpurnius who escaped, though he had been wounded many times and was covered with corpses.[93]

4. The Carthaginians once again put the Elder Hannibal in charge of their fleet. He fought a sea battle with the Romans to no avail and was defeated.[94] Afterwards a mutiny broke out in his army and he was stoned to death by his own men.[95] **5.** The consul Atilius[96] then cruised round and ravaged the famous Sicilian islands of Lipara and Malta.

6. The consuls were ordered to take the war to Africa and made for Sicily with 330 ships where they were met by Hamilcar, the Punic commander, and Hanno, who was in command of their fleet. There was a concerted naval action in which the Carthaginians were put to flight and lost 64 ships.[97] The victorious consuls crossed over to Africa where the city of Clipea was the first of all those that surrendered to them.[98] **8.** After this, they marched on

91 Orosius's main source in this chapter is Livy, 17 and 18. See also Florus, 1.18.

92 This town was abandoned in the Classical period. It was located near the modern Scoglitti.

93 This incident was well known in antiquity and is mentioned in Livy, *Per.* 17; Florus, 1.18.13–14, where Calpurnius is compared to Leonidas and the stand of the Spartans at Thermopylae; and Frontinus, *Stratagems*, 1.5.15 and 4.5.10. Lazenby (1996) 75–76 is sceptical as to whether the incident took place at all.

94 The Battle of Cape Tyndaris in 257 BC. The Roman fleet was commanded by Atilius Regulus; see Polybius, 25.1.

95 According to Livy, *Per.* 17, Hannibal was crucified by his men.

96 C. Atilius Regulus, consul in 257 BC.

97 The battle of Ecnomus, 256 BC. See Eutropius, 2.21.1, who gives identical casualty figures. For detailed discussion of the battle, see Tipps (1985) and Lazenby (1996) ch. 6.

98 Known as Aspis in Greek, the present-day Kelibia in Tunisia.

Carthage, plundering 300, or more, strongholds, and surrounded Carthage with their hostile standards. **9.** The consul, Manlius, left Africa with the victorious fleet and brought 27,000 captives and an immense amount of plunder back to Rome.[99] **10.** Regulus, who had been allotted control of the war against Carthage, marched forward with his army and pitched camp not far from the river Bagras.[100] Here a serpent of incredible size devoured a great number of soldiers when they went down to the river in need of water. Regulus advanced with his army to flush out the beast. **11.** The javelins and all the spears they threw at its back had no effect at all, falling from its horrible, scaly backbone as they would have from a slanting 'tortoise' of shields and in this incredible fashion they were deflected by the creature's hide so that its body should come to no harm. When Regulus saw his great host being whittled down by the creature's bites, worn out by its attacks, and killed by its disease-ridden breath, he ordered the catapults to be brought up. A millstone hurled by one of them struck the creature's backbone and so paralysed its entire body.

12. For this is the nature of the serpent: while it seems to lack feet, its ribs and scales, which run in equal measure from the top of its throat down to the lowest part of its bowels, are so arranged that it can move by using its scales as claws and its ribs as legs. **13.** It is not like the worm which has no backbone and which moves by extending one by one the contracted parts of its small body in the direction in which it is lying and then contacting the parts it has extended; rather it moves its sinuous flanks around with alternating motions in order to keep rigid the line of its ribs along the side where its spine curves outwards and dig in the hooks of its scales where its ribs are naturally upright at their ends. By performing this action quickly on alternate sides, it not only glides over flat surfaces, but even climbs slopes, taking as many steps as it has ribs. **14.** It is for this reason that if it is struck in anyway on any part of its body from the bowels up to its head, it is left helpless and unable to move, because wherever the blow strikes, it breaks the spine which is from where the serpent moves its foot-like ribs and hence its body.

Therefore, this serpent which had remained invulnerable from so many javelins for such a long time, fell helpless when struck by a single stone and was soon easily surrounded and speared to death. **15.** Its skin was carried to Rome and for a time remained an object of wonder to all – they say it was

---

99 L. Manlius Vulso Longinus, consul in 498 *AUC*/256 BC. Eutropius, 2.21.2, gives an equal number of prisoners.

100 The river Mejerdah. For Regulus's campaign, see Tipps (2003).

120 feet in length.[101]

16. Regulus waged a terrible war against three generals, namely the two Hasdrubals and Hamilcar who had been recalled from Sicily. In this campaign 17,000 Carthaginians were killed, 5,000 taken prisoner, 18 elephants were captured, and 82 towns[102] surrendered unconditionally to the Romans.

9[103]

1. The Carthaginians, their forces shattered and disheartened by their reverses, sought peace from Regulus. But when they heard his harsh, unreasonable terms, they thought it safer to die in arms than live in misery, hiring not only Spanish and Gallic mercenaries of whom they already had large numbers, but also engaging some Greeks.

2. And so they summoned Xanthippus, the king of the Lacedaemonians, and his troops and made him their war-leader.[104] Xanthippus inspected the Punic troops, led them down onto the plain, and there joined battle against the Romans with a much-improved army. **3.** This place saw the great ruination of Roman might, for 30,000 Roman soldiers were laid low in this engagement. Regulus himself, a noble leader, was taken prisoner with 500 men, thrown into irons, and finally gave the Carthaginians in the tenth year of the Punic War a glorious triumph.[105] **4.** Xanthippus, *conscious of his audacious deed*,[106] and fearing a turn for the worse in this unstable situation,

---

101 Described as 'splendidly absurd' by Lazenby (1996) 100, the story of this serpent was popular in antiquity, being found in Livy, *Per. 18*; Valerius Maximus, 1.8; Aulus Gellius, *Attic Nights*, 6.3; Florus, 1.18.20; and Silius Italicus, 6.151–293. Orosius takes pains to give a naturalistic explanation of the snake, whereas Florus, and perhaps therefore Livy, hint that there was something supernatural about it. The largest known snake, the anaconda, can grow to 25 feet in length; the largest extinct snake, Titanoboa Cerrejonensis, reached 50 feet. For a full discussion of giant snake stories in antiquity, see Stothers (2004).

102 Eutropius, 2.21.3, has 74, not 82 towns.

103 Orosius's main source for this chapter is Livy, 18.

104 Xanthippus was a Spartan mercenary general, not the king of Sparta. Eutropius, 2.21.4, correctly describes him as such. Polybius, 32.1, describes him somewhat ambiguously as 'a man who had undertaken Spartan training', leading Lazenby (1996) 102–03, to suggest that he may have been a *mothax*, i.e. the son of a helot mother rather than a Spartiate proper.

105 Eutropius, 2.21.5, gives identical figures. The battle, which is described at length by Polybius, 1.32–34, probably took place on the plain of Tunis, though there are problems with identifying its location; see Lazenby (1996) 104.

106 Virgil, *Aeneid*, 11.812. The quotation is singularly apt as it refers to Arruns who flees after killing Camilla.

immediately returned to Greece from Africa.[107]

5. On the news that Regulus had been captured and of the disaster that had befallen the Roman army, the consuls Aemilius Paulus and Fulvius Nobilior,[108] who had been ordered to cross over to Africa with a fleet of 300 ships, made for Clipea.[109] Straightaway the Carthaginians made for the same place with an equal number of ships[110] and a naval battle became inevitable. **6.** 104 Carthaginian ships were sunk, 30 were captured along with their marines, and, apart from this, 35,000 of their troops were killed. Roman casualties were nine ships sunk, and 1,100 men killed.[111] **7.** The consuls then pitched camp by Clipea. The Punic generals, the two Hannos, once again gathered a great army, joined battle, and lost 9,000 men. **8.** But at that time good fortune never stayed long among the Romans, and whatever success they had was immediately overwhelmed by a great mass of disasters. For while the Roman fleet was returning to Italy loaded with plunder, it suffered a set of terrible shipwrecks: out of the 300 ships, 220 perished and the other 80 only just survived after jettisoning their cargo.[112]

9. Hamilcar, the Punic leader, was sent with an army to Numidia and Mauretania. He behaved cruelly, like an enemy, to all the people there, since they were said to have given Regulus a friendly reception, and condemned what remained of them to a fine of 1,000 talents of silver and 20,000 cattle. He had all their tribal leaders impaled.[113]

10. Two years later – as unrestrained frenzy is always forgetful of danger – the consuls of the year, Servilius Caepio and Sempronius Blaesus,[114] crossed over to Africa with 260 ships and ravaged all the seacoast that lies around the Syrtes. Then, advancing inland, they captured and razed a great number of cities, bringing back a vast amount of booty to their fleet. **11.** Subsequently while they were returning to Italy, 150 of their cargo ships

---

107 Orosius follows the version of Polybius, 1.36.2, and probably Livy. According to Valerius Maximus, 9.6, he was arrested at sea by the Carthaginians, while Jerome, *On Daniel*, 11.7.9, states that he entered the service of the Egyptian king Ptolemy Euergetes.

108 The consuls of 499 *AUC*/255 BC.

109 The modern Kelibia in Tunisia. Polybius, 1.36.10, has 350 ships.

110 Polybius, 1.36.8–9, has 200 ships.

111 Eutropius, 2.22.2, omits the Roman casualties and says only 15,000 Carthaginians were killed or captured.

112 The fleet was wrecked off Camarina in 255 BC. Orosius suppresses Livy's comment, found in Eutropius, 2.22.4, that this disaster did not break the Romans' spirit.

113 This information is only found in Orosius.

114 The consuls of 501 *AUC*/253 BC.

were dashed onto the rocks around the promontory of Palinurus[115] where the Lucanian mountains run down to the sea, and they sadly lost their glorious, but cruelly gained, plunder.

12. For a time the enormity of their sufferings overcame the Romans' disgraceful greed, for the Senate, which was disgusted by naval affairs, decreed that Italy should have a fleet of no more than 60 ships for its defence,[116] but seduced by their irrepressible greed, they immediately broke their decree.

13. Moreover, the consul Cotta[117] crossed over to Sicily, fought many battles, both by sea and on land, against the Punic forces there and the Sicels,[118] and left piles of unburied dead, some of the enemy, but others of his own allies, all across Sicily.

14. In the consulate of Lucius Caecilius Metellus and Gaius Furius Placidus,[119] Hasdrubal, the Carthaginians' new general, came from Africa to Lilybaeum[120] with 130 elephants and more than 30,000 infantry and cavalry, and straightaway engaged the consul Metellus at Panormus.[121] **15.** However, Metellus, while he feared the great power of these beasts, used a clever strategy and put them either to flight or to death.[122] In this way, he easily defeated the enemy despite their great numbers. 20,000 Carthaginians died in this battle, in addition 26 elephants were killed and 104 captured.[123] These were paraded through Italy giving an unrivalled spectacle to the Italian peoples.[124] Hasdrubal fled with a few men to Lilybaeum and was condemned to death by the Carthaginians in his absence.

---

115 The modern Capo Palinuro.

116 cf. Eutropius, 2.23.2, and Polybius, 1.39.7–8.

117 C. Aurelius Cotta, consul in 502 *AUC*/252 BC.

118 The native inhabitants of Sicily as opposed to Greek or Punic colonists.

119 The consuls of 503 *AUC*/251 BC. Orosius has misspelt Pacilus as Placidus.

120 The modern Marsala.

121 The modern Palermo.

122 Metellus dug a deep trench outside the town and then told some of his troops to advance, throw their javelins at the elephants, and immediately retreat. The mahouts pursued the retreating Romans, but had their charge halted by the trench and the elephants were then exposed to missile fire from the entire Roman army; see Frontinus, *Stratagems*, 2.5.4.

123 Pliny, *Natural History*, 8.6.16, gives the number captured as 142 or 140.

124 Quite how the elephants were taken to Italy is a mystery. Frontinus, *Stratagems*, 1.7.1, has them floated across the straits of Messina on rafts built to look like courtyards and buoyed up by jars. Eutropius, 2.24.1, speaks of them jamming the roads into Rome. Perhaps Orosius has misread his source at this point and assumed that this implied that the elephants were being deliberately led through all of Italy. Their fate was to be slaughtered in the games. Members of the family who were subsequently moneyers used the elephant on their coins to commemorate the battle.

10[125]

1. After this, the Carthaginians, worn down by so many misfortunes, decided that they must seek peace from the Romans. To this end, they thought that it was especially important to send along with their other envoys the former Roman commander, Atilius Regulus, whom they had now held in captivity for five years. When he returned from Italy having failed to secure peace, *they murdered him by cutting off his eyelids and tying him to a torture engine that stopped him sleeping.*[126]

2. The other Atilius Regulus and Manlius Vulsco, who were both consuls for the second time,[127] then advanced on Lilybaeum with a fleet of 200 ships and four legions. The Romans were trying to besiege this town which lies on a promontory, when they were defeated by the intervention of Hannibal, Hamilcar's son. The two consuls themselves escaped with some difficulty, but the greater part of their army was lost.[128]

3. After them, the consul Claudius[129] advanced against the enemy to the port of Drepanum[130] with a fleet of 120 ships, where he was soon cut off and defeated by the Punic fleet. Claudius himself fled with 30 ships to his camp at Lilybaeum. All the other ships, that is 90 of them, were either captured or sunk. 8,000 soldiers were killed and 20,000 taken prisoner.[131] Gaius Junius, Claudius's colleague, also lost his entire fleet through shipwreck.

4. In the following year, the Punic fleet crossed over to Italy and laid

125 Orosius's main source for this chapter is Livy, 18 and 19.

126 The embassy took place in 250 BC. The italicised section is a direct quotation from Cicero, *Against Piso (In Pisonem)*, 19.43. It is closely paralleled by Valerius Maximus, 9.2.ext.1, and the two may draw on a common source. Regulus's fortitude was commemorated by Horace, *Odes*, 3.5, and his story was a favourite topic of Augustine, see *City of God*, 1.15 (where the sleep-preventing engine is described), 1.24, 2.23, 3.18, and 5.18.

127 The consuls of 504 *AUC*/250 BC. G. Atilius Regulus Serranus was the son of the Regulus whom the Carthaginians put to death.

128 According to Polybius, 1.44.2, Hannibal's relief force was 10,000 men strong.

129 P. Claudius Pulcher, consul in 505 *AUC*/249 BC.

130 The modern Trapani.

131 P. Claudius Pulcher was consul in 249 BC. Drepanum lies some 15 miles from Palermo. For a description of this battle, see Lazenby (1996) 133–36. Frontinus, *Stratagems*, 2.13.9, says Claudius escaped with his remaining ships by decorating them as if he had won the battle. Orosius has suppressed the most famous event about this battle, namely Claudius throwing overboard the sacred chickens when they gave a poor omen for the following battle; see Livy, *Per.* 19; Florus, 1.18.29; and Eutropius, 2.26.1. This incident, which seemingly confirms the truth of paganism, would not have been at all germane to his purposes. Eutropius gives the size of the Roman fleet as 220 ships and says 90 were captured with their marines and the rest sunk. Only Orosius gives numbers for those killed or taken prisoner.

waste to most of it far and wide.

5. Meanwhile, Lutatius had crossed over to Sicily with a fleet of 300 ships.[132] He was badly wounded in the thigh while fighting in the front rank at Drepana[133] and on the point of capture, when he was snatched from harm's way. **6.** Then the Punic troops advanced on Sicily with 400 ships and large number of troops under the command of Hanno. Lutatius was equal to them and, indeed, anticipated the Punic plans with remarkable speed. After both sides' fleets had spent the entire night off the Aegades,[134] lying so close to one another that their anchors almost became entangled. When dawn broke, Lutatius was the first to give the signal for battle. **7.** As the fighting grew fiercer, Hanno was defeated, turned his ship away and, though the leader, was the first to flee. Some of his army went with him to Africa,[135] others fled to Lilybaeum. 63 Punic ships were captured, 125 were sunk, 32,000 men were captured, and 14,000 were slaughtered. Twelve Roman ships were sunk.[136] **8.** Lutatius then marched on the city of Erycina[137] which was held by Punic forces, and joining battle there, killed 2,000 Carthaginians.

11[138]

1. After this, the Carthaginians sent with all haste to the consul Lutatius and then to Rome. They begged for peace and at once obtained it on the conditions previously proposed. **2.** These were that they should leave Sicily and Sardinia and pay 3,000 Euboean talents[139] of refined silver in equal instalments over twenty years as reparations for the war. **3.** These peace terms were made twenty-three years after the Punic war first broke out.

---

132 G. Lutatius Catulus, consul in 512 *AUC*/242 BC. Eutropius, 2.27, also gives the number of ships as 300, though Polybius has 200. According to Polybius, 1.59.8, these ships were modelled on captured Carthaginian vessels.

133 The modern Trapani.

134 These three islands, Maretimo, Favignana, and Levanzo lie to the west of Sicily.

135 Where he was crucified, see Zonaras, 8.17.

136 Lutatius was elected consul in 242 BC. The Battle of Aegates took place on 10 March 241 BC. Eutropius, 2.27.3, gives identical casualty figures except for the Carthaginian dead whom he places at 13,000. Polybius, 1.61.6 and 1.61.8, gives a much lower figure of 10,000 Carthaginians captured, and gives the losses in ships as 50 sunk and 70 captured for Carthage and apparently none for Rome. Diodorus Siculus, 24.11.1, however, says 30 Roman ships were sunk and 50 disabled.

137 The modern Santo Giuliano.

138 Orosius's main source for this chapter is Livy, 19 and 20.

139 A standard measure, weighing some 57 lb.

4. *Whose tongue can tell,*[140] I ask, of a single war waged by two cities for three and twenty years and the number of Carthaginian kings, Roman consuls, columns of troops, and numbers of ships, that it brought together, threw aside, and destroyed?[141] Only when these matters have finally been weighed up thoroughly, will our times be able to be judged.

5. 507 years after the foundation of the City, a sudden reversal of fortune in Rome itself forestalled the Romans' triumph. I have not spoken flippantly, for it was no moderate joy at Rome that this grief, as sudden as it was terrible, destroyed. **6.** In the consulate of Quintus Lutatius Catulus and Aulus Manlius,[142] two contrary disasters caused by fire and flood almost destroyed the city. The Tiber, swollen by unusually heavy rain, broke its banks to a degree and for a length of time that no one had thought possible, and laid low all the buildings of Rome built on the plain. **7.** All these areas, whatever they were like, came to a common end, since where the flood rose more slowly, it soaked things through and crumbled them away, while where it came in a rushing torrent, it struck them and knocked them flat.

8. This terrible flood was followed by a fire that caused even more terrible devastation. It is unclear where the fire began, but it snaked through most of city, causing a pitiable loss of life and property; indeed, more was consumed by this single blaze than could be restored by the great number of victories won abroad. **9.** After ravaging everything around the forum, it took hold of the temple of Vesta and, since the gods did not even come to their own rescue, the fire that was thought to be eternal was extinguished by this temporal fire. Metellus when he carried his gods out of the temple as they were about to go up in flames, hardly escaped alive and had his arm half burnt away.[143]

10. In the consulate of Tiberius Sempronius Gracchus and Gaius Valerius Falco, the Romans waged war on the Faliscians of whom 15,000 fell in the ensuing battle.[144]

---

140 Virgil, *Aeneid*, 2.361.

141 This list of rhetorical questions bears a close resemblance to that found in Augustine, *City of God*, 3.18.

142 513 *AUC*/241 BC. There are two errors by Orosius here. He has placed the date of this disaster six years too late and has corrupted the name of the first consul involved who in reality was Q. Lutatius Cerco.

143 L. Caecilius Metellus, the *pontifex maximus*. Augustine, *City of God*, 3.18, also uses this incident to demonstrate the impotence of the pagan gods. Orosius has perhaps misread him, as Augustine says that Metellus was 'half-burnt' with no qualifications. The incident is also described by Ovid, *Fasti*, 6.437–54.

144 516 *AUC*/238 BC. Orosius has misspelt the second consul's name which should be Gaius Valerius Falto. Eutropius, 2.28, gives identical casualty figures.

12[145]

1.[146] In the same year, the Cisalpine Gauls became restive again.[147] The war against them had varying fortunes. In the first battle the consul Valerius and 3,500 of his men were killed; in the second 14,000 Gauls were slain and 2,000 captured. However, because of the initial disaster, the consul was not allowed to celebrate a triumph.

2. In the consulate of Titus Manlius Torquatus and Gaius Atilius Bubulcus,[148] Sardinia rebelled with Punic encouragement, but the Sardinians were soon defeated and crushed. War was then declared on the Carthaginians on the grounds that they had violated the peace for which they themselves had asked. **3.** In response, the Carthaginians immediately became suppliants and sued for peace. After the two delegations they sent achieved nothing, and then after ten of their leading citizens had gone to Rome twice, asking for peace with equal humility, but had failed to gain their request, they finally got their wishes through the oratory of Hanno, the least distinguished of their ambassadors. **4.** In this year, the gate of the temple of twin-faced Janus was closed, because that year there was no war anywhere. This had only happened before in the reign of King Numa Popilius.[149]

5. Now I must hold my tongue, as it is better to pass over in silence times which can in no way be compared to our own so as not to rouse up by my shouting those who find fault with times in which they live to exult – but in fact over themselves. **6.** Behold, the gates of Janus were closed, the Romans had no wars to fight abroad, Rome held all her sleeping offspring in her bosom and did not breathe a sigh of care. **7.** When did this happen? After the First Punic War. After how long did it happen? After 450 years of war. How long did it last? A single year. And what followed? The Gallic War, to pass over other events, and Hannibal, along with the Second Punic War.

8. Woe is me! How it shames me to have come to know about and uncovered these events. Was that year's peace, or rather that shadow of peace, a respite for their sufferings or an incitement for sins? Did that drop of oil falling in the middle of a great flame extinguish the source of this great fire

145 Orosius's source for the historical sections of this chapter is Livy, 20.

146 This is an artificial section break established by the Bolsving edition of Cologne in the sixteenth century. In fact, this section belongs with 4.11.10.

147 The Gauls concerned are the Boii who had allied with the Gauls of the Po Valley and the Ligurians.

148 519 *AUC*/235 BC. Orosius has misspelt Bulbus as Bubulcus, see Eutropius, 3.3.

149 cf. Eutropius, 3.3. Orosius has previously omitted any mention of Numa in his account of the early history of Rome.

or feed it? Did that tiny sip of cold water taken in high fever cure the patient or make him burn all the more?[150] **9.** For almost 700 years, namely from Hostilius Tullius to Caesar Augustus, there was just one year when Roman bowels did not sweat blood. Through the long passing of so many lengthy generations, the wretched City, which in truth is our wretched mother, has had scarcely a moment's rest from fear of suffering, not to mention from her sufferings themselves. **10.** If any man had enjoyed so little peace in his life, could he have been said to have lived at all? If someone lived for an entire year in pain and sorrow, but had passed just one day in the middle of that year in peace and without strife, surely he would not feel that this day had lightened his troubles, or consider that, because of it, the whole year had not been one of sorrows?

11. 'But these men,' he says,[151] 'have set up this year as a glorious symbol of Rome's unflagging courage' – would that they had passed over it and left in oblivion Rome's endless disasters.

12. Leprosy is finally diagnosed in a man's body if a different colour appears in patches between the healthy parts of the skin, but if the disease has spread everywhere to the degree that it makes the whole body this colour, albeit an unnatural one, this form of diagnosis is impossible. In the same way, if a life of continual hard work rolls on its way and is born with equanimity and without a wish for a rest, this would be said to be a willing choice and a chosen way of life. **13.** However, if the pleasures of our ancestors and the enthusiasm of their descendants rest on this tiny time of repose, it immediately becomes clear what joy this short time, and what bitterness, the rest of time brought: that is how agreeable this rest would have been, had it been long-lasting, and how this unending misery ought to have been avoided, if it could any way have been avoided.

13[152]

1. 517 years after the foundation of the City, Hamilcar, the leader of the Carthaginians, was killed by the Spaniards during a war, while he was secretly planning another war – one against Rome.[153]

150 cf. 3.8.4.

151 The 'men' are Orosius's pagan opponents and the speaker, the sick man of the previous sentence.

152 Orosius main source for this chapter is Livy, 20 and 21.

153 This is Hamilcar Barca, the father of Hannibal. He died in 525 *AUC*/229 BC; Orosius's date is therefore eight years awry.

2. In the following year some Roman ambassadors were killed by the Illyrians. After this, a bitter war was waged with this people in which, after the destruction of many towns and peoples, the remnant surrendered unconditionally to the consuls Fulvius and Postumius.[154]

3. Two years later, the *pontifices*[155] who were powerful, but wicked, brought death to the City through their sacrilegious rites. For the *decemviri*,[156] following the demands of an ancient superstition, buried alive a Gallic man and woman at the same time as a Greek woman in the cattle market.[157] **4.** But straightaway this occult ritual brought about the reverse of what was intended, for they atoned for the terrible death they had worked on these foreigners through having their own people horribly slaughtered.

5. In the consulate of Lucius Aemilius Catulus and Gaius Atilius Regulus,[158] the Senate was greatly troubled by the rebellion of Cisalpine Gaul. It was also reported that a huge army made up mainly of *Gaesati*,[159] which is not the name of a tribe, but that given to Gallic mercenaries, was arriving from further Gaul.[160] **6.** The consuls in their fright gathered together the forces of all Italy to defend the empire. When this had been done, it is said that each consul's army had 800,000 men under arms – this is what the historian Fabius, who took part in the war, has written.[161] **7.** Out of these, the Romans and Campanians provided 348,200 foot and 26,600 cavalry. The rest of the host was provided by the allies.

8. Battle was joined near Arretium.[162] The consul Atilius was killed and

154 L. Postumius Albinus and Gn. Fulvius Centumalus, the consuls of 525 *AUC*/229 BC who celebrated their triumph the following year. Orosius has continued his chronological error from the previous section.

155 Rome's official pagan priesthood and thus a natural target for Orosius.

156 The *decemviri* (later *Quindecemviri*) *sacris faciundis* were another part of Rome's official pagan religion. Their main function was to guard the Sibylline Books, to consult them in times of emergency, and suggest the appropriate religious remedies from them.

157 The Forum Boarium.

158 529 *AUC*/225 BC. Orosius has mistaken Lucius Aemilius's *cognomen* which was Papus.

159 The *Gaesum* is the name of a Gallic javelin; see Caesar, *Gallic War*, 3.4. Whether the *gaesati* were mercenaries *per se* rather than a form of the Germanic warband, or *comitatus*, is disputed; for a full discussion, see Walbank (1970) 194–95. Units of Gaesati were found in the Roman Imperial army; see *Roman Inscriptions of Britain* 1235 and CIL 13.1041.

160 i.e. Transalpine Gaul.

161 Q. Fabius Pictor, the early Roman annalist who wrote in Greek, but whose works were later translated into Latin. Orosius has taken his information at second-hand, probably from Livy. Eutropius, 3.5, makes the point in very similar language.

162 The modern Arezzo.

his 800,000 Romans, after part of their number were cut down, fled, even though the slaughter on their side ought not to have panicked them, for historians record that only 3,000 of them were killed.

9. The flight of so great an army with such small losses was all the more infamous and shameful because the Romans betrayed that in their previous triumphs they had been victorious not so much though the strength of their courage as through war's hazards. Who, I ask, would believe that there had been this number in the Roman army, let alone that they fled?

10. After this, a second battle was fought against the Gauls in which at least 40,000 of them were slaughtered.[163]

11. In the following year, the consuls Manlius Torquatus and Fulvius Flaccus were the first to lead Roman legions across the Po. There they fought with the Insubrian Gauls, killing 23,000 of them and capturing 6,000 more.[164]

12. Then in the year that followed on from this one, grim prodigies terrified the wretched City. Wretched it was indeed, being terrorised on the one side by the cries of its enemies, and on the other by the wickedness of demons. For in Picenum a river ran with blood, among the Etruscans the sky seemed to be in flames, and at Ariminum[165] a bright light shone out in the depths of the night and three moons appeared to rise in different regions of the heavens. **13.** At that time too, the islands of Caria and Rhodes were struck so hard by an earthquake that, as buildings fell down everywhere, even the famous Colossus came crashing down.[166]

14. In this same year, the consul Flaminius defied the omens that forbade him to wage war, attacked the Gauls and defeated them. In this war, 9,000 Gauls were killed and 17,000 were captured.[167]

15. After this, the consul Claudius annihilated 30,000 *Gaesati*: he himself went into the front line and killed their king Virdomarus.[168] Among the many towns of the Insubrians, whom he forced to surrender, he captured

---

163 The Battle of Telamon (the modern Telamone) fought in 529 *AUC*/225 BC.

164 The consuls of 530 *AUC*/224 BC.

165 The modern Rimini.

166 One of the seven wonders of the ancient world, the Colossus fell in an earthquake in either 228 or 226 BC. Orosius has drawn his information from Jerome, *Chronicle, A Abr.* 1793 = 529 *AUC*/225 BC.

167 Gaius Flaminius, consul in 531 *AUC*/223 BC. Orosius is happy to mention the defiance of omens when they are proved wrong – a striking contrast to his suppression of the reports of omens which proved to be correct at Drepanum, see 4.10.3 above.

168 M. Claudius Marcellus, consul in 532 *AUC*/222 BC. The battle took place at Acerrae, the modern Acerra.

was the flourishing city of Milan.[169]

16. Then a new enemy, the Histri, roused themselves up to fight. The consuls Cornelius and Minucius subdued them though after the loss of much Roman blood.[170] **17.** At this time, there emerged once again a little of that old Roman appetite for iniquitous fame even when it involved parricide. **18.** For Fabius Censorius killed his own son, Fabius Buteo, who had been charged with theft – a crime worthy of a name which his father considered should be punished by death, even though it was something for which the law would not sentence any man whatever to more than a fine, or at most exile.[171]

14[172]

1. 534 years after the foundation of the City,[173] the Punic general Hannibal first marched on Saguntum, a flourishing town in Spain and a friend of the Roman people, then besieged it, reduced it to starvation, and finally, after eight months, during which by looking to the support that Rome had promised, it had bravely endured everything foul and fair, destroyed it.[174] **2.** He refused in a most insulting fashion even to see the ambassadors sent to him from Rome.

3. This came from his hatred of Rome, a hatred he most faithfully vowed to his father at their altars, although he was the most faithless of men in other matters. In the consulate of Publius Cornelius Scipio and Publius Sempronius Longus,[175] he crossed the Pyrenean mountains, opening a way by the

---

169 M. Claudius Marcellus, consul in 532 *AUC*/222 BC; cf. Eutropius, 3.1–2. Orosius's comment on Milan appears to be a reference to the city of his own day rather than that of the third century BC.

170 P. Cornelius Scipio Asina and M. Minucius Rufus, consuls in 533 *AUC*/221 BC. The Histri, or Istrians, lived on the Adriatic coast of Croatia and were defeated at the battle of Clastidium, the modern Casteggio.

171 This incident is only preserved in Orosius. The force of 'any man whatever' is to emphasise the horror Orosius feels at Censorius executing his own son.

172 Orosius's main source for this chapter is Livy, 21.

173 220 BC. Orosius's date is one year out; Hannibal in fact attacked the town in 535 *AUC*/219 BC.

174 Now once again renamed Sagunto, previously Murviedro. Rome made a somewhat provocative alliance with this town in 220 BC after interfering in local politics there; see Polybius, 3.15. Augustine, when discussing Saguntum, *City of God*, 3.20, makes much more of Rome's failure to help her ally and the impotence of the pagan gods than does Orosius here.

175 536 *AUC*/218 BC. This Scipio is P. Cornelius Scipio, cousin of the consul of 221 BC and father of P. Cornelius Scipio Africanus, who defeated Hannibal. Orosius has mistaken Longus's *praenomen* which was in fact Tiberius.

sword through the fiercest of the Gallic tribes, and in only nine days had advanced from the Pyrenees up to the Alps. **4.** Here he suffered four days' delay, while he defeated the mountain-dwelling Gallic tribes who tried to stop his ascent, and cut through the impassable rocks with fire and iron, but on the fifth day, with a huge effort he descended into the plain.

5. They say that at this time his army comprised 100,000 infantry and 20,000 cavalry.[176] **6.** The consul Scipio was the first to oppose Hannibal. Battle was joined at Ticinum,[177] Scipio was badly wounded, but escaped death through the help of his son, Scipio, who had not yet reached manhood, but would afterwards be given the name 'Africanus'. Almost the entire Roman army was killed here.

7. A further battle was fought under the leadership of the same consul at the river Trevia,[178] and again the Romans were defeated in a similarly disastrous fashion. The consul Sempronius, on learning of his colleague's defeat, returned from Sicily with his army. He met Hannibal in the same fashion by the same river, lost his army, and was almost the sole survivor. Hannibal too, however, was wounded in this battle.

8. Later when Hannibal crossed into Etruria at the beginning of spring, he was caught in a storm on the top of the Apennines and, trapped and burdened by the snow, froze there, unable to move, for two entire days. It was here that a large number of his men, even more of his pack animals, and almost all his elephants died from the severity of the cold.

9. Meanwhile, the other Scipio, the brother of Scipio the consul, fought many battles in Spain where he defeated and captured the Punic general, Mago.[179]

15[180]

1. Dire portents terrified the Romans at this time. The sun's orb seemed to shrink; targes were seen in the sky at Arpi;[181] the sun also seemed to be

---

176 These are the highest figures listed by Livy, 21.38.2. Livy gives the lowest figures as 20,000 foot and 6,000 cavalry. These latter figures are cited by Polybius, 3.46.4, who says that Hannibal gives them on an inscription that he erected at Lacinium. Lazenby (1978) 48 believes them to be correct.

177 The modern Pavia.

178 Normally spelt Trebia, this river is a tributary of the Po which it joins near Placentia.

179 Gn. Cornelius Scipio who captured Hanno, not Mago.

180 Orosius's main source for this chapter is Livy, 22.

181 The modern Arpa in Apulia.

fighting with the moon; at Capena two moons rose during daylight;[182] in Sardinia two shields sweated blood; among the Faliscians the sky was seen to be torn asunder as if it were gaping open;[183] and at Antium when men were harvesting, bloodstained ears of corn fell in their baskets.[184]

2. Hannibal, knowing that the consul Flaminius[185] was alone in his camp, advanced at the beginning of spring along the nearer, but marshy, road in order to catch him off-guard and overrun him all the quicker. By chance, the Sarnus[186] had overflowed its banks far and wide, leaving the fields boggy and marshy. This phenomenon is described by the line:

and those plains the Sarnus waters.[187]

3. Hannibal advanced into these fields with his army, had his view completely cut off by mist that rose up from the marsh, and lost a great number of his allies and pack animals. He himself, sitting on the one elephant which had survived, barely escaped from the difficulties caused by his route, but lost an eye which had already become diseased because of the harshness of the cold, his lack of sleep, and his exertions.

4. After Hannibal had drawn close to the camp of the consul Flaminius, he roused Flaminius to battle by laying waste to the surrounding area. **5.** This battle took place by Lake Trasumennus.[188] Here the Roman army had the misfortune to be surrounded by Hannibal's skill[189] and was slaughtered to a man. The consul himself was killed and it is said that in this battle 25,000 Romans were laid low and a further 6,000 captured. 2,000 of Hannibal's army fell.[190] **6.** The battle at Lake Trasumennus was famous as being a great disaster for Rome, and all the more so because the fervour of those fighting was such that as they fought they did not notice a severe earthquake which happened at this time and which was so powerful that it is said to

182 The ancient town lay some two and a half miles from the modern town of the same name.

183 The Faliscians' largest town was Falerii Veteres, the modern Civita Castellana.

184 The modern Anzio.

185 Gaius Flaminius, consul in 537 *AUC*/217 BC.

186 The modern river Sarno, but the river involved here was the *Arnus* (the modern Arno) not the *Sarnus*. Orosius has either misread Livy, 22.2.2, 'fluviusarnus', here, or had a poor manuscript.

187 Virgil, *Aeneid*, 7.738.

188 Lake Trasimene. The battle was fought on 21 June 537 *AUC*/217 BC. The lake lies near the modern town of Passignano.

189 Presumably a reference to Hannibal forming up in the mist out of sight of the Romans; see Florus, 1.22.13, and Frontinus, *Stratagems*, 2.5.25.

190 Livy, 22.7.2, gives the Roman casualties as 15,000. Eutropius, 3.9, like Orosius, gives 25,000.

have laid low cities, displaced mountains, split open rocks, and forced rivers back in their courses.[191]

7. What happened at Trasumennus was followed by the battle at Cannae, although the dictatorship of Fabius Maximus who stalled Hannibal's onset by delaying tactics, fell between the two.[192]

<h2 style="text-align:center">16[193]</h2>

1. 540 years after the foundation of the City,[194] the consuls Lucius Aemilius Paulus and Publius Terentius Varro who had been despatched against Hannibal unhappily lost, through the consul Varro's impatience, almost all the resources upon which the Romans had placed their hopes at Cannae, a village in Apulia **2.** For 44,000 Romans were killed in this battle, although a large part of Hannibal's army was lost too.[195] But in no other battle against a Punic enemy were the Romans brought so close to total annihilation. **3.** The consul Aemilius Paulus perished in the fight, as did 20 men of consular or praetorian rank. Thirty senators were captured or killed, along with 300 men of noble family,[196] 40,000 infantrymen, and 3,500 cavalry. The consul Varro fled to Venusium[197] with 500 cavalry. **4.** There can be no doubt that this would have been the last day of the Roman state, if Hannibal soon after his victory had marched on to enter the City. **5.** As a testimony of his victory, Hannibal *sent three modii of gold rings to Carthage that he had taken off the hands of Roman knights and senators.*[198]

6. Despair for the republic reached such depths among the surviving Romans that the Senate thought that a plan to abandon Italy and seek a new

191 Normally spelt Trasimene. Despite mentioning the earthquake, Orosius suppresses the ill omens that preceded the battle as they would suggest that paganism had some validity; see Florus, 1.22.14.

192 Q. Fabius Maximus, dictator in 537 *AUC*/217 BC. Orosius's use of *cunctando*, 'delaying tactics', here recalls a line of Ennius, *unus homo nobis cunctando restituit rem*, 'By delaying, one man restored our fortunes'; see Skutsch (1985) fr. 361.

193 Orosius's source for this chapter is Livy, 22–25.

194 i.e. 214 BC. Orosius's date is two years out; Cannae was fought on 2 August 538 *AUC*/216 BC.

195 The same figures are given by Eutropius, 3.10.3. Livy, 22.49.15, says 47,500 died, Polybius, 3.117.4, 70,000. Polybius, 3.117.6, lists the Carthaginian losses as 5,500 infantry and 200 cavalry.

196 i.e. families numbering a consul among their ancestors.

197 The modern Venosa.

198 Taken virtually verbatim from Eutropius, 3.11.1, except that Eutropius says the rings came from knights, senators, *and soldiers*. Three *modii* is approximately six gallons.

home ought to be considered. This motion, proposed by Caecilius Metellus, would have been passed, had not Cornelius Scipio, the same who was afterwards to be called *Africanus*, but who at that time was a military tribune, drawn his sword, frightening them from putting the motion to the vote and forcing them instead to swear to defend their country. **7.** The Romans, daring to hope for life, *just as if they had come to life again from the dead*,[199] appointed Decimus Junius as dictator.[200] He held a levy of 17-year-olds and gathered together four legions of under-age and ill-disciplined troops from all over Italy. **8.** He even administered the soldiers' oath immediately after they had gained their liberty to slaves of undoubted strength or eagerness who had been given to him by their masters, or been bought with public funds if necessary. The arms they lacked, they took from the temples,[201] and private wealth replenished the treasury in its hour of need. In this way, the Equestrian Order and the panic-stricken plebs forgot their own interests and looked to the common good.[202] **9.** To increase the army's numbers, the dictator Junius, resurrecting an old custom at Rome in times of troubles, issued an edict that offered asylum to any man who was on the run because of crimes he had committed or debts he had incurred, and promised immunity in return for military service.[203] The number of such men came to 6,000. **10.** Campania, or rather all of Italy, in complete despair that Rome would ever regain her position, defected to Hannibal. **11.** After this happened, the praetor Lucius Postumius who had been sent to fight the Gauls was killed along with his army.

12. Then, in the consulate of Sempronius Gracchus and Quintus Fabius Maximus,[204] Claudius Marcellus, a former praetor and proconsul designate, fought Hannibal's army and put it to flight.[205] After so many disasters had been suffered by the republic, he was the first to give hope that Hannibal could be beaten.

13. In Spain the Scipios crushed the Punic general Hasdrubal in a great battle while he was gathering an army to take to Italy.[206] He lost 35,000 men,

199 Taken virtually verbatim from Florus, 1.22.23.

200 An error on Orosius's part, the dictator was Marcus Junius Pera; see Livy, 23.14.2.

201 Strangely, Orosius, perhaps because of his Roman patriotism, avoids commenting on the propriety of keeping arms in a place of worship, or on the lack of respect pagans had for their temples.

202 As usual, Orosius takes an aristocrat's view of Roman politics.

203 This had been done by Romulus soon after the foundation of Rome, see 2.4.3.

204 539 *AUC*/215 BC.

205 Livy, 23.16.8–16. This action forced Hannibal to raise the siege of Nola.

206 P. Cornelius Scipio, the father of Scipio Africanus and his brother Gn. Cornelius

either captured or killed, from his army. **14.** They brought over into their own camp some Celtiberian troops whom they bribed to desert from the enemy. These were the first foreign troops that the Romans enrolled in their army.[207]

15. The proconsul Sempronius Gracchus was led by a Lucanian guest-friend of his into an ambush and killed.[208] **16.** The centurion Centenius Penula sought of his own free will command of the war against Hannibal by whom he was killed along with the 8,000 troops he had led out to battle. **17.** After him, the praetor Gnaeus Fulvius was defeated by Hannibal, lost his army, and barely escaped with his own life.[209]

18. O, the shame of recording these things! Should I speak more of the Romans' depravity than of their wretchedness? Or rather I should talk of their depraved wretchedness or their wretched depravity? **19.** Who would believe that at a time when the treasury of the Roman people was asking for pitiful contributions from private individuals, when there was not a soldier in the camp who was not a boy or a slave or a criminal or a debtor, and there were not enough even of them, when almost every senator in the house seemed to be a new member, and finally, when everything had been so depleted and broken down that they reached such a state of desperation that a motion to leave Italy was submitted; **20.** who can believe that at a time, when, as we have said, they could in no way sustain one war at home, they undertook three more abroad? One was against Philip, the powerful king of Macedonia,[210] the second in Spain against Hasdrubal, Hannibal's brother, and the third in Sardinia against the Sardinians and the other Hasdrubal, the Carthaginians' general. Apart from these, there was the fourth war against Hannibal by whom they were being hard pressed in Italy. **21.** Nevertheless, a courage born of despair in each of these fields turned things out for the better. For in all these places they fought from despair, and from their fighting emerged victorious, by which we can clearly see that the times then were not any calmer from their being at leisure, but rather that men were braver in their misfortunes.

Scipio. The battle was fought on the line of the Ebro in 216 BC; see Livy, 23.28–29.

207 See Livy, 24.49.7–8. The Celtiberians were the racial group found in central Spain. These events have been compressed, as the mercenaries were not hired until 213 BC. Orosius may be noting the fact that that the first non-Italians in the Roman army were from Spain out of a sense of local pride.

208 In 542 *AUC*/212 BC. Sempronius was taking troops to Capua at the time. See Livy, 25.15–16.

209 Gn. Fulvius Flaccus, who was defeated in 542 *AUC*/212 BC; see Livy, 25.20–21.

210 A reference to the First Punic War, 215–205 BC. The Philip concerned is Philip V of Macedon (220–179 BC).

17

1. 543 years after the foundation of the City,[211] Claudius Marcellus captured, with some difficulty and on his second attempt, Syracuse, the wealthiest city of Sicily. When he had previously besieged it, he was driven back by machines built by Archimedes, a citizen of Syracuse endowed with a remarkable genius, and so was unable to storm the town. **2.** In the tenth year after Hannibal had come to Italy, in the consulate of Gnaeus Fulvius and Publius Scipio,[212] Hannibal moved his army from Campania and moved along the *Via Latina*[213] through the lands of the Sedicini and Suessani – a great disaster for all concerned – and pitched camp by the river Anio, three miles from the City, producing tremendous fear throughout the entire state. **3.** While the Senate and people saw to their different concerns, the women too, driven wild by panic, rushed along the battlements, carrying stones up to the walls, and were the first to get ready to fight for the walls. **4.** Meanwhile, Hannibal advanced menacingly with his light cavalry up to the Colline Gate, and then drew up all his troops into battle array, and the consuls and the proconsul, Fulvius, did not refuse battle. **5.** But when both battle lines were drawn up in sight of Rome, which would be the victor's prize, so great a rainstorm mixed with hail suddenly poured down from the clouds that it threw the columns into confusion, and the troops, who could scarcely hold onto their arms, retired to their camps. **6.** Then, after it had become fine again and the troops had returned to their battle-lines, the storm returned, more violent than ever, curbing the audacity of mortal men with an even greater fear and forcing the terrified armies to flee back to their tents. **7.** It is said that at this point Hannibal turned to his religion and declared that at times the wish, and at others the ability, to take Rome had not been given to him.[214]

8. Now let the detractors of the True God give me a reply here, was it Roman courage or Divine mercy that stood in the way of Hannibal seizing and sacking Rome? Perhaps those who were saved think it unworthy to admit that even though Hannibal was triumphant, he became afraid and made this evident by retreating. **9.** If it is clear that Divine protection came in the shape of rain from heaven, I think it can be seen with clear certainty of the same type, and impossible to deny, that this rain was opportunely brought

211 Syracuse was in fact captured in 542 *AUC*/212 BC.
212 543 *AUC*/211 BC.
213 The main road running from Rome into Campania.
214 See Livy, 26.11.2–4, and Florus, 2.6.

at a time of necessity by None other than Christ who is the True God.[215]
10. This is especially the case when now we can add to the proof of His
powers. For when a drought wreaked havoc, they prayed continuously for
rain, the gentiles on some days and the Christians on others, and the longed-
for downpour never came, as even the gentiles themselves bore witness,
except on the day when it was permitted for Christ to be approached and an
approach to be made by the Christians.[216] **11.** So there can be no doubt that
the city of Rome was saved by this same True God, Who is Christ Jesus,
Who orders things according to the decrees of His ineffable judgment, and
that it was then saved on account of its faith which was to come and is now
being punished for the faction there who do not believe.

12. Meanwhile in Spain, the two Scipios were killed by Hasrubal's
brother, and in Campania Capua was taken by the proconsul Quintus
Fulvius.[217] The leading men of Campania committed suicide by taking
poison, while Fulvius put all the Senate of Capua to death, despite the
Senate of Rome forbidding him to do so.

13. After the death of the Scipios in Spain, everyone was frozen by panic,
but then Scipio, although only a youth, put himself forward as commander
of his own free will. The treasury's lack of funds was a disgrace **14.** and,
on the motion of Claudius Marcellus and Valerius Laevinus,[218] the consuls
of the day, all the senators brought out in public for the quaestors[219] their
coined gold and silver as a contribution to state funds. They left nothing for
themselves and their sons except a single ring and *bulla*,[220] along with an
ounce of gold and no more than a pound of silver each for their wives and
daughters

<h1 style="text-align:center">18</h1>

1. Scipio at the age of 24 was allotted the proconsular command in Spain.
With his mind set, above all, on avenging his father and uncle, he crossed
the Pyrenees and with his first attack captured New Carthage[221] where the

---

215 For further rain miracles, see 5.15.15–16 and 7.15.8–11.

216 A reference to the 'rain miracle' which occurred during Marcus Aurelius's German
Wars; see 7.15.9.

217 These events occurred in 543 *AUC*/211 BC.

218 Consuls of 544 *AUC*/210 BC.

219 The financial officials of Rome.

220 The *bulla* was an amulet worn by youths before they reached manhood.

221 The modern Cartagena

Punic forces kept most of their pay, a strong garrison, and large amounts of silver and gold. It was here that he captured Hannibal's brother, Mago, whom he sent along with the rest of the prisoners to Rome.[222]

2. On his way back from Macedonia, the consul Laevinus stormed the city of Agrigentum in Sicily and captured Hanno, the Africans' commander. He received the surrender of 40 cities and stormed 26 more.

3. In Italy, Hannibal killed the proconsul Gnaeus Fulvius, along with 11 tribunes and 17,000 men.[223] **4.** The consul Marcellus fought a battle lasting three whole days with Hannibal. On the first day, the result was indecisive, on the second the consul was vanquished, on the third he emerged the victor, killing 8,000 of the enemy and forcing Hannibal to flee to his camp with what remained of his troops.[224]

5. The consul Fabius Maximus once more stormed Tarentum, which had defected from the Romans, captured it, and wiped out great numbers of Hannibal's troops along with their commander, Carthalo, there.[225] He sold 30,000 men into slavery, giving the proceeds to the treasury.

6. In the following year,[226] the consul Claudius Marcellus was killed along with his army by Hannibal in Italy.[227]

7. In Spain, Scipio defeated the Punic leader Hasdrubal and sacked his camp.[228] Besides this, he brought 80 cities under his control, either receiving their surrender or reducing them in battle. He sold the Africans into slavery, but sent the Spaniards back to their homes without demanding a ransom.

8. Hannibal ensnared separately both of the consuls, Marcellus and Crisipinus, in ambushes and killed them.[229]

222 In fact, this Mago was not the same Mago who had defeated the two Scipiones in Spain in 212 BC. This error is also found in Eutropius, 3.15, who is Orosius's source here.

223 Gn. Fulvius Centumalus, a consul of 211 BC and proconsul in 210 BC. He died in an ambush near Herdonea, the modern Ordona in Apulia. Orosius's casualty figures are far too high; Eutropius, 3.14.5, says 8,000 Romans died. Livy, 21.1.13, presents a variety of figures ranging from 7,000 to 13,000.

224 The Battle of Canusium fought in 209 BC. M. Claudius Marcellus was a proconsul, not a consul. See Livy, 22.12.7ff, who gives the same casualty figures, for a detailed account of the battle. Lazenby (1978) 175 casts doubts on the size of the engagement.

225 Q. Fabius Maximus Verrucosus, consul in 545 *AUC*/209 BC.

226 546 *AUC*/208 BC.

227 M. Claudius Marcellus, 'the sword of Rome' (Plutarch, *Marcellus*, 9.4), who died in a small action near Petelia (the modern Strongoli).

228 The Battle of Baecula, perhaps the modern Bailén in northern Andalusia, 208 BC. For a detailed description of the battle, see Livy, 27.18–19.

229 Orosius seems to have repeated himself, as he referred to the death of Marcellus in section 6 of this chapter. M. Claudius Marcellus and T. Quinctius Crispinus, consuls for 208

9. In the consulate of Claudius Nero and Marcus Livius Salinator,[230] Hannibal's brother, Hasdrubal, was ordered by the Carthaginians to unite his forces with those of his brother and crossed from Spain into Italy, travelling through Gaul and bringing a great number of Spanish and Gallic auxiliaries with him. After he had revealed to the consuls by his hasty arrival that he already descended the Alps, he was, without Hannibal's knowledge, cut off by the Roman army and killed along with his army.[231] **10.** For a long time the outcome of this battle was uncertain. The elephants in particular posed a threat to the Roman battle-line. These were driven back by Roman soldiers called the *flying squad* because they flew from one place to another.[232] **11.** This type of soldier had been devised a short while before: they were a group of youths picked for their agility, who were armed and mounted behind cavalry troopers. On reaching the enemy, they leapt down from the horses and immediately engaged as infantrymen in one position, while the cavalry who had brought them fought in another, thus throwing the enemy into confusion.[233] **12.** When the elephants had been driven back by the *flying squad*, as their own side were now unable to control them, they were killed by having a woodworker's chisel driven in between the ears. This method of killing these beasts, when it was necessary, had been devised by this very general, Hasdrubal, himself.

13. This battle at the Metaurus river where Hasdrubal was killed was the Punic Lake Trasumennus and the town of Cesena in Picenum, their village of Cannae: **14.** for 58,000 men out of Hasdrubal's army were killed there, and a further 5,400 captured.[234] Moreover, 4,000 Roman citizens were found and brought back to their own. This provided some solace for the victorious consuls, for 8,000 men from their own army had fallen. **15.** The head of his brother, Hasdrubal, was thrown down before Hannibal's camp. On seeing it, Hannibal immediately realised the disaster that had befallen the Punic army and, now in his twelfth year since he had arrived in Italy, retreated among the Bruttii.[235]

16. After these events, there seemed to be a whole year's lull in the storm

---

BC, were both killed in separate actions near Petelia.

230 547 *AUC*/207 BC.

231 The Battle of the Metaurus River, 23 June 207 BC.

232 The *velites*.

233 According to Livy, 26.4.10, the *velites* were formed in 211 BC, although in fact he also mentions them in 218 BC (21.55.11). Orosius's etymology of the word is correct.

234 The figures are drawn from Livy, 27.49.6, who has 56,000 killed and 5,400 captured. Polybius, 11.3.3, gives the much lower figure of 10,000 killed and puts Roman losses at 2,000.

235 The inhabitants of modern Calabria.

of war between Hannibal and the Romans, for their camps were troubled by disease and both armies were afflicted by a terrible plague.

17. Meanwhile, after having reduced all of Spain from the Pyrenees to the Ocean into a Roman province, Scipio returned to Rome.[236] He was elected consul along with Licinius Crassus, crossed over to Africa, killed the Punic general, Hanno, the son of Hamilcar, and scattered his army, killing some of them and selling others into slavery. 11,000 Punic soldiers died in this battle.[237]

18. The consul Sempronius engaged with Hannibal, was defeated, and fled back to Rome.[238]

In Africa Scipio advanced on the winter quarters of the Punic troops and those of the Numidians, both of which were not far from Utica, and had them burnt soon after nightfall. **19.** The panicking Punic troops thought that the fire had started by accident, ran out without their arms to extinguish it, and so were easily defeated by the armed Romans. In each of these two camps 40,000 men were lost to the sword and fire, and 5,000 captured.[239] Their leaders were piteously burnt and scarcely escaped with their lives.

20. The supreme commander, Hasdrubal, managed to reach Carthage as a fugitive. And so Syphax[240] and Hasdrubal soon reformed an enormous army, met Scipio in battle again, and were defeated and put to flight.[241] **21.** Laelius and Masinissa captured Syphax as he fled; the rest of the Carthaginian host escaped to Cirta, which Masinissa attacked and forced to surrender. Masinissa took the defeated Syphax to Scipio in chains. Scipio then handed him over to Laelius to take to Rome along with an enormous amount of booty and a host of prisoners.

---

236 Scipio returned to Italy in 549 *AUC*/205 BC. Orosius exaggerates wildly the extent of his conquests. Two provinces were formally established in Spain in 557 *AUC*/197 BC, but these merely bordered the Mediterranean coast of the peninsula.

237 Scipio landed at near Cap Farina. The battle was near Utica, the modern Utique in Tunisia, see Lazenby (1978) 205.

238 P. Sempronius Tuditanus, consul in 550 *AUC*/204 BC. His flight to Rome is recorded only by Orosius.

239 The figures are drawn from Livy, 30.6.8. Lazenby (1978) 208 believes them to be highly exaggerated.

240 The king of the Massaesyli, a tribe located in western Numidia.

241 The 'Battle of the Great Plains' fought by the Bagradas river, the modern river Medjerda, in 551 *AUC*/203 BC.

19

1. Hannibal, who had been ordered to return to Africa to help the weary Carthaginians, first killed all his Italian soldiers who did not want to follow him and then left Italy in tears.[242] As he approached Africa, a sailor, whom he had ordered to climb the mast and look from there at what region they were approaching, told him he had seen a tomb in ruins. Horrified by this, Hannibal changed course and disembarked his troops by the town of Leptis.[243]

2. After allowing his host to recuperate, he immediately went to Carthage and sought an interview with Scipio. The two famous generals looked on one another for a long time with mutual admiration, but as their peace negotiations came to nothing, battle was joined. **3.** This engagement had long been planned with great skill by the generals concerned.[244] It was waged with great numbers of men, fought with great spirit by the troops – and it brought victory to the Romans. 80 elephants were captured or killed on that field and 25,500 Carthaginians were slain. Hannibal, who had tried every stratagem both before and during the battle, escaped in the confusion with a few men, in fact with hardly more than four horsemen, and fled to Hadrumentum.[245]

4. Afterwards, he returned to Carthage 36 years after he had left her as a small child with his father, and persuaded the Senate, which was debating what to do, that there was no hope left except to seek peace.

5. In the consulate of Gnaeus Cornelius Lentulus and Publius Aelius Paetus,[246] the wish of the Senate and people was that Scipio grant peace to the Carthaginians. However, more than 500 of her ships were sailed out onto the deep and burnt in sight of the city. **6.** Scipio, who now received the surname 'Conqueror of Africa', returned to the City in a triumph.[247]

---

242 Hannibal abandoned Italy in late 203 BC. Diodorus Siculus, 27.9, puts the number of Italians killed by Hannibal at 20,000. No number is mentioned by Livy, 30.20, and it is unlikely Orosius would have omitted the figure had he known it. The incident may be entirely fictional. Orosius suppresses Livy's comment that the Italians were killed in the temple precinct of Juno Lacinia, as he wishes to retain the notion of Hannibal's cruelty, but does not wish to associate it, or Hannibal's downfall, with pagan notions of sacrilege.

243 Leptis Parva, the modern Lamta in Tunisia.

244 The Battle of Zama fought in 202 BC. The modern site of the battle is disputed; see Lazenby (1978) 218–27.

245 The modern Sousse in Tunisia.

246 Consuls in 553 *AUC*/201 BC.

247 Scipio was given the *cognomen* 'Africanus'.

Terence, the comic poet, as he was later to become, followed behind the triumphal chariot, among the noble Carthaginian prisoners. He was wearing a Phrygian cap – the sign that he had been given his freedom.[248]

20

1. 546 years after the foundation of the City, the Second Punic War, which had lasted 17 years, came to an end.[249] It was immediately followed by the Macedonian War in which the consul Quinctius Flaminius was allotted command.[250] After many severe battles in which the Macedonians were defeated, he granted peace terms to Philip.[251] **2.** After this, he fought against the Lacedaemonians, and on defeating Nabis,[252] their leader, paraded two most illustrious captives, Philip's son, Demetrius, and Nabis's son, Armenes, in front of his chariot. **3.** All the Roman prisoners who had been sold into slavery in Greece by Hannibal were recovered and followed the *triumphator*'s chariot with their heads shaven to show that they had been purged of their slavery.

4. At the same time, the Insubres, Boii, and Cenomanni united under the leadership of the Punic general Hamilcar who had remained in Italy, and laid waste to Cremona and Placentia. They were defeated after a hard battle by the praetor Lucius Fulvius.[253]

5. After this, the proconsul Flaminius fought and subdued King Philip and, along with him, the Thracians, Macedonians, Illyrians, and many other tribes besides who had given him their support.[254] **6.** The defeated Macedonians had their camp captured and Polybius writes that 8,000 of the enemy were slain that day and 5,000 captured. Valerius says that 40,000 were

248 Orosius has confused the playwright Terence (a popular author in late antiquity) with the senator Q. Terentius Culleo. His error is probably the result of a careless reading of Livy, 30.45.5.

249 Orosius's chronology is too early and contradictory. 546 *AUC* is 208 BC. The Second Punic War ended in 553 *AUC*/201 BC. Moreover, according to this account, the Second Punic War should have begun in 530 *AUC*, but at 4.14.1 Orosius dates its beginning to 534 *AUC*.

250 The so-called Second Macedonian War (200–196 BC). Flaminius obtained his command in 556 *AUC*/198 BC.

251 Philip V of Macedon (221–179 BC). The most important battle was that at Cynoscephalae fought in 557 *AUC*/197 BC.

252 King of Sparta from 207–192 BC.

253 The Battle of Cremona fought in 554 *AUC*/200 BC. Orosius has garbled the praetor's name which was Lucius Furius Purpurio.

254 The Battle of Cynoscephalae, the modern Chalkodonion in Thessaly.

butchered, while Claudius records that 32,000 were killed.[255]

7. These differing figures found in these writers are clearly a mark of deceit, and that deceit assuredly has its roots in flattery. For they took pains to heap up the victor's praise and extol the courage of their country either for their contemporaries or for posterity. Besides had there been no inquiry about the numbers, none of any sort would have been given. **8.** But if it is glorious for a general and his country to have killed a great number of the enemy, how much more joyful it is for a country, and for the general a blessing, to be able to be seen to have lost none or only a few of their own men. **9.** In this way, it is crystal-clear that a shameless method of reckoning similar to that which increased the number of the enemy's losses, also reduced the numbers of losses suffered by their allies, or suppressed them altogether.

10. Sempronius Tuditanus was defeated in battle in Hither Spain[256] and killed along with the entire Roman army there.

11. The consul Marcellus was defeated in Etruria by the Boii and lost a large part of his army. Afterwards, the second consul, Furius, came to his aid and together they laid waste to the entire tribe of the Boii by fire and sword, destroying them almost to the point of annihilation.[257]

12. In the consulate of Lucius Valerius Flaccus and Marcus Porcius Cato,[258] Antiochus, the king of Syria, prepared for war against the Roman people and crossed over from Asia into Europe.[259] **13.** At this time, Hannibal was ordered to be brought to Rome by the Senate, because of the rumours about him that were being spread among the Romans, saying that he was inciting the war. Hannibal then secretly left Africa, fled to Antiochus, whom he found vacillating at Ephesus, and soon spurred him on to wage war.

14. It was at this time too that the law passed by the tribune Oppius which forbade a woman to own more than half an ounce of gold, a coat of many colours, or to ride in a carriage in the City, was repealed after being in force for 20 years.[260]

255 Polybius, 18.27.6. Orosius is referring to Valerius Maximus, who composed a *Handbook of Memorable Deeds and Sayings* in the reign of the emperor Tiberius, and to Quintus Claudius Quadrigarius, an annalistic historian whose *floruit* was the 70s BC.

256 One of the two provinces in Spain in the republican period. Hither Spain was based on Catalonia and extended westwards to Aragon and Old Castile. Tuditanus was defeated in 558 *AUC*/196 BC.

257 M. Claudius Marcellus and L. Furius Purpurio, consuls in 558 *AUC*/196 BC.

258 Consuls in 559 *AUC*/195 BC.

259 Antiochus III 'the Great' 223–187 BC.

260 Orosius makes no comment here, but perhaps the reader is intended to see the law's

15. In the second consulate of Publius Cornelius Scipio and that of Tiberius Sempronius Longus,[261] 10,000 Gauls were slain near Milan and a further 11,000 in a second battle. 5,000 Romans were cut down.

16. The praetor Publius Digitius almost lost his entire army in Hither Spain.[262] The praetor Marcus Fulvius defeated the Celtiberians and their neighbouring tribes, capturing their king.[263] **17.** Minucius was brought into very great danger by the Ligurians, being rescued with difficulty by the courage of his Numidian cavalry after he had been surrounded by the enemy in an ambush.[264]

18. Scipio Africanus was sent with the other envoys to Antiochus, and even had a friendly conversation with Hannibal there, but after his peace negotiations broke down, he left the court.[265]

19. In both Spains the praetors, Flaminius and Fulvius, waged horrible, bloodstained wars against their inhabitants.[266]

20. In the consulate of Publius Cornelius Scipio and Marcus Acilius Glabrio,[267] Antiochus, despite having captured Thermopylae, whose fortified site made him more secure from the fickle outcomes of war, was nevertheless defeated after he engaged in battle with the consul Glabrio.[268] He escaped from the fighting with difficulty along with a few of his men and fled to Ephesus. **21.** He is said to have had an army 60,000 strong out of whom 40,000 are said to have been killed and more than 5,000 captured.

The other consul, Scipio, fought against the Boii and killed 20,000 of the enemy in battle.

22. The following year Scipio Africanus fought a naval battle with his ally Eumenes, the son of Attalus, against Hannibal who was at that time in

repeal as part of the moral weakening which befell at Rome after the fall of Carthage; see 4.23.9–10 below.

261 560 *AUC*/194 BC.

262 Orosius gives the wrong *praenomen* for Digitius – it was in fact Sextus. Digitius was propraetor in *Hispania Citerior* in 561 *AUC*/193 BC.

263 Fulvius was praetor in the other Spanish province, *Hispania Ulterior*, 'Further Spain', in 561 *AUC*/193 BC. *Hispania Ulterior* was centred on the Guadalquivir valley in modern Andalusia and extended to the Mediterranean coast to the south and towards Extremadura, Portugal, and New Castile to the north and west.

264 Consul in 561 *AUC*/193 BC.

265 The meeting is said to have taken place at Ephesus; see Livy, 35.14.5–12. In fact, it is doubtful whether Scipio was a member of the Roman legation. See Holleaux (1913).

266 In 562 *AUC*/192 BC. While Orosius's horror of war is a feature of his entire work, the impassioned description here may reflect his Spanish background.

267 563 *AUC*/191 BC.

268 The Battle of Magnesia, 190 BC.

command of Antiochus's fleet.[269] Hannibal was defeated, driven into exile, having lost all his army, while Antiochus sued for peace and returned of his own volition Africanus's son whom he had captured in unclear circumstances, either while the youth was on a scouting mission or in the battle itself.[270]

23. In Further Spain,[271] the proconsul Lucius Aemilius was cut down by the Lusitanians along with all his army.[272]

24. Lucius Baebius was surrounded by the Ligurians as he advanced towards Spain and was cut down along with all his army. It is generally agreed that this slaughter was so great that not even a sole survivor was left to tell of the defeat, and that it was, therefore, the people of Marseilles who saw to it that this massacre was reported at Rome.[273]

25. The consul Fulvius[274] crossed from Greece into Gallograecia, which is now called Galatia,[275] and penetrated as far as Mount Olympus[276] whither all the Gallograeci had fled with their women and children. Here he fought a bitter battle, for the Romans suffered heavy casualties as they were struck from above by arrows, slingshots, rocks, and every other sort of projectile, before they finally forced their way into hand-to-hand combat with the enemy. It is said that 40,000 Gallograeci were killed in this battle.[277]

26. The consul Marcius[278] advanced on the Ligurians, was defeated, lost 4,000 men, and, had he not swiftly fled back to his camp on his defeat, would have suffered the same sort of massacre as Baebius had a short while before at the hands of the same enemy.

27. In the consulate of Marcus Claudius Marcellus and Quintus Fabius Labeo,[279] King Philip, who had executed some Roman envoys, earned his

269 The Battle of Side, 190 BC.

270 This incident happened during the Battle of Magnesia.

271 See n. 263.

272 An exaggeration by Orosius. Although Paulus did suffer reverses in 564 *AUC*/190 BC, he went on to avenge them the following year with a victory; see Livy, 37.57–58.

273 L. Baebius Dives, praetor in 565 *AUC*/189 BC, died of his wounds at Marseilles; see Livy, 37.57.1–2.

274 M. Fulvius Nobilior, consul in 565 *AUC*/189 BC.

275 An area of central Anatolia, including Ankara.

276 This is not the Mt Olympus of Thessaly, but the hill of that name in the Taurus mountains near Antalya in Turkey; see 1.2.26.

277 Augustine, *City of God*, 3.21, mentions this campaign but assigns it to Gn. Manlius. While Orosius dwells on the numbers killed, Augustine asserts that this was when Asian decadence began to spread to Rome.

278 Q. Marcius Philippus, consul in 568 *AUC*/186 BC.

279 The consuls of 571 *AUC*/183 BC.

pardon through the heartfelt pleas of his son, Demetrius, whom he had sent as his ambassador.[280] **28.** Philip at once murdered him as a supporter of the Romans and a traitor to himself. His brother was an accomplice in this murder perpetrated by his own father. The wretched Demetrius died by poison, suspecting no ill from either of them.[281]

29. In the same year, Scipio Africanus, who had long been in exile from his ungrateful City, died of disease at Amiternum.[282] In these same days, Hannibal, who was the court of Prusias, the king of Bithynia, committed suicide by poison when his extradition was demanded by Rome, and Philopoemen, the leader of the Achaeans, was captured and killed by the Messenians.[283]

30. It was at that time that the island of Vulcan which had previously not existed, suddenly emerged from the sea off Sicily to the amazement of all and has endured down to the present day.[284]

31. Quintus Fulvius Flaccus, the praetor in Hither Spain, put to flight 23,000 men and captured a further 4,000 in a great battle. **32.** In Further Spain, Tiberius Sempronius Gracchus forced 105 towns that had been emptied and reduced to ruins by wars to surrender. **33.** That same summer Lucius Postumius in Hither Spain killed 40,000 of the enemy in battle and in the same province the praetor Gracchus stormed and captured a further 200 towns.[285]

34. In the consulate of Lepidus and Mucius,[286] the savage tribe of the Bastarnae who had been aroused by Philip's son, Perseus, through hope of gaining plunder and the possibility of crossing the Hister, were destroyed without a battle being fought or being opposed by any foe. For it happened that at that time the Danube, which is also called the Hister, was covered by a thick layer of ice that allowed an easy crossing on foot. **35.** But when a great column, composed of a countless host of men and cavalry, began

280 The mention of the murder of these envoys is only found in Orosius.

281 Demetrius died in 180 BC.

282 A town which still retains its Roman name in Campania. Augustine, *City of God*, 3.21, comments on Rome's ingratitude to Scipio. For a modern assessment of Scipio, see Scullard (1970) 210–43.

283 Philopoemen was the leader of the Achaean League. Orosius has a great love of synchronised events. The parallelism of the deaths here is meant perhaps to point up various morals. First, that the paths of glory lead but to the grave; second, that fame does not last even for a single lifetime; and third, that earthly success and failure lead to the same end.

284 The modern Vulcano.

285 These campaigns in Spain were fought between 181 and 178 BC.

286 Consuls in 583 *AUC*/175 BC.

to cross it in a single body, the frozen, icy crust, groaning beneath their enormous weight and the beating of their marching feet, suddenly snapped apart. The ice, now at long last broken and worn away, thus let the entire column, whose weight it had carried for a long time, fall into the middle of the river. It then resurfaced in pieces that got in the men's way, drowning them. Very few out of the entire tribe managed to struggle out on either bank, and they had been ripped to shreds by the ice.

36. In the consulate of Publius Licinius Crassus and Gaius Cassius Longinus, the Macedonian War was fought.[287] This ought to be ranked among the great wars, as Rome was first supported by all Italy, then Ptolemy, the king of Egypt,[288] along with Ariarathes of Cappadocia,[289] Eumenes of Asia,[290] and Masinissa of Numidia,[291] while the Thracians and their king, Cotys, and all the Illyrians along with their king, Gentius, supported Perseus and the Macedonians.

37. Perseus confronted the consul Crassus as he advanced. Battle was joined, and the Romans were defeated and put to flight in a pitiable fashion. The following battle proved an equal disaster for both sides and they departed to their winter quarters. **38.** Perseus, after wearing down the Roman army's strength in a long series of battles, crossed over into Illyricum and captured by arms the town of Sulcamum[292] which was defended by a Roman garrison. Some of the great host of Romans in this garrison he killed, others he sold into slavery, while yet others he took back with him to Macedonia.

39. After this, Perseus was engaged and defeated by the consul, Lucius Aemilius Paulus, who killed 20,000 of his infantry in battle.[293] The king fled with his cavalry, but was immediately captured and paraded in triumph before Paulus's chariot along with his sons. He later died in custody at Alba. **40.** His younger son learnt to be a bronze-smith at Rome in order to alleviate his poverty and lived out his life there. There were many other wars of varying success fought against a host of peoples dwelling all over the world, but I have passed over them for the sake of concision.

---

287 Consuls in 171 BC. The war is the Third Macedonian War, 171–168 BC.
288 Ptolemy VI Philometor, 180–145 BC.
289 Ariarates IV, 220–163 BC.
290 Eumenes II, king of Pergamum, not Asia, 197–159 BC.
291 Masinissa ruled Numidia, roughly modern Algeria, from 206 to 148 BC.
292 In fact Uscana (see Livy, 43.19.1). The site of the town is unknown.
293 The Battle of Pydna, 586 *AUC*/168 BC.

21

1. 600 years after the foundation of the City, in the consulate of Lucius Licinius Lucullus and Aulus Postumius Albinus,[294] a great fear of the Celtiberians overcame all Rome and no one, either soldier or commander, dared to go to Spain. Then Publius Scipio, who was afterwards called 'the conqueror of Africa',[295] although he had already been allotted Macedonia, put himself forward of his own free will to campaign in Spain. **2.** So he set off to Spain and slaughtered great numbers of people there, often behaving more like a private soldier than a commander: for he fought and killed a barbarian who challenged him to single combat.[296]

3. The praetor Sergius Galba, however, was defeated in a great battle against the Lusitanians and lost all his army, barely escaping himself along with a few of his men.

4. It was at this time that the censors decided that a stone theatre should be built in the City. In order to stop this happening, Scipio Nasica delivered a powerful speech, stating that this plan would be extremely harmful to a fighting nation, as it would encourage idleness and licentiousness.[297] He swayed the Senate to such a degree that they not only ordered that everything which they had acquired for the theatre be sold, but also forbade benches to be set up at the games.

5. So let our generation, to whom anything apart from the enjoyment of their lusts is irksome, know this: that if they feel and admit themselves to be weaker than their enemies, they ought to lay the blame on the theatre, not the age they live in, **6.** nor ought they to blaspheme the True God Who has prohibited such things up to the present day, but to abhor their gods, or rather their demons, who require these performances.[298] Their demands for such sacrifices are sufficient proof of their malignity, for they feed no more

---

294 Orosius's dating is three years awry. Lucullus and Albinus were consuls in 603 *AUC*/151 BC.

295 P. Cornelius Scipio Aemilianus, the son of Lucius Aemilius Paulus and hence by adoption the grandson of the Scipio Africanus who defeated Hannibal. He obtained his title after the Third Punic War. For a modern study of Aemilianus, see Astin (1967).

296 This incident occurred in 151 BC at Intercatia, the modern Villalpando; see Livy, *Per.* 48; Florus, 1.33.11; and Pliny, *Natural History*, 37.4.9.

297 169 BC. Scipio was a curule aedile at the time. This minor magistracy was mainly involved with municipal administration. The curule aediles were so-called because they were allowed, unlike other aediles, to use the cural chair normally reserved for higher magistrates.

298 Theatrical performances in antiquity were normally held in honour of one of the pagan gods; see Tertullian, *On Entertainments* (*De Spectaculis*), 10.

on the blood of animals than they do on the ruined virtue of men. **7.** For then there was no lack of enemies, famine, disease, or portents, indeed, they were all there in abundance, but there were no theatres: places where, incredible as it is to relate, men butcher their virtue as a sacrifice on the altar of luxury.

8. Once the Carthaginians thought it right to perform human sacrifices, but they soon abandoned this practice that they had wickedly begun. The Romans, however, demand to pay for their own damnation. **9.** This was done in the past and is done now. It pleases them and they cry out that it be done. They are like men who would be offended by the sacrifice of animals from their own herd, yet rejoice in the destruction of their own heart's virtue. Those who think that the Christians are at fault ought rather to be ashamed of Nasica, and not complain at us about enemies which they have always had, but rather at that famous man about the theatre he stopped them having.[299]

10. In Spain, the praetor, Sergius Galba, criminally slew the Lusitanians who lived on the near side of the Tagus and had voluntarily surrendered to him. He pretended that he was going to act for their well-being, but surrounded them with troops and laid them all low when they were unarmed and off their guard. This act of Roman treachery afterwards provoked a great uprising throughout all of Spain.[300]

22

1. 602 years after the foundation of the City, in the consulate of Lucius Censorinus and Marcus Manilius,[301] the Third Punic War broke out. After the Senate had decided that Carthage must be destroyed, the consuls and Scipio, who was at that time a military tribune, advanced to Africa and occupied the camp of the Elder Africanus near Utica.[302]

2. It was hither they summoned the Carthaginians and ordered them to hand over their arms and ships without delay. The quantity of weapons that were immediately handed over was such that all Africa could easily have been armed with them. **3.** But after the Carthaginians had handed over their

---

299 Orosius is attempting to portray Christianity as the natural culmination of Rome's tradition of austerity.

300 Galba's actions led to him being prosecuted at Rome, though he was acquitted. His behaviour sparked off Viriathus's uprising against Rome.

301 Orosius's dating is awry. Censorinus and Manlius were consuls in 605 *AUC*/149 BC.

302 The *Castra Cornelia* which survived at least to Caesar's day; see Caesar, *Civil War*, 2.24; 2.25; 2.30; 2.37.

arms, they were then ordered to abandon their city and move ten miles inland. Their anguish made them desperate. They decided to defend their city or be buried with, and under, her, elected the two Hasdrubals as their leaders, **4.** and straightaway set out to manufacture arms, making up for their lack of bronze and iron with gold and silver.[303]

The consuls decided to attack Carthage. The town's characteristics are said to have been as follows: **5.** it was surrounded by a wall 22 miles long and almost entirely ringed by the sea, apart from the 'jaws' where three miles lay open to the land. Here there was a wall of squared masonry 30 feet wide and 40 cubits high. **6.** Its citadel, which is called the Byrsa, had a circumference of a little over two miles. On one side, the city and the Byrsa shared a common wall overlooking the sea. They call this part of the sea 'The Pool' as it is calm, being protected by a projecting mole.[304]

7. Although they destroyed a part of the wall with their siege engines, the consuls were defeated and driven off by the Carthaginians. Scipio defended them as they fled, forcing the enemy back within their walls. Censorinus returned to Rome, while Manlius abandoned the siege of Carthage and turned to deal with Hasdrubal's army.

8. Meanwhile, Masinissa died and Scipio divided the kingdom of Numidia between his three sons.[305]

When Scipio had returned to the outskirts of Carthage, Manlius stormed and sacked the city of Tezaga.[306] 12,000 Africans were killed there and 6,000 captured. The Punic commander, Hasdrubal, Masinissa's grandson, was killed by his own people with broken fragments of benches in the council chamber because he was suspected of treachery.

9. The praetor Juvencius fought against the false Philip in Macedonia and was killed in a great disaster encompassing the entire Roman army.[307]

---

303 One Hasdrubal was a general who had recently fought unsuccessfully against Masinissa, the predatory king of Numidia, and had been condemned to death for his pains, but had escaped. The other was, on his mother's side, a grandson of Masinissa.

304 Orosius's mixture of past and present tenses in his description of Carthage shows that he had visited the city himself.

305 Masinissa died in 148 BC. His three sons were Gulussa, Mastanabal, and Micipsa.

306 The modern Henchir-Techga in Tunisia.

307 The defeat occurred in 148 BC. The false Philip was a Thracian named Andriscus who posed as the son of Perseus. Orosius suppresses the fact that in the same year the praetor Q. Caecilius Metellus defeated Andriscus, bringing the war to a successful conclusion.

23

1. 606 years after the foundation of the City, namely in the fiftieth year after the Second Punic War, in the consulate of Gnaeus Cornelius Lentulus and Lucius Mummius,[308] Publius Scipio, the consul of the previous year, advanced to Cothon,[309] intending to destroy Carthage completely.[310] **2.** When he had fought there for six continuous days and nights, the depths of despair brought to Carthaginians to surrender. They asked only that those who had survived the disasters of the war be allowed to live on as slaves.

3. First, a column of women came down from the citadel which was pitiable enough, but it was followed by a much more wretched column of their menfolk. Tradition says that the women numbered 25,000 and the men 30,000. **4.** Their king,[311] Hasdrubal, surrendered of his own free will. The deserters who had occupied the temple of Aesculapius decided to fling themselves into the fire and were consumed by it.[312] Hasdrubal's wife, possessing the sorrow of a man, but a woman's wildness, cast herself and her two sons with her into the midst of the inferno and so the last queen of Carthage died in the same way as once had her first.[313] **5.** The city itself burnt for seventeen days without ceasing, offering to its conquerors a pitiable spectacle of the fickleness of the human condition.

6. 700 years after its foundation, Carthage was destroyed and every stone in its walls reduced to dust. **7.** All the great host of captives, excepting a few of the leading citizens, was sold into slavery. And so the Third Punic War came to its end in under four years after it had begun.[314]

8. But although I have investigated the matter carefully, though, admittedly, I am not a quick-witted man, the cause of the Third Punic War – the thing that Carthage inflamed to such a degree that it was just to decree that she be destroyed – has never been clear to me. What interests me most of all

---

308 146 BC, which is in fact 608 *AUC*.

309 This is the Punic term for a harbour. Here it indicates the famous circular harbour of Carthage lying close to the Brysa hill.

310 As Orosius has said that the Second Punic War ended in 546 *AUC*, his interval of time should be 60 years, not 50 as he states here. The date also contradicts what he has said about the history of Carthage which he says was founded 72 years before Rome, 4.6.1, and endured for 700 years, 4.23.6. This would date its fall on Orosius's own prior reckoning to 629 *AUC*. In actual fact, the gap is 55 years.

311 Hasdrubal was the chief magistrate of the town, not its king.

312 These were Roman deserters. The temple was probably that of the Punic god Eshmun.

313 i.e. Dido, see Virgil, *Aeneid*, 4.504ff.

314 For a detailed discussion of the war, see Caven (1980) 273–94.

is that if, as in previous conflicts, a self-evident reason and grievance against a rising power inflamed them, there would have been no need for a debate.

9. But while some of the Romans proposed that Carthage had to be destroyed in order to safeguard Rome's continuing security, others declared that Carthage ought to be allowed to exist in safety as she was in order to ensure the continuing existence of Roman martial prowess, something which had always been fostered by the suspicion that another city was her rival, and in order that Roman vigour, which had always been schooled in war, should not dissolve into feeble idleness, if Rome obtained her security effortlessly. I think, therefore, that the cause stemmed not from an injury done to them by the Carthaginians, but from the inconstancy of the Romans as they began to decline into idleness.[315] **10.** If this is the case, why do they blame on these Christian times their sluggishness and decay which leaves them bloated on the outside and eaten away within? They are the men who lost almost 600 years ago, as their wiser and more fearful compatriots predicted, that great whetstone of their splendour and glory, namely Carthage.[316]

11. And so I shall put an end to this volume, in case it should turn out that while arguing too fiercely about this matter, I should remove my opponents' sluggishness for a moment, but then encounter mindless hostility where I am unable to draw forth from them the insight which they need – though I would be in no way afraid of confronting such hostility, if I could find some hope of creating that deeper insight.

---

315 This idea is also found in Augustine, *City of God*, 2.18-18, who quotes Sallust, *The War against Catiline*, 9. For a discussion of the *metus punicus*, the fear engendered by Carthage at Rome, see Bonamente (1975).

316 cf. Augustine, *City of God*, 1.30.

BOOK FIVE

1

1. I know that a number of men could be influenced after my description of these events on the grounds that through the slaughter of many states and nations Rome's victories grew greater. Nevertheless, if they look carefully, they will discover that the City suffered more harm than good. For so many wars waged against slaves, her allies, her own citizens, or runaway slaves ought not to be seen as of little account, as they yielded no fruits of victory, but only great suffering.

2. But I shall ignore this fact in order that this period can seem to have been just as they wish it to have been. At this point I think they will say, 'What more blessed times were there than these in which there were never-ending triumphs, famous victories, rich booty, glorious parades, and mighty kings and long columns of conquered nations driven before the victor's chariot?' **3.** I will reply briefly that they are accustomed to plead the case for these times and I have written a tract about the same times, and it is agreed that they concern the whole world, not just one city. See then that Rome's good fortune in her conquests is matched by the misfortune of those outside Rome whom she conquers.

4. How highly should we rate this scintilla of happiness, won at such a cost, to which is ascribed the good fortune of a single city amid such a great mass of misfortune which has laid the entire world in ruins? Or, if these times are thought so happy because one city's wealth increased, why should they not rather be judged as the most unhappy of times in which mighty kingdoms fell in the piteous devastation of many, well-governed nations?

5. Are perhaps these things were viewed differently at Carthage when after 120 years,[1] during which at times she trembled at the disasters of war and at others at the terms of peace, when as both a rebel and a suppliant

---

1 In fact, in Orosius's account there are 123 years from the outbreak of the First Punic War to the end of the Third Punic War.

by turns, she swapped peace for war and war for peace, and finally the whole town became one huge funeral pyre, as all her people in the depths of despondency flung themselves indiscriminately into the fire? Now, a small town stripped of her walls, part of her suffering is to hear of her former greatness.[2]

6. Let Spain give her opinion. When for 200 years[3] she watered her own fields everywhere with her own blood, while she could neither repel nor endure her persistent foe who, with no provocation, restlessly moved as it were from door to door, and when in various towns and places,[4] her people, broken by the slaughter of war and emaciated from the hunger of being besieged, killed their women and children and cured their sufferings by cutting one another's throats in mutual slaughter in a conclave of misery – what then did she feel about these times?

7. Finally, let Italy herself speak. Why did she quarrel with, oppose, and fight back against the Romans, who are one of her own, for 400 years,[5] unless good times for Rome signalled bad times for herself, and that the common good was harmed by Rome becoming the dominant power?

8. I need not ask what the countless nations of divers peoples, previously long free, but then conquered in war, dragged from their homelands, priced, sold, and scattered far apart into slavery,[6] would have preferred for themselves at that time, what they thought of the Romans, or what was their verdict on this period of history. **9.** I shall say nothing of those kings of great wealth, resources, and glory, who had long enjoyed great power, but were then captured, loaded with chains as slaves, forced under the yoke, paraded before the victor's chariot, and finally butchered in gaol.[7] It would be as stupid to ask their opinion, as it would be hard-hearted not to grieve at their sufferings.

10. Now, I say, let us look now at ourselves, and the life that we have chosen and with which we are comfortable. Our ancestors waged war and

2 Orosius is being highly disingenuous here. Carthage grew to be the largest town in the Western empire, save Rome herself.

3 The figure of 200 years is repeated by Orosius at 6.21.1. The period involved begins with Hannibal's attack on Saguntum and ends with Augustus's subjugation of Cantabria.

4 See 5.7.16 below.

5 See 5.22.1–4 below.

6 An echo of the fate of ancient Israel is present here.

7 The normal fate of an enemy leader paraded in a triumph at Rome was to be strangled in the Tullianum, an underground prison located on the edge of the Capitol.

wearied by it, sought peace and paid tribute: for tribute is the price of peace.[8]
11. We pay tribute to avoid suffering war and for this reason have put in and
stayed at anchor in the port to which they finally fled to escape the storms
of evil.

Therefore, I would look at our own days to see if they are happy.
Certainly, I think them happier than the past, for what our ancestors finally
chose for themselves, we have all the time. **12.** The tribulation of war that
wasted them away is unknown to us. We are born into, and grow old in,
that peace of which they had only the first taste after the rule of Caesar[9]
and the birth of Christ. What for them was a compulsory levy of slavery, is
for us a voluntary contribution for our defence. **13.** The enormous difference between past and present can be seen in the fact that what Rome once
extorted from us at sword-point to satisfy her own extravagance, now she
contributes with us for the good of the state we share. And if anyone says
that the Romans were more tolerable enemies for our ancestors than the
Goths are for us, let him hear and discover how different the things going
on around him are to what he believes is the case.

14. Once the entire world was ablaze with war: each province had its
own king, laws, and customs, nor was there any common fellow-feeling
as the different powers quarrelled with one another. What then could draw
together these scattered barbarian tribes whom even religion divided as they
had different sacred rites?

15. If at that time someone, overcome by the burden of his sufferings,
abandoned his country along with its enemies, to what strange land could
he, a stranger, go? What people, who, in the main, were his enemies, could
he, an enemy, ask for pity? Whom could he, a man who had not been invited
in as an ally, nor attracted by a commonality of laws, nor feeling secure in
religion's communion, trust on first meeting them? **16.** Or do Busiris, that
impious sacrificer of travellers who had the misfortune to reach Egypt,[10]
the cruelties practised on strangers by the shores of Taurian Diana and the
still crueller rites found there,[11] and the crimes of Thrace and Polymestor[12]

8 Orosius speaks here from the view-point of a provincial.

9 i.e. Augustus.

10 See 1.11.2.

11 The Tauri were a Crimean tribe who indulged in human sacrifice to placate a goddess
identified as Diana in the classical world. Like the story of Busiris, this myth was common
currency in antiquity, most famously embodied in Euripides' play *Iphigenia in Tauris*.

12 Polymestor, the king of Thrace, murdered Priam's son Polydorus at the end of the Trojan
War in order to obtain the treasure sent with him. The most famous instance of the legend is
Euripides' *Hecuba*. Orosius is likely to have known the legend from Virgil, *Aeneid*, 3.22ff.

towards guests who were their blood-relatives give us too few examples of this? And lest I seem to be lingering among events of the distant past, Rome is my witness in the case of Pompey's murder, and Egypt my witness in the case of his murderer, Ptolemy.[13]

2

1. However, when I flee at the first sign of any sort of trouble, I do this secure in the knowledge that I have a place to which I can flee, for I encounter my country, religion, and laws everywhere. **2.** Now Africa has received me with the liberality I expected when I confidently came to her.[14] Now, as I say, Africa has received me into her undisturbed peace, to her very bosom, under laws common to both of us. A land of which it was once, and rightly, said:

> *It shuts up a desert Shore to drowning men*
> *And drives us to the cruel Seas again.*[15]

now opens her broad bosom with genuine goodwill to receive freely allies who share her religion and common peace, freely inviting in the weary so that she can succour them.

3. Because I come as a Roman and Christian to Christians and Romans, I find my laws and nation in the broad sweep of the east, in the north's expanses, in the southern reaches, and in the safe refuges of the great islands.[16] **4.** I do not fear my host's gods, I do not fear that his religion will bring my death, I have no land to dread where the resident is allowed to do what he will and the rover not allowed to ask for what he needs: a place where my host's law is not my own. **5.** The One God, loved and feared by all, has ordained in these times when He wished to be acknowledged, this united kingdom. Everywhere the same laws, subject to the One God, hold sway. Wherever I should arrive as a stranger, I have no fear of being suddenly attacked like a friendless man. **6.** For, as I have said, as a Roman among Romans, as a Christian among Christians, and as a man among men, I can call on the state's laws, a common knowledge of religion, and our

13 A reference to the murder of Pompey, 28 September 48 BC, when he fled to the Egypt of Ptolemy XIII. See 6.15.27–28.

14 The 'now' of the text suggests that this is a reference to Orosius's return to Africa after he found himself unable to return to Spain rather than his original flight from Spain to Africa.

15 Virgil, *Aeneid*, 1.540–41.

16 The list covers the four points of the compass as the 'great islands', Britain and Ireland, lie in the west.

common nature. For the short time that I am here,[17] I have all the earth as if it were my homeland, for the place that is truly my homeland and which I love is far from the earth. **7.** I have lost nothing, where I love nothing, and have everything when He Whom I love is with me, especially because He, Who is the same among all people, makes me not merely known, but a neighbour to all, nor does He leave me in need *for the Earth and Fullness thereof are His*,[18] from which He has commanded that all be shared by all.

8. These are the blessings of our days: a peaceful present, hope for the future, and a common refuge.[19] These things our ancestors never enjoyed fully and because of this, they waged incessant wars, and being unable to change their homes, they remained in them to be wretchedly slaughtered or shamefully enslaved. This will become clearer and more obvious when deeds of old are revealed in chronological order.

3

1. 606 years after the foundation of the City – that is in the same year in which Carthage was destroyed – the ruin of Carthage was followed by the destruction of Corinth in the consulate of Gnaeus Cornelius Lentulus and Lucius Mummius.[20] In this one short space of time, the piteous flames of two of the most powerful towns lit up different parts of the world.

2. The praetor Metellus[21] defeated the joint forces of the Achaeans and Boeotians in two battles, the first at Thermopylae and the second in Phocis. **3.** The historian Claudius records that 20,000 men were killed in the first battle and 7,000 in the second.[22] Valerius and Antias agree that a battle was fought in Achaea and that 20,000 Achaeans fell along with their leader,

---

17 i.e. Orosius's earthly life, as opposed to his coming life in heaven.

18 A close paraphrase of Psalm 24.1.

19 Orosius has artfully transposed to Christianity the common pagan topos, found, for example, in Aelius Aristides (*To Rome* (*Ad Romam*), 100), that the Roman Empire has made the world one. However, his intention in so doing is not to supplant the notion that Rome is the world's unifier, but to make Christianity an integral part of this process in order to show that Rome's God-given destiny has always been to be a Christian empire. For a translation and commentary on Aristides, see Oliver (1953).

20 Orosius's dating is two years out; Lentulus and Mummius were the consuls of 608 *AUC*/146 BC.

21 Q. Caecilius Metellus Macedonicus, praetor in 148 BC, who held a propraetorian command in Greece until 146 BC. It is this command to which Orosius is referring.

22 The annalist Q. Claudius Quadrigarius who wrote in the 70s BC. Orosius is probably citing him second-hand via Livy.

Diaeus.[23] Although the Achaean Polybius was in Africa with Scipio at that time, he could not ignore the disaster that was occurring in his homeland. He states that there was one battle in Achaea, the Achaeans being led by Critolaus,[24] adding that Diaeus was recruiting troops from Achaea when he was defeated along with his army by the praetor Metellus.[25] **4.** We have already listed a number of disagreements found among historians,[26] about which suffice it to say that the things uncovered here, a poorly noted note of their lies, clearly show that men who differ even when recording events at which they were present are hardly to be trusted in the rest of their accounts. **5.** After the destruction of garrisons throughout Achaea, and while the praetor Metellus was thinking of razing its abandoned cities to the ground, the consul Mummius suddenly arrived at his camp with a few men. Straightaway he dismissed Metellus and stormed Corinth without delay. At that time this town was by far the wealthiest in the entire world, as for many centuries in the past it had been a workshop for all kinds of crafts and craftsmen and a common marketplace for both Asia and Europe.

6. Mummius cruelly gave permission to plunder even to his prisoners and so the entire town was filled with fire and slaughter to such a degree that the fire surged up from the city walls narrowing to a single flame, as if came from a furnace. Most of the population were put to the sword or consumed by the flames, the rest were sold into slavery. After the city had been burnt down, its walls were razed to their foundations and their stones ground to dust. An enormous amount of booty was stolen.

7. Indeed, because of the great number and sorts of statues and idols found in the burning city, gold, silver, bronze, and all metals melted at the same time, and a new kind of metal was created. It is for this reason that to this day, as the tradition has come down to us, things made of it, or in imitation of it, are called Corinthian bronze and Corinthian vases.[27]

---

23 Orosius has here mistaken Valerius Antias, an historian of the first century BC, for two separate individuals. This error is likely to have stemmed from a misreading of the now-lost Livy, 52. Livy often cites Valerius, normally to disagree with him.

24 Critolaus was defeated by Metellus at Scarpheia in Locris.

25 Orosius has quoted Polybius at second-hand via Livy, 52.

26 At 4.20.7–9.

27 See Pliny, *Natural Histories*, 34.3.6 and Florus, 1.32.7, for Corinthian bronze.

4

1. In Spain, during the same consulate, Viriatus, a shepherd and robber born in Lusitania, began as a highwayman, then laid waste to the provinces there, and finally by his defeat, rout, and subjugation of armies commanded by both praetors and consuls caused great terror to all of Rome.[28] **2.** The praetor Gaius Vetilius faced him as he wandered far and wide, passing through the land between the Ebro and the Tagus, two great, widely separated rivers. Almost all of Vetilius's army was slaughtered to the point of utter annihilation, while the praetor himself, along with a few men, only managed to flee with difficulty.[29]

3. Viriatus then broke the praetor Gaius Plautius in a long series of battles and put him to flight.[30] After this, Claudius Unimammus, who had been despatched with a great force against Viriatus in order to wipe out the stain of Rome's past humiliation, only made her disgrace more shameful.[31] **4.** For when he met Viriatus, he lost all the troops that he had brought with him who were the flower of the Roman army. Viriatus set up a trophy of Roman robes of state, *fasces*, and other insignia of office in the mountains of his own country.[32] **5.** At the same time, 300 Lusitanians fought a battle against 1,000 Romans in a glen. Claudius tells us that 70 Lusitanians and 320 Romans fell. **6.** After the triumphant Lusitanians had dispersed in safety, one became greatly separated from his colleagues. He was surrounded by cavalrymen, but though he was on foot, he ran through one of their horses with his javelin and beheaded the trooper with a single blow of his sword. In this way he struck them all with fear and walked away in a contemptuous and leisurely fashion as they looked on.

7. In the consulate of Appius Claudius and Quintus Caecilius Metellus,[33] Appius Claudius fought the Salassian Gauls,[34] was defeated, and lost 5,000

---

28 A similar version of Viriatus's rake's progress is found in Florus, 1.33.15, and Eutropius, 4.16. The conceit derives from Livy, 52. For a detailed account of Viriatus's life which asserts that he was a Lusitanian aristocrat, not a peasant, see Pastor Muñoz (2004).

29 Vetilius was praetor in 607 *AUC*/147 BC. He was ambushed near Tribula (the modern Trevoens). Orosius is probably drawing on Livy, 52, at this point.

30 Praetor in 608 *AUC*/146 BC.

31 More correctly Unimanus, praetor in 609 *AUC*/145 BC.

32 This detail is taken from Florus, 1.33.16. The mountain is probably the so-called *Mons Veneris* in central Spain. Its location is uncertain.

33 Consuls in 611 *AUC*/143 BC.

34 This tribe lived in the Val d'Aosta.

men. The battle was rejoined and he then killed 5,000 of the enemy.[35] But when he sought a triumph according to the law which, as then constituted, stated that anyone who had killed 5,000 of the enemy was entitled to hold a triumph, he was refused because of the losses he had suffered in the first battle. He then held a triumph at private expense in an infamous display of shamelessness and ambition.[36]

8. In the consulate of Lucius Caecilus Metellus and Quintus Fabius Maximus Servilianus,[37] among the other prodigies seen at Rome was a hermaphrodite.[38] It was thrown into the sea by order of the *haruspices*,[39] but the performance of this profane act of expiation served no purpose, for so great a plague suddenly arose that at first there were not enough undertakers to conduct funerals, and soon there were none at all. Great houses were left empty of the living, but full of the dead. Within there were great inheritances, but nowhere was an heir to be found. **9.** In the end, it was not merely impossible to live in the City, but even to approach it, so horrendous was the stench exuding through the whole City from the rotting corpses found in their houses and beds.

10. The cruel expiation that through one man's death opened up a way for men to die,[40] finally taught the Romans how wretched and meaningless it had been, and they felt shame in the midst of their sufferings. For the sacrifice had been held to ward off coming disaster – and the plague had followed on its completion, finally subsiding after it had spent its corrupting force in accordance with secret laws, and without the need for any more expiating sacrifices. **11.** Now if the *haruspices*, those masters of deceit, had held the ceremony when the force of the disease was waning, as is their custom, there can be no doubt that they would have claimed the glory for

35 Orosius suppresses the fact that after the initial defeat, the *decemviri* consulted the Sibylline Books which recommended that a sacrifice be made on enemy territory. This was done, and the Romans were then triumphant; see Livy, *Per.* 53. This anecdote is also found in Julius Obsequens, 21. Obsequens compiled his *Book of Prodigies* (*Liber de Prodigiis*) from Livy's history. He was probably active in the mid-fourth century AD.

36 Claudius's triumph was a by-word for extravagance and arrogance; see Cicero, *Speech in defence of Caelius* (*Pro Caelio*), 34; Valerius Maximus, 5.4.6; Suetonius, *Tiberius*, 2.

37 Consuls in 612 *AUC*/142 BC.

38 Orosius appears to have transposed this account of the hermaphrodite and the plague that followed to Rome from Luna (near the modern Sarzana in Etruria); see Julius Obsequens, 22. Death by drowning was the normal fate of such prodigies.

39 The *haruspices* (lit. gut-gazers) were a prestigious college of diviners at Rome, hence Orosius's extreme hostility towards them.

40 Reading *viam mortibus hominum morte hominis instruens* with Zangemeister and Torres Rodríguez. Arnaud-Lindet reads *mortibus hominem morte hominis instruens*.

bringing back health to the city for themselves, their gods, and rites. And so, the wretched City, wrongly pious to the point of sacrilege, was made sport of by their lies from which it could not escape.[41]

12. The consul Fabius fought against the Lusitanians and Viriatus, driving off the enemy and freeing the town of Buccia which Viriatus was besieging.[42] He accepted its unconditional surrender along with that of many strongholds. Then he perpetrated a crime that would have disgusted even the furthest-flung barbarians of Scythia, let alone the Roman sense of fidelity and moderation. He cut off the hands of 500 of their leading men whom, in accordance with the law of surrender, he had summoned in order to form an alliance with him.[43]

13. The following year's consul, Pompey, advanced into the lands of the Numantines and retreated after suffering a great disaster, for not only was almost his whole army destroyed, but many nobles who were serving with him were also killed.[44]

14. Viriatus, after harrying Roman armies and generals for fourteen years, was killed by a plot formed by his own people. It was in this matter alone that the Romans behaved nobly towards him, for they judged his assassins unworthy of a reward.[45]

15. Now, not only at this point, but frequently in what I have already said, I have been able to weave into my account the complex wars of the East which rarely begin or end without criminal acts, but the crimes of the Romans with which we are now dealing were so great that those of other peoples can be justly ignored.

16. At this time Mithridates, the Parthian king who was sixth in line from Arsaces, defeated the prefect Demetrius, entered the city of Babylon,

41 Perhaps Orosius here wants his readers to see Rome as an essentially pious but deceived city. She is held captive here because Christianity had not yet exposed the *haruspices* as liars.

42 Q. Fabius Maximus Servillianus, consul in 142 BC. 'Buccia' is probably a garbled version of Tucci – the modern Martos in Andalusia

43 Orosius's account of this incident betrays his Spanish background and is in sharp contrast to that of Valerius Maximus, 2.7.11, who portrays it as the just punishment of fugitives and deserters.

44 Q. Pompeius, consul in 613 *AUC*/141 BC. Orosius suppresses his successes against the Numantines' neighbours, the Termestini (see Livy, *Per.* 54), nor does he mention that Pompey made a treaty with the Numantines which was rejected at Rome, though later at 5.4.21 he confusingly alludes to it.

45 Viriatus was murdered in 139 BC. Orosius follows Livy, *Per.* 54, Florus, 1.33.15, and Eutropius, 4.16, in stating that he had fought Rome for fourteen years. In fact, his campaigns lasted for eight years.

occupied all its territory in triumph, and went on to subdue all the peoples who live between the Hydaspes and Indus rivers.[46] He also extended his bloodstained rule to India. **17.** When Demetrius marched against Mithridates a second time, he was defeated and captured.[47] After he was captured, a certain Diodotus and his son, Alexander, usurped his throne and the royal title. **18.** Afterwards, Diodotus killed his son, who had shared in the dangers of seizing the kingdom, to avoid sharing the throne with him.[48]

19. In the consulate of Marcus Aemilius Lepidus and Gaius Hostilius Mancinus,[49] a variety of prodigies occurred, and were dealt with in the traditional manner to the best of the Romans' abilities. But things did not always turn out well for those watchers of events and devisers of lies, the *haruspices*.

20. For the consul Mancinus, after assuming command of the army at Numantia from Popilius,[50] fought all his battles so badly and was reduced to such a degree of despair that he was forced to make a highly shameful treaty with the Numantines.[51] **21.** Although a short time before Pompey too had also made an equally dishonourable treaty with these same Numantines,[52] the Senate ordered that the treaty be abrogated and Mancinus handed over to the Numantines. He was stripped, his hands bound behind his back, and set before the gates of Numantia. There he remained until nightfall, abandoned by his own people, yet not taken in by the enemy, offering a pitiable spectacle to both sides.

---

46 Mithridates I 'the Great'. The Demetrius concerned is Demetrius I Soter, not a prefect but the king of Syria 162–150 BC.

47 Orosius has confused two Demetriuses. This is Demetrius II Nicator, king of Syria 145–139 BC and 129–125 BC.

48 Orosius's account of these events, derived from Livy, 52 and 55, is confused. Diodotus Tryphon 'the Idler', commander of the garrison in Apamea, proclaimed the son of Alexander Balas as king in Antioch in 145 BC. The pretender took the name of Antiochus VI. Demetrius failed to deal with this rebellion before he marched east to fight the Parthians. He was captured by the Parthians in 139 BC and it was then that Diodotus killed 'Antiochus VI', who was not his own son as Orosius states.

49 Consuls in 617 *AUC*/137 BC.

50 M. Popillius Laenas, proconsul in 138 BC who suffered a heavy defeat at the hands of the Numantines; Livy, *Per.* 55.

51 Orosius suppresses Livy's account of the ill omens that preceded Mancinus's departure for Spain; see Livy, *Per.* 55. The treaty is noted briefly by Augustine, *City of God*, 3.21.

52 See 5.4.13 above, though Orosius neglects to mention the treaty.

5

1. My pain forces me to cry out at this point. Why, Romans, do you falsely attribute to yourselves the great names of Justice, Good Faith, Courage, and Mercy?[53] Learn the truth from the Numantines. **2.** Was there need of courage? The Numantines won the fight. Was Good Faith required? The Numantines, believing that others would act as they did, released those whom they could have killed after the treaty was made. **3.** Did Justice have to be put to the test? It was – by the silence of the Senate, when the Numantines' ambassadors demanded that the peace be kept inviolate or that those whom they had freed alive as a pledge of that peace be returned to them. **4.** Must we look at mercy? They gave enough proof of this when they spared the lives of the enemy's army and when they did not take back Mancinus to punish him.

5. My question is ought Mancinus, a man who warded off the impending slaughter of his defeated army with the shield-boss of the treaty he made, and who preserved the endangered resources of his country for better days, to have been handed over at all? **6.** If the treaty he made displeased them, why were the troops redeemed on such conditions? When they returned, why were they received? And when they were demanded back, why were they not returned? On the other hand, if they thought it right to save their troops on whatever terms possible, why was Mancinus, who had made this treaty, the only one to be handed over?

7. In the recent past, Varro had forced his reluctant colleague Paulus to rush into battle prematurely, hurling forward his trembling troops. At Cannae, a place now notorious for the disaster Rome suffered there, he did not draw up his men for battle, but set them face to face with death. It was solely his impatience, on which Hannibal had long relied to bring him victory, that cost the lives of more than 40,000 Roman soldiers.[54] **8.** Finally this shameless man, on the death of his colleague Paulus, and what a man he was, had the nerve to return almost alone to the city – and got a reward for his shamelessness. **9.** For the Senate publicly thanked him because he had not despaired of the republic, though it was he himself who had plunged the republic into despair. **10.** But later, Mancinus, who had taken pains that

---

53 A strong reminiscence of Augustus's *clipeus virtutis*, or 'shield of virtue'. This was awarded to the emperor by the Senate in 27 BC and recorded Augustus's four cardinal virtues of justice, piety, courage, and clemency. It was thereafter hung permanently in the senate-house.

54 See 4.16.2.

he should not lose his army after the fortunes of war had led to it being surrounded, was condemned to be handed over to the enemy by that same Senate.[55]

11. So Romans, you disapproved of Varro's actions, but because of the circumstances forgave them, yet approved of Mancinus's actions, but through circumstances annulled them. By acting like this, you have from the very beginning brought it about that no citizen thinks to help such an ungrateful race and that no enemy places any faith in such a faithless people.

12. Meanwhile, Brutus in Further Spain crushed an army of 60,000 Galicians who had come to help the Lusitanians. The battle was hard and desperate, even though Brutus had surrounded his enemy when they were off their guard. 50,000 were killed in this battle and 6,000 taken prisoner; a few others managed to flee.[56]

13. In Hither Spain, the proconsul Lepidus, although the Senate forbade it, persistently tried to conquer the Vaccaei, a harmless tribe that had sued for peace.[57] Soon he was involved in a great disaster and paid the price for his wicked persistence. Almost 6,000 Romans were justly slain in this unjust war, the remainder had their camp taken from them and even lost their own weapons, but escaped. **14.** This disaster suffered under Lepidus's command was no less disgraceful than that suffered under Mancinus.[58]

So let them now say that these were happy times for them, and I am not speaking of the Spaniards who had been routed and put to flight[59] so many times in battle, but, indeed, of the Romans who were so ground down by unending disasters and defeated so very many times. **15.** In order not to be reproachful, I shall not go over how many of their praetors, commanders, consuls, legions, and armies were lost, but merely return again to one point:

55 Orosius takes a rather more forgiving attitude towards Mancinus here in order to make his point, than he did at 5.4.19.

56 D. Junius Brutus celebrated his triumph for this victory in 136 or 135 BC and was awarded the *cognomen* 'Callaicus' for his campaigns. Jerome, *Chronicle, A Abr.* 1875 (= 140 BC), says that Brutus subdued Spain 'as far as the Ocean'. It is odd, given Orosius came from this area, that he does not include this comment in his account.

57 A Celtiberian tribe centred round Burgos and Valladolid.

58 M. Aemilius Lepidus Porcina, consul in 137 BC, and proconsul in 136 BC, when he conducted this campaign on his own initiative. He was subsequently recalled and fined. The sentiment that his disaster was as great as that suffered by Mincinus is derived from Livy, 56.

59 Reading *fugati* with Arnaud-Lindet. The majority reading, followed by Zangemeister, *fatigati*, 'exhausted' is also possible. However, the two near synonyms, *pulsati* and *fugati* parallel those used of the Romans which follow, *subacti* and *superati*, and this reading seems more consonant with Orosius's style.

namely that the Roman soldier was so gripped by unreasoning fear that he was not able to stand his ground or steel his soul to make even an offer of battle, and soon he fled on simply seeing a Spaniard, if he seemed hostile, thinking himself defeated almost before the enemy was seen.

16. From this it is clear that both sides thought these times wretched: the Spanish because, although they were able to conquer, they had, against their will, to abandon their pleasant life of leisure and endure wars that came from abroad; the Romans because the more shamelessly they imposed themselves on the peace of others, the more shamefully they were defeated.

6

1. In the consulate of Servius Fulvius Flaccus and Quintus Calpurnius Piso,[60] a slave woman bore a son at Rome with four feet, four hands, four eyes, as many ears, and two sets of male members.

2. In Sicily Mount Etna spewed out and poured forth vast amounts of lava which flowed headlong like a torrent over the nearby lowlands, burning them up with its flames. More distant regions too were scorched by hot cinders that flew far and wide in a cloud of thick smoke. This sort of horror, which is native to Sicily, normally does not portend troubles, but rather brings them.

In the fields of Bononia wheat grew on trees.[61]

3. A slave rebellion then arose in Sicily. The numbers of slaves involved, who were drawn up like an army in great force, made it so serious and bitter that, quite apart from the Roman praetors who were utterly routed, it terrified the consuls. **4.** For 70,000 slaves were said to be in the army of the conspirators, except in the town of Messana, which kept its slaves, who were liberally treated, at peace.[62]

5. Sicily found herself in an even more wretched state because of this

---

60 Consuls in 619 *AUC*/135 BC.

61 The eruption of Etna and the tree-wheat at Bononia, the modern Bologna, are found in Julius Obsequens, 26. Obsequens also mentions a prodigious birth, but lists the deformity as a boy lacking an anus. Orosius is careful to give a naturalistic explanation for what the eruption presages. He has taken the prodigy of the child with too many organs from Obsequens' list of prodigies for the previous year (618 *AUC*/136 BC). Obsequens connects this with Lepidus's defeat by the Vaccaei. Oddly, Pliny says the only instance of 'tree-wheat' he knows of occurred in 202 BC; see Pliny, *Natural History*, 18.46.166, and Varro, *On Country Matters* (*De Re Rustica*), 1.9.4.

62 See Livy, *Per.* 56. The rebellion was suppressed by G. Fulvius Flaccus, consul in 134 BC.

fact too: namely that while being an island, she never had laws which fitted this state, falling now into the power of tyrants and then into that of slaves. The formers' evil rule produced the slaves, while the latter with perverse presumption reversed who was slave and who was free.[63] This was made all the worse as, since she is surrounded by sea on all sides, she cannot easily drive out troubles grown from within. **6.** She nursed a viper's brood for her own downfall, fed by her own lust, and destined to triumph through her own death.[64] The trouble caused by a slave rebellion is proportionately more violent as it is rarer than other disturbances, for a crowd of freemen are moved by ideas of helping their country, but one of slaves with the notion of destroying it.

7

1. 620 years after the foundation of the City, when the peace made at Numantia had loaded the Romans' brows with almost more shame than the one once struck at the Caudine Forks,[65] Scipio Africanus was made consul by a unanimous vote of the tribes and sent with an army to attack Numantia.[66] **2.** Numantia lies in Hither Spain, not far from the Vaccaei and Cantabrians on the edge of Gallaecia in the borderlands of the Celtiberians.[67] **3.** This town had not only resisted 40,000 Roman troops with only 4,000 of her own for fourteen years, but had even defeated and forced a shameful treaty on them.[68] **4.** When Scipio Africanus arrived in Spain, he did not immediately march on his enemy with the aim of trapping them off their guard. For

63 See 2.14.1–6.

64 The image of the snake's suicidal generation, originally found in Herodotus, 3.109, is taken from Pliny, *Natural History,* 10.62.169–70. It became a popular image in early Christian writing, being found in Clement of Alexandria, *Miscellany (Stromata)*, 4.16; Prudentius, *On the Genesis of Sin (Hamartigenia)*, 581–636; Ambrose, *On Tobit (De Tobia)*, 12.41; Basil of Caesarea, 3rd *Homily on Psalm 14 (Homilia 3 in Psalm 14)*; and John Chrysostom, *Homily on Matthew (Homilia in Matteum)*, 2.2.

65 This sentiment is found in Florus, 1.33.7. Orosius's account of Numantia is heavily informed by Florus's version of events.

66 Orosius's date is correct. The Scipio Africanus here is the adopted son of the victor of Zama and more commonly known as Scipio Aemilianus. He was elected consul in 134 BC.

67 The late Roman province located in NW Spain, see Torres Rodríguez (1949 and 1953). The ancient Numantia is found by the village of Garray, not far from the modern Soria. After its destruction the town was rebuilt, but appears to have been abandoned in the mid-fourth century AD.

68 This *datum* is found in Livy, *Per.* 54, and Florus, 1.34.2.

he knew that this race never allowed their body or spirit to relax to the degree that they would not prove, even in their everyday way of living, to be stronger in war than even carefully-trained opponents. Scipio therefore exercised his troops in their camp for a period of time as if they were attending a gymnasium. **5.** Although he spent part of the summer and all the winter in this way, and did not offer battle even once, his hard work brought him little by way of reward.

6. For, when the moment of battle came, the Roman army was overwhelmed by the Numantines' charge and turned in flight. Finally, angered by the consul, who flung himself into their midst, rebuking and threatening them, and holding them back with his hands, they turned on the enemy again and forced their foe, who had put them to flight, to flee.[69] It is difficult to believe the account – the Romans put the Numantines to flight and saw this while they themselves fled. **7.** For this reason although Scipio was delighted and rejoiced in his victory, which had exceeded his expectations, he nevertheless admitted that he dared not continue the battle further against them.

8. So he decided that he should take advantage of his unexpected success, besieged the town, and even surrounded it with a ditch 10 feet in width and 20 feet deep.[70] **9.** He then fortified the rampart he had built out of stakes with a large number of towers, so that wherever the enemy should attack it when they sallied forth, he would fight not as the besieger against the besieged, but rather as the besieged against the besieger.

10. Numantia is set on a hill not far from the river Duero, and surrounded by a wall three miles in circumference, although there are some who say that it occupies a small area and has no walls.[71] **11.** Because of this discrepancy, it is likely that the Numantines enclosed this larger area to feed and guard their herds and even to till the land when troubled by war, while they themselves occupied only a small, naturally fortified, citadel. If they had acted otherwise, such a large city would not have given protection to such a small group of men, but would rather have endangered them.

12. After a long siege, the Numantines were decimated by hunger and offered to surrender if they were given fair terms, often even asking for the chance of a fair fight so that they could die like men. **13.** Finally,

69 Florus's account, 1.34.11, of the battle dwells on the effects of Scipio's discipline and makes no mention of the Romans' wavering.

70 For Scipio's siegeworks, see Schulten (1945), Campbell (2006) 122–28, and Dobson (2008).

71 A reference to Florus, 1.34.2.

they all made a sudden sally out of two gates, having drunk beforehand a deep draught not of wine, as that country does not bear vines, but a potion manufactured from wheat which they call 'hot-stuff' because it is made by being heated.[72] **14.** The wet grain is made to germinate by heating it. It is then dried, ground into flour, and mixed with a sweet juice. As it ferments, it becomes bitter and produces the heat that goes with drunkenness. Fired up by this potion after their long hunger, they came out to battle.

15. The struggle was long, fierce, and dangerous for the Romans who, had they not been fighting under Scipio, would have again shown that they were fighting against the Numantines by fleeing from them.[73] When their bravest men had fallen, the Numantines withdrew from the battle, but returned to their town in good order, not in flight. They refused to accept the bodies of the dead that were brought to them for burial.[74]

16. As they were all doomed to die, in a last frenzy of desperation they barred the gates of their city and set fire to it while they were still inside, all alike perishing by poison, sword, or fire.[75]

17. The Romans gained nothing from defeating these men, save their own security. Indeed, when Numantia fell, they considered that the Numantines had escaped rather than that they had defeated them. **18.** The victor's chain held not one Numantine captive and Rome saw no reason for which she could grant a triumph. These poor folk had no gold or silver that would have been able to survive the fire, and the fire had destroyed their arms and clothing.[76]

8

1. While these things were going on at Numantia, the sedition of the Gracchi was taking place at Rome. After destroying Numantia, Scipio made peace with the rest of the Spanish tribes. He asked Thyresus, a Celtic chieftain, how

---

72 A form of beer, see Pliny, *Natural History*, 22.82.164. Orosius derives the name of this drink, *caelia*, from the verb *calefacere*, to heat. Florus only mentions the drink in passing. Orosius's details may be born of personal experience, but his comments on the lack of wine in Spain are false and perhaps intended to emphasise the Numantines' lack of *luxuria*.

73 This detail is mentioned neither by Livy nor Florus.

74 These details of the battle and its aftermath are not mentioned by either Livy or Florus.

75 See Livy, *Per.* 59.

76 These sentiments on Rome's empty victory are drawn from Florus, 1.34.17. Florus says that the triumph was only over the town's name. Contrary to Orosius's implications, a triumph was indeed held by Scipio in 132 BC; see Livy, *Per.* 59. For a discussion of Numantia and its impact on Spanish historiography, see Jimeno Martínez and De La Torre Echávarri (2005).

Numantia had at first avoided defeat for so long and how then it had been overthrown. Thyresus replied, 'Concord made it invincible, discord was its downfall.'[77] **2.** The Romans took this as advice for, and about, themselves, as they had just been told that the whole City was seething with discord.

After Carthage and Numantia were destroyed, beneficial co-operation to look to the future died at Rome and there arose instead shameful political in-fighting born of personal ambition.[78]

3. Gracchus, a tribune of the plebs, was furious at the nobility because he had been listed as one of the architects of the Numantine treaty.[79] He therefore decided that land which had been held up to that time in private hands should be divided up among the people.[80] He deprived Octavius, a tribune of the plebs who opposed him, of his power and appointed Minucius as his successor.[81] These were the reasons that anger took hold of the Senate and arrogance, the people. **4.** By chance, it happened that Attalus,[82] Eumenes' son, died at this moment and had ordered in his will that the Roman people succeed as heir to his Asian empire.[83] Gracchus, seeking to buy public popularity, passed a law that Attalus's money be distributed to the public.[84] Nasica opposed this law and Pompey promised that he would indict Gracchus as soon as he left his magistracy.[85]

---

77 This anecdote is only found in Orosius. It is difficult to see what relationship it bears to his account of Numantia where disunity among the Numantines does not feature at all.

78 cf. Florus 1.34.19 where Numantia is seen as the turning point in the decline of Roman public morality. For a modern discussion of the impact of the Numantine War on Roman politics, see Astin (1967) 155–60.

79 Tiberius was elected tribune in 133 BC. The treaty concerned is that made by Mancinus, see Florus, 2.2.2–3. Florus, however, is prepared to concede that Tiberius may have acted for the common good, something Orosius will not countenance. This negative attitude, which differs markedly from the more sympathetic attitude of Augustine (see *City of God*, 3.24), is drawn from Livy, 58.

80 In fact the land concerned was public land that had been encroached on by wealthy landowners; however, Orosius may not have known this.

81 Orosius seems to have confused this tribune, named Mucius by Plutarch, *Tiberius Gracchus*, 13.2, and Q. Mummius by Appian, *Civil Wars*, 54, with the tribune who succeeded Tiberius's brother, Gaius, as tribune in 121 BC.

82 Attalus III Philometor, king of Pergamum 139–133 BC.

83 Attalus's bequest is noted by Jerome, *Chronicle, A Abr.* 1887 (= incorrectly, 128 BC). In contrast to Orosius's extended account, Jerome makes no mention of the Gracchi at any point in his *Chronicle*.

84 In fact, Gracchus wanted the money to finance his commission to redistribute the confiscated land. This had been starved of funds by the vengeful Senate.

85 P. Cornelius Scipio Nasica, consul in 138 BC and Pontifex Maximus. The identity of this Pompey is not clear, but is likely to be Q. Pompey, consul in 141 BC.

9

1. When Gracchus strove to remain tribune of the plebs for the following year[86] and kindled sedition among the people on the day of the elections, the nobility were enflamed by Nasica and, using broken bench ends as their weapons, put the plebs to flight. **2.** Gracchus had his cloak ripped off and was knocked over by a bench while fleeing along the steps which lie above the arch of Calpurnius. He was killed by another blow of a club to his head as he tried to get up again. **3.** 200 others were killed in this seditious uprising. Their bodies were thrown into the Tiber, which is where the unburied corpse of Gracchus rotted away.[87]

4. Meanwhile, the slave war that had arisen in Sicily went on to infect many other provinces far and wide.[88] 450 slaves were crucified at Minturnae[89] and up to 4,000 slaves were crushed by Quintus Metellus and Gnaeus Servilius Caepio at Sinuessa.[90] **5.** A slave rebellion in the mines at Athens was also put down by the praetor Heraclitus. On Delos too, the slaves attempted to rise again, but their actions were anticipated and crushed by the citizenry. It was from that first flare-up of trouble on Sicily that sparks, as it were, shot out and kindled these divers fires. **6.** In Sicily the consul Piso,[91] who succeeded the consul Fulvius, stormed the town of Mamertium[92] where he killed 8,000 runaways. Those whom he was then able to capture, he crucified. **7.** He was succeeded by the consul Rutilius who took Tauromenium[93] and Henna,[94] the runaways' strongest refuges, by force.[95] More than 20,000 slaves are said to have been slaughtered at that time.[96] **8.** Certainly such a war as this had tragic, complex causes. Their masters would have perished had they not marched on the insolent slaves with the sword, but as regards the terrible

86 This was not technically illegal, but was a flagrant breach of accepted constitutional practice.

87 See Livy, *Per.* 58.

88 See Livy, *Per.* 58, 59.

89 The modern Trajetto.

90 The modern Mondragone.

91 L. Calpurnius Piso, consul in 621 *AUC*/133 BC.

92 The modern Messana.

93 The modern Taormina.

94 The modern Castro Giovanni in central Sicily. Florus, 2.7.8 attributes this victory to Perperna.

95 Orosius has garbled the consul's name which was in fact Rupilius; see Livy, *Per.* 59.

96 The uprising in Sicily is noted by Jerome, *Chronicle, A Abr.* 1890 (= 125 BC), who comments that the besieged slaves were forced to indulge in cannibalism. This detail has been suppressed by Orosius.

losses in the fighting and the even worse prizes from victory, the victors lost as much as numbers of the vanquished that perished.[97]

10

1. 622 years after the foundation of the City,[98] the consul and high priest, Publius Licinius Crassus, was despatched with a superbly equipped army against Attalus's brother, Aristonicus, who had invaded Asia, which had been left in his brother's will to Rome.[99] **2.** Crassus was supported by a group of powerful kings, namely Nicomedes of Bithynia, Mithridates of Pontus and Armenia, Ariarathes of Cappadocia, and Pylaemenes of Paphlagonia, and was reinforced by a great number of their troops.[100] Nevertheless, when battle was joined, he was defeated.[101] **3.** When, after great bloodshed, his army turned to flee, Crassus was himself surrounded by the enemy and nearly captured. He then poked the crop, which he used on his horse, into the eye of a Thracian, and the barbarian, blazing with pain and anger, ran Crassus through the side with his sword. In this way having chosen the manner of his death, he avoided both disgrace and slavery.[102]

4. The consul Perpenna,[103] who had succeeded Crassus, flew with all haste to Asia on hearing of Crassus's death and the disaster suffered by the Roman army. He attacked Aristonicus by surprise, while he was feasting to celebrate his recent victory and away from all his troops, putting him to flight. **5.** He besieged the city of Stratonice[104] to which Aristonicus had fled, and starved him into surrender. The consul Perpenna became ill and died at Pergamum, while Aristonicus was strangled in gaol at Rome by order of the Senate.

6. In the same year, the miserable life of Ptolemy, the king of Alexan-

97 In other words the victors destroyed their own property. Here again, Orosius shows that he has no qualms about the institution of slavery *per se*.

98 Orosius is one year out; these events happened in 623 *AUC*/131 BC.

99 See Livy, *Per.* 59. Aristonicus was Attalus's half-brother and claimed the throne on his death. His support was drawn mainly from the rural non-Greek-speaking population of Pergamum.

100 Nicomedes II of Bithynia (149–128 BC), Mithridates V Eupator of Pontus (150–120 BC), Ariarathes V of Cappadocia (163–130 BC), Pylaemenes II of Paphlagonia (*fl.* c.130 BC).

101 At Levke near Foca in Turkey.

102 See Florus, 1.35.5, for this story, which perhaps derives ultimately from Livy, 59. Florus incorrectly gives Crassus's rank as that of a praetor. Perhaps the reader is meant to contrast Crassus's behaviour here with that of the Athenian general Nicias in Sicily; see 2.15.22.

103 M. Perperna, consul in 130 BC. Orosius has slightly garbled his name. For Perperna's campaigns, see Livy, *Per.* 59.

104 Normally Stratonicea, the modern Eskihisar in Turkey.

dria, came to a still more miserable end. He had committed incest with, and then married, his own sister. Finally, he divorced her – an act more disgraceful than his marriage of her had been.[105] **7.** He then married his step-daughter, that is to say the child of his sister and wife, and killed both his own son whom he had sired by his sister and his brother's son as well. This litany of incest and parricide made him hated by the Alexandrines and he was expelled from his kingdom.[106]

8. At the same time, Antiochus, not being content with Babylon, Ecbatana, and all the empire of the Medes, attacked Phraates, the king of the Parthians, and was defeated. Although he appears to have had 100,000 troops in his army, he dragged along with him an additional 200,000 camp-followers and servants among whom were prostitutes and actors. Because of this, he was easily defeated along with all his army by the might of the Parthians and lost his life.[107]

9. In the consulate of Gaius Sempronius Tuditanus and Marcus Acilius,[108] Publius Scipio Africanus, who had told a public meeting that he was in danger of his life because he had discovered that he would be accused in court by wicked, ungrateful men, while working for his country, was discovered dead in his bedroom the following morning. It is not thoughtlessly that I would number this among the greatest of the Romans' misfortunes, especially since Scipio's reputation for dynamism and personal modesty was so strong in the City that it was easily believed that while he lived there could not be a civil war nor one with Rome's allies.[109] **10.** Men say that he

105 Presumably because of the state this left his sister in, or perhaps because of his conse-quent aggravated murder of his son whose head, hands, and feet Ptolemy sent to his former wife; see Livy, *Per.* 59.

106 Ptolemy VIII Euergetes, but more popularly Physcon, 'pot-belly', had a terrible reputa-tion in antiquity; see Green (1990) 538. He fled from Egypt in 132/1 BC. Incestuous marriage was not an uncommon Pharoanic practice and was adopted by the Ptolemies. Ptolemy VIII's sister, Cleopatra II, whom he married on coming to the throne in 145 BC had been his prede-cessor's, Ptolemy VI, wife. He divorced her to marry his niece, who became Cleopatra III, in 142 BC. His brother's son whom he murdered was Ptolemy VII Neophilopator. Orosius omits to mention that Ptolemy returned to Egypt in 130 BC, basing his rule at Memphis and recap-turing Alexandria in 126/5 BC. Ptolemy died on 26 June 116 BC.

107 Antiochus VII Euergetes Sidetes (138–129 BC). His intended victim was Phraates II (c.139–129 BC). Orosius, eager to moralise here, suppresses the fact that initially Antiochus had great success in his campaign. Antiochus's campaign is recorded by Justin, 38.10.8–10.

108 Consuls in 625 *AUC*/129 BC. Orosius has garbled Manlius Aquillius's name to produce Marcus Acilius.

109 Augustine also expresses shock at Rome's ingratitude towards Scipio, but not at such great length (*City of God*, 3.21). For a modern assessment of Scipio, see Scullard (1970) 210–43.

was treacherously killed by his wife, Sempronia, who was the sister of the Gracchi, so that this criminal, as I believe, family, born for the destruction of their own country, should, amid the godless sedition of its menfolk, become all the more detestable through the criminal deeds of its women.[110]

11. In the consulate of Marcus Aemilius and Lucius Orestes,[111] Etna was struck by a great tremor and poured forth balls of fire. On another day, the island of Lipara and the sea around it seethed with so much heat that rocks were burnt up and dissolved, ships' planks were scorched as their wax caulking melted, and roasted, dead fish floated on the surface. Even men, apart from those able to flee far from the scene, were suffocated, their vitals seared by the hot air they breathed in and out.[112]

11

1. In the consulate of Marcus Plautius Hypsaeus and Marcus Fulvius Flaccus,[113] a horrible and unaccustomed disaster befell Africa when she had hardly recovered from the ravages of war. **2.** Great swarms of locusts gathered all over Africa, not only destroying any hope of a crop, but also eating every sort of grass, including part of their roots, and the leaves of tress along with their younger branches. They even gnawed through bitter bark and dry wood. Then, suddenly, they were swept up into bunches by the wind, and, after being carried through the air for a long time, were drowned in the African Sea. **3.** After the currents had driven great heaps of them onto the shore far and wide along the coast by the action of the waves, these decaying, putrid masses exuded a stench so foul that it could not be imagined. From it so great a plague descended on all of animal-kind alike that everywhere the rotting corpses of birds, domesticated, and wild animals which had been killed by the disease as it was borne through the air, increased the disease's potency. **4.** My whole body trembles as I record how many men perished. Indeed, in Numidia, where at that time Micipsa was king,[114] 800,000 men are said to have perished, along with some 200,000

110 Livy, *Per.* 59, merely records the suspicion of murder and says no trial was held. Orosius has embroidered Livy's original account to fit his own hostile view of Sempronia.

111 Consuls in 628 *AUC*/126 BC.

112 These portents are taken from Julius Obsequens, 29. Orosius has suppressed Obsequens' comment that the eruption prophesised coming civil war. He has also diminished the impact of the dead fish and increased that of the volcano's fumes. Augustine, *City of God*, 3.31, mentions these events in passing.

113 Consuls in 629 *AUC*/125 BC.

114 Micipsa reigned from 148–118 BC.

who lived on the coast, especially in the areas around Carthage and Utica. In the city of Utica itself, 30,000 soldiers who had been stationed there to protect all Africa were killed and blotted out. **5.** This disaster befell them with such sudden violence that it is said that at Utica more than 1,500 corpses of the young were taken out for burial through a single gate in a single day.

6. Notwithstanding this, I want to state that through the grace and peace of Omnipotent God – about Whose mercy and in Whose faith I am writing these things – although in our times too swarms of locusts have appeared from time to time in divers places, usually causing harm, though normally at a tolerable level, there has never occurred in Christian times such a violent attack of inescapable ills as this ruin brought by the locusts, which was unbearable while they were alive and caused even more harm when they were dead. For during the long period when the locusts were alive, everything was on the point of death, but after the locusts had died, and everything began to die all the more, they were forced to wish that the locusts had not died.[115]

12

1. 627 years from the Foundation of the City, in the consulate of Lucius Caecilius Metellus and Quintus Titius Flaminius,[116] Carthage was ordered to be rebuilt in Africa twenty-two years after her destruction. She was rebuilt and populated by Roman families sent there to work her land.[117] Before this happened, a great prodigy occurred. **2.** For the surveyors sent out to mark out the Carthaginians' land found that the poles they had fixed in the ground to mark out its boundaries had been torn up and bitten through by wolves in the night. After this, there was some hesitation as to whether refounding Carthage would help Rome be at peace.

3. In the same year, Gaius Gracchus, the brother of the Gracchus who had already been killed while raising sedition, was made tribune of the plebs during a riot and proved a disaster for the state.[118] **4.** For by his bribes and

115 The account of the locusts is drawn from Augustine, *City of God*, 3.31. It is also found in Julius Obsequens, 30, and Livy, *Per.* 60.

116 Orosius's date is incorrect; these two were consuls in 631 *AUC*/123 BC. The names of the consuls have also been garbled and should read Quintus Caecilius Metellus and Titus Quinctius Flaminius.

117 See Eutropius, 4.21, and Livy, *Per.* 60.

118 *Pernicies* used here of Gracchus is the same word used of the plague of locusts in the preceding chapter, 5.11.6. Orosius's hostile treatment of Gaius Gracchus shows heavy influence from Livy, see *Per.* 60.

excessive promises he often roused the people to violent sedition, princi-
pally in support of the agrarian law over which his brother had been killed.
Finally he left the tribunate and was succeeded by Minucius.[119]

5. When as tribune, Minucius tore up most of the statutes of his predecessor, Gracchus, and repealed his laws, Gracchus, accompanied by Fulvius
Flaccus[120] and surrounded by a great crowd, went up to the Capitol where
a public meeting was being held. There an enormous riot broke out and
Gracchus's supporters killed a herald giving, as it were, the signal for battle.
6. Flaccus, flanked by his two armed sons and accompanied by Gracchus
who, although wearing a toga, was hiding a short sword in his left sleeve,
vainly sent out a herald to call on the slaves to fight for their freedom and
occupied the temple of Diana as his stronghold. **7.** He was attacked by
the former consul Decimus Brutus who launched an attack with a great
column of men from Publician Hill.[121] Flaccus held his ground for a long
time, fighting tenaciously. Gracchus retreated to the temple of Minerva and
wanted to fall on his sword, but was stopped by Laetorius. For a long time
the battle hung in the balance, but in the end the close-packed crowd was
put to flight by a group of archers sent by Opimius.[122] **8.** The two Flacci,
father and son, leapt down from the temple of Luna into a private house
and barricaded its doors. But the wattle walls were torn apart and they were
then run through. While his supporters continued to fight and die for him,
Gracchus made his way with some difficulty to the Sublician bridge, where,
not wishing to be taken alive, he had one of his slaves behead him.[123]

9. Gracchus's severed head was brought to the consul, while his body
was taken to his mother, Cornelia, in the town of Misenum. As I have
already said, this Cornelia, the daughter of the elder Scipio Africanus,
had withdrawn to Misenum after the death of her elder son.[124] Gracchus's
possessions were seized by the state, the young Flaccus was done to death in

119 Gracchus was elected as tribune for 123 and 122 BC, a striking breach of normal
practice.

120 The former consul of 125 BC. By letting slip this detail, Orosius unwittingly destroys
the image he wished to create of Gracchus as a rabble-rouser and reveals that he had support
from some senior members of the Roman establishment.

121 Consul in 138 BC.

122 One of the consuls of the day, 121 BC.

123 The location is significant, as on the Ides of May the *pontifices* threw 30 straw figures
called *argei* into the Tiber from this bridge for the well-being of Rome. Orosius has suppressed
any resonance of this that may have been in his sources. See Ovid, *Fasti*, 5.621, and Varro, *On
the Latin Language* (*De Lingua Latina*), 7.44.

124 Orosius has made no mention of this previously.

prison, while 250 members of Gracchus's cabal are said to have been killed on the Aventine Hill. **10.** The consul Opimius proved to be as cruel in the subsequent inquiry as he had been brave in the fighting, for he punished by execution over 3,000 men, the majority of whom were innocent and had not even been allowed to state their case.[125]

13

1. During the same period, Metellus passed through and conquered the Balearic islands, and, by slaughtering the majority of the inhabitants, put an end to their infestation by pirates which had grown up at this time.[126]

2. The proconsul Gnaeus Domitius defeated the Allobrogian Gauls[127] near the town of Vindalium[128] in a costly battle: the enemies' horses and the enemy themselves scattered in terror on seeing elephants for the first time. 20,000 Allobroges are said to have been killed in this battle and 3,000 were captured.[129]

3. At this same time, there was a greater than usual eruption of Etna. Torrents of fire poured out and flowed far and wide round about, causing such damage to the city of Catina and its territory that house roofs, burnt through and weighed down with hot ash, collapsed. To alleviate this catastrophe, the Senate decreed that Catina have a ten years' exemption from taxes.[130]

14

1. 628 years after the foundation of the City, the consul Fabius attacked Bituitus,[131] the king of the Arverni, a Gallic tribe. Bituitus had prepared for war, gathering together an enormous force of men, so that when Fabius attacked him with his small army, Bituitus boasted that he would hardly

125 Orosius's hostile account of Gaius Gracchus probably derives from Livy, 60–61. It is striking in that Fulvius Flaccus is seemingly given a greater role than in his sources. For Nasica's action after Gracchus's death, see Augustine, *City of God*, 3.24.

126 Metellus conquered the Balearics in 123–122 BC, celebrating a triumph in 121 BC; see Livy, *Per.* 60.

127 See Livy, *Per.* 61. The Allobroges lived in the lands between the Rhône and Isère.

128 Port de la Traille at the confluence of the Rhône and Sorgue.

129 Gn. Domitius Ahenobarbus, consul in 122, held proconsular command in Gaul in 121 BC.

130 Drawn from Augustine, *City of God*, 3.31, where the tax remission is for only one year. The eruption is also mentioned by Julius Obsequens, 32. Catina is the modern Catania.

131 Normally spelt Betultus.

be able to feed the dogs which he had in his column on so few Romans. **2.** When he realised that one bridge would not be sufficient to take his troops over the Rhône, he built another made of small boats lying side by side and lashed together with chains, laying and nailing down planks above them. **3.** Battle was joined and the fight was long and bitter; finally the Gauls were defeated and put to flight. Because each of them was thinking of his own safety, their columns massed together with no thought at all, so that their uncontrolled crossing broke the chains that held the bridge together and they soon fell down among the boats. There are said to have been 180,000 troops in Bituitus's army, of whom 150,000 were killed or drowned.[132]

5. The consul Quintus Marcius attacked the race of Gauls who live at the foot of the Alps. After seeing that they had been surrounded by the Romans and were too weak to fight them, they killed their women and children and flung themselves into the flames.[133] **6.** Those who had been captured by the Romans before they had a chance of taking their lives later killed themselves by stabbing or hanging themselves, or refusing to eat. Not one of them, not even a small child, was found who would endure slavery from a love of life.[134]

15

1. 635 years after the foundation of the City, in the consulate of Publius Scipio Nasica and Lucius Calpurnius Bestia,[135] the Senate, with the agreement of the Roman people, declared war on Jugurtha, the king of the Numidians.

2. I shall discuss Jugurtha only briefly for the sake of preserving the order of my work and to note his presence, since both his fickle, insupportable character and his deeds, which were carried out with a treachery that matched his vigour, are very well known to us all through the excellent, enlightening works of previous writers.[136]

3. Now Jugurtha, the adopted son of King Micipsa of Numidia, was

---

132 Orosius's dating is five years out; Q. Fabius Maximus was consul in 633 *AUC*/121 BC. See Livy, *Per.* 61, and Florus, 1.37, neither of whom mentions the incident of the bridge.

133 Of their families' funeral pyres.

134 Q. Marcius Rex, consul in 118 BC. Orosius's account is drawn from Livy, *Per.* 61. The tribe were the Styni who lived in Liguria.

135 Orosius's date is eight years out. Scipio and Calpurnius were the consuls of 643 *AUC*/111 BC.

136 A reference to Livy and, above all, Sallust.

made one of his heirs along with Micipsa's natural sons. First, he dealt with his co-heirs, that is he killed Hiempsal, and after defeating Adherbal in battle, drove him from Africa. **4.** Then, he bribed Calpurnius, the consul who had been sent to wage war on him and obtained a peace treaty on scandalous terms. **5.** Moreover, when he came to Rome, he immersed himself in sedition and conspiracies, bribing or attempting to bribe everyone. As he left the city, he well characterised it with his infamous aphorism: 'O City for sale and doomed to die – if only you can find a buyer.'[137]

6. In the following year, he defeated Aulus Postumius, the brother of the consul Postumius[138] who had put him in command of an army of 40,000 troops, near the city of Calama,[139] as he lusted for the royal treasure which lay hidden there. On his defeat, Jugurtha imposed a shameful treaty on him, and went on to annex almost all of Africa as it defected from Rome to his kingdom. **7.** Afterwards, however, Jugurtha was contained by the consul Metellus, who was a model of integrity and military discipline.[140] He was defeated twice and saw his homeland Numidia laid waste before his own eyes, being powerless to defend it. Forced to surrender because of this, he handed over 300 hostages, promised to supply grain and other provisions, and returned over 3,000 deserters. **8.** Then when he showed himself untrustworthy in peace as he did not stop his criminal raids, he was crushed by the cunning of the consul Gaius Marius, which was hardly less than that with which he himself was endowed, and his Roman forces.[141] Marius showed this above all when he cleverly surrounded and captured the town of Capsa, which, they say, was founded by the Phoenician Hercules,[142] and was, at that time, packed full of the king's treasure.[143]

9. After this, Jugurtha, despairing of his circumstances and resources, made an alliance with Bocchus, king of the Moors. Greatly strengthened by Bocchus's cavalry, he harried Marius's army with continual raiding. **10.** He

137 Taken from Sallust, *The War against Jugurtha*, 35.20; see also Livy, *Per.* 64.

138 Sp. Postumius Albinus, consul in 664 *AUC*/110 BC. Orosius has continued his chronological error from the beginning of the chapter.

139 The modern Guelma in Algeria. Sallust, *The War against Jugurtha*, 37.3, calls the town Suthul.

140 Q. Caecilius Metellus, consul in 109 BC and proconsul in 108–107 BC. He was awarded the *cognomen* 'Numidicus' for his actions.

141 Marius had previously fought Jugurtha under Metellus. After an acrimonious break with Metellus, not mentioned by Orosius, he was elected consul for 107 BC and returned to Africa as commander-in-chief of Rome's forces.

142 i.e. the Punic god, Melqart. Capsa is the modern Gafsa in Tunisia.

143 See Florus, 1.36.14.

finally faced the Romans in battle with a force of 60,000 cavalry, as they prepared to storm the ancient city of Cirta which was the seat of Masinissa's throne.[144]

11. Never had Roman troops fought in a more confused or terrible battle. So much dust was raised by the circling, whinnying horses as they whirled round and attacked that it covered the sky, turning day into night. Such a great cloud of javelins rained down that no part of the body was safe from their blows, for because of the darkness, they could not see ahead and, as they were all crushed together, they were unable to move to avoid them. **12.** It would have been no effort at all for the Numidian and Moorish cavalry to tear apart their foe, who lay ideally placed, with aimed volleys of javelins, but they preferred to throw their spears without being sure of their target, for they were sure that wounds would surely follow. In this way, the Roman infantry were forced together into one dense mass. Night gave them a respite from their great peril. **13.** On the following day, the battle took the same form and brought the same dangers. Although they drew their swords, the troops could not charge into the enemy as they were driven off at long range by their javelins, nor could they flee, as the horsemen, who were quicker than them, had surrounded them on all sides.

14. The third day came and there was no help from anywhere, while everywhere death's terrible visage stared them in the face. Finally, by his bold desperation the consul Marius opened up a path of hope. Forming up all his men into a column, he broke out from his fortifications, entrusting himself to the plains and battle. **15.** The enemy poured round them again not only cutting the column's wings to pieces, but also, throwing their javelins from afar, bringing slaughter into its centre too. The heat of the sun, the unbearable thirst, and the nearness of death reduced the disordered Romans to the depths of despair. Then, suddenly, the Romans' famous support against Africans, storms and rain, was sent down from heaven, bringing them an unhoped-for salvation.[145] **16.** For this sudden rain gave refreshment and drink to the thirsty, sweating Romans, but it made the Numidians' javelin shafts, which they threw by hand without using any thongs, slippery and hence useless.[146] **17.** Moreover, their light and effective shields made

144 The modern Constantine in Algeria. The battle was fought in 106 BC.

145 cf. 4.17.5-11 and 7.15.9. Orosius deliberately uses a passive verb here to imply that the rain was a result of divine aid.

146 The standard way of throwing the javelin in antiquity was to use a thong wrapped round its shaft. This increased the leverage of the thrower and, by spinning the weapon, made it more accurate.

of stretched, hardened elephant hide became unusable and useless, as this material soaks up the rain like a sponge and so they suddenly became too heavy to manage, and, because they were unable to be carried around, no use for defence. And so, as their Moors had, against their expectations, been thrown into chaos and left helpless, Bocchus and Jugurtha fled.

18. After this, these same kings threw 90,000 armed men into one last battle. It is said that the Romans cut them down to the point of annihilation. The outcome made Bocchus despair of the war and seek peace. To buy this, he sent Jugurtha, whom he had captured by treachery, loaded in chains to Marius through the agency of his lieutenant, Sulla.[147] **19.** Jugurtha, along with his two sons, was driven before Marius's chariot in his triumph.[148] He was strangled in prison soon afterwards.

20. At this time, an obscene, tragic prodigy occurred. A Roman knight, Lucius Helvius, was returning with his wife and daughter to Apulia from Rome. He was caught in a storm and when he saw that his daughter was terrified, he abandoned his coaches and took to the horses so that they might reach the neighbouring houses more quickly, sitting his maiden daughter on a horse in the middle of his party. **21.** The girl was at once struck dead by a bolt of lightning. All her clothes were stripped from her, though none of them were torn, her girdle and the straps of her sandals were broken loose, and her necklace and rings scattered far and wide. Her body too remained untouched, though in an obscene posture, lying naked and with the tongue sticking out a short way. The horse on which she had been riding lay dead a good way off with its saddle, reins, and harness undone and scattered about.[149]

22. A little after this, another Roman knight, Lucius Veturius, polluted the Vestal Virgin Aemilia by secretly having sex with her. This same Aemilia offered and gave to the companions of her own seducer two other Vestal Virgins whom she had enticed into taking part in this pollution. Their

---

147 See Livy, *Per.* 66.

148 Marius celebrated his triumph in 104 BC.

149 Orosius gives no explicit reason for recording this portent. It is found in Julius Obsequens, 37, where it is dated to 114 BC and probably derives from Livy, 63. Obsequens gives the name of the knight as Publius (H)Elvius. The same account is found in Plutarch, *Roman Questions*, 83. Here the girl's name is given as Helvia. In both cases, the explanation given is that the portent revealed adultery between Vestal Virgins and knights and that subsequently three Vestals and several knights were executed precisely for this offence. Orosius records these executions in the following section, but suppresses the link between the two events in order not to concede the efficacy of omens concerning pagan religion.

actions were betrayed by a slave and they were all executed.[150]

23. At the same time as the Jugurthine War was taking place, the consul Lucius Cassius[151] pursued the Tigurini in Gaul as far as the Ocean, but was then surrounded and killed by them in an ambush.[152] **24.** Lucius Piso, Cassius's lieutenant, and a former consul, was also killed.[153] Cassius's other lieutenant, Gaius Publius, made a disgraceful treaty with the Tigurini, handing over hostages and half of all the army's baggage train.[154] He did this to stop the remnants of the army, which had fled to their camp, being wiped out. On his return to Rome, Publius was indicted by a tribune of the plebs, Caelius, on the grounds that he had given hostages to the Tigurini, and fled into exile.[155]

25. The proconsul Caepio captured a Gallic city named Tolosa[156] and took 100,000 pounds of gold and 110,000 pounds of silver from the temple of Apollo there. He sent this under guard to Marseilles, a town friendly to Rome, but some sources relate that he had those whom he had sent to guard and escort it secretly killed, and so, it is said, that by perpetrating this crime he stole the entire treasure. Because of these allegations, a major inquiry was later held at Rome.[157]

16[158]

1. 642 years after the foundation of the City, the consul Gaius Manlius and the proconsul Quintus Caepio were despatched against the Cimbri, Teutonae, Tigurini, and Ambronae: Gallic and German tribes who were at that time conspiring to bring Rome's rule to an end.[159] They divided their

---

150 According to Plutarch, *Roman Questions*, 83, the slave was owned by one of the Vestals' lovers, Vetutius Barrus. Plutarch also names the three Vestals: Aemilia, Licinia, and Marcia.

151 Consul in 107 BC.

152 The Tigurini were a branch of the Helvetii tribe. Orosius exaggerates slightly as Caepio defeated this tribe in the land of the Nitiobroges, who were centred on Agen in Aquitaine, some way inland from the coast. See Livy, *Per.* 65.

153 Consul in 112 BC.

154 See Livy, *Per.* 65.

155 Orosius has garbled the name of G. Popillius Laenas into Gaius Publius. The tribune involved was G. Coelius Caldus.

156 The modern Toulouse.

157 Caepio was stripped of his command in 105 BC after his defeat at Orange (see 5.16.2–3 below) and was indicted by the tribune G. Norbanus in 103 BC, leading to his conviction and exile.

158 Orosius has drawn the bulk of this chapter from Livy, 67–68.

159 Orosius's date is seven years awry; the campaign took place in 649 *AUC*/105 BC. He

command, making the river Rhône the division between them. **2.** Then, while they were quarrelling against one another with great envy and bitterness, they were defeated, bringing both great disgrace and danger to Rome. In this battle Marcus Aemilius, a former consul,[160] was captured and killed, and two of the consul's sons were also slain. **3.** Antias writes that 80,000 Romans and their allies were slaughtered in this storm of battle, along with 40,000 camp-followers and bearers.[161] **4.** And so out of this entire army, they say that merely ten men survived and that they were spared in order to tell the grim news to their fellow-countrymen and so worsen their grief.[162] **5.** After capturing the two Roman camps and a vast amount of booty, the enemy destroyed everything that they had laid their hands on in some new, unexpected form of curse. **6.** Clothing was ripped up and discarded, gold and silver thrown into the river, the men's armour was torn apart, the horses' harness scattered and the horses themselves drowned in the river, while the men had nooses tied round their necks and were hanged from trees. In this way the victor knew no booty nor the vanquished any mercy.[163] **7.** At Rome there was not only great grief, but also great fear that the Cimbri would straightaway cross over the Alps and devastate Italy.

8. At this time, Quintus Fabius Maximus[164] banished his adolescent son to his country estate and killed him there, using two slaves to carry out the act whom he immediately freed as a reward for their crime. He was indicted by Gnaeus Pompey[165] and found guilty.

9. Marius, now consul for the fourth time,[166] pitched his camp by the confluence of the rivers Isère and Rhône. The Teutones, Cimbri, Tigurini, and Ambrones, after attacking the camp continually for three days to see if they could *drive the Romans from the ramparts and flush them out onto the plains,*[167] then decided to march on Italy in three columns.

has also garbled the names of the two men involved who were Gn. Mallius Maximus and Q. Servilius Caepio. Their campaign took place in 649 *AUC*/105 BC.

160 Suffect, i.e. replacement, consul in 108 BC.

161 This information and the reference to Antias is taken from Livy; see *Per.* 67.

162 The Battle of Arausio (the modern Orange) fought on 6 October 105 BC. Orosius suppresses the commonly held view that the defeat was the result of Caepio's sacrilegious stripping of precious metals from the temple of Apollo in Toulouse; see 5.15.25 above.

163 For a discussion of this form of sacrifice, see Ellis Davidson (1964) 54–61.

164 See Valerius Maximus, 6.1.5. This is probably Q. Fabius Maximus Eburnus, the censor of 108 BC.

165 Gn. Pompeius Strabo, the father of Pompey the Great and quaestor in 104 BC.

166 652 *AUC*/102 BC.

167 A strong verbal reminiscence of Virgil, *Aeneid,* 9.68.

10. After the enemy had left, Marius moved camp and occupied a hill that dominated the plain and the river where the enemy had spread out. When his army ran out of drinking water and everyone began to complain to him, he replied that there was, in fact, water in front of them, but that it would have to be won by the sword. The camp-followers were the first to charge screaming into battle, followed by the army. Soon the ranks were drawn up, a battle was fought in good order, and the Romans were victorious. **11.** Three days later, both sides again drew up their battle-lines on the plain and they fought to mid-day without either side gaining any great advantage. However, after the sun grew hot, the Gauls' bodies began to give way like melting snow and the action, which dragged on until nightfall, became more of a massacre than a battle. **12.** 200,000 armed men are said to have been killed in this battle, 80,000 captured, and scarcely 3,000 to have escaped.[168] The enemy's leader, Teutobodus, was also slain. **13.** Their womenfolk, showing a firmness of spirit greater than it would have been had their men-folk been victorious, counselled the consul that if they were allowed serve the Vestal Virgins and the gods with their chastity inviolate, they would not take their own lives.[169] When they were refused, they battered their children to death on the rocks and took their own lives by the sword or by the noose.

This is what was done concerning the Tigurini and Ambrones.

14. However, the Teutones and Cimbri crossed the snows of the Alps with their forces intact and surged across the lowlands of Italy. Here, when this hardy race had long grown soft through the warmer climate, food, drink, and baths,[170] Marius, now consul for the fifth time, and Catulus were despatched against them.[171] When the day and place for battle had been decided, they followed Hannibal's cunning, forming up in the mist, but fighting in the sun.[172] **15.** The first surprise for the Gauls was to come up against a fully formed Roman battle-line before they realised it had arrived.

---

168 The Battle of Aquae Sextae (the modern Aix-en-Provence). Eutropius, 5.1.4, gives the same casualty figures, though does not mention the numbers of those who escaped. Jerome, *Chronicle, A Abr.* 1915, also has these figures. Livy, *Per.* 68, gives the number of prisoners as 90,000.

169 See Valerius Maximus, 6.1.

170 Florus, 1.38.13, probably drawing on Livy, mentions the climate, food, and drink, but makes no mention of baths. These could be a moralising addition by Orosius, the early Christians being deeply suspicious of the baths, but bath-houses were already a topos for *luxuria*; see Seneca, *Letters*, 86, and Tacitus, *Agricola*, 21.

171 652 *AUC*/102 BC.

172 A reference to the Battle of Lake Trasimene, see 4.15.4–6.

Then, when the mauled Gallic cavalry were pushed back into their own people, the whole mass of Gauls who were still coming onto the field of battle and not yet formed up were thrown into confusion. After that, the sun rose and shone in their eyes and the wind blew in their faces, so that they were blinded by dust and exhausted by the heat. **16.** In this way this huge, terrifying host was cut down almost to a man, while the Romans lost hardly anyone. They say that 140,000 of them fell in this battle and that a further 60,000 were taken prisoner.[173]

17. Their women forced a battle which was almost more severe than that fought by the men. They made a sort of fort by drawing their wagons into a circle and drove off the Romans for a long time, fighting themselves from the top of its ramparts. But after the Romans had terrified them by a new way of dealing out death – stripping the skin and hair from their heads and leaving them disgraced by this dishonourable sort of wound – they turned the swords which they had taken up against the enemy on themselves and their children. **18.** Some cut each others' throats, others throttled one another, others tied ropes round their horses' legs and, after tying those same ropes which they had tied to the horses' legs around their own necks, urged the horses on and so were dragged to their deaths. Yet others pushed up the yoke-poles of their wagons and hanged themselves from them. **19.** They found one woman who had placed a noose round the necks of her two sons and attached it to her feet, so that when she flung herself down to be hanged, she dragged her children to their doom with her. **20.** Among these manifold, wretched ways of dying, it is said that two minor chiefs drew their swords and ran each other through. Kings Lugius and Boiorix fell in battle, while Claodicus and Caesorix were taken prisoner.

21. So in these two battles 340,000 Gauls were killed and 140,000 captured, quite apart from the innumerable multitude of women who with a woman's frenzy, but a man's strength, slaughtered themselves and their little children.

22. However, Marius's great triumph and Rome's victory were overshadowed when an unbelievable crime, previously unknown to the Romans, was suddenly perpetrated at Rome and plunged all the city into horror-stricken grief. **23.** Publicius Malleolus killed his own mother with his slaves' aid. He was convicted of parricide and thrown into the sea sewn up in a sack. **24.**

---

173 The Battle of the Raudian Plain. The same casualty figures are found in Livy, *Per.* 68. Florus, 1.38.14, has much lower casualties, giving the numbers of the dead as 65,000 Gauls and fewer than 300 Romans. Jerome, *Chronicle*, *A Abr.* 1916, notes the battle but gives no casualty figures.

The Romans had managed both a crime and a penalty for which even the Athenian Solon had not dared legislate because he did not believe such a thing was possible. But the Romans, who knew they were descended from Romulus, knew that even this could happen and sanctioned a unique penalty for it.[174]

<h1 style="text-align:center">17[175]</h1>

1 645 years after the foundation of the City, in the year after the war with the Cimbri and Teutones and Marius's fifth consulate, it was reasonably assumed that Rome's power was safe, but in the sixth consulate of that same Gaius Marius,[176] Rome endured such a fall that she nearly put an end to herself through internal dissent. **2.** To me it seems a long and tedious task to run through and explain the twists of this strife and the labyrinthine reasons that produced this sedition. **3.** Let it suffice that I have briefly pointed out that Lucius Apuleius Saturninus was the first to incite disturbances. He was a bitter enemy of Quintus Metellus Numidicus, who was indisputably one of Rome's foremost men.[177] After Numidicus was made censor, Saturninus dragged him from his house, and when he had fled to the Capitol, besieged him there with a mob of armed men. He was forced from there by the anger of the Roman knights, after a great many had been killed at the foot of the hill.[178] After this, through

---

174 Livy, *Per.* 68, asserts Malleolus was the first to be punished in this way, though Valerius Maximus, 1.1.13, states that the punishment was used as a form of expiation for religious offences by Tarquin the Proud. For Orosius the purpose of mentioning this incident is to diminish the lustre of Rome's victories over the Gauls and to blacken the Romans' character.

175 Orosius's main source for this chapter is Livy, 69–70.

176 Orosius's date is nine years out; Marius held his sixth consulate in 654 *AUC*/100 BC.

177 Saturninus was one of the tribunes of the plebs in 100 BC. His hatred of Metellus was due to the fact that Metellus, when censor in 102 BC, had tried to expel him and his supporter, Glaucia, from the Senate.

178 This is an extremely confused passage. The incident reported here is not mentioned in any other source. Arnaud-Lindet (1991) 255–56 n. 2, suggests that Orosius has confused Metellus Numidicus with Q. Caecilius Metellus Macedonicus whom a tribune, G. Atilius Labeo, ordered to be thrown from the Tarpeian rock in 131 BC. The account of this incident is found in Livy, *Per.* 59, but we are also told that the rest of the college of tribunes, not the *equites*, prevented the order being carried out. The two incidents are therefore quite distinct, although the verb *deicere* is found in both. It is more likely that Orosius is referring to the riots that broke out in 102 BC when Metellus refused to allow Lucius Equitius, the self-styled son of Tiberius Gracchus, who was supported by Saturninus, onto the census roll; see Cicero, *Speech in defence of Sestius (Pro Sestio)*, 101. Orosius's cryptic reference to the anger of the *equites* may well be a product of him misreading *Equitius* in his source.

the treachery of the consul of the day, Gaius Marius, Saturninus and Glaucia killed Aulus Nunius, their rival for office.[179]

4. The following year, Marius who was consul for the sixth time, Glaucia, now a praetor, and Saturninus, a tribune of the plebs, plotted to use any force necessary to drive Metellus Numidicus into exile. A trial was held, and Metellus, though innocent, was criminally condemned by a jury suborned by this faction and departed into exile to the grief of the entire city.[180] **5.** This same Saturninus feared that Memmius, an active and honourable man, would be made consul and had his henchman, Publius Mettius, kill him with a rough club as he fled from a sudden riot.[181]

6. The Senate and people were now in an uproar about the great troubles afflicting the republic, so the consul Marius, changing his views to fit the circumstances, allied himself with the views of the better sort and calmed the plebs with a soothing speech. Saturninus, after daring to do these disgraceful acts, held a rally at his house at which he was acclaimed as king by some, and as commander-in-chief by others. **7.** Marius formed the people into maniples,[182] stationed the other consul[183] on the hill with a garrison, while he fortified the gates. The battle was fought in the forum. Saturninus was driven from the forum by Marius's supporters and fled to the Capitol. Marius then cut the pipes that took water there. **8.** A grim enough battle followed at the entrance to the Capitol and many men were cut down around Saufeius and Saturninus, while Saturninus kept shouting out aloud to one and all, proclaiming that Marius had been behind all his schemes. **9.** Then Marius forced Saturninus, Saufeius, and Labienus to flee into the senate-house; the doors were forced open, and they were killed by Roman knights.[184] Gaius Glaucia was dragged from Claudius's house and hacked to pieces.[185] **10.** A tribune of plebs, Furius,[186] passed a law confis-

179 Nunius was murdered just before the elections for the tribunate at the end of 101 BC.

180 This is a highly garbled version of events. Metellus was, in fact, outwitted by Marius and Saturninus and went into exile after refusing to swear an oath to respect the provisions of Saturninus's agrarian legislation in 100 BC.

181 The name of Memmius's assassin only appears in Orosius, though it may well have featured in Livy, 69.

182 A subdivision of the legion, containing around 60 men. It was effectively abolished by Marius and certainly obsolete in Orosius's day. Livy, *Per.* 69, notes that Saturninus was put down in a 'war of sorts'. Perhaps the full version of the text made a reference to maniples.

183 L. Valerius Flaccus.

184 These events took place on 10 December 100 BC.

185 Nothing is known of this Claudius.

186 P. Furius, tribune in 99 BC, and a supporter of Marius.

cating the property of all Saturninus's supporters. Saturninus's brother, Gnaeus Dolabella, was killed with along with Lucius Giganius, as he fled through the vegetable market. And so, on the deaths of the leaders of this great sedition, the people became quiet. **11.** At this point, to the delight of the whole city, Cato[187] and Pompeius[188] proposed that Metellus Numidicus return to Rome, but the factions of the consul, Marius, and of the tribune of the plebs, Furius, intervened to stop this happening.

12. Rutilius, too, being a man of such constant loyalty and rectitude, did not, from the time his trial was set by his accusers up to the very time of his appearance in court, grow his hair or beard long or, by wearing dirty clothing and by behaving humbly, win over the jury, appease his enemies, or placate his judges. On the contrary, after he was given permission to speak by the praetor, he was no more submissive than his spirit had ever been. **13.** Although he had been arrayed on a self-evidently trumped-up charge and all the best men thought he should rightly be acquitted, he was found guilty by a perjured jury. He emigrated to Smyrna and grew old pursuing his literary studies.[189]

18

1. 659 years after the foundation of the City, in the consulate of Sextus Julius Caesar and Lucius Marcius Philippus,[190] a war with the allies that had started through internal disputes convulsed all Italy. **2.** Livius Drusus, a tribune of the plebs, had seduced all the Latins with the prospect of freedom and, when he was unable fulfil his promise, roused them to arms.[191]

3. In addition to this, dire portents terrified the sorrowing city. At sunrise, a ball of fire leapt up in the northern sky accompanied by a great crash in the heavens. **4.** At Arretium,[192] when the bread was broken at a banquet,

187 The younger Cato, tribune of the plebs in 99 BC.
188 Q. Pompeius Rufus, one of Cato's fellow tribunes.
189 Smyrna is the modern Izmir in Turkey. Although Orosius implies that Rutilius's trial came soon after Saturninus's conspiracy, in fact it did not occur until 92 BC. Orosius has abbreviated his account to the degree that it makes little sense. A fuller version is found in Livy, *Per.* 70, where we learn that Rutilius was unpopular with the knights because as deputy governor of Asia, he stopped tax extortion in Asia. He was convicted of extortion, but his retirement to Izmir in that province gave the lie to the verdict.
190 Orosius's date is four years out; Caesar and Philippus were in fact consuls in 663 *AUC*/91 BC.
191 Drusus had attempted to make the Latins full Roman citizens, but his proposals were rejected.
192 The modern Arezzo.

blood flowed out of the middle of it as if it came from a wounded body. **5.** Moreover, a hail of stones mixed with shards of tiles lashed the earth far and wide for seven days without stopping. In the land of the Samnites, a flame burst out from a great chasm in the ground and was seen reaching up as far as the sky. **6.** Many Romans as they journeyed saw a golden-coloured globe come down from heaven to earth, grow in size, and then rise from the ground back into the air. It was carried towards the rising sun, and, through its size, blotted out the sun itself.

7. Drusus, troubled by this great number of evil portents, was killed in his house by an unknown assailant.

8. Then, while they were still secretly plotting to defect, *the Picentes, Vestini, Marsi, Paeligni, Marrucini, Samnites, and Lucanians,*[193] killed the praetor Gaius Servius, who had been sent as an ambassador to them, at Asculum.[194] They straightaway closed the city gates, condemned all the Roman citizens to death, and slaughtered them.

9. Immediately the most appalling portents possible then foreshadowed the coming horrendous disaster. For every species of animal which had been accustomed to endure the hand of man and live among men left their byres and pastures and fled with piteous bleating, or whinnying, or lowing, to the woods and hills. The dogs too, whose nature makes them unable to live outside men's company, wandered around like wolves, howling sorrowfully.[195]

10. The praetor Gnaeus Pompey was ordered by the Senate to wage war on the Picenes and was defeated.[196] After this, the Samnites made Papius Mutilus their commander-in-chief, while the Marsi chose the notorious pirate, Agammemnon. Julius Caesar fled after he was defeated and his army slain in a battle against the Samnites.[197] The consul Rutilius chose his

---

193 This list is taken verbatim from Livy, 72. Jerome, *Chronicle, A Abr.* 1928, lists only the Picentes, Marsi, and Paeligni.

194 The modern Ascoli Piceno. The war that follows is normally known as the Social War, see 5.19.1.

195 Orosius has drawn the portents in sections 3–6 and 9 from Julius Obsequens, 54. Augustine, *City of God*, 3.23, drawing on the same source, discusses the portent of the animals found in section 9. Orosius has suppressed two overtly pagan portents involving a statue of Apollo and the temple of Pietas, and changed the portent in section 9 where, according to Obsequens and Augustine, domestic animals attacked their masters rather than fleeing from them. Orosius is also more vague about the earlier portents he lists than Obsequens, who tells us that flame coming from the ground was seen at Aenaria, and the golden globe at Spoletium.

196 Gn. Pompeius Strabo, the father of Pompey the Great.

197 L. Julius Caesar, consul in 90 BC and father of G. Julius Caesar.

kinsman Marius as his lieutenant.[198] Marius continually warned him that the war would profit from a delay and that his recruits ought to be trained for a while in their camps. **12.** Rutilius thought that he was doing this through treachery, spurned his advice, and flung himself along with his entire force into a Marsian ambush. The consul himself died, while many nobles were killed and 8,000 Roman soldiers were cut down. **13.** The river Tolenus[199] carried the arms and bodies of slain past the eyes of his lieutenant, Marius, bearing them away as a testimony to the disaster. Marius immediately gathered his forces together and fell unexpectedly on the victors, killing 8,000 of the Marsi. **14.** But Caepio was lured into an ambush by the Vestini and Marsi, and butchered along with his army.[200]

On the other hand, Lucius Julius Caesar, on fleeing after his defeat outside Aesernia,[201] gathered together troops from all sides, and fought the Samnites and Lucanians, killing many thousands of the enemy. **15.** After he was hailed as commander by his troops[202] and had sent messengers to Rome to report his victory, the Senate, as hope smiled upon them, took off their sagas (this is the dress of mourning that they had put on at the beginning of the Social War) and put on the ancient glory of the toga once more. Marius then killed 6,000 of the Marsi and stripped another 7,000 of their arms. **16.** Sulla was despatched with 24 cohorts to Aesernia, where Roman citizens and troops were being closely besieged, and, after a great battle and much slaughter of the enemy, rescued the city and Rome's allies.

17. Gnaeus Pompey put the Picenes to flight after a hard battle. After this battle, the Senate started wearing the broad stripe and the rest of the marks of their rank again.[203] After Caesar's victory, their first respite from defeat, they had merely resumed wearing their togas. The praetor, Porcius Cato, defeated the Etruscans, and his lieutenant, Plotius, the Umbri. Both battles were hard-fought and cost much blood.

18. In the consulate of Gnaeus Pompey and Lucius Porcius Cato,[204] Pompey undertook a lengthy siege of the town of Asculum; nor would he have taken it, had the populace not sallied forth onto the plain and been

198 P. Rutilius Lupus, consul 90 BC.

199 The modern river Turano.

200 The praetor Q. Servilius Caepio who had taken over Rutilius's command on the consul's death. See CIL 1²708.

201 The modern Isernia.

202 A traditional honour given to successful generals by their troops.

203 After his death, Pompey had taken over Caepio's command. The victory and the resumption of wearing the *latus clavus*, the tradition mark of a senator, are found in Livy, *Per.* 74.

204 Consuls in 665 *AUC*/89 BC.

defeated with very heavy losses. 18,000 of the Marsi were killed in this battle along with their commander, Fraucus. 3,000 were captured.[205] **19.** 4,000 Italians who fled from this slaughter gathered into a single column, and then, as fortune would have it, climbed up onto a mountain. There they were afflicted and then killed by the snow, wretchedly freezing to death. **20.** They stood there as if they had been startled by the enemy. Some were sitting on stakes or rocks, others leaning on their weapons, all had open eyes and showed their teeth, as if they were still alive. For those looking on them from a distance, there was no sign that they were dead, except for an endless stillness that would have been impossible for the life-force of a man to endure long.

21. On the same day, the Picentes came to battle and were defeated. Their leader, Vidacilius, summoned together his leading men and, after a great banquet and some heavy drinking, called on all of them to follow his example, drank a cup of poison, and died. His deed was praised by all, but no one followed it.

22. 661 years after the foundation of the City,[206] a Roman army marched out to besiege Pompeii. Because of his unbearable arrogance, Postumius Albinus, a former consul who was at that time Lucius Sulla's lieutenant, earned the hatred of all his troops and was stoned to death.[207] **23.** The consul Sulla declared that a citizen's death could only be expiated by enemy blood.[208] Moved by a bad conscience over what they had done, the army entered battle with every man feeling that unless he triumphed, he ought to die. 18,000 Samnites fell in this battle. The army then pursued the enemy, killing Juventius, the Italians' leader, and a great number of his people.

24. The consul Porcius Cato was in charge of Marius's men with whom he performed some glorious deeds. After this, he boasted that Marius had not done anything better himself. Because of this, he was killed, allegedly by an unknown hand, in the heat of battle, while fighting against the Marsi by Lake Fucinus, by Gaius Marius's son.[209]

25. His lieutenant, Gaius Gabinius,[210] was killed while storming the

---

205 The battle is noted without detail in Livy, *Per.* 76.

206 Orosius continues to be four years out. These events in fact happened in 665 *AUC*/89 BC.

207 According to Livy, 75, he was suspected of treason.

208 An error of fact – Sulla did not become consul until 88 BC.

209 The Lago di Fucino/Lago di Celano in central Italy. It has been substantially drained since antiquity. There is no hint of foul play concerning Cato's death in Livy, *Per.* 75.

210 Livy, *Per.* 76, has Aulus Gabinius.

enemy's camp. The Marrucini and Vestini were harried and their lands laid waste by Pompey's lieutenant, Sulpicius.[211] The Italian commanders, Popaedius and Obsidius, were defeated and killed by this same Sulpicius in a grim battle by the river Theanum.[212]

26. Pompey entered Asculum and had the prefects, centurions, and all their leading men beaten with staves and executed by the axe.[213] He auctioned their slaves and everything else he had plundered. He decreed that those who remained could indeed leave as freemen, but stripped of their clothes and possessions. The Senate had hoped that some help for public expenditure would come from this booty, but Pompey gave none of it to the treasury in its moment of need.[214] **27.** For at this time the treasury was completely empty and there was not enough money to pay for corn. This lack of provisions forced the public spaces around the Capitol which had been allocated to the priests, augurs, and decemvirs[215] to be sold off, raising a sufficient amount of money to help deal with this time of shortages.

28. So at a time when the wealth ripped from all the towns she had overthrown and lands she had stripped bare was being piled up in the very heart of the state, Rome herself was compelled by her shameful lack of resources to auction off her most precious places. **29.** Let Rome therefore contemplate that part of her past, when, like an insatiable stomach, she consumed everything, but was ever greedy. Yet she was more miserable than all the cities she had reduced to misery. She left nothing, yet gained nothing, being goaded by her pangs of hunger at home to prolong the troubles of war.

30. At this time, King Sothimus invaded Greece with a large number of reinforcements from Thrace.[216] After he had ravaged all of Macedonia, he was finally defeated by the praetor, Gaius Sentius,[217] and forced to retreat to his own kingdom.

211 P. Sulpicius Rufus. He became a tribune of the plebs the following year. Cicero, *Brutus* 55, praises his oratorical skills.

212 The battle of Trinius, 89 BC. Orosius, or his source, has corrupted the name of the river Trinius (the modern river Trigno) to Theanus.

213 A symbolic execution using both elements of the *fascis*.

214 Livy, *Per.* 76, simply notes that Pompey took the town.

215 The *decemviri sacris faciundis*, one of the four main colleges of Roman priests. They were charged with the care of the Sibylline Books and with consulting them when asked to do so by the Senate.

216 Sothimus, normally Sithimus, was in fact a Thracian king. His campaigns appeared in Livy, 76. These wars lasted from 93–88 BC.

217 Praetor in 94 BC, but at the time of this command a propraetor.

19

1. 662 years after the foundation of the City,[218] when the Social War had not yet ended, *the first civil war broke out at Rome and in the same year the Mithridatic War began[219] – a war which, while it was less shameful, was no less dangerous to the City.* **2.** We have various accounts of its duration, depending on whether it should be measured from when it broke out or from when it began to become serious. The two main lines of thought say that it lasted either thirty or forty years. Although at this one time events loaded with a perplexing variety of evils blazed up, I shall set them down individually, though concisely, one after the other.

3. When Sulla was consul and, though still in Campania dealing with the remnants of the Social War, was about to set off with an army to fight Mithridates in Asia, Marius tried to gain a seventh consulate and command of the war against Mithridates. **4.** When he learnt of this, wild rage overcame Sulla, who was, in point of fact, an impatient young man. He first pitched camp in front of the City with his four legions. This was where he killed Marius's envoy, Gratidius, who was in a way the first victim of civil war. He soon broke into the City with his army, calling for torches with which to fire the City. Everyone hid in terror as he marched with his swift column along the Sacred Way to the forum. **5.** Marius, after he had tried in vain to persuade the nobility, rouse up the people, or, finally, arm the Equestrian Order, to oppose Sulla, as a last resort persuaded some slaves to take up arms by promising them freedom and plunder. He did not dare resist Sulla though, and fell back to the Capitol. But when Sulla's troops forced their way in there, after his supporters had suffered heavy losses, he fled. **6.** It was here that Marius's colleague, Sulpicius, was betrayed by one of his own slaves and laid low. The consuls decreed that this slave be freed because he had indeed denounced an enemy of the state, but also that he be hurled from the Tarpeian Rock because he had betrayed his master.[220]

7. Marius fled, but was cornered by the persistence of his pursuers. After hiding in the marshes of Minturnae, he had the bad luck to be dragged out of them in the most shameful fashion, covered in mud. He was taken to Minturnae, providing a spectacle that added to his disgrace, and was thrust into the gaol there, but simply his face was enough to reduce to terror the executioner who had been despatched to deal with him.[221] **8.** After this, he

---

218 Orosius's chronology is four years awry; these events in fact occurred in 666 *AUC*/88 BC.
219 Taken virtually verbatim from Eutropius, 5.4.1.
220 This story was notorious in antiquity and is found in Livy, 77.
221 Livy, *Per.* 77, adds the detail that the executioner was a Gallic slave.

escaped from his chains and fled to Africa. Here, after summoning his son from Utica, where he had been kept in custody,[222] he immediately returned to Rome and joined the consul Cinna in a criminal conspiracy.[223]

9. They divided their army into four parts so that they could lay waste to the entire state. Three legions were given to Marius. Gnaeus Carbo[224] was put in charge of another group of their troops, and Sertorius received command of a further group. This was the Sertorius who had already stirred up and been involved in civil war and who, after the end of this war, stirred up a further war in Spain that was to inflict very heavy losses on the Romans for many years to come.[225] The rest of their army had Cinna as its leader. **10.** At this point Gnaeus Pompey who, along with his army, had been summoned by the Senate to help the state, but had remained inactive for a long time, merely watching the revolution, was spurned by either Marius or Cinna, took himself off to the other consul, Octavius, and was soon in action against Sertorius.[226] **11.** Night put an end to this unhappy conflict in which 600 soldiers on each side were hacked down.

12. On the following day, when the bodies, which were all mixed together, were identified for burial, one of Pompey's soldiers recognised the corpse of his own brother whom he had killed himself, for in the battle their helmets had denied them sight of each other's face, and frenzy their wish to look for them. Although there is little guilt attached to things done in ignorance and while it appears that he did not know that it was his brother, it is nevertheless clear he knew it was a citizen he was killing. **13.** And so the victor was more unfortunate than the vanquished and when he recognised his brother's body and his act of parricide, he drove his sword into his own breast on the spot, cursing civil war and, with his tears and blood flowing, flung himself down on his brother's corpse.

14. But of what use was this tale, whose terrible news spread abroad at the very beginning of the civil wars – namely that two men, ignorant that they were brothers, but knowing that each was a citizen, had fought one

---

222 G. Marius the younger, who was perhaps Marius's nephew rather than his son. He had fled to Numidia where Hiempsal II had put him in under arrest while he watched developments in Rome.

223 Consul in 87 BC.

224 Gn. Papirius Carbo, a leading supporter of Marius. He was consul in 85, 84, and 82 BC. On Sulla's triumph he fled to Sicily (see 5.24.16), was captured by Pompey, and executed at Lilybaeum

225 For a detailed discussion of Sertorius, see Spann (1987).

226 Gn. Pompeius Strabo. His army was a private one. Livy has a much more negative attitude towards Pompeius than Orosius shows here.

another and that the brother who had triumphed in his crime then wanted to strip the spoils from the brother he had slain, and soon, after finding himself guilty of such an atrocity, using the self-same sword and the self-same hand, avenged with his own death the parricide he had committed – to confound this cruel undertaking? **15.** Did such a sad story assuage nothing of the zeal of the factions eager to fight? Did the terror of making such a mistake do nothing to repel anyone from the danger of committing this crime? Did piety and reverence born of the nature which we share even with wild beasts count for nothing? <Was there no one>[227] who feared that what one man had done in killing first another and then himself could happen to him and, overcome by his conscience, remove himself from an undertaking of this sort?[228] **16.** Rather, for almost the next forty years there was continual civil war on such a scale that the size of a man's praise was thought to depend on the size of his crimes. For unless they had wished to commit parricide, after such a tale everyone would have fled from the danger of parricide present in this type of soldiering.

17. Marius forced his way into the colony of Ostia and indulged in every kind of lust, avarice, and cruelty there. **18.** Pompey was struck by a thunderbolt and perished,[229] his army fell victim to plague and was almost completely destroyed, for 11,000 men from Pompey's camp perished and 6,000 of Octavius's command fell victim to a malign star.[230] **19.** Marius broke into the towns of Antium and Aricia like a foreign enemy, killing everyone in

227 There is a lacuna in the text at this point.

228 The incident was widely discussed in antiquity. Orosius would have known it from Livy, 79, and from Augustine, *City of God,* 2.25. Unlike Orosius, Augustine says that many men *were* moved by the incident and goes on to discuss how the pagan gods, demons to him, got round their consequent reluctance to fight. Sadly, our summary of Livy makes no mention of the reaction to the incident and so we cannot be sure whether it is Augustine or Orosius who has changed the tale for their own purposes.

229 Pompeius Strabo died in September 87 BC. The manner of his death is a little mysterious. Julius Obsequens, 56a, presumably drawing on Livy, tells us that Pompeius was 'blasted by a star', *afflatus sidere*. Orosius appears to have drawn the same conclusions, describing Pompeius as *flumine adflatus*. Others, for example Mommsen, however, have suggested that Obsequens and Orosius have misread their source and that Livy was in fact referring to plague not lightning. Plague was often connected with ill-omened stars in antiquity. Velleius Paterculus, 2.21, explicitly states that plague was the cause of Pompeius's death. For a full discussion, see Watkins (1988) and Hillard (1996).

230 Reading *siderata* 'afflicted by the stars' with Zangemeister. Orosius here sees the stars as bringing plague and not as reference to lightning. Arnaud-Lindet reads *desiderata* which would produce a translation 'and the lost of 6,000 men from Octavian's command was to be regretted'.

them, except those who had betrayed the towns to him, and letting his men plunder the townsfolk's possessions.[231] Afterwards, the consul Cinna entered the City with his legions, along with Marius and his runaway slaves. The two of them killed all the noblest men in the Senate and many former consuls.[232] **20.** But how much space should be given to demonstrating their suffering? **[233] Could I have delineated in a single word this slaughter of good men, so great were their numbers, so great was the length of time it went on, so great the cruelty, and so great the number of forms it took? **21.** Yet it is more reasonable that I should discard some evidence which is useful for my theme rather than pile up such a great list of horrors in my account, whether it be placed before those whose know about these events or are ignorant of them. **22.** We are talking about things which concern our country,[234] its citizens, and our ancestors who, tormented by these troubles, did such horrendous deeds that their descendants shudder even on hearing of them. They certainly do not wish these things to be exaggerated to excess, either through moderation from having sufficient acquaintance with them, if they know of them, or through respectful and sympathetic contemplation, if they do not.

23. Marius piled up the heads of the citizens he had killed as a decorative spectacle, having them taken in to his banquets, taken up to the Capitol, and taken onto the rostrum.[235] But when he had embarked on his seventh consulate, alongside Cinna, who was consul for the third time, death finally carried him off at the beginning of his term of office.[236]

24. Cinna then added to his murder of the good by slaughtering the wicked. For since the band of runaway slaves[237] Marius had brought to the city had an insatiable appetite for plunder and gave none of it to the consuls who had initiated the plundering, he summoned them to the forum, pretending that he would pay them. Here he surrounded them with soldiers and wiped them out while they were unarmed. 8,000 runaways were killed in the City's forum that day. Cinna himself was killed by his own army during his fourth consulate.[238]

---

231 The modern Porto d'Anzio and La Riccia. Livy, *Per.* 80, adds a third town, Lanuvium.
232 Marius and Cinna entered Rome at the end of 87 BC.
233 There appears to be a lacuna in the text at this point.
234 Orosius here firmly identifies himself with Rome.
235 Livy, *Per.* 80, only has the heads taken to the rostrum.
236 Marius died on 15 January, 86 BC.
237 The *Bardyaei*; see Plutarch, *Marius*, 43.
238 Cinna was lynched at Ancona in the spring of 84 BC; see Livy, *Per.* 83.

20

1. Meanwhile, the remnants of the Senate, who had fled to escape from the despotism of Cinna, Marius's cruelty, the madness of Fimbria,[239] and Sertorius's arrogance, crossed over to Greece and through their pleading forced Sulla to bring aid to their country which was now in danger, or rather on the brink of destruction. **2.** Sulla, soon after landing on the shore of Campania, defeated the consul Norbanus in battle.[240] On that day, Romans killed 7,000 Romans, and 6,000 more were taken prisoner by their own countrymen. 124 of Sulla's men perished.

3. Fabius Hadrianus, who had the powers of a praetor, tried to take control of the kingdom of Africa with a band of slaves. The masters of those slaves burnt him alive along with all his family on a pyre of wood at Utica.[241]

4. The praetor Damasipus, incited by the consul Marius,[242] summoned Quintus Scaevola, Gaius Carbo, Lucius Domitius, and Publius Antistius to the senate-house on the pretext of wanting their advice and then cruelly killed them. The bodies of the slain were dragged away on hooks by their butchers and thrown into the Tiber.[243]

5. At the same time, Sulla's generals waged many battles against Marius's men with most unfortunate good fortune. For Quintus Metellus[244] destroyed Carrinas's[245] forces and entered his camp, while Gnaeus Pompey

---

239 G. Flavius Fimbria, a partisan of Marius, took control, illegally, of the army sent from Rome to Asia Minor. He fought Mithridates with a degree of success, but Sulla succeeded in seducing his army to desert and he committed suicide in 85 BC. The 'madness' may be a reference to his sack of Ilium discussed at length by Augustine, *City of God*, 3.7, who describes Fimbria as the 'Vilest of the Romans', *vir spurcissimus Romanorum*.

240 Sulla landed in Italy in 83 BC. Norbanus was defeated near Mt Tifata to the east of Capua.

241 Drawn from Livy, 86. Hadrianus had been appointed by Cinna's supporters as governor of Africa, probably in 85 BC. Orosius is our only witness for Hadrianus's attempted usurpation and use of slaves; other sources simply speak of his rapacious government. Valerius Maximus asserts that the lynching had the approval of the Senate and popular opinion at Rome According to Cicero, *Second Discourses against Verres* (*2 Verrine*), 1.70, and Valerius Maximus, 9.10.2, the 'masters' who lynched Hadrianus were Roman citizens living in Utica. However, Diodorus Siculus, 31.11.1, states that it was the Uticans who killed Hadrianus. Being burnt alive was a common Punic form of punishment.

242 The Younger G. Marius, consul in 82 BC.

243 See Livy, *Per.* 86. Orosius suppresses Livy's comment that Scaevola, the *Pontifex Maximus*, was cut down as he was entering the Temple of Vesta. This detail would have added to the horror for Livy's original readers, but not for Orosius nor, he would hope, for his readers. Augustine, *City of God*, 3.28, on the other hand, does give these details.

244 Son of the Metellus mentioned at 5.15.7.

245 A praetor in 82 BC.

cut Carbo's cavalry to pieces.[246]

6. The largest battle was that between Sulla and the young Marius at Sacriportus[247] in which, according to Claudius,[248] 25,000 of Marius's army were cut down.

7. Pompey drove Carbo from his camp and pursued him as he fled, depriving him of the greater part of his army, either by killing them or forcing them to surrender.[249] Metellus crushed Norbanus's troops, slaying 9,000 of Marius's faction.

8. Lucullus[250] was besieged by Quintius,[251] made a sally, and annihilated the besieging army with his sudden attack. More than 10,000 are said to have been slain in that battle.

9. Finally, Sulla fought the Samnites' general, Camponius, and the remnants of Carrinas's troops before the City itself at the Colline Gate at the ninth hour of the day. After a fierce battle, he finally emerged triumphant. 80,000 men are said to have perished there. 12,000 surrendered.[252] The unquenchable wrath of those citizens who had triumphed put an end to the rest after they turned to flee.

21

1. Soon after he had entered the City in triumph, Sulla, contrary what was right and what he had promised, executed 3,000 men who had surrendered themselves via envoys and were unarmed as they felt themselves secure. Then many more, they say more than 9,000, were also cut down: men whom I would not say were merely innocent, but in fact belonged to Sulla's own faction. In this way, unrestrained slaughter was unleashed on the city.[253] Murderers wandered wherever greed or anger took them. **2.** While all were already openly complaining about what each one of them feared would

---

246 Gnaeus Pompey is Pompey the Great. Carbo was consul in 82 BC.

247 Unknown, but near Praeneste.

248 Claudius Quadrigarius, a contemporary of these events. Orosius is most likely to have recorded this second-hand via Livy, 87.

249 In 82 BC; see Livy, *Per.* 88.

250 M. Terentius Varro Lucullus who would be consul in 73 BC; see 5.24.1.

251 Probably one of Carbo's lieutenants.

252 The battle took place on 1 December 82 BC. Eutropius, 5.8, gives the losses as 58,000 dead, with 12,000 taken prisoner.

253 Livy, *Per.* 88, has 8,000 victims and implies that they were those who had surrendered on trust. Augustine, *City of God*, 3.28, has 7,000 victims with a similar implication. Orosius has probably misread Livy here.

happen to himself, Quintus Catulus said to Sulla's face, 'In the end, if we slay the armed in battle, and the unarmed in peacetime, with whom will we live?'

3. It was then that Sulla, at the suggestion of a chief centurion, Lucius Fursidius, first published his infamous list of proscriptions. At first 80 men were proscribed, including four former consuls, Carbo, Marius, Norbanus, and Scipio.[254] Among the rest was Sertorius, the man he feared most. **4.** Another list of 500 names was then posted. While Lollius was reading this, feeling secure and unaware of having done anything wrong, he suddenly came across his own name – he was killed while slinking from the forum in terror with his head covered.[255] **5.** But not even these lists could be trusted or put an end to these crimes – for some who had been proscribed had their throats cut, while others had their throats cut and then were proscribed. **6.** *Nor was their death an easy one or the only suffering which was inflicted on them.*[256] Nor in this murder of citizens was even the law between enemies kept – namely that the victors require nothing of the vanquished save their lives.

7. After Marcus Marius had been dragged from a goat-house, Sulla ordered that he be bound, taken across the Tiber to the tomb of the Lutatii, and be butchered by having his eyes gouged out and his limbs cut off, or rather broken, piece by piece.[257] **8.** After this, the senator Publius Laetorius[258] and the triumvir Venuleius were slain.[259] Marcus Marius's head was sent to Praeneste and, on seeing it, Gaius Marius fell into to the depths of despair. In the place where he was being besieged by Lucretius,[260] he made a suicide pact with Telesinus[261] in order to avoid falling into the hands of the enemy **9.** However, he drove his sword too fiercely into Telesinus as he came on against him and the wound weakened the hand of his assailant.

---

254 L. Cornelius Scipio Asiaticus, consul in 83 BC.

255 Lollius is otherwise unknown.

256 A strong verbal reminiscence of Virgil, *Georgics*, 3.482. The previous line is quoted at 7.27.10.

257 Marius's adopted nephew, M. Marius Gratidianus. He had prosecuted Q. Lutatius Catulus in 87 BC, forcing him to commit suicide.

258 Orosius seems to have misread Plaetorius (see Valerius Maximus, 9.2.1, and Florus, 2.9.26) as two names.

259 Venuleius was probably a *triumvir capitalis*, a minor official concerned with executions. He may have been a *triumvir monetalis*, an official concerned with minting, but as no coins bearing his name have been found this is unlikely.

260 Q. Lucretius Ofella, a Marian who had changed sides.

261 The brother of the Samnites' leader.

Telesinus died, but Marius suffered only a light wound and so offered his neck to a slave.[262]

10. Sulla also murdered the praetor Carrinas. He then set out for Praeneste and ordered that all the principal members of Marius's army, namely its lieutenants, quartermasters, prefects, and tribunes be slain.

11. Pompey dragged Carbo, who was trying to flee from the island of Cossura[263] to Egypt, back into his presence in Sicily, and slew him along with many of his friends.[264]

12. Sulla was made dictator in order to protect and mask his lust for power and cruelty through the reverence due to a noble and exceptional title.[265]

13. Pompey crossed to Africa, made a thrust around Utica and killed 18,000 men. Domitius,[266] the Marians' leader, fought in the front rank in this battle and was killed. **14.** The same Pompey went on to attack Hiertas,[267] the king of Numidia, and engineered that as he fled, he was stripped of all his troops by Bogud, the son of Bocchus, king of the Moors. Hierbas was brought back to Bulla[268] and Pompey killed him as soon as this town surrendered to him.

22

1. When Publius Servilius and Appius Claudius were made consuls, Sulla was finally to be seen as a private citizen.[269] **2.** This brought to an end two calamitous wars: the Social War waged against the Italians and the Civil War waged by Sulla.[270] These had dragged on for ten years and taken the lives of more than 150,000 Romans. **3.** Rome lost as many of her best men and home-born soldiers in this civil war as the numbers which in a previous age when she reviewed herself with an eye to Alexander the Great, the census enrolled in their distinct age groups.[271] **4.** Moreover, 24 former consuls were

---

262 Marius died in November 82 BC; see Livy, *Per.* 88.

263 The modern Pantelaria, which lies between Sicily and Africa.

264 Orosius oddly suppresses Livy's detail that Carbo died 'weeping like a woman'; see *Per.* 89.

265 Sulla was elected dictator at the end of 82 BC.

266 Gn. Domitius Ahenobarbus, proscribed by Sulla; see Livy, *Per.* 89.

267 Normally spelt Iarbas.

268 Bulla Regia, whose ruins are in the Bagradas valley in western Tunisia.

269 675 *AUC*/79 BC.

270 Similar phrasing is found in Eutropius, 5.9.2.

271 According to Livy, 9.19.2, this was a total of 250,000 men.

killed along with six former praetors, 60 former aediles, and almost 200 senators, quite apart from innumerable settlements all over Italy that were destroyed out of hand.[272] Who then would deny, if he is sane, that Rome in her triumph suffered the same loss as Italy did by her defeat.

5. For shame! Is there any need here too for an ambiguous comparison between these two ages? 'A very great need,' they say, 'for what could be more appropriate as to compare a civil war with a civil war? Or perhaps it will be asserted that there have been no civil wars in our times?'

6. To these critics we will reply that it would indeed be more accurate to call them wars against allies, but it will be to our advantage if they are called civil wars. For if the causes, names, and practice of all these wars are held to be the same, then reverence for the Christian religion can make all the greater claim for itself in these events as the enraged violence of the victors has been all the less presumptuous.

7. Many wicked tyrants have been created and armed by the peoples of Britain and Gaul and, rashly invading the republic and usurping its royal name, broken the body of the Roman Empire asunder, and so they have provoked just wars waged against them or fought unjust wars among themselves.[273] **8.** What can these wars, which are as similar to conflicts with foreigners as they are dissimilar to those against fellow-citizens, be justly called except wars against allies, especially since the Romans have never even called the war against Sertorius, or those against Perpenna,[274] Crixus, or Spartacus,[275] civil wars?

9. During such a defection, or act of treason, by our allies, there would be less hatred now if it came to a fierce battle or a bloody victory. **10.** For in our time all these things are brought about more by necessity and so are less shameful. These are the reasons for our battles and victories: to end the arrogance of tyrants, to stop our allies defecting, or to underline an act of vengeance.[276] **11.** Who can doubt that the so-called civil wars of today are fought with more mildness and mercy, or indeed suppressed rather than fought?

272 cf. Eutropius, 5.9, who gives almost identical figures, save for the giving the number of murdered ex-praetors as seven. He makes no mention of the destroyed settlements.

273 Orosius may have in mind Magnus Maximus's usurpation of AD 383–88 and that of Constantine III in AD 408–11, and the latter's consequent dispute with his field marshal or *magister militum*, Gerontius.

274 More correctly Perperna, a lieutenant and, later, murderer of Sertorius.

275 Crixus was associated with Spartacus's uprising for which see 5.24 below.

276 Orosius's reasons do not seem that far away from that famously given by Virgil to Aeneas by Anchises at *Aeneid* 6.853 – *debellare superbos*, 'to humble the haughty by war'.

12. Who has heard of one civil war in our times that lasted for ten years, or a war when 150,000 were slain waged even between enemies, let alone between fellow citizens?

13. Who has known a host of the great and good, lengthy to recite, to be butchered in peacetime? Finally, who has feared, read, or even heard of those notorious lists of men condemned to death? **14.** Rather is it not clear to all that everyone, united in a single peace and secure in the same state of security, victors and vanquished alike, rejoices in a shared joy and that, indeed, in the many provinces, towns, and peoples of the Roman Empire there is hardly anyone who has at any time been condemned to just vengeance and that against the wishes of their conqueror.[277] **15.** And so as not to load more words onto what I have already said, I would not be rash if I said that at all events that the numbers of the nobility slain in peace-time in those times equals the number of common soldiers who have died in battle in our days.[278]

16. Now on the death of Sulla, a supporter of the Marian faction, Lepidus, attacked Catulus, the leader of Sulla's supporters, and rekindled the embers of civil war.[279] Twice there was a fight with battle-lines drawn up, and great numbers of Romans, already wretchedly poor, but still possessing the frenzy of madmen, were cut down. The town of Alba, besieged and brought to the edge of starvation, was saved only by the surrender of those wretches who still survived. It was here that Lepidus's son, Scipio,[280] was captured and killed. Brutus[281] fled to Cisalpine Gaul with Pompey in pursuit and was killed at Rhegium. **18.** So this civil war, like a fire in the stubble, burnt out as quickly as it started, not so much because of Catulus's clemency as through loathing at Sulla's cruelty.[282]

23

1. 673 years after the foundation of the City, the clamour of war could be heard everywhere. One war was being waged in Spain, another in Pamphylia, a third in Macedonia, and a fourth in Dalmatia. And yet at this time the Roman Republic, lifeless and exhausted from its internecine strife

---

277 Perhaps a reference to Honorius sparing the life of the usurper Attalus; see 7.42.9.
278 cf. Orosius's comments on the Gallic sack of Rome, 2.19.14
279 M. Aemilius Lepidus and Q. Lutatius Catulus were the consuls of 78 BC.
280 Cornelius Scipio Aemilianus; see 5.24.16.
281 M. Junius Brutus, one of Lepidus's lieutenants and the father of Caesar's assassin.
282 A baroque version of the events listed in Livy, 90.

as if suffering from fever, was forced to drive back with her arms the strongest of the western and northern races.

2. Sertorius, a man who excelled in cunning and daring, after fleeing
from Sulla out of Africa, since he belonged to the Marian faction, had ended
up in the Spains and roused the most bellicose tribes there to armed rebellion. **3.** To give a brief account, two commanders, Metellus and Domitius,
were despatched against him.[283] Out of these, Domitius was destroyed along
with his army by Sertorius's general, Hirtuleius. **4.** Manlius, the proconsul in
Gaul,[284] crossed into Spain with three legions and 1,500 horse, and fought an
unequal battle against Hirtuleius. After Hirtuleius had stripped him of both
his camp and his army, he fled, almost by himself, to the town of Ilerda.[285]

5. Metellus was weary after fighting many battles, but, by moving
through remote areas, wore down his enemy with delaying tactics until he
reached Pompey's camp.[286]

6. Pompey had raised an army at Palencia and tried to defend the town
of Lauro[287] which was being attacked by Sertorius, but was defeated and
fled. **7.** Sertorius, on defeating and routing Pompey, captured Lauro and laid
waste to it in a bloody fashion. He dragged off the remnants of Lauro's
population, who had survived the slaughter, into slavery in Lusitania. **8.** He
bragged about his defeat of Pompey – Rome's famous general, who come to
fight this war full of confidence, *whom Rome had despatched not in place of
a consul, but in the place of both consuls.*[288] **9.** Galba[289] writes that Pompey
had 30,000 men and 1,000 cavalry at the time, and notes that Sertorius had
60,000 infantry and 8,000 cavalry.[290]

10. After this, Hirtuleius met with Metellus outside Italica, a city in
Baetica,[291] lost 20,000 men and, on his defeat, retreated with what few men

283 Q. Caecilius Metellus Pius, consul, and M. Domitius Calvinus, praetor, in 80 BC.

284 The proconsul of Transalpine Gaul in 676 *AUC*/78 BC.

285 The modern Lerida.

286 Pompey's campaign in Spain began in early 76 BC.

287 Probably Liria in the province of Valencia.

288 A close paraphrase of Cicero, *Speech in favour of the Manilian Law* (*Pro Lege Manilia*),
21.62.

289 Ser. Sulpicius Galba, historian and grandfather of the emperor Galba. Suetonius, *Galba*,
3.3, praises his historical writing.

290 Orosius has a strong dislike of Sertorius and this comment serves to underline his boast-
fulness.

291 The modern Santiponce, just outside Seville. Orosius's use of Baetica is anachronistic
as this province, roughly the area of modern Andalusia, was not created until the reign of
Augustus.

he had left into Lusitania.

11. Pompey captured Belgida, a famous town in Celtiberia.[292] Sertorius then fought Pompey and killed 10,000 of his men. Sertorius almost lost as many men on the opposite flank of the battle where Pompey was fighting with success.[293]

12. Many other battles were fought by these two. Memmius, Pompey's quarter-master and husband of his sister, was killed, as were Hirtuleius's brothers, and Perpenna who had thrown his lot in with Sertorius, suffered heavy losses.

13. Finally in the tenth year after the war had begun, the death of Sertorius, who was killed, like Viriatus, by the treachery of his own men, brought the war to a close and gave the Romans victory, though no glory.[294] Although part of Sertorius's army then followed Perpenna, he was defeated and killed along with all his troops by Pompey.

14. All the towns of Spain were recovered, as they surrendered immediately of their own free will. Only two resisted: Uxama[295] and Calagurris.[296] Pompey destroyed Uxama, and Afranius[297] destroyed Calagurris with fire and slaughter, after exhausting it in an interminable siege that forced its inhabitants in their wretched state of starvation to turn to vile forms of sustenance.[298]

15. Sertorius's assassins did not even consider asking for a reward from the Romans as they remembered that such a reward had been denied to Viriatus's assassins. **16.** Although these murderers gave security to Rome, but gained no reward for themselves, nevertheless Spain, ever loyal and mighty, though she has given excellent, invincible kings to the republic has never, from the earliest days down to our own, sent her a home-born tyrant or let any foreign tyrant who came to her leave alive or with any power.[299]

17. Meanwhile, Claudius, who had been allotted the Macedonian War,[300] attempted to drive out by force the various tribes who lived round

---

292 An error for Segeda, located near Calatayud.

293 See Livy, *Per.* 92.

294 Sertorius was murdered in 72 BC.

295 Uxama's ruins lie just outside the modern Burgo de Osma.

296 The modern Calahorra.

297 A lieutenant of Pompey who was to reach the consulate in 60 BC.

298 A euphemism for cannibalism. See Valerius Maximus, 7.6. *ext.* 3.

299 This is probably an allusion to the demise of Gerontius, Constantine III's one-time *magister militum*, who, on falling out with his former master, attempted to set up an independent regime in Spain; see 7.42.4–5.

300 Ap. Claudius Pulcher, the consul of 79 BC, and proconsul of Macedonia in 76 BC.

the Rhodope mountains[301] and who were at that time were laying waste to Macedonia in a horrendous fashion. **18.** Among the rest of the tortures that they inflicted on their prisoners, which are terrible both to speak, and listen, about, when they needed a cup, they happily used, as if they were genuine cups and with no sense of repulsion, blood-stained bones that they took from human skulls, with hair still sticking to them and their insides smeared with badly scraped out brains. The cruellest and most savage of these tribes were the Scordisci.[302] **19.** It was these tribes, as I was saying, that Claudius attempted to drive out from the borders of Macedonia and brought a great number of troubles on his own head. As a result, while he was sick at heart and surrounded by cares, he fell ill and died. **20.** His successor, Scribonius,[303] declined to force the issue with the tribes his predecessor had fought, turned his arms on Dardania instead, and captured it.[304] **21.** The former consul Publius Servilius[305] set about Cilicia and Pamphylia in a terrible fashion through his eagerness to subdue them, and almost destroyed them altogether. **22.** He also captured Lycia, besieging and destroying its cities. In addition to this, he crossed Mount Olympus,[306] razed Phasis to the ground,[307] sacked Corycus,[308] and combing the flanks of Mount Taurus where it borders on Cilicia, he broke the Isaurians in battle and brought them under Roman control. He was the first Roman to march an army through the Taurus mountains and open up a road through them. In the third year of the war, he received the name Isauricus.[309]

23. The proconsul Cosconius[310] was allotted the Illyrian War. He wore down and subdued Dalmatia, and finally, after two years, took by storm and captured the flourishing town of Salonae.[311]

---

301 These mountains lie on the borders of the Republic of Macedonia and Bulgaria.

302 A Thracian/Illyrian tribe living in what is now Serbia. For the savagery of the Scordisci and their use of skulls, see Florus, 1.39.2-3.

303 G. Scribonius Curio, consul in 76 BC and proconsul in Macedonia from 75 to 72 BC.

304 The modern Kosovo; see Livy, *Per.* 92.

305 P. Servilius Vatia, consul in 79 BC and proconsul in Cilicia in 78 BC.

306 The Mount Olympus of Asia Minor; see 1.2.26.

307 The modern Poti in Georgia.

308 The modern Ghorghos in Turkey.

309 See Eutropius, 6.3, and Livy, *Per.* 93.

310 Proconsul in Illyria from 78 to 76 BC.

311 Near modern Split in Croatia; see Eutropius, 6.3.

24

1. 679 years after the foundation of the City, in the consulate of Lucullus and Cassius, *64 gladiators fled from the barracks of Gnaeus Lentulus at Capua.*[312] Under the leadership of the Gauls, Crixus and Oenomaus, and a Thracian, Spartacus, they immediately occupied Mount Vesuvius. Sallying forth from here, they captured the camp of the praetor Clodius who was besieging them. After putting Clodius to flight, they carried off everything in his camp.

2. Then, marching round by Consentia[313] and Metapontum,[314] in a short time they gathered together a great body of men: for Crixus is said to have commanded a host of 10,000 men, and Spartacus three times that number. Oenomaus had already been killed in the first engagement. **3.** When they had thrown everything into confusion through their slaughter, arson, pillage, and rape, they behaved more like gladiatorial managers rather than commanders of soldiers, holding gladiatorial games at the funeral of a matron they had taken prisoner and who had killed herself in shame after being raped. They used 400 prisoners as participants, and so turned those who used to provide a spectacle into the spectators of one.

4. After this, the consuls Gellius and Lentulus were despatched with an army against them.[315] Gellius defeated Crixus who fought fiercely, but Lentulus was defeated and put to flight by Spartacus. Afterwards, the consuls joined forces, but in vain: they suffered a heavy defeat and were put to flight. Following this, Spartacus also defeated and killed the proconsul Gaius Cassius.[316]

5. The City was hardly less afraid than it had been when it had trembled with Hannibal thundering in arms before its gates.[317] The Senate despatched Crassus[318] with the consuls' legions and a new batch of reinforcements. **6.** He soon came to battle with the runaways, killing 6,000 of them and capturing another 900. Then before he attacked Spartacus himself, who was encamped by the head of the river Silarus,[319] he defeated his Gallic and

312 Orosius's date is two years out; these events in fact occurred in 681 *AUC*/73 BC. The italicised phrase is taken virtually verbatim from Livy, 95.
313 The modern Consenza.
314 The modern Metaponto.
315 The consuls of 681 *AUC*/72 BC.
316 Consul in 73 and proconsul in 72 BC.
317 cf. Eutropius, 6.7.
318 M. Licinius Crassus, propraetor in 72 BC and future triumvir.
319 The modern river Sala.

German allies, killing 30,000 of them along with their leaders.[320] **7.** Finally, he drew up his line of battle and came to grips with Spartacus himself, striking him down along with the vast majority of the runaways. They say that 60,000 were cut down,[321] 6,000 captured, and 3,000 Roman citizens rescued. **8.** The remaining runaways who had escaped from this battle and were now wandering about aimlessly, were quickly encircled and destroyed by a host of commanders.

9. I now, once again, return to my habitual question, is there really, even at this point, a need to compare these times with ours? Who, I ask, would not shudder to hear not of such wars, but merely of their very names: wars against foreigners, wars against slaves, wars against allies, wars against fellow-citizens, wars against fugitives? **10.** Nor do they follow on from one another, huge though they are, like the waves of a stormy sea, but roused and piled up by differing causes, pretexts, natures, and evils, they rush together from all sides at once. **11.** To sum up what I have just discussed, and omitting the shameful war against slaves, the thunder from the Jugurthine War in Africa had not yet ceased, when the Cimbrian War descended like lightning from the north-west. **12.** While the storm clouds of the Cimbrian War were still raining down great, foul torrents of shed blood, poor Italy breathed forth the fog of the Social War that would soon coalesce into great clouds of wrong. **13.** Even after the endless, frequent storms of the Italian War,[322] it was not at all possible to travel safely through Italy, where everyone, quite apart from in the dangerous whirlpools of their enemies' cities, struggled to keep their footing in the treacherous and slippery peace. **14.** And while Rome was giving birth herself to the destruction wrought by Marius and Cinna, she was menaced by another war, which rose up from the divers regions of the east and the north: namely the Mithridatic War. For while the war with Mithridates had begun in an earlier period, it extended down into later ones.

15. Marius was the torch that lit the funeral pyre of Sulla's disastrous regime and from that most baleful of pyres, the Sullan and Civil Wars, blazing sparks were scattered all over the world, spreading many fires from this single source. **16.** For Lepidus and Scipio in Italy, Brutus in Gaul, Domitius, Cinna's son-in-law, in Africa, Carbo in Cossura and Sicily, Perpenna in Liguria and afterwards with Sertorius in Spain, and Sertorius,

320 Livy, *Per.* 97, states that these Germans and Gauls were fugitive slaves. Perhaps Orosius has misread Livy here.
321 Livy, *Per.* 97, gives the same figure.
322 The Social War.

the most brutal of all of them, also in Spain, stirred up these civil wars, or whatever else they should be called, making many wars out of one war, and out of one great war, many great wars. **17.** Apart from these three enormous wars, which were at that time called 'the foreign wars', namely the Pamphylian, Macedonian, and Dalmatian Wars, there was the longest, bitterest, and most dangerous of them all, though this was not apparent at the time, the great Mithridatic War. **18.** At that time, the war in Spain against Sertorius was not yet finished; indeed, while Sertorius himself was still alive, the war against runaways, or, to speak more correctly, gladiators, made the state shudder.[323] For it was not a thing to be watched by a few, but rather one to be feared everywhere. **19.** Although it was called a war against runaways, no one ought to think it a trifling affair because of its name. Often in it, both consuls were defeated individually and, at times, together, after they had combined their forces in vain. Many nobles were butchered, and more than 100,000 of the fugitives themselves were cut down.[324]

20. From all this we can say that while at present she suffers vexations from foreigners, Italy can console herself by thinking of her past troubles, which were born of her, turned themselves on her, and which tore her to pieces with incomparable cruelty.

21. I shall, therefore, now put an end to my fifth volume, so that the civil wars, everywhere mixed in with foreign wars, that I have talked about and which will follow on in my account, because they cling together through the passing of time, wrong following on from wrong, may at least be separated from each other by the end of this book.

---

323 This is the term used by Jerome, *Chronicle*, *A Abr.* 1944, in his brief notice of Spartacus's uprising.

324 Orosius's Spanish origins are perhaps betrayed by his dwelling on the war with Sertorius. Oddly, despite being deeply hostile to Sertorius, Orosius makes no mention of his many atrocities which are listed in Livy, *Per.* 92.

BOOK SIX

1

1. All men, whatever their beliefs, way of life, or country, are always drawn through a gift of nature to look on matters with common sense, so they know that the reasoning of the mind ought to be chosen over the pleasures of flesh in their judgment, even if in their acts they do not chose to do this. The mind, enlightened by its guide, reason, sees, in the midst of the virtues by which it rises up through an innate disposition, though it is turned from its path by vices, the knowledge of God as its citadel.[1] **2.** For any man may spurn God for a time, but it is impossible to be completely ignorant of Him. This is why some men while knowing God in many things, devise in their unreasoning terror many gods. However, at the present time this attitude has been totally dispelled both through the workings of authoritative truth and the refutations of reason. **3.** For their philosophers, to pass over our saints, when inquiring into and observing everything with all their mental energy, have found that One God is the Author of all and that all things ought to be traced back to This One. So now even the pagans, whom the manifest truth now convicts of insolence rather than ignorance, when they debate with us, say that they do not follow many gods, but rather venerate many agents who are ruled by one great god.[2] **4.** There remains a confused discrepancy about the apprehension of the True God because of the many theories about how to apprehend Him, nevertheless one opinion is held by almost everyone – namely that there is One God. This is the point, albeit with difficulty, to which man's investigations have been able to bring him,[3] *but where reasoning fails, faith comes to his aid.* **5.** For unless we have come to believe, we shall not understand.[4] The truth you want to know about God,

---

1 Perhaps an allusion to Romans 7.7–8.

2 An allusion to neoplatonism.

3 This phrase contains an echo of Virgil, *Aeneid*, 11.823.

4 This is Augustine's position, famously summarised by Anselm of Canterbury (1033–1109) as *Neque enim quaero intelligere ut credam, sed credo ut intelligam*, 'For I do not seek to understand in order to believe, but I believe in order to understand'.

you must hear from Him Himself and believe Him.

Now this One, True God Whom, as we have said, every sect, albeit using different arguments, agrees exists, Who transforms kingdoms, orders history, and punishes sins, *choosing the weak of the world in order to throw the mighty into confusion,*[5] founded the Roman Empire using a shepherd of the lowest degree.[6] **6.** After this empire had prospered for a long time under its kings and consuls and come into possession of Asia, Africa, and Europe, by His ordinances He gathered everything into the hands of one emperor who was both the bravest and most merciful of men. **7.** Under this emperor whom almost every people justly honoured with a mixture of fear and love, the True God Who was worshipped through unsettling superstitions by those in ignorance, revealed the great fountain of coming to know Him.[7] Using a man in order to teach men more swiftly, He sent forth His Son to perform miracles that surpassed the ability of men and to denounce demons whom some thought to be gods, so that those who did not believe in the Man might nevertheless believe that His works were those of God. **8.** He also did this in order that the glory of His New Name and news of the Salvation that it proclaimed could spread swiftly and without hindrance in great silence over a land that was at peace far and wide and, indeed, so that his disciples as they travelled among the divers peoples of the empire, freely offering all of them the gift of salvation, should have peace and freedom to meet with others and spread their message as Roman citizens among Roman citizens.[8] **9.** I thought it right to mention these things since this sixth book runs down to the time of Augustus Caesar who is the subject of these comments.

10. But in case anyone thinks that this lucid reasoning is wrong and gives their own gods the credit, saying that they first carefully chose them, and then enticed them in with lavish worship with the result that through them they obtained for themselves this great and glorious empire – **11.** for they boast that they became the gods' favourites by performing the best sorts of religious rite and that after these were banned and abandoned, they then left *after their shrines and altars were abandoned, all the Gods through whom this empire has stood.*[9] **12.** For this reason, although your reverend Holiness

---

5 1 Corinthians 1.27.

6 i.e. Romulus. It is difficult not to see an implicit comparison with Christ being drawn here.

7 A reminiscence of Exodus 17 with Christ as the new Moses.

8 Orosius appears to be unaware that prior to Caracalla's grant of universal citizenship in AD 212 the bulk of the population of the Roman Empire were not Roman citizens. See also 6.22.8.

9 Virgil, *Aeneid*, 2.351–52, cf. 6.1.23 below.

has spoken at length most powerfully and correctly on this matter,[10] circumstances require me to make some small observations about their argument. **13.** If the Romans won the favour of the gods by worshipping them and lost it by not worshipping them, whose worship brought the reward that Romulus, the father of Rome, should have been saved from all the ills that surrounded him from his birth? Was it his grandfather Amulius,[11] who by exposing him tried to murder him? Or his father, whoever that was?[12] Or his mother, Rhea, regaled with adultery?[13] Or his relatives from Alba who persecuted the name of Rome from its earliest beginnings?[14] Or all of Italy, which for 400 years yearned, whenever it dared, for the destruction of Rome? **15.** 'Not at all,' they say, 'it was the gods themselves who, because they knew they would be worshipped, protected their future worshippers.' These gods therefore knew what was to come. **16.** If they knew what was to come, why then, among all the ages they could have chosen, did they bring this empire to the height of its power at precisely the moment when He chose to be born and be known as a man – He after Whose Name they themselves were counted for naught and those whom they had exalted[15] collapsed along with their whole world. **17.** 'But He crept into the world in a mean fashion,' they say, 'and made His entrance in secret.' Then whence came the great fame of this mean and secretive Man, His undoubted following, and manifest power? 'Through some signs or other and miracles He captured and held the minds of those ensnared by superstition,' is their reply. But if it was a man that did these things, the gods ought to have been able to do yet more. **18.** Or is it that He foretold that this power had been given to Him by the Father, and so at last it was possible to know this Known yet Unknown God, something which, as I have said, no one can attain save through Him? And no one can do this, save, after looking at, and despising, himself, he turns to the wisdom of God and abandons entirely the logic of a seeker for the faith of a believer.

19. To put matters briefly: it is openly agreed that those gods whom they say are so powerful that they appear to have furthered the cause of the Roman state when they looked on it propitiously, and to have afflicted it

---

10 A reference to Augustine's *City of God*, which also uses this quotation (2.22 and 3.17). See 1, *Preface* 11.

11 Amulius was in fact Romulus's grandfather's brother.

12 Pious pagan legend held that Mars was Romulus's father, but Orosius will not countenance this. Augustine, *City of God*, 18.21, later returned to this theme.

13 Orosius puns Rhea with *rea*, accused.

14 A reference to the legend of the Horatii and Curiatii; see Augustine, *City of God*, 3.14.

15 Perhaps a reference to pagan priests.

when they were hostile to it, were most devoutly and sincerely worshipped at that time when Christ willed Himself to be born and began to be known to the nations. **20.** So why were they unable to look to their own and their worshippers' interests and restrain or repel that 'superstition' concerning Him by which they saw that they would be spurned and their worshippers left destitute? If men adhered to it unwillingly, the gods ought to have pardoned them and not abandoned them, while if they did it willingly, the gods ought to have used their knowledge of the future and not helped them prior to this. **21.** 'This was done,' they say, 'for we roused up the nations, inflamed kings, passed laws, sent out judges, prepared our punishments of execution and crucifixion, we combed the whole world to see if the name of Christian and Christian worship could in any way be obliterated from the entire earth.' **22.** This was indeed done until this prolific savagery advanced it among, and through, its tortures until it seized the only thing that could restrain it, the heights of royalty. **23.** And what happened then? 'Christian emperors,' they say, 'commanded an end to sacrifices and that the temples be closed so that *there then departed after their shrines and altars were abandoned, all the Gods through whom this empire has stood.*'[16]

24. O how powerful and lucid is the light of Truth, if only the feeble eyes to which It freely offers Itself were not tragically closed against It. There was no way of suppressing the Christian faith in the centuries gone by when nations, kings, laws, murder, crucifixion, and death raged against it from all sides; rather, as I have said, it flourished among and because of these things. The cult of idols that was already failing of its own accord and ashamed of itself, ceased, without any fear of punishment, on one merciful command.[17] **25.** Who can doubt that through revelation of apprehending Him that His creation finally learnt about their Creator the things which up to that time had been sought by various reasoning processes of the mind and which, though the mind was eager, had been obscured by other matters, and that because of this it at once cleaved to the love of Him Whom it had desired even in its ignorance? **26.** It is no wonder if some slaves are found in a great household who, after becoming accustomed to the habits and lasciviousness of those led astray, abuse the patience of their master to the extent of treating him with contempt. And so God rightly chastises with a variety of punishments the ungrateful, disbelievers, and, indeed, the contumacious. **27.** We must admit that this has always been the case, but was

---

16 Virgil, *Aeneid*, 2.351–52, see 6.1.11 above.

17 A reference to the edict of Theodosius the Great on 24 February AD 391 which banned pagan worship, *Theodosian Code*, 16.10.10.

especially so at the time when there was still no Church in any part of the world which could, through the intervention of the prayers of the faithful, temper the punishment the world deserved and the just judgment of God by appealing to His mercy. So things of whatever kind that seem bad to men, were, without a doubt, worse in the past, as will be shown by the order in which they occurred.

28. The Mithridatic War or, I should say more correctly, the disaster of the Mithridatic War, which entangled many provinces, dragged on for forty years.[18] **29.** It flared up 661 years after the foundation of the City at the time of the first civil war, as I have mentioned,[19] and to quote the words of the greatest of poets *was only finished with barbarian poison* in the consulate of Cicero and Antonius.[20] **30.** In the records of those times one finds that the war lasted for thirty years, so it is not easy to see why the majority of authors speak of it lasting for forty.[21]

2

1. After Mithridates, the king of Pontus and Armenia, attempted to deprive Nicomedes, the king of Bithynia and a friend of the Roman people,[22] of his kingdom, he was warned by the Senate that if he tried to do this, he would bring down war with Rome on himself. He then immediately invaded Cappadocia in his fury, expelling its king, Ariobarzanes, and laying waste to the whole province with sword and fire.[23] **2.** He then seized Bithynia causing a similar catastrophe and subjected Paphlagonia to a like end, driving out her kings, Pylaemenes and Nicomedes.[24] After Mithridates had reached Ephesus, he promulgated a cruel edict that any Roman citizens found across

18 For a full account of Mithridates, see Reinach (1980).

19 5.19.1. Here the date given is 662 *AUC.* Orosius has either forgotten himself or the manuscript tradition has become corrupt.

20 Lucan, *Pharsalia,* 1.337, a reference to Mithridates' suicide. Cicero and Antonius were consuls in 63 BC.

21 cf. 5.19.2. Eutropius, 5.5, and Florus, 1.40.2, speak of 40 years, Justin, 37.1.7, of 46 years. Orosius calculates the war as starting in 662 *AUC* and ending in 691 *AUC.*

22 Nicomedes IV Philopator, c. 94–74 BC.

23 Ariobarzanes I Philoromanus, c. 95–c. 62 BC, who had been placed on his throne by Rome.

24 Orosius has drawn this section from Eutropius, 5.5, but has misread his source, making both Pylaemenes and Nicomedes kings of Paphlagonia. In fact, Eutropius is referring here to Nicomedes IV of Bithynia, mentioned in the previous sentence. Pylaemenes was an honorific name taken by all kings of Paphlagonia; see Justin, 37.4.

all of Asia[25] should all be murdered on a single day. And this was carried out. [26] **3.** It is impossible in any way either to describe, or conceive, in words the multitude of Roman citizens slain at that time, the sorrow that befell a great number of provinces, or the cries which rose up from those killed and their killers alike – for one and all were forced to betray their innocent guests and friends or risk suffering the penalty intended for their guests themselves.[27]

4. Archelaus, Mithridates' general, was despatched with 120,000 cavalry and infantry to Achaea[28] and captured Athens and all of Greece, in part by force and in part through its surrendering to him. **5.** Sulla, who had obtained the command of the Mithridatic war after his consulate, subjected Archelaus to a long siege in the Piraeus, Athens' port, which was fortified with seven walls, and took the city of Athens by force.[29] He then fought Archelaus in open battle: 110,000 men from Archelaus's army fell – scarcely 10,000 are said to have survived.[30] **6.** After he learnt of this disaster, Mithridates sent 70,000 of his best troops to Archelaus from Asia as reinforcements. 50,000 of these were killed in a second battle in which Diogenes, Archelaus's son, was hacked to death.[31] **7.** *A third battle destroyed all Archelaus's forces,*[32] for 20,000 of his soldiers were driven into the marshes[33] and, although they pleaded for mercy to Sulla, the victor's implacable anger destroyed them.[34] An equal number were driven into the river and slaughtered.[35] The wretched remnants of the army were butchered as they scattered.

8. Then, Mithridates decided to kill the leading men of the most important towns of Asia and confiscate their property. After he had already killed 1,600

25 i.e. the Roman province of that name comprising western Turkey.

26 Sections 1 and 2 closely follow and simplify Europius, 5.5.

27 cf. Augustine, *City of God*, 3.22.

28 The figures are taken from Eutropius, 5.6. Achaea is the Roman province of that name which comprised south and central Greece.

29 Sulla entered Athens on 1 March 86 BC.

30 The Battle of Chaeronea, April 86 BC. Orosius follows Eutropius's, 5.6, account of the battle. Livy, *Per.* 82, says Archelaus lost 100,000 men.

31 Eutropius, 5.6, has the same number of reinforcements sent by Mithridates, but states that 15,000, not 50,000, died in the battle. Orosius, following Eutropius, mistakenly says that Archelaus's nephew Diogenes was his son.

32 Taken almost verbatim from Eutropius, 5.6.

33 Lake Copaïs.

34 Orosius following Eutropius, 5.6, has turned the two days of the Battle of Orchomenus, fought in the autumn of 86 BC, into two distinct battles. In Eutropius's account, it is Archelaus, rather than his men, who hides in the marshes.

35 The river Cephisus which flows into Lake Copaïs.

in this way, the Ephesians, fearing the example that had been set, expelled Mithridates' garrison and barred their gates against him. Smyrna, Sardis, Colophon, and Trallia did likewise. **9.** Mithridates, his plans in confusion, made peace with Sulla though his general Archelaus.[36]

Meanwhile, Fimbria, a henchman in Marius's crime, who was capable of anything,[37] killed the consul Flaccus, with whom he had come as his lieutenant, at Nicomedia. **10.** Soon, after usurping command of the army, he sent Mithridates' son fleeing from Asia to the town of Miletopolis.[38] He attacked the king's position, drove him from Pergamum, pursued him as he fled, and besieged him at Pitana.[39] He would have certainly captured him, had Lucius Lucullus put the republic's interests above those of internal factionalism and wished to block him off from the sea with his fleet.[40] **11.** Fimbria then became enraged with the people of Ilium who, as they supported Sulla, openly rejected him and barred their gates against him. He went on to raze to the ground with slaughter and fire the famous city of Ilium, Rome's ancient kinsman, though Sulla at once rebuilt it.[41] This same Fimbria, after he was besieged by Sulla's army at Thyatira,[42] fell into despair and died by his own hand in the Temple of Aesculapius.[43]

12. Two refugees from Fimbria's army, Fannius and Magius, joined Mithridates, and on their advice Mithridates sent envoys to Spain and made a pact with Sertorius. Sertorius sent Marcus Marius to him to ratify the treaty. The king kept Marius with him and in a short time made him general instead of Archelaus who had taken himself off to Sulla along with his wife and children.

13. Mithridates despatched his generals Marius and Eumachus against Lucullus. They quickly mustered a great army and met Publius Rutilius at Chalcedon, killing him along with most of his army.[44]

36 The negotiations for the Peace of Dardanus. Once again, Orosius is strikingly favourable in his attitude towards Sulla here – the peace was generally regarded as a disgrace.

37 This judgment is drawn from Livy, 82.

38 A town in Mysia, the modern Hammamli in Turkey.

39 The modern Sanderli in Turkey.

40 L. Licinius Lucullus, consul in 74 BC.

41 85 BC.

42 The modern Ak-Hissar in Turkey.

43 Orosius, no doubt, wants the reader to savour of the irony of Fimbria dying in a temple of a pagan god of healing. His suicide would have underlined his worthlessness in Orosius's eyes and appears to be an embroidery by him – according to Livy, *Per.* 84, Fimbria commanded one of his slaves to kill him.

44 P. Rutilius Nudus. Rutilius was one of the other consul Marcus Aurelius Cotta's lieutenants. Orosius appears to have confused his defeat with the major defeat of the consul

14. While Mithridates was besieging Cyzicus, Lucullus hemmed him in with a ditch and so forced him to suffer what he was making others suffer. To keep the Cyzicenes in good heart, he sent them as a messenger one of his troops who knew how to swim. This man held onto a central pole with an inflated bladder on either side and, using his feet like oars, covered a distance of seven miles.[45] **15.** As he was suffering from lack of supplies, Mithridates ordered part of his army to be marshalled under arms and march home. They were caught by Lucullus and completely destroyed – for it is said that more than 15,000 men were killed in this action.

16. After this Fannius, who had allied himself with Mithridates, and Metrophanes, the king's praetor, were defeated by Mamercus. They fled to Mysia with 2,000 cavalry and crossing Maeonia came to the hills and fields of Inarime. **17.** Here not only the mountains look burnt up and the rocks as if they are covered by a sort of black soot, but the very fields themselves lie neglected and covered with burnt soil for a distance of 50 miles, though there is no trace of a fire or furnace. They lie there crumbling away with ash extending deep down into the ground; in three places parched craters that the Greeks call 'physae' can be seen.[46] **18.** After wandering across this land for a long time, they were finally delivered from their unexpected dangers and came secretly into the king's camp.

Deiotarus, the king of the Gallograeci,[47] killed the king's prefects in battle.

19. Meanwhile, Mithridates, besieged at Cyzicus, endured the same length of blockade as those he was besieging and reduced his army to the straits of great hunger and disease. He is said to have lost more than 300,000 men through starvation and disease in this siege. He himself seized a ship and secretly fled from his camp with a few men.[48] **20.** Lucullus watched the disaster from afar without a drop of his own men's blood being spilled and so won a new form of victory. Soon afterwards, he attacked and defeated Marius, putting him to flight. In this battle, more than 11,000 of Marius's troops are said to have been killed. **21.** Afterwards, Lucullus engaged the

---

himself at Chalcedon; see Livy, *Per.* 93.

45 Cyzicus was joined to the mainland by an artificial causeway. This was occupied by Mithridates, thus forcing Lucullus's messenger to swim a great distance to reach the besieged town. Orosius is our only source that this distance was seven miles. Frontinus, *Strategems*, 3.13.6, adds that Lucullus's messages were placed in the bladders

46 The Kula volcanic field in north-west Turkey. For Inarime, see Servius, *Ad Virgilii Aeneidos*, 9.715 22, which shows Orosius drew his details from Livy, 94. Orosius's 'physae' are shallow volcanic craters known as 'maars'.

47 The Galatians. Orosius's source for this campaign is Livy, 94.

48 The account of the siege of Cyzicus is taken from Livy, 95.

same Marius in a naval battle and sank or captured 32 of the king's ships and a great number of merchantmen. Many of those whom Sulla had proscribed perished here.[49] **22.** On the following day, Marius was dragged out of the cave where he was hiding and rightly paid the price for being an enemy of the state. **23.** Lucullus went on in this same campaign to attack and lay waste to Apamia,[50] and storm, capture, and sack the heavily defended city of Prusa that lies below Mount Olympus.[51] **24.** Mithridates marshalled his fleet and sailed against Byzantium, but was caught in a storm and lost 80 warships. As his own ship was battered by the storm and sinking, he leapt onto a skiff that belonged to the pirate Seleucus, the pirate giving him a helping hand in person. He then with great difficulty went to Sinope and on to Amisus.[52]

3

1. In the same year,[53] Catiline was accused of immorality at Rome. The charge was that he had committed this with Fabia, a Vestal Virgin. However, with Catulus's aid he escaped conviction.[54]

2. Lucullus laid siege to Sinope with the intention of storming it. The pirate king Seleucus and the eunuch Cleochares, who had been placed in charge of its defence, sacked and burnt the town, and then abandoned it. **3.** Lucullus was moved by the disaster his wretched enemies had brought upon themselves, and, after advancing swiftly, put out the fire that had been started there. In this way, the wretched town had its enemies and friends reversed: when it ought to have been defended, it was ruined, and when it ought to have been ruined, it was saved. **4.** Marcus Lucullus, who was Curio's successor in Macedonia, waged war on the Bessi and received the surrender of the whole tribe.[55]

---

49 The land battle was fought at the confluence of the Esopus and Granicus rivers, the sea battle off the island of Lemnos.

50 The modern Afamia in Syria.

51 The modern Bursa in Turkey. For Mount Olympus, see 1.2.26.

52 The modern Sinop and Samsun in Turkey. The account of Lucullus's campaigns is drawn from Livy, *Per.* 95.

53 73 BC.

54 The former consul of 78 BC, Q. Lutatius Catulus. There is a brief mention of this incident in Sallust, *The War against Catiline,* 15, but the Vestal is not named there. Fabia was Cicero's sister-in-law; see Asconius, *Commentary on the speech 'The Candidate'* (*Commentarius in orationem In Toga Candidata*), 91.

55 M. Terentius Varro Lucullus, consul in 73 BC and proconsul in Macedonia in 72 BC. He celebrated his triumph in 71 BC. Sections 1–4 of this chapter are drawn from Livy, 97.

5. At the same time, Metellus, the praetor of Sicily, discovered that Sicily had suffered terribly during the shameful praetorship of Gaius Verres and was being torn apart all the more by the infamous depredations and murders of the pirate king Pyrganio, who had seized the port of Syracuse after defeating the Roman fleet. By fighting him on land and sea, Metellus soon wore down this man's resources and forced him to leave Sicily.[56]

6. Meanwhile, Lucullus had crossed the Euphrates and Tigris and came to battle with Mithridates and Tigranes outside the city of Tigranocerta.[57] He killed a great number of the enemy with his tiny band: for 20,000 men are said to have been slaughtered in that battle.[58] **7.** Tigranes threw away his diadem and tiara to avoid being recognised and fled accompanied by scarcely 150 cavalry. After this, suppliant ambassadors came to Lucullus from almost all the East. As winter was coming on, he retired through Armenia storming and capturing Nisibis, a town which was then famous in those parts.[59]

4

1. In those same days, pirates were found scattered across every sea and not only attacked shipping, but had also begun to lay waste to islands and provinces. Their numbers increased enormously as the impunity of their crimes openly combined with their avidity for plunder. After a long period when they had wrought devastation by land and sea, Gnaeus Pompey crushed them with remarkable speed.[60]

2. At the same time, Metellus threw the island of Crete into turmoil for two years. After this long war, he finally subdued it and substituted Roman laws for those of Minos.[61]

56 In fact L. Caecilius Metellus was propraetor of Sicily in 70 BC, two years after Lucullus's command in Macedonia; see Livy, *Per.* 98.

57 Tigranes II of Armenia (95–55 BC) was Mithridates' son-in-law. Tigranocerta, which merely means 'built by Tigranes', was Tigranes's royal capital. The town was later known as Martyropolis. It should be identified with the modern Silvan in Turkey.

58 Fought in 69 BC. Eutropius, 6.9, gives more details of the battle and puts the size of the king's army at 107,500, but records no casualty figures.

59 The modern Nusaybin in Turkey. 'Then' perhaps alludes to the fact that Nisibis was lost to the Persians in AD 363. Orosius draws his account from Livy, but suppresses the fact that Lucullus was unable to purse Mithridates because of a mutiny in his army; see Livy, *Per.* 98.

60 Pompey's campaign against the pirates took place in 67 BC and was completed within forty days.

61 Q. Caecilus Metellus, proconsul in Crete 68–66 BC who obtained the title *Creticus* for his actions. Metellus's command was part of Rome's war against the pirates. Orosius suppresses his quarrels with Pompey; see Livy, *Per.* 99. The comments about the exchange of

3. After these events, Lucullus's successor, Pompey, surrounded the king's[62] camp in Lesser Armenia[63] by Mount Dastracus.[64] The king made a sally with all his troops by night. He had decided to drive back his pursuer in battle, while Pompey was pressing on to pursue them as they fled. And so battle was joined at night. **4.** The moon had risen and was at the Romans' backs. The king's men, seeing the length of their enemies' shadows, thought that they were close to them and threw all their javelins in vain. After this, the Romans advanced upon them when they were almost unarmed and easily defeated them. **5.** 40,000 of the royal army were captured or killed, while 1,000 Romans were wounded and scarcely 40 killed.[65] **6.** The king fled, escaping in the confusion of battle and helped by the faint light of the night. After being abandoned by all his friends, philosophers, writers of chronicles or poems, and his doctors, he led his horse by hand through the wilderness alone, trembling at every nocturnal sound. He finally came to a fortress and thence journeyed to Armenia.

7. Pompey, before setting off to pursue the king, founded the city of Nicopolis for the old, the camp-followers, and the sick in his train who wished to stay behind.[66] The city was founded between two rivers, namely the Euphrates and Araxes, which flow from a single mountain, but from different springs. **8.** Pompey pardoned Tigranes, who begged for mercy, and then defeated the army and prefects of Horodes, the king of Albania,[67] three times in battle. Afterwards, he was happy to receive the letters and gifts that Horodes sent in order that he restore peace with the Albanians. He routed Artaces, the king of Iberia,[68] in battle and received the surrender of all Iberia. **9.** Then, after he had set the affairs of Armenia, Colchis, Cappadocia, and Syria in order, he marched from Pontus into Parthia and in 50 days reached the city of Ecbatana, the capital of the Parthian kingdom.[69]

---

laws are probably drawn from Livy, 100.

62 i.e. Mithridates.

63 Armenia to the west of the Euphrates, now in north-east Turkey.

64 Sometimes spelt Dasteira, possibly the modern Kizil Dağ.

65 The Battle of Nicopolis, 66 BC where Pompey ambushed Mithridates in the Belgazi gorge. Orosius's account is probably drawn from Livy, 101. Eutropius, 6.12.2, agrees that Mithridates lost 40,000 men, but reduces the Roman casualties to 22.

66 The modern Purkh in Turkey.

67 Albania was located in what is now northern Azerbaijan. Horodes is more commonly known as Oroeses.

68 The eastern part of modern Georgia.

69 Orosius probably took his account of Pompey's campaigns from Livy, 101, but see also Eutropius, 6.13–14. In fact, Pompey never reached Ecbatana.

5[70]

1. While Mithridates was celebrating the rites of Ceres on the Bosphorus,[71] there suddenly occurred such a severe earthquake that it is related to have caused great damage to both cities and the countryside. **2.** At this time too Mithridates' prefect, Castor, who was in command at Phanagorium,[72] killed the king's supporters, occupied the town's citadel, and sent four of Mithridates' sons to the Roman garrison.[73] **3.** Mithridates was burning with anger and this soon blazed forth into crime. For it was then that he killed many of his friends and his own son, Exipodra – he had already committed parricide by butchering another of his sons, Machares. **4.** His other son, Pharnaces, was terrified by what had happened to his brothers, won over the army that had been sent against him, and soon led it against his father. **5.** For a long time Mithridates pleaded in vain with his son from the top of the highest wall, but when he saw that Pharnaces was implacable, he is said to have cried out on the point of death, 'Since Pharnaces commands my death, I beg you, gods of my fathers, if you exist, that someday he too might hear this command from his own children'.[74] He then at once went down to his wives, concubines, and daughters and gave them all poison. **6.** He was the last to drink it, but, because of the antidotes that he had often used to fortify his vitals against noxious potions, the poison could not kill him. He wandered back and forth, hoping in vain that the fatal draught would at last spread through his veins if he exercised his body. Then he summoned a Gallic soldier who was fleeing from the breached wall and held out his throat to be cut. **7.** This was how Mithridates ended his life. He is said to have been the most superstitious of men and has left us a clear statement of his opinions. He was 72 at his death and had always surrounded himself with philosophers and the most skilled practitioners of all the arts. **8.** 'Gods of my fathers, if you exist,' he said, showing that he, who had long cultivated them and enquired into this matter, saw that it was not clear that those thought to be gods were in fact gods. This king had seen much of life and lived to an old age, but did not come to know the True God, apprehension of Whom comes only by listening in faith. However, by the light of pure reason he had

---

70 The historical material in this chapter is drawn from Livy, 102.

71 At his capital Panticapeum, the modern Vospro in the Crimea.

72 The modern Taman in Russia.

73 Implicit in the text is that pagan worship far from bringing aid to its practitioners, brings positive harm to them.

74 This curse is only found in Orosius.

seen that these gods were false, deducing this in part from experience and in part from his own intelligence. **9.** 'If you exist, gods,' he said, meaning 'I know that above man is a power more powerful than man himself. As I have need to pray, I commend my perseverance in searching for it and ask mercy for my ignorance, I call upon the God Who is, while coming before one who is not.' **10.** This matter must be considered in both sorrow and fear: for what penalty and judgment will those deserve who, contrary to what widespread, manifest truth forbids, follow and worship those gods whose existence even men of those past times, who were unable to know anything other than them, were able to doubt?

11. I shall put forward this brief observation: what was the whole of the East like at this time? For forty years the wretched nations there were ground down by the depredations of an endless procession of generals; any city which lay in the middle of these conflicts was inevitably in danger and the actions it took to placate one side merely inflamed another, so that what was once a remedy soon itself became an affliction. **12.** Meanwhile panic-stricken delegations from the different provinces went off to successive Roman commanders and to Mithridates, who was harsher even than his reputation, taking their dubious excuses from one side to the other as the chances of war dictated and so making the danger they were trying to avert still worse.

13. Now I will set out in a few words what Pompey, and Pompey was one of the most moderate of the Romans, achieved throughout great areas of the east after the Mithridatic War had come to an end.[75]

6

1. 689 years after the foundation of the City, in the consulate of Marcus Tullius Cicero and Gaius Antonius,[76] Pompey, on receiving news that Mithridates had been killed, invaded Syria Coele[77] and Phoenicia. He first subdued the Ituraeans and Arabs, and captured their city which they call Petra.[78] **2.** From there, he despatched Gabinius with an army to Jerusalem against the

---

75 Orosius's favourable attitude towards Pompey is probably influenced by Livy whose support for Pompey was notorious. See Tacitus, *Annals*, 4.34.

76 Orosius has contradicted himself. At 6.1.29 he dates Mithridates' suicide to 691 *AUC*/63 BC. which is, in fact, the correct date of Cicero and Antonius's consulate.

77 'Hollow Syria', the name given to the valley lying between the Lebanon and anti-Lebanon mountains in the modern state of Lebanon.

78 In present-day Jordan.

Jews. They were led by Aristobulus who had expelled his brother, Hyrcanus, and become the first man to rise to the throne from the priesthood. Pompey swiftly followed after Gabinius, and while he was received in the town by its senate, he was driven from the walls of the temple by the people, and decided to storm it. **3.** Though he threw legion after legion by day and night into the fray without ceasing, it took him almost three months to capture it, fortified as it was not merely by its location, but also by a great wall and enormous ditch. 13,000 Jews are said to have been slaughtered there, the rest submitted to Rome.[79] **4.** Pompey commanded that the walls of the city be destroyed and levelled to the ground and, after executing some of the Jews' leaders, restored Hyrcanus to the priesthood and took Aristobulus as a captive back to Rome.[80] Pompey himself gave an account of this war that he had waged in the east against 22 kings at a public meeting.

5. Meanwhile, Catiline's conspiracy against his country was devised and then betrayed in the City,[81] but it was put down in a civil war in Etruria. The accomplices of the conspiracy were executed at Rome. **6.** It is enough for us to have sketched its history briefly as everyone knows about these things which were done by Cicero and described by Sallust.[82]

7. A rebellion in Paelignia engineered by the Marcelli, father and son, was betrayed by Lucius Vettius.[83] It was, as it were, ripped up by the roots after Catiline's conspiracy had been uncovered, being suppressed by Bibulus in Paelignia and by Cicero in Bruttium.

7

1. 693 years after the foundation of the City, in the consulate of Gaius Caesar and Lucius Bibulus,[84] the three provinces of Transalpine Gaul, Cisalpine Gaul, and Illyricum along with seven legions were allotted to Caesar for a period of five years by the Vatinian Law.[85] Afterwards the senate

---

79 Eutropius, 6.14, gives the figure as 12,000.

80 Orosius's information is drawn from Jerome, *Chronicle, A Abr.* 1950 (= incorrectly, 65 BC).

81 63 BC, in fact Pompey returned to Rome after the Catilinarian conspiracy.

82 A reference to Sallust's *The War against Catiline*. Both Cicero and Sallust were both important authors in the education curriculum of Orosius's day.

83 Orosius is our only source for this rebellion.

84 Orosius's chronology is two years out, Caesar and Bibulus were consuls in 695 *AUC*/59 BC.

85 So named as it was proposed by one of Caesar's supporters, the tribune P. Vatinius.

added 'long-haired' Gaul to his command.[86] **2.** Suetonius Tranquillus has expounded these events at length and I have followed him, making appropriate excerpts from his account.[87]

3. A certain Orgetorix, a leading light among the Helvetii, had inflamed the spirits of his people to rise up in arms with hopes of attacking all of Gaul.[88] The Helvetii were the bravest of the Gallic tribes, above all because they were almost always at war with the Germans from whom they were separated only by the river Rhine. **4.** The other nobles seized Orgetorix and put him to death, but they were unable to restrain their people once they had been roused by an opportunity for plundering. After devising their plot and deciding on a day to act, they burnt their homes and villages so that there could be no question of a wish of going back, and so set out. **5.** Caesar met them at the river Rhône, defeated them twice in a major and close-run campaign, and, after defeating them, forced them to surrender. When this horde, which comprised all the men and women of the Helvetii, Tulingi, Latobogii, Rauraci, and Boii, first set out, they numbered 157,000. Out of these 47,000 fell in battle and the remainder were sent back to their own lands.[89]

6. After this, Caesar defeated King Ariovistus in the land of the Sequani.[90] He was stirring up and gathering to his side an enormous number of Germans with whom he boasted that he had recently subjugated all the peoples of Gaul because Caesar's army had long declined battle through fear of his Germans' numbers and their courage. **7.** Ariovistus at once stole a small boat and, crossing the Rhine, fled into Germany, but his two wives and two daughters were captured.[91] Ariovistus's army had been composed of the

86 The modern France, named 'longed-haired', *comata*, after the native fashion of wearing hair long there.

87 An extraordinary statement as in fact Orosius appears to draw exclusively on Caesar's *Gallic War* for his account of the Gallic Wars. Suetonius (*Caesar*, 25) provides only a brief résumé of Caesar's campaigns in Gaul.

88 The account of the Helvetian War that follows is drawn, in a highly abbreviated form from Caesar, *Gallic War*, 1.2–29.

89 This list is taken from Caesar, *Gallic War*, 1.29. Some names have become slightly corrupted: Orosius has Latobogii for Latovici and Rauraci for Raurici. Orosius's total of 157,000 for those migrating is much lower than that given by Caesar (368,000). This is likely to be the result of a corrupt manuscript rather than Orosius deliberately changing his source material.

90 The Battle of Alascia, fought in the autumn of 57 BC. The account of the war is again drawn, in a highly abbreviated fashion, from Caesar, *Gallic War*, 1.31–53.

91 According to Caesar, *Gallic War*, 1.53, both Ariovistus's wives were killed, was one of his daughters, the other being captured.

Arudes, Marcomanes, Triboci, Vangiones, Nemetes, Eduses, and Sueves.[92] **8.** The battle had been especially hard because of the phalanx[93] used by the Germans. They formed this in advance when they gathered into one column and linked their shields together over their heads in order to be protected on all sides as they attacked the Romans' lines. **9.** However, some of the Roman troops known for their daring and agility, leapt on top of their *testudo*,[94] and pulled the shields away one by one, like tearing off scales. They then stabbed down from above on the exposed shoulders of those whom they had surprised and deprived of their defence. The enemy were terrified by this new threat of death and broke their threatening formation. **10.** They were then put to flight and slaughtered without mercy over a distance of 50 miles.[95] It is impossible to guess at the number of Germans who fought or were killed in this battle.

11. After this, the Belgae, who occupy one third of the Gauls, rose up against Caesar.[96] **12.** Their forces were as follows:[97] the Bellovagui who appeared to be the largest in number and most courageous, had 60,000 picked men under arms; the Suessones had 50,000, drawn from their twelve towns; **13.** the Nervii similarly had 50,000 men – it was said that they were so ferocious that up to that time they had never allowed merchants to bring them wine or any other goods through which imported pleasures could weaken their courage;[98] **14.** the Atrebates and Ambiani had 10,000 men;[99] the Morini, 25,000; the Menapii, 9,000;[100] the Caleti, 10,000; the Velocasses and Veromandi, another 10,000; the Atuatuci, 18,000;[101] the Condurses, Eborones, Caerosi, and Caemani, who are collectively referred to as the Germans, 40,000. **15.** So in total they are said to have had 282,000 picked

92 This list is identical to that found in Caesar, *Gallic War*, 1.51, Orosius's 'Eduses' are a corruption of Caesar's Sedusii.

93 A striking term to use of barbarians. Orosius has taken it from Caesar, *Gallic War*, 1.52.

94 Or 'tortoise'. This terminology, normally reserved for the Roman army, and the rest of the incident have been taken from Caesar, *Gallic War*, 1.52.

95 Caesar says the pursuit was over 15 miles. Orosius's error could be a result of having a corrupt version of Caesar; see Pain (1937).

96 While what follows is drawn from the second book of Caesar's *Gallic War*, Orosius has chosen to add this piece of information drawn from *Gallic War*, 1.1, here.

97 Orosius's list is taken from Caesar, *Gallic War*, 2.4. Some of the tribal names have become slightly corrupt.

98 Taken from Caesar, *Gallic War*, 2.15.

99 Orosius has misread his text and failed to notice that Caesar says that the Atrebates had 15,000 men of their own and the Ambiani a further 10,000.

100 Caesar has 7,000.

101 Caesar has 17,000.

men under arms. **16.** Caesar's army was thrown into confusion and put to flight with very heavy losses when these men suddenly burst out of the woods. Finally, urged on by its commander, the army stood firm, attacked those who had defeated them, and slaughtered them almost to a man.[102]

8

1. After performing these great deeds in Gaul, Caesar decided to go to Italy and despatched Galba[103] with the 12th legion to the lands of the Veragri and Seduni.[104] **2.** Galba stopped to winter in the village belonging to the Veragri called Octodurus,[105] leaving the half of the town, which was separated from him by a stream, to its inhabitants. One day, he saw that these had left by night and were encamped on a neighbouring hill. **3.** They had done this because they had contempt for his small force of scarcely half a legion and believed that there was booty that would fall into their hands with no effort whatsoever. They also had summoned their neighbours to join in the slaughter and plunder.

4. While Galba was surrounded by this pressing danger, afraid, and unclear how to take a clear decision about the various plans put to him, the Gauls suddenly swept down from the hill, poured round his unfinished camp, surrounding it and raining javelins and rocks on the troops scattered along on the ramparts. **5.** When they were already breaking into the camp, the entire Roman force, on the advice of the chief centurion Pacuvius[106] and the tribune Volusenus, sallied forth from its gates. Their sudden attack caught the enemy off-guard, and they first threw them into confusion and then routed them with pitiable carnage – more than 30,000 barbarians are said to have been slaughtered.[107]

6. And so Caesar was forced back to fight a new and bigger war after he had thought that all the Gallic tribes had been pacified. **7.** *For while the young Publius Crassus was wintering by the Ocean with the 7th legion in the*

---

102 The Battle of the Sambre, fought in 57 BC. Orosius's account is a highly abbreviated version of Caesar, *Gallic War*, 2.19–28.

103 Ser. Sulpicius Galba, later one of Caesar's assassins.

104 Caesar, *Gallic War*, 3.1 adds the Nantuates to these two tribes.

105 The modern Martigny in Switzerland. Orosius does not note that Galba divided his legion when going into winter quarters; see Caesar, *Gallic War*, 3.1.

106 This name has become very corrupt – Caesar, *Gallic War*, 3.5, calls the centurion P. Sextius Baculus.

107 The figure is taken from Caesar, *Gallic War*, 3.6.

lands of the Andicavi,[108] the Veneti and all their neighbours suddenly formed an armed conspiracy, imprisoned some Roman envoys, and told the Romans that they would release them only if they received their own hostages back. **8.** They gathered as allies for their war the Osismi, Lexovi, Namnetes, Ambivariti, Morini, Diablintes, and Menapii, and also summoned help from Britain.[109]

9. Caesar was told by Crassus about this rebellion of tribes who had previously surrendered. Although he knew how great the difficulty of engaging in war would be, he did not think such an important task should be shirked lest this example should offer a stimulus for other tribes to dare to act in the same way. **10.** Therefore after he had set out to attack his enemies by land but in vain – because the enemy were protected by tidal estuaries and inaccessible bays which lay safe along the winding coast – he ordered that warships be built on the river Loire. **11.** Soon, when the enemy saw them brought down the river to the Ocean, they immediately fitted out 220 vessels of their own and, after arming them with every kind of weaponry, put out from their port to face him.

12. As Brutus[110] looked round, he saw that the battle between the two fleets was far from equal, as the barbarians' ships were built of solid timbers with stout hulls which beat back the blows of his ships' rams as if they were striking rocks. **13.** His first line of defence was to lash sharp scythes loosely onto long poles and then tie them onto ropes. Using these weapons, they could, when necessary, catch and cut their enemies' rigging at a distance, by hauling in the poles and pulling back the blade with the rope. **14.** These preparations were quickly made and Brutus ordered his men to cut the tackle on the enemy's yard-arms. In this way as their yards fell, he immediately rendered most of the enemy's ships immobile, as if they had already been captured. **15.** The others, terrified by the danger they were in, raised their sails and tried to flee to wherever the wind took them, but the wind soon failed, leaving them as a laughing-stock for the Romans.[111] **16.** And so, after all their ships had been burned and those who resisted had been killed, all

---

108 Caesar, *Gallic War*, 3.7, calls the tribe the Andes. This phrase is drawn virtually verbatim from Caesar, *Gallic War*, 3.7.2.

109 This list is taken from Caesar, *Gallic War*, 3.9. Some of the names have suffered minor corruption, e.g. Namnetus for Nemetes, Lexovi for Lixovii.

110 D. Junius Brutus, the prefect of Caesar's fleet in 56 BC and later to be one of his assassins.

111 The description of Brutus's ploy and its effect is taken from Caesar, *Gallic War*, 3.14–15.

the remaining Gauls gave themselves up.

17. However, Caesar, mainly because of the insult to his ambassadors, and also in order, by way of example, to sear with a terrible brand a race that was eager to embrace any kind of plot, had all their leaders tortured to death[112] and the rest sold into slavery.

18. At the same time, Titurius Sabinus made a sally against, and wiped out with incredible slaughter, the Aulerci, Eburovices, and Lixovii, who had killed their leaders because these had not wished to renew the war.[113]

19. When Publius Crassus reached Aquitania, he was welcomed with a war.[114] For the Sotiates attacked the Romans with great numbers of cavalry and strong groups of infantry, causing them serious problems for a long period of time. **20.** On being defeated and driven into the Sotiates' town where they were put under siege,[115] they saw that it would be taken by storm, and so handed over their weapons and surrendered. **21.** The Aquitanians were stirred up by this disaster and gathered an army from all sides, even summoning help from Hither Spain. They chose as their overall commanders men who had served with Sertorius.[116] **22.** Crassus overwhelmed and obliterated them in their own camp while they were plotting to besiege him. 38,000 out of the Aquitanians and Cantabrians, 50,000 of whom had come to their aid, are said to have been killed.[117]

23. Caesar attacked and slaughtered to a man the Germans who had crossed the Rhine with huge forces and were preparing to bring all of Gaul under their control. They say their numbers reached 440,000.[118]

112 Orosius's amplification of the verb *necare* (to murder) used by Caesar, *Gallic War*, 3.16.

113 These tribes lived on the Cotentin peninsula. The incident is taken from Caesar, *Gallic War*, 3.17. Orosius however has missed out the main target of Sabinus's raid, the Venelli, and gives only the list of their allies.

114 Crassus's adventures are drawn from Caesar, *Gallic War*, 3.19–21.

115 The modern Sos.

116 Hither Spain was the province of Spain which lay closest to Gaul. This information, and that about the involvement of Sertorians in the Aquitanian revolt, is drawn from Caesar, *Gallic War*, 3.23.

117 Crassus's campaigns are taken from Caesar, *Gallic War*, 3.20–21. Orosius has omitted his further actions in the region. See Caesar, *Gallic War*, 3.22–27.

118 The Usipetes and Tenecteri. Orosius's note is a highly abbreviated version of Caesar, *Gallic War*, 4.1–16. The extent of the massacre has been overstated by Orosius. Caesar, *Gallic War*, 4.15, gives the number of Germans as 430,000 and makes it clear that not all of them were killed.

9

1. Caesar then built a bridge and crossed into Germany.[119] He struck terror into the Sugambri and also, to raise the siege of the Ubii, into the Sueves, Germany's largest and fiercest tribe whom many have said are composed of 100 lands and peoples,[120] and, indeed, into all of Germany by his coming. Soon he retired back into Gaul and tore down his bridge.

2. He then advanced into the lands of the Morini from where the shortest and swiftest crossing to Britain can be made.[121] He fitted out around 80 transport and fast ships and made the passage to Britain.[122] Here, he was first worn down by fierce fighting and then caught in bad weather, losing the greater part of his fleet, along with a good number of his troops and almost all his cavalry.

3. On returning to Gaul, he sent his troops into winter quarters and ordered 600 ships of these two kinds to be built.[123] **4.** He crossed over to Britain again with these at the beginning of spring.[124] As he was marching on the enemy with his army, his ships were caught in a storm while riding at anchor. They ran into one another or broke up as they ran aground on the sand. In all, 40 were completely lost and the rest were repaired only with great difficulty.[125] **5.** Caesar's cavalry was defeated by the Britons in its first engagement where the tribune Labienus lost his life.[126] In a second battle, the cavalry, after putting themselves into great danger, defeated and routed the Britons.

6. Caesar then advanced to the river Thames which they say is fordable only at one point. A huge force of the enemy under the leadership of

119 The information of Caesar's incursion into Germany is drawn from Caesar, *Gallic War* 4.16–19.

120 Taken from Caesar, *Gallic War*, 1.37.

121 See 1.2.76.

122 The figure is drawn from Caesar, *Gallic War*, 4.22. Orosius reduces Caesar's account of his first incursion into Britain (*Gallic War*, 4.21–36) to a mere note.

123 i.e. transports and warships. This comment stems from a mis-reading of Caesar, *Gallic War*, 5.1, where Caesar describes in detail a single type of new warship with two distinct capabilities. Orosius has taken this as a description of two separate sorts of ship, hence the confusion in his text here. The figure of 600 ships is drawn from Caesar, *Gallic War*, 5.2.

124 54 BC; that Caesar sailed in spring is an embellishment in Orosius's text not found in Caesar.

125 The storm and the losses it caused are drawn from Caesar, *Gallic War*, 5.10–11.

126 Orosius, perhaps because his manuscript was corrupt, has confused Labienus with Q. Laberius Durus; see Caesar, *Gallic War*, 5.15.

Cassovellaunus[127] had encamped on the far bank and fortified the riverbank and almost all the ford beneath the water with sharp stakes. **7.** After the Romans detected and avoided these obstacles, the barbarians were unable to bear the onslaught of the legions and hid themselves in the woods whence they frequently sallied forth causing severe losses to the Romans.

8. Meanwhile, the well-defended town of the Trinovantes and their leader, Androgius,[128] surrendered to Caesar, giving him 40 hostages. **9.** Many other cities followed their example and made treaties with the Romans. With these acting as his guides, Caesar, after a fierce battle, finally captured Cassovellaunus's town[129] which lay between two marshes, defended above all by its cover of trees, and filled with every kind of provision.[130]

10

1. Caesar immediately returned from the Britains[131] to Gaul. After he had sent his troops into winter quarters, he was suddenly surrounded by the storms of war and accosted on all sides. For Ambiorix conspired with the Eburonates and Atuatuci, and, inspired by a plan devised by the Treveri, surrounded and killed Caesar's lieutenants Cotta and Sabinus in an ambush near Eburonae with the loss of an entire legion.[132]

2. Elated by his victory, Ambiorix summoned the Atuatuci, the Nervii, and many others to arms and marched on Caesar's lieutenant, Cicero, who was also in charge of a legion in winter quarters.[133] **3.** It is possible to deduce

127 More properly Casivellaunus; see Caesar, *Gallic War*, 5.18.

128 The town is probably Colchester. Androgius is more properly Mandubracius; see Caesar, *Gallic War*, 5.20.

129 Probably the *oppidum* of Wheathampstead in Hertfordshire.

130 Orosius appears to have misunderstood Caesar's comments on Cassivellaunus's stronghold where he states, *Gallic War*, 5.21: 'For the Britons call impassable woodland they have fortified with a rampart and a ditch, a town'. Caesar's description of the *oppidum*'s capture does not indicate particularly stiff resistance. The end of the campaign, which included an attempt to stir up resistance in Kent by Casivellaunus (see *Gallic War*, 5.22–23), has been suppressed by Orosius.

131 Orosius is anachronistically thinking of the Britain of his day – a *diocese* comprising several provinces.

132 The ambush took place near Tongres. The demise of Cotta and Sabinus is drawn from Caesar, *Gallic War*, 5.26–37, though there is no mention of the Treveri being involved here. Orosius has either misread Caesar or used a corrupt manuscript as he has created a town 'Eburonae' out of a tribe, the Eburones.

133 Q. Tullius Cicero, the brother of the orator Cicero. He was encamped among the Nervii. The account of his troubles is drawn from Caesar, *Gallic War*, 5.38–52.

the size of the enemy from the following facts. Their Roman prisoners had taught them that they ought to surround the camp's rampart, if they wanted to besiege it. They had no farm tools, yet by cutting into the earth with their swords and carrying it away in their cloaks, in less than three hours they constructed a rampart 10 feet high and a ditch 15 feet deep, 15 miles in circumference. Besides this, they built 120 towers of astounding height.[134] **4.** After the enemy were exhausted by fighting in their assault formations for seven days and nights, a strong wind suddenly arose. They then used their slings to throw red-hot tiles into the camp,[135] along with javelins that they set alight in their fires and were soon blazing with flames. **5.** The wind, rushing over the reed roofs, quickly fanned these scattered fires. But even so the Romans did not yield, although they were overwhelmed on all sides by wounds, toil, lack of sleep, hunger, and fire.

6. Finally, Caesar was told that one legion had been lost and another was on the point of destruction. **7.** On his arrival with two legions, the enemy raised their siege, gathered all their forces, and attacked him. Caesar deliberately hid himself in a very small camp and sent his cavalry forward, instructing them to pretend to flee in order to tempt the enemy, who would then despise them, to cross the valley that lay between the two sides and which he thought was a position full of danger. **8.** When they arrived, Caesar ordered the gates to be barricaded. The Gauls, when they saw this, assuming that they had already won the battle, abandoned their attack in order to build a rampart outside the fort. Caesar then unleashed his army, which he had held in readiness, from all the gates of the fort and put the Gauls to flight with great slaughter. **9.** They were said to have numbered 60,000 out of whom a few survived by fleeing into impassable marshland.[136]

10. After the leader of the Treveri, Indutiomarus, who had a large force of armed men, on being told that he had the support of all of Gaul, decided to destroy the camp and legion which Labienus commanded – something he thought could easily be done – and then to join up with the Eburones and

---

134 These details are taken from Caesar, *Gallic War*, 5.42. The number of towers is only found in Orosius, and Caesar does not make use of the fortifications to point to the size of his opponents' army.

135 The Gauls' use of the wind is drawn from Caesar, *Gallic War*, 5.43. Caesar makes no mention of the Gauls growing weary. Orosius's use of *cuneus*, 'assault formation' may well be an anachronism as irregular cavalry units in the late Roman army were often given this title; see *Roman Inscriptions of Britain*, 1594. Orosius's rather improbable picture of tiles being thrown from slings derives from an over-hasty reading of Caesar, *Gallic War*, 5.43, where we are told that the Gauls fired red-hot bullets made of clay into the Romans' camp.

136 The figure is drawn from Caesar, *Gallic War*, 5.49.

Nervii and march off to crush Caesar. **11.** Labienus used what devices he had at hand to pretend that he was afraid, and in this way crushed Indutiomarus in a sudden sally after the Gaul failed to take sufficient care while he and his troops were wandering across the front of Romans' fortifications, taunting them.

12. Labienus's victory put an end to the Gauls' remaining attempts at rebellion, and Caesar passed the remainder of the winter a little more quietly.[137] **13.** Nevertheless, he knew that the worst part of the war was still to come, especially since he had lost the greater part of his army and his other troops had been badly wounded which meant he felt that he was not able to sustain, not to mention be able to contain, the Gauls' attacks. He therefore asked the proconsul Pompey to raise some legions and send them in his support. And so three legions arrived at his camp before the end of the winter.[138]

14. Caesar therefore got ready to attack and crush his enemies at the beginning of spring before they could gather their forces together and while they were still afraid and scattered in their own lands. He first ravaged the lands of the Nervii, allowing his men to plunder the vast quantities of booty to be found there.[139] **15.** He then formed his army up into three columns and attacked the Menapii who seemed to be the best protected of the tribes because of the great marshes and impenetrable forests in their lands. After horrendous slaughter on all sides, he accepted the surrender of those who had survived when they came to sue for peace.[140]

16. In the battle that followed, Labienus cunningly lured all the troops of the Treveri into a fight, killed them before they could join with the Germans who were coming to meet them, and straight after this captured their city.[141] **17.** Caesar who wished to avenge the deaths of his lieutenants, Sabinus and Cotta, learnt that Ambiorix and the Eburones, who had destroyed his legion,

137 The attack on Labienus that took place at the end of 54 BC is drawn from Caesar, *Gallic War*, 5.55–58.

138 This material is drawn from Caesar, *Gallic War*, 6.1, where there is no mention of Caesar's losses or his feeling embattled. Pompey is Pompey the Great, Caesar's fellow triumvir.

139 Caesar, *Gallic War*, 6.3, merely mentions a 'large amount' of booty in the form of cattle and prisoners.

140 This account is taken from Caesar, *Gallic War*, 6.5–6. Caesar speaks of taking much booty and of burning buildings and villages, but there is no mention of the 'great slaughter' found in Orosius. Similarly, in the *Gallic War* there is no hint that the envoys who make peace with Caesar are representatives of a tiny surviving remnant of the tribe as Orosius implies here.

141 This account is taken from Caesar, *Gallic War*, 5.7–8. It is possible that Orosius has failed to understand Caesar here and interpreted *civitas* as meaning city when 'tribe' was intended.

had fled to the Ardennes forest **18.** *which is the largest in Gaul and runs from the Rhine and the lands of the Treveri as far as those of the Nervii – a distance of more than 50 miles.*[142] **19.** Calculating that it would be a terrible danger to his own men if they were divided up across this broad, difficult, and unknown woodland to search for an enemy who knew the lie of the land perfectly, he sent heralds across all of Gaul inviting anyone to seek out and seize the booty hidden in the Ardennes forest as he saw fit. **20.** By doing this, as the Gauls fought one another, he avenged the great wrong done to Rome without putting a single Roman in danger. **21.** And so applying this, the safest style of conquering his enemy, he returned safely to Italy.[143]

11

1. When Caesar returned to Italy, Gaul once again plotted to rise up in arms and many tribes gathered together. Their leader was Vercingetorix, on whose advice all the Gauls at once burnt their own towns.[144] **2.** The first to be burnt by its own people was Biturigo.[145] They then launched an attack on Caesar, who, by using forced marches, had secretly rushed back through Narbonensis to his army.

    3. Caesar had already laid siege to a town called Caenapum.[146] After it had been invested for a long time and the Romans had suffered many set-backs, it was finally captured and destroyed by using siege towers on a rainy day when the ropes of the enemies' war engines and their bow strings were slack. **4.** There are said to have been 40,000 men in the town, scarcely 80 of whom escaped by flight and reached the nearest Gallic camp.[147]

    142 A very close paraphrase of Caesar, *Gallic War*, 6.29.4.

    143 At the end of 53 BC. Orosius's account is drawn from Caesar, *Gallic War*, 6.34, where the invitation is to plunder the Eburones rather than the Ardennes forest. This is compression on Orosius's part, as Caesar previously noted in the same chapter that the Eburones had scattered into the Ardennes. Orosius's point here is that man's natural greed will overcome social solidarity. To underline this, he suppresses Caesar's final campaign in Gaul (Caesar, *Gallic War*, 6.37–44, especially ch. 43) this year to give the false impression that his attempt to pit Gaul against Gaul had relieved him of any further need to fight.

    144 While Vercingetorix soon became the leader of the uprising, it had in fact started elsewhere under the different leaders; see Caesar *Gallic War*, 7.1–4. Perhaps this is excusable compression on Orosius's part.

    145 Orosius has misread Caesar, *Gallic War*, 7.15, which reads 'more than 20 towns *of the Bituriges* were burnt in a single day'.

    146 Normally Cenabum, the modern Orleans.

    147 Orosius is highly confused here. According to Caesar, *Gallic War*, 7.3,11, Caenapum was the site of a massacre of Roman citizens, after which it was then recaptured. However,

5. Then the Arverni and all their neighbours – they even persuaded the Aedui to join them[148] – fought against Caesar in a long series of battles. **6.** When they were wearied of the fighting, they withdrew to a strongpoint, which Caesar's troops, eager for booty, were determined to storm, while Caesar in vain pointed out the danger of the position.[149] Because of this, Caesar was hard pressed by the enemy who sallied out from above him, lost a great part of his army, and withdrew in defeat.[150]

7. *While this was going on at Alesia,*[151] Vercingetorix, whom they had all chosen as their king by common consent, urged everyone in all of Gaul who could bear arms to be at hand to fight in this war. This one war, he declared, would either bring everlasting freedom, perpetual slavery, or the death of them all. **8.** In this way, apart from the countless horde that he had already amassed, he managed to collect around 8,000 cavalry and 250,000 infantry.[152] **9.** After this, the Romans and Gauls occupied two hills facing one another. They frequently fought each other in various engagements with varied outcomes, until the Romans were finally triumphant, mainly because of the courage of their German cavalry. These were long-standing allies whom they had now recruited as auxiliary troops.[153]

10. On another day, Vercingetorix summoned all those who had escaped in the battle and declared that it was in good faith that he had instigated them to break the treaty to defend their freedom, and that he was ready in his heart either for all the Gauls to offer themselves up to the Romans to die or for them to offer himself up on behalf of all of them. **11.** The Gauls then took, as if on the king's advice, the choice which they had for sometime concealed through shame and immediately, while asking for pardon for themselves, delivered him up alone as the instigator of this great crime.[154]

Orosius's account of the town's capture is drawn from the later siege of Avaricum (Caesar, *Gallic War*, 7.27, where the heavy rain is portrayed as a hindrance, not a help for the Romans). Orosius's casualty figures, drawn from Caesar, *Gallic War*, 7.28, also refer to Avaricum.

148 Prior to this, the Aedui had been Caesar's staunchest Gallic allies.

149 Gergovia, near the modern Clermont-Ferrand.

150 This incident is drawn from Caesar, *Gallic War*, 7.47–53.

151 Drawn verbatim from Caesar, *Gallic War*, 7.75.1. Alesia is the modern Alise-Sainte-Reine, some 32 miles north-west of Dijon. Orosius is either guilty of a terrible misunderstanding of Caesar here or of over-compression, as his use of this phrase implies that the previous sections dealt with affairs at Alesia which is not the case.

152 Vercingetorix's sentiments and the numbers of his levy are drawn from Caesar, *Gallic War*, 7.76.

153 The incident with the German cavalry is drawn from Caesar, *Gallic War*, 7.80. The comment on their recruitment is Orosius's own.

154 Vercingetorix's surrender is drawn from Caesar, *Gallic War*, 7.89. Orosius has

12. The Gauls themselves believed that the Bellovagui were the bravest of their tribes.[155] Under the leadership of Correus they renewed the war, made an alliance with the Ambiani, Aulerci, Caleti, Velocasses, and Atre-bates,[156] and occupied a position that was surrounded on every side by impassable marshland. When battle was joined, they butchered a great band of the Remi who were supporting the Romans.[157] **13.** They then occupied a position that they had previously decided was ideal for an ambush. The Romans, however, had learnt about this and advanced to the place of the ambush drawn up in battle order. When battle was joined, the Romans closed off the Gauls as they fled against the very fortifications in which they had enclosed themselves and slew them to a man. **14.** It was here that Correus, who refused either to flee or surrender, forced the Romans to kill him as he killed those who were pressing forward to take him alive.[158]

15. Now when Caesar thought that he had pacified all of Gaul and that the country would not dare to attempt any more uprisings, he sent his legions into winter quarters, while he himself laid waste with horrendous slaughter the lands of Ambiorix who had stirred up so many of these wars.[159]

16. Caesar's lieutenant, Gaius Caninius, however, found himself in a war when he arrived in the lands of the Pictones:[160] a great host of the enemy surrounded a legion while it was bogged down on the march and placed it in the greatest danger. **17.** Another lieutenant, Fabius, set out for the Pictones' lands on receiving Caninius's despatches, and there, since he had learnt about the lie of the land from his prisoners, he crushed his enemy while they were off-guard. After indulging in much slaughter, he carried off an even greater amount of booty.[161] **18.** Then, when he had signalled to Caninius that

---

compressed Caesar's account of the fighting at Alesia, but still chosen awkwardly to paraphrase Caesar's, *postero die*, 'on the following day' to introduce his account of the collapse of Gallic resistance. There is no reference to a treaty in Caesar. It must therefore be either an invention of Orosius or something he found in another source. The former option seems the most likely. For a modern discussion of the siege, see Campbell (2006) 148–54.

155 Normally the Bellovaci. The sentiment is drawn from Hirtius, *Gallic War*, 8.6 (Aulus Hirtius, a close ally of Caesar, composed the eighth, and final, book of the *Gallic War*).

156 This list is drawn from Hirtius, *Gallic War*, 8.7.

157 The incident with the Remi is drawn from Hirtius, *Gallic War*, 8.12. The 'great band' is a deduction from *Gallic War*, 8.11 where Hirtius says Caesar levied great numbers of cavalry from the Remi, Lingones, and 'other tribes'. Nothing is said of the casualties in the actual fighting and Hirtius implies that this was a skirmish more than a major battle.

158 The battle and death of Correus are drawn from Hirtius, *Gallic War*, 8.17–19.

159 Caesar's attack on Ambiorix is drawn from Hirtius, *Gallic War*, 8.24–25.

160 The Pictones were centred around the modern Poitiers.

161 Drawn from Hirtius, *Gallic War*, 8.27.5. The comment about 'even more' booty is

he had arrived, Caninius suddenly sallied forth with all his men and flung himself on the foe. In this way an innumerable number of the Gallic host were butchered in a great and lengthy battle, being attacked on one side by Fabius, and on the other by Caninius. **19.** Fabius then advanced into the land of the Carnutes; for he knew that Domnacus, their leader and the one of the longest-standing instigators of the whole rebellion, had escaped from this battle and would stir up more great rebellions in Gaul if he could join up with the Armorican tribes. However, he subdued these with great courage and rapidity, while they were still frightened by the change in the state of things.[162]

20. Meanwhile, after they saw Caninius and his legions invade their territory, Draptes together with Lycterius[163] gathered troops together from all sides and occupied the town of Uxellodunum.[164] **21.** This town hangs from the top of a high mountain citadel with its steep slopes flanked on two sides by a river of no small size. With a secure water supply from an abundant spring half-way down the slope and a large supply of corn safely stored within, it could look down with contempt from afar at the futile manoeuvres of its enemies.[165] **22.** Caninius, doing what only a Roman could do by foresight, lured both their leaders and most of their army out onto the plain and defeated them in a great battle. One of them was killed and the other fled with a few survivors: not one returned to the town.[166] But it was left to Caesar to attack the town itself.

23. When he had been told what had happened, Caesar rushed to the spot and after investigating every possibility, saw that if he tried to take the town by force, it would be child's play and mere entertainment for the enemy to wipe out his army. He had only one route to success: he had in some way to cut off the enemy's water supply. **24.** Caesar could not do this, if the spring that they used for drink continued to flow from half-way down the hill's slope. Caesar ordered mantelets[167] to be moved up close to the spring

---

Orosius's own embroidery: Hirtius simply states that Fabius's men obtained 'a great amount of booty after killing many of the enemy'.

162 Canninus's and Fabius's campaigns are drawn from Hirtius, *Gallic War*, 8.26–31.

163 Slightly corrupted forms of Drappes and Lucterius; see Hirtius, *Gallic War*, 8.30.

164 Probably the Puy d'Issolu in the Dordogne.

165 The description of Uxellodunum is drawn from Hirtius, *Gallic War*, 8.40–41.

166 A rather confused version of the events described in Hirtius, *Gallic War*, 8.35–36. Orosius has collapsed two engagements into a single battle. The comments about the Romans' superior ability are Orosius's own gloss.

167 Latin, *vinea* – the wooden sheds constructed by a besieging army to allow them to advance under cover. See Vegetius, 4.15.

and a tower to be built there. Straightaway there was a great sally from the town. Although the Romans stubbornly pressed on against their opponents who fought with no danger to themselves, and had many successes, a great number of them were butchered. **25.** Therefore, they constructed a mound and a 60-foot-high tower whose top was level with the spring so that they were able to throw their javelins from the same level as the enemy and have no fear that great rocks would be rolled down on them from above.

26. When the townsfolk saw not only their herds, but also the old and the young suffering from thirst, they filled barrels with pitch and tallow, set them alight, rolled them down the hill, and then poured out of the entire town close behind them.[168] **27.** When his siege engines caught fire, Caesar saw that the battle would be hard and dangerous for his men, he therefore ordered his cohorts to go round the town swiftly by a secret route and then suddenly to raise a great cry on all sides. When this happened, the townsfolk were alarmed and wanting to rush back to defend the town, abandoned their attack on the tower and efforts to destroy the mound.

28. Meanwhile the Romans who were safely digging tunnels to cut off the source of the spring beneath the cover of the mound, found the water's source in the depths of the earth and weakened it by dividing it into many channels and turning it back on itself. When they saw their spring run dry, the townsfolk were seized with uttermost despair and surrendered. **29.** Caesar *took the hands from all of them who had lifted a weapon, but left them their lives so that the punishment of the wicked might be all the clearer to future generations*, **30.** for a visible form of punishment has great power to curb insolence, as the very appearance of the wretched, living victim before their eyes reminds those who know about the crime, and compels those who do not, to learn about it.[169]

12

1. When the Gauls had been ground down and conquered, Caesar returned safely to Italy with his legions. He had no fear of Gallic uprisings occurring behind him, knowing that he had left there very few who would dare to rebel or who were to be feared if they did.

168 The fighting around the siege-tower is drawn from Hirtius, *Gallic War*, 8.41–43. Orosius has misunderstood Hirtius's account where the siege-tower is part of Caesar's initial plan, not a response to the fierce resistance he encountered.

169 Caesar's ploy, the end of the siege, and the punishment of the Gauls are drawn from Hirtius, *Gallic War*, 8.43–44, the last being a very close paraphrase of *Gallic War*, 8.44.1. The *sententia* which follows is Orosius's own.

2. I now wish to set before the reader's eyes a bloodless and exhausted Gaul, her state after these blazing fevers and inner seethings had roasted the better part of her vitals, how emaciated and how pale she was, how she lay crushed and undone, how she feared even to conduct necessary business in case it brought back the same onset of woes again. **3.** For the Roman army had fallen on her in a sudden onslaught like disease that is stronger than even the strongest body and which flares up all the more strongly the less patiently it is endured. **4.** The wretched land thirsted as she was forced at sword point to pledge herself to everlasting slavery, and had hostages taken from her besides. She thirsted, as I have said, for the well-known, sweet taste of liberty, something which refreshes us all like a drink of cool water, and the more she realised that it was being taken away from her, the more fervently she desired it. **5.** It was this that produced her frequent attempts to gain what was forbidden to her; she was seized by an ill-opportune freedom to defend her freedom and there grew up an unrestrained lust for endless conquest because this seemed to put an end to the malady that she had unfortunately caught.[170] **6.** Because of this, the Roman was more cunning and devious before battle, a more savage foe in it, and a more heartless victor after it. Hence came every escalation designed to curb the Gauls' restiveness and the lack of belief in any remedy for it.[171]

7. And so, if I could ask this nation which we are talking about,[172] what she thought about those times when she bore these ills, she would reply, I think, as follows: 'That fever has left me so bloodless and cold that even the events of today, which have afflicted almost all the world, neither warm my blood or move me. The Romans have left me in such a state that I cannot rise up even against the Goths.'[173]

8. Nor did even Rome herself escape the disaster that she inflicted. The power of the commanders and might of the legions which had increased and been exercised in every corner of the world and coming into conflict with one another their victories were at her expense, and their defeats at her peril. For it was civil war that accompanied Caesar's return from Gaul and this was heralded by other dire evils, such as the slaughter of Crassus and his army in Parthia.[174]

---

170 A particularly obscure passage. Orosius's point seems to be that the Gauls' enthusiasm to defend themselves had led to a wish to conquer others.
171 Therefore, the Gauls, according to Orosius, were the authors of their own misfortune.
172 i.e. the Gauls.
173 At the time of writing Gaul had been lost to the Roman Empire.
174 Crassus and his army were wiped out by the Parthians at Carrhae in 53 BC, see 6.13.

13

1. 697 years after the foundation of the City,[175] Crassus, the colleague of Pompey in the consulate, was allotted the command against the Parthians. He was a man of insatiable greed and when he heard of the riches of the temple of Jerusalem that Pompey had left untouched, he diverted his course to Palestine, came to Jerusalem, burst into the temple, and ransacked its treasures.[176] **2.** He then marched through Mesopotamia to Parthia, exacting levies and demanding monies from Rome's allies all along his route. Soon after crossing the Euphrates, he encountered Vagenses, the envoy who had been sent to him by Horodes, the king of the Parthians.[177] Vaganses rebuked him furiously, demanding to know why he had been lured by his greed across the Euphrates, breaking the treaty made by Lucullus and Pompey, and said that, because of this, very soon he would be loaded down not with the gold of Parthia, but with Chinese iron.[178]

3. When he arrived near Carrhae, the Parthians led by their prefects Surenas[179] and Silacea[180] suddenly fell upon the Romans and overwhelmed them with their arrows.[181] Very many senators fell there, including even a number of former consuls and praetors. Crassus's son, Crassus, an outstanding youth, was killed fighting in the battle-line.[182] In addition to this, four cohorts along with Crassus's lieutenant, Vargunteius, were caught and killed in the middle of the countryside. **4.** Surenas took his cavalry from the battle and pressed on after Crassus. He surrounded and killed him as he vainly sought a parley, though he would rather have taken him alive. A few men, given their chance by nightfall, fled to Carrhae.

5. After the catastrophe that the Romans had suffered became known, many of her eastern provinces would have reneged on their allegiance or pledges of loyalty to Rome had not Cassius rallied those few who had fled

The notion of Caesar's Gallic Wars being a harbinger of disasters for Rome is also found to some degree in Eutropius, 6.18–19.

175 Orosius's date is two years out; Pompey and Crassus were consuls in 699 *AUC*/55 BC.

176 Orosius is the only evidence for Crassus's actions in Jerusalem. It allows him to imply that Crassus's subsequent downfall was a product of divine vengeance.

177 Orodes II (57–38 BC).

178 Perhaps an allusion to the belief that some of Crassus's army were sold as slaves to China. For a modern version of this fanciful notion, see Dobbs (1957).

179 Orosius has mistaken this title for a personal name.

180 The Parthian satrap of Mesopotamia.

181 The Battle of Carrhae, 9 June 53 BC.

182 A reference to the death of Crassus's son in Livy, *Per.* 106, suggests that Livy is the source for Orosius's account of Crassus's campaign.

and with exceptional presence of mind and moderation secured a restive Syria. He defeated Antiochus and his huge army in a great battle and drove out the Parthians who had been despatched by Horodes to Syria and had already managed to enter Antioch, killing their leader, Osages.[183]

14

1. Rome's place in the world was, therefore, always changing, like the Ocean's swell which is different every day.[184] For seven days it rises steadily and then falls back for the same number of days, being absorbed into itself with a loss that is part of its nature **2.** To put what I have just described in order, a Roman army perished at the hands of the Cimbri and Tigurini by the river Rhône, causing a great panic at Rome. But when the threat of the Cimbri receded, immediately she was overjoyed at her great successes and forgot her previous failings. **3.** The Italian War[185] and Sulla's depredations were her punishment for this boasting about her recent good fortune. Yet after this internecine domestic turmoil that ate her away and eviscerated her down almost to the very marrow of her bones, in an almost equal space of time she was not only restored to her old state, but even extended her boundaries. Lucullus took Asia; Pompey, Spain; and Caesar, Gaul; and the Roman Empire was extended almost to the furthest ends of the earth. **4.** Great disaster followed on from this great expansion. A Roman consul was killed and a Roman army wiped out in Parthia. The seeds of a horrendous civil war between Pompey and Caesar were sown and, while these events were happening, Rome herself was suddenly seized by a great fire and reduced to ashes. **5.** For in the 700th year after the foundation of the City, a fire whose origins were unclear took hold of the greater part of the City. They say that never before had the City been affected or devastated by such a conflagration. For it has been recorded that 14 districts were burnt down along with the Iugarium district.[186] At this point, the civil war, for which dissension and rebellion had long paved the way, began.

---

183 G. Cassius Longinus, Crassus's quaestor, and later one of Caesar's assassins. Orosius has turned the town of Antigoneia, where Cassius defeated the Parthians, into a non-existent general, Antiochus. The account of Cassius's campaigns is probably drawn from Livy, 108.

184 The bulk of this chapter is recapitulation to illustrate Orosius's metaphor.

185 i.e. the Social War.

186 An area of Rome adjacent to the forum, see Livy, 27.37.13. Orosius mentions this fire again at 7.2.11 where he gives Livy as his source. This should be Livy, 109. Orosius dates the fire to 52 BC; however, our only other extant source for it, Julius Obsequens, 65, dates it to 50 BC and notes that it was seen as a prodigy. This is implicit in Orosius's account.

15

1. While returning in triumph from Gaul, Caesar asked that another consulate be decreed for him in his absence. This was denied him by the consul Marcellus who was supported by Pompey. The Senate then decreed that Caesar could not enter the City unless he dismissed his army, and, on the authority of the consul Marcellus, Pompey was sent to take command of the legions at Luceria. **2.** Caesar went to Ravenna. The tribunes of the plebs, Mark Antony and Publius Cassius,[187] who had intervened on Caesar's behalf, but whom Marcellus had banned from the senate-house and forum, came to join him there, accompanied by Curio and Caelius.

3. Caesar crossed the river Rubicon, soon reached Arimium[188] and told the five cohorts, who were the only troops he had, what they had to do. It was with these five cohorts, as Livy says,[189] that he set out to fight the world. He lamented the wrongs done to him and declared that the reason for the civil war was the need to restore the tribunes to their country. **4.** Then through Antony's actions he obtained from Lucretius the seven cohorts that were at Sulmo,[190] and won over to his side the three legions that were under the command of Domitius at Corfinum.[191] Pompey and the entire Senate were terrified by Caesar's growing strength and, as if they had been driven from Italy, they crossed over to Greece and chose Dyrrachium[192] as their headquarters for waging the war.

5. On entering Rome, Caesar broke down the doors of the treasury and took the money he had been refused. He carried off 4,135 pounds of gold, and almost 900,000 pounds of silver.[193] **6.** He then returned to his legions at Ariminum and soon after crossed over the Alps to Marseilles. As this town did not receive him, he left Trebonius there with three legions to storm it, and marched on into the Spains which were held by the Pompeian commanders Lucius Afranius, Marcus Petreius, and Marcus Varro and their legions. There, after many battles, he defeated Petreius and Afranius and let them

---

187 In fact, the second tribune was Quintus Cassius.

188 The Rubicon marked the boundary between Caesar's province and Italy proper; its location is disputed. Ariminum is the modern Rimini. Orosius's chronology is awry here as Ariminum was taken before the crossing of the Rubicon.

189 Livy, 109.

190 The modern Sulmona. These troops defected from their Pompeian commander Lucretius to Caesar when they were approached by Antony.

191 The modern Corfinio.

192 The modern Durazzo in Albania.

193 Up to this point in the chapter, Orosius's main source is Livy, 109.

go after making terms with them.[194] **7.** In Further Spain too, he took two legions from Marcus Varro. His commanders fared equally well, that is to say Curio drove Cato from Sicily, Valerius Cotta from Sardinia, and Tubero was ejected from Africa by Varus. Caesar returned to Marseilles which had been captured after being besieged. He gave the townsfolk merely life and liberty and destroyed everything else there.

8. On the other hand, Dolabella,[195] Caesar's supporter in Illyricum, was defeated by Octavius, and Libo lost his troops and fled to Antony.[196] Basillus[197] and Sallust,[198] each in command of a single legion, Antony, who likewise had one legion, and Hortensius,[199] who came to join them from the Inner Sea,[200] all marched together on Octavius and Libo, but were defeated by them. **9.** Antony and his 15 cohorts surrendered to Octavius and these were all taken to Pompey by Libo. When Curio crossed into Africa from Sicily with his army, King Juba immediately came out to face him and butchered him along with all his troops. Octavius tried to storm Salonae and lost almost all his troops.[201] **10.** Caelius defected from Caesar and joined the exile Milo; they were both cut down when they tried to seize Capua with a band of slaves. On Corfu Bibulus was overcome by his shame because the enemy made a mockery of the defences he had thrown up in the town and along the sea, and killed himself by refusing to eat or sleep.[202]

11. Appius Claudius Censorinus, who had been ordered by Pompey to guard Greece, wished to make trial of the already discredited Pythian oracle. The prophetess whom he forced to go down into the cave is said to have replied to him as follows when he asked about the war: 'This war does not concern you, Roman. You will take the Hollows of Euboea.' The Euboean Gulf is called the Hollows. So Appius departed confused by this perplexing reply.[203]

12. This questioner reminds us to ask a question of our detractors. They

194 A reference to the Ilerda, the modern Lérida, campaign in Catalonia. Afranius and Petreius surrendered on 2 August 49 BC.

195 P. Cornelius Dolabella, later consul in 44 BC.

196 Orosius may have created two individuals out of one here. Florus, 2.13.31, speaks of a lieutenant of Pompey named Octavius Libo. Gaius Antony was the younger brother of Mark Antony.

197 Mentioned by Florus, 2.13.32, and Lucan, *Pharsalia*, 4.416, but otherwise unknown.

198 Perhaps Sallust the historian.

199 The son of the great orator, and Cicero's rival, of the same name.

200 The Adriatic.

201 Sections 6–9 of this chapter are drawn from Livy, 110.

202 The Bibulus involved was Caesar's fellow consul and opponent of 59 BC.

203 The 'Hollows' was a name for the Gulf of Euboea (see Livy, 31.47.1), but is also the name of a region of Euboea between Ramnunta and Carystus.

complain that because of the Christians' faith their holy rites are forbidden, their ceremonies ended, and, especially, that now divination from entrails and prophecy have ceased, it is impossible to avoid future calamities as they cannot be foreseen.[204] **13.** Why then, as their own authors attest, had belief in the Pythian oracle vanished long before Caesar's[205] rule or the birth of Christ? It vanished because the oracle was despised. And why was it despised, save that it was wrong, empty, or ambiguous? Whence the poet wisely warned:

> *Thus many not succeeding, most upbraid*
> *The madness of the visionary maid*
> *And with loud curses leave the mystic shade.*[206]

14. Nor should they think it a small thing that both the god and his seat have become ignored through contempt and are now part of the past.[207] This was the famous Pythian Apollo whom they say after killing the great serpent Pytho, the author and chief practitioner of all prophecy, became heir to the snake's abode, its prophetic powers, and name.[208] He chose, they go on, to give his oracles there because this is where divination and its creator seem to have arisen. **15.** Moreover, his name is spewed forth in other parts of the world from the frothing mouths and wild rants of every wild madman. A great number of kings have rushed to consult the oracle, as if it were the living voice of a wise divinity, and very often Romans too have sent it luxurious gifts.[209]

16. But if the notorious Pythian Apollo has gradually fallen into contempt as experience has exposed him, been abandoned, and had an end put to him, what life can we expect from a dead animal or what truth from a mad girl? Finally, *when at the altars the bloated Tuscan blows his horn*[210] and the innards of a splendid beast are set before him, what lies will the greedy oracle not tell, if, as they admit, Apollo himself leads men astray with obscure and false statements.

17. So, while in the meantime they are unwilling to follow us, let them bear with equanimity the fact that we forbid with truthful judgment a

204 A reference to Theodosius the Great's ban on paganism, promulgated in AD 391, *Theodosian Code*, 16.10.10.

205 i.e. Augustus.

206 Virgil, *Aeneid*, 3.452.

207 Orosius is contrasting the 'antiquity' of Apollo with the 'new times' of Christianity.

208 'Great serpent' carries clear Christian overtones of the devil.

209 Orosius implies that Romans ought to have known better than these kings.

210 Virgil, *Georgics*, 2.193.

practice that the majority of their ancestors despised after experiencing it.

18. Meanwhile at Dyrrachium, a large number of Oriental kings came bringing support for Pompey.[211] When Caesar arrived, he besieged Pompey in vain, for although he dug a ditch 15 miles long, the seas lay open to Pompey. **19.** Pompey destroyed a strongpoint by the sea guarded by Marcellinus[212] and killed Caesar's garrison posted there. Caesar set out to take Torquatus and his single legion by storm. **20.** Pompey, realising his allies' danger, concentrated his forces here, upon which Caesar abandoned his siege and immediately marched against him. Torquatus then sallied forth and attacked his rearguard. **21.** This led to Caesar's troops panicking at their sudden danger and they fled, while Caesar vainly tried to rally them. Pompey, whom Caesar admits was the victor, then recalled his army. 4,000 of Caesar's troops, 22 centurions, and a good number of Roman knights were killed in this battle.[213] **22.** After this, Caesar swiftly marched through Epirus into Thessaly. Pompey followed him with an enormous force and battle was joined.[214]

23. The lines of battle on both sides were drawn up as follows: Pompey ordered his 88 cohorts into three lines. He had 40,000 infantry and 600 cavalry on his left wing, and 500 on his right. There were also many kings, and a greater number of Roman knights and senators, besides which there was a large force of light infantry. **24.** Caesar ordered his 80 cohorts into a similar threefold line; he had fewer than 30,000 men and 1,000 cavalry.[215] **25.** One could not help groaning on seeing the might of Rome gathered on the fields of Pharsalia to destroy itself, for if harmony had reigned over these armies, no people or king would have been able to resist them.[216]

26. In the first exchange, Pompey's cavalry was put to flight, exposing his left flank. Then, after long, inconclusive slaughter, Pompey stood on one side urging his men 'to spare the citizens', but not practising what he preached, while Caesar, on the other, did precisely that, as he urged his troops on, shouting 'soldier, strike at the face'.[217] In the end, all Pompey's

---

211 Pompey's conquest of the east had given him a large number of clients in Asia Minor.

212 P. Cornelius Lentulus Marcellinus, Caesar's quaestor in 48 BC.

213 Caesar, *The Civil War*, 3.71; 3.73. Caesar is a little less explicit than Orosius merely remarking that he was 'forced to revise his previous plans'. His casualty figures are also lower – he says he lost 960 men along with 32 tribunes and centurions.

214 The Battle of Pharsalus, 9 August 48 BC.

215 These figures are taken from Eutropius, 6.20.

216 A similar sentiment is found in Eutropius, 6.21.

217 See Plutarch, *Caesar*, 45.2. According to Plutarch, Caesar was playing on the vanity of Pompey's troops who would not want facial scars.

army fled and his camp was ransacked. **27.** 15,000 of Pompey's troops and
33 of his centurions were killed in the battle. This was the end of the battle
at Old Pharsalus.[218]

Pompey fled to the mouth of the river Peneus,[219] commissioned a
merchantman, and crossed over to Asia. **28.** Thence he went to Egypt via
Cyprus and as soon after he had come ashore was killed on the orders of the
young Ptolemy in order to placate the triumphant Caesar.[220] Pompey's wife
and sons fled, the rest of his fleet was destroyed and everyone in it cruelly
butchered. It was here that Pompey Bithynicus died,[221] while the former
consul Lentulus was killed at Pelusium.[222]

29. After setting the affairs of Thessaly in order, Caesar came to Alexandria and wept when Pompey's head and signet ring were brought out for
him to see. When he came to the palace, he was outwitted by the king's
guardians[223] who, in order to stop Caesar taking their money and to stir
up their people to hate him, had cunningly stripped the temples to create
the impression that even the royal treasury was empty. **30.** Moreover the
royal commander, Achillas, whose hands had already been stained with
Pompey's blood, was, in the meantime, plotting Caesar's death too. After he
was ordered to dismiss the army that he commanded which was composed
of 20,000 armed men, he did not merely disregard his orders, but drew his
men up in order of battle.

31. In the battle that followed, the command to burn the royal fleet,
which happened to be beached at the time, was given. The flames reached
part of the city and destroyed 400,000 books that were housed in a building
that happened to be close by, a singular monument to the study and labours
of our ancestors who had gathered together this great collection of famous
works of genius. **32.** And so although there are, as I have seen myself,
bookshelves in the temples which they say were plundered and emptied by
our own people[224] in our own time – which is indeed true[225] – it would be

218 The name of the acropolis of Pharsalus. Sections 10–27 of this chapter are drawn from
Livy, 111, though the moralising excursus on oracles is no doubt Orosius's own.
219 The modern river Pineios, the main river of Thessaly.
220 Ptolemy XIII Dionysius, aged 13.
221 Orosius just seems to be wrong here. A. Pompeius Bithynicus was killed by Sextus
Pompey on Sicily in 42 BC, Cicero, *Letters to his Friends* (*Ad Familiares*), 6.16 and 6.17;
Livy, *Per.* 123.
222 L. Cornelius Lentulus Crus, consul in 49 BC.
223 The eunuch Pothinus, the orator Theodotus of Chios, and the general Achillas.
224 i.e. Christians.
225 Some commentators, e.g. Sánchez Salor (1982a) 135 n. 267, believe that this phrase is

more reasonable to believe that they sought out other books which imitated the studies of old rather than that there had been some other library apart from this one of 400,000 books and which had escaped destruction.[226]

33. After this, Caesar took control of the island where the Pharos is found.[227] Achillas advanced on him here with Gabinius's troops.[228] A great battle was fought: an enormous number of Caesar's troops fell and all of Pompey's killers were killed here. **34.** Hard pressed by the force of his enemy's advance, Caesar boarded a launch that soon was weighed under and sunk by the weight of those following him. Caesar swam 200 yards to a ship, holding his papers aloft in one hand. Soon afterwards, he was forced to fight at sea and had the great fortune to sink or capture the ships of the royal fleet.[229]

16

1. At the Alexandrians' request, Caesar restored their king to them, warning him that he ought to seek to experience Rome's friendship rather than her arms. However, when he was freed, he immediately declared war and was straightaway annihilated along with all his army. 20,000 are reported to have

an interpolation into the text. Certainly, the admission is not consonant with Orosius's normal aggressive defence of all things Christian or with what follows in his account.

226 Canfora (1989) 70, 93, reads the Latin *proximis forte aedibus condita* as 'stored by chance' in the neighbouring buildings and therefore thinks that the books were in a warehouse destined for export (or potentially which had just been imported – Galen, *Commentary on the Hippocratic book 'Concerning the nature of man'* (*Commentarium in Hippocratis librum De Natura Hominis*), 1.44, notes that books were not immediately taken to the library but stored in warehouses rather than in a library), a view with which Barnes (2005) 72 is cautiously inclined to agree. Plutarch, *Caesar*, 25, on the other hand, is explicit that the library was destroyed, a statement corroborated by Aulus Gellius, *Attic Nights*, 8.17.3. Orosius's figure of 400,000 is likely to be corrupt. Seneca, *On an Untroubled Mind* (*De Tranquilitate Animi*), 9.4–5, speaks of Livy, Orosius's source, recording that 40,000 books were burnt at Alexandria and this is probably the true number. Orosius is being disingenuous in his account. There was another great library in Alexandria, the Pergamene, housed at the Serapeum. This collection of 200,000 volumes was created by the kings of Pergamum and later given by Antony to Cleopatra. It was destroyed by the Christian patriarch of Alexandria, Theophilus, with the support of Theodosius the Great. It is this act of vandalism by Christians, and, by proxy, Spanish Christians, that Orosius is trying to talk away.

227 The lighthouse which was one of the Seven Wonders of the World. The island is now known as El Sayyala.

228 These were the Roman troops Aulus Gabinius had left in Egypt in 57 BC after restoring Ptolemy XI Auletes to his throne.

229 Sections 10–34 of this chapter are drawn from Livy, 112.

been killed in this battle. 12,000 are said to have surrendered along with 70 warships. 500 of the victor's men are said to have fallen.[230] **2.** The young king boarded a launch in order to escape, but he was pushed under water by the numbers jumping onto it and killed. His body when it was washed up onto the shore was recognised by its golden breastplate. Caesar sent this on ahead of him to Alexandria and so forced all the Alexandrians to surrender to him in despair. He then gave the kingdom of Egypt to Cleopatra.[231] **3.** After this, he crossed through Syria and defeated Pharnaces in Pontus.[232]

He then returned to Rome, was made dictator and consul, and crossing over to Africa, fought Juba and Scipio at Thapsus,[233] killing a great host of men. Both Juba and Scipio's camps were ransacked and 60 elephants were captured. **4.** Cato committed suicide at Utica,[234] while Juba paid an assassin to cut his throat, and Petreius used that self-same sword to run himself through.[235] Scipio cut his throat on the ship on which he had been trying to flee to Spain, but which had been forced by the wind to return to Africa. **5.** Titus Torquatus died on the same ship.[236] Caesar ordered Pompey the Great's[237] grandsons and his daughter Pompeia to be killed along with Faustus Sulla[238] and Afranius and his son, Petreius.[239]

6. Then he entered the City in a four-fold triumph,[240] arranged the affairs of the republic he had won back, and immediately set off for the Spains to fight the Pompeys, Pompey's sons.[241] Seventeen days after he had left the City, he reached Saguntum and at once began to fight a long series of battles with varying outcomes against the two Pompeys, Labienus, and Attius Varus.

230 The Battle of the Nile, 27 March 47 BC.

231 Sections 1–2 of this chapter are drawn from Livy, 112.

232 Pharances was Mithridates' son and attempting to re-establish his father's kingdom. He was defeated in a lightning campaign, culminating in the Battle of Zela, 2 August 47 BC. It was on this occasion that Caesar coined the phrase, *veni, vidi, vici* – 'I came, I saw, I conquered.'

233 The modern Ras Dimas in Tunisia.

234 The modern Utique in Tunisia.

235 According to Livy, *Per.* 114, Petreius killed Juba and then himself. Orosius may have misread Livy here. [Caesar], *The African War*, 94, has Juba running Petreius through and then committing suicide.

236 More correctly Manlius Torquatus.

237 This is Orosius's only use of this epithet.

238 The son of the former dictator and Pompey's son-in-law.

239 The first sentence of section 3 is drawn from Livy, 113, the remainder of sections 3–5 from Livy, 114.

240 On 25 July 46 BC. The triumphs celebrated were over Gaul, Egypt, Pontus, and Africa.

241 Gnaeus and Sextus Pompey.

7. The final battle was fought by the river Munda.[242] The forces engaged were so large and the slaughter that followed so great that Caesar too, seeing his lines cut down and forced back and that even his veterans were not ashamed to retreat, was thinking of forestalling his coming disgrace on defeat by suicide, when suddenly the Pompeys' army broke and fled. **8.** The battle was fought on the same day that the Elder Pompey had fled from the City to wage war; for four years since that day civil war had thundered without ceasing around the whole world. Titus Labienus and Attius Varus were killed in action, Gnaeus Pompey fled with 100 cavalry. **9.** His brother Sextus Pompey swiftly mustered a not inconsiderable band of Lusitanians, attacked Caesonius, was defeated, and then killed while fleeing. Caesar attacked the town of Munda and eventually took it after very heavy losses.[243]

17

1. Caesar returned to Rome. Here, while he was restoring the constitution of the state in a merciful fashion, contrary to the examples set by his predecessors,[244] he was run through 23 times in the senate-house and died. The ring-leaders of the plot were Brutus and Cassius, but most of the Senate knew of it. **2.** They say that there were more than 60 participants in the conspiracy.[245] The two Brutuses, Gaius Cassius, and the other conspirators withdrew to the Capitol with daggers drawn. For a long time, there was a debate whether the Capitol should be burnt along with those who had perpetrated the murder. **3.** The people, stricken with grief, took Caesar's body to the forum and cremated it on a pyre made from magistrates' benches and seats.

4. Rome covered the breadth of her realm with her troubles and, turning to slaughter herself, avenged each nation in the self-same place where

242 On 17 March 45 BC. Orosius refers to Munda more correctly as a town at 6.16.9.

243 Orosius has reversed the fates of the two Pompeys. Munda is normally taken as a city, see Eutropius, 6.24. Its site perhaps lay near Bailén in Andalusia. Again, Orosius seems to have misread Livy (116, though our extant summary of this book lacks any mention of these Spanish campaigns) here.

244 Orosius uses *maiores* here. He wants the reader to think both of Caesar's immediate political predecessors, such as Sulla, but also of the Roman political tradition as a whole. Augustine took the same view of Caesar's death; see *City of God*, 3.30.

245 Orosius is likely to have drawn the details of Caesar's death from Livy, 116. Eutropius, 6.25, perhaps drawing on the same source, also states that there were 'sixty or more' senators and equestrians involved in the plot.

she had conquered them. In Asia, Africa, and Europe – I am not merely speaking of the three parts of the world, but of every corner of these three parts – Rome exhibited her own people as gladiators, producing a heart-breaking performance of vengeance for an enemy's holiday.

5. However, it was not enough that the causes of this strife were consumed along with their authors. Their seeds fell in the same field and took root there: seeds that would bring a great crop of troubles producing much sweat for those who reaped them.[246] Caesar, the victor of a war between citizens, was killed by citizens, and a great column of conspirators was implicated in the murder of this one single man. **6.** It was clear that, given his unjust death, Caesar would have many avengers, but the majority of Rome's nobility had bound themselves with the chains of this crime in order that this great source of evil should swell up to the scale of a war, rather than be brought to a close by a speedy act of vengeance.[247]

7. Stories tell us how the famous Medea once sowed the teeth of a slain serpent from which armed men, a crop befitting the sowing, came forth from the earth and at once began to fight and lay each other low. **8.** This story was devised by poets' imagination,[248] but how many armies did our Rome after Caesar's death give birth to from his ashes, and how many wars did she fight to show her fecundity in producing misery? And these were not childrens' stories, but spectacles for entire peoples.

9. However, it is pride that was the root of all these ills, it is this that made civil wars flare up, and it is this that made them multiply.[249] Therefore, it is not unjust to kill those who seek to kill unjustly as long as such ambition and rivalry are punished by the same men who indulge in them. This will be so until those who have refused to share power learn to endure being ruled and supreme power is vested in the hands of one man so that all men might enter into a very different way of life where all try in humility to please and not arrogantly to give offence.[250] **10.** However, a teacher of this

246 Orosius has in mind the aphorism, 'for whatsoever a man soweth, that shall he also reap', Galatians 6.7.

247 A tortured reference to Cicero's proposal to the Senate for a political amnesty at the meeting convened immediately after Caesar's murder; see 7.6.4–5.

248 Orosius is probably thinking of Ovid, *Metamorphoses*, 7.121–30.

249 See Proverbs 13.10 and 16.18. Orosius has taken this notion from the teaching of Augustine, who states it explicitly at *City of God*, 19.1. This book of *City of God* had not been composed when the *Histories* were written, but the perils of *superbia* are an underlying theme of Augustine's approach to history and so Orosius is likely to have been aware of the notion. See Corsini (1968) 68.

250 Given the context, this appears to be an argument for the providential nature of

doctrine of humility is needed for us to reach this healthy state. Therefore when Augustus Caesar's rule had been opportunely set in place, the Lord Christ was born. He, although He was in the form of God, humbly took the form of a slave[251] so that the teaching of humility might finally become more fitting, at a time when the punishment of pride already served as an example for all throughout the world.

18

1. 710 years after the foundation of the City,[252] after Julius Caesar was killed, Octavian, to whom his uncle had bequeathed in his will both his estate and name, and who was later, after he had assumed power, called Augustus, came to Rome and, though he was but a youth, devoted himself to waging civil war. **2.** For, to outline briefly this mass of ills, *he waged five such wars: at Mutina,[253] Philippi, Perusia, on Sicily, and at Actium. Two of these, the first and last, he fought against Mark Antony; the second against Brutus and Cassius; the third against Lucius Antonius; and the fourth against Gnaeus Pompey's son, Sextus Pompey.[254]*

3. On being proclaimed a public enemy by the Senate, Antony had blockaded Decimus Brutus, besieging him at Mutina. Caesar[255] was sent along with the consuls Hirtius and Pansa to free Brutus and defeat Antony. Pansa arrived first and fell into an ambush. In the midst of his army's defeat he was gravely wounded by a javelin and died of his wounds a few days later. Hirtius, on bringing reinforcements for his colleague, destroyed Antony's great army with enormous slaughter.[256] Caesar merely guarded their camp. **5.** In a second battle against Antony, both sides suffered heavy losses. It was then that the consul Hirtius was killed, Antony was defeated and put to flight, and Caesar emerged victorious.[257] Decimus Brutus confessed to him

---

Augustus's rise to power. For Orosius's belief in the necessity of one kingdom to rule the world, see 2.1.4.

251 See Philippians 2.6–7.

252 44 BC. Orosius's date is correct.

253 The modern Modena.

254 Taken verbatim, save one word, from Suetonius, *Augustus*, 9.

255 i.e. Octavian, who styled himself Gaius Julius Caesar Octavianus.

256 14 April 44 BC.

257 21 April 44 BC. In fact, the Senate awarded a triumph to Decimus Brutus and only an ovation to Octavian. This is underlined by Livy, *Per.* 119, who goes on state that this was the reason for Octavian's and Antony's reconciliation. Perhaps Orosius has read his Livy too hastily here.

his part in the plot to kill Caesar, pouring out entreaties of repentance.[258]

6. At Zmyrna Dolabella killed Trebonius, who had been one of Caesar's killers. Dolabella was proclaimed to be a public enemy by the Senate.

Both the armies of the dead consuls began to obey Caesar.

7. After this, Decimus Brutus was captured and killed by the Sequani in Gaul, and Basillus, another of the assassins, was killed at the hands of his own slaves.[259]

8. Through Lepidus's careful diplomacy, Caesar became a friend of Antony and, as a pledge of their friendship and reconciliation, was given his daughter in marriage.[260] **9.** They then went to the City and rumours began that proscriptions would follow. The former praetor Gaius Thoranius paid no attention to these and was killed when soldiers burst into his house. Many others were also butchered. **10.** Because of this, the names of 132 senators were posted up to stop unlicensed killing spreading further and out of control.[261] Lepidus's authority and signature appeared at the top of the list, followed by Antony, and finally Caesar. **11.** It was on this list that Antony proscribed his personal enemy Tullius Cicero[262] and also his uncle, Lucius Caesar, a crime made worse by the fact that his mother was still alive.[263] Lepidus cast his brother Lucius Paulus into the numbers of the proscribed. **12.** Afterwards 30 knights were added to the proscription list. There followed a long period in which many and various forms of murder occurred. The houses of the proscribed were destroyed after everything there had been stolen.[264]

13. Meanwhile, Dolabella was fighting a sequence of battles with Cassius in Syria in which he was defeated and committed suicide. Brutus and Cassius gathered large armies and united their forces at Athens, having laid waste to all of Greece. Cassius attacked the Rhodians by land and sea and compelled them to surrender, leaving them nothing but their lives.[265] **14.** Caesar and Antony with their enormous war machine chased these two into

258 Sections 1–5 of this chapter are drawn from Livy, 117–18.

259 These three lapidary sections almost appear to be notes intended to be worked up at a later date.

260 Antony's step-daughter, Claudia. Orosius is dealing with the negotiations that led to the creation of the Second Triumvirate in November 43 BC.

261 Orosius's figure is taken from Livy, *Per.* 120. Florus, 2.16.3, says 140 senators were proscribed.

262 Orosius makes no previous mention of this animosity.

263 Caesar was his mother's brother.

264 Sections 6–12 are drawn from Livy, 119–20.

265 This section is drawn from Livy, 121.

Macedonia and forced them to commit suicide, though it is very clear that it was not bravery on Antony's part, but Caesar's good luck, that brought this battle to a close. **15.** At the time Caesar was ill and had decided to stay in the camp to take some rest; however, urged on by the entreaties of his doctor, who said that he had received a warning in a dream to take Caesar out of the camp that day for good of his health, he went out with some difficulty onto the field and mixed with the troops. Soon afterwards, his camp was taken by the enemy. On the other hand, his troops captured Cassius's camp. **16.** This reduced Brutus and Cassius to despair, and they decided on a premature death before the battle was over. Having summoned their assassins, Cassius offered them his head and Brutus, his flank.²⁶⁶

17. Meanwhile at Rome, Antony's wife and Caesar's mother-in-law, Fulvia, exercised power in the way one would expect of a woman. As she transformed consular into regal power, it is unclear whether she should be counted as the last of the old order or the first of the new,²⁶⁷ but what is clear is that she acted with arrogance towards those who had worked to allow her assume her arrogant position. **18.** She even attacked Caesar on his return to Brundisium,²⁶⁸ insulting him and stirring up factional plots against him. When she was driven out of Rome by Caesar, she fled to Antony in Greece.²⁶⁹

19. After he found he was on the list of the proscribed, Sextus Pompey turned to piracy and laid waste to all the coast of Italy with his murdering and pillaging. He captured Sicily, blocking Rome's food and reducing her to starvation. **20.** Soon after this, the triumvirs, or rather tyrants,²⁷⁰ namely Lepidus, Caesar, and Antony, made peace with him. But immediately Pompey, contrary to the agreement, allowed fugitives to join his army and was declared an enemy again.

21. Pompey's freedman, Mena, defected to Caesar with a fleet of 60

266 The battle at Philippi in northern Greece lasted two days; Cassius committed suicide after the first day, and Brutus after the second. Orosius has elided the two events. Sections 14–16 are drawn from Livy, 123–24. Orosius indulges in bold revisionism as normally Antony is rightly credited with winning the battle by ancient authors.

267 A striking statement, which shows that by late antiquity the principate was regarded as a form of monarchy. See also 6.20.2 below.

268 The modern Brindisi.

269 Sections 17–18 are drawn from Livy, 125–26. Although he has alluded to it at 6.18.2, Orosius suppresses any description of the bloody siege of Perusia, the modern Perugia, which reflected very badly on Octavian.

270 This is Orosius's first mention of the second triumvirate. The gloss of 'tyrants' appears to be his own.

ships and was put in charge of it on Caesar's command. He and Statilius
Taurus[271] at once fought at sea against Pompey's commander, Menecrates.
22. Then Caesar himself fought a bloody sea-battle against these same
Pompeians, but after triumphing, he lost almost all his victorious fleet by
shipwreck off Scylaceum.[272]

23. In three great battles Ventidius[273] routed the Persians[274] and Parthians
who had invaded Syria, and killed the Parthian king, Pacorus, in combat.[275]
This happened on the self-same day that Crassus had been killed by the
Parthians. After hardly taking a single strongpoint, Antony made peace with
Antiochus in order that he should seem to have been the one to have brought
this great affair to a close. **24.** He made Ventidius governor of Syria and
instructed him to make war on Antigonus who had at that time defeated the
Jews, captured Jerusalem, pillaged the temple there, and given their kingdom
to Herod. Ventidius defeated him at once and accepted his surrender.[276]

25. The freedman Mena fled back to Pompey with six ships. He was
received with mercy and then set fire to Caesar's fleet. Shortly before this,
Caesar had lost a second fleet through shipwreck. Afterwards, this same
Mena was ensnared in a naval battle by Agrippa[277] and defected to Caesar
with six triremes. Caesar spared this three-times-a-turncoat's life, but left
him without a command. **26.** Agrippa then fought a victorious sea-battle
against Demochas and Pompey between Mylae and the Liparae islands,
sinking or capturing 30 ships and leaving the rest badly damaged. Pompey
fled to Messana. Meanwhile, Caesar had crossed over to Tauromenium,[278]
27. but Pompey then launched a sudden attack on him. Caesar had many
of his ships sunk, lost a great number of his men, and fled to Italy, but he
returned without delay to Sicily. **28.** Here he met Lepidus who had come
from Africa and was trying through terror, threats, and arrogance to win back

271 A leading member of Octavian's entourage who later became consul in 26 BC and City
Prefect or *Praefectus Urbi* in 16 BC.

272 The Gulf of Squillace off Calabria, notoriously treacherous for shipping; see Virgil,
Aeneid, 3.553.

273 Ventidius Bassus, one of Antony's lieutenants.

274 Orosius is here thinking anachronistically of his own day.

275 Pacorus was, in fact, the son of the Parthian king, Orodes II.

276 Sections 19–24 are drawn from Livy, 127–28. Antigonus is the Jewish Hasmonean
pretender Mattathias Antigonus who allied with the Parthians to establish a kingdom in 40 BC.
He was crushed in 37 BC and subsequently killed in Antioch. He is also mentioned by Jerome,
Chronicle, A Abr. 1978 (= correctly, 37 BC).

277 M. Vipsanius Agrippa, Octavian's right-hand man.

278 The modern Taormina on the east coast of Sicily.

supreme command for himself. **29.** A few days later Agrippa fought a fierce sea-battle against Pompey at Caesar's command. Caesar stood watching on the shore with his army drawn up in battle array. Agrippa defeated Pompey, sinking or capturing 163 ships. Pompey only just escaped with 17 vessels.

30. Lepidus, swollen with pride because he had 20 legions, plundered Messana which he had turned over to his troops, and then spurned Caesar twice when he came to meet him, indeed, he ordered that javelins to be thrown at him. **31.** Caesar gathered his cloak around his left arm and so managed to ward off these weapons. Soon, after spurring his horse on and returning to his own men, he marshalled his army and marched against Lepidus. After a few casualties, he won over the majority of Lepidus's legions to his side. **32.** When Lepidus finally realised where his vanity had led him, he took off his general's cloak, put on mourning, and went as a suppliant to Caesar. He succeeded in keeping his life and property, but was sent into perpetual exile. Caesar's prefect, Taurus,[279] marched through almost all of Sicily with the sword, and cowed it into loyalty.[280]

33. Caesar then had 44 legions under his sole command. The troops, made more restive by their numbers, started to riot and demand that land be given to them. Caesar kept his nerve, discharged 20,000 soldiers, restored 30,000 slaves to their masters, and crucified another 6,000 whose masters could not be found. **34.** He entered the City to an ovation[281] and the Senate decreed that he should have the power of a tribune permanently.[282] It was at this time that a spring of oil came out of the earth in a lodging house across the Tiber and flowed copiously for the whole day.[283]

19

1. After he had crossed the Araxes,[284] Antony was assailed on all sides by every kind of trouble, and finally returned with difficulty to Antioch with a few men. In every battle, and he had provoked most of them, he fled, defeated by a host of horse-archers.[285] His movements were hindered by his lack of

---

279 i.e. Statilius Taurus.
280 Sections 25–32 are drawn from Livy, 129.
281 A minor, but official, triumph.
282 See 6.20.7 below.
283 This miracle is recorded by Jerome, *Chronicle. A Abr.* 1976 (= 39 BC).
284 The river Aras in Armenia.
285 According to Plutarch, *Antony*, 50, Antony in fact won 18 victories. Nevertheless, Orosius is right to see his campaign as a disastrous defeat.

knowledge of these parts of the world, and the extremes of hunger drove him to use unspeakable food.[286] The majority of his troops surrendered to the enemy.[287] **2.** After this, he crossed over to Greece and ordered Pompey, who was readying an army for battle after his defeat by Caesar, to come to him with a small escort. Pompey fled, and after many defeats by land and sea at the hands of Antony's generals, Titius and Furnius, was captured, and, soon after, put to death. **3.** Caesar subdued Illyricum, Pannonia, and part of Italy by force, bringing then under his control.

Antony captured Artabanes,[288] the king of Armenia, by treachery and deceit. He was bound with silver chains and forced to reveal the whereabouts of the royal treasury. Antony then stormed the city where the king had betrayed that the treasure was hidden and carried off a great amount of gold and silver.[289] **4.** Elated by obtaining this money, he ordered that war be declared on Caesar, and divorce proceedings be begun against his wife, Octavia, who was Caesar's sister. He also commanded that Cleopatra should come from Alexandria to meet him. **5.** He himself set out to Actium where he had stationed his fleet. When he found almost a third of his rowers had died of starvation, he was unmoved and said, 'Just keep the oars safe, for as long as there are men in Greece, there will be no lack of rowers.'

6. Caesar advanced from Brundisium to Epirus with 230 warships. Agrippa, who had been sent on ahead by Caesar, captured a great number of merchantmen sailing from Egypt, Syria, and Asia, loaded with grain and arms for Antony. Cruising round the Peloponnesian Gulf, he stormed the fortified city of Mothona, which was held by Antony's strongest garrison.[290] **7.** He then captured Corfu, chased and crushed in a sea-battle those who fled, and, after performing many bloody deeds, returned to Caesar. Antony, troubled because his soldiers were deserting and starving, decided to force the issue. He suddenly marshalled his army, marched on Caesar's camp, and was defeated.

8. Two days after this battle, Antony moved his camp to Actium and made ready to fight at sea. There were 230 warships, and 30 ancillary ships – triremes equal in speed to Liburnians[291] – in Caesar's fleet. Eight legions

---

286 There is a hint of cannibalism here.

287 A description of Antony's disastrous expedition against the Parthians in 36 BC. Orosius has drawn his account from Livy, 130.

288 Livy, *Per.* 131, gives the king's name as Artavasdes.

289 Sections 2 and 3 are drawn from Livy, 131.

290 The modern Methoni.

291 At the time of Actium the standard warship was the quinquereme. The Liburnian was

along with an additional five praetorian cohorts were embarked on the fleet.
9. Antony's fleet numbered 170 ships, but what it lacked in numbers it made
up for in size, for his vessels stood ten feet proud from the waterline. **10.** The
great and famous battle took place at Actium.[292] From the fifth to the seventh
hour its outcome was in the balance, and both sides suffered very heavy
casualties. During the rest of the day and the following night, things turned
in Caesar's favour. **11.** First, Queen Cleopatra fled with 60 of the swiftest
ships, then, Antony pulled down the standard from his flagship and followed
his wife as she fled. As the dawn came up, Caesar brought his victory to
completion. **12.** 12,000 men are said to have been killed on the defeated side
and 6,000 taken prisoner of whom 1,000 later died while receiving medical
treatment.[293]

13. Antony and Cleopatra decided to send the children that they had had
together to the Red Sea along with some of the crown jewels, while they
themselves established garrisons at the two horns of Egypt, Pelusium and
Parethonium, and prepared a fleet and army to renew the war.

14. Caesar was acclaimed general for the sixth time, and went to
Brundisium as consul for the fourth time along with his colleague in office,
Marcus Licinius Crassus. There he divided his legions into garrisons to
station around the world. He then advanced to Syria and soon after came
to Pelusium, where Antony's garrison received him of their own free will.
15. Meanwhile, Cornelius Gallus, who had been sent on ahead by Caesar,
received a pledge of loyalty from the four legions that Antony had stationed
as a garrison in Cyrene. He then defeated Antony, captured Parethonium,
which is the first city in Egypt after the Libyan border,[294] and then defeated
Antony again by the Pharos.

16. Antony engaged Caesar in a cavalry battle in which he fled after
being defeated in a pitiable fashion. On the first of Sextilis,[295] Antony went
down to the port at dawn to draw up his fleet, when suddenly all his ships
defected to Caesar. Deprived of his only protection, he retreated in panic
with a few men to the palace. **17.** Then, with Caesar's approach imminent
and rioting in the city, Antony ran himself through with his sword and was
carried half-dead to Cleopatra into the tomb where she, determined to die,

a light bireme originally developed on the Illyrian coast that was widely used as a scouting
vessel; see Morrison (1995) 72–73.

292 2 September 31 BC.
293 Sections 4–12 are drawn from Livy, 132.
294 See 1.2.88.
295 Later renamed August. Here 1 August 30 BC.

had hidden herself away. **18.** Cleopatra, after she learnt that she was to be kept alive for Caesar's triumph, committed suicide of her own free will, and was found lifeless, having been bitten, it is believed, by a snake on her left arm. The Psylli, who are accustomed to drink snake venom out of men's wounds by sucking and drawing it forth,[296] were summoned to her aid by Caesar, but in vain.

19. Caesar, triumphant, was left master of Alexandria, the greatest and wealthiest city in the world. Rome was so enriched by her wealth that because of the abundance of cash, the price of land and other saleable commodities doubled from the price they had been up until to that time. **20.** Caesar ordered Antony's eldest son to be killed, along with Publius Candidus, who had always been a bitter enemy to Caesar and had proved a traitor to Antony as well; Cassius Palmensis, who was the last victim to atone for the violence done to Caesar's father;[297] and Quintus Ovinius, who was executed above all for not having been ashamed, despite being a Roman senator, at the disgusting disgrace of being in charge of the queen's spinning and weaving workshops. **21.** Caesar then marched with his infantry into Syria and thence sent them into winter quarters in Asia, after which he returned to Brundisium via Greece.[298]

20

1. 725 years after the foundation of the City, when Emperor Caesar Augustus himself was consul for the fifth time along with Lucius Apuleius,[299] Caesar returned in triumph from the east. On the sixth of January, he entered the city in a triple triumph and then closed the gates of Janus for the first time, now all the civil wars had died down and come to an end.[300] **2.** This day was the first on which he was called Augustus.[301] This title, previously left unclaimed, and which no other ruler up to our own times has dared to use, proclaimed that he had legitimately taken up the mantle of power over the world, and that from that day ultimate power was vested and remained in the

296 See Pliny, *Natural History*, 7.2.14.
297 i.e. Julius Caesar who had adopted Octavian in his will.
298 Sections 13–21 are drawn from Livy, 133.
299 29 BC. Orosius's date is correct, but Lucius should read Sextus.
300 A concatenation of errors – Augustus's triumphs were held in the August of this year, but the gates of Janus had been previously closed by decree of the Senate on 11 January (see the *Fasti Praenestini*) while Augustus was absent from Rome.
301 In fact, this title was awarded two years later in 27 BC. Livy may have elided these two events, see *Per.* 134, and Orosius has seemingly misread him because of this.

hands of one individual – a system that the Greeks call monarchy.[302]

3. No believer, nor even anyone who opposes the faith, is ignorant of the fact that we keep on this same day, the sixth of January, the feast of Epiphany, that is the appearance or manifestation of the Lord's sacrament. **4.** At present, there is no reason, nor does the context demand, that I speak more fully concerning this sacrament which we observe with the utmost devotion. I shall keep this for those who are interested and not foist it upon those who are not.[303] Nevertheless, it is right carefully to have underlined this point to show that Caesar's rule had been ordained in advance entirely to prepare for the future coming of Christ.

5. The first proof is that when he entered the City, returning from Apollonia, after his uncle, Gaius Caesar's[304] murder, at around the third hour, a circle of light like a rainbow surrounded the sun in a clear, serene sky as if to mark him as the one, mightiest man in this world and by himself the most glorious man on the earth in whose days would come He Who by Himself made and rules over the sun and the whole world.[305] **6.** The second proof is that when the legions of Antony and Lepidus came over to him in Sicily, and he had restored 30,000 slaves to their masters and had stationed the 44 legions over which he had sole command in positions to keep the

302 An interesting side-light on the political thought of the later Roman Empire. Augustus tried very hard indeed to persuade his people he was *not* a monarch. Cassius Dio writing in the third century, however, was of the opinion that a monarchy was established at this time, *History*, 53.17.1. Jerome, *Chronicle*, *A Abr.* 1968 (= 47 BC), unlike Orosius, sees Julius Caesar as the first of the emperors. This would be impossible for Orosius, as it would destroy his important synchronism between the change in Rome's political system and the epiphany. Orosius's comment on the use of 'Augustus' as a title is very odd. Augustus remained a standard part of the nomenclature of emperors after Octavian. Presumably, Orosius means no one dared to use the name standing by itself which is true: there was no 'Augustus II'.

303 This synchronisation appears to be unique to Orosius. The actual date of Augustus's proclamation was 11 January. The combination is ideal for Orosius, as it is further evidence that Augustus is the divinely ordained secular precursor to Christ. This strange form of words Orosius uses about the epiphany shows that he knows that his interpretation of it is at odds with that of Augustine, and increasingly that of the Western church as a whole. While Augustine saw the epiphany as purely a commemoration of the visit of the magi to the infant Christ, others, including the Eastern church and, from Orosius's words, we may assume a substantial part of the Spanish church (cf. Isidore of Seville who combines the two meanings, *Etymologies*, 6.18.6–7), saw the epiphany primarily as the commemoration of Christ's own baptism and that baptism's revelation of His mission on earth. See Mommsen (1959).

304 i.e. Julius Caesar.

305 This portent is found in Livy, *Per.* 117; Julius Obsequens, 68; Suetonius, *Augustus*, 95; and Velleius Paterculus, 2.59. It is also found in Dio, 45.4.4.

world safe,[306] entering the city to an ovation, he decreed that all previous debts of the Roman people be rescinded, and even ordered the records of them to be destroyed.[307] At that time, as I have already mentioned, a spring of oil flowed all day out of a lodging house.[308] What could be more obvious than that this sign declared that the birth of Christ would occur when Caesar ruled the whole world? For Christ in the language of that race into which and from which he was born, means 'the anointed'.[309]

7. So at the time when permanent tribunician power was granted to Caesar, a spring of oil flowed all day at Rome.[310] These clearest of signs were set forth in heaven and on earth for those who did not heed the voices of the prophets. They tell us that in the principate of Caesar in the Roman Empire for a whole day – interpreted this means that as long as the Roman Empire endures – Christ and, after him, the Christians – that is the oil and those anointed by it – will march from a lodging house – that is the welcoming and bountiful Church – in great and inexhaustible numbers to restore, with Caesar's aid, all slaves who acknowledge their master and hand over the rest who are found to have no master to death and punishment. The debts from their sins are to be redeemed in Caesar's reign in that city whence the oil flowed of its own accord.

8. The third proof is that when he entered the city holding a triumph as consul for the fifth time, on that very day that we have named above, he closed the temple of Janus for the first time in 200 years,[311] and took the glorious name of Augustus. What could be more plausibly or credibly believed than that, given this co-incidence of the peace, his name, and the date, this man been predestined by the secret ordering of events in order to prepare the way for His coming when he took up the banner of peace and assumed the title of power on the same day on which He would shortly make Himself known to the world?

---

306 A confused argument. At 6.18.33, Orosius speaks of Augustus having sole command of 44 legions after Lepidus's surrender, but only at 6.19.14, i.e. after the Battle of Actium, says that they were stationed round the world. This is a key part of his argument here, as it shows that Augustus was master of the world.

307 36 BC. Orosius may intend his reader to draw a parallel with the Hebrew practice of a 'Jubilee'.

308 6.18.34.

309 An odd statement as 'Christos' does indeed mean 'the anointed one', but in Greek.

310 An error, but perhaps an excusable one. Augustus did not obtain tribunician power until 23 BC; however, he was awarded the *sacrosanctitas* of a tribune in 36 BC. Orosius in his enthusiasm has probably failed to make the distinction.

311 See 3.8.2–4.

9. What happened to prove the truth of the faith which we profess when Caesar returned to the City for the fourth time at the end of the Cantabrian War, when he had pacified every nation is better set down at the right time in my history.[312]

21

1. 726 years after the foundation of the City, when the Emperor Caesar Augustus was consul for the sixth, and Agrippa for the second, time,[313] Caesar, realising that little would have been achieved in Spain over the last 200 years, if the Astures and Cantabrians, the two sturdiest Spanish tribes, were left to live by their own devices, opened the gates of the temple of Janus and marched to the Spains himself at the head of an army.[314] **2.** The Cantabrians and Astures live in the northern part of the province of Gallaecia by the end of the Pyrenees, not far from the second Ocean.[315] **3.** These tribes were not only ready to defend their own freedom, but even dared to take away that of their neighbours, frequently raiding the Vaccaei, Turmogi, and Autrigonae.

Caesar pitched his camp at Segisama[316] and by using three columns surrounded almost all of Cantabria. **4.** A long period elapsed when the army was worn out for no purpose and often found itself in danger. Finally, Caesar ordered a fleet to cross the Ocean from the Aquitanian Gulf[317] and land troops before the enemy realised what was happening. **5.** The Cantabrians then fought a great battle under the walls of Attica,[318] were defeated, and fled to Mount Vinnius, a natural stronghold.[319] Here they were besieged and almost starved to death. Then the town of Racilium[320] was finally captured

312 See 6.21.11.

313 28 BC, Orosius's chronology is correct.

314 Orosius devotes a striking amount of space to the Cantabrian Wars, betraying a personal interest here. His account draws heavily on Florus, 2.33.

315 After previously using archaic divisions of Spain, Orosius oddly chooses to use those of his own day here. The province of Gallaecia, comprising north-west Spain, was only created in the late third century AD by Diocletian. The phrase 'second Ocean' is striking. Orosius perhaps means the ocean stream to the north of Spain rather than that to its west.

316 The modern Sasamón.

317 The Bay of Biscay.

318 The text is corrupt here. The town concerned was Bergida (Florus, 2.33.49), the location of which is disputed; see Pastor Muñoz (1977) and Ramírez Sádaba (1999). The best account of the war in English is Syme (1970).

319 The location of this mountain, normally spelt Vindius, is disputed; see n. 318 above.

320 Probably the modern Aradillos.

and sacked after long and fierce resistance. **6.** At the same time, Caesar's lieutenants, Antistius and Firmus,[321] subdued by heavy and serious fighting the further-flung parts of Gallaecia whose mountains and woods run down to the Ocean. **7.** Digging a ditch 15 miles long, they besieged Mount Medullius[322] which towers over the Minius river,[323] and where a great host of men had taken refuge. **8.** Then, when this naturally savage and indomitable race discovered that they had neither sufficient means to survive the siege nor were equal to fighting a battle, their fear of slavery led them willingly to commit suicide, and so almost all of them killed themselves with fire, sword, or poison.[324]

9. Now the Astures, who had pitched their camp by the river Astura,[325] would have overwhelmed the Romans with their great numbers and cunning plans, had they not been betrayed and forestalled. They made a sudden attack intending to overwhelm Caesar's three lieutenants, who were separated with their legions into three camps, with three equally-matched columns of their own, but they were betrayed by their own people and discovered.[326] **10.** Afterwards, Carisius brought them to battle and, after heavy Roman losses, defeated them. Some of them escaped from the battle and fled to Lancia.[327] When the troops had surrounded the town and were preparing to fire it, their commander, Carisius, persuaded his men not to do this and got the barbarians to surrender voluntarily. He made great efforts to leave the town safe and undamaged, so it could bear witness to his victory.[328] **11.** Caesar accorded this honour to his victory in Cantabria: he ordered that the gates of war be closed once more. And so, the gates of Janus were then closed for a second time by Caesar, this being the fourth time they had been closed since the foundation of the City.[329]

12. After these events, Caesar's stepson, Claudius Drusus,[330] was allotted

321 More correctly Furnius; see Dio, 45.13.6. Manuscripts of Florus are corrupt at this point and Orosius's error may well be a product of this.

322 Again, the location of this mountain is disputed; see n. 318 above.

323 The modern river Minio.

324 Compare the end of the siege of Numantia at 5.7.16.

325 The modern river Esla.

326 According to Florus, 2.33.56, the Astures were betrayed by the philo-Roman Brigaecini.

327 See n. 318 above.

328 The incident with Carisius is not found in Florus. It is striking that Orosius refers to the Spaniards as barbarians here.

329 25 BC.

330 Normally known as Drusus, the empress Livia's son by her previous husband. He died on campaign in Germany in 9 BC.

the provinces of Gaul and Raetia[331] and subdued by arms the greatest and fiercest of the German tribes.

13. For at that time, all these tribes, hurrying as if to set a day to make peace, came in waves to take their chance in battle or discuss peace terms. Their intention was to accept terms if they were defeated, or enjoy their freedom in peace if they should be victorious. **14.** It was then that the Noricans, Illyrians, Pannonians, Dalmatians, Moesians, Thracians, Sarmatian Dacians, and most of the Germans,[332] including the most powerful tribes, were defeated or checked by a variety of commanders, or cut off from the empire by those great rivers the Rhine and Danube.[333]

15. In Germany Drusus first subdued the Usipetes and then the Tencteri and Catti.[334] He almost annihilated the Marcomani. **16.** After this, he defeated together in a single battle, though one that went hard with his men, the most powerful peoples to whom nature has granted strength, and their way of life, the ability to make use of that strength – the Cherusci, Sueves, and Sygambri. **17.** Their courage and ferocity can be judged from the following fact: whenever their womenfolk were trapped among their carts by a Roman advance and they ran out of weapons or anything that could in their fury be used as a weapon, they would dash their own small children to the ground and then fling them into the faces of their enemy, becoming parricides twice over for the murder of each of their children.[335]

18. It was at this time too that Caesar's general, Cossus, tightened the over-wide range of the nomadic Musolani and Gaetuli in Africa, forcing them through fear not to molest Rome's frontiers.[336]

19. Meanwhile, envoys from the Indians and Scythians, after crossing the whole world, finally found Caesar at Tarragona in Hither Spain, beyond which they would have been unable to seek him. They reinvested Caesar with the glory of Alexander the Great, **20.** for just as an embassy from the Spaniards and Gauls had come to Alexander seeking peace when he

331 Raetia occupied what is now Switzerland and the Tyrol.
332 This list is taken from Florus, 2.21.
333 Orosius implies that Augustus was looking for 'safe boundaries' for his empire. For a modern, contrary view, see Brunt (1963).
334 Normally spelt Chatti.
335 Drusus's campaigns against the Germans are drawn from Florus, 2.30. Orosius has extrapolated the near annihilation of the Marcomanni from Florus's comments that Drusus erected a *tropaeum* (a monument composed of the arms and armour of the enemy and dedicated to the Gods) in their territory. He has also transposed the account of the German women from Florus's account, 2.22, of the women of Alpine tribes. cf. 5.16.13 and 5.16.19.
336 This section is drawn from Florus, 2.31.

was in the middle of the east at Babylon, so now the Indian from the east and the Scythian from the north begged him in the utmost west, in Spain, for peace, coming as suppliants with gifts from their peoples.[337] **21.** After waging war in Cantabria for five years and inclining and restoring all of Spain to everlasting peace, thus giving it some rest from its weariness, Caesar returned to Rome.

22. In those days he waged many wars himself and through his commanders and lieutenants. Among these, Piso was despatched to fight the Vindelici and, after defeating them, returned victorious to Caesar at Lyons.[338]

23. Caesar's stepson, Tiberius,[339] put an end to a new uprising of the Pannonians with great slaughter.[340] **24.** The same man then immediately went on to fight the Germans, carrying off 40,000 prisoners in triumph from them.[341] **25.** This great, fearful war was fought over three years by 15 legions; there had hardly been a greater war, according to Suetonius, since that against Carthage.[342]

26. At the same time,[343] Quintilius Varus, who behaved with incredible arrogance and greed towards his subjects, was completely annihilated along with three legions by rebellious Germans.[344] **27.** Caesar Augustus took this disaster for the republic so seriously that the strength of his sorrow often made him bang his head against the wall, crying out, '*Quintilius Varus, give back the legions.*'[345]

28. Agrippa overcame the Bosphorans and forced them after their defeat

337 Indian embassies are mentioned by Augustus in his *Res Gestae*, 31. For the comparison with Alexander, see 3.20.1–3. Tarragona, though on the Mediterranean coast of Spain, is used as a symbol of Rome's most westerly possessions, so preserving the parallel with Alexander. The account of the embassies has been drawn, and embroidered, from Florus, 2.34.62. See also Suetonius, *Augustus*, 21. Given Orosius's love of parallelism, it is difficult not to think of the three magi at the nativity in this context.

338 The Vindelici were an Alpine tribe. Orosius has made an error here – these operations were in fact carried out by Drusus; see Florus, 2.22.

339 The empress Livia's son by her former husband, Ti. Claudius Nero, and the future emperor Tiberius.

340 In AD 8.

341 The figure of 40,000 is found in Suetonius, *Tiberius*, 9.

342 Suetonius, *Tiberius*, 16, but this is a specific reference to the Illyrian War.

343 At the same time as the Illyrian War, not the expedition into Germany. Orosius has misread Suetonius; see Suetonius, *Tiberius*, 16–17.

344 The disaster of Teutoburgerwald in AD 9. The comment on Varus's arrogance is drawn from Florus, 2.30.31.

345 Quoted verbatim from Suetonius, *Augustus*, 23.

to surrender, recovering in battle the Roman standards that they had once captured under Mithridates.[346]

29. The Parthians, thinking that all the eyes of the conquered, pacified world were on them, that the whole might of the Roman Empire would be turned on them alone, and because they were already gnawed by a guilty conscience over the death of Crassus which they knew would be avenged, returned to Caesar of their own free will the standards that they had captured when they killed Crassus. After handing over members of their royal family as hostages, and through their sincere supplications, they then earned a firm treaty for themselves.[347]

22

1. So in the 752nd year after the foundation of the City, Caesar Augustus, after giving every nation from east to west, from north to south, and all around the encircling Ocean an all-embracing peace, closed the gates of Janus for a third time.[348] **2.** That they remained shut in perfect peace from that time for almost the next twelve years was shown by the rust on them nor were the gates pushed open again until the sedition at Athens and the troubles in Dacia in Augustus's extreme old age.[349] After he had closed the gates of Janus, Caesar endeavoured to nourish and propagate by peace the state that he had sought out by war. He promulgated many laws through which he inculcated the custom of discipline in the human race through a respect that was freely given.

4. He rejected being called 'master' on the grounds that he was only a man. *Indeed, when he was watching the games, the line 'O good and fair master' was spoken in one of the mimes and everyone broke out into enthusiastic applause as if it referred to him, but he at once suppressed this unbecoming flattery by gesturing with his hand and through the expression on his face. The following day he put an end to it by issuing a stern edict and after this would not let either his children or grandchildren call him master*

346 The campaign, though not the recovery of the standards, is noted by Jerome, Chronicle, *A Abr.* 2003 (= 12 BC).

347 The standards were returned in 20 BC. The hostages were the four sons of the Parthian king, Phraates IV.

348 i.e. the third time Augustus had personally closed the gates and the fifth time in all Roman history that they had been closed. See Augustus, *Res Gestae*, 13, and Suetonius, *Augustus*, 22. The date of this event is impossible to determine accurately. Orosius's date conveniently coincides with the birth of Christ.

349 The problems in Dacia broke out in AD 10, those in Athens in AD 14.

even as a joke.[350] **5.** Now at that time, namely in the year when Caesar, through God's decree, had established the most secure and stable peace on earth, Christ, for Whose coming that peace was a servant and upon Whose birth angels exultantly sang to listening men, *'Glory to God in the Highest, and on the Earth peace towards men of good will'*,[351] was born. At that same time he to whom all earthly power had been granted, did not suffer, or rather did not dare, to be called master of mankind, since the True Master of all the human race was then born among men. **6.** So in the same year when Caesar, whom God in His deep mysteries had marked out for this task, ordered that the first census be taken in each and every province and that every man be recorded, God deemed it right to be seen as, and become, a man.[352] Christ was therefore born at this time and at His birth was immediately recorded on the Roman census. **7.** This census in which He Who made all men wished to be listed as a man and numbered among men was the first and clearest statement which marked out Caesar as the lord of all and *the Romans as masters of the world*,[353] both individually and as a people. Never since the beginning of the world or the human race had anyone been granted to do this, not even Babylon or Macedon, not to mention any of the lesser kingdoms.[354] **8.** Nor can there be any doubt since it is clear to all from thought, faith, and observation that Our Lord, Jesus Christ brought to the apogee of power this city which had grown and been defended by His will, vehemently wishing to belong to it when He came and to be called a Roman citizen by decree of the Roman census.[355]

9. Now, therefore, as we have arrived at that time when the Lord Christ first enlightened the world with His coming and gave Caesar a kingdom entirely at peace, I shall make this the end of my sixth book. **10.** In the seventh, if, with God's aid, I am equal to the task, I shall deal with the times when the Christian faith germinated, the times when it grew all the more

350 A very close paraphrase of Suetonius, *Augustus*, 53.

351 Luke 2.14.

352 cf. Luke 2.1.

353 A quotation from Virgil, *Aeneid*, 1.282, where Jupiter predicts the coming greatness of Rome to Venus. Orosius may just be displaying his learning here, but it is possible that he wants to show his readers that a prophecy made by a pagan god has in fact been brought about by the True God.

354 Orosius's theory of the four kingdoms appears to have broken down here. There is no mention of Carthage, and the allusion to other kingdoms sits very uneasily with the theory.

355 Orosius is unaware that prior to Caracalla's grant of universal citizenship in AD 212, most provincials, though listed on the census, would not have been Roman citizens. Nevertheless, this is a bold move by Orosius which turns the Romans into the new chosen race.

amid the hands of those who would have stopped it, and how, after having advanced to its present position, it is still gnawed at by the abuse of those against whom we are forced to make this reply. **11.** And since from the beginning of this work I have not passed over in silence the fact that men sin and are punished for those sins, now too I shall expound what persecutions were inflicted on Christians, what vengeance followed them, and from this that all men are as a whole predisposed to sin and so are chastised individually.

BOOK SEVEN

1

1. Enough material has been gathered together, I believe, from which it is shown openly, without using that secret which belongs to the faithful few,[1] that the One, True God Whom the Christian Faith proclaims created the world and, when He willed it, both dispersed His creation widely, though He was widely unknown, and also united it into one when He was proclaimed by His Only Son, and that at the same time His power and patience have shone forth through many proofs of different kinds.

2. As regards this matter, I have come to realise in a short time that the narrow-minded and dispirited are offended that such great power mingles with patience that is so great. 'If He is powerful enough to create the world, to set the world at peace, and to introduce His Worship and news of Himself throughout the world,' they say, 'what need is there of this great (or pernicious, as they hold it) patience which means there eventually comes to pass through men's failings, disasters, and suffering, the thing which this God Whom you proclaim could rather have brought about immediately through His power?' **3.** To such objections I could truthfully answer that the human race was at first created and devised so that by living religiously, at peace, and without any labours, it would earn eternal life as the fruit of its obedience, but after abusing the liberty given by the goodness of its Creator, it turned its licence into contumacy and descended from contempt towards God to forgetting Him altogether. **4.** Now God's restraint is just, and just in both regards: for He has not, though spurned, utterly destroyed those to whom He wishes to show mercy, and He allows them to be afflicted with trials while He should wish it, as, though spurned, He is mighty. From this it follows that He ever justly guides man, unaware though he is, to whom one

---

1 This is an obscure remark, but is probably an attack on pagan mystery religions, or Gnostic Christian sects that retained an inner set of secrets; see Augustine, *City of God*, 2.6. However, Raymond (1936) 318 n.1 believes it is a reference to inner knowledge kept secret by orthodox Christians.

day, on his repentance, He will loyally restore possession of His grace of old.

5. But since these matters, though expounded in a true and compelling fashion, nevertheless demand faith and obedience, and as at present my business is clearly with those who disbelieve (although I shall see if one day they will believe), I shall swiftly put forward arguments with which, even if they do not wish to agree, it is impossible to disagree. **6.** Now, so far as human understanding is concerned, both our groups live a religious life, granting that there is a higher power and worshipping it. On the other hand, our faiths are distinct: ours declares that everything came from, and is sustained through, One God, whereas theirs thinks that there are as many gods as there are things in the world.[2] **7.** 'If it was the power of the God you preach that made the Roman Empire so great and sublime,' they say, 'why then did His restraint stop Him from bringing this about earlier?' One can reply in the same vein to these objectors: if it was the power of those gods whom you preach that made the Roman Empire so great and sublime, why then did their restraint stop them from bringing this about earlier? **8.** Were they not yet gods? Or did Rome not exist at that time? Or were they not worshipped then? Or did she not seem ripe for empire yet? If these gods did not yet exist, then the argument is at an end,[3] as what purpose would there be in delaying to discuss beings whose very nature cannot be discovered? But if they were indeed gods, then either their power, as my opponents hold it, or their restraint is at fault – their restraint, if it was present, their power, if it was absent. **9.** Or, if it seems more plausible that there were then gods who were able to further the empire, but the Romans whom they could, and justly, make mightier did not yet exist, we will reply that we are seeking for the power that brings things into being, not the knowledge of how to shape what is already there. Our search is for mighty gods as they consider them, not for base craftsmen whose art fails when they have no material to work on.[4] **10.** If these beings always had the knowledge of the future and the will to act –

2 This statement contradicts Orosius's previous statement at 6.1.3–4 that the vast majority of pagans concede that there is only one god.

3 For two reasons – first, because for Orosius it necessarily follows that if the pagan gods did not exist, then God must have been responsible for Rome's rise, and second, because, given the general belief in antiquity that the truly authentic had always existed, any concession that there was a period of time when the pagan gods did not exist would be a concession that the Christian God was superior to them.

4 The distinction is a common one in both Christian and pagan thought – the manipulation of pre-existing matter, as opposed to the creation of matter itself, is a mark of the 'demiurge', rather than God or the gods.

and we should assume that they had knowledge of the future, since, where omnipotence is concerned, to foreknow and to will one's acts are one and the same thing – whatever their will demanded and was foreseen by them ought not to have been put off, but to have been created. This is especially so since they tell us that their Jupiter was in the habit of turning anthills into races of men as a game.[5]

11. Nor do I think that we need to consider the care that they took to perform religious ceremonies, since amid their endless sacrifices there was no end or respite from endless disasters until Christ, the Saviour of the World, shone forth. The peace of the Roman Empire was preordained for His coming, and, although I think I have already demonstrated this satisfactorily, I shall try to add a few proofs more.

2

1. At the beginning of my second book,[6] when I sketched out Rome's beginnings, I noted the many points of similarity between the Assyrian city of Babylon, which was the leading nation at the time, and Rome, which dominates the nations in a similar way today. **2.** I showed that the former had the first, while the latter has the last, empire; that the former slowly declined, while the latter gradually grew; that the former lost her last king at the same time the latter gained her first; that while, when Cyrus invaded, Babylon fell as if dead, Rome was confidently rising and, after expelling her kings, began to be governed by the counsels of freemen; **3.** and that, most of all, at the time when Rome won her freedom, at that time too the Jewish people who had been enslaved under the kings at Babylon received their freedom, returned to holy Jerusalem and rebuilt the temple of the Lord as had been foretold by the prophets.[7]

4. Moreover, I have noted how in between the kingdom of Babylon in the east and that of Rome which was rising in the west and nourished by her eastern inheritance, came the Macedonian and African kingdoms and that that these, one to the south and the other to the north, briefly held the role of guardian[8] and attorney.[9] **5.** Now I know that no one has ever doubted that

5 See Ovid, *Metamorphoses*, 7.622, and Hyginus, *Fables*, 52.

6 See 2.1–3.

7 See *Esdras*, 1.1–6. The parallelism between Rome and the Jews is of interest here. Orosius is anxious to show Rome, even at this early date in her history, plays an equally important part as Israel in God's plans for mankind.

8 A *tutor* in Roman law oversaw the affairs of a minor.

9 cf. 2.1.4–5. A *curator* in Roman law oversaw the affairs of one incapable of acting on

the kingdoms of Babylon and Rome are rightly called the kingdoms of the east and west. Its position under the heavens and the altars, which endure to this day, set up by Alexander the Great by the Riphaean mountains,[10] teach us that the Macedonian kingdom was in the north. **6.** And what can be seen both in history books and in cities themselves tells us that Carthage surpassed all of Africa and extended the boundaries of her realm not only to Sicily, Sardinia, and the rest of the islands adjacent to her, but even to Spain. **7.** It has also been stated how both kingdoms endured for an equal number of years before Babylon was laid waste by the Medes and Rome invaded by the Goths.[11]

8. I shall now add to those facts this point in order to make it clearer that God is the sole Ruler of all ages, kingdoms, and places. **9.** The kingdom of Carthage stood a little over 700 years from its foundation to its destruction.[12] Equally, the kingdom of Macedon lasted a little less than 700 years from the reign of Caranus to that of Perses.[13] However, the number seven, by which all things are judged, put an end to both of them.[14]**10.** Even Rome herself, although she reached the advent of the Lord Jesus Christ with her empire intact, was nevertheless also affected when she came to this number **11.** to the point that in the 700th year after her foundation, a fire of unknown origin rose up and consumed 14 of her districts. According to Livy, Rome had never suffered as great a fire with the result that some years later Caesar Augustus spent a great deal of money from the public treasury to make good

---

their own behalf.

10 See 1.2.52.

11 See 2.3.3.

12 Orosius has used the figure from Jerome that he feels suits his purpose. Jerome, *Chronicle, A Abr.*1871, states that Carthage endured 678 years from her foundation to her fall, adding that 'others' believe the figure to be 749. Oddly, the former figure would have made a better fit for Orosius's theory, as Carthage's lifespan would then be closer to Macedon's, but he chooses not to use it. His manuscript may have been corrupt, or perhaps his arithmetic was at fault. Alternatively, he may not have been able to resist making a verbal contrast between 'a little over', *paulo amplius*, and 'a little less', *paulo minus*.

13 According to Jerome, Caranus began his reign in *A Abr.* 1204 and the kingdom fell in *A Abr.*1850, making a total of 646 years.

14 For Orosius seven is the number of completion as evinced by the seven days of creation. The composition of the *Histories* in seven books is also influenced by this view. The classical biblical example of the destructive power of completion is the fall of the walls of Jericho accomplished by seven trumpets on the seventh day they were paraded around the town walls, Joshua 6.13–17. For another example of the power of the number seven on the earlier Christian imagination, see Cyprian. *Treatise* 3 (*De Lapsis /On the Lapsed*), 1.20.

the areas that had been burnt down.[15] **12.** Were I not recalled by consideration of the present, I could demonstrate that Babylon lasted for twice this number of years, when she was finally captured by Cyrus after existing for a little more than 1,400 years.[16]

13. I freely add this fact – that the famed holy man, Abraham, to whom divine promises were given and from whose seed Christ was promised to come forth, was born in the 43rd year of the rule of Ninus, the first of Babylon's kings, albeit his father Belus too is said, on no good evidence, to have been the first king.[17] **14.** Then in the present epoch Christ, Who had been promised to Abraham in the reign of Ninus, the first king, was born at almost the end of the 42nd year of the rule of Augustus Caesar,[18] the first of all Rome's emperors, although his father, Caesar, too distinguished himself, though rather as the architect of the empire than as an emperor.[19] **15.** He was born on 25 December, the date when all the increase of the coming year first begins to grow.[20] And so it has come to pass that while Abraham was born in the 43rd year, Christ's nativity came at the end of the 42nd year, so that instead of coming forth in part of this 43rd year, it should come forth from Him.[21] **16.** I believe that it is well enough known how much that year abounded with both new and unaccustomed blessings without me listing them: an all-embracing peace came to all the lands of the globe, there was not a cessation but an abolition of all wars; the gates of Janus of the two faces were closed as the roots of war were not pruned, but torn out; this was when the first and greatest census was held, when all God's creation of great nations unanimously swore loyalty to Caesar alone, and, at the same time, by partaking of the census were made into one community.[22]

---

15 See 6.14.5.

16 See 2.2.

17 Augustine, *City of God*, 18.2, lists Belus as the Assyrians' first king.

18 Jerome, *Chronicle, A Abr*. 2015.

19 i.e. Julius Caesar. Caesar is mentioned here in order to create a Roman parallel to the Ninus–Belus dispute. It was convenient for Orosius in this respect that Julius Caesar was at times viewed as the first 'emperor'; he is the first subject, for example, of Suetonius's *Lives of the Caesars* and Jerome notes that in 47 BC (*A Abr*. 1968) 'Julius Caesar was the first Roman to obtain sole power from which the leaders of the Romans are called Caesares'.

20 Christ therefore is the symbol of a new epoch.

21 An ingenious way of preserving the parallelism between Abraham and Christ in the face of the chronological evidence and, at the same time, of emphasising Christ's superiority to Abraham.

22 Orosius wishes us to see the census creating a community in the same way that the Eucharist did among Christians.

3

1. So 752 years after the foundation of the City, Christ was born and brought to the world the faith that gives salvation. Truly, He is the Rock set at the heart of things, where there is ruination for whoever strikes against Him, but where whoever believes in Him is saved.[23] Truly, He is the blazing Fire that lights the way for whoever follows Him, but consumes whoever makes trial of Him.[24]

2. He is the Christ, the Head of the Christians,[25] the Saviour of the good, the wicked's Castigator, the Judge of all men, Who sets forth both in word and deed an example for those who will follow Him, through which to teach them all the more that it is necessary to endure the persecutions which they undergo in return for eternal life. He began His own sufferings soon after He came into the world through a virgin birth. For when Herod, the king of Judaea, learnt of His birth, he immediately decreed that He be murdered, and in his pursuit of this one child, killed a host of little children. **3.** Hence we see that just punishment befalls the wicked who vilely pursue their paths of evil;[26] hence we see that the degree to which the world is at peace is due to the grace given to believers and that the degree to which it is troubled is due to the punishment of blasphemers, though however things stand, faithful Christians have security as they either are at rest in the safety of the life eternal or profit even from this life on earth. I shall show this more readily, using the facts themselves to do so, as I reach these events in sequence.

4. After the Lord Jesus Christ, the Redeemer of the World, came down to earth and was enrolled as a Roman citizen in Caesar's census,[27] the gates of war were kept closed, as I have mentioned, for twelve years in the blessed calm of peace. Caesar Augustus then sent his grandson Gaius to govern the provinces of Egypt and Syria.[28] **5.** As Suetonius Tranquillus tells us,[29] on

---

23 The rock of Salvation is a common Old Testament theme: see 2 Samuel 22.47, and Psalm 18.46. The rock is interpreted as Christ by St Paul: see 1 Corinthians 10.4. For the rock as a stumbling block to the wicked, see Isaiah 8.14, and Romans 9.33.

24 A reference to the pillar of fire that guided the Israelites through Sinai (Exodus 13.21) and the refiner's fire of Malachi 3.2; 3.3.

25 'Head' here is metaphorical, referring to Christ's role as the leader of the Christians, and actual, referring to His position as the head of the mystical body of the Church.

26 For the massacre of the innocents, see Matthew 2.16, and Jerome, *Chronicle, A Abr.* 2019. For Herod's death, a particularly gruesome affair that we are meant to remember here, see Josephus, *Antiquities of the Jews*, 17.174–78.

27 6.22.6–8.

28 The son of Augustus's daughter, Julia, and Agrippa. He was given proconsular power over the east in 1 BC.

29 Suetonius, *Augustus*, 93.

crossing into Palestine from Egypt, he disdained to pray in the holy, much-visited, temple of God at Jerusalem. After he told Augustus what he had done, the emperor in an error of judgment praised him, saying that he had acted prudently. **6.** And so in the 48th year of Caesar's rule such a terrible famine befell the Romans that Caesar commanded that troupes of gladiators, all foreigners, and great masses of slaves, apart from doctors and teachers, be expelled from the City.[30] So when the prince sinned in God's holy place and the people were beset by famine, the degree of the offence was made clear by the severity of its punishment.

7. After this, to quote the words of Cornelius Tacitus: *When Augustus was an old man, the gates of Janus were opened and new peoples at the furthermost ends of the earth were sought out, sometimes with profit and sometimes with loss. This went on until the reign of Vespasian.*[31] Thus Cornelius. **8.** However, when at that time the city of Jerusalem had been taken and destroyed, as the prophets had foretold, and the Jews exterminated, Titus, who had been ordained by God's Judgment to avenge the blood of the Lord Jesus Christ,[32] closed the temple of Janus on celebrating his triumph along with his father, Vespasian.

9. Therefore, although the temple of Janus was opened in Caesar's last years, nevertheless for many years afterwards, though the troops were girt for battle, no sounds of war were to be heard.[33] **10.** It was for this reason that in the Gospels when the Lord Jesus Christ was asked by His disciples, at a time when all the world was enjoying the profoundest calm and a single peace lay over every people, about the end of days which was to come, He said, among other things: **11.** *And ye shall hear of wars and rumours of wars: see that ye be not troubled: for all these things must come to pass, but the end is not yet. For nation shall rise against nation, and kingdom against kingdom: and there shall be famines, and pestilences, and earthquakes, in divers places. All these are the beginning of sorrows. Then shall they deliver you up to be afflicted, and shall kill you: and ye shall be hated of all nations*

30 Jerome, *Chronicle, A Abr.* 2022. For the expulsions, see Suetonius, *Augustus*, 42.

31 A fragment from a lost section of Tacitus's *Histories*. Orosius has presumably doctored this passage, as we know that Nero closed the gates of Janus in AD 66 (Suetonius, *Nero*, 13) and Tacitus is unlikely to have made the error attributed to him here. For Orosius it would be impossible to present a persecutor of Christians such as Nero as a bringer of peace. He was either unaware of Nero's closing of the gates or suppressed it.

32 See Daniel 9.26, and, perhaps, Zachariah 14.2.

33 Given the quotation from Tacitus cited above, this is a striking statement. Orosius appears to have become carried away with his own rhetoric.

for my name's sake.[34] **12.** He taught this from His divine foresight, strengthening the faithful by His warning and confounding unbelievers through His prophecy.

4

1. 767 years after the foundation of the City, Tiberius Caesar obtained the empire after the death of Augustus Caesar and remained in power for 23 years.[35] **2.** He neither waged war himself nor even engaged in any significant war through his lieutenants,[36] except to anticipate and crush some local rebellions in a number of places, **3.** though it is true that in the fourth year of his reign, Germanicus, who was Drusus's son and Caligula's father, celebrated a triumph for his campaign against the Germans against whom he had been despatched by Augustus in his old age.[37]

4. However, Tiberius for most of his reign presided over the state with such great and grave moderation that *he wrote to some governors who were urging him to increase the tribute from the provinces that 'the mark of good shepherd is to shear, not flay, his flock'.*[38]

5. After Christ the Lord had suffered, risen from the dead, and sent forth His disciples to preach, Pilate, the governor of the province of Palestine, made a report to the emperor Tiberius and the Senate concerning Christ's suffering, resurrection, and the miracles which then followed, both those performed by Himself in public and those performed by His disciples in His name. He also reported that He was believed to be God by the growing faith of a great number of men. **6.** Tiberius proposed, and strongly recommended, to the Senate that Christ be considered as God, but the Senate was angry that this matter had not been brought to its notice first, as was the custom, in order that it might be the first to decree that a new cult be adopted. Therefore, it refused to consecrate Christ and passed a decree that Christians be

---

34 Matthew 24.6–9.

35 Orosius's date is correct. Tiberius reigned from AD14–37. Jerome, *Chronicle, A Abr.* 2030, is one year out at this point placing the beginning of Tiberius's reign in AD 13.

36 Eutropius, 7.11, states that while Tiberius did not go to war, he waged war through his lieutenants. As Orosius wants to depict the early empire as a time of peace, he has chosen to downplay the nature of fighting under Tiberius.

37 Drawn from Jerome, *Chronicle, A Abr.* 2033. Jerome has Germanicus triumph over the Parthians, but the German campaign is intended. For the beginning of these campaigns, see Syme (1974) ch. 4 and Wells (1972) ch. 7.

38 A close paraphrase of Suetonius, *Tiberius*, 32. Tiberius's words are taken verbatim.

completely extirpated from the City,[39] above all because Tiberius's prefect, Sejanus, strongly opposed adopting the religion.[40] **7.** Tiberius then passed a decree threatening death to those who denounced Christians.[41] Because of these events, Tiberius gradually abandoned his praiseworthy moderation in order to take revenge on the Senate for opposing him – for whatever the king did by his own choice was pleasing to him, and so from the mildest of princes there blazed forth the most savage of wild beasts. **8.** He proscribed great numbers of the Senate and forced them to their deaths; he left scarcely two of the 20 noble men whom he had chosen as his councillors alive, murdering the others on a variety of charges;[42] he killed his prefect, Sejanus, when he was plotting revolution;[43] **9.** left obvious signs of having killed both his natural son, Drusus and his adopted son, Germanicus,[44] with poison, and killed the sons of his own son, Germanicus.[45] **10.** It would cause horror and shame to go through his deeds one by one. So great was his seething frenzy of lust and cruelty that those who had spurned salvation under Christ the King were punished by king Caesar.[46] **11.** In the 12th year of his reign, a new and unbelievable kind of calamity befell the city of Fidenae. While the people were watching a gladiatorial show the amphitheatre's seating collapsed, killing more than 20,000 people.[47] **12.** This is indeed a worthy

39 See Jerome *Chronicle, A Abr.* 2051; similar material occurs in the fourth-century *Acts of Pilate*. The story first appears in Tertullian, *Apology*, 21. It is possible that Tertullian may have seen an earlier, lost, version of the *Acts of Pilate*, but Barnes (1971) 108–9, 149 is inclined to believe that he invented the story himself. If a pagan source were involved, the original meaning of the text could be 'that Christ be considered *a* God'. The Latin (*christus deus haberetur*) is potentially ambiguous, but a straight-forward Christian reading is the most likely.

40 Sejanus was Tiberius's Praetorian Prefect, i.e. commander of the Praetorian Guard. He had an extremely black reputation in antiquity and fell spectacularly from grace in AD 31. It was a wise apologetic move by Orosius to link him to opposition to Christianity which would appear in a favourable light simply because it was disliked by Sejanus. However, the grounds for Orosius's assertion are difficult to discover. Jerome, *Chronicle, A Abr.* 2050, notes that Sejanus continually urged Tiberius to extirpate the Jews, but makes no mention of a similar animus against Christians. Orosius has either drawn on another source or misread/manipulated this passage.

41 Sections 5–7 use material drawn from Rufinus, *Ecclesiastical History*, 2.2.

42 See Jerome, *Chronicle, A Abr.* 2052, and Suetonius, *Tiberius*, 55.

43 Taken from Suetonius, *Tiberius*, 5.

44 Germanicus was the son of Tiberius's brother, Drusus.

45 cf. Suetonius, *Tiberius*, 54.

46 Orosius has ingeniously managed to present Tiberius's change for the worse, a *topos* of ancient writers, as almost a product of divine vengeance.

47 Modern Castel Giubileo. The disaster happened in AD 27. Orosius has taken his

example for future generations of the great punishment inflicted on the men of that time who had eagerly gathered together to watch the death of their fellow men at the very time God had willed Himself to become a man for man's salvation.

13. It was in the 17th year of the same emperor's reign, when the Lord Jesus Christ voluntarily gave Himself up to suffer, though it was the Jews who blasphemously arrested and fixed Him to the cross.[48] Rocks in the mountains were torn apart by the greatest earthquake the world has known, with great parts of the biggest cities being laid low by its hitherto unknown violence.[49] **14.** On the same day at the sixth hour, the sun's light was completely effaced, a hellish darkness suddenly fell over the earth,[50] and, as the saying goes, *impious mortals fear'd eternal night.*[51] **15.** The darkness was so great that it was clear that neither the moon nor the clouds had cut off the sun's light, for it is said that on that day the moon was in its 14th station at the opposite side of the heavens and as far as it could be from the sun, and that stars shone over all the heavens during the hours of the day, or rather of that terrible night. This is testified to not only by the faith of the Holy Evangelists, but also by a number of Greek books.[52]

16. Now from the time after the passion of the Lord which the Jews prosecuted with all their might, ceaseless disasters roared around them until finally, emptied of all strength and scattered, they passed away.[53] **17.** Tiberius, using the pretext of military service, deported their youth to provinces with poor climates, while he expelled the remainder of the race, and those who were members of similar sects, from the City, threatening those who disobeyed with life-long slavery.[54] **18.** He certainly remitted the

---

information from Suetonius, *Tiberius*, 40, who gives the same number of casualties. The incident is also mentioned by Tacitus, *Annals*, 4.62, who gives the number of dead as 50,000.

48 Jerome, *Chronicle, A Abr.* 2047, has the eighteenth year. Orosius attempts to exonerate the Roman authorities of responsibility for Christ's death, but only the Roman governor had the power of execution in Judaea.

49 See Matthew 27.51, though the implication here is that the earthquake was local.

50 See Luke 23.44–45.

51 Virgil, *Georgics*, 1.468.

52 The bulk of this material is drawn from Jerome, *Chronicle, A Abr.* 2047. Jerome mentions that the earthquake is found in the works of several pagan writers. This is no doubt from where Orosius has drawn his comment to this effect. Orosius has also embroidered Jerome's account of substantial earthquake damage in Nicaea into damage in 'the biggest cities' (7.4.13).

53 An embroidered version of Jerome, *Chronicle, A Abr.* 2048.

54 Drawn from Suetonius, *Tiberius*, 36, where Jews, astrologers, and devotees of Egyptian cults are mentioned. Tiberius deported 4,000 Jews to Sardinia; Tacitus, *Annals*, 2.85.

tribute and even gave their freedom to the cities of Asia destroyed in the earthquake.[55] On his death, there were hints that he had been poisoned.[56]

5

1. 790 years after the foundation of the City, Gaius began his reign. He was the second emperor after Augustus, and remained in power for fewer than four years.[57] He was more deeply steeped in crime than all who had preceded him, and seemed to have been set up as a truly worthy castigator for the blaspheming Romans and persecuting Jews. **2.** This man, to encapsulate the breadth of his cruelty in a few words, is said to have cried, '*If only the Roman people had one neck*',[58] and often to have complained about the state of the world in his day on the grounds that it was not distinguished by any great calamities.

3. O blessed seeds of the Christian epoch! How great was your strength in human affairs that man's cruelty was more able to wish for disasters, than to find them! Behold, how brutality, when starved, laments universal peace:

within remains
Imprison'd Fury, bound in brazen chains:
High on a trophy rais'd of useless arms;
He sits, and threats the World with vain Alarms[59]

4. Once slaves in rebellion and fugitive gladiators terrified Rome, brought ruin to Italy, and laid waste to Sicily. Indeed, they were feared by almost every race across the face of the earth. However, in these days of well-being, that is to say the Christian Epoch, not even a Caesar who hated it could tear up the peace. **5.** He set out with an almost unbelievably great retinue to seek out an enemy for his idle troops and, after rushing through Gaul and Germany, finally paused for breath on the shore of the Ocean, near where one can see across to Britain.[60] After he had received the surrender there of Minocynobelinus,[61] the son of the king of the Britons, who had been

55 This earthquake occurred in AD 17. See Suetonius, *Tiberius*, 48, where we are told that tax was remitted for three years, and also Tacitus, *Annals*, 2.47 and 4.13.

56 See Suetonius, *Tiberius*, 73.

57 Gaius, normally known as Caligula, ruled from AD 37–41. Orosius's date is correct.

58 Suetonius, *Gaius*, 30.

59 Virgil, *Aeneid*, 1.294–96.

60 See Suetonius, *Gaius*, 43–47. The emperor's rush to Germany was in order to forestall Gaetulicus's rebellion in Upper Germany.

61 Orosius has read Suetonius carelessly here. The original text (Suetonius, *Gaius*, 44) reads, 'Adminius, Cunobelinus's son'; Orosius has elided the two words.

expelled by his father and was wandering in exile with a few followers, the emperor returned to Rome, having failed to find grounds for waging war.

6. At the same time, the Jews, who had been justly afflicted by disasters on all sides because of Christ's suffering, were killed in a riot that had broken out in Alexandria and driven from the city. They sent a certain Philo, undoubtedly one of the most learned men of his time, as an envoy to Caesar to lay their grievances before him.[62] **7.** But Caligula, since he hated all mankind, and especially the Jews, ignored Philo's embassy and commanded that all the Jews' holy places and, above all, the famous sanctuary at Jerusalem be profaned by the gentiles' sacrifices, be filled with statues and idols, and that he himself be worshipped as a god there. **8.** The governor Pilate, who had pronounced the death sentence on Christ and dealt with, and provoked, a great deal of rioting in Jerusalem, was so tormented by Gaius's orders that he ran himself through with his own hand and sought an end to his catalogue of woes by a quick death.[63]

9. Gaius Caligula even added this crime to his lusts: he first committed incest with his sisters and then exiled them.[64] After he had ordered that everyone he had exiled was to be killed at the same time, he himself was killed by his own bodyguards.[65] **10.** Two notebooks were discovered among his secret papers; one was called 'The Dagger', the other 'The Sword'. Both contained the names and notes on the most distinguished members of the Senatorial and Equestrian orders whom he had marked down for death. A great chest full of various poisons was also found. It is said that soon afterwards, when these were flung into the sea on Claudius Caesar's orders, the sea became infected, a great number of fish died, and that their bodies were washed up all over the nearby shore by the tide.[66] **11.** How great a host of men escaped from the death that had been prepared from them could be seen from the host of dead fish, and it became clear to everyone what this great quantity of poison, made even worse by artifice,[67] could have wrought in the City, given that it polluted the very seas when it was poured into them

62 For the embassy, see Philo, *The Embassy to Gaius* (*De Legatione ad Gaium*). The riot happened in AD 38.

63 See Jerome, *Chronicle, A Abr.* 2055, and Rufinus, *Ecclesiastical History*, 2.5–7.

64 Drawn from Jerome, *Chronicle, A Abr.* 2056. For the charge of incest, see also Suetonius, *Gaius*, 24. Two of Caligula's three sisters, Livilla and Agrippina, were exiled in AD 39; see Suetonius, *Gaius*, 29. The emperor's third, and favourite, sister Drusilla had already died in AD 38.

65 The material in this section is drawn from Jerome, *Chronicle, A Abr.* 2056.

66 The material in this section is drawn from Suetonius, *Gaius*, 49.

67 i.e. Caligula's agents had augmented the strength of natural poisons.

with no plan at all. All this, indeed, is great proof of God's mercy which He showed by extending His grace to a people who, in part, were on the point of believing in Him and by tempering His wrath against a people who were at that time obstinate in their unbelief.

6

1. 795 years after the foundation of the City, Tiberius Claudius became the third man to obtain the kingdom after Augustus. He remained in power for fourteen years.[68] **2.** At the beginning of his reign, Peter, the apostle of the Lord Jesus Christ, came to Rome and with his trustworthy words preached the Faith that brings salvation to all who believe, proving its truth with his mighty miracles. From that time there began to be Christians at Rome.[69]

3. Rome felt the benefit from her faith, for, although after the death of Caligula, the Senate and consuls had made many decrees to abolish the empire, restore the republic to its old form of government, and sweep out the family of the Caesars in its entirety, **4.** Claudius, soon after securing his power, acted with great clemency, something previously unknown at Rome. In order to stop vengeance raging against such a large number of nobles, as would have happened, had it once begun, he obliterated all record of those two days on which the unfortunate debates and decrees about the constitution of the state had occurred and decreed that everything said or done at that time be pardoned and forgotten for ever.[70] **5.** In this way the Athenians' glorious and famous custom of amnesty which the Senate, on Cicero's advice,[71] had tried to introduce at Rome after Julius Caesar's death, but which failed when Antony and Octavian burst in upon the scene to avenge the death of Caesar, was now established, without anyone asking him, by Claudius through his innate sense of mercy, although he had an even more compelling motive to put these conspirators to death.[72]

68 Now normally known as Claudius. Orosius's date is one year out. Claudius's rule began in 794 *AUC*/AD 41.

69 Jerome, *Chronicle, A Abr.* 2058. Jerome merely mentions that Peter founded the church at Rome and was bishop there for twenty-five years.

70 The material in sections 3 and 4 is drawn from Suetonius, *Claudius*, 10–11. The two days referred to are those immediately after the assassination of Caligula when the Senate debated the possibility of restoring a Republic at Rome. See also Dio, 60.1.

71 See 6.17.6, where a more negative view of Cicero's amnesty proposal is taken.

72 Orosius takes a more negative view of the Athenian amnesty when he first mentions it at 2.17.15. There it fails because of human nature. Orosius therefore could be hinting that its success here shows God's favour towards Rome. Claudius's motive for revenge was stronger

6. At the same time, a great miracle attesting the presence of God's grace occurred. Furius Camillus Scribonian, the governor of Dalmatia, plotted civil war and seduced many powerful legions to change their oath of allegiance.[73] **7.** But on the appointed day when they were all to come and rally together to their new emperor, the troops were unable to crown their eagles, or to take up, or move, their standards in any way at all.[74] The army's confidence was so shaken by their belief in such a great and unexpected miracle that they repented, deserted and killed Scribonian four days after his coup began, and remained loyal to their old allegiance. **8.** It is clear enough that nothing has ever been more woeful or destructive to Rome than civil war. So can anyone who denies that this incipient tyranny and impending civil war were crushed by the Divinity because of Peter's arrival in the City and the few tender Christian seedlings that were scarcely yet budding to profess their faith, give a similar example from previous times of a civil war put down in this way?

9. In the fourth year of his reign, Claudius wanted to show that he was a prince of some use to the state and looked everywhere for a war and a victory to come from it. He therefore launched an expedition against Britain which appeared to be in a state of chaos because some fugitives had not been returned there. He crossed over to the island where no one either before, or after, Julius Caesar had dared to go, **10.** and there, in the words of Suetonius Tranquillus, '*within but a few days he received the surrender of most of the island without having fought a battle and without any blood being shed.*'[75] He even added the Orkney Islands, which lie beyond Britain in the Ocean, to the Roman Empire and then returned to Rome in the sixth month after beginning his journey.[76]

---

than that of Octavian and Antony because the 'conspiracy' (i.e. the Senatorial debate about the possibility of restoring a Republic at Rome) had been directed at himself rather than a relative or political ally.

73 Scribonian's abortive coup took place in AD 42; see Suetonius, *Claudius*, 13.

74 A legion's standards were normally garlanded, the *coronatio signorum*, at the beginning of a major campaign, see Suetonius, *Claudius*, 13. For an in-depth discussion of honours given to military standards, see Hoey (1937).

75 The account of Claudius's British campaign is taken from Suetonius, *Claudius*, 17. Suetonius mentions the bloodless nature of Claudius's campaign to disparage him, but for Orosius it is another sign of divine grace.

76 Claudius's invasion of Britain took place in AD 43. Orosius has probably drawn the implausible detail about the Orkneys (for which see 1.2.78) from Eutropius, 7.13.2–3. Jerome, *Chronicle*, *A Abr.* 2061, when noting Claudius's triumph for his British conquests, also states that the emperor added the Orkneys to the empire. However, claims that Claudius conquered the Orkneys are also found as early as Claudius's contemporary, Pomponius Mela (3.49–54).

11. Now let anyone who wants to do so, make a comparison concerning this single island between the one time and the other; between the one war and the other; and between the one Caesar and the other. I shall say nothing about the outcome, since the latter produced the happiest of the victories, but the former the bitterest of disasters.[77] In this way, Rome might finally realise that the share of good fortune that she had in her past deeds was due to the hidden providence of Him through Whose recognition she enjoys a plenitude of good fortune in so far as she is not besmirched by the stains of blasphemy.

12. In the same year of Claudius's reign, a severe famine that had been foretold by the prophets broke out in Syria.[78] But Queen Helena of Adiabene, a convert to the faith of Christ, generously ministered to the needs of the Christians of Jerusalem by importing grain from Egypt.[79]

13. In the fifth year of Claudius's reign, an island 30 stades long rose from the deep between Thera and Therasia.[80]

14. In the seventh year of his reign, when the procurator Cumanus was governor of Judaea, such a violent riot broke out in Jerusalem during the days of the *azyma*[81] that it is said that 30,000 Jews were trampled or suffocated to death when the people were crushed together at the gates as they attempted to leave.[82]

15. In the ninth year of the same emperor's reign, Josephus tells us that the Jews were expelled from the City by Claudius. However, I am more interested by Suetonius who speaks as follows: '*Claudius expelled the Jews from Rome as they were continually rioting because of Christ*'. **16.** It is not at all clear whether he ordered the Jews to be restrained and suppressed because they were rioting against Christ, or whether he wished to expel the

77 Orosius deals with Caesar's invasion in Britain at 6.9.2–9 where he makes no negative comments.

78 Jerome, *Chronicle*, A Abr. 2061. Jerome names the prophet as Agabus of *Acts*, 11.28, 21.10.

79 Drawn from Rufinus, *Ecclesiastical History*, 2.12. Adiabene lies in Northern Iraq. Queen Helena did visit Jerusalem between AD 46 and AD 48, but was a convert to Judaism, not Christianity; see Josephus, *Antiquities of the Jews*, 20.1–5.

80 AD 46; see Jerome, *Chronicle*, A Abr. 2064. The islands mentioned are the two main islands of the Santorini group. The island formed at this time is now known as Mikra Kammeni.

81 The Passover, *azymus* meaning 'unleavened'; see Luke 22.1.

82 This incident occurred in AD 49. Orosius has taken the numbers of the dead and the manner of their death from Jerome, *Chronicle*, A Abr. 2064. See also Rufinus, *Ecclesiastical History*, 2.19.

Christians at the same time on the grounds that they had a related religion.[83]

17. It is the case, however, that in the following year, a great famine occurred at Rome and the emperor was surrounded by his people in the forum and, to his great disgrace, set upon with insults and bits of bread. It was only with difficulty that he escaped the rage of the aroused plebs, fleeing back to his palace through a secret gate.[84]

18. A little later, he killed, on the slightest of pretexts, 35 senators along with 300 Roman knights. His own death showed evidence of poisoning.[85]

7

1. 808 years after the foundation of the City, Nero Caesar became the fourth man to reach the principate after Augustus and remained in power for almost fourteen years.[86] He was a follower of his uncle Gaius Caligula in all his crimes and vices[87] and, indeed, surpassed him, for he practised *wantonness, lust, extravagance, greed, and cruelty*[88] with every kind of crime. He was so overcome with depravity that he went round almost all the theatres in Italy and Greece, putting on the shame of motley clothing and often dreaming that he had defeated trumpet-players, harpists, tragedians, and charioteers.[89] **2.** He was so driven by lust that it is said he did not hold back from his mother or his sister through any reverence for blood-ties, that he took a man to wife, and that he himself was received as a wife by another man. **3.** He was so given to unbridled extravagance that he fished with nets of gold towed by lines of purple, and *bathed in hot and cold*

---

83 There is no mention of an expulsion of the Jews under Claudius in Josephus's works. The quotation is taken from Suetonius, *Claudius*, 25. Orosius rightly notes that the passage can bear more than one reading. For a detailed discussion of this passage, see Riesner (1998) 180–87.

84 Jerome, *Chronicle, A Abr.* 2065 (= AD 51). Tacitus, *Annals*, 12.43, also dates this famine to AD 51. The details of Claudius's treatment are taken from Suetonius, *Claudius*, 18. Given that in the *Histories* divine vengeance inevitably follows anti-Christian actions, Orosius's notice of this incident suggests strongly that his own reading of this passage was that Claudius had ordered the expulsion of Christians from Rome in the previous year.

85 For the death of the nobility, see Suetonius, *Claudius*, 29; for Claudius's own death, see Suetonius, *Claudius*, 44.

86 Orosius is one year out. Nero's reign began in 807 *AUC*/AD 54. Nero ruled until AD 68.

87 Orosius has drawn the bulk of his account of Nero's crimes from Eutropius, 7.13–14.

88 The list of crimes is taken verbatim from Suetonius, *Nero*, 26.

89 An abbreviated form of information found in Jerome, *Chronicle, A Abr.* 2082. While Jerome says that Nero was crowned as the victor in these games, Orosius, following Suetonius, *Nero*, 24, denigrates him further by implying that in fact he was defeated.

unguents.[90] It is even said that he never made a journey accompanied by fewer than 1,000 carriages. **4.** Finally, he set the city of Rome alight to create a spectacle for his own delight: for six days and seven nights the royal gaze feasted on the burning city.[91] **5.** The granaries made of squared stones and the famed blocks of flats of yesteryear that the rushing flames could not reach were demolished by engines that had once been got in readiness for wars against foreigners, and set ablaze. The wretched plebs were forced to use tombs and mausolea as their lodgings. **6.** Nero himself watched the scene from the top of highest tower of Maecenas's villa[92] and is said, in his delight at the flames' beauty, to have sung the *Iliad* dressed in a tragic actor's robe.[93] **7.** His greed was so pronounced that after this fire in the City which Augustus boasted that he had found made of brick and left made of marble,[94] he forbade anyone to return to the ruins of their home and stole everything that had in some way survived the flames. **8.** He commanded that the Senate grant him 10,000,000 *sestertii* for his expenses every year[95] and confiscated the property of many senators for no given reason, wiping out the entire wealth of all Rome's merchants in a single day, torturing them into the bargain. **9.** His wild cruelty was so unrestrained that he killed the greater part of the Senate and almost annihilated the Equestrian order. He did not even hold back from parricide, but had no hesitation in murdering his mother, brother, sister, wife,[96] and all his other blood relations and kin.

10. He added to this mound of iniquities his rash impiety towards God. For he was the first to execute and put to death Christians at Rome and command that they be hunted out and tortured in the same way throughout all the provinces.[97] He tried to extirpate the very name of Christian, killing the blessed apostles of Christ, Peter and Paul, crucifying the former and

90 Taken virtually verbatim from Eutropius, 7.14.1.
91 The fire of Rome occurred in AD 64.
92 Found on the Esquiline Hill.
93 Orosius's account of the fire of Rome is drawn from Suetonius, *Nero*, 38. Orosius has amplified Suetonius's account by adding the gloss that the war engines which demolished the *insulae* had been prepared for foreign wars, hence what had been got ready for Rome's increase was used to destroy her.
94 Suetonius, *Augustus*, 28.
95 Jerome, *Chronicle, A Abr.* 2083.
96 Respectively: the younger Agrippina (murdered AD 59); Britannicus (in fact Nero's step-brother, murdered in AD 55 by Agrippina rather than Nero); Claudia Octavia (again Nero's step-sister, murdered in AD 62); and Poppaea Sabina, who died after a miscarriage provoked by an assault on her by Nero in AD 65.
97 An embroidered version of Jerome, *Chronicle, A Abr.* 2084, and Rufinus, *Ecclesiastical History*, 2.24–5; cf. Tertullian, *Apology*, 5.

putting the latter to death by the sword.[98] **11.** Soon great numbers of disasters piled up and beset the wretched City from all sides. For the following
autumn, such a great plague broke out in the City *that 30,000 funerals were
entered on Libitina's books.*[99] *On its heels disaster occurred in Britain,
where the two main towns were sacked amid a stupendous slaughter of
Roman citizens and their allies.*[100] **12.** *Moreover, in the east the important provinces of Armenia were lost,*[101] *Roman legions passed beneath the
Parthian's yoke,*[102] *and Syria was only retained with great difficulty.*[103] In
Asia, three cities, namely Laodicea, Hierapolis, and Colossae, were levelled
by an earthquake.[104]

13. Nero, when he learnt that Galba had been proclaimed emperor by his
army in Spain, abandoned all hope and courage. As he had devised unbelievable evils to trouble, nay rather destroy, the state, the Senate proclaimed
him a public enemy. He killed himself four miles from the City, while, to
his great disgrace, he was running away. His death put an end to the entire
family of the Caesars.[105]

98 Also drawn from Jerome, *Chronicle, A Abr. 2084.* Orosius knows, but suppresses, the
fact that Suetonius, *Nero,* 16, includes the persecution of Christians among Nero's good deeds.
For the details of Peter and Paul's death, see Sulpicius Severus, *Chronicle,* 2.29. Paul escaped
the grimmer form of death by virtue of being a Roman citizen, whereas Peter was merely a
free non-Roman. However, Orosius would not have understood this distinction, which was
extinct in his day.

99 Perhaps because Orosius has drawn this phrase virtually verbatim from Suetonius, he is
happy to mention Libitina, the pagan goddess of funerals.

100 Boadicea's uprising of AD 60. Following Suetonius, *Nero,* 39, Orosius speaks of two
towns when in fact three, Colchester, London, and St Albans, were sacked; see Tacitus, *Annals,*
14.32–33.

101 An anachronistic embroidery of Suetonius's comments. In this period Armenia,
sandwiched between the Roman and Parthian empires, enjoyed a precarious independence.
It was partitioned by Rome and Persia in AD 384, Rome annexing her portion as a province.
The campaigns in Nero's reign under Corbulo were an attempt to reinstate a client ruler in the
country.

102 This military disaster occurred at Rhandeia, the modern Kharput, in AD 62; see Dio,
62.21. The legions involved were *XII Fulminata* and *IIII Scythica,* commanded by L. Caesen-
nius Paetus.

103 This list of disasters is a close paraphrase, in a simplified form, of Suetonius, *Nero,* 39.

104 Laodicea is the modern Denizli Ladik, Hierapolis, the modern Pamukkale, and the site
of Colossae lies near the modern Chonae; all are located in Turkey; see Jerome, *Chronicle,
A Abr.* 208. Orosius has pushed the earthquake forward in time so that it follows, rather than
precedes, as it does in Jerome's account, Nero's persecution of the Christians. In this way, it
becomes part of God's vengeance for persecution – one of Orosius's favourite themes.

105 The details of Nero's death and the fact he was the last of the 'Caesars', i.e. the Julio-
Claudian dynasty, are drawn from Jerome, *Chronicle, A Abr.* 2084.

8

1. 824 years after the foundation of the City, Galba usurped the empire while he was in the Spanish provinces.[106] Soon, on hearing that Nero was dead, he came to Rome and, after angering everyone by his greed, brutality, and idleness, adopted Piso, a noble and hard-working youth, as his son and heir to the throne, with whom in the seventh month of his rule he was murdered by Otho.[107]

2. Rome paid for the wrongs she had recently inflicted on the Christian religion with the death of princes and the outbreak of civil war, and those legionary standards which God had held fast in place on the arrival of the apostle Peter in the City so that it was impossible to raise them to begin the civil war which Scribonian had planned, were now, after Peter was killed in the City and Christians butchered in all sorts of ways, loosened throughout the world. **3.** Galba at once rebelled in Spain, and soon after he had been quashed, Otho at Rome, Vitellius in Germany, and Vespasian in Syria all seized command and their arms at the same time.[108] **4.** Now let those who moan about our Christian times witness, albeit unwillingly, both God's might and His clemency, as they recall with what speed the flames of these great wars were kindled and then extinguished; previously great and continual disasters had come from the smallest of reasons, but now these, the greatest of thunderclaps, which rang out on all sides, portending great ills, were calmed with least amount of trouble. **5.** For the Church, though troubled by persecution, was already to be found at Rome and made supplication to Christ, the Judge of all men, even on behalf of her enemies and persecutors.[109]

6. Therefore, when Otho, who had waded through riot and slaughter to the purple after the death of Galba and Piso at Rome, learnt soon afterwards that Vitellius had been declared emperor in Gaul by the German legions,

106 Orosius's date is three years awry. Galba, the governor of Hither Spain, proclaimed himself emperor in Cartagena at the beginning of April 821 *AUC*/AD 68. There is no mention in Orosius's account of Vindex's previous rising in Gaul which set in motion the events that led to the fall of Nero.

107 L. Calpurnius Piso Frugi Licianus, a distant descendent of Pompey who was adopted by Galba on 10 January AD 69. Otho murdered him and Galba in Rome on 15 January AD 69.

108 Otho proclaimed himself emperor on 15 January AD 69, Vitellius, the governor of Lower Germany, on 2 January AD 69. Vespasian, whom Nero had placed in command of suppressing the Jewish revolt, made his claim to the purple first in Alexandria on 1 July AD 69 and was soon after hailed as emperor by his troops in Syria.

109 cf. Matthew 5.44 and Luke 6.28, 6.35.

he began a civil war. He first engaged Vitellius's generals *in three small encounters: one in the Alps, one near Placentia, and a third near a place which is called Castores, from which he emerged victorious.*[110] But after he heard that his troops had been defeated in a fourth battle near Bedriacum, he took his own life three months after he had begun his reign.[111]

7. The victorious Vitellius entered Rome where, while performing many cruel and vile acts and heaping opprobrium on human nature through his incredible gluttony, after learning about Vespasian, he first tried to abdicate; then, after some hangers-on had bolstered his courage, he forced Sabinus, Vespasian's brother, who had not suspected any trouble,[112] and the other Flavian supporters to flee to the Capitol. He then set fire to the temple. The flames and the building's collapse gave them all a common funeral and a common tomb.[113] **8.** Abandoned, after his army defected to Vespasian, and panicking, as the enemy was now approaching, he hid himself in a tiny hut near the palace. To his great shame, he was dragged out and led naked along the Via Sacra to the forum with people on all sides throwing dung in his face. In the eighth month after he had seized the kingdom, he was flayed at the Gemonian Stairs by a death of a thousand tiny cuts, dragged away thence on a hook, and flung in the Tiber without being given even a pauper's burial.[114] **9.** Vespasian's men then turned on the Senate and people of Rome for many days, indulging in indiscriminate slaughter and all types of murder.

9

1. 825 years after the foundation of the City, after this short, but turbulent, storm of tyrants had passed, a serene tranquillity returned under the leadership of Vespasian.[115]

2. For, to go back a little in time in my account, the Jews, who, after Christ's suffering, had completely lost God's grace, on being beset by troubles on all sides, were seduced by certain oracles on Mount Carmel

110 A close paraphrase of Suetonius, *Otho*, 9. Castores is 12 miles from Cremona; see Tacitus, *Histories*, 2.24. The name suggests a rural shrine to the Dioscuri is intended.

111 16 April AD 69. Otho's death is drawn from Jerome, *Chronicle*, *A Abr.* 2084. Bedriacum lay between Cremona and Verona, and is perhaps the modern S. Lorenzo Guazzone.

112 Sabinus, Vespasian's elder brother, was Prefect of the City at the time.

113 19 December AD 69.

114 20 December AD 69.

115 Orosius's date is three years awry. Vespasian's rule began in 822 *AUC*/AD 69. Vespasian reigned until AD 79.

which declared that there would rise up in Judaea leaders who would take control of the world. As they believed that the oracle applied to themselves, they blazed forth in rebellion, annihilating the Roman garrisons in their country and routing the lieutenant-governor of Syria when he came with reinforcements, capturing his eagle and killing his troops.[116]

3. Vespasian was despatched by Nero to deal with these matters. Among his lieutenants he took his eldest son, Titus, and brought many powerful legions with him to Syria. After he had captured many of the Jews' towns and besieged them in Jerusalem where they had gathered in large numbers for their feast day,[117] on learning of Nero's death, he declared himself emperor, urged on by a great number of kings and rulers. He took especial notice of the views of the Jewish leader, Josephus, who was at that time a prisoner in chains and had steadfastly declared, as Suetonius records,[118] that he would be freed immediately by the same man who had captured him, but by then that man would be the emperor. Vespasian left his son, Titus, in the camp to oversee the siege of Jerusalem, while he himself set out for Rome via Alexandria; however, on learning of Vitellius's death, he stayed in Alexandria a short while.[119]

4. Titus crushed the Jews in a great and long siege.[120] He finally breached the walls of the city, though not without heavy losses among his men, with engines and all the other devices of war. However, it took more time and more force to storm the inner fortifications of the temple which were defended by a mass of priests and the leading men who had withdrawn there. **5.** When it was finally in his power, he observed its skilful construction and antiquity, and pondered for a long time whether he ought to burn it down, as it was an incitement for Rome's enemies to rebel, or whether he should preserve it as evidence of his triumph. But as the Church of God was now springing up in abundance throughout the whole world, God decided this building now it was exhausted from giving birth, empty, and fit for no good purpose, ought to

116 The revolt broke out in AD 66. The governor killed was G. Cestius Gallus. This material is drawn from Suetonius, *Vespasian*, 4. Tacitus, *Histories*, 2.78, also notes that Mount Carmel was the site of an oracle. The consensus view in antiquity was that the oracle referred to Vespasian.

117 i.e. the Feast of the Passover. This detail is probably drawn in a confused fashion from Jerome, *Chronicle, A Abr.* 2086. Oddly, Orosius does not use Jerome's point that divine justice arranged for the Jews to be besieged at the same of time of the year that they had crucified Christ.

118 Suetonius, *Vespasian*, 5.

119 Taken from Jerome, *Chronicle, A Abr.* 2085.

120 Jerusalem was captured in AD 70.

be removed. **6.** So Titus, after being hailed as a victorious commander by his troops, fired and demolished the temple at Jerusalem. It had endured 1,102 years from its first foundation down to the day of its final destruction.[121] Titus then levelled all the town-walls to the ground. **7.** Cornelius and Suetonius say that 600,000 Jews were killed in this war.[122] Josephus, a Jew himself who had been a commander in the war and earned Vespasian's pardon and friendship because he had predicted that he would become emperor, writes that 111,000 Jews perished either in the fighting or through famine.[123] What remained of them suffered various plights and were scattered throughout the world – the story goes that they numbered up to 90,000.

8. The emperors Vespasian and Titus entered the City, leading a magnificent triumph for their war against the Jews. A father and son riding in the same triumphal chariot, bringing home their glorious victory over those who had opposed the Father and Son – this was a beautiful spectacle which had never previously been seen by any man in the 320 triumphs which had been celebrated up to that time from the foundation of the City.[124]

9. These two, now that all wars and sedition, both at home and abroad, had been ended, immediately proclaimed peace throughout the world and decreed that Janus of the two faces be kept behind closed doors for only the sixth time since the foundation of the City;[125] for it was just that the same honour was paid to the avenging of the Lord's suffering as had been given to His birth.[126]

10. After this, the Roman state greatly expanded without any trouble or wars. Achaea, Lycia, Rhodes, Byzantium, Samos, Thrace, Cilicia, and Commagene were at this time reduced to the status of provinces for the first time and obeyed the Romans' judges and laws.[127]

11. In the ninth year of Vespasian's reign, three cities in Cyprus were struck by an earthquake and a great plague broke out at Rome.[128]

121 This time span is taken from Jerome, *Chronicle, A Abr.* 2088.
122 Cornelius is Tacitus, *Histories*, 5.13; Suetonius gives no figures.
123 Orosius has taken Josephus's comments via Jerome, *Chronicle, A Abr.* 2086.
124 Orosius's account of the destruction of Jerusalem was to have a profound impact on the medieval and early modern mind; see Hook (1988) and Lupher (2003) 35–42.
125 See 7.3.7–8.
126 Orosius is drawing a parallel with the beginning of Augustus's reign, see 6.22.1.
127 This bloodless expansion parallels Orosius's account of the bloodless expansion in the early Julio-Claudian period. The list of conquests is drawn from Suetonius, *Vespasian*, 8, but is also found in Eutropius, 7.19, and Jerome, *Chronicle, A Abr.* 2090. The first four areas lost their 'free' status, the latter four were client kingdoms that were absorbed into the empire.
128 Jerome, *Chronicle, A Abr.* 2093.

12. In this ninth year of his reign, Vespasian died of dysentery at his villa in the Sabine country.[129]

13. 828 years after the foundation of the City, Titus, if we exclude Otho and Vitellius from the ranks of the emperors, became the seventh man to rule after Augustus, ruling for two years after Vespasian.[130] His rule was so peaceful that it is said that he spilt absolutely no one's blood while governing the state.[131] **14.** It was then, however, that a fire suddenly broke out at Rome and burnt down the majority of its public buildings. We are also told that the summit of Mount Bebius broke asunder and poured out great fires, destroying the neighbouring regions along with their towns and inhabitants in torrents of flame.[132] Titus, to the great grief of all, died of disease in the same villa where his father had died.

10

1. 830 years after the foundation of the City, Titus's brother, Domitian, succeeded his brother as the eighth ruler of the kingdom after Augustus.[133] For fifteen years his cruelty, which gradually scaled every level of crime, finally reached the stage where he dared to uproot the Christian church, which was now firmly established throughout the world, issuing edicts everywhere that enjoined the cruellest persecution.[134] **2.** He fell into such a state of pride that he commanded that he be called, be described, and be worshipped as men's master and their god.[135] He killed the noblest in the Senate out of both envy and at the same time greed. Some he murdered openly, others he thrust into exile, giving commands that they be cut down

129 24 June AD 79.

130 A striking contradiction. At 7.9.1, Orosius states that Vespasian began his reign in 825 *AUC*, and at 7.9.12 that he ruled for nine years. Therefore the date given here is impossible. Titus's rule began in 832 *AUC*/AD 79.

131 cf. Eutropius, 7.21.

132 A reference to the eruption of Mount Vesuvius and the destruction of Pompeii, Herculaneum, and Stabia on 24 August AD 79. Orosius, following Jerome, *Chronicle, A Abr.* 2095, calls Vesuvius Bebius. The information about the fire at Rome is also drawn from Jerome, *Chronicle, A Abr.* 2096.

133 Orosius's date is four years awry. Domitian began to rule in 834 *AUC*/AD 81. Domitian ruled until AD 96.

134 The idea of Domitian's rake's progress is found in Eutropius, 7.23.1, but Orosius changes its culmination to his persecution of Christians. See Jerome, *Chronicle, A Abr.* 2107, and Rufinus, *Ecclesiastical History*, 3.17, for Domitian as the second persecutor of Christians after Nero.

135 An embroidered version of Jerome, *Chronicle, A Abr.* 2107.

there.[136] His intemperate lust drove him to perpetrate whatever acts he had
been able to imagine. He built many public buildings in the City, funding
them from his destruction of the Roman people's wealth.[137]

3. The war he waged through his lieutenants against the Germans[138] and
Dacians[139] was equally damaging to the state. For while he ripped apart
the Senate and people in the City, abroad his enemies continually slaughtered his badly led armies. **4.** I would have described at great length the
great battles fought by the Dacians' king, Diurpanus, against the Roman
commander Fuscus[140] and the extent of the disasters that befell Rome, had
not Cornelius Tacitus, who recorded these events with the uttermost care,
stated that Sallustius Crispus and a vast number of other writers had decided
not to speak about the numbers killed and that he himself had decided that
this was the best policy.[141] Domitian, however, full of the most disgusting
conceit, held a triumph for killing his own legionaries, on the pretext that
it was for defeating his enemies.[142] **5.** Driven wild by the pride that made
him wish to be worshipped as a god, he was the first emperor after Nero
to command that Christians be persecuted. At this time too the blessed
apostle John was exiled to the island of Patmos.[143] **6.** It was also decreed
that among the Jews the race of David be sought out by harsh torture and
bloody inquisitions, and killed. He did this because he hated, but believed
the holy prophets, thinking that someone who would be able to take his
kingdom might still come from the seed of David.[144]

7. However, straight after this, Domitian was cruelly murdered by his
servants in the Palace. His body was carried out in a pauper's coffin by the
public pall-bearers and given an ignominious burial.[145]

136 An embroidered version of Eutropius, 7.23.2. See also Suetonius, *Domitian*, 10.

137 Jerome, *Chronicle, A Abr.* 2105, where there is no mention of financial harm.

138 A campaign against the Chatti in AD 83.

139 AD 86–89.

140 Cornelius Fuscus, Domitian's Praetorian Prefect, who was killed at the beginning of
the war. Diurparnus is normally known as Decebalus (ruled AD 87–106).

141 An odd comment which presumably refers to a lost section of Tacitus's *Histories*,
though conceivably it is a reference to Tacitus, *Annals*, 1.6, where Sallustius Crispus, the great
nephew of the historian Sallust, warns Tiberius at the beginning of his reign not to make state
secrets public.

142 Held in AD 89. Jerome, *Chronicle, A Abr.* 2106, merely states that Domitian celebrated
a triumph over the Dacians and Germans.

143 The persecution and detail about St John the Divine are drawn from Jerome, *Chronicle,
A Abr.* 2110.

144 Drawn in an extremely abbreviated fashion from Rufinus, *Ecclesiastical History*, 2.19.

145 Domitian's persecution of the Jews and his death are drawn from Jerome, *Chronicle, A*

11

1. In the 846th year after the foundation of the City, though Eutropius says this year was the 850th year, Nerva, who was already a very old man, was made emperor by Petronius, the Praetorian Prefect, and the eunuch Parthenius, Domitian's murderer.[146] He was the ninth emperor after Augustus and adopted Trajan as the heir to his kingdom. In this, he truly looked to his troubled country's interests with the aid of God's foresight.[147] **2.** With his very first edict, he recalled all those who had been exiled. It was in this way that the apostle John, freed by the general amnesty, returned to Ephesus. After a year of his rule had passed, Nerva fell sick and died.[148]

12

1. 847 years after the foundation of the City, Trajan, a Spaniard by race, took the rudder of state from Nerva, becoming the tenth emperor after Augustus, and ruled for nineteen years.[149]

2. He put on the insignia of power at Agrippina, a city in Gaul,[150] and soon afterwards reduced Germany across the Rhine to its old status. He subjugated many tribes across the Danube, made the regions lying beyond the Euphrates and Tigris into provinces, and occupied Seleucia, Ctesiphon, and Babylon.[151] **3.** Nevertheless, he was the second emperor after Nero to be

---

Abr. 2112. Orosius's chronology here underlines that the emperor's death was a direct consequence of his persecution of the Christians.

146 Eutropius, 8.1.1. In fact neither date given is correct, Nerva came to the purple in 849 *AUC* = AD 96. Nerva's old age and the names of the two kingmakers are found in Eutropius, but the information that Pathenius was a eunuch is an addition by Orosius.

147 Trajan was adopted by Nerva on 27 October AD 97. The old emperor may have been helped as much by the mutinous mood of Trajan and the size and proximity of army that he commanded (he was governor of Upper Germany at the time) as he was by God to adopt Trajan. Orosius is clearly proud that Trajan came from Spain; however, the notion of divine aid is not his own but taken from Eutropius, 8.1.2.

148 The return of the exiles and John is drawn from Jerome, *Chronicle, A Abr.* 2113. Nerva died on 7 January AD 98.

149 Orosius's chronology is four years awry. Trajan became emperor in 851 *AUC*/AD 98. He was born in Italica, the modern Santiponce, just outside Seville. It is normally thought that he was descended from Roman settler stock whose ancestors came from Tuder. However, Orosius's adjective *Hispanus* means rather native Spaniard. This was also the view of Cassius Dio who describes him as 'alloethnes', i.e. a non-Roman. For a discussion of this issue, see Canto (2003).

150 Colonia Agrippinensis, the modern Cologne.

151 This potted account of Trajan's career draws heavily on Eutropius, 8.2–3; Jerome, *Chronicle, A Abr.* 2117–2118 has also been used as a source. Trajan stabilised the German

ensnared by the error of persecuting Christians, ordering that they be sought out everywhere and forced to sacrifice to idols. His command was that those who refused be killed, and very many were killed. On being advised by the report of Pliny Secundus, who had been chosen as prosecutor out of Rome's judges, that these men, apart from confessing their belief in Christ and holding small, harmless meetings, did nothing contrary to Roman law and that because of their unobjectionable faith none of them thought that death was a serious or frightening matter, the emperor straightaway issued some more merciful rescripts to mitigate his decree.[152]

4. But in Rome immediately after these events, the Golden House, which Nero had built by spending all his private funds along with those of the state, was suddenly burnt down to make it known that although this particular persecution had been begun by another, its punishment fell most fiercely on the buildings of the man who had begun the persecutions and so on their true author.[153]

5. Four cities in Asia, Elea, Myrina, Pitane, and Cyme along with two in Greece, those of the Opuntii and Oriti,[154] were destroyed by an earthquake that also ruined three cities in Galatia. At Rome, the Pantheon was struck by lightning and burnt down, while an earthquake in Antioch almost levelled the entire city.[155]

---

limes, but did not recreate the old trans-Rhine province as Orosius implies. The Dacians were defeated in two wars in AD 101–02 and AD 105–06. Trajan's campaigns into Parthia in AD 114–17 resulted in the creation of the short-lived provinces of Armenia, Mesopotamia and Assyria.

152 A reference to Pliny, *Letters*, 10.96–97. Pliny was governor of Bithynia and Pontus at the time, not, as Orosius thinks, an official concerned with persecuting Christians. His weak understanding of the letters suggests that he had never seen a copy of them at first hand, but is probably relying on the account given by Rufinus, *Ecclesiastical History*, 3.33. When dealing with the letters, Orosius has again altered the dates that he found in Jerome to fit his preferred pattern of natural disasters following persecution rather than preceding it. Here the date of Pliny's correspondence given by Jerome, *Chronicle, A Abr.* 2124 (= AD 110), has been pushed back in time in order that all the natural disasters listed should follow Trajan's persecution and hence demonstrate God's just vengeance.

153 Drawn from Jerome, *Chronicle, A Abr.* 2120.

154 Opus, the chief city of the Opuntian Locrians, is perhaps the modern Kardhenitza in modern Greece. Oricum, a port in Illyricum, is the modern Erikha in Albania.

155 The destruction of the Golden House is drawn from Jerome, *Chronicle, A Abr.* 2120. Orosius tries nobly to absolve his compatriot and hero, Trajan, from the blame of initiating a persecution in his account. The earthquake in Asia and Greece is taken from Jerome, *Chronicle, A Abr.* 2121. Orosius disingenuously elides this with the earthquake in Galatia to make God's vengeance seem the greater. In fact, Jerome dates the earthquake in Galatia and the burning of the Pantheon six years after the Asian earthquake, *A Abr.* 2127 (= AD 113), and

6. Then, the Jews in a wild rage blazed forth in an incredible rebellion that extended across different parts of the world all at the same time. They waged a brutal campaign throughout all Libya against its inhabitants, slaughtering its peasants and leaving it so desolate that had the emperor Hadrian not afterwards brought in men from other lands and settled them there in colonies,[156] it would have remained an empty land, as those living there had been completely wiped out. **7.** Then the Jews' bloodstained sedition threw Egypt, Cyrene, and the Thebaid into chaos. In Alexandria, however, they were brought to battle, defeated, and annihilated. In Mesopotamia too, the emperor ordered that war be waged on the rebels and so many thousands of them were slaughtered and killed. **8.** Nevertheless, they razed the city of Salamis in Cyprus to the ground and killed all its inhabitants. Trajan died of dysentery, according to some accounts, in the city of Seleucia in Isauria.[157]

13

1. 867 years after the foundation of the City, Hadrian, Trajan's cousin, became the 11th emperor after Augustus, and ruled for twenty-one years.[158] **2.** Through the agency of Quadratus, a student of the apostles, Aristides of Athens, a man full of faith and wisdom, and his lieutenant-governor, Serenus Granius, he was taught by, and learned from, books written about the Christian religion. He therefore decreed in a letter to Minucius Fundanus, the governor of Asia, that no one could condemn a Christian without charging them of a crime or presenting proof.[159] **3.** He was immediately proclaimed Father of his Country in the Senate,

---

gives a third date for the earthquake at Antioch, *A Abr.* 2130.

156 Jerome, *Chronicle, A Abr.* 2137.

157 The details of the Jewish rebellion are drawn from Jerome, *Chronicle, A Abr.* 2130–2132. The account of Trajan's death in AD 117 is taken from Jerome, *Chronicle, A Abr.* 2132. Here Orosius may have misread Jerome who mentions Seleucia as the possible scene of Trajan's death, but prefers, correctly, Selennutis which was renamed Traianopolis in the deceased emperor's honour.

158 Orosius's date is three years awry. Hadrian became emperor in 870 *AUC*/AD 117. He ruled until AD 138.

159 Orosius's account of Christianity and Hadrian is drawn from Jerome, *Chronicle, A Abr.* 2142. Quadratus and Aristides were Christians and said to have presented Hadrian with apologies when he visited Athens to participate in the Eleusinian mysteries; see also Jerome, *Letters,* 70 and *Famous Men (De Viris Illustribus)*, 19 and 20. Jerome notes that Granius wrote a letter of protest about the execution of Christians to Hadrian. Orosius, while not stating it as a fact, goes beyond Jerome and implies that Granius was a Christian. The disputed rescript of Hadrian to Fundanus is preserved (in Latin) with the *1st Apology* of Justin Martyr.

something without precedent, and his wife was proclaimed Augusta.[160] Hadrian ruled his country with the justest of laws and waged war on, and defeated, the Sauromatae.[161] **4.** He also finally exterminated and subdued the Jews, who, roused up by troubles caused by their own crimes, were at that time laying waste to the province of Palestine which had once belonged to them. In this way, Hadrian avenged the Christians whom the Jews, under their leader Cocheba, had tortured because they would not join them in opposing Rome. **5.** The emperor decreed that no Jew be allowed to enter Jerusalem and that only Christians be permitted in the city. He rebuilt its walls to their former glory and named it Aelia after his own name.[162]

14

1. 888 years after the foundation of the City, Antoninus, who was known as the Pious, was made the 12th emperor after Augustus. He governed the state so peacefully and respectfully for almost twenty-three years along with his sons, Aurelius and Lucius, that he was deservedly called 'the Pious' and 'Father of his Country'.[163] **2.** It was in his reign that the haeresiarch Valentinus and Marcion's teacher, Cerdo, came to Rome. However, the philosopher Justin gave Antoninus the book he had written in support of the Christian religion and made him look favourably on Christian men. Antoninus was taken ill and died 12 miles from the City.[164]

160 Jerome, *Chronicle, A Abr.* 2144. Orosius has arranged his text to imply, falsely, that Hadrian's acclamation as *pater patriae* was a consequence of his letter to Fundanus. It is difficult to see why this event is described as 'without precedent', *ultra morem maiorum*, as the title was commonly held by emperors, being first awarded to the emperor Augustus in 2 BC.

161 A reference to Hadrian's successful defence against an incursion on the Danube frontier in AD 117.

162 The account of the Bar Cochba rebellion of AD 132–35, including the note about Jewish persecution of Christians, is drawn from Jerome, *Chronicle, A Abr.* 2149–2152. After the suppression of the rebellion, Hadrian refounded Jerusalem as a pagan city, Aelia Capitolina. Jerome makes no mention, however, of Jews being banned from Jerusalem or Christians being allowed there. Orosius's text is deliberately opaque. It probably means that only Christians out of the Jews and Christians were allowed into Jerusalem, but could be taken as meaning that the city was given to the Christians.

163 The comment about Marcus's co-rule with his sons, Marcus Aurelius and Lucius Verus whom he adopted on the orders of Hadrian, is drawn from Jerome, *Chronicle, A Abr.* 2153. That concerning Antoninus's acclamation as *pater patriae* is taken from Jerome, *Chronicle, A Abr.* 2155. However, Orosius's chronology is again three years awry; Antoninus Pius became emperor in 891 *AUC*/AD 138.

164 Valentinus was a Gnostic heretic; a Coptic version of his *Gospel of Truth* has been

15

1. 911 years after the foundation of the City, Marcus Antoninus Verus became the 13th man to assume the throne after Augustus. He ruled with his brother Aurelius Commodus and remained in power for nineteen years. These men were the first to oversee the state with each having equal power.[165] **2.** They then waged a war against the Parthians with admirable courage and good fortune. Annius Antoninus Verus set out to prosecute this war. The Parthians' king, Vologaesus, made a serious incursion into the empire and laid waste to Armenia, Cappadocia, and Syria.[166] **3.** But Antoninus, after great deeds were performed by his generals who acted with great vigour, captured Seleucia in Assyria, a town which lies on the banks of the river Hydaspes, along with 400,000 of the enemy. He celebrated the triumph for this victory over Parthia with his brother, but not long afterwards, while he was sitting with his brother in a carriage, he was afflicted by the onset of the disease which the Greeks call apoplexy and choked to death.[167]

4. On Verus's death, Marcus Antoninus was left in sole charge of the state. During the Parthian War, the third set of persecutions after those of Nero was carried out at Marcus's command and fell heavily on the Christians in

---

found at Nag Hammadi. Both Irenaeus, *Against Heresy* (*Adversus Haereses*), and Tertullian, *Against the supporters of Valentinian* (*Adversus Valentinianos*), provide an orthodox perspective on his work. For discussions of Valentinus's theology, see Bermejo (1998) and Thomassen (2005). Marcion regarded the god of the Old Testament as the evil demiurge and thus discarded the Old Testament and a substantial part of the New. Irenaeus, *Against Heresy*, 1.27 and 3.4, states that Cerdo was his mentor. See Salter-Williams (1984) for an in-depth discussion of Marcion and his impact. The philosopher, so described by Jerome, Justin is Justin Martyr (c. AD 100–65). His *First Apology* is dedicated to Antoninus Pius, though there is no proof that the emperor ever received or read the work. Orosius's details are taken from Jerome, *Chronicle, A Abr.* 2156, 2157. The details of Antoninus's death are taken from Jerome, *Chronicle, A Abr.* 2176.

165 Marcus Antoninus Verus is known to history as Marcus Aurelius. Orosius's chronology remains three years awry: Marcus Aurelius became emperor in AD 161/914 *AUC*. Orosius has drawn his information from Jerome, *Chronicle, A Abr.* 2177, but appears to have misread his source. Jerome speaks of 'Marcus Antoninus qui et Verus et Lucius Aurelius Commodus'. Orosius has read *qui et* as 'who was also called' when in fact it means 'who along with'. Verus is Lucius Verus, Marcus Aurelius's co-emperor from AD 161–69.

166 Vologaeses IV, AD 148–92. His incursions are noted by Jerome, *Chronicle, A Abr.* 2179.

167 The account of this war, which lasted from AD 162–66, and of Verus's death (for which see also Jerome, *Chronicle, A Abr.* 2185) draw heavily on Eutropius, 8.10. Statius Priscus recovered Armenia in AD 163, while Seleucia, which lies 18 miles south of Baghdad in Iraq, was captured and sacked by G. Avidius Cassius in AD 164. The joint triumph was held in AD 166. Verus died of a stroke near Altinum while returning from the German front.

Asia and Gaul. Many of the saints were crowned with martyrdom. **5.** There followed a plague which swept over most of Rome's provinces and such a great pestilence laid waste to all of Italy that farms, fields, and towns everywhere were stripped of their tillers and inhabitants and turned into ruins and woodland.[168]

6. It is said that the Roman army and all its legions stationed far and wide in their winter quarters lost so many men that the Marcomannic war which broke out at this time could not be have been waged without the fresh levy of troops which Marcus Antoninus held at Carnuntium for three years running.[169]

7. A great amount of evidence makes it absolutely clear that this war was guided by divine providence. The most important piece is a letter written by this sober and serious emperor. **8.** For when an innumerable host of savage barbarian tribes, that is the Marcomanni, Quadi, Vandals, Sarmatians, Sueves, and almost all of Germany, rose in rebellion, the army advanced up to the frontier with the Quadi and were surrounded by the enemy. They then found themselves in more immediate danger from their lack of water than the enemy. **9.** When some soldiers, showing their great constancy of faith, suddenly poured forth their prayers, openly calling on the name of Christ, the rain fell with such violence that it more than made good the Romans' supplies at no danger to themselves,[170] but the constant lightning bolts terrified the barbarians, especially as many of them were killed, and forced them to flee. **10.** As they turned their backs in flight, the Romans fell on them and slaughtered them to a man, winning with a few untrained troops, but also with the mighty aid of Christ, a glorious victory that outshone almost all those of old. **11.** The majority of authors say that Antoninus's report, in which he admits that it was the invocation of Christ's name by his Christian soldiers that remedied his lack of water and won the victory, is still extant to this day.[171]

---

168 The persecutions are drawn from Jerome, *Chronicle, A Abr.* 2183, the heavily embroidered account of the plague from Jerome's entry for the following year.

169 Carnuntium, more correctly Carnuntum, is the modern Petronell in Austria which lies on the south side of the Danube. Orosius has drawn his account from Eutropius, 8.12–13, but has misinterpreted his source – Eutropius makes no mention of levies, but simply says that Marcus worked hard here for three years. The Marcomanni were a German tribe living in what is now Bohemia. The First Marcomannic War lasted from AD 166–73. For an attempted modern reconstruction of this war, accounts of which in our ancient sources are highly confused, see Birley (1987) ch. 8.

170 cf. 4.17.9.

171 The 'rain miracle' is depicted on the Column of Marcus Aurelius. The incident

12. This same Antoninus made his son, Commodus, ruler of the kingdom with him.[172] He remitted the tribute, even that which was outstanding from the past, in all the provinces and at the same time ordered that every forged document dealing with taxation be heaped together in the forum and burnt. He also tempered Rome's harsher laws with new rulings.[173] He finally died, after suddenly being taken ill in Pannonia.[174]

16

1. 930 years after the foundation of the City, Lucius Antonius Commodus succeeded his father to the kingdom, the 14th to do so after Augustus, and remained in power for thirteen years.[175] **2.** He waged a successful war against the Germans. In all else, however, he became depraved through his disgraceful extravagance and obscene behaviour.[176] He often fought as a gladiator in their training schools and frequently pitted himself against wild beasts in the arena.[177] He killed a great number of senators, especially those whom he saw were outstanding by birth or ability. **3.** The City's punishment followed in the wake of the king's wrong-doing. The Capitol was struck by lightning which started a fire-storm that gripped and burned down, along with some buildings adjacent to it, the library which their ancestors had taken great care to build.[178] After this, another fire then broke out at Rome

---

produced a great deal of legendary material, including an 'official' version which held that the rain came in response to the emperor's prayers to pagan gods; see Dio, 71.8 and *SHA Marcus Aurelius*, 24.4. Orosius's statement that the emperor explicitly thanked the Christians in his army for bringing about the miracle is drawn from Jerome, *Chronicle, A Abr.* 2189. See also Rufinus, *Ecclesiastical History*, 5.5. For a detailed discussion of the rain miracle and the Marcomannic Wars in general, see Kovács (2009)

172   In AD 176, see Jerome, *Chronicle, A Abr.* 2193.

173   Jerome, *Chronicle, A Abr.* 2194.

174   Orosius presumably had no knowledge of Marcus Aurelius's *Meditations* which contain scathing criticisms of Christianity, as his picture of the emperor is generally favourable.

175   Orosius's chronology remains three years awry: Commodus's rule began in 933 *AUC/* AD 180.

176   A reference to the end of the Second Marcomannic War in AD 180. Commodus ended the war that had begun three years earlier at the price of abandoning newly conquered Roman territory. He held a triumph over the Marcomanni at the end of AD 180. Commodus's decision was probably a wise one, but Orosius, perhaps misled by the notice of a triumph, seems to think that the emperor was more successful than was in fact the case. SHA *Commodus*, 13.5, is more generous than Orosius, and speaks of triumphs against the Moors and Dacians.

177   This potted account of Commodus draws heavily on Eutropius, 8.15.

178   This library is known only from Orosius and his source, Jerome, *Chronicle, A Abr.* 2204.

and razed to the ground the temple of Vesta, the Palace, and a good part of the City.[179] **4.** Commodus, who incommoded everyone, is said to have been strangled to death in the Vestilian Hall.[180] Even when he was alive, he was condemned as an enemy of mankind.[181]

5. After Commodus's reign, the elderly Helvius Pertinax was made Augustus's 15th successor by the Senate. He was killed after ruling for six months by the criminal acts of the lawyer Julian.[182]

6. After killing Pertinax, Julian seized power, but soon he was defeated at the Mulvian Bridge in a civil war and killed by Severus in the seventh month of his reign. Pertinax and Julian's rule took up a year.

17

1. 944 years after the foundation of the City, Severus, a Tripolitanian of African descent from the town of Lepcis, who wanted to be called Pertinax after the name of the emperor whose death he had avenged, took over the ruler-less empire as Augustus's 16th successor, and held power for seventeen years.[183] **2.** He had a naturally vicious character and was always troubled by a multiplicity of wars, but nevertheless ruled the state with great courage, though also with great brutality. At Cyzicus, he defeated and killed Pescennius Niger, who had aspired to establish himself as a usurper in Egypt and Syria.[184] **3.** He also used the sword to coerce the Jews and Samaritans when they tried to rebel, and conquered the Parthians, Arabs, and Adiabeni.[185] He

179 The fires took place in AD 188 and 189; see Jerome, *Chronicle, A Abr.* 2207.

180 Here, surprisingly, disaster, and, by implication, divine vengeance, follows the persecution of a pagan group. The details of this, the disasters which followed it, and Commodus's death are drawn from Jerome, *Chronicle, A Abr.* 2207–2208. Vestilian is Jerome's error for Vectilian. The Vectilian villa was a gladiatorial school to which Commodus had transferred his palace; see SHA *Commodus* 16.3.

181 Orosius has drawn this sentiment from Eutropius, but awkwardly reversed it. Eutropius reads: 'even when he was *dead*, he was condemned as an enemy of the human race'.

182 M. Didius Julianus, who famously purchased the Roman Empire from the Praetorian Guard for a donative of 6,250 *denarii* per soldier.

183 Orosius's chronology is two years awry. Severus's rule began in 946 *AUC*/AD 193. These details are drawn from Jerome, *Chronicle, A Abr.* 2210, which places the beginning of Severus's rule in AD 196.

184 Pescennius proclaimed himself emperor in May AD 193. Orosius has garbled his account of this coup. It was Pescennius's deputy, Asellius Aemilianus, who was defeated at Cyzicus. Pescennius was defeated soon afterwards at Issus.

185 Jerome, *Chronicle, A Abr.* 2213 (Jews and Samaritans), 2214 (Parthians, Arabs, the Adiabeni).

subjected the Christians to their fourth persecution after that of Nero, and a great number of the saints in a wide number of provinces were crowned as martyrs.[186] **5.** Divine vengeance followed on the heels of Severus's impious presumption against Christians and the Church of God. For Severus was at once snatched, or rather dragged back, from Syria to Gaul to fight a third civil war. **6.** For he had already fought one in Italy against Julian, another in Syria against Pescennius, and now Clodius Albinus, who had connived in the murder of Pertinax with Julian and proclaimed himself Caesar in Gaul, started a third. This war spilt much Roman blood on both sides. However, Albinus was defeated and killed near Lyons.[187]

7. Severus, though the victor, was forced to go to the British provinces as almost all his allies there had rebelled.[188] On recovering part of the island after frequent, heavy, and severe fighting, he decided to divide this from the other unconquered tribes with a rampart. He therefore built a great ditch and stout rampart fortified with many towers across from one sea to the other – a distance of 132 miles.[189] **8.** He died of disease in Britain in the town of York.[190] He left two sons, Bassianus and Geta. Geta was condemned as an enemy of the state and put to death,[191] while Bassianus obtained the kingdom and took the name Antoninus.

186 An embroidered version of Jerome, *Chronicle, A Abr.* 2218.

187 Caesar here is the title of the subordinate ruler under the emperor whose own title was Augustus. Severus recognised Albinus as Caesar in AD 194, which allowed him to deal with Niger without having to fight a war on two fronts. However, it is highly unlikely that he ever intended to allow Albinus to continue in such a rôle. Albinus's army was defeated by Severus on 19 February AD 197.

188 Orosius has drawn his information about Albinus and the British campaigns from Jerome, *Chronicle, A Abr.* 2221. He has assumed, and Jerome's terse text perhaps implies, that Severus's British campaigns immediately followed on after his defeat of Albinus in AD 197, whereas in fact he did not enter the province until AD 208. Orosius would have been eager to make such an error, as it would strengthen the notion that these wars were divine vengeance for the emperor's persecution of the church.

189 The information on Hadrian's Wall is drawn from Jerome, *Chronicle, A Abr.* 2221. Severus made extensive repairs to the wall from AD 205 onwards. Orosius, following Jerome and Eutropius, 8.19, appears to be completely unaware of who built the wall in the first place. The figure of 132 miles given is incorrect: the wall was 76 Roman miles long. It has been suggested that the original figure intended was 32 and that it referred to the western section of the wall running from the River Irthing to the Solway Firth. However, a more elegant solution is to assume that manuscript corruption has taken place with CXXXII being written for LXXXII which would yield a figure close to the correct length of the wall.

190 Severus died in AD 211. Orosius has drawn his information about York from Jerome, *Chronicle, A Abr.* 2225.

191 In AD 212.

18

1. 962 years after the foundation of the City, Aurelius Antoninus Bassianus, namely Caracalla, became the 17th emperor after Augustus and remained in power for just under seven years.[192] **2.** He was a harsher man than his father, and more intemperate than any man in his lusts, even marrying his own stepmother, Julia. He died while fighting against the Parthians after he had been surrounded between Edessa and Carrhae.[193]

3. After Caracalla, Ophilus Macrinus, who had been his praetorian prefect, was, along with his son, Diadumen, the 18th man after Augustus to seize power. However, a year later he was killed in a soldiers' mutiny at Archelais.[194]

4. 970 years after the foundation of the City, Marcus Aurelius Antoninus became the 19th man after Augustus to gain power and held it for four years. **5.** This man was a priest in the temple of Heliogabal and left nothing to remember him by, save the infamy of his perversions, outrages, and all kinds of obscenity. He was killed at Rome, along with his mother, in a military uprising.[195]

6. 974 years after the foundation of the City, Aurelius Alexander was, by the wishes of both the Senate and the troops, created the 20th emperor after Augustus.[196] He ruled for thirteen years, rightly obtaining a reputation for justice. **7.** His mother, Mamea, was a Christian and took pains to be taught by the presbyter Origen.[197] Alexander at once launched an expedition

192 Orosius's chronology is two years awry: Caracalla's reign began in 964 *AUC*/AD 211.

193 Orosius's account of Caracalla is drawn mainly from Eutropius, 8.20, and that of his death from Jerome, *Chronicle, A Abr.* 2233. SHA Caracalla, 7, tells us that Caracalla was murdered while relieving himself on the road between Carrhae and Edessa. Orosius has suppressed the building of the Baths of Caracalla which is mentioned by both Eutropius and Jerome.

194 Orosius's account of Macrinus is drawn from Eutropius, 8.21, and Jerome, *Chronicle, A Abr.* 2234. Achelais is the modern Khirbat al-Bayudat in Palestine. *SHA* Macrinus, 10.3, places the site of Macrinus's death, along with that of his son, in an unnamed village in Bithynia.

195 Antoninus is normally known as Elagabalus/Heliogabalus. Orosius's chronology is one year in error: Elagabalus began to rule in 971 *AUC*/AD 218. Orosius's account is informed by Eutropius, 8.22, and Jerome, *Chronicle, A Abr.* 2235–2238 (where Elagabalus's accession date is correct). The cult of Elagabal was an Eastern orgiastic religion centred on a betyl (an aniconic sacred stone) that Elagabalus had brought to Rome from the cult's home, Emesa, the modern Homs in Syria. His mother was Julia Sohaemias, the daughter of Julia Maesa, who was the sister of Julia Domna, the wife of Septimius Severus.

196 Normally known as Severus Alexander. Orosius's chronology is one year out: Severus Alexander's reign began in 975 *AUC*/AD 222.

197 Normally Julia Mamaea. Like Julia Sohaemias, she was a daughter of Julia Maesa. The assertion that Mamaea was a pupil of Origen is drawn from Rufinus, *Ecclesiastical History*,

against the Persians and defeated their king, Xerxes, in a great battle.[198] He employed Ulpian as his advisor and showed the utmost moderation in ruling the state. He was, however, killed in a mutiny near Mainz.[199]

19

1. 987 years after the foundation of the City, Maximin was made the 21st emperor after Augustus by the army, though the Senate opposed him. After he had waged a successful war in Germany, he carried out the fifth persecution of Christians after that of Nero. **2.** But straightaway, that is to say in the third year of his reign, he was killed at Aquileia by Pupienus, putting an end both to his persecutions and his life. He had specifically persecuted priests and clergymen, that is to say the teachers of doctrine, either because the family of Alexander whom he had succeeded and Alexander's mother were Christians, or because he had a special hatred of the presbyter Origen.[200]

3. 991 years after the foundation of the City, Gordian was made the 22nd emperor after Augustus and stayed in this office for six years, for Maximin's killer, Pupienus, and his brother, Balbinus, who had seized power were killed soon afterwards in the Palace.[201] **4.** Though still a boy, Gordian when he was about to set off to the east to wage war against the Parthians, opened, according to Eutropius, the gates of Janus which I cannot recall any writer saying that anyone had closed after the time of Vespasian and Titus, while

---

6.21. Orosius amplifies the comment that he found in Rufinus that Mamaea was a 'devout' woman into the positive assertion that she was a Christian. Overall, this is a curious detail, as Origen was not well thought of by the church of the fifth century – see Augustine, *City of* God, 11.23 and 21.17. Presumably, Orosius thought any hint of imperial sponsorship of Christianity outweighed the awkwardness of Origen's problematic orthodoxy.

198 The campaign began in AD 231. 'Xerxes' is Ardachir I, the founder of the Sassanid dynasty.

199 Orosius's account of Alexander Severus is informed by Eutropius, 8.18.6–8, and Jerome, *Chronicle, A Abr.* 2238–2251. Ulpian was the great lawyer of the third century, much of whose work is preserved in Justinian's *Digest.* Alexander Severus made him Praetorian Prefect in AD 222. However, the following year he was lynched by the Praetorian Guard with whom he commanded no respect. For a general account of Ulpian, see Honoré (2002).

200 Orosius's chronology is one year out: Maximin 'the Thracian' began to rule in 988 *AUC*/AD 235. Orosius's account is drawn mainly from Jerome, *Chronicle, A Abr.* 2252–2254, though his German war is derived from Eutropius, 9.1. The speculations on why Maximin persecuted priests are Orosius's own.

201 This is Gordian III; Orosius truncates the political squabble that spawned the short-lived emperors Gordian I and II. His source is Jerome, *Chronicle, A Abr.* 2255. The date for Gordian's accession is correct.

Cornelius Tacitus tells us that Vespasian opened them in the second year of his reign.[202] **5.** Gordian, after successfully fighting some great battles against the Parthians, was treacherously killed by his own men not far from Circessus on the Euphrates.[203]

20

1. 997 years after the foundation of the City, Philip was made the 23rd emperor after Augustus. He made his son, Philip, his co-ruler and reigned for seven years.[204] **2.** He was the first of all the emperors to be a Christian, and after two years of his rule the 1,000th year after the foundation of Rome was completed. So it came to pass that this most pre-eminent of all her previous birthdays was celebrated with magnificent games by a Christian emperor.[205] **3.** There can be no doubt that Philip dedicated the gratitude and honour expressed in this great thanksgiving to Christ and the church, as no author speaks of him going up to the Capitol and sacrificing victims there as was the custom.[206] **4.** Nevertheless, the two Philips died in a mutiny and through Decius's treachery, though in different places.[207]

202 For Gordian III, see Eutropius, 9.2.2, and also SHA Gordian, 26.3. The comments by Tacitus are in a lost part of his *Histories*.

203 Jerome, *Chronicle, A Abr.*2257 and Eutropius, 9.2.3. Circessus is modern Qarqisiya which lies at the junction of the Euphrates and Khabur rivers.

204 Orosius's date for Philip's accession is correct. Philip 'the Arab' ruled from AD 244–49, his son, Philip II, from AD 247–49. Orosius suppresses the view found in many of our sources that Philip the Arab was involved in the murder of the Gordians as it is not germane to his purpose to have the first Christian emperor reach the purple by treachery. See Zosimus, 1.18; Zonaras, 12.18, and SHA Gordian, 29.2–30.9.

205 Perhaps an odd comment, given Orosius's hostility to the games. Jerome, *Chronicle, A Abr.* 2262, gives more detail, speaking of 'innumerable' animals killed in the Circus Maximus, games celebrated in the Campus Martius, and three days and nights of theatrical performances.

206 This is a striking claim and not made by other Latin authors. Eusebius, *Ecclesiastical History*, 6.34, claims Philip was a Christian, but says nothing about Rome's millennium. For Orosius, the link he has made shows that Rome and its empire are an integral part of God's plan. Orosius suppresses Eutropius's, 9.3, comment that the two Philips were deified after their deaths, which would have destroyed his case. See Pohlsander (1980) for a sceptical, and Shahîd (1984), for a more accepting, approach to Philip's possible Christian beliefs.

207 Decius claimed that he was 'forced' to declare himself emperor by his troops and promised to lay aside his claim on entering Italy. In fact, he met the elder Philip in battle at Verona, where he defeated and killed him. When news of the battle spread, the Praetorian Guard lynched the younger Philip in their barracks at Rome. See Jerome, *Chronicle, A Abr.* 2267, who notes the place of death of both Philips, and Eutropius, 9.3. Orosius seems puzzled at these Christian emperors' fate, but offers no explanation for it.

21

1. 1,004 years after the foundation of the City, Decius, who had both started and finished a civil war, became, on the death of the two Philips, the 24th man after Augustus to seize power and retained it for three years.[208] **2.** He immediately – and in so doing revealed that this was why he had killed the Philips – became the sixth emperor after Nero to issue death-laden edicts for the persecution and murder of Christians, and sent very many of the saints from their crosses to their crowns in Christ.[209] **3.** He chose his son as his Caesar, and it was with him he was killed immediately afterwards when in the midst of a barbarian horde.[210]

4. 1007 years after the foundation of the City, Gallus Hostilian became the 25th man after Augustus to obtain the kingdom which he ruled for scarcely two years along with his son, Volusian.[211]

5. Vengeance for the defiling of Christians now made itself manifest. And wherever Decius's edict to cast down churches had reached, there fell a plague of inconceivable ills. There was hardly a province of the Roman Empire, a city, or a home that was not seized and emptied of its inhabitants by this universal plague. **6.** Gallus and Volusian, whose rule was distinguished only by this disaster, were killed while fighting a civil war against the pretender Aemilian. Aemilian had embarked on the third month of his usurpation when he too was killed.[212]

208 G. Messius Quintus Decius 'Traianus'. Orosius's chronology is two years awry. Decius began to reign in 1002 *AUC*/AD 249.

209 Jerome, *Chronicle, A Abr.* 2268. Jerome states here that Decius launched his persecution because he hated the Philips. This had possibly led Orosius to conclude that the Philips were Christians. Decius's persecution, AD 249–51, is normally accepted as the first widespread, systematic persecution of Christianity. For a discussion of Decius's religious policy, see Pohlsander (1986) and Rives (1999).

210 Decius's Caesar was Herennius Etruscus. The two died while fighting the Goths at Arbito in Dobruja; Jerome, *Chronicle, A Abr.* 2268. The pagan historian Zosimus, 1.23, is full of praise for Decius whom he sees as attempting to rectify problems on the frontier created by Philip's inactivity and who he asserts was killed by Gallus Hostilian's treachery.

211 Orosius's chronology is three years awry; Hostilian and Volusian's reign began in 1004 *AUC*/AD 251.

212 For the plague, see Jerome, *Chronicle, A Abr.* 2269. The comment that Gallus and Volusian's reign was memorable only for the plague is drawn from Eutropius, 9.5. The two were killed in August AD 253. The plague is also recorded by Zosimus, 1.26, who also, 1.27–28, speaks of major incursions into the empire in both Europe and Asia. The material on Aemilian is found in Eutropius, 9.6, and Jerome, *Chronicle, A Abr.* 2270.

22

1. 1,010 years after the foundation of the City, two emperors, the 26th since Augustus, were created: Valerian was hailed Augustus by his army in Raetia, while at Rome Gallienus was made Caesar by the Senate.[213] Gallienus remained in power for a miserable fifteen years, during which the human race slowly recovered from the severe plague, one worse and more long-lasting than is normally the case. Wickedness blithely calls forth its own punishment, and though impiety, when scourged, feels the whip, being hard of heart she does not perceive by Whom she is being whipped. **2.** In order to avoid going over the points I have already made: after Decius persecuted Christians, the whole Roman Empire was tormented by a great plague. However, iniquity, ensnared, to her own loss, by her perverse belief, lied to herself that this plague was of the common type, and that the death which came from these diseases was simply in accordance with nature and not a punishment at all.

3. Once again, therefore, and soon after, Rome provoked God's anger by her sinful actions and was to receive a lashing whose effects she was forced to remember for some time. Valerian as soon as he seized power became the seventh emperor after Nero to order that Christians be tortured into idolatry and that those who refused be killed, and so the blood of the saints poured far and wide over the breadth of the Romans' kingdom. **4.** Straightaway the author of this vile decree, Valerian, was captured by Sapor, king of the Persians, and the emperor of the Roman people grew old as the lowliest of slaves among the Persians, condemned as long as he lived to perform the shameful office of helping the king to mount his horse, not with his hand, but with his back as he lay on the ground.[214]

5. Gallienus was terrified by God's manifest judgment, and, troubled by his colleague's wretched fate, restored peace to the empire's churches

---

213 Orosius's chronology is four years awry; Valerian and Gallienus were proclaimed emperors in 1006 *AUC*/AD 253. See also Jerome, *Chronicle, A Abr.* 2271 (incorrectly dating these events to AD 254) and Eutropius, 9.7.

214 Valerian's persecution took place in AD 257–58; he was captured in AD 260. His captor was Shapur I, 'The Great' (AD 241–72) of Sassanid Persia who commemorated his triumph on a rock relief carving at Behistun in Iran. Orosius's main source for the persecution and Valerian's demise is Jerome, *Chronicle, A Abr.* 2274, though the details of the emperor's slavery may be drawn from Lactantius, *On the Deaths of the Persecutors* (*De Mortibus Persecutorum*), 5.2–3. Valerian's demise is also noted by Zosimus, 1.36, who attacks his loose morals and effeminacy, points omitted by Orosius.

by way of panic-stricken reparation.[215] However, the incarceration of one impious man, albeit that it was forever and of a particularly vile kind, did not compensate for the wrong or provide sufficient recompense for the torture of so many thousands of the saints. The blood of the just cried out to God to be avenged in the selfsame land where it had been spilled. **6.** It was required by just judgment that not only the individual author of the decree be punished, but it was also just that those who had carried it out, been informers and accusers, judges or jurymen, or, finally, all those who had given assent to this most unjust cruelty, even silently – for God knows men's secrets – the greatest body of whom were to be found throughout all the provinces, be enveloped in the same stroke of vengeance.

Therefore with God's consent, suddenly and everywhere the tribes left around the edge of the empire for this purpose broke their chains and invaded all Rome's domains. **7.** The Germans crossed the Alps, Raetia, and Italy, arriving at Ravenna; the Alamanni ranged through the Gallic provinces until they too crossed into Italy; Greece, Macedonia, Pontus, and Asia were wiped out by a deluge of Goths; Dacia across the Danube was lost forever;[216] the Quadi and Sarmatians ransacked the Pannonian provinces; the furthest-flung German tribes took hold of Spain and stripped it bare;[217] the Parthians seized Mesopotamia and drained Syria of all its wealth. **8.** In various provinces, small, poor villages lying in the ruins of great cities still give evidence of what was suffered and preserve memories of their past names. Among these, we too in Spain can show our town of Tarragona to reconcile us to our recent troubles.[218] **9.** Then, in case some part of the Roman body politic should escape from this dismemberment, usurpers conspired within, civil wars commenced, and everywhere rivers of Roman blood were spilt as Roman and barbarian vented their rage. The wrath of

---

215 Gallienus issued an edict of tolerance in AD 260.

216 In fact, Dacia was not abandoned until the reign of Aurelian (AD 270–75).

217 The Frankish invasion of Spain took place in AD 267.

218 This list of invasions is found in Jerome, *Chronicle, A Abr.* 2278–2280 and Eutropius, 9.8.2. Zosimus, 1.30–37, also describes the incursions into the empire in detail. Both Jerome and Eutropius state that Gallienus started his reign well, but lapsed into debauchery. However, Orosius is unwilling to attack Gallienus as he passed an edict of tolerance and so is forced to see the invasions as punishment for Valerian's persecution. The use of 'our' to describe Tarragona (understandably mentioned both by Jerome and Eutropius as it was the provincial capital of Hither Spain, but with no 'our') has been seen as marking the town as Orosius's birth-place, but merely marks his Spanish, not his Catalan, sympathies. The 'recent troubles' is probably a reference to the sack of Rome, but may relate to Orosius's enforced exile in Africa. In all events, the intention of the text is to demonstrate that the troubles of the present are nothing compared to those of the past.

God, however, swiftly turned to mercy and held that merely beginning their chastisement was better than meting out punishment in full measure.

10. First, therefore, Genuus, who had usurped the purple, was killed at Myrsa.[219] Postumus proclaimed himself emperor in Gaul which proved of great benefit to the state, for he ruled with great courage and moderation for ten years, driving out the enemies who had taken power,[220] and restoring the lost provinces to their old state of affairs; he was nevertheless killed when his troops mutinied.[221] **11.** Aemilian was suppressed while plotting revolution at Mainz.[222] After Postumus's death, Marius usurped the purple in the same area, but was killed immediately.[223] Then, of their own free will, the Gauls made Victorinus emperor, but he was killed soon after.[224] **12.** He was succeeded by the governor of Aquitania, Tetricus, who endured many mutinies from his troops.[225] In the east, the Persians were defeated and driven back by a band of peasants rallied together by a man called Odenatus. He managed to defend Syria, recover Mesopotamia, and the peasants of Syria marched in triumph with Odenatus as far as Ctesiphon.[226] **13.** Gallienus was killed when he abandoned the duties of state and gave himself up to his lusts at Milan.[227]

219 Normally Ingenuus, who attempted a usurpation, probably in AD 258. Myrsa is the modern Eszek in Turkey.

220 See Jerome, *Chronicle, A Abr.* 2284, who also lists the other Gallic emperors Victorinus and Tetricus. See also Eutropius, 9.9.1.

221 Given his dislike of civil strife, Orosius has a surprisingly positive view of Postumus (AD 260–69). This may simply reflect the opinions found in Eutropius, 9.9.1, but could also be because Spain, along with Gaul and Britain, formed part of his breakaway Gallic Empire. This would also account for the interest shown in Postumus's successors seen in the rest of the chapter. The Gallic Empire was finally re-absorbed into the Roman state in AD 274.

222 Normally Laelian; see Eutropius 9.9.1.

223 According to Eutropius, 9.9.2, Marius ruled for only two days. However, as coins were struck in his name, this seems unduly pessimistic.

224 See Eutropius, 9.9.3, though Orosius uses none of the uncomplimentary material found there. Victorinus ruled the Gallic Empire from AD 269 to AD 271.

225 Eutropius, 9.10. In AD 274, Tetricus handed back control of the Gallic Empire to the emperor at Rome, Aurelian.

226 Orosius's main source is Jerome, *A Abr. Chronicle,* 2282, where we are told that Odenatus was a town councillor of Palmyra; see also Eutropius, 9.10 and Zosimus, 1.39. In c. AD 250 Odenatus made Palmyra an independent kingdom, though one closely allied to Rome, receiving the title *corrector totius Orientis,* 'supervisor of the whole East' from the emperor Gallienus. He launched two attacks on the Persians, one in AD 263, the other in AD 266/7. For a general discussion of Palmyra and its relations with Rome, see Stoneman (1992).

227 Jerome, *Chronicle, A Abr.* 2285 and Eutropius, 9.11. Orosius chooses this point to accuse Gallienus of debauchery, but both Jerome and Eutropius place his neglect of duty earlier

23

1. 1,025 years after the foundation of the City, Claudius, who had the approval of the Senate, became the 28th man to take power.[228] He immediately waged war on the Goths who had been laying waste to Macedonia and Illyricum for fifteen years and annihilated them with great slaughter. The Senate awarded him a golden shield to hang in the senate-house and a statue, also made of gold, to be placed on the Capitol. However, before he had finished the second year of his reign, he succumbed to disease and died at Sirmium.[229]

2. *On the death of Claudius, his brother, Quintillus, was made emperor by the army. He was a man of outstanding moderation and the only man who could be preferred to his brother, but after seventeen days of his reign he was killed.*[230]

3. 1,027 years after the foundation of the City, Aurelian became the 29th emperor and ruled for five years and six months.[231] He was of man of outstanding military ability, **4.** who undertook a campaign on the Danube, shattered the power of the Goths in a series of great battles, and restored the writ of Rome to her old frontiers.[232] Then he turned east, and brought Zenobia back under control, more by threatening to wage war on her, than by actually doing so. After her husband, Odenatus, had been killed, she had begun to take over the province of Syria, which he had recaptured, for herself.[233] **5.** He had no difficulty in defeating Tetricus who was unable

---

and make it the cause of the barbarian invasions. In contrast to Orosius's debauched emperor, Zosimus, 1.40, has Gallienus murdered in a palace conspiracy when returning from the wars in the Balkans. See also SHA *The Two Gallieni*, 14. In the following chapter, the author of the SHA biography records that the troops of the day thought that Gallienus 'had been useful and indispensable to them, courageous and competent'.

228 Although giving no warning in his narrative, Orosius now goes back in time to deal with the emperors at Rome as opposed to those of the Gallic Empire.

229 Claudius II Gothicus. Orosius's chronology is four years awry. Claudius came to the purple in 1021 *AUC*/AD 268. Orosius's sources are Jerome, *Chronicle, A Abr.* 2286 (who places Claudius's accession incorrectly in 1022 *AUC*/AD 272) and Eutropius, 9.11. Claudius defeated the Goths at Naissus, the modern Niš in Serbia. According to Zosimus, 1.43, 50,000 Goths were killed. Claudius's golden shield parallels the *clipeum virtutis* awarded to Augustus by the Senate in 27 BC. Sirmium is near the modern Mitrovica in Serbia.

230 Orosius repeats virtually verbatim Eutropius's, 9.12, comments on Quintillus.

231 Orosius's chronology is four years awry. Aurelian's rule began in 1023 *AUC*/AD 270.

232 Orosius suppresses, or is ignorant of, the fact that it was in Aurelian's reign that the province of Dacia across the Danube was abandoned.

233 This is the Odenatus of 7.22.12. For Aurelian's campaigns against Zenobia, see Zosimus, 1.50–60. For modern discussions of the queen, see Stoneman (1992) and Southern (2009).

to hold out against the mutinies of his own soldiers in Gaul and wrote to Aurelian saying: *free me, invincible as you are, from these troubles,* and in this way betrayed his own army.[234] Aurelian therefore held a triumph in glory as the man who had recovered both the east and the north. He also surrounded the city of Rome with stronger walls. **6.** But in the end, after he became the eighth emperor after Nero to order that Christians be persecuted, a thunderbolt fell in front of him to the great terror of those standing nearby, and soon afterwards he was killed while making a journey.[235]

24

1. 1,032 years after the foundation of the City, Tacitus became the 30th man to obtain imperial power. He was killed in Pontus in the sixth month of his reign. After him came Florian, who had similar luck with his reign – he was killed after three months in Tarsus.[236]

2. 1,033 years after the foundation of the City, Probus became the 31st man to rule the kingdom and reigned for six years and four months.[237] After many fierce battles, he destroyed his enemies and completely liberated the Gallic provinces that had been occupied by barbarians.[238] **3.** He then fought two extremely bloody civil wars: one in the east in which he crushed and captured the usurper Saturninus, and another in which he defeated and killed Proculus and Bonosus in fierce fighting near Cologne. He himself was killed at Sirmium in an iron tower during a mutiny of his troops.[239]

234 Taken, including the quotation of Virgil, *Aeneid*, 6.365, from Eutropius, 9.13.1. See also Jerome, *Chronicle, A Abr.* 2289, and 7.22.12 above.

235 Aurelian's double triumph, walls, persecution, the portent of his death, and death are all drawn from Jerome, *Chronicle, A Abr.* 2290–2292. Aurelian was assassinated at Caenophrurium, the modern Erégli in Turkey, in AD 275. Orosius has suppressed Jerome's, *Chronicle, A Abr.* 2291, notice that Aurelian built a temple to the sun god and is generally favourable to him, suppressing Eutropius's, 9.13.1 and 9.14, comments on his brutality, and presenting him as behaving badly only at the end of his reign. He also suppresses Eutropius's, 9.15.2, notice of his deification. For modern discussions of the emperor, see Watson (1999) and White (2004).

236 Orosius's chronology is four years awry; Tacitus began to rule in 1028 *AUC*/AD 275, Florian's brief rule was in 1029 *AUC*/AD 276. Orosius's source for these two emperors is Eutropius, 9.16 and Jerome, *Chronicle, A Abr.* 2293.

237 Orosius's chronology is four years awry; Probus began to rule in 1029 AUC/ AD 276. Orosius also fails to mention that Probus was declared emperor in the east by his troops while Florian was still emperor at Rome.

238 Jerome, *Chronicle, A Abr.* 2294. See also SHA *Probus*, 13–14.

239 For the rebellions, see SHA *Probus* 18. Orosius's main source for Probus is Eutropius, 9.17. Eutropius also refers to an 'iron tower'. Jerome, *Chronicle, A Abr.* 2299, is perhaps more

4. 1,039 years after the foundation of the City, Carus from Narbonensis became the 32nd man to rule the empire and held on to power for two years. After he had made his sons, Carinus and Numerian, joint rulers, he fought a Parthian war in which, after capturing two of the Parthians' finest cities, Coche and Ctesiphon, he was struck by lightning and killed in his camp by the Tigris.[240] Numerian, who was with his father, was treacherously killed by his father-in-law, Aper, while returning to Rome.[241]

25[242]

1. 1,041 years after the foundation of the City, the army chose Diocletian as the 33rd emperor and he held power for twenty years. Immediately he obtained full power, he killed Numerian's killer, Aper, with his own hand. Then, through great effort in a most difficult war, he overcame Carinus who was living a disgraceful life in Dalmatia where Carus had left him as Caesar.[243] **2.** After this, Amandus and Aelian gathered together a band of peasants whom they called the Bagaudae and sparked off damaging disturbances in Gaul. Diocletian made Maximian, who was surnamed 'the Herculean',[244] Caesar, and despatched him to the Gallic provinces. Maximian, with his soldier's training, easily put down this unskilled and ill-disciplined peasant band.[245]

---

correct when he talks of 'a tower called the iron tower'. The tower is not mentioned by either the author of SHA or Zosimus.

240 Orosius's account of Carus and his sons is drawn from Jerome, *Chronicle, A Abr.* 2300. Both he and Jerome are incorrect about the date of Carus's accession which was in 1035 *AUC/* AD 282. Orosius is four years out placing it in 1039 *AUC/*AD 286 and Jerome in 1038 *AUC/* AD 285. Coche and Ctesiphon are also paired by Gregory Nazianzus, *Discourses against Julian (Orationes in Julium)*, 2. Ctesiphon is the modern Al-Madain which lies some 20 miles south-east of Baghdad. Its importance in this period can be seen from the still extant remains of the palace built by Shapur I, the Tagh-e-Kasra. Coche, a refoundation of Seleucia-on-the-Tigris, lay opposite it. The lightning bolt is also mentioned by the author of SHA, *Lives of Carus, Carinus, and Numerian* 8–9.

241 See Jerome, *Chronicle, A Abr.* 2301, and Eutropius, 9.18.2. It has been suggested that Aper was innocent of this crime; see Bird (1976).

242 Sections 1–12 of this chapter follow Eutropius, 9.20–25, closely.

243 Orosius's chronology is four years awry. Diocletian was proclaimed emperor by his army at Nicomedia on 20 November 1037 *AUC/*AD 284. He ruled until AD 305. Orosius's account of his rise is drawn from Eutropius, 9.19–9.20.1, and Jerome, *Chronicle, A Abr.* 2301 (who erroneously places his accession in 1040 *AUC/*AD 287).

244 Maximianus Herculius.

245 'Bagaudae' is a Celtic word for 'vagabonds'; see Sánchez-León (1996). Orosius's account is taken from Eutropius, 9.20.3. Orosius has drawn his account from Jerome, *Chronicle, A Abr.* 2303.

3. Then one Carausius, who, while of very lowly birth, was of great intelligence and ability, after being posted to watch over the Ocean's shores which were at that time infested with Franks and Saxons, began to act in a way that was more pernicious than profitable to the state. His policy of not returning any part of the plunder seized by these brigands to its owners but keeping it entirely for himself aroused the suspicion that he allowed his enemies to make their incursions into his domains through a deliberate policy of negligence. For this reason, Maximian ordered him to be put to death. He then usurped the purple and seized control of the British provinces.²⁴⁶ **4.** So at that time rumblings of unforeseen trouble could be heard all round the frontiers of the Roman Empire. Carausius had rebelled in the British provinces, Achilles in Egypt,²⁴⁷ while the Quinquegentians²⁴⁸ plagued Africa, and even Narseus, the king of the Persians, was waging war in the east.²⁴⁹ **5.** Troubled by this danger, Diocletian promoted Maximian Herculius from Caesar to Augustus and chose Constantius and Maximian Galerius as Caesars.²⁵⁰ Constantius took Maximian Herculius's step-daughter, Theodora, as his wife, by whom he fathered six sons who were the brothers of Constantine. **6.** Carausius, after laying claim to Britain, bravely held on to it for seven years, but finally was treacherously killed by his associate Allectus,²⁵¹ who kept hold of the island for three years after he had snatched it from Carausius. He was crushed by Asclepiodotus, the Praetorian Prefect, who recovered Britain ten years after it had been lost.²⁵² **7.** The Caesar Constan-

---

246 Jerome, *Chronicle, A Abr.* 2305. Carausius began his usurpation late in AD 286.

247 Jerome, *Chronicle, A Abr.* 2306. Achilles was a barbarian *corrector*, probably a Saracen, who set up Domitius Domitianus as a puppet emperor in Egypt in AD 297.

248 Jerome, *Chronicle, A Abr.* 2305. The Quinquegentians were a tribe of Mauretania Caesariensis.

249 Jerome, *Chronicle, A Abr.* 2305. Narseus is Narseh, the son of Sapor I, AD 293–302. He broke the treaty made with Rome by his predecessor, Vahram II, invading Armenia, Osrhoene, and Syria in AD 297.

250 Orosius has abbreviated these events to increase his reader's sense of danger. Maximian was made Augustus in AD 286, but the Caesars were appointed seven years later in AD 293. The Constantius here is Constantius Chlorus, the father of Constantine the Great.

251 Allectus was Carausius's *rationalis*, i.e. his chief financial official. The assassination took place in AD 293. Orosius is surprisingly sympathetic to Carausius, perhaps betraying his western origins. For a modern discussion of Carausius and Allectus, see Casey (1995).

252 Drawn from Jerome, *Chronicle, A Abr.* 2316. His absence from Jerome's note may explain why Orosius does not mention Constantius Chlorus's rôle in this campaign, despite the fact that it was widely publicised at the time, with Constantius being described as the 'restorer of eternal light' to Britain. See, in particular, the gold medallion struck in Trier and found near

tius was defeated by the Alamanni in his first battle in Gaul, lost his army, and was only spirited to safety himself with difficulty. His second battle, however, provided him with a satisfactory victory, for in only a few hours 60,000 of the Alamanni are said to have been slaughtered. **8.** Meanwhile, the Augustus Maximian conquered the Quinquegentians in Africa.[253] Then Diocletian captured and killed Achilles after besieging him in Alexandria for eight months. He was not, however, restrained in his triumph, for he gave Alexandria up to be plundered and soiled all of Egypt with his proscriptions and slaughter.[254] **9.** After fighting two battles against Narseus, Galerius Maximian met him in a third between Callinicus and Carrhae, where he was defeated.[255] After losing his army, he fled to Diocletian, who gave him a most arrogant reception: it is said that he was forced to run in front of Diocletian's chariot for several miles while clad in his imperial robes.[256] Nevertheless, he used this insult to hone his courage and in this way was able to sharpen his wits by grinding away the rust brought on by regal arrogance. He soon gathered together troops from all over Illyricum and Moesia, swiftly returned to face his foe, and defeated Narseus through his superior tactics and manpower.[257] **11.** After annihilating the Persians' troops and putting Narseus to flight, Galerius entered his camp and captured his wives, sisters, and children, seizing as plunder a vast number of Persian gems and taking the vast majority of the Persian nobility prisoner.[258] On his return to Mesopotamia, he was received with great honour by Diocletian. **12.** After this, these two commanders fought a bitter war against the Carpi and Basternae.[259] They then defeated the Sarmatians, scattering a great number of their prisoners throughout the outposts of the Roman world.

13. Meanwhile, Diocletian in the east and Maximian Herculius in the west ordered that churches be destroyed and Christians be attacked and killed in the ninth persecution after that of Nero. This persecution lasted longer and was more brutal than almost all the previous ones. For ten

---

Arras bearing this legend and depicting Constantius entering London. It is now on display in the Musée des Beaux Arts in Arras.

253 Maximian campaigned in Africa between AD 296 and 298.

254 The siege took place in the winter of AD 296/7. Orosius has drawn his information from Jerome, *Chronicle, A Abr.* 2314.

255 AD 298.

256 Drawn from Jerome, *Chronicle, A Abr.* 2317. See Seston (1946).

257 In AD 298.

258 Drawn from Jerome, *Chronicle, A Abr.* 2318.

259 In fact, these campaigns predate those just mentioned by Orosius. See Jerome, *Chronicle, A Abr.* 2311, who notes that the two tribes were translated into Roman territory.

years there was no end to the burning of churches, the proscription of the innocent, and the slaughter of martyrs.[260] **14.** An earthquake in Syria followed in which many thousands of men in Tyre and Sidon were killed by falling buildings.[261] In the second year of the persecution, Diocletian forced Maximian against his will jointly to lay aside the purple and their power, leaving younger men in charge of the state while they retired into private life. And so on the same day, Diocletian laid down his imperial power and its trappings at Nicomedia, while Maximian did the same at Milan.[262]

15. The Augusti Galerius and Constantius were the first to divide the Roman Empire into two parts. Galerius Maximian received Illyricum, Asia, and the East; Constantius, Italy, Africa, Spain, and the Gallic provinces. But Constantius was a most easy-going individual, content to rule merely Gaul and Spain, and he handed over the rest of his portion to Galerius.[263] **16.** Galerius picked two Caesars, Maximin, whom he appointed to be in charge of the East, and Severus, to whom he entrusted Italy, while he himself stayed in Illyricum.[264] The Augustus Constantius, a most mild and civil man, then died in Britain, leaving his son Constantine, whom he had fathered by his concubine Helena, as emperor of the Gallic provinces.[265]

26

1. 1,061 years after the foundation of the City, Constantine became the 34th man to steer the ship of state, taking its rudder from his father and holding on to it for thirty-one prosperous years.[266]

---

260 For a discussion of this persecution, see Williams (1985) ch. 14 and MacMullen (1969) ch. 1.

261 The persecution and earthquake are drawn from Jerome, *Chronicle, A Abr.* 2320. This persecution began in AD 303 and lasted until Constantine's edict of Milan in AD 313.

262 The two abdicated on 1 May AD 305. Orosius's account is a much-abbreviated version of Eutropius, 9.27.1–2.

263 An abbreviated version of Eutropius, 10.1. However, while Eutropius mentions the division of the Roman world, it is Orosius who makes the point that this was the first time that this had happened.

264 Maximin Daïa, Galerius's nephew, and Flavius Valerius Severus. Orosius's account draws on Eutropius, 10.2.1.

265 Orosius, unlike Jerome, *Chronicle, A Abr.* 2322, suppresses the fact that Constantine usurped power at York after his father's death. Jerome, like Orosius, names Helena, but Orosius's main source, Eutropius, 10.2.2, gives no name to Constantine's mother, merely noting that he was born 'from an obscure marriage'.

266 Orosius's chronology is two years awry. Constantine became emperor in 1059 *AUC*/ AD306.

2. Now all of a sudden someone will come up and dance, leaping round me, saying, 'Aha, *long-awaited one, you have come*²⁶⁷ at last into our snares! Here we were waiting for you to go too far! Here you have stumbled and we have seized you! Here we caught you in your confusion! Up to this point we have borne with you, as, in a rather forced and sly way, you have linked together the fortuitous changes that have happened in these Christian times with the vengeance worked on the Christians' behalf. **3.** While you did this, troubled by these plausible parallels, we grew pale with fear, like men who were ignorant of the secrets of heaven. But now our Maximian has cleared out the mummery of your stories and shone forth as an unassailable pillar of our old faith.²⁶⁸ **4.** For ten years, as even you yourself admit, your churches were demolished, and Christians were wracked with torture and their numbers depleted by death throughout the whole world. We have your clear testimony that no previous persecution had been as serious or as long. **5.** Yet, behold, amid these good, peaceful times, the unexpected felicity of the very emperors who performed these deeds: there was no famine at home or any plague, and no wars abroad save those they wished to wage – wars in which they were able to train their forces rather than endanger them. **6.** Moreover, something as yet unknown among the human race happened – a group of kings ruling at the same time exercised joint rule, tolerating one another, showing great harmony, and holding a common power, which now, as it had never done before, looked to the common good. **7.** And after this, those great emperors and persecutors did something that up to that time men had never known. They set aside their office and peacefully retired as private citizens: the thing which men judge to be the most blessed and highest reward of a good life. This, then, was what the authors of the persecution obtained as their prize so to speak, at a time when the persecution that they had kindled was raging throughout the world. **8.** Or are you going to assert that the good fortune of this epoch was a punishment and try to terrify us with that too?'

9. To such objections I would humbly reply that, girt with an overwhelming concern to be pious, I am warning them with the truth, not frightening them with falsehood. The Church of Christ suffered ten persecutions from Nero to Maximian.²⁶⁹ Nine times vengeance, as I have put it,

267 A quotation from Virgil, *Aeneid*, 2.283.

268 'Pillar' here is *columna*, which is used in the account of Samson bringing down the Philistines' palace; see Judges 16.26–31. It is hard not to see this as a deliberate piece of sarcasm on Orosius's part.

269 The number of persecutions suffered by the Church was an issue for debate within the

or disaster, as they would not deny, followed in their wake. I will not argue about words and debate whether the things both of us call disasters were due punishment or unfortunate changes of circumstance. **10.** These poor blind folk think that my argument falters at the tenth persecution, not realising that the vengeance that fell on them was all the greater for going unperceived. For the impious man is scourged yet does not feel the whip.[270] When this is expounded, given the simple truth of the matter, they will confess, though unwillingly, that their greatest wounds have come from their greatest punishment – that given for Maximian's persecution. It is over these wounds that they grieve even now, and grieve over to such a degree that they cry out and provoke me to shout back in return that I am concerned to find a way to silence them.

27

1. In the first book I showed how Pompeius Trogus and Cornelius Tacitus had recorded, though not fully, and how our Moses, a trustworthy source even according to them, had explained in a trustworthy and ample way that the Egyptians and their king were troubled by ten terrible plagues when they summoned back the people of God, who were intent on serving and obeying God, to mud and straw in order to hinder their devotion.[271] **2.** Then, that overcome by the violence of their sufferings,[272] the Egyptians not only forced the Jews to hurry on their way, but even loaded them down with vessels made of gold and silver that belonged to themselves. And that after this, heedless of their punishment, lusting to plunder what did not belong to them, and, above all, hating this foreign religion, they pursued the innocent Jews with all their might, but, while doing so, were finally all sucked into the Red Sea and drowned. I recall and return to this story now, which, even if it is not believed through faith, can be proved to have occurred by its outcome, because *these things were our examples.*[273] **3.** Both people who suffered were the people of the One God, and both upheld the same cause. The synagogue of the Israelites was in thrall to the Egyptians, the Church

---

Church itself. Sulpicius Severus, *Chronicle*, 2.28.31, believed that there had been nine persecutions and a final tenth would come with the arrival of the Antichrist. Orosius adds a further temporal persecution and this version became the standard for Western Christendom.

270 An echo of Jeremiah 5.3.

271 1.10.1–18.

272 i.e the ten plagues.

273 1 Corinthians 10.6.

of the Christians to the Romans, and the Egyptians were persecutors and the Romans too were persecutors. Ten refusals were sent to Moses in Egypt, ten edicts against the Christ were proclaimed at Rome. There, the Egyptians suffered from plagues of different sorts; here, the Romans suffered from different sorts of disasters.

4. I shall compare these plagues to one another in as far as their different forms allow comparison. There, the first reproof was that blood appeared everywhere, dripping from wells and running in rivers; here, the first plague came under Nero, when the blood of the dying which had either been corrupted by disease in the City or spilt in wars around the world, was to be found everywhere.[274] **5.** There, the second plague was of croaking, leaping frogs which penetrated every innermost place, reducing the inhabitants to the verge of starvation and exile; here, the second punishment which happened under Domitian, produced similar effects, as the shameless, unchecked forays of his flunkeys and soldiers, carried out under the orders of this cruellest of princes, reduced almost all the citizens of Rome to a state of want, and scattered them into exile. **6.** There, the third trouble was that of the *sciniphnes*: extremely small and extremely vicious flies which are often accustomed in the middle of summer to gather together in thick, buzzing clouds in filthy places and then worm their way between men's hair and beasts' bristles, inflicting stinging bites on them.[275] In the same way, here, the third plague under Trajan roused up the Jews who, after they had been completely scattered across the world, lived so quietly that it was as if they did not exist. However, then all of them were suddenly aroused in anger and raged against those among whom they lived across the entire world. In addition to this, many great cities were ruined after being cast down by the frequent earthquakes which happened at that time.[276] **7.** There, the fourth plague was of dog-flies, which are truly the children of filth and the worms' mothers; here, the fourth plague in the time of Marcus Antoninus was of the same sort. Disease spread to most of the provinces and also brought a death of rotting in filth and worms to the whole of Italy, including the City of Rome, along with the Roman army stationed in its winter quarters along the extensive frontiers of the empire. **8.** There, the fifth reproof brought about the sudden death of flocks and draught animals; similarly, here, the fifth act of vengeance in the time of the persecutor Severus brought about,

274 See 7.7.11 above.
275 See 1.10.10.
276 The earthquakes rather spoil Orosius's parallel with the plague of flies, but he simply cannot resist mentioning them.

through frequent outbreaks of civil war, a weakening of the state's very vitals and workhorses: namely the people of the provinces and the troops of the legions. **9.** There, the sixth source of trouble was suppurating blisters and oozing ulcers; here, in the same way, the sixth punishment which came after the persecution of Maximin, who ordered bishops and priests, that is to say the leaders of churches, be attacked and slaughtered while leaving the people alone, breathed forth its oft-swelling anger and hatred in the slaughter not of the common people, but in the wounding and killing of leading, powerful men of the state.[277] **10.** There, the plague ranked as the seventh was the hail that condensed out of the air to such degree that it could kill men, animals and crops; here, a similar seventh plague happened in the reign of Gallus and Volusian who soon succeeded the persecutor Decius on his death. Disease came forth from the corrupted air and poured over all the bounds of Rome's kingdom from east to west, killing almost the whole race of men and beasts – *poys'ning the Standing Lakes and Pools Impure.*[278] **11.** There, the eighth thing that made the Egyptians repent was the locusts which rose up on all sides, colonising, consuming, and covering everything; here, equally the eighth punishment was the tribes who were roused up on every side to overturn the Roman world, laying all the provinces waste with their arson and slaughter. **12.** There, the ninth disturbance was the darkness which lasted for days and was so thick that you could almost touch it. It threatened danger more than caused it. Here, the ninth reproof was the same – a terrible and terrifying thunderbolt fell in a horrifying whirlwind at Aurelian's feet as he was in the act of proclaiming his persecution. This thunderbolt showed what so powerful an Avenger could do, when there was so great a call for vengeance, were He not both merciful and restrained. Nevertheless, within six months of this happening, three emperors, namely Aurelian, Tacitus, and Florian, were killed in succession in diverse ways. **13.** There, finally the tenth and last plague of all was the death of everyone's first-born sons; here, this tenth, that is to say final, punishment was no less than the destruction of all the idols which were their first creation and their first love.

14. There, the king saw, felt, and feared the power of God, and, because of this, allowed the people of God to go free; here, the king saw, felt, and believed in the power of God and because of this allowed the people of God

277 Orosius struggles to keep a parallel here, but with little success. In the end, he tries by using adjectives and verbs for the anger of civil war which could be applied to blisters or buboes.
278 Virgil, *Georgics,* 3.481. The succeeding line is quoted at 5.21.6.

their freedom. There, the people of God were never again dragged back into slavery; here, never, after these troubles, have the people of God been forced into idolatry. There, the precious vessels of the Egyptians were given to the Hebrews; here, the most glorious pagan temples became Christian churches. **15.** I certainly think, as I have already said, that this must be stated – namely that just as eternal damnation fell upon the Egyptians when the sea was poured over them as they set out to pursue the Hebrews whom they had let go after the ten plagues, so there remains for us at some time in the future as we go freely on our way a persecution from the gentiles, until we cross the Red Sea, that is the fire of judgment, with Our Lord Jesus Christ Himself as our leader and judge.[279] **16.** Truly, these men, who have taken the place of the Egyptians, will rage against and persecute Christians with terrible tortures in the moment of power that is allowed to them. But it is also true that all these enemies of Christ, along with their king, the Antichrist, are destined to damnation for forever and to burn in everlasting torment, falling into the lake of eternal fire which, because it is hidden with billows of thick smoke, is entered without being seen.

28[280]

1. On the death, as I have recorded, of Constantius in Britain, Constantine was made emperor. With the exception of Philip, whose short rule as a Christian emperor seems to me to have occurred simply so that Rome's millennium could be said to have happened under the rule of Christ rather than that of idols, Constantine was the first Christian emperor. **2.** After Constantine, however, all those made emperor up to the present day have always been Christians, with the exception of Julian whose cursed life left him, they say, while he was devising blasphemies.

3. This is that slow, but sure, punishment of the pagans. Because of it, they utter madness while they are sane; because of it, though they have no bodily wounds, they suffer the goad; because of it, while they laugh, they are groaning in pain; because of it, while they live, they are dying; because

279 Orosius's parallels were a commonly held Christian interpretation of persecution, as was the belief, based on the Egyptians' pursuit of the Israelites, that there would be only one further persecution which would be led by the Antichrist just before the second coming. Both of these views are denounced by Augustine, *City of God*, 18.52, who perhaps wrote in part to answer what is written here.

280 The bulk of this account, except for the specifically Christian elements, follows closely, but abbreviates, Eutropius, 10.2.2–10.8.

of it, though no one persecutes them, they suffer torments in secret; because of it, although no persecutor has subjected them to punishment, now very few of them are left at all.[281] **4.** Now I shall set out what sort of end awaited these persecutors in whose immunity from punishment my opponents not only glory, but even use to insult me.

5. While Constantine strained to look after the interests of the state in the Gallic provinces, the Praetorian Guard at Rome proclaimed Herculius's son, Maxentius, who was at that time living as a private citizen in Lucania, Augustus. **6.** Maximian Herculius, although he had retired from the throne into private life, still remained in public life as a persecutor. He was now roused up by what had happened to his son, and so a man who had set aside his legitimate power set himself up as a usurper.[282] **7.** The Augustus Galerius sent his Caesar, Severus, to Rome with an army to fight Maxentius. **8.** When he besieged the city, he was wickedly deserted and betrayed by his troops, and killed at Ravenna as he fled. [283] **9.** Maximian Herculius, the persecutor and former emperor turned usurper, now tried to strip his son, who had by this time been established as emperor, of his royal robes and power. However, the open insults and mutinous nature of the troops terrified him, and he set out for Gaul in order to take away power from his son-in-law, Constantine, with whom his connection was equally treacherous. **10.** After being discovered and betrayed by his daughter, he fled towards Marseilles, but was caught and killed.[284]

11. After the death of Severus, Galerius made Licinius emperor.[285] **12.** He then intensified the persecution begun by Diocletian and Maximian by issuing even harsher edicts himself. When, after ten years, he had emptied the provinces of their populations, his breast began to rot away within and his vitals to dissolve. In addition to the usual horrors caused by human suffering, he began to cough up worms and often ordered his doctors, who were unable to bear the stench, to be put to death. **13.** After he was rebuked by one doctor whose desperation had given him courage and who told him

281 A pious exaggeration in order to contrast the resilience and growth of Christianity under persecution with the feeble nature of paganism even when not persecuted.

282 Diocletian had forced Maximian against his will to abdicate as Augustus in AD 305. He now attempted to re-assert himself.

283 The rise of Maxentius and the demise of Severus occurred in AD 307. See Jerome, *Chronicle, A Abr.* 2323.

284 Maximian in fact committed suicide at Marseilles. Constantine had married his daughter, Fausta, in AD 307. Maximian was killed in AD 310; see Jerome, *Chronicle, A Abr.* 2324. For his failed attempt to re-assert himself, see Zosimus, 2.10–11.

285 At the Conference of Carnuntum, 11 November AD 308.

that this was the punishment that the wrath of God had brought down on him and so impossible for doctors to cure, he sent edicts far and wide recalling Christians from their exile. However, he was unable to bear the agony he was suffering and took his own life.[286]

14. At that time, therefore, the state was under the control of four new rulers: Constantine and Maxentius, the sons of the Augusti, and the parvenus, Licinius and Maximin. **15.** Constantine gave the churches peace after the ten years during which they had been plagued by persecutors. **16.** Then civil war broke out between Constantine and Maxentius. Maxentius's strength was weakened after many battles and he was finally defeated and killed at the Mulvian Bridge.[287] **17.** Maximin, the worst inciter and perpetrator of persecutions against the Christians, died at Tharsus while he was preparing to wage civil war against Licinius.[288] **18.** Licinius, overtaken by a sudden madness, ordered that all Christians be expelled from his court, and soon war broke out between him and Constantine.[289] **19.** Constantine first defeated Licinius, who was his sister's husband, in Pannonia, then vanquished him at Cibalae[290] and, after gaining control of all of Greece, finally forced Licinius, who had launched many unsuccessful attacks on him by land and sea, to surrender. **20.** However, because he remembered the example set by his father-in-law, Maximian Herculius, Constantine ordered Licinius to be killed secretly in order to stop him taking up once more to the detriment of the state the purple that he had laid down. **21.** So although all the participants in this notorious persecution were dead, just punishment also befell this man who had also persecuted Christians when he had had the power to do so.[291] **22.** Constantine's sons, Crispus, and Constantine, along

286 AD 311. The nature of Galerius's death bears a pleasing resemblance to that of Herod. The gruesome details of his death are not found in either Jerome, *Chronicle, A Abr.* 2325, or Eutropius, 10.4.2, both of whom merely note it. Eutropius has a positive view of Galerius, describing him, 10.2.1, as 'a man of proven good character and great military ability'.

287 28 October AD 312. Orosius makes no mention of the vision that urged Constantine to paint Christian symbols on his troops' shields. The battle is noted by Jerome, *Chronicle, A Abr.* 2328. For Maxentius's campaign, see Zosimus, 2.12–17. Zosimus notes that the Temple of Fortune at Rome caught fire while Maxentius was in the city. This is not mentioned by Orosius, probably to avoid any hint that pagan omens could convey the future accurately.

288 Tharsus is Tarsus; see Jerome, *Chronicle, A Abr.* 2327. According to Zosimus, 2.17, the war between Maximin and Licinius was already underway when Maximin died.

289 Socrates, *Ecclesiastical History*, 1.4, also sees Licinius's maltreatment of Christians as the reason why war broke out between him and Constantine.

290 Modern Vinkovci in Croatia. The battle is noted by Jerome, *Chronicle, A Abr.* 2329.

291 Orosius has misread Eutropius, 10.6.1, who refers to only one battle fought on both land and sea at Nicomedia. Orosius also takes great pains to excuse Constantine's murder of

with the young Licinius, who was the son of the Augustus Licinius and a nephew of Constantine's on his sister's side, were made Caesars.[292]

23. It was at this time that Arrius, a priest in the city of Alexandria, strayed from the truth of the Catholic faith and established a dogma that was to prove fatal for very many men.[293] **24.** At first, he became famous, or rather infamous, among his supporters and opponents at Alexandria who mixed indiscriminately. He was excommunicated from the church by Alexander who was the then bishop of this town.[294] **25.** Then, after he had roused up into rebellion those whom he had seduced into error, a council of 318 bishops was convened in Nicaea, a town in Bithynia. These bishops openly proclaimed their denunciation of Arrius's doctrine as something that a great amount of evidence showed to be both dangerous and deplorable.[295]

26. In the middle of these affairs, it remains unclear why, the emperor Constantine was moved to turn his avenging sword and the punishment he had devised for blasphemers against his own kin. For he killed his son, Crispus, and his sister's son, Licinius.[296] Besides this, he embroiled many peoples in war. **27.** He was the first, or rather the only, Roman king to found a town which took his own name.[297] This town, the only one free of

---

Licinius which both Eutropius, and significantly Jerome, *Chronicle, A Abr.* 2340, state was done despite a sworn oath that his life would be spared. The pagan historian Zosimus, 2.28, also notes that Licinius died in this way and adding that Constantine habitually broke the oaths he had sworn.

292 See Jerome, *Chronicle, A Abr.* 2333.

293 Arius (spelt Arrius in our manuscripts) is said to have held that the son was a separate and subordinate god to God the Father, though whether in fact he believed this is open to doubt. See Williams (1987).

294 At the Synod of Alexandria in AD 318.

295 The Council of Nicaea, AD 325. Orosius has drawn his account from Jerome, *Chronicle, A Abr.* 2338.

296 Crispus was executed in AD 326, Licinius in c. AD 336. Both deaths are listed as occurring in the same year by Jerome, *Chronicle, A Abr.* 2341, who describes the two's execution as 'most cruel'. Unlike Orosius, Jerome does not suppress the fact that Constantine also executed his wife Fausta; see *Chronicle, A Abr.* 2344. Eutropius, 10.6.3, mentions all three killings in succession, stating that Fausta was executed because of the number of lovers she had taken. The murder of Crispus led to a pagan allegation that Constantine had only become a Christian in order to purge his guilt for this action; see Zosimus, 2.29, and Sozomen, *Ecclesiastical History*, 1.5.

297 Constantinople. Constantine decided to build his new capital soon after defeating and deposing his co-emperor Licinius in AD 324, naming it Constantinople on 8 November that year. However, the official foundation date of the town was 11 May AD 330, when building works were complete.

idolatry,[298] reached, very soon after its foundation by a Christian emperor, such a size that it was the only town able to rival Rome, a town which had grown to this size in beauty and power only through many centuries of suffering.[299] **28.** Then Constantine was the first to change the old order to a new and just disposition of affairs. He decreed by edict that the pagans' temples be closed down, without killing a single man.[300] **29.** Soon afterwards, he annihilated the teeming, powerful tribes of the Goths in the very heart of the barbarian lands themselves, namely Sarmatia.[301] **30.** He crushed Calocaerus who attempted to launch a revolution on Cyprus.[302] On the 30th anniversary of his reign, he chose Dalmatius as his Caesar.[303] **31.** He died in the state residence close to Nicomedia while on campaign against the Persians, leaving the state in good order for his sons.[304]

29[305]

1. 1,092 years after the foundation of the City, Constantius, along with his brothers, Constantine and Constans, became the 35th man to obtain the empire.[306] He held power for twenty-four years. Constantine's successors had also included his brother's son, the Caesar Dalmatius, but he was killed straightaway in a military conspiracy.[307]

298 It was *de rigueur* to believe this in the early Church (see Eusebius, *Life of Constantine*, 3.47), but Constantine's attitude to paganism was more ambiguous than Orosius implies. Zosimus, 2.31, notes that Constantine erected a shrine to the Dioscuri in the Hippodrome at Constantinople and two pagan temples in the forum.

299 Orosius echoes the sentiments of Augustine, *City of God*, 5.25.

300 See Jerome, *Chronicle, A Abr.* 2347. The ban is also noted by Socrates, *Ecclesiastical History*, 1.18, and Sozomen, *Ecclesiastical History*, 1.8.

301 Orosius sees this victory, drawn from Jerome *Chronicle, A Abr.* 2348, as a consequence of Constantine's suppression of paganism. He does not, however, attribute Constantine's victory directly to his faith, as does Socrates, *Ecclesiastical History*, 1.18, or impute any direct divine aid to Constantine as does Sozomen, *Ecclesiastical History*, 1.8.

302 Jerome, *Chronicle, A Abr.* 2350. Calocaerus's uprising took place in AD 334.

303 Dalmatius the Younger, son of Constantine's brother, Dalmatius the Elder. He was made Caesar on 15 September AD 335.

304 For a much more negative assessment of Constantine's reign, see Zosimus, 2.32–39. For a modern discussion of the controversies his reign has generated see Lieu and Monserrat (1998).

305 The bulk of this chapter follows closely, though abbreviates, Eutropius, 10.9–10.15.2.

306 Orosius's chronology is two years awry. At the Council of Viminacium, held on 9 September 1090 *AUC*/AD 337, the three brothers all took the title Augustus and divided the empire between them.

307 In AD 337. See Jerome, *Chronicle, A Abr.* 2354. According to Socrates, *Ecclesiastical*

2. Meanwhile the Devil's never-ending malign hostility to the True God which from the beginning of time down to the present day has confused the fickle hearts of men, leading them from the true faith and the path of religion by pouring forth clouds of error, after Christian emperors had reached the heights of royal power and were changing things for the better, ceased to persecute the Church of Christ by means of love of idolatry and devised a different instrument by which it could use these selfsame Christian emperors to do damage to the Church of Christ. **3.** Therefore, a quick and easy way was found whereby Arrius, the deviser of a new heresy, and all his disciples should become confidants of the emperor Constantius.[308] Constantius was then persuaded that there were different parts of the Godhead, and so a man who had left the error of idolatry by the front door was, so to speak, inveigled back into its bosom through a secret passage, as he began to seek for gods in the Godhead itself. **4.** His deranged power became armed with a misguided zeal, and violent persecution was begun under the name of piety. There was discussion about choosing a new name so that the church should be called Arian rather than Catholic. **5.** These events were followed by a terrible earthquake that razed vast numbers of towns in the east to the ground.[309]

Constantine through foolish rashness brought himself into danger while fighting against his brother Constans and was killed by Constans' generals.[310] **6.** Constans fought nine battles with little success against the Persians and Sapor, who had laid waste to Mesopotamia. Finally, he was forced by his mutinous and ill-disciplined troops to attack the Persians at night. He lost the battle when victory was in his grasp and went on to be defeated himself.[311] **7.** After he had given himself up to insufferable vices[312] and was

---

History, 2.25, Dalmatius was lynched by his troops, 'Constantius having neither commanded his demise, nor forbidden it'. Zosimus, 2.40, places the blame for Dalmatius's murder firmly on Constantius.

308 According to Socrates, *Ecclesiastical History*, 2.2, and Sozomen, *Ecclesiastical History*, 3.1, the Arians suborned Eusebius, the chief eunuch of the imperial bed-chamber, who first spread Arianism to the empress and then to the emperor himself.

309 Orosius's account of the rise of Arianism is a much-embroidered version of Jerome, *Chronicle, A Abr.* 2355. The subsequent earthquake, again embroidered, is drawn from Jerome, *Chronicle, A Abr.* 2357.

310 At Aquileia in the spring of AD 340; see Jerome, *Chronicle, A Abr.* 2356. Sozomen, *Ecclesiastical History*, 2.5, says Constantine was killed by his own generals.

311 Orosius has confused Constans here with Constantius II; see Jerome, *Chronicle, A Abr.* 2363.

312 A reference to sodomy, see Aurelius Victor, *Lives of the Caesars*, 41.23–24, and Zosimus, 2.42.

currying favour with the troops at the expense of the people of the provinces, Magnentius cunningly killed him in a town on the borders of Spain called Helena.³¹³ **8.** Magnentius usurped imperial power at Autun³¹⁴ and swiftly brought Gaul, Africa, and Italy under his control.

9. Meanwhile, in Illyricum the troops proclaimed the elderly Vetranio as their emperor.³¹⁵ He was a simple-minded soul and kind to all, but had never been given even the first elements of an education. **10.** Because of this, it happened that while the old emperor was begrudgingly learning the alphabet and the syllables found in words, he was ordered to give up his power by Constantius, who was burning to take vengeance on Magnentius for his brother and preparing for war. Vetranio cast aside his studies along with the purple, and content with the quiet life of a private man, left both the palace and the schoolroom.³¹⁶

11. At this point in time, Nepotian, Constantine's sister's son, seized power with a band of gladiators, but after his wickedness was seen and he had become universally hated because of it, he was suppressed by Magnentius's generals.³¹⁷

12. There then followed a terrible battle between Constantius and Magnentius which was fought by the city of Mursa. The squandering of Roman might there weakened even future generations.³¹⁸ **13.** Magnentius, though defeated, escaped; however, he killed himself soon afterwards at Lyons.³¹⁹ His brother Ducentius, whom he had made Caesar and put in

313 The modern Elne in the Pyrenees. Constans' tomb may be the striking mausoleum at Centcelles near Tarragona in Spain. See Jerome, *Chronicle, A Abr.* 2366, and Zosimus, 2.42. Socrates, *Ecclesiastical History*, 2.25, places Constans' death 'in the Gallic provinces', Sozomen, *Ecclesiastical History*, 4.1, in 'Western Gaul'.

314 18 January AD 350.

315 At Naissus on 1 March AD 350; see Jerome, *Chronicle, A Abr.* 2367. Vetranio was the *magister militum*, i.e. field marshal, of the army in Pannonia.

316 This splendid phrase is Orosius's own. Sozomen, *Ecclesiastical History*, 4.4, has a much more prosaic account of Vetranio's demise, stating that the usurper threw himself on Constantius's mercy and that the emperor, after stripping him of all official ranks, provided for his retirement from the official treasury. Zosimus, 2.44, has Constantius depose Vetranio by trickery and notes that his enforced retirement was in Bithynia.

317 3 June AD 350. Nepotian's usurpation lasted a week. Orosius suppresses Jerome's comments, *Chronicle, A Abr.* 2366, that his head was paraded around Rome on a pike and that his death was followed by proscriptions.

318 Mursa is the modern Osijek in Croatia. The battle was fought on 28 September AD 351. Orosius's comment about the squandering of Roman might is drawn from Jerome, *Chronicle, A Abr.* 2367. For a description of the battle, see Zosimus, 2.50.

319 Orosius is a little disingenuous; 'soon afterwards' was in fact almost two years later:

charge of the Gallic provinces, also hanged himself at Sens.[320] **14.** Constantius immediately appointed his cousin, Gallus, Caesar, but killed him shortly after his elevation as he behaved in a cruel and tyrannical fashion.[321] He also took care quickly to encircle and suppress Silvanus who was eager to begin a revolution in the Gallic provinces.[322]

15. On the death of Silvanus, Constantius made Julian, his cousin and Gallus's brother, Caesar and despatched him to the Gallic provinces. Caesar Julian acted vigorously to restore the Gallic provinces that had been ravaged and plundered by the enemy. He put to flight a great host of Alamanni with his small forces and bound the Germans back behind the Rhine.[323] **16.** Elated by his success, he usurped the title of Augustus, soon crossed into Italy and Illyricum, and snatched part of Constantius's kingdom from him while he was occupied with fighting the Parthians.[324]

17. When he learnt of Julian's treachery, Constantius abandoned his Parthian expedition and turned back to fight a civil war. He then died on the march between Cilicia and Cappadocia.[325] **18.** So this man, who had ripped apart the peaceful unity of the Catholic faith and rent asunder the

---

Magnentius committed suicide on 10 August AD 353; see Jerome, *Chronicle, A Abr.* 2369. Just prior to his suicide, he had been defeated a second time by Constantius at 'Mons Seleucus', an unknown hill in the south of France.

320 18 August AD 353. The detail about hanging is drawn from Jerome, *Chronicle, A Abr.* 2369; it is also mentioned by Zosimus, 2.54.

321 Gallus was executed at Istria towards the end of AD 354. See Jerome, *Chronicle, A Abr.* 2370. For Gallus's cruelty, see Ammianus Marcellinus, 14.1.1–10; 14.7.1; 14.9.1–9. For his execution by Constantius, see Ammianus Marcellinus, 14.11.23. Zosimus, 2.55, notes Gallus's execution, but sees this as evidence of Constantius's brutality, making no mention of Gallus's cruelty.

322 A Roman commander of Frankish extraction, who proclaimed himself emperor at Cologne on 11 August AD 354. According to Jerome, *Chronicle, A Abr.* 2370, his usurpation lasted 28 days.

323 Julian's campaigns date to AD 357–59. Orosius is thinking in particular of Julian's victory at the Battle of Strasbourg, fought in AD 357. For these campaigns, see Ammianus Marcellinus, 16.2–16.4; 16.11–16.12; 17.1–17.2; 17.8–17.10; and 18.2.

324 February AD 360. Orosius has twisted his sources to Julian's disadvantage. While Orosius sees Julian's *pronunciamiento* as the product of personal pride, Ammianus Marcellinus, 20.4.17, tells us that he was proclaimed emperor against his will by his troops. This is also the view of Eutropius, 10.15.1 and Zosimus, 3.9. The use of 'treachery' in the following sentence is also Orosius's own; Eutropius merely says, 'when he learnt this'.

325 Constantius died in AD 361 at Mopsucrene; see Jerome, *Chronicle, A Abr.* 2377. Mopsucrene lay under the Taurus mountains, 12 miles from Tarsus. Ammianus Marcellinus, 21.15.3, has the emperor die of fever on 5 October, Socrates, *Ecclesiastical History*, 2.47, of apoplexy on 3 November.

limbs of the Church by arming Christians against Christians in, so to speak, a civil war, employed, eked out, and ended all of his unquiet reign and troubled life in civil wars which had been stirred up even by his relatives and kinsmen.[326]

30

1. 1,116 years after the foundation of the City, Julian, who had already been Caesar, became the 35th man after Augustus to take control of affairs, ruling alone for one year and eight months. **2.** He attacked the Christian faith more through cunning than violence, trying to lure men with honours rather than force them by torture to deny the faith of Christ and take up the worship of idols. **3.** He openly decreed that no Christian could be a teacher of the liberal arts, but, as we have learnt from our forefathers, almost everywhere all those affected by this edict chose to abandon their office rather than their faith.[327]

4. Julian prepared to fight a war against the Parthians and when he had gathered together Roman troops from all over the empire to drag down with him to his foreordained destruction, he dedicated the blood of the Christians to his gods, promising that he would openly persecute the Church, if he were able to win a victory.[328] **5.** He ordered an amphitheatre to be built in Jerusalem where, on his return from Parthia, he intended to throw the bishops, monks, and all the saints of that place to beasts which had been deliberately enraged and watch them be torn apart.[329] **6.** After he marched

326 In contrast to Orosius's religiously motivated criticisms, Eutropius, 10.15.2, gives a generally favourable view of Constantius, saying that he deserved to be deified. Ammianus Marcellinus, 21.16, is equivocal, listing both virtues and vices.

327 Orosius has placed Julian's accession in 1116 *AUC*/AD 363, two years too late. The bulk of Orosius's information is drawn from Jerome, *Chronicle, A Abr.* 2378–2379. See also Rufinus, *Ecclesiastical History*, 1.32.258–59. Orosius suppresses Jerome's comment that Julian's approach enjoyed a considerable amount of success. For the comment on schoolmasters, see Augustine, *Confessions*, 8.10. Socrates, *Ecclesiastical History*, 3.12, 3.16, Sozomen, *Ecclesiastical History*, 5.18, and Theodoret, *Ecclesiastical History*, 3.4, state that Julian banned the children of Christians from attending schools of higher education.

328 For Julian's campaign, see Ammianus Marcellinus, 23.2–23.6; 24.1–24.8; 25.1–25.3; and Zosimus, 3.12–28.

329 This implausible detail appears to be Orosius's invention. While Jerome mentions that Julian had vowed to offer Christian blood to his gods, there is no mention of the amphitheatre at Jerusalem. Both this and the 'blood vow' appear simply to be attempts to besmirch Julian's reputation. Eutropius, 10.16.3, states that while Julian was a zealous persecutor of Christians, on principle he abstained from spilling blood. Julian did attempt to refound the temple at Jerusalem, but failed in his attempt. This is noted by Ammianus Marcellinus, 23.1.2–3;

from Ctesiphon, he was treacherously led into the desert by a Parthian deserter. As his troops became exhausted from their overpowering thirst and the heat of the sun, in addition to the effort of having to march through the sand, and began to die, the emperor became so concerned by the state of things that, taking no precautions, he wandered through the vast desert.[330] There he came across an enemy horseman, was run through by his lance, and died. Thus God's mercy ended these blasphemous plans through the blasphemer's death.[331]

31[332]

1. 1,117 years after the foundation of the City, Jovian was created the 37th emperor by the army at a time of great peril.[333] Since he had no chance of escaping, being both trapped by unfavourable terrain and surrounded by the enemy, he made a treaty with the Persian king, Sapor, which, though men thought it was lacking in dignity, was nevertheless certainly required by necessity.[334] **2.** To keep the Roman army safe and sound not just from enemy attacks, but also the dangers of the place itself, he handed over Nisibis[335] and part of Upper Mesopotamia to the Persians. **3.** While he was marching through Galatia on his way back to Illyricum, he retired to a new bedroom to sleep and was overcome and suffocated by the overpowering heat from

Socrates, *Ecclesiastical History*, 3.20; and Sozomen, *Ecclesiastical History*, 5.22. All of these accounts include references to miraculous fires which would have seemed useful for Orosius, but he does not include the incident.

330 Perhaps there is a slight hint here of Daniel 4.31–33, where God forces the unbelieving Nebuchadnezzar to wander through the wilderness.

331 Julian died near Samarra on the Tigris on 26 June AD 363. The account of his Parthian campaign and death is drawn from Jerome, *Chronicle, A Abr.* 2379. For another account of Julian's death, see Ammianus Marcellinus, 25.3.3–23. Orosius makes no mention of the pious legend that a Christian in his own army killed Julian. Socrates, *Ecclesiastical History*, 3.21, states that most 'current opinion' in his day believed that one of the emperor's own men had killed him, but gives no motive. Sozomen, *Ecclesiastical History*, 6.1, and Theodoret, *Ecclesiastical History*, 3.20, echo this and give the motive not as religious, but simply anger at having been led into great danger.

332 This chapter is drawn mainly, though in abbreviated fashion, from Eutropius, 10.17–18. For a more detailed account of Jovian's reign, see Ammianus Marcellinus, 25.2–5–10.

333 Orosius's chronology is one year awry; Jovian was proclaimed emperor in 1116 *AUC*/ AD 363. See *PLRE* 1 Jovianus 3. Jovian had been a *protector domesticus*, i.e. one of the emperor's bodyguard.

334 See Zosimus, 3.32.

335 The modern Nezib in south-east Turkey.

the braziers and the fumes from its newly whitewashed walls. His life came to an end in the eighth month of his reign.[336]

32

1. 1,118 years after the foundation of the City, Valentinian was made the 38th emperor at Nicaea by agreement of the troops and remained in power for eleven years.[337] **2.** Although he was a Christian, under Julian he fulfilled his soldier's oath as a commander of the emperor's bodyguard[338] while keeping his faith intact. When he was ordered by that sacrilegious emperor either to sacrifice to his idols or leave the service, he knew as a true believer that God's judgments are more severe and His promises better than an emperor's, and left the service of his own free will.[339] **3.** And so after a short interval had passed, when Julian was killed and Jovian died soon afterwards, this man, who for the sake of Christ had lost his command, was recompensed by Christ and took over the empire in place of his persecutor. **4.** After he had made his brother, Valens, a partner in his rule,[340] he killed the usurper Procopius and afterwards a great number of that man's followers.[341]

5. An earthquake which struck the entire earth also stirred up the sea so much that, it is said, as the water flowed back, it struck and submerged a

336 Orosius's information is drawn from Jerome, *Chronicle*, *A Abr.* 2380. Jovian died at Dadastana on 17 February AD 364. For theories about his strange demise, see Ammianus Marcellinus, 25.10.13, and Duval (2003).

337 See *PLRE* 1 Valentinianus 7. Orosius's chronology is one year awry; Valentinian was proclaimed emperor by his troops at Nicaea on 26 February 1117 *AUC*/AD 364.

338 The *scutarii*, or 'shield-bearers'.

339 Theodoret, *Ecclesiastical History*, 3.4, states that Julian passed a law expelling Christians from the army. Orosius's comments here contrast with those of Rufinus, *Ecclesiastical History*, 2.268C, who states that Julian dismissed Valentinian from the service; see also Sozomen, *Ecclesiastical History*, 6.6. Sozomen states that Valentinian was reinstated in his rank by Jovian. Socrates, *Ecclesiastical History*, 4.1, suggests that Valentinian wished to resign his commission, but that Julian refused to accept his resignation, recognising his value to the state. Ammianus Marcellinus, 26.1.5, merely notes that Valentinian was in command of the 2nd Schola (imperial bodyguard unit) of shield-bearers when he was acclaimed emperor. Orosius also fails to mention that Valentinian's brother, Valens, also made a similar sacrifice for his faith. As Valens was an Arian Christian, this information would not have been germane to Orosius's intentions. See Socrates, *Ecclesiastical History*, 4.1.

340 See *PLRE* 1 Valens 8. Valens was proclaimed Augustus on 28 March AD 364 at Constantinople.

341 Drawn from Jerome, *Chronicle*, *A Abr.* 2382. Procopius proclaimed himself emperor in Constantinople on 28 September AD 365. Valens executed him on 27 May AD 366. For a full account of Procopius's uprising, see Ammianus Marcellinus, 26.5–9 and Zosimus, 4.4–8.

great number of island cities that lay by the coast, destroying them.[342]

6. Valens was baptised by Eudoxius, a partisan of Arrius's dogma, and was persuaded by him to descend into this most brutal of heresies,[343] but for a long time he hid his malign partisanship and never used his power to enforce his wishes, as his brother's authority, while he was alive, restrained him. **7.** For he was mindful how much power Valentinian could wield to avenge the faith as an emperor, when he had showed such constancy in keeping it when a soldier.

8. In the third year of their rule, Gratian, Valentinian's son, was made emperor.[344] In the same year, real wool mixed in with the rain fell from the clouds among the Atrebates.[345]

9. At this time, the king of the Goths, Athanaric,[346] cruelly persecuted the Christians among his people and raised many barbarians killed for the faith to a martyr's crown. However, very many more fled, because they confessed Christ, to Roman soil. They did not come trembling, as if to enemies, but with confidence because they were coming to their brothers.[347]

10. Valentinian crushed the Saxons, a race that lives by the Ocean's shores and impenetrable marshland and which causes terror because of its courage and mobility, in the lands of the Franks when they were plotting to make a dangerous incursion in large numbers into Roman territory.[348] **11.**

342 For the earthquake, see also Socrates, *Ecclesiastical History*, 4.3.

343 The baptism of Valens into Arianism is drawn from Jerome, *Chronicle, A Abr.* 2382 (Orosius cannot abide to call Eudoxius a bishop as does Jerome), as is the account of the earthquake which struck on 21 July AD 365; see Kelly (2004). For Orosius, though not Jerome, the two follow naturally from one another, as the latter presaged the troubles that then flowed from the rule of the heretic Valens. Theodoret, *Ecclesiastical History*, 4.11, draws a parallel with the Garden of Eden, claiming that Valens was won over to Arianism by his wife, Alba Domenica, who in turn had been converted by Eudoxius.

344 Gratian was raised to the purple in AD 367. See Jerome, *Chronicle, A Abr.* 2383. *PLRE* 1 Gratianus 2.

345 Jerome, *Chronicle, A Abr.* 2383. The Atrebates were a tribe based in north-west Gaul. Oddly, Orosius does not mention the other prodigy mentioned by Jerome here – that many were killed in a hailstorm at Constantinople. See also Socrates, *Ecclesiastical History*, 4.11, and Sozomen, *Ecclesiastical History*, 6.10, where both prodigies are mentioned.

346 See *PLRE* 1 Athanaricus.

347 Jerome, *Chronicle, A Abr.* 2385. The moralising is Orosius's own; see his comments at 5.1.14–16 and 5.2.1–6. Athanaric's persecution lasted from AD 369 to AD 372. Its most famous victim was St Saba; see Heather and Matthews (1991) ch. 4. For the persecution among the Goths, see also Socrates, *Ecclesiastical History*, 4.33, and particularly Sozomen, *Ecclesiastical History*, 6.37.

348 The campaign took place in AD 370; see Jerome, *Chronicle, A Abr.* 2389. Jerome adds that the decisive battle took place at Deuso. The details about the Franks are Orosius's own.

Meanwhile, the Burgundians, a new name for a new enemy and numbering over 80,000 it is said, settled on the bank of the Rhine.[349] **12.** This tribe was scattered into camps when the interior of Germany was subjugated by Caesar's adopted sons, Drusus and Tiberius.[350] They then coalesced as a great people and even took their name from this process since they set up many small settlements along their frontier that are commonly called 'burgs'. They are a powerful and dangerous group, as the Gallic provinces, of which they have assumed ownership and where they have settled, bear witness to this day. **13.** However, through the providence of the Christian God, they have recently all become Catholics, received priests from us whom they obey, and live peacefully, calmly, and causing no harm with the Gauls, looking on them not as their subjects, but truly as brother Christians.[351]

14. In the eleventh year of his reign, while Valentinian was preparing war against the Sarmatians who had poured into the Pannonian provinces and laid waste to them, he was overcome in the town of Brigitio by a sudden effusion of blood, which the Greeks call apoplexy, and died.[352]

For an extended account of this campaign, see Ammianus Marcellinus, 28.5.1–8. In his brief account of campaigns in Valentinian's reign, Orosius has omitted the near loss of Britain in AD 367 when the provinces there suffered attacks on three sides and a Roman army was lost (see Ammianus Marcellinus, 26.8), as he wishes to portray the orthodox Valentinian's reign as one of unblemished success, in contrasts to the disasters suffered under the Arian Valens.

349 Jerome, *Chronicle*, *A Abr.* 2389, including the numbers involved.

350 A reference to campaigns in Germany during the reign of Augustus. Orosius seems to be attributing the tactics of his own times to these campaigns which in fact led to an attempt to bring the Germans together into towns rather than to disperse them; see Dio, 56.18.2. According to Ammianus Marcellinus, 28.5.11, the Burgundians believed themselves to be descendants of the Romans. For a discussion of the Burgundians in this area, see Schutz (2001) 35–42.

351 Orosius omits the fact that Valentinian used the Burgundians as allies in his wars against the Allemanni; see Ammianus Marcellinus, 28.5.9–15. The Burgundians entered the empire as a result of the usurpation of Jovinus in AD 411; see 7.42.6 below and Prosper, *Chronicle*, *A Abr.* 2430 = PL 27 709. Orosius's claim that the tribe converted to Trinitarian Christianity is striking and likely to be false. The Burgundians were originally converted to Arianism and Gregory of Tours states they were Arians in the early sixth century, when their king, Gundobad, finally converted to Trinitarianism (*History of the Franks*, 2.32–34). Given Orosius's championing of Honorius, this assertion that the Burgundians are now controlled by Roman priests is the only way he can save the emperor's face and disguise the fact that Honorius had allowed this piece of the empire to slip out of Roman control. For a general discussion of the Burgundians in this period, see Drinkwater (2007).

352 Drawn from Jerome, *Chronicle*, *A Abr.* 2391. Brigitio, the spelling found in Jerome, is normally spelt Brigetio and is the modern Komarom-Szony in Hungary; see also Socrates, *Ecclesiastical History*, 4.31. Valentinian died in on 17 November AD 375. Sozomen, *Ecclesiastical History*, 6.36, erroneously places the site of Valentinian's death in 'a fortress in Gaul'.

15. After his death, his son Gratian took power in the west, while his uncle Valens held it in the eastern regions.[353] Gratian also shared his power with his brother Valentinian who was still merely a child.[354]

33

1. 1,128 years after the foundation of the City, Valens became the 39th emperor and held power for four years after the death of Valentinian – the only man who could make him blush when he behaved in his impious fashion.[355] Straightaway, as if he were now free with the bridle being taken off his arrogance, he passed a law that monks – that is, Christians who put aside their various earthly tasks to dedicate themselves to the single work of the Faith – should be forced to join the army.[356] **2.** At that time, the great sand-covered wastes of Egypt which had never known human company because of their lack of water, infertility, and dangerous abundance of serpents, had been filled by a great host of monks who dwelt there. **3.** Tribunes and soldiers were sent here to drag away these holy men who were true soldiers of Christ. This was persecution, but under another name, and there many battalions of the saints were killed. **4.** Let my decision to keep silent about the details of what was done at that time by this, and similar, commands against Catholic churches and people of the True Faith in all various provinces speak for itself.[357]

5. Meanwhile in Africa, Firmus stirred up the Moorish tribes, set himself up as king, and laid waste to Africa and Mauretania.[358] He took Caesarea,

353 The Sarmatian war, Valentinian's death, and Gratian's succession are drawn from Jerome, *Chronicle, A Abr.* 2391. See also Ammianus Marcellinus, 30.5–9, for an account of these events and an assessment of his reign. Strikingly, Ammianus does not portray Valentinian as a resolute orthodox Christian as does Orosius, but rather notes that the emperor 'was especially remarkable during his reign for his moderation in this respect – that he kept a middle course between the different sects of religion'.

354 See *PLRE* 1 Valentinianus 8. Valentinian II was proclaimed Augustus at Aquincum on 22 November AD 375. He was four at the time; see Zosimus, 4.19.

355 Orosius's date for the beginning of Valens' sole rule is correct.

356 This law is only otherwise known from Jerome, *Chronicle, A Abr.* 2391: 'Valens passed a law that monks should serve in the army and commanded that those who refused be clubbed to death'.

357 Details of the persecutions are given by Socrates, *Ecclesiastical History*, 4.24, and Sozomen, *Ecclesiastical History*, 6.20.

358 See *PLRE* 1 Firmus 3. This extremely serious rebellion broke out in AD 372. Its origins lay in dynastic squabbling after the death of the Moorish prince, Nubel. Firmus was one of his sons who murdered another, Zammac, who had enjoyed good relations with the Count in

the finest city of Mauretania, by treachery and then filled it with fire and slaughter, giving it to his barbarians to plunder.[359]

6. Therefore, Count Theodosius,[360] the father of the Theodosius who later became emperor, on being dispatched by Valentinian, scattered the Moorish tribes, breaking them in a series of battles, and forced the despondent, defeated Firmus to commit suicide. **7.** Then, after, with his foresight born of great experience, he had returned all Africa and Mauretania to a better state than it had been in before, he was condemned to death – a sentence provoked by growing and unexpected envy towards him. He chose to be baptised and have his sins pardoned at Carthage, and after taking this sacrament of Christ that he had desired, sure, after a glorious life on earth, of the life eternal, he willingly offered his throat to the executioner.[361]

8. Meanwhile, the emperor Gratian, who was still a youth, on seeing an innumerable host of enemies pouring round Rome's borders, relying on the power of Christ, engaged the enemy, though he had far fewer troops than them, and with astounding good fortune won a terrible battle near Argentaria, a town in the Gallic provinces. For it is said that more than 30,000 Alamanni were killed in that battle with minimal losses to the Romans.[362]

9. In the 13th year of Valens' reign, that is shortly after Valens had hacked apart churches and slaughtered the saints throughout the east, this root of our sufferings brought forth abundant fruit. **10.** For the race of the Huns, which had been long hidden behind inaccessible mountains, suddenly rose up in anger and fell upon the Goths, scattering and driving them from their old homes. The Goths fled across the Danube and were received by Valens

Africa, Romanus. After being denounced to Valentinian by Romanus, Firmus decided there was no alternative but to rebel. A detailed account of the rebellion is given by Ammianus Marcellinus, 29.5. According to Zosimus, 4.16, the local population rose up against Romanus because of his rapacity and proclaimed Firmus emperor.

359 The modern Cherchel in Algeria.

360 See *PLRE* 1 Theodosius 3.

361 Jerome, *Chronicle*, *A Abr.* 2391, though Jerome gives only a bald statement of fact. For the circumstances of Theodosius's death, see Demandt (1969). Valens' hostility towards Theodosius may have been influenced by a prophecy which predicted his nemesis would have a name beginning 'Theod...'; see Ammianus Marcellinus, 29.1.29; Socrates, *Ecclesiastical History*, 4.19; Sozomen, *Ecclesiastical History*, 6.35.

362 Argentaria is the modern Colmar in France. This material, including the casualty figures, is drawn from Jerome, *Chronicle*, *A Abr.* 2393. For Gratian's campaign, see Ammianus Marcellinus, 31.10.5–18. Ammianus places the Germans' force at between 40,000 and 70,000 men strong. He also says that Gratian's victory was obtained 'by the favour of the eternal deity' (*sempiterni numinis nutu*) which perhaps suggests that the emperor did indeed lay stress on his faith during the campaign.

without any treaty being signed – they did not even hand over their arms to the Romans, which would have made it safer to deal with these barbarians.[363] **11.** After this, because of the intolerable greed of Duke Maximus,[364] their hunger and the insults they suffered forced them to rise in arms. They defeated Valens' army, and poured into Thrace, enveloping everything with murder, arson, and pillage.[365]

12. Valens set out from Antioch to be led to his ultimate destiny in that luckless war. He finally felt the need to repent for his great sins and ordered that the bishops and all of the rest of the saints be recalled from exile.[366]

13. So in the 15th year of his reign, Valens waged *a war full of tears*[367] in Thrace against the Goths who were now well prepared with a trained army and an abundance of resources. The Romans' cavalry squadrons were routed by the Goths' first charge and fled, leaving the infantry exposed. **14.** Soon these infantry legions were hemmed in on all sides by the enemies' cavalry. They were first overwhelmed by clouds of arrows, and then, as they fled in scattered groups and out of their minds with fear across the pathless countryside, they were wiped out by the swords and lances of their pursuers.[368]

15. The emperor himself was wounded by an arrow and turned to flee. He was carried with some difficulty to an outhouse on a small farm to hide, but was found by the pursuing enemy who killed him by burning it down. So that his punishment should bear even greater witness to, and provide an even more terrible example of, Divine Wrath for future generations, he did not even have a common grave.[369]

363 See Ammianus Marcellinus, 31.3–4, who describes the migration as being of enormous proportions. For a discussion of these events, see Heather (1991) 122–42.

364 See *PLRE* 1 Maximus 24. Similar comments are made by Ammianus Marcellinus, 31.4.9–11, and Zosimus, 4.20.6.

365 This material is drawn from Jerome, *Chronicle, A Abr.* 2393. See also Ammianus Marcellinus, 31.8.6–9.

366 Valens' repentance is drawn from Jerome, *Chronicle, A Abr.* 2393. According to Socrates, *Ecclesiastical History*, 4.32, and Sozomen, *Ecclesiastical History*, 6.36–37, Valens' moderation was due to a speech delivered before him by Themistius. Sadly, this speech has not survived. For the possibility that Themistius was merely echoing a change in imperial policy determined by *realpolitik*, rather than expressing his known opinion, see Heather and Moncur (2001) 29–42.

367 The phrase is drawn from Jerome, *Chronicle, A Abr.* 2395.

368 The Battle of Adrianople, 9 August AD 378. For an ancient account of the battle, see Ammianus Marcellinus, 31.13. For modern discussions, see Heather (1991), 142–47, and Barbero (2007).

369 The core of Orosius's description of the battle and Valens' death is drawn from Jerome, *Chronicle, A Abr.* 2395. For a more balanced ancient assessment of Valens, see Ammianus

16. The gentiles' stubbornness and misery can take this, but this alone, for its consolation – that in Christian times and under Christian kings such a great mountain of disasters were heaped all at one time on the republic's neck with provinces turned upside down, armies destroyed, and an emperor burned alive. This, it is true, caused us sorrow and all the more so because it had never happened before. **17.** But how does this help to console the pagans, as they can clearly see that here too a persecutor of the Church was being punished? One God gave One Faith, and spread one Church over all the earth. It is this Church that He watches over, cherishes, and defends. Whosoever hides under whatever name, if he does not associate with this Church, he is a stranger to it, and if he attacks it, he is its enemy. **18.** Let the gentiles takes as much consolation as they please in the punishment of the Jews and heretics, but let them confess that there is One, Sole God Who is not made up of separate 'persons' – the greatest proof of which is the demise of Valens. **19.** Prior to this, the Goths had sent envoys, humbly asking that bishops be sent who could teach them the principles of the Christian faith. In his cursèd wickedness, the emperor Valens sent them teachers of Arrius's dogma and the Goths clung to the rudiments of this, the first faith they had received.[370] So it was by the righteous judgment of God that they burnt alive the man because of whom they would burn when dead for the error of heresy.[371]

34

1. 1,132 years after the foundation of the city, Gratian became the 39th man to hold power after Augustus, succeeding on the death of Valens and ruling for six years,[372] though he had already previously been joint ruler with his uncle

Marcellinus, 31.14. For a modern, and sympathetic, discussion of the emperor, see Lenski (2002).

370 Orosius is referring to the Arian bishop, Ulfila (died AD 383), who translated the Bible into Gothic. See Socrates, *Ecclesiastical History*, 4.33, and Sozomen, *Ecclesiastical History*, 6.37. For a modern discussion of Ulfila's work, see Heather and Matthews (1991) ch. 5.

371 Orosius, through his emphasis on the Goths' ultimate fate, shows his dislike of barbarians here. His near contemporary, Salvian, *De Gubernatione Dei* (*On the Guidance of God*), 5.3, is much more generous and stresses how God will eventually bring a worthy people to the true faith.

372 Orosius's chronology is one year awry: Gratian's sole rule began in 1131 *AUC*/AD 378. A devout Christian (Rufinus, *Ecclesiastical History*, 2.13, describes him as 'excelling almost all previous emperors in his piety and religious devotion'), Gratian was the first Roman emperor to refuse the title of *pontifex maximus* (see Zosimus, 4.36), and deprived pagan cults

Valens and his brother Valentinian.[373] **2.** When he saw the state afflicted and close to collapse, with the same foresight through which Nerva had once chosen a Spaniard, Trajan, by whom the state was restored,[374] he, too, chose another Spaniard, Theodosius, and because of the need to rescue the state, invested him with the purple at Sirmium and placed him in charge of the east and Thrace.[375] **3.** When he did this, he acted with even better judgment than Nerva, because while Theodosius was Trajan's equal in all the virtues of human life, he excelled him without compare in his allegiance[376] to the Faith and in the practice of religion. For the one was a persecutor of the Church,[377] while the other helped it grow. **4.** And so while the former was granted not even one son of his own in whose succession he might rejoice, the glorious progeny of the latter have ruled both east and west through succeeding generations down to our own day.

5. Theodosius, therefore, believing that a state afflicted by God's wrath

---

of their traditional state subsidies. His most memorable act was to remove the statue of Victory from the enate-house in Rome, provoking Symmachus's famous protest, *Reports (Relationes)*, 3.10. Vegetius, 1.1.20, believes that the decline in the quality of Roman infantry began during Gratian's rule.

373 From AD 367, see 7.32.8 above.

374 7.11.1.

375 See *PLRE* 1 Theodosius 4. For the rise of Theodosius, see Matthews (1975) ch. 4. Theodosius had already made his military mark in AD 374 with a successful campaign against the Sarmatians while holding the rank of Duke of Moesia, Ammianus Marcellinus, 29.6.15. After the execution of his father, Count Theodosius, in AD 376, he had lived in 'voluntary' retirement in Spain. Gratian rehabilitated him in AD 378, promoted him to the rank of field marshal, *magister militum*, and sent him to campaign once more against the Sarmatians; see Theodoret, *Ecclesiastical History*, 5.5. After a successful expedition, Theodosius was proclaimed Augustus on 19 January AD 379. Apart from the areas listed by Orosius, he was also assigned the provinces of Dacia and Macedonia. The entire Balkans region was in turmoil following the Roman defeat at Adrianople; see Ambrose, *Letters*, 14 and 15 (= *PL* 16 955, 956). Orosius may be echoing the official propaganda of the Theodosian regime, or simply showing his own local patriotism, by marking out the Spanish origins of Theodosius and Trajan. However, he refrains from trying to place Theodosius's family in the same town as that of Trajan, Italica near Seville (for such an attempt, see Themistius, *Oration* 16). Theodosius's family in fact hailed from Coca in Old Castile; see Hydatius, *Chronicle*, 1. Despite Orosius's fulsome praise of his Christian pedigree, Theodosius's first imperial decree, *Theodosian Code*, 10.1.12, issued on 17 June AD 379 forbade the felling of sacred cypress trees at the shrine of Daphne near Antioch.

376 Orosius's use here of *sacramentum*, the standard term for the military oath, is carefully chosen. It alludes to the common metaphor of Christians being soldiers of Christ, but also underlines, and perhaps implies a judgment about, the martial aspects of these two emperors for which they were popularly remembered.

377 See 7.12.3.

must be set aright by God's mercy, placed all his trust in Christ's aid and straightaway attacked the mighty Scythian tribes, who had been a terror to all our ancestors, and were, as Pompeius and Cornelius[378] bear witness, avoided by Alexander the Great himself. In a great sequence of battles, he defeated these tribes, namely the Alans, Huns, and Goths, who were well supplied with Roman horses and weapons after the destruction of the Roman army,[379] **6.** entered the city of Constantinople in triumph,[380] and, in order not to wear out the small band that now comprised the Roman army by constant fighting, struck a treaty with Athanaric, king of the Goths. **7.** Athanaric, however, died as soon as he arrived in Constantinople. On the death of their king, all the tribes of the Goths, seeing the courage and kindliness of Theodosius, surrendered themselves to the power of Rome.[381]

8. At the same time, the Persians who, after the death of the persecutor Julian, had often defeated the emperors who succeeded him, and now, after putting Valens to flight, were belching forth with boorish insults their satiety at this recent victory, nevertheless humbly sent ambassadors of their own free will to Theodosius at Constantinople to seek peace. A treaty was then struck, and from that time the entire east has enjoyed tranquility down to the present day.[382]

---

378 i.e. Trogus and Tacitus, cf. 1.16.2.

379 See Zosimus, 4.25, who suggests that campaigning here was easier than Orosius implies. This is also true of Theodoret, *Ecclesiastical History*, 5.5, who does so to imply that Theodosius enjoyed divine favour. Sadly the bulk of the details concerning these campaigns fought in AD 379–380 has been lost; see Thompson (1966) 22 and n. 2. Orosius's comments on the destruction of the Roman army are a reference to the battle of Adrianople

380 In November AD 380. Prior to this, Theodosius had used Salonica as the base for his operations. Zosimus, 4.33, states that Theodosius's victory celebrations were groundless and that his presence in Constantinople was marked by continual debauchery. He goes on to imply that Roman successes were due to the generals Bauto and Argobastes sent by a frustrated Gratian rather than to Theodosius. Significantly Orosius makes no mention of Theodosius's edict of 27 February 380 issued at Constantinople which imposed Nicaean Christianity on all his subjects (*Theodosian Code*, 16.1.2) nor his illness and baptism later that year; see Ensslin (1953) 17f. These actions and Theodosius's attacks on pagan shrines may well explain Zosimus's hostility to the emperor.

381 Athanaric fled to Constantinople on 11 January AD 381 as a result of a civil war between himself and Fritigern (*Consularia Constantinopolitana* s.a. 381, 382). After his death on 25 January, Theodosius gave him a lavish, Roman-style funeral (see Ammianus Marcellinus, 27.5.10, and Zosimus, 4.34) and a funerary monument. Orosius, however, is being disingenuous, as a formal peace with the Visigoths was not signed until 3 October AD 382. The treaty allowed the Goths to settle within the empire as *foederati*, i.e. as an autonomous people.

382 This treaty, made in AD 387, partitioned Armenia. Rome gained the smaller part, but one that filled a dangerous salient in her frontier with Persia. Roman rule was nominal in the six

9. Meanwhile, while Theodosius, after subduing barbarian tribes in the east, was finally liberating the Thracian provinces, and made his son, Arcadius, his consort,[383] Maximus, a vigorous man of proven ability, and worthy of the purple, had he not broken his oath and dyed himself as a usurper,[384] was, almost against his will, declared emperor by the army in Britain, and crossed into Gaul.[385] **10.** There, through treachery, he captured and put to death the emperor Gratian, who had been terrified by his sudden incursion and was intending to retreat to Italy.[386] He also drove Gratian's brother, the emperor Valentinian,[387] from Italy.[388] Valentinian fled to the east where Theodosius received him with a father's piety and soon even restored him to his throne.[389]

satrapies she gained – the Armenians retained their own laws and local rulers were to command any levies raised for the Roman army.

383 See *PLRE* 1 Arcadius 5. Arcadius was declared Augustus on 19 January AD 383.

384 See *PLRE* 1 Maximus 39. It is hard not to detect here an echo of Tacitus's famous judgment on Galba 'that it would have been believed that he was capable of ruling, had he not ruled', *Histories*, 1.49.

385 In AD 383. Magnus Maximus, who was of Spanish origin, was Count of the British provinces at the time of his usurpation. The favourable assessment of Orosius contrasts sharply with the wholly negative account of Gildas, *On the Destruction and Conquest of Britain* (*De Excidio et Conquestu Britanniae*), 13, for whom Maximus was nothing more than a brutal usurper. Orosius is motivated first by Magnus's Spanish origins, but, above all, because he put to death the controversial Spanish cleric Priscillian whom Orosius regarded as an arch-heretic and against whom he wrote his *Defence* (*Liber Apologeticus*). For a discussion of the usurpation and its possible motives, see Matthews (1975) 173ff.

386 Gratian was captured at Lyons and put to death by Maximus's general, Andragathius, on 25 August AD 383. According to Socrates, *Ecclesiastical History*, 5.11, Andragathius disguised himself in a litter decorated like that used by the empress, leapt out from it, and assassinated the unsuspecting emperor. A similar account is found in Sozomen, *Ecclesiastical History*, 7.13, where we are told that the young emperor on seeing the litter, being 'passionately attached to his wife, hastened incautiously across the river, and in his anxiety to meet her, fell without forethought into the hands of Andragathius.' He was executed soon afterwards. Zosimus, 4.35, states that Gratian had alienated his troops by showing excessive favouritism to the Alans at his court.

387 Aged 12 at the time.

388 The situation was more complex than Orosius suggests. Initially, Maximus was content with Gaul and Spain, leaving Valentinian in charge of Italy. Valentinian recognised Maximus as an official Augustus in AD 384. It was only in AD 387 that Maximus finally invaded Italy and expelled Valentinian. See Zosimus, 4.42–43.

389 For similar 'paternal' sentiments on the part of Theodosius, see Augustine, *City of God*, 5.26.

35

1. 1,138 years after the foundation of the City, Theodosius was the 40th man to obtain sole power over the Roman Empire after the murder of Gratian by Maximus.[390] He remained in power for eleven years and had already ruled for six years in the east while Gratian was alive. **2.** So roused by just and necessary reasons to wage civil war,[391] since of the two imperial brothers, the spilt blood of one demanded vengeance and the wretchedness of the other in exile begged for his restitution, and placing his faith in God, he took himself off against the usurper Maximus, being his superior only in faith – for he was by far his inferior in every sort of supplies needed for war.[392] **3.** At that time, Maximus had established his court at Aquileia to view his victory. Andragathius, his count, saw to the necessities of war.[393] Using an enormous body of troops and tactics that counted for more than the strength of his forces, he blocked off in an astounding fashion all the entrances to the Alps and river estuaries. But, through the ineffable will of God, while he was preparing a naval expedition to surprise and overwhelm his enemy unawares, of his own free will he abandoned those very gates that he had barred. **4.** So Theodosius, without anyone realising, let alone resisting, crossed the abandoned Alps and unexpectedly advanced upon Aquileia. Without any trickery or opposition, he surrounded, captured, and killed his great enemy, Maximus, a brutal man, who had exacted tribute and taxes from the most savage German tribes merely through the terror of his reputation.[394] **5.** Valentinian, his power restored, took control of Italy. Count Andragathius, after learning that Maximus was dead, hurled himself from

390 Orosius's chronology is two years awry. Theodosius's sole rule began in 1136 *AUC*/ AD 383.

391 Given Orosius has already stated, 7.6.8, that Civil War was the worst of the Romans' ills, he needs this escape clause for his hero, Theodosius, cf. 5.22.5–12.

392 Theodosius's response to Maximus's usurpation was not immediate as Orosius implies, though this could have been because his own position in the east initially precluded serious warfare in the west. In 384, he led a western expedition, allegedly to avenge Gratian (Themistius, *Oration* 10, 220d–221a), but it came to nothing. In fact by 386 at the latest Theodosius had recognised Maximus as an official Augustus; see Zosimus, 4.37. For Theodosius's decisive campaign in 388, see Zosimus, 4.45–47, who states that Theodosius was in fact reluctant to go to war and was induced to do so only out of sexual lust.

393 See *PLRE* 1 Andragathius 3. Zosimus, 4.3.6, gives Andragathius rank as the *magister equitum*, i.e. commander of horse.

394 28 July AD 388; see Hydatius, *Chronicle*, 10.17. Orosius seems to have rapidly changed his mind about Maximus. For Maximus's cruelty, see also Sulpicius Severus, *Dialogues*, 3.15, and Pacatus, 25–26.

his ship into the waves and drowned.[395] Through God's protection, Theodosius had won a bloodless victory.

6. Behold, how in Christian times and under Christian rulers civil wars are waged, when they cannot be avoided. Matters ended triumphantly, the city was taken, and the usurper seized. And this is the least of these wonders. Behold, in another place, the enemy army defeated and the usurper's count, more brutal than the tyrant himself, forced to commit suicide, the great number of snares undone and evaded, and the great preparations that were in vain. **7.** But no one practised treachery, no one drew up a line of battle, indeed, no one, if I may say so, drew his sword from its scabbard. That most terrible war was consummated to the point of victory without bloodshed, and that victory by the deaths of only two individuals. **8.** And in case anyone thinks that this was brought about by chance rather than by the power of God, through which all things are ordered and judged and which, proclaimed through its clear testimony, may either reduce the minds of doubters to confusion or compel them to Faith, I shall refer to a thing that everyone knows and yet is unknown to everyone: **9.** namely that after this war in which Maximus was slain, many wars as we all know, both foreign and civil, pursued Theodosius and his son, Honorius[396] down to the present, but, nevertheless, almost all of these, right down to the present day, have ended with the fruit of a clear-cut and holy victory, and with very little, or no, shedding of blood.

10. On the death of Maximus and his son Victor, whom Maximus had left as emperor of the Gauls,[397] the younger Valentinian's rule was restored and he himself crossed over into Gaul.[398] Here, while he ruled this tranquil state peacefully, he was strangled at Vienne, through the treachery, men say, of his count, Arbogastes,[399] and then hanged up on a noose in order that he might be thought to have willingly taken his own life.[400]

---

395 If we to believe Socrates, *Ecclesiastical History*, 5.14, and Sozomen, *Ecclesiastical History*, 7.14, this death was on a river. However, Zosimus, 4.47, like Orosius, more plausibly places Andragathius's death at sea.

396 See *PLRE* 1 Honorius 3.

397 Flavius Victor, AD 384–88, see *PLRE* 1 Victor 14. Victor was hunted down and killed by Theodosius's general Argobastes, Zosimus, 4.47. On the other hand, Theodosius treated Maximus's mother and daughters with great leniency. See Ambrose, *Letters*, 40.32.

398 Theodosius's presence in Italy meant that Valentinian's passage to Gaul was one of virtual internal exile.

399 See *PLRE* 1 Arbogastes.

400 15 May AD 392. According to Zosimus, 4.54, Argobastes openly murdered Valentinian. Socrates, *Ecclesiastical History*, 5.25, is of the same opinion, as is Zosimus, 4.53–54.

11. On the death of the Augustus Valentinian, Arbogastes soon found the nerve to set up Eugenius as a usurper.[401] He picked a man to whom he could give the title of emperor, but he, a barbarian overly endowed with audacity and might in mind, council, and deed, intended to run the empire. He gathered together from all sides a vast number of undefeated troops, both garrisons of Romans and barbarian auxiliaries, trusting in his rank to influence one group and his kinship to influence the other. **12.** There is no need to describe at length events that many witnessed and that those who actually saw them know better than myself. Arbogastes himself, on both occasions, is the best proof that Theodosius always triumphed through the power of God and not through trusting in man's ingenuity. For when he served Theodosius, Arbogastes captured Maximus, even though that man had the stoutest defences, with the minimum of effort. But then when he rushed out against the same Theodosius, with the united strength of the Gauls and Franks, and placing reliance on his devoted worship of idols, he was very easily laid low. **13.** Eugenius and Arbogastes drew up their line of battle on the plains. They cunningly placed forward ambush parties on the narrow slopes of the Alps and in the passes which Theodosius had to cross, planning that, though they were weaker in numbers and strength,[402] they would triumph simply by their tactics.

Sozomen, *Ecclesiastical History*, 7.22, perhaps knowing that Valentinian had been frustrated in his attempt to cashier Arbogastes (see Zosimus, 4.53), also states that the emperor committed suicide, but also notes that 'some' asserted that the Valentinian had committed suicide out of frustration that he was not allowed to act as he wished, perhaps implying he was under a form of *de facto* house arrest. Matthews (1975) 238 is inclined to believe that Valentinian did indeed commit suicide, see also Croke (1976). Valentinian was buried in Milan and his funeral oration delivered by St Ambrose, *On the Death of Valentinian (De Obitu Valentiniani)* = CSEL 73 329–67.

401 See *PLRE* 1 Eugenius 6. Eugenius, a teacher of rhetoric, was the *magister* of one of the imperial *scrinia*, (or state secretarial bureaux). He was proclaimed emperor at Lyons on 22 August AD 392, *Consularia Constantinopolitana* s.a. 392. Whether or not the rebellion began as a pagan reaction to Theodosius's aggressive Christian politics, it rapidly took on pagan overtones. Eugenius himself professed Christianity, but was said to have been a crypto-pagan; see Sozomen, *Ecclesiastical History*, 7.22. On their departure from Milan to confront Theodosius, Argobastes and Eugenius threatened to stable their horses in the town's Christian basilica when they returned; Paulinus, *Life of Ambrose*, 31 = *PL* 14 37. For the use of pagan symbolism at the Battle of Frigidus itself see Augustine, *City of God*, 5.26, and Theodoret, *Ecclesiastical History*, 5.24.4; 5.24.17. Eugenius's rule lasted until September AD 394. He is much praised by Zosimus, 4.54.

402 Orosius, in order to make a pious point, contradicts himself. After previously stating that Arbogastes had more troops than Theodosius, 7.35.11–12, he now admits that he was the weaker party.

14. But Theodosius, standing on the summit of the Alps, devoid of food and sleep, knowing that he had been abandoned by his men, though not knowing that he was surrounded by his enemies, lay with his body on the ground and, with his mind fixed on heaven, prayed to the Lord Christ: one man praying to the One God Who can bring about all things. **15.** Then, after he had passed a sleepless night in constant prayer[403] and left as witnesses almost lakes of tears through which he purchased the protection of heaven, alone he loyally took up his arms, knowing that he was not alone. He gave the sign of the Cross as the sign for battle and marched to war assured of victory regardless of whether anyone should follow him.[404] **16.** Arbitio, the Count of the enemy forces, was *his first step on the road to salvation.*[405] Although he had trapped the unwitting emperor in an ambush,[406] he was moved to reverence in the presence of his Augustus, and not only freed him from danger, but even gave him support.

17. However, when he arrived within range to give battle, straightaway a great, ineffable whirlwind[407] blew in his enemies' faces. Our javelins were carried through the air further than they can be thrown by human hands and, born over the void, were almost never allowed to fall before they had found their mark. **18.** Moreover, the incessant whirlwind at one moment lashed the enemies' breasts and faces, beating their shields heavily against them, at another rendered them immobile by pressing their shields hard against them, at another laid them bare, violently snatching their shields away, and at another forced them to turn their backs to their opponents, spinning their shields around. Even the spears that the enemy threw with all their might, were caught up by the blast of the wind, had their strength reversed, and were forced back again, transfixing their unfortunate owners.[408] **19.** In a

---

403 Orosius wishes his reader to draw a parallel with the Agony in the Garden; see Matthew 26.36–46; Mark 14.35–41; and Luke 22.39–46.

404 A parallel with Christ's journey to Calvary, the *Via Dolorosa*, is implied. According to Socrates, *Ecclesiastical History*, 5.25, Theodosius's recourse to prayer happened after his vanguard, composed of Gothic auxiliaries, had been severely mauled by Eugenius's troops. Given Orosius's attitude to the Goths, see 7.35.9 below, it is unsurprising that he suppresses this detail.

405 Virgil, *Aeneid*, 6.96.

406 Arbitio's troops had sealed off Theodosius's line of retreat.

407 The wind known as the 'Bora'.

408 For this miraculous aid, see Claudian, *Panegyric on the Emperor Honorius's third consulate* (*Panegyricus de Tertio Consulatu Honorii Augusti*), 93–95 and Ambrose, *Explanation of the Psalms*, 36.25.2–4 = *CSEL* 64.91. Apart from this miracle, Theodoret asserts that St John and St Philip accompanied Theodosius's army.

panic produced by human conscience,[409] they looked to their own safety and, after a small group of them had been routed, the enemy army straight-away prostrated itself before the triumphant Theodosius.[410] Eugenius was captured and executed, while Arbogastes fell by his own hand.[411] And so the civil war was ended by the deaths of these two men, apart from the 10,000 Goths who, it is said, were Theodosius's advance guard and were completely wiped out by Arbogastes. But to lose them was a gain and their defeat was a victory.[412]

20. I am not insulting my detractors,[413] but let them produce from any time since the foundation of the City one example of a war begun through such pious necessity which was so easily brought to a close by such Divine aid and calmed though such good-will and forgiveness; where battle did not produce much slaughter[414] nor victory blood-stained vengeance. Then, perhaps, I will concede that these things do not seem to have been granted because of the faith of a Christian leader. **21.** But I have no fears of their testimony, since one of them, a famous poet, though a notorious pagan, has left a record of the event for God and for man in these verses:

> *O deeply beloved of God, for you the sky joins battle*
> *And the winds banded together come to the trumpet's call.*[415]

409 i.e. the miracle, as Orosius would have it, of the whirlwind showed Eugenius and Arbogastes' men that God was against them.

410 The Battle of the River Frigidus, (the modern Wippach) fought on 5 and 6 September AD 394. Orosius's account closely parallels that of Ambrose, *Explanation of the Psalms*, 36.25. Zosimus, 4.58, gives a very different account in which Eugenius gave his troops leave to feast after they had defeated Theodosius's Gothic troops and Theodosius fell upon them unawares the following morning.

411 Eugenius was beheaded and his head paraded through Italy on a spear; Zosimus, 4.58, and John of Antioch, *fr.* 187. According to Socrates, *Ecclesiastical History*, 5.25, and Sozomen, *Ecclesiastical History*, 7.24, Eugenius was beheaded by Theodosius's troops as he grovelled at the emperor's feet. For Argobastes' suicide, see the passages from Zosimus, Socrates, and Sozomen cited above, and also Claudian, *Panegyric on the Emperor Honorius's Third Consulate,* 102f.

412 This is the nearest Orosius comes to mentioning the inconclusive first day of fighting when half of Theodosius's 20,000 Gothic *foederati* and his Iberian general, Bacurius, were killed; see Jordanes, *History of the Goths*, 28. Orosius seems to have forgotten his maxim that all Christians are brothers at this point.

413 Orosius's pagan critics.

414 The 10,000 slain Goths may have disputed this point.

415 Claudian, *Panegyric on the Emperor Honorius's Third Consulate*, 96–98. The quotation is a bowdlerised version given by Augustine, *City of God*, 5.26. In the original, Claudian attributes the miracle of the whirlwind to the god Aeolus. 'O deeply beloved of God, *for whom Aeolus pours forth armed storms from his caves*, for whom the sky joins battle and the

22. This was Heaven's judgment between the party which had no human help, but humbly placed its hope in God alone, and that which had the arrogant presumption to trust in its own strength and idols.

23. Theodosius having set the state at peace and rest died at Milan.[416]

36

1. 1,149 years after the foundation of the City, Arcadius Augustus, whose son, Theodosius, now rules the east, and Honorius Augustus, his brother, whom the state obeys today, began their joint rule as the 41st emperors; they were divided only by where they lived.[417] Arcadius lived for twelve years after the death of his father and, when on his deathbed, gave his supreme power to his son Theodosius, who was still a child.[418]

2. Meanwhile Count Gildo,[419] who had been governor of Africa at the beginning of the two's reign, as soon as he learnt of Theodosius's death, either motivated by envy, as some say, tried to join Africa to the eastern part of the empire,[420] **3.** or, as another opinion holds, believing that there was little hope to be had in the rule of two young boys, above all, because, apart from these two, no boy who had previously been left with supreme power had had an easy journey to maturity and adulthood, and these two were virtually alone (for divided from one another and abandoned, it was only Christ's protection which guarded them for the sake of their father's, and their own, great faith), he dared to cut Africa off from the state and take it for

---

winds banded together come to the trumpet's call.' It is unclear whether Orosius knew these verses other than from Augustine, but even had he done so, their modification would not have troubled him.

416 Theodosius's funeral oration was delivered by Ambrose, *On the Death of Theodosius* (*De Obitu Theodosii*) = CSEL 73 371–401. His body was finally buried in Constantinople beside those of Constantine and his successors in the Church of the Apostles. For a hostile ancient assessment of Theodosius, see Zosimus, 4.59. For a modern discussion of Theodosius's reign, see Friell and Williams (1994).

417 Orosius's chronology is one year awry. The two brothers began their reigns in 1148 *AUC*/AD 395. Honorius ruled from AD 395–423, Arcadius from AD 395–408. Despite Orosius's insistence on their unity, the rule of Honorius and Arcadius in AD 395 is normally taken as the beginning of the division of the Roman Empire into two separate units and relations between the two courts were far from ideal.

418 Orosius is wrong about Arcadius's son, Theodosius II. Arcadius made him co-ruler in AD 403, long before his death in AD 408.

419 See *PLRE* 1 Gildo.

420 This is the view of Zosimus, 5.11, who states that the most powerful of Arcadius's court eunuchs, Eutropius, supported Gildo precisely to bring this about.

himself. He did this more because he enjoyed the licentious pagan life there than through being puffed up with hopes of becoming emperor.[421] **4.** He had a brother, Mascezil, who was horrified at his preparations for revolution and returned to Italy, leaving his two young sons with the African army. Gildo, seeing the absence of his brother, but the presence of his sons, as suspicious, captured them by treachery and killed them.[422]

5. His brother Mascezil was then dispatched to wage war on him as an enemy of Rome, for his recent sorrow at his family bereavement held out the promise that he was the right man to look after the state's interests.[423] Now Mascezil already knew from Theodosius's example how much a man's prayers made in the Faith of Christ obtain from God's mercy in desperate circumstances, and he went to the Isle of Capraria[424] whence he took with him some holy servants of God who were moved by his prayers. With them he spent his time in praying, fasting, and singing psalms, ceasing neither by day and nor by night, and so earned a victory without fighting and Africa's reconquest without bloodshed.[425]

6. There is a river called the Ardalio, which flows between the cities of

421 Gildo was a Moorish prince, a son of king Nabul, who was appointed Count of Africa in AD 385 and promoted to supreme military command in Africa as *Commander of both Arms* (i.e. infantry and cavalry) in Africa, *Magister utriusque militiae per Africam*, at some time before 30 December AD 393 (*Theodosian Code*, 9.7.9), receiving this title for his help in suppressing the rebellion of his brother, Firmus, in Africa; see 7.33.5–6 above. He had been restive prior to his rebellion, refusing to send support to Theodosius in his campaign against Eugenius. Gildo appears to have been a strong supporter of the schismatic Donatist church as Augustine brands the Donatist bishop Optatus as Gildo's man, 'Gildonianus' (*Arguments on Baptism opposing the Donatists (De Bapistismo contra Donatistas*, 2.11 = PL 43 137). The death of Theodosius may have been a catalyst for Gildo's outright rebellion in AD 397 which cut Rome off from its major food supply. Of the two motives that Orosius suggests for the rebellion, the most likely is that Gildo wanted to attach Africa to the eastern empire. This is the view of Zosimus, 5.11, who states that Gildo was urged to rebel by the influential eunuch at Constantinople, Eutropius.

422 See Claudian's unfinished poem *The War against Gildo (De Bello Gildonico)*, 1.390–98. Zosimus, 5.11, has a more self-interested account in which Gildo conspires against his brother in a 'barbarian frenzy' and forces him to flee to Stilicho in Italy.

423 See *PLRE* 1 Mascezel. Ironically Mascezil had fought with Firmus against Rome and Gildo in the uprising of AD 372–73; see Ammianus Marcellinus, 29.5.11.

424 Capraja, lying between Corsica and Tuscany. See also Claudian, *The War against Gildo*, 415–23. Sánchez Salor's (1982), 258 n. 483, identification of the island as Cabrera should be resisted. The island was a singularly appropriate destination for Mascezel, as the main article of manufacture on the island was a coarse goat-hair shirt, used at times of penance (see Augustine, *Letters*, 48).

425 cf. the comments on Theodosius's victory at 7.35.20.

Thebeste and Ammedera.[426] He camped here with a small band, some 5,000 soldiers they say,[427] facing an enemy 70,000 strong. After a short delay, he decided to leave his position and cross the narrow pass of a valley lying in front of him. **7.** As night fell, the blessed Ambrose, the bishop of Milan who had died shortly before,[428] appeared to him in a dream, beckoning to him with his hand and striking the ground three times with his staff saying, 'Here, here, here.' Mascezil wisely interpreted this as meaning that victory had been assured him through the merits of the man who had brought him the news; through his words, its place; and through their number, the day. **8.** He stayed in his position and finally on the third day after a night-vigil of hymns and prayers, he set forth from the mysteries of the Holy Sacraments against the enemy who had surrounded him. **9.** As he hurled his pious words of peace at the first enemies he encountered, Mascezil struck on the arm with his sword a standard-bearer, who arrogantly stood in his way and was on the point of starting the battle. The man's hand was paralysed by the blow and he was forced to lower his standard to the ground. **10.** When they saw this, the rest of the enemy's army thought that their vanguard had surrendered, turned their banners round, and fought to surrender themselves to Mascezil. The great host of barbarians whom Gildo had brought to fight, after being abandoned by the defection of his regular troops, fled in all directions.[429] **11.** Gildo himself fled, seizing a ship to put out to sea, but he was summoned back to Africa and strangled to death a few days later.[430]

12. If the testimony of those who were there did not come to our aid, we would be in danger of being accused of presumptuous, shameless lying when speaking about such great miracles. There was no ambush, nor any bribery – 70,000 of the enemy were defeated almost without a fight. The vanquished fled in a timely fashion lest the enraged victor dare to do more, and Gildo was spirited away to a different place so that his brother would not know he had been killed and that he had been avenged by his death.

13. It is true that this same Mascezil became puffed up with arrogance by his success, forgot his association with the saints with whose help he had beforehand triumphantly fought for God, and dared to desecrate a church; not hesitating to drag some men out of it. Punishment followed this

---

426 The modern Tebessa and Haïdra in Algeria.
427 The units are listed by Claudian, *The War against Gildo*, 1.415–23.
428 St Ambrose died in AD 397.
429 The battle took place on 31 July AD 398.
430 According to Zosimus, Gildo hanged himself immediately after the battle to avoid capture.

sacrilege, for after some time had passed, he alone was punished while those whom he had dragged from the church to punish were still alive and derided him. And so he made himself an example that divine judgment always has two sides, for when he placed his hope in it, he was helped, when he spurned it, he was killed.[431]

37

1. Now after the care of the two children and the affairs of the two palaces had been entrusted by the old emperor Theodosius to the two most powerful men in the state: namely Rufinus at the court of the east and Stilicho in the western empire, their ends show what each did and tried to do.[432] One tried to take royal power for himself,[433] the other to take it for his son.[434] The former brought barbarians into the empire and the latter helped him to do so in order that after the state had suddenly been thrown into disorder, their criminal ambitions could be covered up by pleading the necessity of the state.

2. I shall say nothing about how King Alaric and his Goths were often defeated and often trapped, but always allowed to go free.[435] I shall say nothing about those terrible acts done at Pollentia,[436] when supreme

431 Zosimus, 5.11, holds that Mascezil was a victim of Stilicho's envy and drowned by being pushed off a bridge in Rome. Orosius probably collected some of the details of his account of Gildo's rebellion during his stay in Africa.

432 For Rufinus, see *PLRE* 1 Rufinus 18. A Gaul by origin, Rufinus was made Praetorian Prefect of the east in AD 392. He had been *de facto* ruler of the east since Theodosius has marched from Constantinople to face Maximus in AD 394. For Stilicho, see *PLRE* 1 Stilicho. Stilicho, is spelt Stilico in our manuscript tradition, but for ease of reference the standard spelling has been retained in this translation. Stilicho was half-Vandal and had married Theodosius's niece, Serena, in AD 393 when he was made *magister militum*. Theodosius made him Honorius's guardian and put him in command of the western empire after the Battle of Frigidus, but before the onset of his illness. For the two's dominance of the state, see Zosimus, 5.1.

433 Zosimus, 4.51, hints that Rufinus may have been tempted to usurp the eastern empire. He was killed through the machinations of Stilicho and Arcadius's court eunuch, Eutropius, on 27 November AD 397; see Zosimus, 5.7–8. According to Zosimus, 5.5, Rufinus had invited Alaric and the Visigoths to invade the empire. However Socrates, *Ecclesiastical History*, 6.1 and Sozomen, *Ecclesiastical History*, 8.1, state that he had been conspiring with the Huns. Orosius displays no interest or knowledge of the affairs of the eastern empire after Rufinus's death.

434 Stilicho, see 7.38.1 below.

435 See *PLRE* 1 Alaricus. This is a reference to Alaric's first invasion of Italy AD 401–403.

436 The modern Pollenzo.

command was given to a barbarian, pagan general, namely Saul,[437] who in his wickedness violated the most revered days of the year and Holy Easter, forcing the enemy, who had withdrawn in respect for religion, to fight. Then God showed in a brusque judgment what His favour can do and what His vengeance exacts, for we won the battle, but were vanquished in our victory.[438] **3.** I shall say nothing about the savage fighting between the barbarians themselves, when two formations of Goths, followed by the Vandals and Huns, ripped each other apart in varied acts of slaughter.

4. Radagaisus, who was by far the most barbarous of all Rome's present and past foes, suddenly launched an invasion into all of Italy.[439] They say that there were more than 200,000 Goths among his people.[440] **5.** Apart from the incredible size of his host and his own indomitable courage, because he was a pagan and a Scythian,[441] he had vowed, as is the custom among barbarous nations of this kind, to placate his gods by sacrificing every last drop of Roman blood to them. **6.** When this danger loomed over Rome's defences, all the pagans gathered together in the City, saying, 'An enemy has arrived who is powerful because of the size of his forces, but more than this, because he has the protection of the gods, while the City has been abandoned by them and will soon perish because she has lost her gods and their sacred rites.' **7.** This sort of moaning was heard everywhere, and straightaway there was talk of beginning to sacrifice again. The whole City seethed with blasphemy, and everywhere the name of Christ was insulted as if it were the plague of the times.

8. So it was brought about by the ineffable judgment of God that, since among this divided people grace was owed to the pious, but to the impious punishment and it was right to give passage to enemies, though not those that

437 See *PLRE* 1 Saul.

438 The Battle of Pollentia was fought against a Gothic army under Alaric on Easter Day, 6 April AD 402, hence Orosius's disgust. Saul is likely to have been an Alan, Orosius suppresses the fact that he had been one of Theodosius's generals in the campaign leading to the Battle of Lake Frigidus; see Zosimus, 4.57. The *post eventum* defeat was that Alaric was allowed to retreat in good order. In fact, the battle appears to have resulted in a stalemate; see Prudentius, *Against Symmachus (Contra Symmachum)*, 2.717–20.

439 See *PLRE* 1 Radagaisus. Ragadaisus was a pagan who invaded Italy from Pannonia in late AD 405 with a band of Ostrogoths. For the sentiments underlying Orosius's treatment of Radagaisus, see Augustine, *City of God*, 5.23.

440 It also contained Alans and Vandals. Zosimus, 5.26, gives a total number of 400,000. Bury (1958), 1.167 n. 3, would place the number at no more than 50,000, regarding Orosius's figure like others from antiquity as a 'gross exaggeration'.

441 Radagaisus is more likely to have been a German.

would kill everyone by indiscriminate slaughter, so that they could chastise the City, which for the most part was inflexible and hostile to the faith, more severely than usual, at that time two Gothic tribes, led by their two most powerful kings, raged through Rome's provinces. **9.** One of these was Christian, more like a Roman, and, as events have proved, less savage in his slaughter through his fear of God.[442] The other was a pagan and barbarian, a true Scythian, whose insatiable cruelty loved slaughter for slaughter's sake as much as glory and plunder. This man entered the heart of Italy at this time and, drawing near, made Rome tremble and quake with terror. **10.** Now if the power of exacting vengeance had been given to this man whom Rome thought especially dangerous because he had courted the favour of the gods by sacrificing to them, the slaughter would have been all the worse, leaving no chance for repentance, and error would have taken root anew, worse than before. For had they fallen into the hands of a pagan idolator, not only would those pagans who survived indubitably have been convinced to renew the cult of idols, but Christians too would have become dangerously confused, since they would have been terrified by this judgment, while the pagans would have been strengthened in their faith by what had happened. **11.** Therefore, God, the Just Director of the human race, willed the pagan enemy to perish, but allowed the Christian one to triumph so that the pagans and the blasphemous Romans might both be confounded by the destruction of the former and be punished by the onset of the latter. Moreover, the moderation and devout faith, so admirable in a king, of the emperor Honorius earned no small measure of Divine mercy.

12. God granted that the minds of Rome's other enemies be inclined to give her help against Radagaisus, her most terrible enemy: for Uldin[443] and Sarus,[444] the leaders of the Huns and Goths came to defend Rome.[445] But God did not allow what had been brought about by His power to be seen to be the result of human courage, least of all that of the enemy. **13.** For the Godhead drove the terrified Radagaisus into the Fesulanian hills[446] and through overwhelming, all-encompassing panic trapped his 200,000

---

442 Alaric and his people. Orosius goes on to make great play of Alaric's Christianity, conveniently forgetting that Alaric and the Goths were Arians, a heresy that he has ferociously denounced.

443 See Maenchen-Helfen (1973) 59–72.

444 See *PLRE* 2 Sarus.

445 In fact, it was Stilicho who led the resistance to Radagaisus (see Zosimus, 5.26), but Orosius, who has an intense dislike of him, suppresses this fact. Sarus was an independent Gothic chieftain whom Alaric alienated, upon which he allied with Honorius; see Zosimus, 6.13.

446 The modern Fiesole.

men (according to the lowest figure we find among historians[447]): devoid of plans or provisions on a bare, brutal hillside, forcing a host which a short time before all Italy had not seemed big enough to hold onto one small summit in the hope it could hide there. **14.** Why should I delay my account any longer? No battle-line was drawn up, there was none of the uncertainty that the frenzy and fear of battle brings, no murder was done, no blood was spilled, nor, above all, and this is normally regarded as good fortune, were there any losses in the battle which were 'compensated' by its ending in victory.[448] Our men ate, drank, and made merry, while such a barbarous enemy starved, grew thirsty, and languished away. **15.** This, however, was not enough for the Romans, until they knew that they had captured and imprisoned him whom they feared – the idolator whose sacrifices were more feared than his arms – and then sneered at this man whom they had defeated without a battle as they led him under the yoke loaded with chains. For King Radagaisus whose only hope had been to flee, had secretly deserted his own people, but had then fallen into the hands of our own men, who took him captive, held him prisoner for a short while, and then killed him.[449] **16.** It is said that there were so many Gothic prisoners that everywhere herds of men were bought for a single gold coin, just like the poorest sort of cattle. But God did not allow any of that people to survive, for straightaway all those who were bought began to die so that those who had wickedly bought them spent to their sorrow in burying them that which they had saved to their shame in buying them.[450] **17.** Rome was so ungrateful that she did not realise that the indirect working of God's Judgment was not to pardon their presumption in committing idolatry, but to put an end to it, so straightaway she was to suffer God's Wrath, though not in full measure, for He loyally remembered the saints, both living and dead, there. In this way, the incursion of King Alaric, their enemy, though a Christian one,[451]

---

447 See 7.37.4 above.

448 Augustine, *City of God*, 5.23, on the other hand, speaks of 100,000 barbarians being killed, with no Roman casualties. Zosimus, 5.26, too, speaks of a massacre. Orosius also suppresses the fact that some 12,000 of Radagaisus's men were recruited into the Roman army; see Olympiodorus, *fr.* 9.

449 Radagaisus was killed on 23 August AD 406.

450 A triumphal arch was built at Rome to celebrate the victory; see CIL VI 1196. Again, we can see that Orosius has no complaint against slavery *per se*: his complaint is not about the vanquished being enslaved, but about slaves being bought at an unfair price.

451 Orosius deliberately omits the fact that Alaric was an Arian, a heresy that he has previously fiercely denounced (see 7.28.23 above), as this would destroy his comparison of the two enemies of Rome.

was put off for a short while, in case she should repent of her confusion and learn to be faithful from what she had experienced.

38

1. Meanwhile Count Stilicho, offspring of that effete, greedy, treacherous, and sorrow-bringing race, the Vandals,[452] thought it was not enough to rule under a ruler and strove by all means possible to substitute as ruler his own son Eucherius, whom, most historians say even then, while he was a young boy and held no official post, was planning how to persecute Christians.[453] **2.** It was for this reason that he held Alaric and the entire Gothic race in reserve to worry and wear down the state, courting him with a secret treaty, but in public refusing to countenance either war or peace. In fact, Alaric was humbly pleading for no more than peace on good terms and somewhere to settle.[454] **3.** He also roused up other tribes, openly urging them to take up arms and wiping away for the first time their fear of Rome's reputation: tribes whose numbers and forces were irresistible and who now oppress the Gallic and Spanish provinces, namely the Alans, Sueves, Vandals, and also the Burgundians who were stirred up by the movement of these others.

4. The wretch wanted them to shake the banks of the Rhine and attack the Gallic provinces in the hope that under these straitened circumstances he could wrest power from his son-in-law and hand it over to his son, and that the barbarian tribes would prove as easy to suppress as they were to spur on.[455] **5.** When this panorama of high crime was revealed to Honorius and the Roman army, Stilicho, who had offered the blood of the entire human race to cover one boy in the purple, was killed by the army that was quite rightly enraged by his conduct.[456] **6.** Eucherius too was killed. He had

452 Again, Orosius shows a marked dislike for barbarians. His hostility to the Vandals may be due to his personal experience of their depredations in Spain.

453 See *PLRE* 2 Eucherius 1. Eucherius was born in AD 389 and betrothed to Honorius's sister Galla Placidia. Zosimus, 5.34, expressly denies that Stilicho sought illicitly to further his son's career, perhaps to counter allegations like the one made here.

454 Stilicho's willingness to negotiate with Alaric lost him many friends at Rome. His support for paying Alaric 4,000 pounds of gold in AD 407 (see Zosimus, 5.29) was particularly damaging.

455 There is no evidence that Stilicho was active among these tribes. His previous success against Radagaisus probably made his failure to recover Gaul look deeply suspicious in many eyes.

456 Stilicho was beheaded in Ravenna on 22 August AD 408. For a radically different assessment of Stilicho from the hostile one given here, see Zosimus, 5.34.

curried favour for himself by threatening to restore the pagans' temples and demolish churches as soon as he began to reign.[457] A few of their followers who had been party to these deep machinations were also punished along with them. In this way, with minimal effort, the Churches of Christ and a pious emperor were freed from danger and avenged and the punishment of but a few men.

7. However, after such an increase in blasphemy and no sign of repentance, the long-postponed punishment of the City finally arrived.[458]

39

1. Alaric came, besieged, threw into panic, and burst into Rome as she trembled, but he first gave the order that whoever had fled to the holy places, above all to the basilicas of the Holy Apostles Peter and Paul, were to be left safe and unharmed.[459] He also told his men that as far as possible, they must

457 Orosius is the only extant source that makes this claim.

458 This one sentence suppresses the period of chaos that broke out after Stilicho's death. First, the Roman troops in the north of Italy massacred the families of the barbarian *foederati*, provoking 30,000 of these to join Alaric; see Zosimus, 5.36. Alaric then invaded Italy and besieged Rome in the winter of AD 408/9. The siege may have reduced the inhabitants of the city to cannibalism; see Olympiodorus, *fr.* 4. Some 40,000 slaves fled to Alaric and there was an attempted resurrection of pagan rites in the City led by the City Prefect, Gabinius Barbarus Pompeianus, apparently with the complicity of Pope Innocent I; see Zosimus, 5.41–42, and Sozomen, *Ecclesiastical History*, 9.16.3. Orosius could have mentioned this incident, as it would have helped his theme that Rome was justly punished for backsliding from Christianity. However, he must have decided that this would be too damaging to his main point – that Alaric's attack on Rome was negligible compared to the sacks of the pagan past. Alaric was finally bought off for 5,000 pounds of gold, 30,000 of silver, 3,000 of pepper, 4,000 silk tunics, and 3,000 scarlet-dyed fleeces; see Zosimus, 5.41. After the breakdown of further negotiations, Alaric once again besieged Rome at the end of AD 409. This time the City, with his blessing, proclaimed the *praefectus urbi*, Priscianus Attalus (see 7.42.7 below), emperor and appointed Alaric supreme military commander of the empire, *magister utriusque militia*; see Zosimus, 6.7. Our sources imply that the Romans were happy to do this and that these events brought Honorius close to flight to the east (see Zosimus, 6.7–8), facts that Orosius cannot permit to be known about his hero. In AD 410, Alaric fell out with Attalus and had him deposed at Arimmium; see Zosimus, 6.12. It was at this point that Alaric decided to sack Rome. For a modern account of this confused period, see Matthews (1975) ch. 11.

459 Orosius's choice of verb for Alaric's entry into Rome, *inrumpere*, 'to break in', is perhaps chosen to deny any question of treachery. Procopius, *History of the Wars*, 3.2.20–32, explicitly states that the Visigoths entered the city through treachery and perhaps this was also true of Zosimus, 6.7, whose account of the sack is lost, but who hints here that the Anicii family may have betrayed Rome. Alaric entered through the Salarian Gate on 24 August AD 410. For churches as refuges in the sack, see also Augustine, *City of God*, 1.2 and 1.7.

refrain from shedding blood in their hunger for booty.

2. And in order to show all the more that this storming of the City was brought about by God's displeasure rather than the enemy's valour, it came to pass that in the same way as Lot the Just was taken away from Sodom by God's hidden providence, the blessed Innocent, the bishop of the Church of Rome, at that time had his seat at Ravenna in order that he should not see the destruction of his sinful people.[460]

3. As the barbarians rampaged through the City, it happened that in a certain convent one of the Goths, a powerful, Christian man, came across an elderly virgin, who had dedicated her life to God. When he asked her, politely, for gold and silver, **4.** steadfast in her faith, she promised him that she had a great deal and would soon bring it forth, and brought it forth. When she saw that the barbarian was astounded by the size, weight, and beauty of what she had brought out, but had no idea of the nature of the vessels, Christ's virgin said to him, **5.** 'These are the sacred vessels of the Apostle Peter, take them, if you dare, and you will be judged by your act. I dare not keep them, as I cannot protect them.' **6.** The barbarian was moved to religious awe through his fear of God and the virgin's faith, and sent a messenger to tell Alaric about these matters. He immediately ordered that all the vessels should be taken back, just as they had been found, to the basilica of the Apostle **7.** and that the virgin and any other Christians who might join her be taken there with the same degree of protection. They say that her convent was in the other half of the City, far away from the holy sites, **8.** and so each piece was given to a different individual, and they all carried the gold and silver vessels openly above their heads, providing a great spectacle for all to see. This pious parade was protected by drawn swords on every side,[461] **9.** and Romans and barbarians joined together in singing openly a hymn of praise to God. The trumpet of salvation sent its note far and wide as the City fell, calling out and rousing up even all those who were in hiding.[462] **10.** From all sides the vessels of Christ[463] came running to the vessels of Peter – even many pagans joined the Christians,

---

460 See *Genesis*, 19.16. Pope Innocent I held office from AD 402–417. Orosius suppresses the fact that Innocent was in Ravenna as part of an embassy sent from Rome to urge Honorius to negotiate with Alaric; see Zosimus, 5.45.

461 Orosius intends his reader to recall the Israelites' crossing of the Red Sea here; see 1.10.15.

462 See Matthew 24.31 (compare the use of Matthew 24.21 at 1, *pref.* 15) and Revelation 11.15.

463 i.e. Christians.

professing, though not possessing, the faith and in this way managed to save themselves for that time when they would be all the more undone[464] – and the more the Romans gathered here in their flight, the more eagerly the barbarians surrounded and defended them.

11. O sacred and ineffable discernment of Divine Judgment! O what a holy river of salvation, which rose in a small home, and, as it ran its blessed course to the seats of the saints, piously snatched up wandering souls in danger and carried them off to the bosom of salvation![465] **12.** O glorious trumpet of Christ's army, which, while calling all alike to life with its sweet music, does not rouse up the disobedient to salvation, but rather leaves them, devoid of excuses, to death. **13.** This mystery of the parade of vessels, singing of hymns, and leading forth of the people[466] was, I believe, like a great sieve through which out of the assembled population of Rome, just like out of a great mass of corn, living grains set in motion either by circumstances or by the truth, passed through all the hidden gates of the city along all the circumference of its walls.[467] **14.** All those who believed in their present salvation were received from the granary prepared by the Lord, while those left, already condemned because of their lack of belief or disobedience, remained to be burnt and destroyed like dung and straw.[468] Who can fully understand these miracles or praise them as they deserve?

15. On the third day after the barbarians had entered the city, they departed of their own free will.[469] A number of buildings had been set alight, but not on the scale of the disaster that had occurred in the 700th year from the City's foundation.[470] **16.** For, if I were to recall the fire that the Romans' own emperor Nero brought about for his own amusement, it would be beyond doubt that this second fire, started by an emperor's dissipation, could not be likened to this one, brought on by the victor's wrath.[471] **17.** Nor ought I to recall the Gauls' sack of Rome as something similar – they held Rome, treading on the ashes of the burnt, ruined city for almost a year.[472]

---

464 cf. the more charitable comments of Augustine, *City of God*, 1.1.

465 A parallel with the 'oil miracle' of Augustus, 6.18.34, is intended here.

466 Again, a parallel with the Israelites' Exodus from Egypt is intended here.

467 Orosius has in mind Amos 9.9, where we are told that God will sieve Israel through the nations because of her lack of faith, but will still preserve her.

468 An allusion to the parable of the wheat and the tares, Matthew 13.25–30.

469 A parallel with the resurrection is intended here.

470 See 6.14.5.

471 Orosius appears to have elided his great fire of Rome of 52 (50?) BC (see 6.14.4–5 and 7.2.11) with the fire in Rome during Nero's reign that occurred in AD 64; see 7.7.4–7.

472 See 2.19.7–15.

18. And so that no one should doubt that the enemy was allowed to do this in order to punish the arrogant, debauched, blasphemy of the town, at this same time the most famous buildings in the City which the enemy was unable to set alight were destroyed by lightning.[473]

40

1. And so 1,164 years after the foundation of the City, the City was breached by Alaric. Although this deed is of recent memory, if anyone were to see the great numbers of Rome's population and listen to them, he would think, as they themselves say, that 'nothing had happened', unless he were to learn of it by chance from the few ruins which still remain from the fire.

2. During the breach, Placidia,[474] Prince Theodosius's daughter, and sister of the emperors Arcadius and Honorius, was captured and married by Athaulf,[475] a kinsman of Alaric and, as if Divine Judgment had made Rome hand her over as a hostage and, as it were, a special pledge of goodwill, finding herself in an influential marriage to a powerful barbarian was of great use to the state.[476]

3. Meanwhile, two years before the breach of Rome, the Alans, Sueves, Vandals, and many other tribes with them, were, as I have mentioned, roused up by Stilicho,[477] crushed the Franks, crossed the Rhine, invaded the Gallic provinces, and marched straight through them as far as the Pyrenees. They were halted by this barrier for a time and poured back over the neighbouring provinces.

4. While they indulged in an orgy of destruction in the Gallic provinces,[478] in the British provinces Gratian, a citizen of that island, usurped power and was killed.[479] Constantine, a man from the lowest ranks of the army, lacking in any ability, and whose only appeal was in his name, was chosen in his stead.[480] Immediately he had usurped power, he invaded the Gallic

---

473 See 2.19.15.

474 See *PLRE* 2 Placidia 4.

475 See *PLRE* 2 Athaulfus.

476 Orosius is less than truthful here: Galla Placidia was captured before the sack of Rome and was not married by Athaulf until AD 413. She then married against Honorius's wishes. The wedding took place in Narbonne. For Gallia's life in general, see Oost (1968).

477 7.38.3–4.

478 For a contemporary description of the devastation wreaked in Gaul, see Orientius of Auch, *Commonitorium* 2.165–84 = CSEL 16 234.

479 See *PLRE* 2 Gratianus 3. Orosius omits the previous military usurpation of Marcus in Britain; see Zosimus, 6.3.1. Gratian ruled for four months.

480 See *PLRE* 2 Constantinus 21 and Drinkwater (1998). The self-styled Constantine III

provinces where he did great harm to the state, frequently being made a fool of by the barbarians, who broke the treaties they made with him. **5.** He sent governors[481] to the Spanish provinces. These were received obediently, but two young brothers, the noble landowners, Didymus and Verinian, acted not to usurp the usurper, but to defend themselves and their country for their lawful emperor against the usurper and the barbarians.[482] **6.** This was made clear from the order of events, for every usurper plots swiftly, makes his attempt in secret, and then openly defends his gains. The most important thing is to be seen wearing the diadem and purple before being known to have this wish. These two, however, spent a great deal of time gathering together merely their serfs[483] from their own estates, feeding them at their own expense, and, with no attempt to hide their intentions, marched to the passes in the Pyrenees without causing any disquiet.

7. Constantine sent his son Constans[484] to the Spanish provinces to fight them – O, the shame of it! He had been a monk and was made a Caesar – along with some barbarians with whom he had once made a treaty and recruited into his service, calling them the *Honoriaci*.[485] *This was the beginning of the Spanish provinces' downfall.*[486]

8. When they had killed the two brothers who were trying to defend the Pyrenean Alps with their private army,[487] these barbarians were first granted permission to plunder the fields of Palencia as a sort of reward for their

began his usurpation in AD 407. Orosius's sentiments are echoed by Sozomen, *Ecclesiastical History*, 9.11. However, Procopius, *History of the Wars*, 3.2.31, describes Constantine as 'no obscure individual', perhaps suggesting that Constantine the common soldier is a product of Honorius's propaganda.

481 *Iudices.*

482 See *PLRE* 2 Didymus 1 and *PLRE* 2 Verenianus. According to Sozomen, *Ecclesiastical History*, 9.11, Didymus and Verinian were kinsmen of Honorius. This fact is possibly suppressed by Orosius in order to make Honorius's rule seem more popular in Spain. Orosius's defensive tone here suggests that not all Spaniards were content with their emperor. Sozomen notes that the two did not initially act in concert as Orosius implies, but that later they combined their forces, attacked Lusitania, and killed many of Constantine's troops. If true, these comments also imply that Constantine commanded some support in Iberia prior to his invasion of the peninsula.

483 *Servuli.* This is a reference to *coloni*, labourers tied to the land; see *Theodosian Code*, 5.17.1. For a discussion of the institution, see Jones (1958) and Carrié (1982).

484 See *PLRE* 2 Constans 1.

485 For the nature of the *Honoriaci*, see Matthews (1975) 310 and Kulikowski (2004) 363 n. 30 who argues that their title shows they were regular troops not barbarians.

486 A close paraphrase of Virgil, *Aeneid*, 2.97.

487 The two were killed at the beginning of AD 409 by Constantine's *magister militum*, the Briton Gerontius; see 7.42.4.

victory, and then entrusted with the task of guarding the Pyrenees and their passes, this job being taken away from the old and reliable guard composed of the peasantry.[488] **9.** As a consequence, the *Honoriaci*, loaded down with plunder and further tempted by the wealth of the province to let their crimes go all the more unpunished and to have more scope for crime, betraying their watch over the Pyrenees, opened the passes and let all the tribes who were wandering through the Gallic provinces into the Spanish provinces and joined with them.[489] **10.** After indulging for a time there in great and bloody raids and causing destruction of both life and property, things for which they too now have some regret, they drew lots to divide up their gains and settled in those parts which they hold to this day.[490]

41

1. I would now have the opportunity of saying a great deal about matters of this kind, save that, according to all men, the secret voice of conscience speaks only to each man's mind individually. **2.** The Spanish provinces were invaded and suffered devastation and slaughter. But this is nothing new. For during these two years while the enemy's sword raged, they endured from barbarians what they had suffered at the hands of the Romans for some 200 years and what, indeed, they had received at the hands of rampaging Germans for nearly twelve years in the reign of the emperor Gallienus.[491] **3.** Still, what man who fears God's judgment and knows himself, his deeds, and, indeed, his thoughts, would not confess that everything he has suffered, he has suffered justly, and, in fact, endured little? Or, on the other hand, if he does not know himself or fear God, how could he argue that these things were not justly done and of little account?

4. Since this is so, God's clemency through the same piety, which He had long foretold, brought it about, in accordance with His Gospel where He continually gives the advice: *When they persecute you in one city, flee*

488 For the issue of whether a *limes* existed in Spain at this time, see Arce (1982) 66–69 and 165–68.

489 The invasion began on a Tuesday in late AD 409, 28 September or 12 October; see Hydatius, *Chronicle*, 15.42.

490 The Hasding Vandals settled in north-west Galicia, the Siling Vandals in Andalusia, to which they gave their name, (V)andalusia, the Alans in Lusitania and Carthaginiensis, and the Sueves in Southern Galicia.

491 From AD 409 until the treaty of AD 411. Orosius's account is paralleled by that of Hydatius, *Chronicle*, 40. For Spain's suffering under Roman rule, see 5.1.6. For her suffering at the hands of the Germans, see 7.22.7.

to another,[492] that anyone who wished to go out and leave could use the barbarians themselves as paid helpers and defenders. **5.** The barbarians themselves willingly offered to do this and, although they could have killed everyone and carried off all their belongings, they demanded a paltry fee to pay for their services and the task of carrying over the goods. Very many took advantage of this, **6.** but those who insolently disbelieved the Gospel of God or, with twice as much insolence, did not even listen to It, and did not give way to God's wrath, were rightly seized and destroyed by that wrath when it fell upon them.[493] **7.** However, immediately after these events, the barbarians foreswore their swords and turned to the plough,[494] and cherished the remaining Romans as allies of a kind and friends, with the result that some Romans who prefer freedom in poverty to trouble and taxation under Rome can be found among them.[495]

8. Even if the barbarians were sent into the territory of Rome for this purpose alone – that the Churches of Christ throughout the east and west alike should be filled with Huns, Sueves, Vandals, Burgundians, and a countless host of believers of different races – God's mercy should be praised and extolled, seeing that, albeit with some loss on our part, so many peoples came to recognise the Truth Which they would have been unable to find without this opportunity. **9.** For what loss is it to the Christian who yearns for the life eternal to be taken from this world at any time or in any way? Or what gain is it for a pagan who has hardened himself against the Faith in the midst of Christians, if he drags out his days a little longer, since he who gives up hope of conversion will be doomed to die in the end?

10. Now because God's judgments are ineffable and we are neither able to know them all nor explain what we know of them, I would briefly state that the chastisements of God's judgment, in whatever way they are inflicted, are rightly suffered by those who know Him and rightly suffered by those who know Him not.

---

492 In fact this is only said once in the Gospels: at Matthew 10.23. Orosius may well have thought the verse had particular meaning for his own life.

493 Orosius appears to be justifying his own flight from Spain here. Given that he wrote the *Histories* in Africa, the Donatist controversy that centred on what was the appropriate response by Christians to persecution, and which was still a live issue in the region, may also have been in his mind.

494 cf. Isaiah 2.4 and Micah 4.3.

495 See Salvian, *The Guidance of God* (*De Gubernatione Dei*), 5.21–3. Hydatius, *Chronicle*, 41, on the other hand, describes the division of Spain into various areas of barbarian influence and the 'enslavement' of the Spaniards there.

42

1. 1,165 years after the foundation of the City, the emperor Honorius, seeing that with so many usurpers opposing him, he was unable to do anything against the barbarians, ordered that these usurpers be suppressed first. Count Constantius was placed in charge of this campaign.[496] **2.** It was then that the state finally realised what advantages there were to having a Roman leader again and how much she had suffered in the long period when she had been a subject to barbarian counts.[497] **3.** Count Constantius advanced into Gaul with his army and trapped, took, and executed the emperor Constantine in the city of Arles.[498]

4. At this point, to speak about the string of usurpers as briefly as possible, Constantine's count, Gerontius,[499] a man more wicked than treacherous, killed Constans, Constantine's son, at Vienne, putting in his place a certain Maximus.[500] Gerontius was then killed by his own troops.[501] **5.** Maximus was stripped of the purple, forsaken by his Gallic troops, who crossed to Africa and were then summoned back to Italy, and now lives as a poor exile among the barbarians in Spain.[502] **6.** After these events, Jovinus, the highest-ranking man in the Gallic provinces, began a usurpation which failed as soon as it was attempted.[503] His brother, Sebastian, chose but one thing: to die as a

496 See *PLRE* 2 Constantius 17. Constantius went on to marry Galla Placidia who bore him the future Valentinian III. He was elected Augustus in AD 421, but died the same year.

497 A veiled attack on Stilicho.

498 AD 411. 'Constantine' is the usurper Constantine III, see 7.40.4. Olympiodorus, *fr.* 16, and Sozomen, *Ecclesiastical History*, 9.15, have a very different account of Constantine's death. According to these historians, Constantine fled to an oratory and was ordained as a priest. He was then sent with his son, Julian, to Honorius at Ravenna, having been promised his life, but the emperor had the two treacherously murdered before they arrived at the town. Constantine's head was exhibited on a stake at Ravenna on 18 September AD 411; see *Consularia Constantinopolitana*, s.a. 411.

499 See *PLRE* 2 Gerontius 5.

500 See *PLRE* 2 Maximus 4. Maximus was proclaimed emperor in Tarragona; see Sozomen, *Ecclesiastical History*, 9.13.1. His precise status is unknown. Sozomen, describes him as an *oikeos*, while Olympiodorus calls him a *domesticus* of Gerontius. Gregory of Tours, *History of the Franks*, 2.9, simply describes him as one of Gerontius's *clientes*.

501 According to Sozomen, *Ecclesiastical History*, 9.13, Gerontius committed suicide after being trapped by mutinous soldiers.

502 See Prosper, *Chronicle*, a. 415 = PL 27 709. Maximus was to lead a second usurpation, probably in 419. He was defeated by Asterius, the Count of the Spanish provinces, and paraded at Ravenna in Honorius's *tricennalia* celebrations in 422. See the *Ravenna Annals*, s.a. 422 and Marcellinus Comes, *Chronicle*, s.a. 422.

503 See *PLRE* 2 Iovinus 2. Orosius is being disingenuous here. Jovinus's reign lasted for

usurper – for he was killed as soon as he was declared emperor.[504]

7. What should I say of the wretched Attalus for whom it was an honour to be killed amid usurpers and a blessing to die? Alaric laughed at his puppet and watched an imperial farce in which he made, unmade, remade, and reunmade this emperor almost more swiftly than it takes to tell this tale.[505] **8.** Nor is it surprising that this wretched man should be mocked by this pomp and circumstance when his cipher of a consul, Tertullus,[506] dared to say in the senate-house, 'I shall address you, conscript fathers, as consul and high priest, for I hold one of these offices and hope for the other.' But he placed his hope in one who had no hope and was surely cursed for putting his hope in a man.[507] **9.** Attalus was carted off, like a hollow statue of an emperor, by the Goths to the Spanish provinces. He was captured while leaving there by sea to an unknown destination and taken to Count Constantine. He was then brought before the emperor Honorius, who had his hand cut off, but spared his life.[508]

---

two years. A high-born Gallo-Roman aristocrat Jovinus proclaimed himself emperor in Mainz, relying on the support of the Burgundian king, Gundahar (see *PLRE* 2 Guntarius) and the Alan king, Goar (see *PLRE* 2 Goar); see Olympiodorus, *fr.* 17. A result of this usurpation was that the Burgundians moved across the Rhine into Roman territory establishing their capital at Worms. The emperor Honorius later 'officially' granted them this land; see Prosper, *Chronicle*, a. 416 = PL 27 709. Orosius mentions the Burgundian incursion at 7.32.11–13 above. For a discussion of the usurpation, see Drinkwater (1998).

504 Jovinus proclaimed his brother Sebastian co-Augustus in AD 412. Contrary to what is implied here, he was not killed until the following year. Orosius suppresses the fact that this usurpation was not crushed by Roman forces, but by the Visigoths under Athaulf who killed Sebastian and captured Jovinus after besieging him in Valence (*Chronica Gallica 452* 69).

505 See *PLRE* 2 Attalus 2. The Visigoths deposed Attalus in AD 410, but proclaimed him emperor for a second time in AD 414. He was soon discarded by them again; see Olympiodorus, *fr.* 13.

506 See *PLRE* 2 Tertullus 1. Tertullus was consul in AD 410. According to Zosimus, 6.7.4, his appointment was a popular one.

507 As opposed to placing it in God. Tertullus's wish to be *pontifex* has sometimes been seen as a sign that Attalus wished to lead a pagan revival. Until his accession Attalus had been a pagan, but he allowed himself to be baptised by an Arian bishop on becoming emperor; Sozomen, *Ecclesiastical History*, 9.9.1. It seems unlikely therefore that a full-blooded pagan revival was intended. However, many of his senatorial allies were pagan and Tertullus was perhaps expressing a hope that the new regime would be more tolerant than that of the persecuting Honorius. It is odd that Orosius does not make more of Attalus's paganism or Arianism. According to Paul the Deacon, 13.1, Tertullus expressed a wish to become emperor to the Senate and was subsequently executed.

508 This punishment had perhaps been threatened against Honorius by Attalus or his ministers; see Zosimus, 6.8, and Olympiodorus, *fr.* 13. Attalus was exiled to the island of Lipara in AD 416.

10. Meanwhile, Heraclian, who had been dispatched as Count of Africa while Attalus exercised his ghostly reign, vigorously defended Africa against the governors sent there by Attalus and became consul.[509] **11.** His promotion made him arrogant and he made his private secretary,[510] Sabinus, his son-in-law. He was a clever, hard-working man, who would have been called wise, had he used his mental energies for peaceable ends.[511] **12.** It was with him that Heraclian acted when he suspected that he was in some sort of danger and, after illegally holding up the corn supply from Africa, he sailed to Rome with a huge fleet, certainly with one that seemed unbelievably large in our days. **13.** For he is said to have possessed 3,700 ships, a number which history does not record even Xerxes, the famous king of Persia, Alexander the Great, or any other king as possessing. **14.** But as soon as he had disembarked and started towards Rome with his troops, he encountered Count Marinus and fled in terror.[512] Seizing a ship, he returned to Carthage alone, where he was immediately killed by a group of soldiers. His son-in-law, Sabinus, fled to Constantinople from where he was brought back after a period of time and sentenced to exile.[513]

15. The destruction of this entire list of outright usurpers and insubordinate dukes was, as I have said, earned by the outstanding piety and good fortune of the emperor Honorius and was executed by the great speed and energy of Count Constantius. **16.** In those days, under Honorius's leadership[514] and with Constantius's help, peace and unity was deservedly restored to the Catholic Church throughout Africa and the Body of Christ, which is what we are, was healed, with the schism brought back to the fold. The tribune Marcellinus was put in charge of carrying out this sacred command. From the outset, he showed himself a prudent, energetic man and most eager to pursue everything that was good.[515] Count Marinus, either out of jealousy

---

509 See *PLRE* 2 Heraclianus 3. The governorship of Africa was Heraclian's reward for having killed Stilicho in person, Zosimus, 5.37. Honorius in exile at Ravenna ordered him to stop grain and oil supplies from Africa to Rome. Heraclian became consul in AD 413, just after this he rebelled against Honorius.

510 His *domesticus*.

511 See *PLRE* 2 Sabinus 4. For comments on Sabinus, see Jerome, *Letters*, 130.7.10.

512 For Marinus, see *PLRE* 2 Marinus 1. According to Hydatius, *Chronicle*, 56, Heraclian was defeated at Otricoli on the edge of Rome.

513 For Heraclian's rebellion, see Oost (1966).

514 cf. 7.37.11.

515 See *PLRE* 2 Marcellinus 10. Orosius's remarks about Marcellinus's 'pursuit of the good' refer to the Council of Carthage held in May AD 411. The 'schism' is a reference to the Donatist church which had broken away from the Catholics in AD 311 over a dispute

or after being bribed with gold, it is unclear which, had him executed at Carthage.[516] Marinus was immediately recalled from Africa, reduced to the rank of a private citizen, and dismissed to be punished or to look to the repentance of his conscience.

43

1. 1,168 years after the foundation of the City, Count Constantius halted at the city of Arles in Gaul and doing what had to be done with great energy, drove the Goths from Narbonne and forced them to depart into Spain, taking special care to cut them off from any trade by sea and stopping them importing foreign goods.[517] **2.** At this time, Athaulf was the ruler over the Gothic tribes.[518] He became king in Alaric's place, after the breaching of the City and Alaric's death. As I have mentioned, he married the emperor's captive daughter, Placidia.[519] **3.** It has often been heard, and was proved by his end, that he was clearly a keen partisan of peace and chose to fight loyally for the emperor Honorius and use the Goths' might to defend the Roman state.[520]

4. I myself heard a devout, sober, and serious man from Narbonne who had served with distinction under Theodosius, telling the most blessed priest

concerning the legitimacy of Caecilian's ordination as bishop of Carthage. The Council was composed of 284 representatives from each side of the dispute and was presided over by Marcellinus (to whom Augustine dedicated the first books of his *City of God*). Marcellinus ruled in favour of the Catholics and on 30 January AD 412 an imperial edict, *Theodosian Code*, 16.5.52, outlawed the Donatist church. Nevertheless, despite persecution (for which see Augustine, *Letters*, 133) Donatism survived until the Arabs overran North Africa in the eighth century. For the conference *acta*, see Lancel (1974) and for comments on it, Tilley (1991). For a detailed account of the schism, see Frend (1952) and Tilley (1997).

516 Marcellinus was executed in September AD 413. Orosius is our only source for Marinus being responsible for his execution.

517 The winter of AD 414/415. The Vandals made good the Goths' food shortage, selling them grain at highly inflated prices – see Olympiodorus, *fr.* 29.

518 Athaulf established his capital at Barcelona which appears to have surrendered peacefully to him.

519 See 7.40.1. Orosius does not see the union, as did his fellow Spaniard Hydatius, *Chronicle*, 57, as a fulfilment of the prophecy in Daniel 11.6, that a queen of the south would marry a king of the north.

520 Athaulf's philo-Roman attitudes can be seen in his wedding. Both he and Placidia were dressed in Roman style and classical-style wedding hymns, *epithalamia*, were sung for the couple, first by Attalus, the deposed emperor, and then by two other Romans, Rusticius and Phoebadius. The pair had a child, significantly named Theodosius, who died in infancy and was buried in a silver coffin near Barcelona; Olympiodorus, *fr.* 24, 26.

Jerome in Bethlehem, a town in Palestine, that he had been a great friend of
Athaulf in Narbonne and had learnt this about him, often before witnesses:
that when he was too full of confidence, strength, and cleverness,[521] **5.** he
was accustomed to relate that at first he earnestly had wanted to obliterate
the name of Rome and make the Romans' land the Goths' empire in both
word and deed, so that there would have been, to put it in everyday speech, a
Gothia where there had once been *Romania* and that he, Athaulf, would now
be what Augustus Caesar had once been. **6.** But when, after long experience,
he had proved to himself that, because of their wild barbarism, the Goths
were completely unable to obey the law, and because he believed it wrong
to deprive a state of laws (without which a state is not a state at all), he
chose at least to seek for himself the glory of having restored and extended
the Roman Empire by the might of his Goths and, since he could not be her
supplanter, to be remembered by posterity as the author of Rome's renewal.
7. It was for this reason that he strove to avoid war, and for this reason
that he strove to love peace. He was influenced to carry out everything
required to set things in good order by the persuasive advice of his wife,
Placidia, without a doubt a woman of keen intellect and clearly virtuous in
religion.[522] **8.** It is said that he was killed in the Spanish city of Barcelona
through the treachery of his own people, while making every effort to make
and offer peace.[523]

9. After Athaulf, Segeric was made king by the Goths, but although he
was, through God's judgment, inclined to peace in the same way, he was
nonetheless killed by his own men.[524]

10. He was succeeded on the throne by Vallia whom the Goths elected
precisely to break the peace, but who was ordained by God precisely to
strengthen it.[525] **11.** He was especially terrified by God's judgment because
in the previous year when a great band of Goths had mustered themselves
under arms and attempted to cross in their fleet to Africa, they had been
caught up in a storm twelve miles from the Straights of Cadiz and died

521 A euphemism for being drunk?

522 See Oost (1968).

523 Athaulf was murdered in August AD 415. According to Olympiodorus, *fr.* 26, the
king was killed by a retainer named Dubius who was determined to avenge his old master.
According to Jordanes, *History of the Goths*, 31, Athaulf was killed by a Goth named Everwulf
whom he had angered by sneering at his small size.

524 See *PLRE* 2 Segericus. Segeric ruled for only seven days. Orosius suppresses Segeric's
murder of Athaulf's children despite them being under Church protection and his maltreatment
of Galla Placidia; see Olympiodorus, *fr.* 26.

525 See *PLRE* 2 Vallia.

a wretched death.[526] **12.** He was also mindful of the disaster suffered in Alaric's time when the Goths had tried to cross over to Sicily and, under the eyes of their comrades, been carried off by a storm and pitiably drowned.[527] He therefore made a highly favourable peace with the emperor Honorius, giving him nobles of the highest lineage as hostages.[528] He also restored the emperor's sister, Placidia, who had lived in honour and unmolested at his court, to her brother.[529] **13.** He put himself in danger for Rome's security, attacking the rest of the tribes that had settled in Spain – he did the fighting, but conquered for Rome.[530] **14.** Moreover, all the other kings, those of the Alans, Vandals, and Sueves were disposed to make treaties on the same terms with us. They sent ambassadors to the emperor Honorius, 'Make peace with us all, and take hostages from us all,' they begged. 'We ourselves will fight and perish, but we will conquer for you, it would be an everlasting boon for your state, if we were to perish, one and all.'[531] **15.** Who would believe this, if it were not confirmed by the facts? At the present, every day we learn from frequent, reliable reports that in the Spanish provinces these people wage war and slaughter each other, and that Vallia, the king of the Goths, in particular wishes to make peace.[532]

16. For this reason, I would happily grant that this Christian epoch be freely criticised, if anything from the beginning of the world down to the present day can be shown to have been concluded with similar good fortune. **17.** We have shown, I believe, and demonstrated almost as much by pointing, as by my words, that innumerable wars have come to an end, a great number of usurpers have been put down, and the most savage tribes have been defeated, restrained, surrendered, and emptied of their strength with the minimum of bloodshed, no battles, and hardly any killing. **18.** All that remains is for our critics to repent of their efforts, blush at the truth,

---

526 i.e. the Straits of Gibraltar. Orosius is our only source for this incident, for a discussion of which see Kulikowski (2004) 169.

527 At the end of AD 410; see Olympiodorus, *fr.* 15. Orosius perhaps does not discuss the incident at length because Alaric is said to have been turned back by a pagan enchanted statue which would have suggested to his readers that paganism could be efficacious.

528 The treaty was struck in AD 416.

529 See Olympiodorus, *fr.* 31.

530 cf. 1.16.3 and 1.17.3. Vallia defeated the Alans and Siling Vandals in AD 417–18. Orosius is ever the optimist: a more cynical historian might have thought that the Goths, having failed to cross to Africa, were intent on securing Spain for themselves.

531 This speech is a fabrication by Orosius.

532 For these wars, see Hydatius, *Chronicle*, 52, 55, 59–61; *Gallic Chronicle of 511*, 33, 35–6; and Sidonius Apollinaris, *Poems*, 2.362–65.

and believe in, fear, love, and serve the One, True God for Whom all things are possible and learn that His every act, even those that they think wrong, is good.

19. In accordance with your instructions, most blessed father Augustine, I have set down, with Christ's aid, the lusts and punishment of sinful men, the conflicts of our age, and the judgments of God from the beginning of the world to the present day, that is over 5,618 years. I have done this as briefly and as clearly as possible, separating the years which through the nearer presence of Christ's grace are Christian ones from the previous chaos of disbelief. **20.** So now I am secure in the enjoyment of the one thing for which I ought to long – the fruit of my obedience.[533] As for the quality of my little works, you, who commissioned them, must see to that – if you publish them, they must be approved of by you, but if you destroy them, you will have disapproved of them.

---

533 1, *pref.* 2.

BIBLIOGRAPHY

PRIMARY SOURCES

Unless an English title is in common use, Latin titles have been retained for ease of reference. Standard works from the classical period which have only a slight bearing on Orosius's work have not been listed with editions or translations. These works can be found in the Loeb Classical Library. The reader is referred to the Loeb Classical Library or the Oxford Classical Dictionary (3rd edn) for available editions of these authors. Works with a particular relevance to Orosius have been listed with a modern English translation where available.

Anonymous Works

Acta Triumphalia, ed. A. Degrassi, *I fasti consolari dell'Impero romano*, Rome, 1954.

Acts of Pilate, ed. C. von Tischendorf in his *Evangelia Apocrypha*, Hildesheim, 1853; trans. M. R. James, *The New Testament Apocrypha*, Oxford, 1924.

Chronica Gallica 452, ed. and trans. R. Burgess in R. W. Mathisen and D. Shanzer (eds), *Gallic Society and Culture in Late Antique Gaul: Revisiting the Sources*, Aldershot, 2001.

Chronica Gallica 511, ed. and trans. R. Burgess in R. W. Mathisen and D. Shanzer (eds),), *Gallic Society and Culture in Late Antique Gaul: Revisiting the Sources*, Aldershot, 2001..

Codex Theodosianus, ed. Th. Mommsen (3 vols), Berlin, 1905; trans. C. Pharr, *The Theodosian Code and Novels*, Princeton and London, 1952.

Conference of Carthage: Acta. ed. S. Lancel, CCSL 149a, Turnhout, 1974; trans. K. J. von Hefele (vol. 1), *History of the Councils of the Church*, London, 1871.

Consularia Constantinopolitana, ed. and trans. R. Burgess in his *Chronicle of Hydatius and the Consularia Constantinopolitana: Two Contemporary*

Accounts of the Final Years of the Roman Empire, Oxford, 1993.
Consularia Ravennatia ed. Th. Mommsen in MGH Auctores Antiquissimi 9, Berlin, 1892.
Divisio Orbis Terrarum, ed. A. Riese, in *Geographi Latini Minores*, Hildesheim, 1878, 15–20.
Fasti Capitolini, ed. A. Degrassi, *I fasti consolari dell'Impero romano*, Rome, 1954.
Fasti Praenestini, ed. A. E. Gordon, *Album of Dated Latin Inscriptions*, Berkeley, 1958, no. 36.
Ilias Latina, ed. and trans. G. A. Kennedy, Fort Collins, 1999.
Peutinger Table, ed. A. Levi and M. Levi, Rome, 1967.
SHA Lives of the Caesars, ed. H. Hohl (2 vols), Leipzig, 1997; trans. D. Magie (3 vols), Loeb Classical Library: London and Cambridge, MA, 1921–32.
The Zend Avesta. ed. K. F. Geldner, Stuttgart (3 vols), 1885–96; trans. J. Darmesteter and L. H. Mills, Oxford, 1880–87.

Ancient Authors

Aeschines, *Against Ctesiphon*.
Appian, *The Civil Wars*.
Arrian, *Anabasis Alexandri*.
—— *Indica*.
Ambrose, *De Obitu Theodosii*, ed. O. Faller, CSEL 73, Vienna, 1955, 369–401; trans. J. H. W. G. Liebeschuetz, *Ambrose of Milan: Political Letters and Speeches*, Translated Texts for Historians, Liverpool, 2005.
—— *De Obitu Valentiniani*, ed. O. Faller, CSEL 73, Vienna, 1955, 327–67; trans. J. H. W. G. Liebeschuetz, *Ambrose of Milan: Political Letters and Speeches*, Translated Texts for Historians, Liverpool, 2005.
—— *De Tobia*, ed. C. Schenkl, CSEL 32.2, Vienna, 1897.
—— *Explanatio Psalmorum*, ed. M. Petschenig (rev. M. Zelzer), CSEL 64, Vienna, 1999.
—— *Letters*, ed. O. Faller (rev. M. Zelzer), CSEL 82.10.1–4, Vienna, 1968–96; partial translation (book 10), J. H. W. G. Liebeschuetz, *Ambrose of Milan: Political Letters and Speeches*, Translated Texts for Historians, Liverpool, 2005.
Ammianus Marcellinus, *Histories*, ed. W. Seyfarth (2 vols), Leipzig, 1970; trans. J. C. Rolfe (3 vols), Loeb Classical Library, London and Cambridge, MA, 1935–39.

Asconius, *Commentarium in orationem In Toga Candida*, ed. and trans. R. G. Lewis, Oxford, 2006.

Augustine, *City of God*, ed. B. Dombart and A. Kalb (2 vols), Turnhout, 1955; trans. H. Bettenson, Harmondsworth, 2003.

—— *De Baptismo contra Donatistas*, ed. M. Petschenig, CSEL 51, Vienna, 1908; trans. J. R. King and C. D. Hartranft in NPNF 1.4.

—— *De Excidio urbis Romae*, ed. and trans. M. V. O'Reilly, Washington, DC, 1955.

—— *Letters*, ed. A. Goldbacher, CSEL 34, 44, 57, 58, Vienna, 1895–1923; trans. R. J. Teske, *The Works of Saint Augustine, a translation for the 21st Century: – Letters* (4 vols), New York, 2004.

—— *Liber ad Orosium contra Priscillianistas et Origenistas*, ed. K. D. Daur, CCSL 49, Turnhout, 1985.

—— *Sermons*, ed. PL 38, 39, 46, and G. Partoens = CCSL 41, Turnhout, 1961; partial translation, R. J. Teske, *St Augustine: Arianism and other Heresies*, New York, 1995.

Augustus, *Res Gestae,* ed. and trans. P. A. Brunt and J. M. Moore, Oxford, 1969.

Aulus Gellius, *Attic Nights.*

Aurelius Victor, *De Caesaribus,* ed. E. Pichlmayr (rev. R. Gruendel), Leipzig, 1970; trans. H. W. Bird, Translated Texts for Historians, Liverpool, 1994.

Avitus of Braga, *Epistula Aviti ad Palchonium*, ed. S. Vanderlinden, 'Revelatio Sancti Stephani', *Revue des Études Byzantines* 4 (1946) 173–217.

Basil of Caesarea, *Homilies*, ed. PG 29 209–494; trans. A. Clare, *Exegetic Homilies*, Washington, DC, 1963.

Braulio of Saragossa, *Letters*, ed. (and Spanish translation) L. Riesco Terrero, *Epistolario de San Braulio: introducción, edición crítica y traducción*, Seville, 1975.

Caesar, *The Civil War*, ed. S. Mariner Bigorra (2 vols), Barcelona, 1959–61; trans. J. Gardner, Harmondsworth, 2004.

—— *The Gallic War*, ed. T. Rice Holmes, Oxford, 1914; trans. J. Gardner and S. Handford, as *The Conquest of Gaul*, Harmondsworth, 2003.

(Caesar) *The African War*, ed. A. Klotz, Lepizig, 1927; trans. J. Gardner with *The Civil War*, Harmondsworth, 2003.

Cicero, *Ad Familiares.*

—— *Brutus.*

—— *De Divinatione.*

—— *De Fato.*

—— *De Oratore.*

—— *De Republica.*

—— *In Pisonem.*

—— *In Verrem.*

—— *Pro Caelio.*

—— *Pro Lege Manilia.*

—— *Pro Marcello.*

—— *Pro Murena.*

—— *Pro Sestio.*

Claudian, *De Bello Gildonico*, ed. J. B. Hall, Leipzig, 1985; trans. M. Platnauer, *Claudian* (vol. 1), Loeb Classical Library: London and New York, 1922.

—— *De Raptu Proserpina*, ed.and trans. C. Gruzelier, Oxford, 1993.

—— *In Rufinum*, ed. J. B. Hall, Leipzig, 1985; trans. M. Platnauer, *Claudian* (vol. 1), Loeb Classical Library: London and New York, 1922.

—— *Panegyricus de tertio consulatu Honorii Augusti*, ed. J. B. Hall, Leipzig, 1985; trans. M. Platnauer, *Claudian* (vol. 1), Loeb Classical Library: London and New York, 1922.

Clement *Stromata*, ed. O. Stählin and L. Früchtel (2 vols) Berlin, 1960, 1970; trans. A Coxe, as 'Miscellanies' in A. Roberts and J. Donaldson (eds), ANF 2.

Cornelius Nepos, *Life of Iphicrates.*

Cyprian, *Treatises*, ed. R. Weber, M. Bévenot, M. Simonetti and C. Moreschini (2 vols), CCSL 3, 3A, Turnhout, 1972–76; trans. E. Wallis in A. Roberts and J. Donaldson (eds), ANF 5.

Dio, *Histories.*

Diodorus Siculus, *Universal History.*

Ennius, *Annals*, ed. O. Skutsch, *The Annals of Q. Ennius*, Oxford, 1985.

—— *Medea*, ed. H. D. Jocelyn, Cambridge, 1967.

Euripides, *Hecuba.*

—— *Iphigenia in Tauris.*

Eusebius, *Ecclesiastical History*, ed. Th. Mommsen, Liepzig, 1903; trans. K. Lake (2 vols), Loeb Classical Library, London and Cambridge, MA, 1926, 1932.

—— *Life of Constantine*, ed. F. Winkelmann, Berlin, 1975; trans. A. Cameron and S. G. Hall, Oxford, 1999.

Eutropius, *Breviarium*, ed. J. Hellegouarc'h, Paris, 1999; trans. H. W. Bird, Translated Texts for Historians, Liverpool, 1993.

Florus, *Epitome of Roman History*, ed. P. Jal, Paris, 1967; trans. E. Forster, Loeb Classical Library, London and Cambridge, MA, 1929.

Fulgentius, *De Aetatibus Mundi et Hominis,* ed. R. Helm, Leipzig, 1898; trans. L. G. Whitbread, *Fulgentius the Mythographer*, Columbus, 1971.

Galen *Commentarium in Hippocratis librum De Natura Hominum*, ed. G. Helmreich (= *Corpus Medicorum Graecorum* V 9,1), Leipzig and Berlin, 1914.

Gelasius, *Letters*, ed. A. Thiel, *Epistolae Romanorum Pontificum Genuinae* (vol.1), Braunsberg, 1868.

Gennadius, *De Scriptoribus Ecclesiasticis*, ed. C. A. Bernoulli (as *De Viris Illustribus*), Freiburg, 1895.

Gildas, *De Excidio et Conquestu Britanniae*, ed. and trans. M. Winterbottom, Chichester, 1978.

Gregorius Nazianzus, *Orationes in Julium*, ed. P. Gallay, Berlin, 1969.

Herodotus, *Histories.*

Hirtius, *The Gallic War*, ed. T. Rice Holmes, Oxford, 1914; trans. J. Gardner and S. Handford, as *The Conquest of Gaul*, Harmondsworth, 2003.

Gregory of Tours, *A History of the Franks*, ed. B. Krusch and W. Levison (= MGH Scriptores Rerum Merovingicarum 1.1), Hanover, 1951; trans. L. Thorpe, Harmondsworth, 2005.

Horace, *Odes.*

Hydatius, *Chronicle,* ed. and trans. R. Burgess in his *Chronicle of Hydatius and the Consularia Constantinopolitana: Two Contemporary Accounts of the Final Years of the Roman Empire*, Oxford, 1993.

Hyginus, *Fabulae*, ed. J.-Y. Boriaud, Paris, 1997; trans. R. S. Smith and S. M. Trzaskoma, Indianapolis, 2007.

Irenaeus, *Adversus Haereses*, ed. A. Rousseau, L. Doutreleau, B. Hermmerdinger and C. Mercier (5 vols), Paris, 1965–82; trans. R. M. Grant in his *Irenaeus of Lyons*, London, 1997.

Isidore of Charax, *Parthian Stations*, ed. and trans. W. H. Schoff, London, 1914.

Isidore of Seville, *Etymologies,* ed. M. C. Díaz y Díaz, Madrid, 1982; trans. S. Barney, W. Lewis, J. Beach and O. Berghof, Cambridge, 2006.

Jerome, *Commentaria in Daniel*, ed. F. Glorie, CCSL 75A, Turnhout, 1964; trans. G. L. Archer, Grand Rapids, 1958.

—— *Commentaria in Ezekiel*, ed. F. Glorie, CCSL 75, Turnhout, 1964.

—— *Chronicle*, ed. R. Helm (= *Griechischen Christlichen Schriftsteller* 47), Berlin, 3rd edn, 1984; trans. M. Drew Donaldson, Lewiston, 1996.

—— *De Viris Illustribus*, ed. A. Ceresa-Gastaldo, Florence, 1988; trans. E.

Cushing Richardson as *Lives of Illustrious Men* in NPNF 2.3.

—— *Letters*, ed. I. Hilberg, CSEL 54–56; trans. M. A. Fremantle in *Jerome: Letters and Select Works*, repr. Grand Rapids, 1954.

John of Antioch, *Chronicle* (fragmentary), ed. C. Muller, *Fragmenta Historicorum Graecorum*, IV, 535–622 and V, 27–28, Paris,1883.

John Chrysostom, *Homilies on Matthew*, ed. F. Field, Cambridge, 1839; trans. G. Prevost (3 vols), Oxford, 1843, 1844, 1851.

Jordanes *Getica*, ed. Th. Mommsen, (= MGH, Auctores Antiquissimi 5.1) Berlin, 1882; trans C. Mierow, *The Gothic History of Jordanes*, Cambridge, 1966.

Josephus, *Against Apion*.

—— *Antiquities of the Jews*.

—— *The Jewish War*.

Julius Obsequens, *Liber de Prodigiis*, ed. O. Jahn, Leipzig, 1853; trans. A. C. Schlesinger as *A Book of Prodigies after the 505th year of Rome*, in his *Livy Summaries, Fragments, Julius Obsequens, General Index*, Loeb Classical Library, London and Cambridge, MA, 1959.

Justin, *Epitome of Pompeius Trogus*, ed. O. Seel, Stuttgart, 1985; trans. J Selby Watson, London, 1853, partial translation, J. C. Yardley and W. Heckel, *Justin: Epitome of the Philippic History of Pompeius Trogus* (vol. 1), Oxford, 1997.

Justinian, *Digest of Roman Law*, ed. P. Kruger and Th. Mommsen, Berlin, 1870; trans. A Watson, Pennsylvania, 1985 (contains the Kruger and Mommsen text).

Lactantius, *De Mortuis Persecutorum*, ed. and trans. J. L. Creed, Oxford, 1984.

Livy, *History of Rome*. ed. W. Weissenborn et al. (6 vols), Leipzig and Stuttgart, 1887–1986; trans. B. O. Foster et al. (15 vols), Loeb Classical Library, London and New York, 1919–59.

Lucan, *Pharsalia*.

Marcellinus Comes, *Chronicle*, ed. Th. Mommsen, MGH Auctores Antiquissimi 9, Berlin, 1894; trans. B. Croke, Sydney, 1995 (contains the Mommsen text).

Marcus Aurelius, *Meditations*.

Nonnus, *Dionysiaca*.

Orientius, *Commonitorium*, ed. R. Ellis, CSEL 16.1.

Orosius, *Commonitorium de errore Priscillianistarum et Origenistarum*, ed. K. Zangemeister, CSEL 5, Vienna, 1882; trans. C. L. Hanson as 'Inquiry or Memorandum to Augustine on the Error of the Priscillianists and Origenists' in his *The Fathers of the Church: Iberian fathers 3: Pacian of Barcelona and Orosius of Braga,* Washington, DC, 1999.

—— *Liber Apologeticus contra Pelagium de Arbitrii Libertate,* ed. K. Zangemeister, CSEL 5, Vienna, 1882; trans. C. L. Hanson, as 'Book in Defense against the Pelagians', in his *The Fathers of the Church: Iberian fathers 3: Pacian of Barcelona and Orosius of Braga,* Washington, DC, 1999.

—— *Seven Books of History against the Pagans,* ed. M.-P. Arnaud-Lindet, *Orose: Histoires (contre les païens),* 3 vols, Paris, 1990–91 and K. Zangemeister, CSEL 5, Vienna, 1882; trans. I.W. Raymond, New York, 1936; Spanish translation, E. Sánchez Salor, *Orosio, Historias* (2 vols), Madrid, 1982.

Ovid, *Fasti.*

—— *Metamorphoses.*

Pacatus, *Panegyric of Theodosius,* ed. R. A. B. Mynors, in *XII Panegyrici Latini,* no.2, Oxford 1964; trans. C. E. V. Nixon and B. Saylor Rogers, *In Praise of Later Roman Emperors,* Berkeley and Los Angeles, 1994.

Paul the Deacon, *History of the Lombards,* ed. L. Bethmann and G. Waitz in MGH Scriptores Rerum Langobardorum, Hanover, 1878; trans. W. Dudley Foulke, Philadelphia, 1974.

Paulinus of Milan, *Life of St Ambrose,* ed. M. Pellegrino, Rome, 1961; trans. B. Ramsey, in his *Ambrose,* London, 1997.

Pausanias, *The Description of Greece.*

Petronius, *Satyricon.*

Philo, *De Mundo Opificio,* ed. L. Cohn and P. Wendland in their *Philonis Alexandrini Opera quae supers*unt (vol. 1), Berlin, 1915; trans. F. H. Colson and G. H. Whitaker as *On the Account of the World's Creation given by Moses* in Philo (vol. 1), Loeb Classical Library, London and New York, 1929.

Plato, *Timaeus.*

Pliny the Elder, *Natural History.*

Plutarch, *Life of Alexander the Great.*

—— *Life of Gaius Marius.*

—— *Life of Mark Antony.*

—— *Life of Tiberius Gracchus.*

—— *Roman Questions.*

Polybius, *Histories.*

Pomponius Mela, *Geography.*

Procopius, *A History of the Wars,* ed. J. Haury and rev. G. Wirth (3 vols),

Leipzig, 1962–64; trans. H. B. Dewing (5 vols), Loeb Classical Library: London and New York., 1914–28.

Prosper, *Chronicle*, ed. Th. Mommsen, MGH Auctores Antiquissimi 9, Berlin, 1892; trans. A. C. Murray, *From Roman to Merovingian Gaul: a Reader*, Ontario, 2003.

Prudentius, *Harmartigenia*, ed. M. Lavarenne in Prudence (vol. 2), Paris, 1945; trans. H. J. Thomson in Prudentius (vol. 1), Loeb Classical Library, London and Cambridge, MA, 1949.

Ptolemy, *Geography*.

—— *Tetrabiblios*.

Rufinus, *Ecclesiastical History*, ed. E. Schwartz and Th. Mommsen in *Eusebius Werke, II.1* and *II.2: Die* Kirchengeschichte, Leipzig, 1903–09, 951–1040; partial translation (books 10 and 11) P. R. Amidon, *The Church History of Rufinus of Aquileia*, Oxford, 1977.

Rutilius Namatianus, *De Reditu Suo*, ed. J. Vessereau and F. Prechac, Paris, 1961; trans. J. Wight Duff and A. M. Duff in *Minor Latin Poets* (vol. 2), London and Cambridge, MA, 1934, 753–829.

Sallust, *The War against Catiline*.

—— *The War against Jugurtha*.

Salvian, *De Gubernatione Dei*, ed. G. Lagarrigue, Paris, 1975; trans. J. F. O'Sullivan in his *Writings of Salvian, the Presbyter*, Washington, DC, 1947.

Seneca, *De Tranquillitate Animi*.

—— *Letters*.

Servius, *Commentaries on the Aeneid*, ed. G. Thilo and H. Hagen (3 vols), Leipzig, 1881–1902, repr. Hildesheim, 1986.

Severus of Minorca, *Epistola ad Omnem Ecclesiam de Virtutibus ad Judaeorum Conversionem in Minorcensi Insula Factis in Praesentia Reliquarum Sancti Stephani*, ed. and trans. S. Bradbury, as *Severus of Minorca: Letter on the Conversion of the Jews*, Oxford, 1996.

Sidonius Apollinaris, *Carmina*, ed. A. Loyen, Paris, 1960; trans. W. B. Anderson, Loeb Classical Library, London and Cambridge, MA, 1936.

Silius Italicus, *Punica*.

Socrates, *Ecclesiastical History*, ed. G .C. Hansen, Berlin, 1995; trans. A. C. Zenos in NPNF 2.2.

Solinus, *Collectanea Rerum Memorabilium*, ed. Th. Mommsen, Berlin, 1895.

Sozomen, *Ecclesiastical History*, ed. J. Bidez and G. C. Hansen, Berlin, 1995; trans. C. D. Hartranft in NPNF 2.2.

Strabo, *Geography*.

Suetonius, *Lives of the Twelve Caesars*, ed. M. Ihm, Leipzig, 1908; trans C. Edwards, Oxford, 2001.

Sulpicius Severus, *Chronicle*, ed. G. de Senneville-Grave, Paris, 1999; trans. A. Roberts in NPNF 2.11.

—— *Dialogues*, ed. J. Fontaine, Paris, 2006; trans. A. Roberts in NPNF 2.11.

Symmachus, *Relationes*, ed. J. P. Callu, (3 vols), Paris, 1972–95; trans. R. H. Barrow in his *Prefect and Emperor: The Relationes of Symmachus*, Oxford, 1973.

Tacitus, *Agricola*.

—— *Annals*.

—— *Germania*.

—— *Histories*.

Tertullian, *Adversus Valentinianios*.

—— *Apology*.

—— *De Spectaculis*.

Themistius, *Orationes*, ed. G. Downey and A. F. Norman (3 vols), Leipzig, 1965–74; partial translation in P. Heather and D. Moncur, *Politics, Philosophy, and Empire in the Fourth Century: Select Orations of Themistius*, Translated Texts for Historians, Liverpool, 2001; *Orations* 8 and 10, trans. Heather and Matthews (1991); Private Orations, trans. R. J. Penella, Berkeley and Los Angeles, 2000.

Theodoret, *Ecclesiastical History*, ed. L. Parmentier (rev. G. C. Hansen), Berlin, 1998; trans. B. Jackson in NPNF 2.3.

Theophilus, *Apologia ad Autolycum*, ed. J. C. T. von Otto, Jena, 1861; trans. R. M. Grant, Oxford, 1971.

Valerius Maximus, *Memorable Deeds and Sayings*.

Varro, *De Lingua Latina*.

—— *De Re Rustica*.

Velleius Paterculus, *History*.

Virgil, *Aeneid*.

—— *Eclogues*.

—— *Georgics*.

Zonaras, *Epitome of History*, ed. M. Pinder and T. Büttner-Wobst (3 vols), Bonn, 1841–97; partial translation, T. M. Banchich and E. N. Lane, *The History of Zonaras: From Alexander Severus to the Death of Theodosius*, London and New York, 2009.

Zosimus, *New History*, ed. F. Paschoud (3 vols), Paris, 1970–93; trans. R. T. Ridley, Canberra, 1982.

SECONDARY READING

Amagro-Gorbea, M. et al. (1999), *Las Guerras Cántabricas*, Santander.

Anderson, A. R. (1932), *Alexander's Gate, Gog and Magog, and the Enclosed Nations*, Cambridge, MA.

Arce, J. (1982), *El ultimo siglo de la España romana (284–409)*, Madrid.

Arnaud-Lindet, M.-P. (1990), see Orosius, *Seven Books of History against the Pagans.*

—— (1991), see Orosius, *Seven Books of History against the Pagans.*

—— (1991a), see Orosius, *Seven Books of History against the Pagans.*

Astin, A. E. (1967), *Scipio Aemilianus*, Oxford.

Barry, K. (1999), *The Greek Qabalah*, York Beach.

Bhargava, P. L. (1996), *Chandragupta Maurya*, New Delhi.

Barbero, A. (2007), *The Day of the Barbarians*, New York.

Barnes, R. (2005), 'Cloistered Bookworms in the Chicken-Coop of the Muses: the Ancient Library of Alexandria', in Macleod (2005) 61–78.

Barnes, T. D. (1970), 'The Lost Kaisergeschicte and the Latin Historical Tradition', in *Bonner Historia-Augusta-Colloquium 1968/1969: Antiquitas Reihe 4: Beiträge zur Historia-Augusta-Forschung 7*; Bonn, 13–43. Reprinted in Barnes (1985).

—— (1971), *Tertullian: a Historical and Literary Study*, Oxford.

—— (1985), *Early Christianity and the Roman Empire*, London.

Bately, J. M. (1970), 'The Authorship of the Old English Orosius', *Anglia* 88, 289–322.

—— (1980), *The Old English Orosius*, London and New York.

Bately, J. M. and Ross, D. J. A. (1961), 'A Checklist of Manuscripts of Orosius', *Historiarum adversum Paganos Libri septem'*, *Scriptorium* 15, 329–34.

Bauman, R. (1992), *Women and Politics in Ancient Rome*, London and New York.

Bermejo, F. (1998), *La ecisión imposible: lectura del gnosticismo valentiano*, Salamanca.

Bird, H. W. (1976), 'Diocletian and the deaths of Carus, Numerian, and Carinus', *Latomus* 35, 127–32.

Birley, A. (1972), *Septimius Severus: the African Emperor*, London.

—— (1987), *Marcus Aurelius: a Biography* (rev. edn), London.

Bonamente, G. (1975), 'Il metus punicus e la decadenza di Roma in Sallustio, Agostino ed Orosio', *Giornale Italiano di Filologia* 27, 137–69.

Bosworth, A. (1978), 'Eumenes, Neoptolemus, and PSI XII 1284', *Greek,*

Roman, and Byzantine Studies 19, 227–37.

Bosworth, A. (1993), *Conquest and Empire. The Reign of Alexander the Great*, Cambridge.

Bradbury, S. (1996), see Severus of Minorca.

Briant, P. (2002), *From Cyrus to Alexander: a History of the Persian Empire*, Winona Lake.

Brunt, P. A. (1963), Review of H. D. Meyer, *Die Aussenpolitik des Augustus und die augusteische Dichtung, Journal of Roman Studies* 53, 170–76 = Brunt (1990) ch. 5.

—— (1990) *Roman Imperial Themes*, Oxford.

Burgess, R. (1995), 'On the Date of the Kaisergeschichte', *Classical Philology* 90.2, 111–28.

Bury, J. B. (1958) *History of the Later Roman Empire from the death of Theodosius I to the death of Justinian*, New York.

Campbell, D. B. (2006), *Besieged: Siege Warfare in the Ancient World*, Oxford and New York.

Canfora, L. (1989), *The Vanished Library*, Berkeley.

Canto, A. M. (2003), *Las Raíces Béticas de Trajano*, Seville.

Carrié, J-M. (1982), 'Le 'colonat' du Bas-Empire', *Opus* 1.

Casey, P. J. (1995), *Carausius and Allectus: the British Usurpers*, Yale.

Caven, B. (1980), *The Punic Wars*, London.

Christys, A. (2002), *Christians in Al-Andalus*, Richmond.

Corsini, E.(1968), *Introduzione alle 'Storie' di Orosio*, Turin.

Croke, B. (1976), 'Arbogast and the Death of Valentinian II', *Historia* 25, 235–44.

Crone, G. R. (1968), 'New Light on the Hereford Map', *The Geographical Journal,* 131.4, 446–62.

Declercq, G. (2002), 'Dionysius Exiguus and the Introduction of the Christian Era', *Sacris Erudiri* 41, 165–246.

Demandt, A (1969), 'Der Tod des älteren Theodosius', *Historia* 17, 598–626.

Desanges, J. (1978), *Recherches sur l'activité des Méditerranéens aux confins de l'Afrique*, Rome.

Dobbs, H. H. (1957), *A Roman City in China*, London.

Doberentz, O. (1880), 'Die Erd- und Völkerkunde in der Weltchronik des Rudolf von Hohen-Ems', *Zeitschrift für deutsche Philologie* 12, 257–301 and 387–454.

—— (1881) 'Die Erd- und Völkerkunde in der Weltchronik des Rudolf von Hohen-Ems', *Zeitschrift für deutsche Philologie* 13, 29–57 and 165–223.

Dobson, M. (2008), *The Army of the Roman Republic: the Second Century*

BC, Polybius and the Camps at Numantia, Spain, Oxford.

Drinkwater, J. (1998), 'The Usurpers Constantine III (407–411) and Jovinus (411–413)', *Britannia* 29, 269–98.

Drinkwater, J. (2007), *The Alemanni and Rome 213–496: Caracalla to Clovis*, Oxford.

Duval, Y.-M. (2003), *L'Affaire Jovinien: d'une crise de la société romaine à une crise de la pensée chrétienne à la fin du IVè siècle et au début du Vè*, = *Studia Ephemeridis Augustinianum* 83, Rome.

Ellis Davidson, H. R. (1964), *Gods and Myths of Northern Europe*, Harmondsworth.

Enmann, A. (1883), 'Eine verlorene Geschichte der römischen Kaisar und das Buch *de viris illustribus urbis Romae* Quellenstudien.', *Philologus*, sup. 4, 335–501.

Ensslin, W. (1953), *Die Religionspolitik des Kaisers Theodosius der Grosse*, Munich.

Fink-Errera G. (1950), *Paul Orose et sa conception de l'histoire*, Aix en Provence.

Fink-Errera, G. (1952), 'Recherches bibliographiques sur Paul Orose', *Revista de Archivos Bibliotecas y Museos* 58, 271–322.

—— (1954), 'San Agustín y Orosio. Esquema para un estudio de las Fuentes del *De civitate Dei*', *Ciudad de Dios* 167.2, 445–549.

Freeman, P. (2001), *Ireland and the Classical World*, Austin.

Frend, W. H. C. (1952), *The Donatist Church: A Movement of Protest in Roman North Africa*, Oxford.

Friell, G. and Williams, S. (1994), *Theodosius: the Empire at Bay*, London.

Gauge, V (1998), 'Les routes d'Orose et les reliques d'Etienne', *Antiquité Tardive* 6.

Green, P. (1990), *From Alexander to Actium*, London.

Gsell, S. (1915), *Hérodote*, Algiers.

Harris, W. V. (1971), *The Romans in Etruria and Umbria*, Oxford.

Harvey, P. D. A. (1996), *Mappa Mundi: the Hereford World Map*, London.

Hay, D. (1977), *Annalists and Historians: Western Historiography from the Eighth to the Eighteenth Centuries*, London.

Heather, P. (1991), *Goths and Romans 332–489*, Oxford.

Heather, P. and Matthews, J. (1991), *The Goths in the Fourth Century*, Translated Texts for Historians, Liverpool.

Heather, P. and Moncur, D. (2001), see Themistius.

Hillard, T. W. (1996), 'Death by Lightning, Pompeius Strabo and the People', *Rheinisches Museum für Philologie* 139, 135–45.

Hobsbawn, E. J. (1955), Correspondence in the *New Statesman and Nation* 20 August, 217.

Hoey, A. S. (1937), 'Rosaliae Signorum', *Harvard Theological Review* 30.1, 22–30.

Holleaux, M. (1913), 'L'entretien de Scipion l'Africain et d'Hannibal', *Hermes* 48, 75–98.

Hook, D. (1988), 'The Legend of the Flavian Destruction of Jerusalem in Late Fifteenth-Century Spain and Portugal', *Bulletin of Hispanic Studies* 65, 113–28.

Honoré, A. (2002), *Ulpian: Pioneer of Human Rights*, Oxford.

Humphries, M. (2007), 'A New Created World: Classical Geographical Texts and Christian Contexts in Late Antiquity', in J. H. D. Scourfield (ed.), *Texts and Culture in Late Antiquity: Inheritance, Authority, and Change*, Swansea, 33–67.

Hutter, S. and Hauschild, T. (1991), *El Faro romano de La Coruña*, Corunna.

Janvier, Y. (1982), *La Géographie d'Orose*, Paris.

Jimeno Martínez, A and De La Torre Echávarri, J. I. (2005), *Numancia, símbolo e historia*, Madrid.

Johnson, S. (1983), *Late Roman Fortifications*, London.

Jones, A. H. M. (1958), 'The Roman Colonate', *Past and Present* 13.1, 1–13.

Kelly, G. (2004), 'Ammianus and the Great Tsunami', *Journal of Roman Studies* 94, 141–67.

Kelly, J. N. D. (1975), *Jerome: his Life, Writings, and Controversies*, London.

Kovács, P. (2009), *Marcus Aurelius' Rain Miracle and the Marcomannic Wars*, Leiden and Boston.

Kulikowsky, M. (2004), *Late Roman Spain and its Cities*, Baltimore.

Lacroix, B. (1965), *Orose et ses idées*, Montreal.

Lancel, S. (1974), see *Conference of Carthage*.

—— (1995), *Carthage: a History*, Oxford.

Lazenby, J. F. (1978), *Hannibal's War*, Warminster.

—— (1996), *The First Punic War*, London.

Lenski, N. (2002), *Failure of Empire: Valens and the Roman State in the Fourth Century*, Berkeley.

Lieu, S. N. C. and Monserrat, D. (1998), *Constantine: History, Historiography, and Legend*, London and New York.

Liggins, E (1970), 'The Authorship of the Old English Orosius', *Anglia* 88, 289–322.

Lozovsky, N. (2000), 'The Earth is Our Book': Geographical Knowledge in the Latin West ca. 400–1000, Michigan.

Lupher, D. A. (2003), Romans in a New World: Classical Models in Sixteenth-Century Spanish America, Ann Arbor.

Macleod, R. (2005), The Library of Alexandria, London and New York.

MacMullen, R. (1969), Constantine, New York.

Maenchen-Helfen, J. O. (1973), The World of the Huns, Berkeley, Los Angeles, and London.

Matthews, J. (1975), Western Aristocracies and Imperial Court AD 364–425, Oxford.

Menéndez Pidal, R. (1940), Historia de España II, Madrid.

Merrills, A. H. (2005), History and Geography in Late Antiquity, Cambridge.

Milan, A. (1973), 'I socii navales di Roma', Critica Storica 10, 193–221.

Miller, J. I. (1969), The Spice Trade of the Roman Empire 29 BC–AD 641, Oxford.

Miller, K. (1896), Mappaemundi: Die ältesten Weltkarten (vol. 4), Stuttgart.

Mommsen, T. E. (1959), 'Aponius and Orosius on the significance of the Epiphany', in his Medieval and Renaissance Studies (ed. E. F. Rice), New York, 299–324.

—— (1959a), 'Orosius and Augustine', in his Medieval and Renaissance Studies, New York, 265–98.

Moore, E. (1903), 'The Geography of Dante', in his Studies in Dante. Third Series: Miscellaneous Essays, Oxford, 109–43.

Mörner, T. (1844), De Orosii vita eiusque <<Historiarum libris septem adversum paganos>>, Berlin.

Morrison, J. (1995), The Age of the Galley: Mediterranean Oared Vessels since pre-classical Times, London.

O'Donnell, J. (1977), 'Paganus', Classical Folia 31, 163–69.

—— (2004), 'Late Antiquity: before and after', Transactions of the American Philological Association 134.2, 203–13.

Oakley, S. (1998), A Commentary on Livy books VI–XII, Oxford.

Oates, J. (1979), Babylon, London.

Oliver, J. H. (1953), 'The Ruling Power: a Study of the Roman Empire in the Second Century after Christ through the Roman Oration of Aelius Aristides', Transactions of the American Philosophical Society, 43.3.

Oost, S. I. (1966), 'The Revolt of Heraclian', Classical Philology 61, 236–42.

—— (1968), Galla Placidia Augusta, Chicago and London.

—— (1968a), 'Galla Placidia and the Law', Classical Philology 63, 114–21.

Pain, A. (1937), 'À propos de *De Gallo Bellico* I 53', *Revue de Études Latines* 15, 269–72.

Pastor Muñoz, M. (1977), 'En torno a la ubicación del *mons Vindius*', *Durius* 5, 147–55.

—— (2004), *Viriato, el heroe hispano que lucha por su pueblo*, Madrid

Penelas, M. (2001), *Kitāb Hurūšiyūš*, Madrid.

Picard, G. C. and Picard, G. (1968), *The Life and Death of Carthage*, London.

Pohlsander, H. (1980), 'Philip the Arab and Christianity', *Historia* 29, 463–73.

—— (1986), 'The Religious Policy of Decius', *Aufstieg und Niedergang der römischen Welt* II 16.3, 1826–42.

Ramírez Sábada, J. L. (1999), 'La toponimia de la Guerra: utilización y utilidad', in Almagro-Gorbea et al. (1999), 171–200.

Rapson, E. J. (ed.) (1935), *The Cambridge History of India*, Cambridge.

Raymond, I. W. (1936), see Orosius, *Seven Books of History against the Pagans*.

Reinach, T. (1980), *Mithridate Eupator, roi du Pont*, Paris.

Riese, A. (1878), see *Divisio Orbis Terrarum*.

Riesco Terrero, L. (1975), see Braulio of Saragossa.

Riesner, R. (1998), *Paul's Early Period: Chronology, Mission Strategy, Theology*, Grand Rapids.

Rives, J. B. (1999), 'The Decree of *Decius* and the Religion of Empire', *Journal of Roman Studies* 89, 135–54.

Romm, J. (1992), *The Edges of the Earth in Ancient Thought: Geography, Exploration, and Fiction*, Princeton.

Rowley, H. H. (1935), *Darius the Mede and the Four World Empires in the Book of Daniel*, Cardiff.

Salmon, E. T. (1967), *Samnium and the Samnites*, Cambridge.

Sallares, R. (2002), *A History of Malaria in Ancient Italy*, Oxford.

Salter Williams, D. (1984), 'Reconsidering Marcion's Gospel', *Journal of Biblical Literature* 108.3, 477–96.

Sánchez León, J. C. (1996), *Los bagaudas: rebeldes, demonios, mártires. Revueltas campesinas en Galia e Hispania durante el Bajo Imperio*, Jaén.

Sánchez Salor, E. (1982), see Orosius, *Seven Books of History against the Pagans*.

—— (1982a), see Orosius, *Seven Books of History against the Pagans*.

Schutz, H. (2001), *Tools, Weapons, and Ornaments: Germanic Material Culture in Pre-Carolingian Central Europe 400–750*, Leiden.

Schulten, A. (1945), *Historia de Numanica*, Barcelona.

Scullard, H. H. (1970), *Scipio Africanus: Soldier and Politician*, Bristol.

—— (1975), *The Elephant in the Greek and Roman World*, Cambridge.

Seston, W. (1946), *Dioclétien et la Tétrarchie*, Paris.

Shahîd, I. (1984), *Rome and the Arabs*, Dumbarton Oaks.

Skutsch, O. (1968), *Studia Enniana*, London.

Skutsch, O. (1985), see Ennius, *Annals*.

Southern, P. (2009), *Empress Zenobia: Palmyra's Rebel Queen*.

Southern, P. and Dixon, M. (1996), *The Late Roman Army*, London.

Spann, P. O. (1987), *Quintus Sertorius and the Legacy of Sulla*, Fayetteville.

Spedicato, E. (2008), 'Homer and Orosius: a Key to Explain Deucalion's Flood, Exodus and Other Tales', in S. A. Paipetis (ed.), *Science and Technology in the Homeric Epics*, Cassino, 369–74.

Stoneman, R. (1992), *Palmyra and its Empire: Zenobia's Revolt against Rome*, Michigan.

Stothers, R. B. (2004), 'Ancient Scientific Basis of the "Giant Serpent" from Historical Evidence', *Isis* 95, 220–38.

Straub, J. (1966), 'Eugenius', *Reallexikon für Antike und Christentum* 6, 860–77.

Svennung, J. (1922), *Orosiana*, Uppsala.

Syme, R. (1970), 'The conquest of North West Spain', *Legio VII Gemina*, Léon.

—— (1974), *History in Ovid*, Oxford.

Tarn, W. W. (1984), *The Greeks in Bactria and India* (3rd edn), Chicago.

Thomassen, E. (2005), *The Spiritual Seed: the Church of Valentinus*, Leiden.

Thompson, E. A. (1966), *The Visigoths in the Time of Ulfila*, Oxford.

Tilley, M. (1991), 'Dilatory Donatists or Procrastinating Catholics: the Trial at the Conference of Carthage', *Church History* 60.1, 7–19.

—— (1997), *The Bible in Christian North Africa: the Donatist World*, Augsburg.

Tipps, G. K. (1985), 'The Battle of Encomus', *Historia* 34, 432–65.

—— (2003), 'The Defeat of Regulus', *Classical World* 96.4, 375–85.

Torres Rodríguez, C. (1955), 'La *Historia* de Paulo Orosio', *Revista de Archivos, Bibliotecas y Museos* 61, 107–53.

—— (1971), 'Notas preliminaries en torno a la historiografía de Orosio', *Cuadernos de Estudios Gallegos* 26, 329–36.

—— (1985), *Paulo Orosio: su vida y sus obras*, Santiago de Compostella.

Toynbee, P. (1903), 'Dante's Obligations to the *Ormista*', in his *Dante: Studies and Researches*, London, 121–36.

Trevor-Roper, H. (1955), Correspondence in the *New Statesman and Society*, 27 August, 243.

Trompf, G. W. (1979), *The Idea of Historical Recurrence in Western Thought*, Berkeley, Los Angeles, London.

—— (2000), *Early Christian Historiography: Narratives of Retributive Justice*, London.

Vilella, J. (2000), 'Biografía crítica de Orosio', *Jahrbüch für Antike und Christentum* 43, 94–121.

Voeglin, E. (1952), *The New Science of Politics*, Chicago.

—— (1968), *Science, Politics and Gnosticism*, Chicago.

Walbank, F. (1970), *A Commentary on Polybius*, vol. 1, Oxford.

Watson, A. (1999), *Aurelian and the Third Century*, London and New York.

Wells, C. (1972), *The German Policy of Augustus*, Oxford.

Watkins, O. H. (1988), 'The Death of Cn. Pompeius Strabo', *Rheinisches Museum für Philologie* 131, 143–50.

Whitbread, L. G. (1971), see Fulgentius.

White, J. F. (2004), *Restorer of the World: the Roman Emperor Aurelian*.

Williams, R. (1987), *Arius: Heresy and Tradition*, London.

Williams, S. (1985), *Diocletian and the Roman Recovery*, Frome.

Worsfold, T. C. (1934), *A History of the Vestal Virgins of Rome*, London.

Yardley, J.C. (2003), *Justin and Pompeius Trogus: a Study in the Language of Justin's Epitome*, Toronto.

Yardley J. C. and Heckel, W. (1997), see Justin.

Zangemeister, C. (1967), see Orosius.

INDEX

Q.Fabius Maximus Verrucosus 191
Q. Fabius Pictor 181
M. Fabius Vibulanus (consul 480 BC) 82
Fabricius 158
Faliscians 117, 178, 185
Famine 55, 56, 79, 82, 91, 94, 202, 324,
    332, 333, 339, 364
Fannius 267, 268
Faustus Sulla 298
Fesulanian Hills 398
Fidenae 79, 95, 326
    Fidenates 95
'Firmus' (= Furius) 312
Firmus 381, 382
G. Flaminius Nepos 182, 217
G. Flaminius 197
Quinctius Flaminius 195
G. Flavius Fimbria 249, 267
Flood 27, 32, 54, 57, 178
Florian 359, 367
Florus 15
Formiae 160
Franks 361, 379, 390, 404
Fratafernes 147
Fraucus 243
Frigidus 9
Fructuosus 2
Fulvia 303
L. 'Fulvius' (= L. Furius Purpurio) 195
Gn. Fulvius Centumalus 181,
C. Fulvius Flaccus 223
Gn. Fulvius Flaccus 188, 189, 191
M. Fulvius Flaccus 226, 228
Q.Fulvius Flaccus 182, 190
Ser. Fulvius Flaccus 218
M. Fulvius Nobilior (consul 189) 197,
    198
Ser. Fulvius Paetinus Nobilior 174
Furnius 306
P. Furius 239, 240
G. Furius Placidus 175
L. Fursidius 251
Fuscus 341

Gabii 80
A. Gabinius 273, 274, 297
G. Gabinius 243

Gaesati 181, 182
Gaetuli 46, 313
Gallia Placidia 404, 411, 412, 413
Gaius Caesar 323
Gaius Marcius 119
Galatia 198, 343, 377
Galautes 47
Galba 335, 336
Galicia 2, 3
    Galicians 217
Gallaecia 44, 45, 219, 311, 312
Gallia Belgica 42, 43
Gallic Sea 43, 44, 49
Gallic Wars 29, 179
Gallienus 355, 357, 406
Gallograecia 198
    Gallograeci 198, 268
Gallus 375
Gandaridae 41
Gangaridae 138
Ganges 37, 41
Ganymede 62
Garamantes 46
Gaul 9, 29, 43, 44, 45, 192, 234, 253, 255,
    259, 275, 277, 279-287, 289, 291,
    292, 302, 313, 328, 336, 342, 347,
    350, 357, 359, 360, 362, 363, 369,
    374, 387, 389, 408, 411
    Cisalpine 181, 254, 274
    Further 181
    Long-haired 275
    Narbonensis 43, 44, 284, 360
    Transalpine 274
    Gallic provinces 356, 359, 360, 363,
        369, 375, 380, 382, 400, 404, 406,
        408, see also Lugdunensis
Gauls 12, 22, 28, 29, 44, 106, 107, 108,
    110, 118, 119, 140, 142, 145, 179,
    182, 187, 197, 230, 236, 237, 258,
    276, 277, 279, 282, 283, 284, 285,
    286, 288, 289, 313, 357, 380, 389,
    390, 403
    Allobrogian 229
Cisalpine 179
    Insubrian 182
    Salassian 212
    Senonian 106, 145